BIG IDEAS
MATH.
Algebra 2

Resources by Chapter

- Family Communication Letters

- Start Thinking/Warm Up/Cumulative Review Warm Up

- Extra Practice (A and B)

- Enrichment and Extension

- Puzzle Time

- Cumulative Review

BIG IDEAS LEARNING.

Erie, Pennsylvania

Photo Credits

ISBN 13: 978-1-60840-860-3
ISBN 10: 1-60840-860-4

3456789-VLP-18 17 16 15

Contents

About the Resources by Chapter

Family Communication Letters (English and Spanish)

The Family Communication Letters provide a way to quickly communicate to family members how they can help their student with the material of the chapter. They make the mathematics less intimidating and provide suggestions for helping students see mathematical concepts in common activities.

Start Thinking/Warm Up/Cumulative Review Warm Up

Each Start Thinking/Warm Up/Cumulative Review Warm Up includes two options for getting the class started. The Start Thinking questions provide students with an opportunity to discuss thought-provoking questions and analyze real-world situations. The Warm Up questions review prerequisite skills needed for the lesson. The Cumulative Review Warm Up questions review material from earlier lessons or courses.

Extra Practice

The Extra Practice exercises provide additional practice on the key concepts taught in the lesson. There are two levels of practice provided for each lesson: A (basic) and B (average).

Enrichment and Extension

Each Enrichment and Extension extends the lesson and provides a challenging application of the key concepts.

Puzzle Time

Each Puzzle Time provides additional practice in a fun format in which students use their mathematical knowledge to solve a riddle. This format allows students to self-check their work.

Cumulative Review

The Cumulative Review includes exercises covering concepts and skills from the current chapter and previous chapters.

Chapter 1

Chapter 1 Linear Functions

Dear Family,

In this chapter, your child will be graphing based on transformations to parent functions. The transformations to be used are translations, reflections, and horizontal and vertical stretches and shrinks.

These transformations are similar to how television show animators create cartoons. Each frame is drawn with pencil and paper, transferred onto a transparency using ink and color, and then photographed. Each 20-minute cartoon is created by sequencing about 30,000 different frames. When there are slight changes in each frame, using various transformations, the objects appear to be animated.

To make your own flip book at home, follow the steps below:

1. Gather a stack of paper. The more pages or frames you have, the better your animation will look.

2. Determine what you want to illustrate. You can use stick figures and easy-to-draw objects, or you can use objects that have a lot of detail. It's your choice!

3. Draw your first picture at the bottom of the stack. It will make it easier to trace or reference part of the picture that remains the same.

4. Draw the next pages so that objects that do not move are in the same position, and the animated objects move slightly in each frame. Adding translations and rotations gives the illusion of movement. Adding horizontal stretches and shrinks may add some humor to your animation.

5. Flip the pages of your book!

You can make each page as detailed as you want. You can also use the Internet to find many free animation websites that will allow you to create your own personalized animation electronically.

Have fun creating your own animation.

Nombre _____ Fecha_____

Estimada familia:

En este capítulo, su hijo hará gráficas basándose en transformaciones de funciones madre. Las transformaciones que se usarán serán traslaciones, reflexiones y alargamientos y encogimientos horizontales y verticales.

Estas transformaciones se parecen a la manera en que los animadores de programas televisivos crean los dibujos animados. Cada marco se dibuja con lápiz y papel, se traslada a una transparencia usando tinta y color y luego se toma una fotografía. Cada dibujo animado de 20 minutos se crea con una secuencia de aproximadamente 30,000 marcos diferentes. Cuando hay cambios menores en cada marco, mediante el uso de varias transformaciones, los objetos parecen ser animados.

Para crear su propio foliscopio en casa, sigan los siguientes pasos:

1. Busquen una pila de hojas de papel. Cuantas más páginas o marcos tengan, mejor lucirá su animación.

2. Decidan qué quieren ilustrar. Pueden usar monigotes hechos con palitos y objetos fáciles de dibujar o pueden usar objetos que tengan muchos detalles. ¡Es su elección!

3. Dibujen el primer dibujo en la parte inferior de la pila. Será más fácil calcar o tomar como referencia a una parte del dibujo que no cambia.

4. Dibujen las siguientes páginas de manera que los objetos que no se mueven estén en la misma posición y que los objetos animados se muevan levemente en cada marco. Agregar traslaciones y rotaciones da la impresión de que hay movimiento. Agregar alargamientos y encogimientos horizontales y verticales puede sumar algo de humor a su animación.

5. ¡Pasen las páginas de su foliscopio!

En cada página, pueden incluir todos los detalles que quieran. También pueden buscar en Internet muchos sitios web de animación gratis que les permitirán crear su propia animación electrónica personalizada.

Que se diviertan creando su propia animación.

1.1 Start Thinking

Draw a coordinate plane. Tape the middle of a string to the origin to make a V with the ends of the string. Then tape the ends of the string in the coordinate plane. Trace the line formed by the string. Move the ends of the string wider and trace the new lines. What happens as the string ends are stretched wider?

1.1 Warm Up

Plot the ordered pairs from the table in a coordinate plane. Connect them with a line.

1.

x	y
−3	−3
−2	−2
−1	−1
0	0

2.

x	y
−2	−5
0	−3
3	0

3.

x	y
−2	−5
0	0
2	5

4.

x	y
−4	1
−2	3
0	5

1.1 Cumulative Review Warm Up

Find the slope of the line passing through the set of points.

1. $(-4, 4)$ and $(2, 1)$

2. $(-2, 0)$ and $(0, 2)$

3. $(5, 2)$ and $(7, 3)$

4. $(10, 300)$ and $(15, 425)$

Name_____ Date_____

1.1 Practice A

In Exercises 1 and 2, identify the function family to which f belongs. Compare the graph of f to the graph of its parent function.

1.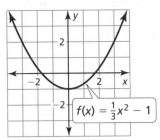

2.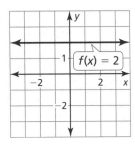

3. You purchased a computer for your business for $800. Using straight-line depreciation, the amount of depreciation allowed for each year after the purchase is given by the function $f(x) = 800 - 114.29x$. What type of function can you use to model the data?

In Exercises 4–9, graph the function and its parent function. Then describe the transformation.

4. $h(x) = x + 2$

5. $f(x) = x - 3$

6. $g(x) = x^2 + 2$

7. $f(x) = (x - 1)^2$

8. $h(x) = |x + 4|$

9. $f(x) = 5$

In Exercises 10–15, graph the function and its parent function. Then describe the transformation.

10. $f(x) = 3x$

11. $g(x) = \frac{1}{2}x$

12. $h(x) = 3x^2$

13. $g(x) = \frac{1}{4}x^2$

14. $h(x) = 2|x|$

15. $f(x) = \frac{5}{2}x$

In Exercises 16–18, use a graphing calculator to graph the function and its parent function. Then describe the transformations.

16. $f(x) = \frac{1}{3}x - 1$

17. $h(x) = 2|x| - 3$

18. $g(x) = \frac{5}{3}x^2 + 2$

19. In the same coordinate plane, sketch the graph of a parent absolute-value function and the graph of an absolute-value function that has no x-intercepts. Describe the transformation(s) of the parent function.

Name _____ Date _____

In Exercises 1 and 2, identify the function family to which *f* belongs. Compare the graph of *f* with the graph of its parent function.

1.
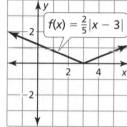
$f(x) = \frac{2}{5}|x - 3|$

2.
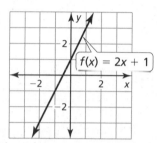
$f(x) = 2x + 1$

In Exercises 3–8, graph the function and its parent function. Then describe the transformation.

3. $h(x) = x + 2$

4. $f(x) = -x$

5. $g(x) = -x^2$

6. $f(x) = (x + 2)^2$

7. $h(x) = |x| - 2$

8. $f(x) = -3$

In Exercises 9–11, graph the function and its parent function. Then describe the transformation.

9. $f(x) = \frac{3}{5}x$

10. $h(x) = \frac{3}{2}|x|$

11. $h(x) = \frac{4}{3}x^2$

In Exercises 12–14, use a graphing calculator to graph the function and its parent function. Then describe the transformations.

12. $g(x) = \frac{1}{10}x^2 + 5$

13. $h(x) = (x - 5)^2 + \frac{4}{9}$

14. $f(x) = -|x + 2| - \frac{1}{3}$

In Exercises 15–18, identify the function family and describe the domain and range. Use a graphing calculator to verify your answer.

15. $h(x) = |x + 5| + 3$

16. $g(x) = -2x - 10$

17. $g(x) = 7x^2 - 3$

18. You are throwing a football with your friends. The height (in feet) of the ball above the ground *t* seconds after it is thrown is modeled by the function
$f(t) = -16t^2 + 45t + 6.$

   a. Without graphing, identify the type of function modeled by the equation.

   b. What is the value of *t* when the ball is released from your hand? Explain.

   c. How many feet above the ground is the ball when it is released from your hand? Explain.

Name_____ Date_____

Parent Functions and Transformations

In the coordinate plane below, graph two trapezoids, one with coordinates of $A(0, 1)$, $B(1, 0)$, $C(4, 0)$, and $D(5, 1)$, and the other with coordinates of $A'(-6, -2)$, $B'(-5, -1)$, $C'(-2, -1)$, and $D'(-1, -2)$.

1. Describe a possible sequence of transformations that take trapezoid $ABCD$ to trapezoid $A'B'C'D'$.

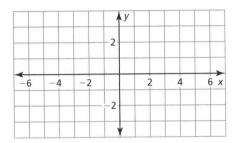

2. You purchase a car from a dealership for $15,000. The trade-in value of the car x years after the purchase is given by the function $f(x) = 15,000 - 300x^2$.

   a. What type of function could be used to model the data?

   b. After how many years will the trade-in value be $0?

   c. In this situation, what is the domain and range?

Using the table given, state the domain and range of each function, and describe the transformation of each function from its parent function. Use a graphing calculator to confirm your answer.

	Domain	Range	Vertical stretch or shrink	Horizontal stretch or shrink	Reflection(s)	Translation(s)
3. $-\frac{1}{2}x + 5$						
4. $-4(x)^2 - 3$						
5. $\left\|-\frac{1}{3}x - 1\right\| + 5$						

1.1 Puzzle Time

Why Didn't The Man Fix Dinner?

A	B	C	D	E	F
G	H	I	J	K	L
M					

Complete each exercise. Find the answer in the answer column. Write the word under the answer in the box containing the exercise letter.

$f(x) = \frac{2}{3}x$

BECAUSE

$f(x) = \frac{1}{2}x - 1$

PEOPLE

$f(x) = -x^2$

DO

$f(x) = |x - 5| + 3$

IT

$f(x) = x^2 - 1$

IF

$f(x) = 5x - 3$

BROKEN

$f(x) = (x + 1)^2 + 2$

FIX

Identify the function that matches the given description of the graph.

A. vertical shrink of the linear function

B. vertical shrink followed by a translation 1 unit down of the linear function

C. reflection in the x-axis followed by a vertical stretch and a translation 3 units right of the absolute value function

D. vertical stretch followed by a translation 7 units down of the linear function

E. translation 1 unit down of the quadratic function

F. vertical stretch of the linear function

G. reflection in the x-axis followed by a translation 1 unit up of the quadratic function

H. reflection in the x-axis followed by a vertical stretch and a translation 4 units up of the absolute value function

I. vertical stretch followed by a translation 3 units down of the linear function

J. reflection in the x-axis of the quadratic function

K. vertical stretch of the absolute value function

L. translation 1 unit left and 2 units up of the quadratic function

M. translation 5 units right and 3 units up of the absolute value function

$f(x) = -2|x| + 4$

NOT

$f(x) = 7x$

IT

$f(x) = -4|x - 3|$

ALWAYS

$f(x) = 9|x|$

NOT

$f(x) = -x^2 + 1$

IS

$f(x) = 2x - 7$

SAY

1.2 Start Thinking

Graph the line $h(x) = \frac{2}{3}x + 2$ in a coordinate plane. What happens if 1 is added to the right side of the equation? What happens if -1 is added? Explain what happens to each point on the line when a number is added to one side of the equation of the line.

1.2 Warm Up

Graph the point and its reflection.

1. point $(5, 2)$ reflected in the x-axis

2. point $(-1, 0)$ reflected in the y-axis

3. point $(1, 2)$ reflected in the y-axis

4. point $(3, -3)$ reflected in the x-axis

5. point $(-3, 3)$ reflected in the line through $(-5, 1)$ and $(-2, 1)$

6. point $(-4, 3)$ reflected in the line through $(2, 2)$ and $(4, 2)$

1.2 Cumulative Review Warm Up

Determine the number of lines of symmetry, if any, for the letter. Draw each line of symmetry.

1. T

2. E

3. L

4. W

5. H

6. R

Name _____ Date _____

In Exercises 1–4, write a function _g_ whose graph represents the indicated transformation of the graph of _f_. Use a graphing calculator to check your answer.

1. $f(x) = x - 2$; translation 5 units left

2. $f(x) = x + 1$; translation 4 units right

3. $f(x) = |3x + 2| + 4$; translation 3 units down

4. $f(x) = 4x - 5$; translation 3 units up

In Exercises 5–8, write a function _g_ whose graph represents the indicated transformation of the graph of _f_. Use a graphing calculator to check your answer.

5. $f(x) = -3x + 7$; reflection in the x-axis

6. $f(x) = \frac{1}{3}x - 2$; reflection in the x-axis

7. $f(x) = |4x| - 6$; reflection in the y-axis

8. $f(x) = |3x - 5| + 3$; reflection in the y-axis

In Exercises 9–12, write a function _g_ whose graph represents the indicated transformation of the graph of _f_. Use a graphing calculator to check your answer.

9. $f(x) = x + 3$; vertical stretch by a factor of 4

10. $f(x) = 4x + 3$; vertical shrink by a factor of $\frac{1}{3}$

11. $f(x) = |3x| + 2$; horizontal shrink by a factor of $\frac{1}{3}$

12. $f(x) = |x + 1|$; horizontal stretch by a factor of 3

In Exercises 13 and 14, write a function _g_ whose graph represents the indicated transformation of the graph of _f_.

13. $f(x) = x$; vertical shrink by a factor of $\frac{1}{3}$ followed by a translation 4 units down

14. $f(x) = |x|$; translation 3 units left followed by a horizontal shrink by a factor of $\frac{1}{2}$

Name_____ Date _____

1.2 Practice B

In Exercises 1–4, write a function *g* whose graph represents the indicated transformation of the graph of *f*. Use a graphing calculator to check your answer.

1. $f(x) = 5x - 2$; translation 5 units right

2. $f(x) = 3x + 6$; translation 4 units up

3. $f(x) = 3 - |x - 2|$; translation 2 units left

4. $f(x) = |2x| + 3$; translation 2 units down

In Exercises 5–8, write a function *g* whose graph represents the indicated transformation of the graph of *f*. Use a graphing calculator to check your answer.

5. $f(x) = -x + 3$; reflection in the *y*-axis

6. $f(x) = \frac{2}{3}x - 4$; reflection in the *x*-axis

7. $f(x) = -5 + |x - 8|$; reflection in the *y*-axis

8. $f(x) = |4x - 1| + 2$; reflection in the *y*-axis

In Exercises 9–12, write a function *g* whose graph represents the indicated transformation of the graph of *f*. Use a graphing calculator to check your answer.

9. $f(x) = 3 - x$; horizontal stretch by a factor of 2

10. $f(x) = 3x + 5$; vertical shrink by a factor of $\frac{1}{3}$

11. $f(x) = |3x| + 2$; horizontal shrink by a factor of $\frac{1}{3}$

12. $f(x) = -2|x - 2| + 4$; vertical stretch by a factor of 2

In Exercises 13 and 14, write a function *g* whose graph represents the indicated transformation of the graph of *f*.

13. $f(x) = x$; translation 5 units up followed by a vertical shrink by a factor of $\frac{1}{4}$

14. $f(x) = |x|$; reflection in the *x*-axis followed by a translation 2 units left

1.2 Enrichment and Extension

Transformations of Linear and Absolute Value Functions

In Exercises 1–6, write a function *g* whose graph represents the indicated transformations of the graph of *f*. Then find the *x*-intercept of the graph of *g*. Use a graphing calculator to check your answers.

$$f(x) = 2x - 1$$

1. translation 3 units right followed by a translation 1 unit down

2. translation 1 unit left followed by a reflection in the *x*-axis

3. vertical stretch by a factor of 3 followed by a translation 3 units down

4. horizontal shrink by a factor of $\frac{1}{3}$ followed by a translation 5 units up

5. translation 3 units right followed by a vertical stretch by a factor of 2

6. translation 1 unit up followed by a reflection in the *x*-axis and a translation 3 units left

In Exercises 7–12, write a function *g* whose graph represents the indicated transformations of the graph of *f*. Then find all *x*-intercepts of the graph of *g*. Use a graphing calculator to check your answers.

$$f(x) = |x + 2| - 1$$

7. translation 3 units right followed by a translation 1 unit down

8. translation 1 unit left followed by a translation 2 units up

9. translation 1 unit up followed by a reflection in the *x*-axis and a translation 3 units left

10. translation 1 unit right followed by a vertical stretch by a factor of 2 and a translation 4 units down

11. horizontal shrink by a factor of $\frac{1}{4}$ followed by a translation 10 units right and 1 unit up, and a reflection in the *x*-axis

12. translation 5 units right followed by a translation 3 units down, a vertical shrink by a factor of $\frac{1}{2}$, and a reflection in the *x*-axis

Name_____ Date _____

 **Puzzle Time**

What U.S. President Died July 4, 1831?

Write the letter of each answer in the box containing the exercise number.

Write a function g whose graph represents the indicated transformation of the graph of f.

1. $f(x) = x + 4$; translation 3 units left

2. $f(x) = x - 7$; translation 5 units right

3. $f(x) = |2x - 5| + 3$; translation 2 units up

4. $f(x) = -4x - 8$; reflection in the x-axis

5. $f(x) = |2x + 1| - 6$; reflection in the y-axis

6. $f(x) = -x + 5$; horizontal shrink by a factor of $\frac{1}{2}$

7. $f(x) = |2x - 4|$; vertical stretch by a factor of 4

Write a function g whose graph represents the indicated transformation of the graph of f.

8. $f(x) = x$; vertical stretch by a factor of 3 followed by a translation 2 units down

9. $f(x) = x$; translation 1 unit up followed by a vertical shrink by a factor of $\frac{1}{4}$

10. $f(x) = |x|$; reflection in the x-axis followed by a translation 2 units right

11. $f(x) = |x|$; vertical shrink by a factor of $\frac{1}{2}$ followed by a translation 5 units up and 1 unit left

Answers

R. $g(x) = \frac{1}{4}x + \frac{1}{4}$

O. $g(x) = -|x - 2|$

A. $g(x) = x - 12$

M. $g(x) = |2x - 5| + 5$

M. $g(x) = -2x + 5$

E. $g(x) = 4x + 8$

E. $g(x) = \frac{1}{2}|x + 1| + 5$

S. $g(x) = |-2x + 1| - 6$

N. $g(x) = 3x - 2$

J. $g(x) = x + 7$

O. $g(x) = 4|2x - 4|$

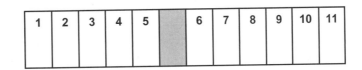

1.3 Start Thinking

Your business is debuting a new product to be sold at $14.99 per unit. Your business produces this product at a cost of $8.50 per unit. Your goal is to make $150,000 in profit from this product in the next year. How could you model this situation with an equation and a graph to "sell" this idea to your employees?

1.3 Warm Up

Determine a reasonable domain and range for the situation. Write your answer in set notation.

1. A professional basketball player earns $150,000 for each game played, and there are 82 games in a season.

2. You eat up to 5 meals a day with an average of 844 milligrams of potassium at each meal.

3. The average amount of money spent on food per person at an amusement park that can accommodate 2500 people is $5.25.

1.3 Cumulative Review Warm Up

Find the mean of the data set. Round to the nearest tenth, if necessary.

1. 5, 2, 7, 4, 6, 6, 6

2. 11, 6, 8, 8, 11, 13, 9, 7, 11

3. 10, 9, 6, 10.1, 10.9, 9.6, 9.8, 16.9, 10.1

4. Salaries at a company: $216,000 $95,000 $80,600

Name_____ Date_____

1.3 Practice A

In Exercises 1 and 2, use the graph to write an equation of the line and interpret the slope.

1.
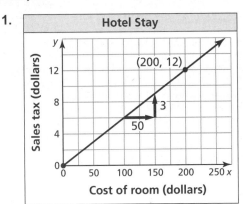

2.
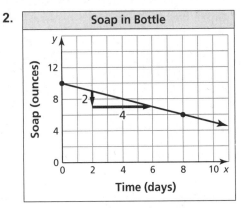

3. Two car washes charge a basic fee plus a fee based on the number of extras that are chosen. The table below shows the total costs for different car washes at Bubbles Car Wash. The total cost y (in dollars) for a car wash with x extras at Soapy Car Wash is represented by the equation $y = x + 9$. Which car wash charges more for the basic fee? How many extras must be chosen for the total costs to be the same?

Number of extras, x	2	4	6	8
Total cost, y	9	12	15	18

In Exercises 4 and 5, determine whether the data show a linear relationship. If so, write an equation of a line of fit. Estimate y when $x = 15$ and explain its meaning in the context of the situation.

4.
Weeks, x	3	6	10	12	16
Height of basil plant (inches), y	1	2	5	9	15

5.
Minutes, x	6	10	14	20	24
Cars washed, y	3	5	7	10	12

6. A set of data points has a correlation coefficient $r = -0.86$. Your friend claims that because the correlation coefficient is close to -1, it is reasonable to use the line of best fit to make predictions. Is your friend correct? Explain your reasoning.

Name _____ Date _____

1.3 Practice B

In Exercises 1 and 2, use the graph to write an equation of the line and interpret the slope.

1.
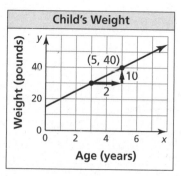

2.
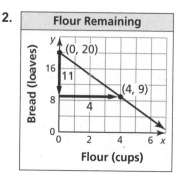

In Exercises 3 and 4, determine whether the data show a linear relationship. If so, write an equation of a line of fit. Estimate y when $x = 15$ and explain its meaning in the context of the situation.

3.

Days, x	3	7	11	14	20
Number of tickets sold, y	76	164	252	318	450

4.

Minutes running, x	6	10	17	25	40
Calories burned, y	70	118	200	295	472

In Exercises 5 and 6, use the linear regression feature on a graphing calculator to find an equation of the line of best fit for the data. Find and interpret the correlation coefficient.

5.
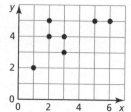

6.
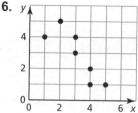

1.3   Enrichment and Extension

Modeling with Linear Functions

In Exercises 1–4, write a linear equation in slope-intercept form.

1. a line that passes through the points $(-1, 4)$ and $(1, 4)$

2. a line whose x-intercept is 3 and y-intercept is -2

3. a line that has a slope of 0 and passes through the point $(2, 7)$

4. a line that has the same slope as $6y + 10 = 3x$ and the same y-intercept as $4x - 3y = 9$

In Exercises 5–10, find the value of A that would make the statement true.

5. The lines $3x - 4y = 6$ and $Ax + 12y = 20$ are parallel.

6. The lines $7x + 2y = 8$ and $Ax + 4y = 11$ are parallel.

7. The lines $6x - 8y = 11$ and $Ax + 2y = 15$ are parallel.

8. The lines $5x + 10y = 40$ and $Ax + 9y = 27$ are perpendicular.

9. The lines $4x - 3y = 10$ and $Ax + 4y = 7$ are perpendicular.

10. The lines $8x + 32y = 14$ and $Ax + \frac{1}{3}y = 12$ are perpendicular.

Use the data in the table to answer the question.

11. The data displayed represents a positive correlation. Use the data in the years 2004 and 2008 to create an equation of a line of fit and estimate the cost of tuition in 2015.

12. Imagine the tuition in 2008 was $\$24,000$. Use the data in the years 2004 and 2008 to create an equation of a line of fit to estimate the cost of tuition in 2015. How much more would the tuition be in 2015 in this situation in comparison to the situation in Exercise 11?

Yearly College Tuition (thousands of dollars)	
Year, x	Cost, y
2004	17
2005	18
2008	22
2011	26
2013	28

Name _____ Date _____

What Do You Call It When A Chicken Stumbles As It Crosses The Street?

Write the letter next to each answer in the box containing the exercise number.

Use the graph to write an equation of the line.

1.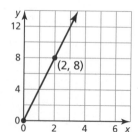

2.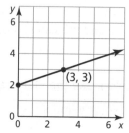

3.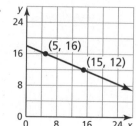

4.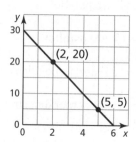

Answers

O. $y = \frac{1}{3}x + 2$

A. $y = -\frac{2}{5}x + 18$

P. $y = \frac{1}{2}x + 3$

R. $y = -\frac{4}{5}x + 8$

D. $y = -5x + 30$

T. $y = -\frac{2}{3}x + 5\frac{1}{3}$

R. $y = 4x$

I. $y = \frac{1}{2}x + 2\frac{1}{2}$

The data in the table show a linear relationship. Write an equation for the line of fit.

5.

x	y
−7	10
−4	8
−1	6
2	4

6.

x	y
5	4
2.5	6
0	8
−2.5	10

7.

x	y
−13	−4
−17	−6
−21	−8
−25	−10

8.

x	y
−6	0
−4	1
−2	2
0	3

1	2	3	4		5	6	7	8

Companies often try out different business models for the same product to determine which generates the most revenue. A graph depicts three business models that intersect at a point. What does the point of intersection represent?

1.4 **Warm Up**

Rewrite the equation in slope-intercept form.

1. $3x - 2y = 3$

2. $2x + 6y = 21$

3. $3x + 2y = 0$

4. $7x + 2y = 13$

5. $x - 4y = 5$

6. $7x - 8y = 19$

1.4 **Cumulative Review Warm Up**

Determine whether the ordered pair is a solution to the equation.

1. $(3, 2); 4x - 3y = 6$

2. $(0, -1); x - 6y = -9$

3. $(5, 2); 6x + y = 15$

4. $(-2, 4); x - 2y = -10$

5. $(3, -4); 2y = x + 8$

6. $(4, -2); y = 3x - 14$

Name _____ Date _____

1.4 Practice A

In Exercises 1 and 2, solve the system using the elimination method.

1. $x - 6y + 2z = 5$

$2x - 3y + z = 4$

$3x + 4y - z = -2$

2. $x + y - z = -2$

$2x - y + z = 8$

$-x + 2y + 2z = 10$

3. Describe and correct the error in the first step of solving the system of linear equations.

$5x + 3y - z = 15$

$-x + 2y + 3z = 10$

$3x - 4y + 3z = 8$

$$\boxed{\quad \times \quad \begin{array}{l} 5x + 3y - z = 15 \\ \underline{-5x + 10y + 15z = 10} \\ \qquad 13y + 14z = 25 \end{array}}$$

In Exercises 4 and 5, solve the system using the elimination method.

4. $x + 4y - 3z = 1$

$3x + 12y - 9z = 8$

$2x + 4y - 4z = -12$

5. $x + y - z = 2$

$x - y - z = 2$

$3x + y - 3z = 6$

6. Three bouquets of flowers are ordered at a florist. Three roses, 2 carnations, and 1 tulip cost $14, 6 roses, 2 carnations, and 6 tulips cost $38, and 1 rose, 12 carnations, and 1 tulip cost $18. How much does each item cost?

In Exercises 7 and 8, solve the system of linear equations using the substitution method.

7. $y = -3$

$2x + y = 5$

$x - 2y + z = 6$

8. $x - y = 5$

$-x + 4y + 2z = 3$

$-x + 3y - 5z = -6$

9. A triangle has a perimeter of 90 centimeters.

a. Write and use a linear system to determine the lengths of sides ℓ, m, and n.

b. Is the triangle a right triangle? Explain.

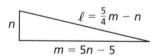

$\ell = \frac{5}{4}m - n$

n

$m = 5n - 5$

1.4 Practice B

In Exercises 1 and 2, solve the system using the elimination method.

1. $3x - y + z = -1$
$3x + 2y - 5z = -16$
$3x + 3y + 2z = 6$

2. $4x + 3y - 5z = -9$
$6x + 6y - 3z = 6$
$3x - 3y + 4z = 19$

3. Describe and correct the error in the first step of solving the system of linear equations.

$5x + 3y - z = 15$
$-x + 2y + 3z = 10$
$3x - 4y + 3z = 8$

$$\begin{array}{r} -15x - 9y - 3z = 45 \\ 3x - 4y + 3z = 8 \\ \hline -12 - 13y = 53 \end{array}$$

In Exercises 4 and 5, solve the system using the elimination method.

4. $x - y - z = 5$
$4x - 4y - 4z = 15$
$3x - y - 4z = -2$

5. $-x + y + z = 3$
$x + y + 3z = 5$
$3y + 6z = 12$

In Exercises 6 and 7, solve the system of linear equations using the substitution method.

6. $2x - y = 6$
$4x - 3y - 2z = 14$
$-x + 2y - 3z = 12$

7. $6x + 3y - 9z = 10$
$-2x - y + 3z = 3$
$x - 2y - z = 1$

8. Your friend claims that she has a bag of 30 coins containing nickels, dimes, and quarters. The total value of the 30 coins is $3. There are twice as many nickels as there are dimes. Is your friend correct? Explain your reasoning.

9. Each equation in this system represents a line.

$x - 2y - 3 = 0$
$2x + y + 1 = 0$
$3x + 4y + 5 = 0$

a. Solve the system of linear equations using either the elimination method or the substitution method.

b. Do the lines intersect at a point? Explain.

1.4 Enrichment and Extension

Solving Linear Systems

Example: Solve the system of four equations using the elimination method.

$3w + 3x + 9y - 6z = 33$
$2w + 5x + 4y - 2z = 20$
$-w + 2x - 3y + z = -1$
$w - 3x + 2y + 3z = -17$

Solution:

Step 1 Rewrite the system as a linear system with two variables.

$$\begin{array}{r} 3w + 3x + 9y - 6z = 33 \\ \underline{-3w + 6x - 9y + 3z = -3} \\ 9x \quad\quad - 3z = 30 \end{array}$$

Add 3 times Equation 3 to Equation 1 (to eliminate w and y).

$$\begin{array}{r} 2w + 5x + 4y - 2z = 20 \\ \underline{-2w + 6x - 4y - 6z = 34} \\ 11x \quad\quad - 8z = 54 \end{array}$$

Add –2 times Equation 4 to Equation 2 (to eliminate w and y).

Step 2 Solve the new linear system for both its variables.

$$\begin{array}{r} 72x - 24z = 240 \\ \underline{-33x + 24z = -162} \\ 39x \quad\quad\quad = 78 \\ x = 2 \\ z = -4 \end{array}$$

Add –3 times the new Equation 2 to 8 times the new Equation 1.
Substitute x to solve for z.

Step 3 Substitute x and z into any of the two original equations. Solve for the remaining variables using elimination.

The solution is $w = 1$, $x = 2$, $y = 0$, and $z = -4$ or $(1, 2, 0, -4)$.

In Exercises 1–3, solve the system of equations using the elimination method.

1. $2w + 4x + 2y - z = 1$
$4w + 3x + 8y - 3z = 19$
$-w - 5x - y + 3z = 8$
$w + 2x + 2y - z = 2$

2. $5w + x + 2y - 2z = -13$
$3w + 2x - 3y - z = -7$
$3w - 2x - 3y + 4z = 25$
$w + 4x - y - 2z = -19$

3. $6w + x + 6y - 9z = 10$
$3w + 7x - y + 9z = 34$
$w + 5x + 4y - 3z = -5$
$2w - x - 3y - 3z = -9$

Name_____ Date _____

1.4 Puzzle Time

Did You Hear About...

A	B	C	D	E	F
G	H	I	J		

Complete each exercise. Find the answer in the answer column. Write the word under the answer in the box containing the exercise letter.

(−2, −3, 3) TALLEST		**Infinite solutions** SIX
(−5, 4, −3) MEASURED		**(0, 0, −3)** HORSE
(1, 3, −3) FEET		**no solution** WHO
(1, 3, 1) LIVING		**(−1, 0, 2)** THE
(5, −1, −4) TEN		**(1, 4, −2)** INCHES

Solve the system using the elimination method.

A. $-2x - 6y - 2z = -2$
$3x + 2y + 5z = 7$
$-3x - 3y + 3z = 9$

B. $-x - 5y - 5z = 2$
$4x - 5y + 4z = 19$
$x + 5y - z = -20$

C. $4x - 4y + 4z = -4$
$4x + y - 2z = 5$
$-3x - 3y - 4z = -16$

D. $x - 6y + 4z = -12$
$x + y - 4z = 12$
$2x + 2y + 5z = -15$

Solve the system using the substitution method.

E. $5x + 4y - 6z = -24$
$-2y + 2z = 0$
$y - z = 2$

F. $-4x + 2z = 14$
$-x + y - z = 12$
$-2x - 4z = 22$

G. $6x - 9y + z = -12$
$2x - 3y - z = -4$
$-8x + 12y = 16$

H. $3x - 3y = -6$
$3x + 3y + z = 9$
$-4x + 5y + z = 8$

Solve the system using the method of your choice.

I. $5x - 4y + 2z = 21$
$-x - 5y + 6z = -24$
$-x - 4y + 5z = -21$

J. $4x - 3y + z = -10$
$2x + y + 3z = 0$
$-x + 2y - 5z = 17$

Chapter 1 Cumulative Review

In Exercises 1–12, tell whether the value is a solution of the inequality.

1. $2x + 8 \geq 13;\ x = 4$

2. $7 - 3x < 9;\ x = 1$

3. $13 - 2x \leq 10;\ x = -4$

4. $1 + 5x < 2;\ x = -4$

5. $-6 < x + 9 < 3;\ x = 3$

6. $-7 \leq 5 - x \leq 11;\ x = -2$

7. $1 \leq 8 - 2x \leq 16;\ x = -9$

8. $3 < 4x + 3 \leq 18;\ x = 2$

9. $5x - 7 > 3$ or $-4x - 1 \leq 6;\ x = -2$

10. $4 - 2x < -1$ or $7x < 28;\ x = -2$

11. $\frac{1}{2}x + 6 \geq 8$ or $\frac{1}{4}x - 2 \leq 2;\ x = 4$

12. $\frac{1}{3}x - 1 < 2$ or $\frac{1}{6}x + 5 \geq 3;\ x = 12$

13. Your slowest time to run a mile is 12 minutes and your fastest time is 10.5 minutes. Write a compound inequality to represent your running times.

14. You plan on visiting relatives. Your vehicle gets about 21 miles per gallon in the city and 25 miles per gallon on the highway.

   a. Write a compound inequality to represent the range of gas mileages for your vehicle.

   b. Your relative lives in the city 31.5 miles away. How many gallons of gasoline do you use on the trip?

   c. To visit another relative who lives 98 miles away, you travel 10.5 miles through the city and 87.5 miles on the highway. How many gallons of gasoline do you use on the trip?

In Exercises 15–28, solve the equation. Check your solution.

15. $2z + 8 = 15 - 5z$

16. $-4c + 13 = -11 + 2c$

17. $2(y - 3) - 4 = 8 + 5y$

18. $-4(2 - h) - 3 = 6 + 3(2h + 1)$

19. $\frac{1}{3}p - 5 = -2$

20. $-\frac{1}{7}b - 4 = 3$

21. $\frac{5}{2}r + \frac{3}{4} = \frac{3}{8} - \frac{1}{2}r$

22. $\frac{2}{3}s + \frac{1}{3} = \frac{3}{4}s - \frac{1}{4}$

23. $|f - 4| = 9$

24. $|-3k + 8| = 17$

25. $|2g + 2| - 1 = 6$

26. $|4v - 1| + 3 = 7$

27. $2|5 - w| - 9 = -1$

28. $4|3d - 1| + 4 = 12$

Chapter 1 **Cumulative Review** (continued)

In Exercises 29–37, solve the equation for y.

29. $3x + y = 2$

30. $9x - y = 8$

31. $2y - 4x = -2$

32. $2y + x = 5$

33. $\frac{1}{3}y + 2x = 4$

34. $x - \frac{1}{5}y = 6$

35. $4x = 3y - 5$

36. $2x - y + 8 = 0$

37. $x + 5xy = 7$

In Exercises 38–41, write an expression that represents the situation.

38. You spend $108 on x DVDs. How much does each DVD cost?

39. You have $55 and spend x dollars. How much money do you have left?

40. You have $32 and your friend loans you x dollars. How much money do you now have?

41. On a boat you cruise 40 miles per hour for x hours. How many miles do you cruise?

42. A taxi company charges a flat fee of $2.50 and then $2.25 per mile for a ride.

    a. Write an expression to show the cost of traveling m miles.

    b. How much does it cost to travel 9 miles?

    c. How much does it cost to travel 11 miles?

    d. You travel 13 miles and give the driver a $3 tip. How much do you spend?

43. Apples cost $2.12 per pound at the local grocery store.

    a. Write an expression for the cost of buying p pounds of apples.

    b. How much does it cost to buy 5 pounds of apples?

    c. You buy 6 pounds of apples and pay with a $20 bill. How much change do you receive?

    d. How many pounds of apples can you buy with $20?

44. A cell phone company charges a monthly fee of $35 and $0.21 per minute for any time used over 400 minutes. Your bill this month is $40.46. How many minutes over the allotted 400 minutes did you use?

45. A cell phone company charges a monthly fee of $35 and $7.50 per gigabyte for any data used over 4 gigabytes. Your bill this month is $57.50. How many gigabytes over the allotted 4 gigabytes did you use?

Chapter 1 **Cumulative Review** (continued)

In Exercises 46–53, tell which property is illustrated by the statement.

46. $4(5 + 2) = 4(5) + 4(2)$

47. $24 + (-24) = 0$

48. $3 \bullet 8 = 8 \bullet 3$

49. $(-4 \bullet 9) \bullet 7 = -4 \bullet (9 \bullet 7)$

50. $13 + 25 = 25 + 13$

51. $8 + (13 + 15) - (8 + 13) + 15$

52. $14 + 0 = 14$

53. $13 \bullet 1 = 13$

In Exercises 54–57, draw a scatter plot of the data.

54.

x	3	4	6	9	12
f(x)	17	15	15	12	9

55.

x	10	12	14	17	18
f(x)	2	5	8	9	10

56.

x	1	1	2	3	5
f(x)	4	5	8	11	14

57.

x	5	7	8	8	11
f(x)	26	24	21	19	17

In Exercises 58–69, solve the system.

58. $x + y = 4$
$-x + 2y = -13$

59. $2x + y = 17$
$-2x + y = 1$

60. $-x + 4y = -27$
$y = 3x - 4$

61. $x = 2y + 2$
$x - 2y = -1$

62. $\frac{1}{2}x - y = -8$
$3x + 2y = 8$

63. $3x - 3y = -12$
$-2x + 2y = -8$

64. $4y = 4x + 4$
$-x + y = -1$

65. $2x + 6y = 2$
$x = 3y + 13$

66. $y = 2x + 1$
$-4x + 2y = 2$

67. $x - 2y = -13$
$4x + 2y = 18$

68. $\frac{1}{4}x + 3y = 2$
$x + 12y = 8$

69. $-\frac{1}{2}x + y = -8$
$-3x + y = -3$

In Exercises 70–77, simplify the expression.

70. $(3a + 2)^2$

71. $(-b + 7)^2$

72. $(9 + 5c)^2$

73. $(8 - 3d)^2$

74. $(-4m + 4)^2$

75. $(-2n - 1)^2$

76. $(6 - 5p)^2$

77. $(q - 2)^2$

In Exercises 78–83, find the x- and the y-intercepts of the graph of the function.

78. $2x + 3y = 6$

79. $-x + 5y = 8$

80. $x - 6y = 7$

81. $-2x + 5 = 3y$

82. $\frac{1}{2}x + 4y = 2$

83. $\frac{1}{3}x = 6y + 3$

26 **Algebra 2**
Resources by Chapter

Chapter 1 **Cumulative Review** (continued)

In Exercises 84–91, write an equation of the line.

84. y-intercept: 3, slope: 2

85. y-intercept: -4, slope: 1

86. y-intercept: 1, slope: $-\frac{1}{4}$

87. y-intercept: -5, slope: $-\frac{3}{4}$

88. y-intercept: 0, slope: 4

89. y-intercept: $\frac{4}{5}$, slope: 0

90. y-intercept: $-\frac{1}{2}$, slope: $-\frac{2}{7}$

91. y-intercept: 2, slope: $\frac{2}{3}$

In Exercises 92–95, write a function g whose graph represents the indicated transformation of $f(x) = |x + 2| - 5$.

92. translation of 2 units up

93. translation of 3 units left

94. vertical stretch by a factor of 3

95. translation of 1 unit down

In Exercises 96–101, solve the system. Check your solution, if possible.

96. $x + y - z = -4$
$2x + 2y + 2z = 4$
$x + y + z = 2$

97. $x - y - z = -9$
$2x + 2y + z = 19$
$x + y - z = -1$

98. $x + y + z = 2$
$-3x - 3y - 3z = -6$
$2x + 2y + 2z = 4$

99. $x - y + z = 13$
$-2x + 2y - 2z = -18$
$3x - 3y + 3z = 36$

100. $-x + y + z = 1$
$2x + 2y - 2z = -18$
$x - 3y + z = 11$

101. $-x - y + z = 10$
$-2x + 2y - 2z = -24$
$x - y + 3z = 26$

102. You are decorating a rectangular picture frame. The length is twice the width. The perimeter of the rectangular picture frame is 18 inches. What are the dimensions of the picture frame?

103. You are making trail mix for an upcoming camping trip. Recipe A requires 3 pounds of peanuts, 2 pounds of raisins, 2.5 pounds of pretzels, and 1.5 pounds of chocolate candy pieces. Recipe B requires 4.5 pounds of peanuts, 1.5 pounds of raisins, 2 pounds of pretzels, and 1.5 pounds of chocolate candy pieces.

   a. You make one batch of each trail mix recipe. How many pounds of each ingredient do you need?

   b. Which recipe weighs more?

   c. You make two batches of each trail mix recipe. How many more pounds of peanuts will you need for Recipe B than for Recipe A?

104. The school spirit store charges $15 for a T-shirt, $25 for a sweatshirt, and $3.50 for a large sticker. Your friend buys two T-shirts, one sweatshirt, and four large stickers. You buy three T-shirts and five large stickers. Who spends more money at the spirit store? How much more?

Chapter 2

Name_____ Date _____

Dear Family,

How warm does the temperature get during the summer months in the city or town where you live? How cold does the temperature get during the winter months? It may surprise you how often you can use a quadratic function to model naturally occurring data such as average monthly high and low temperatures in a city.

Use an almanac or the Internet to research information about the weather in the city or town where you live. Then complete each table below. For each table, let $x = 1$ represent January, $x = 2$ represent February, and so on.

Month, x	1	2	3	4	5	6	7	8	9	10	11	12
Average high temperature (°F), y												

Month, x	1	2	3	4	5	6	7	8	9	10	11	12
Average low temperature (°F), y												

- Make a scatter plot of each data set. Do you notice any patterns? Does the data show a quadratic relationship? How do you know?

- If possible, use a graphing calculator to find a quadratic function that models each set of data. Graph the function on your scatter plot. Is it a good fit? Explain.

- Why do you think average monthly temperature data usually follows a quadratic pattern?

- If average global temperatures are going to increase over time, then how do you think these changes will affect your graphs?

Choose a city you would like to visit in the United States. Then complete the tables and answer the questions above for the city you chose. Compare the graphs to the ones that represent your city. Do the greatest average monthly temperatures occur in the same month?

Think of other naturally occurring data that may follow a quadratic pattern. Does average monthly precipitation or average monthly snowfall follow a quadratic pattern?

Nombre _____ Fecha _____

Capítulo 2 — Funciones cuadráticas

Estimada familia:

¿Cuán cálida es la temperatura durante los meses de verano en la ciudad donde viven? ¿Cuán fría es la temperatura durante los meses de invierno? Quizás les sorprenda saber con qué frecuencia usan una función cuadrática para representar datos que surgen naturalmente, tal como el promedio de temperaturas altas y bajas en una ciudad.

Consulten en un almanaque o Internet para investigar sobre el tiempo en la ciudad donde viven. Luego, completen la siguiente tabla. Para cara tabla, imaginen que $x = 1$ representa enero, $x = 2$ representa febrero, etc.

Mes, x	1	2	3	4	5	6	7	8	9	10	11	12
Temperatura alta promedio (°F), y												

Mes, x	1	2	3	4	5	6	7	8	9	10	11	12
Temperatura baja promedio (°F), y												

- Hagan un diagrama de dispersión para cada conjunto de datos. ¿Observan algún patrón? ¿Los datos muestran una relación cuadrática? ¿Cómo lo saben?

- Si es posible, usen una calculadora gráfica para hallar una función cuadrática que represente cada conjunto de datos. Hagan una gráfica de la función en su diagrama de dispersión. ¿Es un buen ajuste? Expliquen.

- ¿Por qué creen que los datos sobre la temperatura mensual promedio sigue un patrón cuadrático?

- Si las temperaturas promedio globales van a aumentar con el transcurso del tiempo, entonces, ¿cómo creen que estos cambios afectarán a sus gráficas?

Elijan una ciudad de Estados Unidos que les gustaría visitar. Luego, completen las tablas y respondan las preguntas mencionadas anteriormente sobre la ciudad que eligieron. Comparen las gráficas con las gráficas que representan a su ciudad. ¿Las temperaturas promedio más altas ocurren en el mismo mes?

Piensen en otros datos que surgen naturalmente que tal vez sigan un patrón cuadrático. ¿La precipitación mensual promedio o la nevada mensual promedio siguen un patrón cuadrático?

2.1 Start Thinking

Make a table of values and use it to graph the following functions on the same coordinate plane. Use the same x-values for each function.

$f(x) = x^2$

$f(x) = (x - 1)^2$

$f(x) = 2x^2$

$f(x) = x^2 + 1$

Describe how the graphs of the last three functions differ from the graph of $f(x) = x^2$.

2.1 Warm Up

Multiply.

1. $(3x - 2)(2x - 4)$

2. $(5x + 2)(4x + 1)$

3. $(4x + y)(2x - 3y)$

4. $3a(4a + 1)$

5. $(4x + 1)(5x - 2)$

6. $(5y + 4)(3y + 2)$

2.1 Cumulative Review Warm Up

Write a function g whose graph represents the indicated transformation of the graph f.

1. $f(x) = x + 6$; translation 3 units right

2. $f(x) = x - 3$; translation 1 unit left

3. $f(x) = |5x - 2| - 3$; translation 1 unit down

Name _____ Date _____

In Exercises 1–6, describe the transformation of $f(x) = x^2$ represented by g.
Then graph each function.

1. $g(x) = x^2 - 2$
2. $g(x) = x^2 + 1$
3. $g(x) = (x + 1)^2$

4. $g(x) = (x - 2)^2$
5. $g(x) = (x - 5)^2$
6. $g(x) = (x + 2)^2 - 1$

In Exercises 7–9, describe the transformation of $f(x) = x^2$ represented by g. Then
graph each function.

7. $g(x) = -2x^2$
8. $g(x) = (-2x)^2$
9. $g(x) = \frac{1}{4}x^2$

10. Describe and correct the error in analyzing the graph of $f(x) = -\frac{1}{3}x^2$.

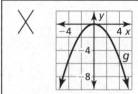

The graph of g is a reflection in the
x-axis, followed by a vertical stretch
by a factor of $\frac{1}{3}$ of the graph of the
parent quadratic function.

In Exercises 11 and 12, describe the transformation of the graph of the parent
quadratic function. Then identify the vertex.

11. $f(x) = 2(x + 3)^2 + 2$
12. $f(x) = -5x^2 - 1$

In Exercises 13 and 14, write a rule for g described by the transformations of the
graph of f. Then identify the vertex.

13. $f(x) = x^2$; vertical stretch by a factor of 3 and a reflection in the x-axis, followed
by a translation 3 units down

14. $f(x) = 4x^2 + 5$; horizontal stretch by a factor of 2 and a translation 2 units up,
followed by a reflection in the x-axis

15. Let the graph of g be a translation 4 units down and 3 units right, followed by a
horizontal shrink by a factor of $\frac{1}{2}$ of the graph of $f(x) = x^2$.

a. Identify the values of a, h, and k. Write the transformed function in
vertex form.

b. Suppose the horizontal shrink was performed first, followed by the
translations. Identify the values of a, h, and k, and write the transformed
function in vertex form.

2.1 Practice B

In Exercises 1–6, describe the transformation of $f(x) = x^2$ represented by g. Then graph each function.

1. $g(x) = x^2 + 3$

2. $g(x) = (x + 5)^2$

3. $g(x) = (x + 6)^2 - 4$

4. $g(x) = (x - 1)^2 + 5$

5. $g(x) = (x - 4)^2 + 3$

6. $g(x) = (x + 8)^2 - 2$

In Exercises 7–9, describe the transformation of $f(x) = x^2$ represented by g. Then graph each function.

7. $g(x) = -\left(\frac{1}{2}x\right)^2$

8. $g(x) = \frac{1}{3}x^2 + 2$

9. $g(x) = \frac{1}{3}(x + 1)^2$

In Exercises 10 and 11, describe the transformation of the graph of the parent quadratic function. Then identify the vertex.

10. $f(x) = -3(x + 6)^2 - 4$

11. $f(x) = \frac{1}{3}(x - 2)^2 + 1$

In Exercises 12 and 13, write a rule for g described by the transformations of the graph of f. Then identify the vertex.

12. $f(x) = x^2$; vertical shrink by a factor of $\frac{1}{2}$ and a reflection in the y-axis, followed by a translation 2 units left

13. $f(x) = (x + 4)^2 + 2$; horizontal shrink by a factor of $\frac{1}{3}$ and a translation 2 units up, followed by a reflection in the x-axis

14. Justify each step in writing a function g based on the transformations of $f(x) = 4x^2 - 3x$.

translation 3 units up followed by a reflection in the y-axis

$h(x) = f(x) + 3$	
$= 4x^2 - 3x + 3$	
$g(x) = h(-x)$	
$= 4x^2 + 3x + 3$	

2.1 Enrichment and Extension

Transformations of Quadratic Functions

Displayed below are 10 parabolas.

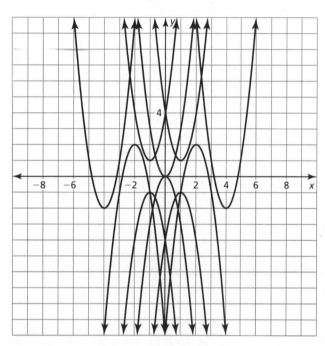

The equations for three of the graphs are as follows.

$$y = -3(x - 1)^2 - 1$$
$$y = 3x^2$$
$$y = 3(x + 4)^2 - 2$$

Find the equations of the other seven parabolas with the help of a graphing calculator.

2.1 Puzzle Time

What Is The Most Densely Populated Country On The Mainland Of The Americas?

Write the letter of each answer in the box containing the exercise number.

Describe the transformation of $f(x) = x^2$ represented by g.

1. $g(x) = -2x^2$

2. $g(x) = (x - 1)^2$

3. $g(x) = x^2 - 1$

4. $g(x) = (x + 1)^2$

5. $g(x) = \frac{1}{2}x^2 - 2$

6. $g(x) = (x - 2)^2 - 1$

Write a rule for g described by the transformations of the graph of f.

7. $f(x) = x^2$; vertical stretch by a factor of 2 and a reflection in the x-axis, followed by a translation 3 units down

8. $f(x) = x^2$; vertical shrink by a factor of $\frac{1}{2}$, followed by a translation 3 units left

9. $f(x) = 4x^2 + 10$; horizontal stretch by a factor of 2, followed by a translation 3 units up

10. $f(x) = (x - 2)^2 - 8$; horizontal shrink by a factor of $\frac{1}{2}$ and a translation 5 units down, followed by a reflection in the x-axis

Answers

O. $g(x) = x^2 + 13$

L. translation 1 unit right

R. $g(x) = -(2x - 2)^2 + 13$

S. translation 1 unit down

V. translation 2 units right followed by a translation 1 unit down

L. vertical shrink by a factor of $\frac{1}{2}$ followed by a translation 2 units down

E. reflection in the x-axis and a vertical stretch by a factor of 2

A. $g(x) = -2x^2 - 3$

D. $g(x) = \frac{1}{2}(x + 3)^2$

A. translation 1 unit left

1	2		3	4	5	6	7	8	9	10

2.2 Start Thinking

Complete the table for the function $f(x) = |x|$. Graph the values from the table on a piece of graph paper.

x	-2	-1	0	1	2
$f(x)$					

What is the shape of the graph? Are opposite integers the same distance from the y-axis on the graph? Is this graph symmetric? Why or why not?

2.2 Warm Up

Give the coordinates of the image of point $P(-5, 3)$ after each reflection.

1. reflection in the y-axis
2. reflection in the x-axis
3. reflection in the line through $(5, -6)$ and $(8, -6)$
4. reflection in the line through $(-1, -1)$ and $(-1, -2)$

2.2 Cumulative Review Warm Up

Determine if the data show a linear relationship. If so, write an equation of a line of fit. Estimate y when $x = 20$ and explain its context in the situation.

1.

Minutes jogging, x	2	5	10	15
Calories burned, y	22	55	110	165

2.

Years, x	10	12	17	21
Height (feet), y	4.2	5.0	6.0	6.1

2.2 Practice A

In Exercises 1–12, graph the function. Label the vertex and axis of symmetry.

1. $f(x) = (x - 2)^2$

2. $f(x) = (x + 1)^2$

3. $g(x) = (x + 2)^2 + 4$

4. $h(x) = (x - 3)^2 - 2$

5. $y = -3(x - 1)^2 + 3$

6. $f(x) = 4(x + 2)^2 - 1$

7. $y = x^2 - 2x + 1$

8. $y = 3x^2 + 6x + 1$

9. $y = -3x^2 + 6x + 4$

10. $f(x) = -x^2 + 6x - 3$

11. $g(x) = -x^2 + 2$

12. $f(x) = 5x^2 - 4$

13. Explain why you cannot use the axes of symmetry to distinguish between the quadratic functions $y = 3x^2 + 12x + 1$ and $y = x^2 + 4x + 5$.

14. Which function represents the parabola with the narrowest graph? Explain your reasoning.

    A. $y = x^2 + 3$

    B. $y = 0.5x^2 - 2$

    C. $y = 3(x + 2)^2$

    D. $y = -2x^2 + 1$

In Exercises 15–18, find the minimum or maximum value of the function. Describe the domain and range of the function, and where the function is increasing and decreasing.

15. $y = 5x^2 + 2$

16. $y = 4x^2 - 3$

17. $y = -x^2 + 4x - 1$

18. $f(x) = -2x^2 + 4x + 9$

19. The number of customers in a grocery store is modeled by the function $y = -x^2 + 10x + 50$, where y is the number of customers in the store and x is the number of hours after 7:00 A.M.

    a. At what time is the maximum number of customers in the store?

    b. How many customers are in the store at the time in part (a)?

2.2 Practice B

In Exercises 1–12, graph the function. Label the vertex and axis of symmetry.

1. $f(x) = -3(x - 2)^2 - 4$

2. $f(x) = 3(x + 1)^2 + 5$

3. $g(x) = -\frac{1}{2}(x + 3)^2 + 2$

4. $h(x) = \frac{1}{2}(x - 2)^2 - 1$

5. $y = 0.6(x - 2)^2$

6. $f(x) = 0.25x^2 - 1$

7. $y = -x^2 + 8$

8. $y = 7x^2 + 2$

9. $y = 1.5x^2 - 6x + 3$

10. $f(x) = 0.5x^2 + 3x - 1$

11. $y = \frac{5}{2}x^2 - 5x + 1$

12. $f(x) = -\frac{3}{2}x^2 - 6x - 4$

13. A quadratic function is decreasing to the left of $x = 3$ and increasing to the right of $x = 3$. Will the vertex be the highest or lowest point on the graph of the parabola? Explain.

14. The graph of which function has the same axis of symmetry as the graph of $y = 2x^2 - 8x + 3$? Explain your reasoning.

   A. $y = -4x^2 + 16x - 5$

   B. $y = 2x^2 + 8x + 7$

   C. $y = 3x^2 - 6x + 7$

   D. $y = -6x^2 + 10x - 1$

In Exercises 15–18, find the minimum or maximum value of the function. Describe the domain and range of the function, and where the function is increasing and decreasing.

15. $y = 3x^2 + 12$

16. $y = -x^2 - 6x$

17. $y = -\frac{1}{3}x^2 - 2x + 3$

18. $f(x) = \frac{1}{2}x^2 + 3x + 7$

19. The height of a bridge is given by $y = -3x^2 + x$, where y is the height of the bridge (in miles) and x is the number of miles from the base of the bridge.

   a. How far from the base of the bridge does the maximum height occur?

   b. What is the maximum height of the bridge?

2.2 Enrichment and Extension

Characteristics of Quadratic Functions

Example: Write the quadratic function in standard form that has a vertex at $(2, 5)$ and passes through the point $(3, 7)$.

Solution:

$y = a(x - h)^2 + k$	Write the vertex form of a quadratic function.
$y = a(x - 2)^2 + 5$	Substitute in the vertex for h and k.
$7 = a(3 - 2)^2 + 5$	Substitute the other point for x and y.
$a = 2$	Solve for a.
$y = 2(x - 2)^2 + 5$	Substitute h, k, and a.
$y = 2x^2 - 8x + 13$	Simplify.

In Exercises 1–6, write the quadratic function in standard form.

1. vertex $(1, -2)$ and passes through point $(3, 10)$

2. vertex $(-1, -2)$ and passes through point $(-4, 7)$

3. vertex $(-2, 9)$ and passes through point $(1, -9)$

4. vertex $(-1, 0)$ and passes through point $(-3, -12)$

5. vertex $(1, 6)$ and passes through point $(2, 5)$

6. vertex $(-2, 0)$ and passes through point $(2, 8)$

7. Could there be a quadratic function that has an undefined axis of symmetry? Why or why or not?

8. The graph of a quadratic function has a vertex at $(3, -6)$. One point on the graph is $(7, 10)$. What is another point on the graph? Explain how you found the other point.

2.2 Puzzle Time

What Is Roz Savage Famous For?

1	2	3	4	5	6
7	8	9	10	11	12

Complete each exercise. Find the answer in the answer column. Write the word under the answer in the box containing the exercise number.

0 minimum **WOMAN**
2 maximum **THE**
$(-1, -9.5)$ $x = -1$ **ROWER**
$f(x) =$ $-2(x + 1)^2 - 1$ **OCEANS**
$f(x) = x^2 - 2$ **ROW**
$(1, -4)$ $x = 1$ **BRITISH**

Find the vertex and axis of symmetry of the function.

1. $f(x) = 9x^2 - 3$ 2. $y = -x^2 + 2x - 5$

3. $g(x) = -0.5x^2 - x - 10$ 4. $f(x) = -2x^2 + 8x - 1$

Find the minimum or maximum value of the function.

5. $f(x) = -3x^2 + 12x - 10$ 6. $y = -x^2 + 8$

7. $g(x) = x^2 - 2x + 1$ 8. $y = 2x^2 - 20x$

Match the graph with its function.

9. 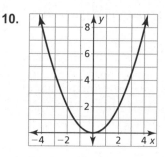   10.

11. 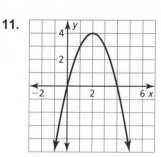   12.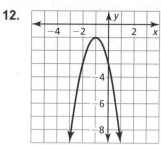

8 maximum **FIRST**
$f(x) =$ $-(x - 2)^2 + 4$ **THREE**
-50 minimum **TO**
$f(x) = \frac{1}{2}x^2$ **ACROSS**
$(0, -3)$ $x = 0$ **THIS**
$(2, 7)$ $x = 2$ **WAS**

On a piece of graph paper, sketch the graph of $y = \frac{1}{2}x^2$.

Draw the line $y = -\frac{1}{2}$ and mark point $P\left(0, \frac{1}{2}\right)$.

Mark any point A on the graph of $y = \frac{1}{2}x^2$. Use a ruler to measure the distance $\left(\text{to the nearest } \frac{1}{4}\text{-inch}\right)$ from point A to point P. Can you find a spot on the line $y = -\frac{1}{2}$ that is the same distance from point A? Try any three additional points B, C, and D for verification. Do you believe this method will always work? Why or why not?

2.3 **Warm Up**

Find the distance between the points. If necessary, round to the nearest tenth.

1. $(7, -3), (13, 7)$ **2.** $(-1, -5), (-4, -4)$

3. $(6, -11), (6, 7)$ **4.** $(-3, 0), (4, -2)$

5. $(-15, -8), (-3, -4)$ **6.** $(-5, 7), (-2, -7)$

2.3 **Cumulative Review Warm Up**

Use the elimination method to solve the system.

1. $4x + y - 2z = 0$
$2x - 3y + 3z = 9$
$-6x - 2y + z = 0$

2. $3x - y + 3z = 8$
$x - 4y - 3z = -18$
$6x - 6y - 2z = 3$

Name _____ Date _____

2.3 Practice A

In Exercises 1–6, use the Distance Formula to write an equation of the parabola.

1. focus: $(0, 2)$

   directrix: $y = -2$

2. focus: $(0, -3)$

   directrix: $y = 3$

3. focus: $(0, -6)$

   directrix: $y = 6$

4. vertex: $(0, 0)$

   directrix: $y = 4$

5. vertex: $(0, 0)$

   focus: $(0, -1)$

6. vertex: $(0, 0)$

   directrix: $y = 2$

7. Which of the given characteristics describe parabolas that open up? Explain your reasoning.

A. focus: $(0, 3)$

   directrix: $y = -3$

B. focus: $(0, -5)$

   directrix: $y = 5$

C. focus: $(0, -10)$

   directrix: $y = 10$

In Exercises 8–10, identify the focus, directrix, and axis of symmetry of the parabola. Graph the equation.

8. $y = \frac{1}{12}x^2$

9. $y = -\frac{1}{16}x^2$

10. $x = \frac{1}{8}y^2$

11. The cross section (with units in inches) of a parabolic satellite dish can be modeled by the equation $y = \frac{1}{48}x^2$. How far is the receiver from the vertex of the cross section? Explain.

In Exercises 12–17, write an equation of the parabola with the given characteristics.

12. focus: $(2, 0)$

   directrix: $x = -2$

13. focus: $(-4, 0)$

   directrix: $x = 4$

14. focus: $\left(0, \frac{3}{4}\right)$

   directrix: $y = -\frac{3}{4}$

15. directrix: $x = -6$

   vertex: $(0, 0)$

16. focus: $(0, 2)$

   vertex: $(0, 0)$

17. directrix: $x = 1$

   vertex: $(0, 0)$

In Exercises 18–21, identify the vertex, focus, directrix, and axis of symmetry of the parabola. Describe the transformations of the graph of the standard equation with vertex $(0, 0)$ and $p = 1$.

18. $y = \frac{1}{12}(x - 1)^2 + 3$

19. $y = -\frac{1}{8}(x + 5)^2 - 2$

20. $x = \frac{1}{4}(y + 4)^2 + 2$

21. $y = -\frac{1}{28}(x + 6)^2 + 10$

Name_____ Date_____

2.3 Practice B

In Exercises 1–6, use the Distance Formula to write an equation of the parabola.

1. focus: $(0, 5)$

    directrix: $y = -5$

2. focus: $(0, -6)$

    directrix: $y = 6$

3. focus: $(0, 4)$

    directrix: $y = -4$

4. vertex: $(0, 0)$

    directrix: $y = 8$

5. vertex: $(0, 0)$

    focus: $(0, -7)$

6. vertex: $(0, 0)$

    directrix: $y = -2$

In Exercises 7–12, identify the focus, directrix, and axis of symmetry of the parabola. Graph the equation.

7. $y = -\frac{1}{32}x^2$

8. $x = \frac{1}{4}y^2$

9. $y^2 = 12x$

10. $-x^2 = 36y$

11. $8x^2 + 2y = 0$

12. $2x^2 - y = 0$

In Exercises 13 and 14, write an equation of the parabola shown.

13.

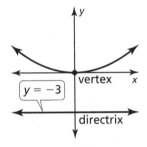

14.

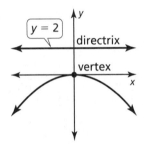

In Exercises 15–20, write an equation of the parabola with the given characteristics.

15. focus: $\left(0, -\frac{1}{4}\right)$

    directrix: $y = \frac{1}{4}$

16. focus: $(-12, 0)$

    directrix: $x = 12$

17. focus: $\left(\frac{3}{5}, 0\right)$

    directrix: $x = -\frac{3}{5}$

18. vertex: $(0, 0)$

    directrix: $y = \frac{2}{3}$

19. vertex: $(0, 0)$

    focus: $\left(-\frac{3}{4}, 0\right)$

20. vertex: $(0, 0)$

    directrix: $x = -\frac{1}{3}$

In Exercises 21–24, identify the vertex, focus, directrix, and axis of symmetry of the parabola. Describe the transformations of the graph of the standard equation with vertex $(0, 0)$ and $p = 1$.

21. $x = -\frac{1}{16}(y - 2)^2 - 3$

22. $y = 8(x + 2)^2 - 1$

23. $x = 5(y + 3)^2 + 6$

24. $y = -\frac{1}{32}(x + 1)^2 + 9$

2.3 Enrichment and Extension

Focus of a Parabola

Write an equation of the parabola with vertex at (0, 0) and the given directrix or focus.

1. focus: $\left(\dfrac{1}{a^2}, 0 \right)$

2. directrix: $y = -\dfrac{2}{n}$

3. focus: $\left(0, \dfrac{3}{b} \right)$

4. directrix: $x = -\dfrac{1}{6n}$

5. Given: Equation $y = x^2$ and parallel line segments $\overline{RS}$ and $\overline{OT}$, where
   $R = \left(r, r^2 \right)$, $S = \left(s, s^2 \right)$, $T = \left(t, t^2 \right)$, and O is the origin. Prove that $r + s = t$.

6. Create another parallel line segment UV, where U and V are two other points on the parabola.

Prove that the midpoints of all three line segments lie on the same line.

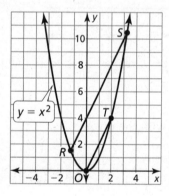

Name_____ Date _____

2.3 Puzzle Time

What National Park In The United States Is Known For Its 10,000 Hot Springs And Geysers?

Write the letter of each answer in the box containing the exercise number.

Use the Distance Formula to write an equation of the parabola.

1. focus: $(4, 0)$
   directrix: $x = -4$

2. directrix: $y = 2$
   vertex: $(0, 0)$

3. focus: $(0, -8)$
   directrix: $y = 8$

4. directrix: $y = -5$
   vertex: $(0, 5)$

5. focus: $(0, -1)$
   vertex: $(0, 0)$

6. focus: $(0, -1.5)$
   vertex: $(0, 0)$

Identify the focus, directrix, and axis of symmetry of the parabola.

7. $y = \frac{1}{6}x^2$

8. $y = -\frac{1}{9}x^2$

9. $x = \frac{1}{3}y^2$

10. $x = -\frac{1}{16}y^2$

11. $10x^2 - 5y = 0$

12. $20x^2 - y = 0$

13. $y = (x + 1)^2 - 4$

14. $x = -\frac{1}{2}(y - 5)^2 + 1$

15. $-x^2 = 24y$

Answers

W. $y = -\dfrac{x^2}{6}$

A. focus: $(-1, -3.75)$ directrix: $y = -4.25$
   axis of symmetry: $x = -1$

Y. $x = \dfrac{y^2}{16}$

T. focus: $(-0, -2.25)$ directrix: $y = 2.25$
   axis of symmetry: $x = 0$

E. $y = -\dfrac{x^2}{8}$ O. $y = -\dfrac{x^2}{4}$

S. focus: $(0, 1.5)$ directrix: $y = -1.5$
   axis of symmetry: $x = 0$

K. focus: $(0, -6)$ directrix: $y = 6$
   axis of symmetry: $x = 0$

O. focus: $(0.75, 0)$ directrix: $x = -0.75$
   axis of symmetry: $y = 0$

L. $y = \dfrac{x^2}{40} + 5$

N. focus: $(-4, 0)$ directrix: $x = 4$
   axis of symmetry: $y = 0$

E. focus: $(0, 0.125)$ directrix: $y = -0.125$
   axis of symmetry: $x = 0$

L. $y = -\dfrac{x^2}{32}$

P. focus: $(0, 0.0125)$ directrix: $y = -0.0125$
   axis of symmetry: $x = 0$

R. focus: $(0.5, 5)$ directrix: $x = 1.5$
   axis of symmetry: $y = 5$

1	2	3	4	5	6	7	8	9	10	11		12	13	14	15

2.4 Start Thinking

Use the graph of the parabola $y = \frac{1}{4}(x - 4)^2$ to label the x- and y-axis and give the graph an appropriate title for a real-life situation. Then find y when $x = 25$ and describe what this signifies in terms of the labels you created.

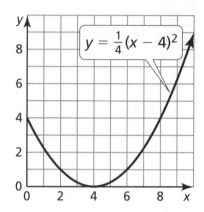

2.4 Warm Up

Write an equation of a line in point-slope form with the information given.

1. passes through: $(6, 0)$; slope: $-\frac{1}{6}$

2. passes through: $(1, 3)$; slope: $\frac{1}{2}$

3. passes through: $(4, -1)$; slope: -2

4. passes through: $(3, -3)$; slope: 3

5. passes through: $(4, -18)$; slope: $-\frac{1}{4}$

6. passes through: $(6, -1)$; slope: -3

2.4 Cumulative Review Warm Up

Use a graphing calculator to graph the function and its parent function. Then describe the transformation.

1. $f(x) = 4x - 1$

2. $h(x) = -2|x|$

3. $g(x) = 2x^2 + 7$

4. $f(x) = -(x - 2)^2 - \frac{2}{3}$

Name_____ Date_____

In Exercises 1–3, write an equation of the parabola in vertex form.

1. passes through $(6, 4)$ and has vertex $(2, -3)$

2. passes through $(-3, -10)$ and has vertex $(3, -8)$

3. passes through $(0, -5)$ and has vertex $(-1, 4)$

In Exercises 4–6, write an equation of the parabola in intercept form.

4. x-intercepts of 10 and 6; passes through $(11, 8)$

5. x-intercepts of 2 and 8; passes through $(0, 3)$

6. x-intercepts of -14 and -2; passes through $(-16, -8)$

7. Use the parabola shown.

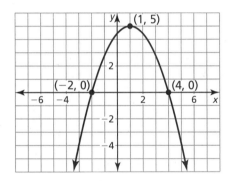

    a. Write an equation of the parabola in vertex form.

    b. Expand the equation in part (a) to the form $y = ax^2 + bx + c$.

    c. Write an equation of the parabola in intercept form.

    d. Expand the equation in part (c) to the form $y = ax^2 + bx + c$.

    e. Do both methods give an equation that represents the parabola? Which method did you find easier? Explain.

8. A basketball is thrown up in the air toward the hoop. The table shows the heights y (in feet) of the basketball after x seconds. Find the height of the basketball after 5 seconds. Round your answer to the nearest hundredth.

Time, x	0	9	18
Basketball height, y	6	10	6

2.4 Practice B

In Exercises 1–3, write an equation of the parabola in vertex form.

1. passes through $(4, -7)$ and has vertex $(1, -6)$

2. passes through $(5, -4)$ and has vertex $(-2, 5)$

3. passes through $(2, 2)$ and has vertex $(-1, -1)$

In Exercises 4–6, write an equation of the parabola in intercept form.

4. x-intercepts of 12 and 8; passes through $(9, 5)$

5. x-intercepts of -7 and -1; passes through $(1, 1)$

6. x-intercepts of -9 and 9; passes through $(0, 4)$

7. Describe and correct the error in writing an equation of the parabola.

> $\times$ Vertex: $(3, -5)$
>
> Passes through $(1, -7)$
>
> $$y = a(x - h)^2 + k$$
> $$-5 = a(3 - 1)^2 + (-7)$$
> $$-5 = 4a - 7$$
> $$2 = 4a$$
> $$\frac{1}{2} = a$$
>
> The equation is $y = \frac{1}{2}(x - 1) - 7$.

8. The graph shows the area y (in square feet) of rectangles that have a perimeter of 200 feet and a length of x feet.

   a. Interpret the meaning of the vertex in this situation.

   b. Write an equation for the parabola to predict the area of the rectangle when the length is 2 feet.

   c. Compare the average rates of change in the area from 0 to 50 feet and 50 to 100 feet.

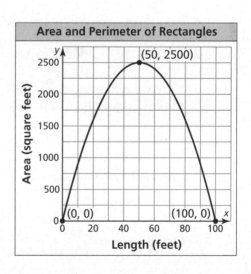

Area and Perimeter of Rectangles

2.4 Enrichment and Extension

Modeling with Quadratic Functions

In Exercises 1–5, analyze the differences in the outputs. Determine whether the data are linear or quadratic. Write an equation that fits the data. If quadratic, write the equation in (a) standard form and (b) vertex form, and (c) state the transformation from the parent function x^2.

1.

Altitude (1000 feet), x	1	1.5	2	2.5	3
Boiling water temperature (°F), y	210.3	209.4	208.5	207.6	206.7

2.

Time (seconds), x	1	2	3	4	5
Height (feet), y	73.5	78.4	73.5	58.8	34.3

3.

Units sold, x	1	2	3	4	5
Profit (thousands of dollars), y	39	60	75	84	87

4.

Depth (feet), x	0	10	20	30	40
Pressure (pounds per square inch), y	14.7	19.03	23.36	27.69	32.02

5.

Time (seconds), x	1	1.5	2	2.5	3
Height (feet), y	12	12.75	11	6.75	0

Name _____ Date _____

2.4 Puzzle Time

Don Featherstone Is Famous For Being The First To Make This Plastic Lawn Ornament In 1957.

Write the letter of each answer in the box containing the exercise number.

Write an equation of the parabola in vertex form.

1. passes through $(-5, 0)$ and has vertex $(-2, 1)$

2. passes through $(4, 10)$ and has vertex $(0, 0)$

3. passes through $(6, -1)$ and has vertex $(14, -20)$

4. passes through $(-5, -3)$ and has vertex $(7, 12)$

5. passes through $(9, 15)$ and has vertex $(-6, 21)$

6. passes through $(0, 0)$ and has vertex $(-10, -4)$

Write an equation of the parabola in intercept form.

7. x-intercepts of 10 and -2; passes through $(1, 4)$

8. x-intercepts of 9 and -3; passes through $(3, 4)$

9. x-intercepts of -5 and -1; passes through $(-10, 2)$

10. x-intercepts of 4 and 6; passes through $(2, 3)$

11. x-intercepts of -10 and 8; passes through $(-6, -4)$

12. x-intercepts of 0 and 4; passes through $(12, -8)$

Answers

I. $y = \frac{5}{8}x^2$

I. $y = \frac{2}{45}(x + 5)(x + 1)$

L. $y = \frac{1}{25}(x + 10)^2 - 4$

N. $y = \frac{19}{64}(x - 14)^2 - 20$

M. $y = -\frac{1}{9}(x - 9)(x + 3)$

F. $y = -\frac{2}{75}(x + 6)^2 + 21$

A. $y = -\frac{4}{27}(x - 10)(x + 2)$

N. $y = \frac{3}{8}(x - 4)(x - 6)$

G. $y = \frac{1}{14}(x + 10)(x - 8)$

K. $y = -\frac{5}{48}(x - 7)^2 + 12$

O. $y = -\frac{1}{12}x(x - 4)$

P. $y = -\frac{1}{9}(x + 2)^2 + 1$

1	2	3	4		5	6	7	8	9	10	11	12

Name_____ Date_____

In Exercises 1–16, solve the proportion.

1. $\dfrac{-6}{4} = \dfrac{x}{12}$

2. $\dfrac{5}{-3} = \dfrac{x}{9}$

3. $\dfrac{-19}{6} = \dfrac{38}{x}$

4. $\dfrac{7}{13} = \dfrac{-14}{x}$

5. $\dfrac{-7}{15} = \dfrac{-35}{x}$

6. $\dfrac{x}{4} = \dfrac{-1}{2}$

7. $\dfrac{-2}{x} = \dfrac{6}{-9}$

8. $\dfrac{-24}{36} = \dfrac{-8}{x}$

9. $\dfrac{3}{-5} = \dfrac{x}{-35}$

10. $\dfrac{12}{x} = \dfrac{60}{45}$

11. $\dfrac{x}{-2} = \dfrac{-80}{20}$

12. $\dfrac{4}{10} = \dfrac{x}{15}$

13. $\dfrac{13}{-17} = \dfrac{x}{-34}$

14. $\dfrac{5}{x} = \dfrac{-40}{56}$

15. $\dfrac{-2}{15} = \dfrac{x}{-60}$

16. $\dfrac{81}{x} = \dfrac{-9}{5}$

17. Your chemistry test has 64 questions. Your teacher rounds to the nearest whole percent.

   a. You have 57 correct answers. What percent of your answers are correct?

   b. You have 61 correct answers. What percent of your answers are correct?

   c. You want to earn at least an 85%. How many correct answers must you have?

   d. You want to earn at least a 93%. How many correct answers must you have?

18. Your English literature test has 28 questions. Your teacher rounds to the nearest whole percent.

   a. You have 25 correct answers. What percent of your answers are correct?

   b. You have 21 correct answers. What percent of your answers are correct?

   c. You want to earn at least an 85%. How many correct answers must you have?

   d. You want to earn at least a 93%. How many correct answers must you have?

   e. You want to earn at least a 77%. How many correct answers must you have?

19. You want to mix leftover yellow and blue paint to make green paint. The ratio to make the green paint is 2 parts yellow paint to 1 part blue paint. You have 6 cups of yellow paint. How many cups of blue paint do you need to make the green paint?

20. You want to make an environmentally friendly carpet cleaner using salt and white vinegar. The recipe ratio of white vinegar to salt is 8:2. You have one cup of white vinegar. How many tablespoons of salt are needed to make the carpet cleaner?

Chapter 2 **Cumulative Review** (continued)

In Exercises 21–35, find the distance between the two points. Round your answer to the nearest hundredth.

21. $(-4, 3)$ and $(-1, -2)$
22. $(3, 7)$ and $(-4, 6)$
23. $(-9, 8)$ and $(-11, 10)$

24. $(2, 5)$ and $(-1, -5)$
25. $(-9, -10)$ and $(1, 6)$
26. $(2, 3)$ and $(1, 10)$

27. $(8, 6)$ and $(-4, 3)$
28. $(-2, -9)$ and $(4, -5)$
29. $(12, -7)$ and $(9, 3)$

30. $(5, -8)$ and $(2, 11)$
31. $(5, 10)$ and $(-1, 2)$
32. $(-3, -2)$ and $(5, 4)$

33. $(7, -3)$ and $(-4, -8)$
34. $(8, 1)$ and $(-9, 2)$
35. $(-2, -1)$ and $(7, 7)$

In Exercises 36–44, find the x-intercept of the graph of the linear equation.

36. $y = \frac{3}{7}x - 5$
37. $y = 12x + 27$
38. $y = -7x + 39$

39. $y = 5(x + 2)$
40. $y = -7(x + 10)$
41. $y = 4(x - 8)$

42. $-6x + 5y = -30$
43. $11x + 7y = -33$
44. $14x - 8y = 28$

In Exercises 45–53, solve the equation for x.

45. $y = 8x + 24$
46. $y = \frac{1}{2}x + 3$
47. $y = -5x + 35$

48. $y = \frac{x - 7}{4}$
49. $y = \frac{-3x + 8}{-6}$
50. $y = \frac{4x + 5}{6}$

51. $3x - 6y = 30$
52. $-8x - 2y = 40$
53. $5x - 15y = -40$

In Exercises 54–65, solve the equation. Check for extraneous solutions.

54. $4\sqrt{x} - 2 = 0$
55. $-7\sqrt{x} - 5 = 0$
56. $6\sqrt{x + 10} + 3 = 0$

57. $-\sqrt{x - 9} - 8 = 0$
58. $3\sqrt{x + 8} - 6 = 4$
59. $7\sqrt{x - 5} - 4 = 3$

60. $\sqrt{2x} - 9 = 0$
61. $\sqrt{3x} - 10 = 0$
62. $\sqrt{4x} - 1 = 1$

63. $\sqrt{9x} - 7 = 3$
64. $\sqrt{2x - 4} = \sqrt{x + 4}$
65. $\sqrt{5x + 10} = \sqrt{x - 6}$

66. You are riding in a car and traveling at an average speed of 65 miles per hour. The destination is 325 miles away. How long does it take you to get there?

67. You are riding in a car and traveling at an average speed of 48 miles per hour. The destination is 108 miles away. How long does it take you to get there?

68. You are on a cruise ship that travels at an average speed of 24 knots per hour. The first port of call is 1449 miles away from where you set sail (1 knot is about 1.15 miles). How long does it take you to get there?

Chapter 2 **Cumulative Review** (continued)

In Exercises 69–83, write an equation for the line that passes through the points.

69. $(11, -2)$ and $(3, -1)$ **70.** $(12, 7)$ and $(11, 3)$ **71.** $(4, 6)$ and $(-4, 2)$

72. $(-5, 8)$ and $(-1, -6)$ **73.** $(8, -6)$ and $(-2, 7)$ **74.** $(-12, 8)$ and $(2, 2)$

75. $(1, 8)$ and $(-9, 2)$ **76.** $(-2, -10)$ and $(6, 9)$ **77.** $(3, 5)$ and $(6, -7)$

78. $(-4, 3)$ and $(8, -12)$ **79.** $(12, 5)$ and $(4, -6)$ **80.** $(11, -3)$ and $(3, 3)$

81. $(-5, 4)$ and $(9, 1)$ **82.** $(6, -3)$ and $(-1, -4)$ **83.** $(9, -6)$ and $(5, -1)$

In Exercises 84–104, factor the trinomial.

84. $x^2 + x - 6$ **85.** $x^2 - x - 42$ **86.** $x^2 + 8x - 48$

87. $x^2 - 4x - 77$ **88.** $x^2 + 13x + 12$ **89.** $x^2 + 6x - 16$

90. $x^2 - 2x - 24$ **91.** $x^2 + 4x - 5$ **92.** $x^2 - 4x + 3$

93. $x^2 + 11x + 30$ **94.** $x^2 - 20x + 96$ **95.** $x^2 + 13x + 40$

96. $2x^2 - 3x - 35$ **97.** $3x^2 - 2x - 40$ **98.** $2x^2 + 19x - 10$

99. $3x^2 - 32x + 20$ **100.** $4x^2 + 36x - 144$ **101.** $5x^2 + 7x - 6$

102. $6x^2 + 10x - 44$ **103.** $4x^2 + 27x - 81$ **104.** $2x^2 + 2x - 40$

In Exercises 105–122, write the quadratic function in standard form.

105. $y = -(x + 8)(x - 4)$ **106.** $y = 4(x + 4)(x - 3)$ **107.** $y = -2(x - 1)(x + 2)$

108. $y = -6(x + 3)(x - 4)$ **109.** $y = -5(x - 3)(x - 8)$ **110.** $y = 3(x + 4)(x - 7)$

111. $y = 6(x - 3)^2$ **112.** $y = -7(x + 1)^2$ **113.** $y = 2(x - 4)^2$

114. $y = (x - 4)^2 + 1$ **115.** $y = (x + 5)^2 - 7$ **116.** $y = (x - 8)^2 + 9$

117. $y = 3(x + 1)^2 + 4$ **118.** $y = -7(x + 5)^2 - 3$ **119.** $y = -9(x - 3)^2 + 7$

120. $y = -4(x + 8)^2 - 5$ **121.** $y = 2(x - 5)^2 + 1$ **122.** $y = 3(x + 1)^2 - 1$

123. You painted a picture that is 18 inches by 24 inches. You want to put wooden pieces around the outside as a frame. There are 648 square inches of wooden pieces. You are using all the material, and you want an even boarder around the entire picture. What should be the width of the border?

124. You want to create a decorative border for your garden that measures 12 feet by 7 feet. You decide to put a 1-foot border around the garden. How many square feet of rocks do you need?

Cumulative Review (continued)

125. You have a piece of canvas that you want to paint. You have enough paint to cover 252 square inches. You know you want one side to be 14 inches. How long should the other side be if you want to use up all the paint?

126. You have a square table and want to create a tablecloth for it using a piece of fabric. The side length of the table is 72 inches. How much fabric do you need?

In Exercises 127–146, use the quadratic formula to solve the equation.

127. $x^2 - 4x + 58 = 0$

128. $x^2 + 2x - 14 = 0$

129. $x^2 + 3x - 16 = 0$

130. $x^2 - 5x + 18 = 0$

131. $x^2 + 6x - 21 = 0$

132. $x^2 - 8x - 18 = 0$

133. $2x^2 + 14x - 45 = 0$

134. $3x^2 - 5x + 6 = 0$

135. $-4x^2 - 7x + 5 = 0$

136. $5x^2 - 4x + 32 = 0$

137. $6x^2 - 7x + 4 = 0$

138. $-4x^2 + 13x - 21 = 0$

139. $2x^2 + 3x = -8$

140. $-2x^2 + 5x = 18$

141. $-3x^2 + 16x = 34$

142. $-4x^2 - 15x = 28$

143. $2x^2 - 12x = -6$

144. $6x^2 + 9x = -12$

145. $5x^2 - 4x + 23 = 3x^2 + 14x + 34$

146. $3x^2 - 4x + 14 = 9x^2 - 7x + 19$

In Exercises 147–152, graph the function and its parent function. Then describe the transformation.

147. $g(x) = 2x$

148. $h(x) = -\frac{1}{2}x$

149. $c(x) = x - 4$

150. $d(x) = 2x^2$

151. $k(x) = |x + 4|$

152. $m(x) = |x - 3| + 2$

In Exercises 153–160, write a function g whose graph represents the indicated transformation of the graph of f.

153. $f(x) = -2x$; translation 3 units down

154. $f(x) = \frac{4}{7}x$; translation 1 unit up

155. $f(x) = |x| + 4$; translation 2 units left

156. $f(x) = \frac{1}{2}|x| - 7$; translation 6 units right

157. $f(x) = |x - 3| + 5$; reflection in the x-axis

158. $f(x) = |x + 1| - 2$; reflection in the x-axis

159. $f(x) = 3x - 1$; reflection in the y-axis

160. $f(x) = \frac{3}{4}x + 5$; reflection in the y-axis

Chapter 3

Name _____ Date _____

Dear Family,

Have you ever noticed that when a baseball is hit, the path of the ball is in the shape of a parabola? Quadratic equations can also be used to model the path of a baseball with respect to time. An example of the path of a baseball is shown in the graph below.

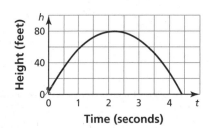

The ball is hit 3 feet from the ground, so the initial height h_o is 3. From the graph, you can also see that the ball is in the air for about 4.4 seconds and reaches a maximum height of about 80 feet.

Working together, list five to ten sports that involve an object whose height with respect to time is in the shape of a parabola. For each sport:

- Determine a reasonable value for the initial position of the object.

- Determine a reasonable domain for the time the object is in the air.

- Determine a reasonable range for the height of the object.

- Graph the path of the object.

Consider the following questions:

- What does the x-intercept represent for each graph?

- What determines how long an object is in the air?

- What determines the height that the object travels?

You can use the Internet to learn more about the applications of quadratic equations in sports. In this chapter, you will find an equation to model the path of an object and learn several techniques for finding the x-intercepts of the graph of a quadratic function.

Next time you are at a sporting event, notice how many different applications of parabolas you see!

Nombre _____ Fecha_____

Estimada familia:

¿Alguna vez se han dado cuenta de que cuando se golpea una pelota de béisbol, la trayectoria de la pelota tiene forma de parábola? Las ecuaciones cuadráticas también pueden usarse para representar la trayectoria de una pelota de béisbol con respecto al tiempo. Un ejemplo de la trayectoria de una pelota de béisbol se muestra en la siguiente gráfica.

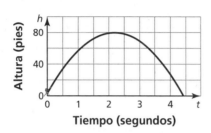

Se golpea la pelota a 3 pies del suelo, entonces la altura inicial ho es 3. Según la gráfica, también pueden ver que la pelota está en el aire durante casi 4.4 segundos y alcanza una altura máxima aproximada de 80 pies.

Trabajen juntos para enumerar entre cinco a diez deportes donde haya un objeto cuya altura con respecto al tiempo tenga forma de parábola. Para cada deporte:

- Determinen un valor razonable para la posición inicial del objeto.

- Determinen un dominio razonable para el tiempo que el objeto está en el aire.

- Determinen un rango razonable para la altura del objeto.

- Hagan una gráfica de la trayectoria del objeto.

Consideren las siguientes preguntas:

- ¿Qué representa la intersección con el eje *x* para cada gráfica?

- ¿Qué determina cuánto tiempo un objeto está en el aire?

- ¿Qué determina la altura que recorre un objeto?

Pueden consultar en Internet para aprender más sobre los usos de las ecuaciones cuadráticas en los deportes. En este capítulo, hallarán una ecuación para representar la trayectoria de un objeto y aprenderán varias técnicas para hallar las intersecciones con el eje x de la gráfica de una función cuadrática.

La próxima vez que vayan a un evento deportivo, ¡fíjense cuántos usos diferentes de las parábolas ven!

Graph equations $y = x^2$, $y = -x^2$, $y = x^2 - 4$, and $y = -x^2 - 4$ in a coordinate plane. Label the equations.

Make a chart to show the number of x-intercepts of each equation, along with the corresponding point(s) of the x-intercept(s). Are there any patterns you notice? What are they? How can you tell when the vertex will be the minimum of the graph? The maximum?

3.1 Warm Up

Use a graphing calculator to find the solution to the system of equations, if possible.

1. $2x + 3y = 2$
$3x - 5y = 22$

2. $2x + 3y = 6$
$2x + y = -2$

3. $2x - y = 1$
$6x - 3y = 12$

4. $2x + 3y = 6$
$6x + 9y = 18$

5. $3x + 2y = -3$
$x - 3y = 6$

6. $2x - 5y = 8$
$-x + 3y = -5$

3.1 Cumulative Review Warm Up

Graph the function. Label the vertex and axis of symmetry.

1. $f(x) = (x + 4)^2$

2. $g(x) = (x - 2)^2 - 6$

3. $y = -5(x + 3)^2 - 3$

4. $f(x) = -x^2 + 4$

Name_____ Date_____

3.1 Practice A

In Exercises 1–6, solve the equation by graphing.

1. $x^2 - 6x + 5 = 0$

2. $x^2 - 6x + 9 = 0$

3. $x^2 - 25 = 0$

4. $x^2 - 4x - 12 = 0$

5. $12 = x^2 - 4$

6. $2x^2 - 3 = 5x$

In Exercises 7–9, solve the equation using square roots.

7. $t^2 = 100$

8. $g^2 = 64$

9. $(y + 2)^2 = 16$

10. Describe and correct the error in solving the equation.

$$\times \quad (x - 2)^2 + 16 = 25$$
$$x - 2 + 4 = \pm 5$$
$$x + 2 = \pm 5$$
$$x = -2 \pm 5$$
$$x = 3 \text{ and } x = -7$$

In Exercises 11–13, solve the equation by factoring.

11. $0 = x^2 - 4x + 4$

12. $x^2 + x = 6$

13. $m^2 + 4m = 0$

In Exercises 14 and 15, find the value of x.

14. Area of triangle $= 27$

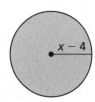

15. Area of circle $= 9\pi$

In Exercises 16–19, solve the equation using any method. Explain your reasoning.

16. $\dfrac{c^2}{8} - 3 = 2$

17. $7v = v^2$

18. $-3(p + 2)^2 = 12$

19. $x^2 - 5x - 24 = 0$

20. Write a quadratic function in the form $f(x) = x^2 + bx + c$ that has zeros 2 and −12.

3.1 Practice B

In Exercises 1–6, solve the equation by graphing.

1. $x^2 - 1 = 0$

2. $6x^2 = 4x + 2$

3. $x^2 - 14 = -5x$

4. $9x - 9 = -4x^2$

5. $\frac{1}{2}x^2 - 2x = 6$

6. $-3x = \frac{1}{3}x^2 + 6$

In Exercises 7–9, solve the equation using square roots.

7. $(k - 3)^2 = 121$

8. $3(x + 1)^2 - 4 = 5$

9. $\frac{4}{3}x^2 = \frac{2}{3}x^2 + 6$

10. Write an equation of the form $(x - a)^2 + b = d$ that has (a) two integer solutions, (b) two irrational solutions, and (c) no real solutions.

In Exercises 11–14, solve the equation by factoring.

11. $0 = x^2 - 121$

12. $3k^2 + 2k = 2k^2 + 11k$

13. $-w^2 - 3w - 7 = -2w^2 + 3$

14. $2y^2 = 6y$

In Exercises 15 and 16, solve the equation using any method. Explain your reasoning.

15. $x^2 - x + \frac{6}{25} = 0$

16. $n^2 - 1.5 = 0.19$

In Exercises 17–20, find the zero(s) of the function.

17. $h(x) = x^2 + 7x - 18$

18. $j(x) = x^2 - 16$

19. $g(x) = x^2 - 13x$

20. $f(x) = 9x^2 - 24x + 16$

21. A local kayak rental shop rents 28 kayaks per week when it charges \$25 per day. For each \$5 increase in price, the shop loses four kayak rentals per week. How much should the kayak rental shop charge to maximize weekly revenue? What is the maximum weekly revenue?

22. You drop a coin into a fountain from a height of 15 feet. Write an equation that models the height h (in feet) of the coin above the fountain t seconds after it has been dropped. How long is the coin in the air?

3.1 Enrichment and Extension

Solving Quadratic Equations

In Exercises 1–14, use square roots or factoring to solve.

1. The hypotenuse of a right triangle is 4 times one of the legs. The other leg is $3\sqrt{15}$ units. Find the length of the hypotenuse.

2. One leg of a right triangle exceeds the other leg by 4 inches. The hypotenuse is 20 inches. Find the length of the longer leg.

3. When a number is added to its square, the result is 6. What is the number?

4. The length of a rectangle is 8 units greater than its width. Find the dimensions when its area is 105 square units.

5. The difference of two numbers is 2 and their product is 224. What are the numbers?

6. The product of two consecutive integers is 72. Find the integers.

7. The product of two consecutive even integers is 528. Find the value of each integer.

8. The sum of two numbers is 25 and the sum of their squares is 337. Find the numbers.

9. In 10 years from now, my age will be the square of my age 10 years ago. How old am I?

10. The dimensions of a rectangle were originally 10 units by 12 units. The area of the rectangle increased by 135 square units, and the dimensions were increased by the same amount. Find the dimensions of the new rectangle.

11. A rectangular pool has a sidewalk around it. The pool measures 6 feet by 10 feet and the total area of the pool and sidewalk is 96 square feet. What is the width of the sidewalk?

12. A rectangular swimming pool is twice as long as it is wide. A small concrete sidewalk surrounds the pool. The sidewalk is a constant 2 feet wide. The total area of the pool and sidewalk is 160 square feet. Find the dimensions of the pool.

13. The area of a rectangle is 250 square inches. The length is 5 more than twice the width. Find the length of the rectangle.

14. The area of a triangle is 80 square centimeters. The base is 4 less than twice the height. What is the height of the triangle?

3.1 Puzzle Time

How Can You Get Four Suits For A Dollar?

Write the letter of each answer in the box containing the exercise number.

Solve the equation using square roots.

1. $(3x - 3)^2 = 36$ 2. $x^2 = 81$

3. $2(x - 2)^2 - 8 = -4$ 4. $5 - 3(2x + 1)^2 = -22$

Solve the equation by factoring.

5. $0 = x^2 + 8x + 16$ 6. $x^2 - 3x = 10$

7. $x^2 - 64 = 0$ 8. $4x^2 - 12 = 2x$

Find the zero(s) of the function.

9. $f(x) = 2x^2 + 7x - 4$ 10. $f(x) = x^2 - 121$

Solve the equation using any method.

11. $x^2 - 7x = 0$ 12. $3x^2 - 4x = 20x + 27$

13. $\frac{1}{2}(x - 1)^2 - 4 = -1$ 14. $2x^2 + 5x = 5x + 50$

15. $-x^2 + 30 + 4x = -2x^2 + 14x + 6$

Answers

D. $x = -4$

U. $x = 9; x = -9$

S. $x = 6; x = 4$

Y. $x = 2 + \sqrt{2}; x = 2 - \sqrt{2}$

A. $x = 1; x = -2$

C. $x = 8; x = -8$

E. $x = 5; x = -2$

K. $x = -\frac{3}{2}; x = 2$

B. $x = 3; x = -1$

F. $x = 11; x = -11$

C. $x = 0; x = 7$

A. $x = -1; x = 9$

D. $x = 5; x = -5$

O. $x = \frac{1}{2}; x = -4$

R. $x = 1 + \sqrt{6}; x = 1 - \sqrt{6}$

1	2	3		4		5	6	7	8		9	10		11	12	13	14	15

3.2 Start Thinking

Enter the following keystrokes on a calculator.

| $\sqrt{}$ | $-$ | 1 | ENTER |

Describe what the calculator gives you as a solution.
Repeat the keystrokes with a different negative number.
Why does the calculator give this answer?

3.2 Warm Up

Simplify.

1. $4(x - 1) + 6(x + 6)$

2. $7(y + 8) + (2 + 3y)$

3. $3\left[x + 3(x + 2)\right]$

4. $-4\left[x - 4(4 + x)\right]$

5. $3x + 2\left[x + (5 + x)\right]$

6. $-6x + 3\left[x + 5(x - 6)\right] + 8$

3.2 Cumulative Review Warm Up

Identify the vertex, focus, directrix, and axis of symmetry of the parabola.

1. $y = \frac{1}{7}(x + 4)^2 - 1$

2. $y = \frac{1}{15}(x + 4)^2$

3. $y = -\frac{1}{8}(x - 3)^2$

4. $y = \frac{1}{4}(x - 4)^2 + 4$

Name _____ Date _____

3.2 **Practice A**

In Exercises 1–3, find the square root of the number.

1. $\sqrt{-25}$ 2. $\sqrt{-81}$ 3. $\sqrt{-32}$

In Exercises 4–7, find the values of x and y that satisfy the equation.

4. $5x + 3i = 15 + yi$ 5. $-6x + 10i = 12 + 2yi$

6. $x + 2yi = 13 + 8i$ 7. $3x + 50i = 18 - 5yi$

In Exercises 8–11, add or subtract. Write the answer in standard form.

8. $(3 + 2i) + (5 + 7i)$ 9. $(4 - 3i) + (9 + 2i)$

10. $(6 + 5i) - (4 + 3i)$ 11. $(7 - 4i) - (10 - 3i)$

12. Write each expression as a complex number in standard form.

   a. $\sqrt{-25} - \sqrt{-9} + \sqrt{-81}$

   b. $\sqrt{-27} + \sqrt{-49} - \sqrt{-64}$

In Exercises 13–16, multiply. Write the answer in standard form.

13. $5i(-4 + 2i)$ 14. $3i(8 - 3i)$

15. $(2 - i)(3 + i)$ 16. $(4 + 6i)(9 - 2i)$

17. Justify each step in performing the operation.

   $14 + (5 - 3i) - 4i$

$\left[(14 + 5) - 3i\right] - 4i$	
$(19 - 3i) - 4i$	
$19 + (-3i - 4i)$	
$19 - 7i$	

In Exercises 18 and 19, find the zeros of the function.

18. $f(x) = 5x^2 + 15$ 19. $g(x) = 3x^2 + 21$

In Exercises 20 and 21, solve the equation. Check your solution(s).

20. $x^2 + 36 = 0$ 21. $x^2 + 6 = -14$

Name_____ Date _____

3.2 Practice B

In Exercises 1–3, find the square root of the number.

1. $3\sqrt{-25}$

2. $2\sqrt{-40}$

3. $4\sqrt{-54}$

In Exercises 4–7, find the values of x and y that satisfy the equation.

4. $2x - 3yi = 14 + 12i$

5. $\frac{1}{3}x - 6i = 8 - 3yi$

6. $22 + \frac{1}{5}yi = 2x - 2$

7. $-1 + 10i = -x + 3yi$

In Exercises 8–11, add or subtract. Write the answer in standard form.

8. $(9 + 6i) - (15 - 7i)$

9. $13 - (5 + i) + 7i$

10. $14 - (17 - 7i) + 8i$

11. $-4 + (9 - 2i) + 3i$

12. The additive inverse of a complex number z is a complex number z_a such that $z + z_a = 0$. Find the additive inverse of each complex number.

   a. $z = 2 + 3i$

   b. $z = 4 - 4i$

   c. $z = -5 + 2i$

In Exercises 13–16, multiply. Write the answer in standard form.

13. $(4 + 7i)(5 + 2i)$

14. $(5 - 3i)(5 + 3i)$

15. $(10 - 7i)(10 + 7i)$

16. $(6 - 4i)^2$

17. Justify each step in performing the operation.

   $(6 - 2i)(8 - 3i)$

$48 - 18i - 16i + 6i^2$	
$48 - 34i + 6i^2$	
$48 - 34i + 6(-1)$	
$42 - 34i$	

In Exercises 18 and 19, find the zeros of the function.

18. $f(x) = -x^2 - 48$

19. $g(x) = -\frac{1}{4}x^2 - 13$

In Exercises 20 and 21, solve the equation. Check your solution(s).

20. $x^2 + 16 = -28$

21. $\frac{1}{3}x^2 = -15$

Name _____ Date _____

3.2 Enrichment and Extension

Complex Numbers

The complex conjugate of a complex number $a + bi$ is $a - bi$. For example, the complex conjugate of $-3 - 2i$ is $-3 + 2i$. The sign only differs on the imaginary part of the complex number.

In Exercises 1–6, use the complex conjugate of the denominator to write the quotient in standard form.

1. $\dfrac{3}{1 + 2i}$

2. $\dfrac{2 + i}{3 - i}$

3. $\dfrac{5 + 3i}{-5 - 3i}$

4. $\dfrac{4 - i}{3i}$

5. $\dfrac{-2 + 2i}{-3 - 4i}$

6. $\dfrac{4 + 2i}{\frac{2}{3} + \frac{1}{2}i}$

Complex numbers can be graphed in a coordinate plane called *the complex plane*. The horizontal axis is called the *real axis* and the vertical axis is called the *imaginary axis*.

To graph a complex number such as $2 + 3i$, represent it with coordinates $(2, 3)$ in the complex plane. Similarly, the point $(-1, -3)$ represents $-1 - 3i$.

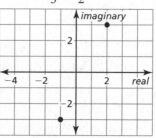

In Exercises 7–18, graph the number and its complex conjugate in the complex plane.

7. $-2 + 3i$

8. $-4 - 3i$

9. $-5i$

10. $4i$

11. $-1 + 5i$

12. $-6 - i$

13. -3

14. $4 + i$

15. $2 - 6i$

16. 4

17. $4 + 3i$

18. $1 + i$

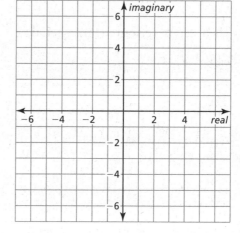

19. Describe the relationship between a complex number and its complex conjugate in the complex plane.

20. If the complex conjugate of $a + bi$ is $-a - bi$, what can you say about the complex number $a + bi$?

3.2 Puzzle Time

What Is The Difference Between A Pterodactyl And A Parrot?

A	B	C	D	E	F
G	H	I	J	K	L
M	N				

Complete each exercise. Find the answer in the answer column. Write the word under the answer in the box containing the exercise letter.

Answer column (left)
$-48i$ **THE**
$3i\sqrt{10}$ **KNOW**
$25i$ **YOU'D**
$16i\sqrt{5}$ **DIFFERENCE**
$x = -3; y = 2$ **IF**
$i\sqrt{2}; -i\sqrt{2}$ **ON**
$11 - i$ **EVER**

Find the square root of the number.

A. $\sqrt{-625}$ **B.** $\sqrt{-90}$

C. $-4\sqrt{-144}$ **D.** $8\sqrt{-20}$

Find the values of x and y that satisfy the equation.

E. $-3x + 4i = 2yi + 9$ **F.** $20 - 5xi = \frac{1}{3}y + 35i$

Add, subtract, or multiply. Write the answer in standard form.

G. $(8 - i) + (3 + i) - i$ **H.** $(12 + 7i) - (8 - 4i)$

I. $4i(-2 + 7i)$ **J.** $(4 - 6i)(4 + 6i)$

Find the zeros of the function.

K. $f(x) = -2x^2 - 30$ **L.** $f(x) = 4x^2 + 8$

M. $f(x) = \frac{2}{3}x^2 + 18$ **N.** $f(x) = 3x^2 + 75$

Answer column (right)
$i\sqrt{15}; -i\sqrt{15}$ **SIT**
$-28 - 8i$ **A**
$3i\sqrt{3}; -3i\sqrt{3}$ **YOUR**
$5i; -5i$ **SHOULDER**
$4 + 11i$ **LET**
52 **PTERODACTYL**
$x = -7; y = 60$ **YOU**

Simplify the expression $(x + 4)^2$. Explain how to find the middle term and the last term of the resulting expression.

Factor the expressions $a^2 + 6a + 9$ and $b^2 + 14b + 49$. If the constant term were missing from each polynomial, how could you use the middle term to determine what the constant term should be?

3.3 **Warm Up**

Factor the expression.

1. $25z^2 - y^2$

2. $25x^2 - 1$

3. $49x^2 + 28xy + 4y^2$

4. $\dfrac{1}{x^2} - 1$

5. $8y^2 - 2$

6. $4rs^2 - 4rs + r$

3.3 **Cumulative Review Warm Up**

Identify the function family and describe the domain and range.

1. $g(x) = |x - 3|$

2. $g(x) = 4x - 3$

3. $f(x) = 6x^2 + 1$

4. $h(x) = |x + 4| - 1$

5. $f(x) = -3x - 10$

6. $f(x) = -x^2 - 5$

Name_____ Date_____

3.3　Practice A

In Exercises 1–4, solve the equation using square roots. Check your solution(s).

1. $x^2 - 4x + 4 = 9$

2. $y^2 - 12y + 36 = 49$

3. $n^2 - 20n + 100 = 40$

4. $p^2 + 14p + 49 = 2$

In Exercises 5–8, find the value of *c* that makes the expression a perfect square trinomial. Then write the expression as the square of a binomial.

5. $x^2 + 8x + c$

6. $x^2 + 14x + c$

7. $y^2 - 18y + c$

8. $y^2 + 26y + c$

In Exercises 9–14, solve the equation by completing the square.

9. $x^2 + 8x + 5 = 0$

10. $h^2 - 10h - 4 = 0$

11. $t^2 - 12t + 10 = 0$

12. $s^2 + 14s - 9 = 0$

13. $y(y + 6) = 2$

14. $g(g + 10) = -6$

In Exercises 15–18, determine whether you would use factoring, square roots, or completing the square to solve the equation. Explain your reasoning. Then solve the equation.

15. $(x - 3)^2 = 25$

16. $x^2 + 5x + 4 = 0$

17. $x^2 - 6x + 9 = 0$

18. $x^2 - 10x - 8 = 0$

In Exercises 19 and 20, find the value of *x*.

19. Area of rectangle $= 64$

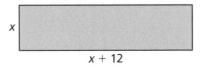

20. Area of parallelogram $= 20$

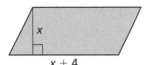

In Exercises 21 and 22, write the quadratic function in vertex form. Then identify the vertex.

21. $f(x) = x^2 + 10x + 32$

22. $g(x) = x^2 - 6x - 2$

3.3 Practice B

In Exercises 1–4, solve the equation using square roots. Check your solution(s).

1. $w^2 - 22w + 121 = 81$

2. $k^2 - 16k + 64 = -8$

3. $t^2 - 30t + 225 = -24$

4. $9p^2 + 6p + 1 = 12$

In Exercises 5–8, find the value of *c* that makes the expression a perfect square trinomial. Then write the expression as the square of a binomial.

5. $x^2 + 16x + c$

6. $x^2 + 7x + c$

7. $y^2 - 3y + c$

8. $y^2 + 20y + c$

In Exercises 9–14, solve the equation by completing the square.

9. $q(q + 6) = 1$

10. $5h^2 - 5h - 15 = 0$

11. $3x^2 + 24x + 15 = 0$

12. $3y(y - 8) = -36$

13. $7t^2 - 18t = 14 + 10t$

14. $2s^2 + 4s = -6s + 3$

In Exercises 15–18, determine whether you would use factoring, square roots, or completing the square to solve the equation. Explain your reasoning. Then solve the equation.

15. $(x + 9)^2 = 49$

16. $3x^2 + 6x - 4 = 0$

17. $x^2 - 144 = 0$

18. $5x^2 - 45 = 0$

In Exercises 19–22, write the quadratic function in vertex form. Then identify the vertex.

19. $f(x) = x^2 + 18x + 100$

20. $g(x) = x^2 - 2x - 26$

21. $h(x) = x^2 + 22x + 96$

22. $f(x) = x^2 - x + 2$

23. The height y (in feet) of a basketball t seconds after it is thrown can be modeled by the function $y = -16t^2 + 32t + 2$.

   a. Find the maximum height of the basketball.

   b. The basketball is caught in its descent when it is 7 feet above the ground. How long is the basketball in the air?

3.3 Enrichment and Extension

Completing the Square

In Exercises 1–6, complete the square to find the vertex of each quadratic function. Continue to solve to find the *x*-intercepts, if any. Use the information to graph and describe the transformation from the parent function $f(x) = x^2$.

1. $f(x) = 4x^2$

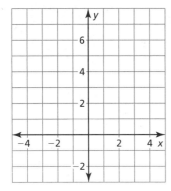

2. $f(x) = -x^2 + 3$

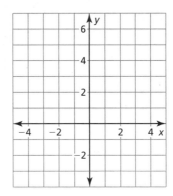

3. $f(x) = x^2 - 5x$

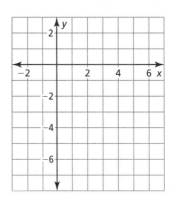

4. $f(x) = x^2 + 8x + 11$

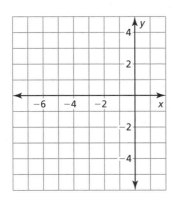

5. $f(x) = -3x^2 + 6x - 9$

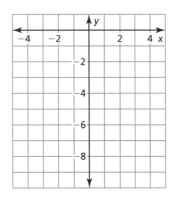

6. $f(x) = 2x^2 + 12x + 13$

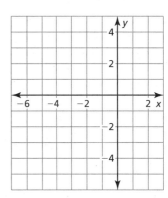

Name _____ Date _____

3.3 Puzzle Time

What Do You Call An Ice Skater Who Chats On The Internet?

Write the letter of each answer in the box containing the exercise number.

Solve the equation using factoring, square roots, or completing the square.

1. $(x + 8)^2 = 25$

2. $2x^2 - 12x + 6 = 0$

3. $x^2 - 8x + 15 = 0$

4. $x^2 - 45 = 0$

5. $3x^2 - x = 10$

6. $9x^2 + 79 = -18x$

7. $3x^2 = -4 + 8x$

8. $x^2 - 2x = 3$

9. $4x^2 + 8x + 80 = 0$

10. $-8 - 8x^2 = -31$

11. $2x^2 - 2 = 6$

12. $-4x^2 + 6x - 16 = -5x^2$

Answers

K. $x = 3; x = -1$

E. $x = 2; x = -2$

N. $x = -\dfrac{5}{3}; x = 2$

N. $x = 3 + \sqrt{6}; x = 3 - \sqrt{6}$

L. $x = 3; x = 5$

I. $x = \pm 3\sqrt{5}$

E. $x = -1 \pm \dfrac{\sqrt{70}}{3}i$

S. $x = 2; x = \dfrac{2}{3}$

A. $x = -1 \pm i\sqrt{19}$

T. $x = \dfrac{\pm\sqrt{46}}{4}$

O. $x = -3; x = -13$

R. $x = 2; x = -8$

1	2	3	4	5	6		7	8	9	10	11	12

3.4 Start Thinking

The four different ways to solve a quadratic function covered thus far are listed below. Explain when you should use each one. Then use your opinion to arrange them in order from the way you are most comfortable using to least comfortable using.

Completing the Square

Factoring

Graphing

Using Square Roots

3.4 Warm Up

Evaluate the expression when $a = -1$, $b = 3$, $c = 0$, and $d = 2$.

1. $\dfrac{b - c}{d}$

2. $\dfrac{b - 3d}{b}$

3. $b - d + 5a$

4. $2(b + a) + bc$

5. $2d + \dfrac{4}{9}b^3$

6. $-\dfrac{2}{5}b - 0(ac - bd)$

3.4 Cumulative Review Warm Up

Write a function g whose graph represents the indicated transformation of the graph of f. Use a graphing calculator to check your answer.

1. $f(x) = -6x - 3$; reflection in the y-axis

2. $f(x) = \dfrac{1}{3}x + 5$; reflection in the y-axis

3.4   Practice A

In Exercises 1–8, solve the equation using the Quadratic Formula. Use a graphing calculator to check your solution(s).

1. $x^2 + 9x + 4 = 0$

2. $2x^2 - 2x - 4 = 0$

3. $2x^2 + 12x + 18 = 0$

4. $-4x^2 = 3x - 1$

5. $-3x^2 + 5x = 4$

6. $x^2 + 144 = 24x$

7. $-7x = 2x^2 + 9$

8. $6x^2 = 4x - 9$

In Exercises 9–12, find the discriminant of the quadratic equation and describe the number and type of solutions of the equation.

9. $x^2 - 4x + 1 = 0$

10. $x^2 + 10x + 25 = 0$

11. $3t^2 - 3t + 18 = 0$

12. $-x^2 - 2x + 3 = 0$

13. What are the complex solutions of the equation $2x^2 - 32x + 178 = 0$?

    A. $8 + 20i,\ 8 - 20i$

    B. $8 + 5i,\ 8 - 5i$

    C. $32 + 5i,\ 32 - 5i$

    D. $32 + 20i,\ 32 - 20i$

In Exercises 14 and 15, find a possible pair of integer values for *a* and *c* so that the quadratic equation has the given solution(s). Then write the equation.

14. $ax^2 + 8x + c = 0$; one real solution

15. $ax^2 - 5x + c = 0$; two imaginary solutions

In Exercises 16 and 17, use the Quadratic Formula to write a quadratic equation that has the given solutions.

16. $x = \dfrac{9 \pm \sqrt{-79}}{8}$

17. $x = \dfrac{-11 \pm \sqrt{97}}{-6}$

In Exercises 18–21, solve the quadratic equation using the Quadratic Formula. Then solve the equation using another method. Which method do you prefer? Explain.

18. $9x^2 + 4 = 12x$

19. $4x^2 - 13x + 3 = 0$

20. $x^2 - 12x + 9 = 0$

21. $x^2 - 4x = 12$

22. Suppose a quadratic equation has the form $x^2 + x + c = 0.$ Show that the constant c must be less than $\dfrac{1}{4}$ in order for the equation to have two real solutions.

Name_____ Date_____

3.4 Practice B

In Exercises 1–8, solve the equation using the Quadratic Formula. Use a graphing calculator to check your solution(s).

1. $x^2 + 3x - 4 = 0$

2. $4x^2 + 8x + 4 = 0$

3. $x^2 + 5x + 20 = 0$

4. $4x^2 - 3x - 5 = 0$

5. $x^2 + 12x = 15$

6. $3x^2 - 6x = -25$

7. $-v^2 = -10v + 4$

8. $-3t^2 = -8t + 6$

In Exercises 9–12, find the discriminant of the quadratic equation and describe the number and type of solutions of the equation.

9. $5x^2 - 4x + 2 = 0$

10. $14x + 49 = -x^2$

11. $-12h = 3h^2 + 1$

12. $-2x^2 + x = 3$

13. Determine the number and type of solutions to the equation $2x^2 - 8x = -15$.

    A. two real solutions

    B. one real solution

    C. two imaginary solutions

    D. one imaginary solution

In Exercises 14 and 15, find a possible pair of integer values for *a* and *c* so that the quadratic equation has the given solution(s). Then write the equation.

14. $ax^2 - 3x + c = 0$; two real solutions

15. $ax^2 + 10x + c = 0$; two imaginary solutions

In Exercises 16 and 17, use the Quadratic Formula to write a quadratic equation that has the given solutions.

16. $x = \dfrac{10 \pm \sqrt{-68}}{14}$

17. $x = \dfrac{-3 \pm 5i}{8}$

In Exercises 18–21, solve the quadratic equation using the Quadratic Formula. Then solve the equation using another method. Which method do you prefer? Explain.

18. $7x^2 + 7 = 14x$

19. $x^2 + 20x = 8$

20. $x^2 + 2 = -x$

21. $8x^2 - 48x + 64 = 0$

22. Suppose a quadratic equation has the form $x^2 + x + c = 0$. Show that the constant c must be greater than $\dfrac{1}{4}$ in order for the equation to have two imaginary solutions.

Name_____ Date _____

Using the Quadratic Formula

For Exercises 1–6, use the Quadratic Formula to solve for x. By looking at the answer, could you have factored?

1. $(2x + 1)^2 = 3x(4x - 1)$

2. $(2x + 5)(x - 3) = (4x - 7)(5 + 2x)$

3. $(x - 3)^2 = 16$

4. $(1 - 4x)^2 = (x - 3)^2$

5. $0.4x^2 - 4.7x = 12.6$

6. $\frac{7}{16}x^2 - \frac{5}{2} = -\frac{3}{8}x$

For Exercises 7–9, determine the number and type of solutions the quadratic equation $f(x) = 0$ will have. Then graph f using the x-intercepts, vertex, and other points.

7. $f(x) = 4x^2$

8. $f(x) = -x^2 + 3$

9. $f(x) = x^2 - 5x$

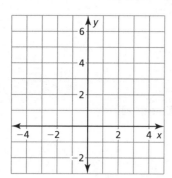
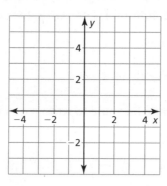
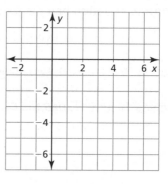

10. Make a statement about the relationship between the x-intercepts of the graph of a quadratic function and the x-coordinate of its vertex.

3.4 Puzzle Time

What Did The Couch Say Halfway Through The Marathon?

Write the letter of each answer in the box containing the
exercise number.

Solve the equation using the Quadratic Formula.

1. $x^2 + 4x - 8 = 0$

2. $10x^2 - 2 = 0$

3. $2x^2 + x - 8 = 0$

4. $-x^2 + 3x + 5 = 0$

5. $4x^2 - 5x = -2$

6. $x^2 + 1 = -2x$

7. $-4x^2 + 6x - 2 = 0$

8. $3x^2 - x = -2$

9. $-x^2 + 2x = 7$

10. $x^2 = x$

Answers

O. $x = 1 \pm i\sqrt{6}$

A. $x = \dfrac{-3 \pm \sqrt{29}}{-2}$

S. $x = -2 \pm 2\sqrt{3}$

F. $x = \dfrac{-1 \pm \sqrt{65}}{4}$

O. $x = \dfrac{\pm\sqrt{5}}{5}$

S. $x = \dfrac{5 \pm \sqrt{7}}{8}$

D. $x = 0; x = 1$

O. $x = -1$

G. $x = 1; x = \dfrac{1}{2}$

O. $x = \dfrac{1 \pm i\sqrt{23}}{6}$

1	2	3	4		5	6		7	8	9	10

3.5 Start Thinking

The solution to a system of linear equations is the point of intersection of the lines. If the lines are parallel, there is no intersection, so there is no solution.

Given the following, sketch a possible graph of the system.

System with one linear equation and one quadratic equation, two points of intersection

System with two quadratic equations, one point of intersection

System with two quadratic equations, two points of intersection

3.5 Warm Up

Solve the system using a graphing calculator.

1. $x - 4y = 9$
   $2x - 3y = 11$

2. $y = 2x$
   $3x + 5y = 0$

3. $x = 2$
   $3x + 2y = 4$

4. $y = -\frac{1}{3}x + 1$
   $2x + 6y = 6$

3.5 Cumulative Review Warm Up

Graph the function.

1. $f(x) = (x - 5)^2$

2. $g(x) = (x + 1)^2 + 7$

3. $y = -6(x - 4)^2 + 2$

4. $f(x) = -2(x - 1)^2 - 5$

Name_____ Date _____

3.5 Practice A

In Exercises 1–4, solve the system by graphing. Check your solution(s).

1. $y = x + 6$

   $y = \frac{1}{2}(x + 6)^2$

2. $y = (x + 2)^2 - 3$

   $y = -3$

3. $y = -x + 3$

   $y = 3x^2 - 4x + 3$

4. $y = 2x^2 - 8x + 5$

   $y = 2x - 3$

In Exercises 5 and 6, solve the system of nonlinear equations using the graph.

5.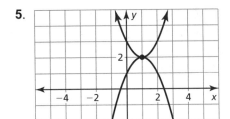

6.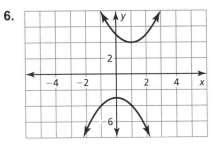

In Exercises 7–10, solve the system by substitution.

7. $y = x - 4$

   $y = x^2 - 4x$

8. $x^2 + y^2 = 25$

   $y = 5 - x$

9. $x^2 + y^2 = 1$

   $x = 1$

10. $y = 7$

    $3x - 6 = 4x^2 - y$

In Exercises 11–14, solve the system using elimination.

11. $x^2 - 5x - y = 2$

    $-x + y = -11$

12. $-4x^2 + x - 7 = y$

    $2x + 8 = -y$

13. $-2x^2 + y = 14x + 16$

    $-2x^2 - y = -14x - 12$

14. $y = x^2 - 4x + 6$

    $y = -5x^2 + 20x - 12$

15. A nonlinear system contains the equation of a constant function and the equation of a circle. The system has two solutions. Describe the relationship between the graphs.

3.5 Practice B

In Exercises 1–4, solve the system by graphing. Check your solution(s).

1. $y = -2x^2 + 4x - 3$
   $y = x^2 - 2x + 3$

2. $y = -3x^2 + 6$
   $y = 3x$

3. $y = -(x + 3)^2$
   $y = x^2 - 9$

4. $y = 3x^2 - 6x + 5$
   $y = (x - 1)^2 + 2$

In Exercises 5 and 6, solve the system of nonlinear equations using the graph.

5.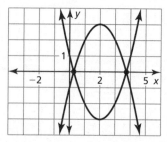

6.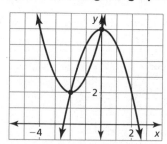

In Exercises 7–10, solve the system by substitution.

7. $y = x^2 - 3$
   $y + 1 = -x^2$

8. $y - 12x + 15 = 3x^2$
   $3x^2 - 16x + 13 - y = 0$

9. $x^2 + y^2 = 6$
   $x + 2y = 12$

10. $x^2 + y^2 = 13$
    $x - y = -1$

In Exercises 11–14, solve the system using elimination.

11. $x^2 - 3x - y = -6$
    $3x - y = 5$

12. $y = x^2 + 3x - 8$
    $-y = 3x - 8$

13. $y = -2x^2 - 18x - 16$
    $y = 3x^2 + 12x + 24$

14. $-6x^2 - y = -32x + 50$
    $12x^2 - y = 64x - 76$

15. A nonlinear system contains the equation of a constant function and the equation of a circle. The system has one solution. Describe the relationship between the graphs.

3.5 Enrichment and Extension

Solving Nonlinear Systems

Conic sections can all be written in the form $Ax^2 + Bxy + Cy^2 + Dx + Ey + F = 0$ where A, B, and C are not all equal to zero.

There are two cases: $B = 0$ (the axes of symmetry are parallel to the x-axis or y-axis) and $B \neq 0$ (the conic sections are rotated).

Type of conic	Coefficients
Parabola: $y = (x - h)^2 + k$	$AC = 0$
Hyperbola: $\dfrac{(x - h)^2}{a^2} - \dfrac{(y - k)^2}{b^2} = 1$	$AC < 0$
Circle: $x^2 + y^2 = r^2$	$A = C, A \neq 0, C \neq 0$

Example: Classify the conic section defined by the equation $4y^2 - 8y = 4 + 4x + x^2$ and write it in standard form. Let $B = 0$.

$-x^2 + 4y^2 - 4x - 8y - 4 = 0$, where $A = -1$ and $C = 4$. Because $AC < 0$, the equation represents a hyperbola.

$$-x^2 + 4y^2 - 4x - 8y = 4$$
Because the equation is a hyperbola, isolate the constant.

$$-(x^2 + 4x + 4) + 4(y^2 - 2y + 1) = 4 - 4 + 4(1)$$
Complete the square for x and y.

$$-(x + 2)^2 + 4(y - 1)^2 = 4$$
Simplify.

$$-\frac{(x + 2)^2}{4} + \frac{(y - 1)^2}{1} = 1$$
Write in standard form.

$$\frac{(y - 1)^2}{1} - \frac{(x + 2)^2}{4} = 1$$
Rearrange.

In Exercises 1–6, let $B = 0$ and classify the conic section as a parabola, hyperbola, or circle. Write the standard equation of the conic section.

1. $9x^2 - 3 = 18x + 4y$

2. $x^2 - 2x = 2y - y^2 + 6$

3. $4x^2 - y^2 - 13 = -16x + 6y$

4. $x^2 + 6x + y^2 + 5 = y^2 + y$

5. $x^2 - 15 + 2x = -6y - y^2$

6. $4x^2 + 8x - 68 = 9y^2 - 36y$

3.5 **Puzzle Time**

What Do You Get When You Cross A Rocket Ship With A Potato?

Write the letter of each answer in the box containing the exercise number.

Solve the system by graphing, substitution, or elimination.

1. $y = 2$
   $y = x^2 - 14$

2. $y = -2x + 1$
   $y = -x^2 + 10$

3. $y = 4x^2 - x + 5$
   $y = 2x^2 + 2x + 4$

4. $2x^2 - 6x - y = -12$
   $-2x + y = 12$

5. $3x^2 + 4x - y = 7$
   $2x - y = -1$

6. $-x + y = 4$
   $x^2 + y = 3$

7. $x^2 + y^2 = 100$
   $y - x = 2$

Answers

U. $(0.5, 5.5);\ (1, 8)$

P. $(4.16, -7.325);\ (-2.16, 5.325)$

N. $(-2, -3);\ \left(\dfrac{4}{3}, \dfrac{11}{3}\right)$

K. $(-8, -6);\ (6, 8)$

S. $(-4, 2);\ (4, 2)$

D. $(0, 12);\ (4, 20)$

I. no solution

1	2	3	4	5	6	7

3.6 Start Thinking

The following steps can be used to graph a linear inequality. Replace the underlined words as needed to explain how to graph a quadratic inequality.

Graph the <u>line</u> with $y = mx + b$. Make the <u>line</u> *dashed* for inequalities with $<$ or $>$ and *solid* for inequalities with $\leq$ or $\geq$.

Test a point (x, y) <u>above</u> the <u>line</u> to determine whether the point is a solution to the inequality.

Shade the region <u>above</u> the <u>line</u> if the point is a solution. Shade the region <u>below</u> the <u>line</u> if the point is not a solution.

3.6 Warm Up

Graph the inequality.

1. $x - y < 5$

2. $2x + y > 10$

3. $y \geq -3$

4. $6x - 3y < 5$

3.6 Cumulative Review Warm Up

Solve the system of linear equations using the substitution method.

1. $-x - 3y + 8z = 43$
   $8x - 5y - 2z = 57$
   $7x - 2y - 3z = 40$

2. $-3x - 3y + 7z = 67$
   $3z = 21$
   $-3x + 2y - 2z = -16$

Name_____ Date _____

3.6 Practice A

In Exercises 1–4, graph the inequality.

1. $y > x^2$

2. $y \le -3x^2$

3. $y \ge x^2 - 5$

4. $y < x^2 - 3x$

In Exercises 5 and 6, use the graph to write an inequality in terms of $f(x)$ so point P is a solution.

5.

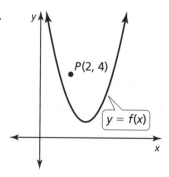

6.

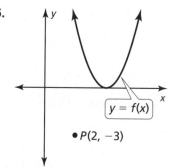

In Exercises 7 and 8, graph the system of quadratic inequalities.

7. $y \le -2x^2$
   $y > x^2 - 3$

8. $y < 4x^2$
   $y < 2x^2 - 4$

In Exercises 9–12, solve the inequality algebraically.

9. $9x^2 > 16$

10. $x^2 - 8x + 7 \ge 0$

11. $x^2 + 10x \le -21$

12. $2x^2 - 11x < -9$

In Exercises 13–16, solve the inequality by graphing.

13. $x^2 - 2x + 2 > 0$

14. $x^2 + 5x - 3 \le 0$

15. $x^2 + 6x \le -5$

16. $x^2 + 4x > -1$

17. An oceanfront lot has a perimeter of 250 feet and an area of at least 2500 square feet.

   a. Write an inequality describing this situation.

   b. Describe the possible widths of the oceanfront lot.

Name_____ Date _____

3.6   Practice B

In Exercises 1–4, graph the inequality.

1. $y \le x^2 + 3$

2. $y > x^2 + 2x - 3$

3. $y < -(x + 1)^2 + 2$

4. $y \ge -x^2 + 4x$

5. Describe and correct the error in graphing $y < -x^2 + 2$.

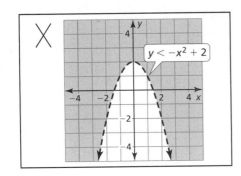

In Exercises 6 and 7, graph the system of quadratic inequalities.

6. $y \le -x^2 + 3$
   $y \ge 2x^2 - 3x + 1$

7. $y > x^2 - x + 4$
   $y < x^2 + 2x - 4$

In Exercises 8–11, solve the inequality algebraically.

8. $2x^2 - 6 > -11x$

9. $2x^2 - 5x + 3 \le 1$

10. $\frac{1}{2}x^2 + 3x \ge 2$

11. $\frac{1}{3}x^2 - 2x < 9$

In Exercises 12–15, solve the inequality by graphing.

12. $2x^2 - 6 > -3x$

13. $4x^2 + 3x - 5 \le 1$

14. $\frac{1}{2}x^2 + x \le 2$

15. $\frac{2}{3}x^2 + 2x > 4$

16. An object is dropped from a building. The height h (in feet) of the object after t seconds can be modeled by $h(t) = -16t^2 - 28t + 25$.

   a. At what height was the object initially dropped? Explain.

   b. Write an inequality that you can use to find the t-values for which the object was in the air.

   c. Based on your results from parts (a) and (b), use a graphing calculator to determine the time intervals in which the object was in the air.

3.6 Enrichment and Extension

Quadratic Inequalities

You are a sales representative for a fashion and accessory wholesaler specializing in handbags. The price per handbag varies based on the number of handbags purchased in each order. Beginning with a price of $368 for one handbag, the price of each additional handbag purchased is reduced by $2.

Fill in the table to represent the prices and revenue of handbags.

Number of handbags purchased	Price per handbag (dollars)	Revenue per order (dollars)
1		
2		
3		
4		
5		
6		
$\vdots$	$\vdots$	$\vdots$
x		

a. Write a function for the revenue.

b. What is the maximum revenue per order?

c. How many handbags must be purchased to attain maximum revenue?

d. Assume that it costs $30 to produce each handbag and that you spend an average of $312 in fixed costs per order. Based on only these two factors, what is the function for the costs?

e. In order to have a profit, the revenue must be greater than the costs. Write an inequality for the profit.

f. How many handbags do you need to sell to make a profit?

g. What is the maximum profit per order? How many handbags must be sold to earn the maximum profit per order?

Name_____ Date _____

 3.6 **Puzzle Time**

If Seagulls Fly Over The Sea, What Flies Over The Bay?

Write the letter of each answer in the box containing the exercise number.

Match the inequality with its graph.

1. $y + 2x^2 < -x^2 - 2$

2. $y \geq \frac{1}{2}x^2 - 5$

3. $-10x^2 - 2y > 4$

4. $4y + 3x^2 \leq -8$

5. $-x^2 - y < -3$

6. $\dfrac{y + 2x^2}{3} \geq -1$

Answers
L. A
G. F
B. D
A. C
E. E
S. B

A.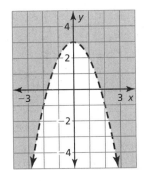

B.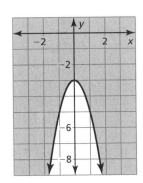

C.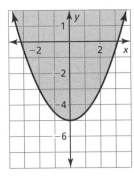

D.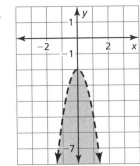

E.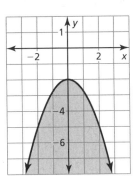

F.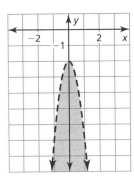

1	2	3	4	5	6

Chapter 3 **Cumulative Review**

In Exercises 1–24, simplify.

1. $\sqrt{50}$

2. $\sqrt{45}$

3. $\sqrt{96}$

4. $\sqrt{192}$

5. $\sqrt{300}$

6. $-\sqrt{54}$

7. $-\sqrt{175}$

8. $-\sqrt{72}$

9. $\sqrt{\dfrac{5}{36}}$

10. $\sqrt{\dfrac{6}{49}}$

11. $\sqrt{\dfrac{3}{4}}$

12. $\sqrt{\dfrac{7}{9}}$

13. $\sqrt{\dfrac{1}{16}}$

14. $-\sqrt{\dfrac{4}{25}}$

15. $-\sqrt{\dfrac{7}{81}}$

16. $-\sqrt{\dfrac{5}{64}}$

17. $\sqrt{7+2}$

18. $\sqrt{-6+9-3}$

19. $\sqrt{15-11}$

20. $\sqrt{-13+22}$

21. $\sqrt{14+9-12}$

22. $\sqrt{16+4-10}$

23. $\sqrt{22+25+20}$

24. $\sqrt{-3-20+24}$

In Exercises 25–34, find the sum or difference.

25. $(-24x-4)+(11-22x-2)$

26. $(17+20x)-(-8x-5)$

27. $(19x^2+12x+5)+(-23-12x^2+10)$

28. $(x-9)-(-x^2-19x+6)$

29. $(18x+2x-21)+(13x+8-11)$

30. $(-16x^2-14)-(21-25x-15x^2)$

31. $(24x^3+23x-7)+(18x-7x^2+3x^3+16)$

32. $(21x^5+5x-17)-(12x+16x^2-4x^4-11+22x^5)$

33. $(9+x^3+22x+25)+(-15+10x^2+7x^3)$

34. $(-10x^4-19x^2+8x+15x^3+3)-(-6x^2-20x^3+23+6x^2)$

35. After you get on the school bus, there are six additional stops before you reach school. The travel time between stops varies. The times (in minutes) between stops are 2.3, 1.4, 2.8, 1.7, 1.9, 2.1, and 3.4, respectively.

   a. Each stop is 0.8 minute long. How long does it take to reach school from where you get on the bus?

   b. Each stop is 0.9 minute long. How long does it take to reach school from where you get on the bus?

   c. The total time you are on the bus is 22.2 minutes. How long is each stop, if all the stops take an equal amount of time?

Chapter 3 Cumulative Review (continued)

In Exercises 36–47, find the product.

36. $4\left(x^2 - 10x + 11\right)$

37. $-5\left(2x^2 - x - 3\right)$

38. $(x + 4)(x + 2)$

39. $(x - 1)(x - 2)$

40. $(5x + 10)(-4x + 9)$

41. $\left(3x^2 - 11\right)(2x - 7)$

42. $(12x + 2)\left(x^2 - 12x + 7\right)$

43. $\left(-5x^2 - 1\right)\left(-6x^2 + 8x - 3\right)$

44. $(-7x - 9)\left(12x^2 + 8x + 1\right)$

45. $\left(x^2 - 8x + 11\right)\left(x^2 + 4x - 9\right)$

46. $\left(-2x^2 + 12x + 1\right)\left(x^3 + 3x - 11\right)$

47. $\left(x^2 + 9x - 6\right)\left(6x^2 + 11x - 10\right)$

In Exercises 48–59, simplify the expression. Write your answer in standard form.

48. $4\left(x^2 + 7x + 3\right)$

49. $-5\left(2x^2 + 5x - 10\right)$

50. $(x + 12)(x + 4)$

51. $-8(x - 9)(x - 11)$

52. $3(x - 1)(x + 3)$

53. $-4(-4x + 7)(x + 1)$

54. $6(-2x - 11)(8x - 7)$

55. $2\left(x^2 + 10x - 11\right) + 12$

56. $(x + 4)(7x - 5) + 3$

57. $9\left(6x^2 + x + 4\right) - 5$

58. $(2x + 9)(-3x - 4) - 12x + 8$

59. $2(x + 7)(2x - 5) + 3x - 17$

60. During a school food drive, your class collects 137 nonperishable food items.

   a. How many total items are collected Tuesday through Friday if you know there are 42 items collected on Monday?

   b. Twenty-nine items are collected on Wednesday, and the number of items collected on each of the remaining three days is the same. How many items are collected on Thursday?

61. You walk your dog each night. To walk the same route and distance, it takes your sister 3 additional minutes and your brother 2 fewer minutes. If it takes you 9 minutes to walk your dog, how long does it take your brother and sister to walk the dog?

62. You are building a fence around a garden. The length is 5 feet more than the width.

   a. The perimeter is 66 feet. What are the length and width of the fence?

   b. Fence material is $16 per linear foot. How much will the fence material cost?

   c. Determine the area of the garden.

Chapter 3 **Cumulative Review** (continued)

In Exercises 63–77, solve the quadratic equation.

63. $x^2 - 3x - 28 = 0$ **64.** $x^2 - 5x + 6 = 0$ **65.** $x^2 - 2x - 63 = 0$

66. $2x^2 - 3x - 5 = 0$ **67.** $4x^2 + 21x + 27 = 0$ **68.** $5x^2 + 13x - 6 = 0$

69. $15x^2 - 11x - 14 = 0$ **70.** $8x^2 - 38x + 35 = 0$ **71.** $24x^2 + 2x - 1 = 0$

72. $84x^2 + 29x = 3$ **73.** $56x^2 + 18x = 8$ **74.** $80x^2 - 74x = 18$

75. $6x^2 = -67x + 60$ **76.** $35x - 50 = -22x^2$ **77.** $52x = 48 - 66x^2$

In Exercises 78–89, solve the equation for y.

78. $y - x = 9$ **79.** $x = 2y - 10$ **80.** $17 = 3x - y$ **81.** $2y + 8 = 4x$

82. $22x - 2y = 46$ **83.** $4y + 3x = 5$ **84.** $15 - 5y = -30x$ **85.** $-3y + 27 = -15x$

86. $\frac{1}{7}y = -2x + 3$ **87.** $\frac{1}{3}y + 8 = 2x$ **88.** $14 - \frac{1}{2}y = x$ **89.** $9x - \frac{1}{5}y = 4$

In Exercises 90–101, evaluate $b^2 - 4ac$ for the given values of a, b, and c.

90. $a = -4, b = 2, c = -7$ **91.** $a = 12, b = -2, c = 11$

92. $a = 8, b = -8, c = -12$ **93.** $a = -7, b = 12, c = 8$

94. $a = 6, b = -9, c = 1$ **95.** $a = 7, b = -5, c = -1$

96. $a = 9, b = 4, c = 1$ **97.** $a = 4, b = -10, c = 8$

98. $a = -12, b = 3, c = -6$ **99.** $a = 6, b = 10, c = 9$

100. $a = 6, b = 5, c = -2$ **101.** $a = 1, b = -6, c = 10$

102. You and your friend are playing basketball. Your friend makes 4 more baskets than you, and the total number of baskets you both make is 18.

   a. Write an algebraic equation to represent the situation.

   b. How many baskets does your friend make?

   c. How many baskets do you make?

103. You travel 165 miles for 3 hours.

   a. What is your traveling rate?

   b. You travel at a rate of 5 miles per hour faster than the original rate. Now how long does it take you to travel 165 miles?

Chapter 3 Cumulative Review (continued)

In Exercises 104–112, solve the absolute value equation. Check for extraneous solutions.

104. $2|x - 1| = 18$

105. $\frac{1}{4}|x + 6| = 7$

106. $-3|x - 2| = -6$

107. $|x + 4| - 1 = 9$

108. $|x + 5| + 3 = 11$

109. $|8 - x| - 5 = 12$

110. $3|x - 4| + 5 = 6$

111. $\frac{1}{5}|x + 3| - 2 = 1$

112. $-\frac{1}{4}|x + 1| - 3 = -2$

In Exercises 113–124, solve the system of linear equations.

113. $x - 2y = 13$
$3x + 2y = 15$

114. $2x + y = -10$
$x - 3y = 2$

115. $x + y = 9$
$-x - y = 7$

116. $x + 3y = -12$
$2x + 2y = 0$

117. $-2x + y = -16$
$2x - y = 16$

118. $-x - 4y = 23$
$-3x + y = -22$

119. $x - y + z = 13$
$x + y - z = -7$
$-2x + 2y + z = -8$

120. $x + y + z = 15$
$x + y + 2z = 13$
$-x + y - 2z = 3$

121. $-x + y - z = 3$
$2x - y + 3z = -7$
$x - 2y - 2z = -4$

122. $x + y + z = 7$
$-x - y - z = -7$
$2x + 2y + 2z = 14$

123. $2x - y + z = 1$
$3x - 2y + 2z = 0$
$-x + y - 2z = 5$

124. $2x - y + 3z = 9$
$-4x + 2y - 6z = -20$
$6x - 3y + 9z = 24$

In Exercises 125–133, add or subtract. Write the answer in standard form.

125. $(12 + 4i) + (-6 + 11i)$

126. $(1 + 15i) - (13 + 5i)$

127. $(-7 + 3i) - (-2 + 8i)$

128. $(4 - 9i) + (3 - 9i)$

129. $(6 - 7i) + (3 + 14i)$

130. $(-5 - 7i) - (7 + i)$

131. $-15 + (9 + 2i) + 8$

132. $7 - (4 - 2i) - 3$

133. $12 - (-10 + 3i) + 4$

In Exercises 134–142, multiply. Write the answer in standard form.

134. $-11i(-2 + i)$

135. $8(2 + 9i)$

136. $6i(-4 + 10i)$

137. $(2 + 7i)(-2 + 5i)$

138. $(-8 + 3i)(-8 - 5i)$

139. $(3 + 5i)(4 - 7i)$

140. $(6 - 3i)^2$

141. $(11 + 12i)^2$

142. $(-9 - i)^2$

143. You buy dog food by the pound. It costs $0.85 per pound.

    a. How many pounds of dog food can you purchase with $20?

    b. How much change will you receive?

    c. There is a 7% sales tax on the dog food. How much is the new cost per pound?

Chapter 4

Name_____ Date_____

Dear Family,

There are many patterns in the world that can be explained using math. Once a pattern is determined, the information can be used to make predictions and simplify problems. One of the most commonly used patterns in mathematics is Pascal's Triangle, named after the French mathematician Blaise Pascal.

> **Pascal's Triangle**
>
> 1 ← Row 0
> 1 1 ← Row 1
> 1 2 1 ← Row 2
> 1 3 3 1 ← Row 3
> 1 4 6 4 1 ← Row 4

To find the next row of Pascal's Triangle, the first and last numbers will be 1. Then each number between each 1 is the sum of the two numbers above it.

Work together to copy the first 5 rows of Pascal's Triangle onto a sheet of paper, and then find the next 10 rows of the pattern. Use the first 15 rows of Pascal's Triangle to answer the following questions.

- What patterns do you notice within the triangle?
- What pattern do you notice when you find the sum of each row?
- What is the relationship between Pascal's Triangle and the powers of 11?

You can use the Internet to verify the rows of the Triangle and the answers to the questions above.

In this chapter, your student will work with polynomial functions. To find the binomial expansion of $(x + y)^n$, your student can use Pascal's Triangle to determine the coefficients of the variables.

There is a lot of interesting information about Pascal's Triangle, including its history and applications in the mathematical and real world, such as in probability and statistics.

Have fun looking for patterns in your daily life!

Nombre _____ Fecha _____

Funciones polinomiales

Estimada familia:

Hay muchos patrones en el mundo que pueden explicarse con matemáticas. Luego de que se determina un patrón, la información puede usarse para hacer predicciones y simplificar problemas. Uno de los patrones más usados en matemáticas es el triángulo de Pascal, que lleva su nombre por el matemático francés Blaise Pascal.

```
Triángulo de Pascal
          1              ← Fila 0
        1   1            ← Fila 1
      1   2   1          ← Fila 2
    1   3   3   1        ← Fila 3
  1   4   6   4   1      ← Fila 4
```

Para hallar la siguiente fila en el triángulo de Pascal, el primer y el último número serán 1. Luego, cada número entre cada 1 es la suma de los dos números que están arriba de el.

Trabajen juntos para copiar las primeras 5 filas del Triángulo de Pascal en una hoja de papel y luego, hallen las siguientes 10 filas del patrón. Usen las primeras 15 filas del Triángulo de Pascal para responder las siguientes preguntas.

• ¿Qué patrones observan dentro del triángulo?

• ¿Qué patrón observan cuando hallan la suma de cada fila?

• ¿Cuál es la relación entre el Triángulo de Pascal y las potencias de 11?

Pueden consultar en Internet para verificar las filas del triángulo y las respuestas a las preguntas mencionadas.

En este capítulo, su hijo trabajará con funciones polinomiales. Para hallar la expansión binomial de $(x + y)^n$, su hijo puede usar el triángulo de Pascal para determinar los coeficientes de las variables.

Hay mucha información interesante sobre el triángulo de Pascal, incluyendo su historia y usos en el mundo matemático y en el mundo real, tal como en probabilidad y estadística.

4.1 Start Thinking

Use a graphing calculator to graph the functions $f(x) = x^3$ and $g(x) = x^4$. Compare and contrast the graphs of the two functions.

Explain why the graph of $g(x) = x^4$ is always positive. Are there any points the two graphs have in common? If so, what are they?

4.1 Warm Up

Evaluate the function for the given value of x.

1. $f(x) = 7x - 6; x = -2$

2. $g(x) = x^2 + 3; x = 6$

3. $f(x) = -3x + 4; x = -2$

4. $g(x) = x^2 - 6x; x = -4$

5. $f(x) = 1.7x - 73; x = 16$

6. $h(x) = 8.49x; x = 4$

4.1 Cumulative Review Warm Up

Determine whether the given characteristics describe a parabola that opens up or down.

1. Focus: $(0, -5)$

Directrix: $y = 5$

2. Focus: $(0, 5)$

Directrix: $y = -5$

3. Focus: $(0, -1)$

Directrix: $y = 1$

4. Focus: $(0, 1)$

Directrix: $y = -1$

Name _____ Date _____

In Exercises 1–4, decide whether the function is a polynomial function. If so, write it in standard form and state its degree, type, and leading coefficient.

1. $f(x) = 4x^2 - 3x + 5x^3 - 7$

2. $h(x) = 5x^3 - 7x^{-2} + x - 1$

3. $g(x) = x^4 - \frac{1}{3}x^2 + 10 - 4x^3 + 2x$

4. $f(x) = 8x^2 - \sqrt{3}x + 2$

In Exercises 5–7, evaluate the function for the given value of *x*.

5. $f(x) = -2x^4 + x^3 + 5x^2 - 3x - 7; \ x = -1$

6. $g(x) = 5x^4 - 2x^3 + 9x - 10; \ x = -6$

7. $h(x) = x^5 - 4x^3 + 3x^2 + 11x - 8; \ x = 7$

In Exercises 8 and 9, describe the end behavior of the graph of the function.

8. $g(x) = 6x^4 - 3x^3 + 12x^2 + 8x + 2$

9. $h(x) = -5x^9 + 6x^7 - 5x^4 + x^2 - 1$

In Exercises 10–13, graph the polynomial function.

10. $q(x) = x^4 - 2$

11. $h(x) = x^3 - 2x + 3$

12. $k(x) = 2x^2 + 3 - x^3$

13. $f(x) = x^5 - 2x^3 + 1$

In Exercises 14 and 15, describe the *x*-values for which *f* is increasing, decreasing, positive, and negative.

14.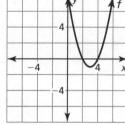

15.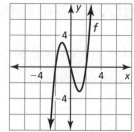

16. Suppose $f(x) \to -\infty$ as $x \to -\infty$ and $f(x) \to -\infty$ as $x \to +\infty$. Describe the degree and leading coefficient of the function.

4.1 Practice B

In Exercises 1–4, decide whether the function is a polynomial function. If so, write it in standard form and state its degree, type, and leading coefficient.

1. $h(x) = 6x^3 - 9x^{-3} + x^2 - 5x - 1$

2. $f(x) = 11x^2 - \sqrt{7} + 12x$

3. $g(x) = 2x^4 - \dfrac{1}{3}x^2 - \sqrt{14}x^3 + 2x - \dfrac{5}{3}$

4. $f(x) = 2x^3 + 9x^2 - 5x + \dfrac{4}{x} - 1$

In Exercises 5–7, evaluate the function for the given value of x.

5. $f(x) = -x^3 + 5x^2 + 9x + 4;\ x = -11$

6. $g(x) = 3x^3 + 6x^2 + 12x - 10;\ x = \dfrac{1}{3}$

7. $h(x) = 9x^3 - 8x^2 + 11x + 8;\ x = -\dfrac{1}{2}$

In Exercises 8 and 9, describe the end behavior of the graph of the function.

8. $g(x) = -5x^4 + 7x^3 - 7x^6 + x^2 - 9x + 2$

9. $h(x) = -2x^3 + 5x^2 + 4x^5 - 3x^4 + 12x^2 - 4$

In Exercises 10–13, graph the polynomial function.

10. $q(x) = x^4 - x^3 - 5x^2$

11. $h(x) = 4 - 2x^2 - x^4$

12. $k(x) = x^5 - 2x^4 + x - 2$

13. $f(x) = x^6 - 3x^5 + 2x^3 + x + 1$

In Exercises 14 and 15, sketch a graph of the polynomial function *f* having the given characteristics. Use the graph to describe the degree and leading coefficient of the function *f*.

14. *f* is increasing when $x < 1$; *f* is decreasing when $x > 1$.

$f(x) > 0$ when $-1 < x < 3$; $f(x) < 0$ when $x < -1$ and $x > 3$.

15. *f* is increasing when $x < -1.1$ and $x > 2.4$; *f* is decreasing when $-1.1 < x < 2.4$.

$f(x) > 0$ when $-2 < x < 0$ and $x > 4$; $f(x) < 0$ when $x < -2$ and $0 < x < 4$.

16. The function $h(t) = -4.9t^2 + 28.62t + 2.4$ models the height *h* of a high pop-up hit by a baseball player after *t* seconds. Use a graphing calculator to graph the function. State an appropriate window to view the maximum height of the ball and when the ball hits the ground.

4.1 Enrichment and Extension

Graphing Polynomial Functions

Quartic regression is a process by which the equation of "best fit" is found for a set of data in the form $y = ax^4 + bx^3 + cx^2 + dx + e$. Consider the data set shown below.

The median monthly rent (in dollars) in the United States for different years between 1950 and 2000 is given in the table below. Find a quartic regression model for the data by using $x = 0$ for 1950.

x	1950	1960	1970	1980	1990	2000
y	257	350	415	481	571	602

To input data, press **STAT** and then **EDIT**. Input x-values starting with 0 and y-values.

```
EDIT  CALC  TESTS
1:1-Var Stats
2:2-Var Stats
3:Med-Med
4:LinReg(ax+b)
5:QuadReg
6:CubicReg
7▪QuartReg
```

To calculate the **Quartic Regression**, press **STAT** and then **RIGHT ARROW** to **CALC**.

Select **7:QuartReg**. After **QuartReg** appears on the screen, press **ENTER**.

The equation $y \approx -0.0002x^4 + 0.0225x^3 - 0.694x^2 + 14.46x + 256.6$ should appear.

In Exercises 1–4, find a quartic regression equation for the data given in the table.

1.

x	1	2	3	4	5
y	1	−2	3	0	1

2.

x	2	4	6	8	10
y	3	−1	4	−3	4

3.

x	−1	0	1	2	3	4
y	6	−1	−3	−1.5	5	1

4.

x	23	42	112	32	98	112
y	32	87	423	23	19	233

Name_____ Date_____

 4.1 **Puzzle Time**

What Do You Get When You Cross An Ear Of Corn With A Spider?

Write the letter of each answer in the box containing the exercise number.

Write the polynomial function in standard form and state its degree, type, and leading coefficient.

1. $f(x) = \frac{3}{4}x^3 - 2x + x^4$

2. $f(x) = 12 - x + 2x^2 - 4x$

3. $f(x) = 3x^2 - x^3 + 7x - 3$

4. $f(x) = \sqrt{4}x^2 - 8$

5. $f(x) = 5 - \frac{2}{5}x^3 + 6x - x^2$

6. $f(x) = \sqrt{\frac{1}{4}}x + 10$

7. $f(x) = -3x^2 + x - x^2 - 6$

Answers

B. $f(x) = -x^3 + 3x^2 + 7x - 3$

degree 3 (cubic)
leading coefficient of −1

W. $f(x) = 2x^2 - 8$

degree 2 (quadratic)
leading coefficient of 2

O. $f(x) = 2x^2 - 5x + 12$

degree 2 (quadratic)
leading coefficient of 2

B. $f(x) = \frac{1}{2}x + 10$

degree 1 (linear)
leading coefficient of $\frac{1}{2}$

E. $f(x) = -\frac{2}{5}x^3 - x^2 + 6x + 5$

degree 3 (cubic)
leading coefficient of $-\frac{2}{5}$

C. $f(x) = x^4 + \frac{3}{4}x^3 - 2x$

degree 4 (quartic)
leading coefficient of 1

S. $f(x) = -4x^2 + x - 6$

degree 2 (quadratic)
leading coefficient of −4

1	2	3	4	5	6	7

4.2 Start Thinking

Use FOIL to multiply $(x + 1)(x - 1)$. Show your steps. Then choose another number to replace the constant 1 in the binomials and multiply. Show your steps. Is there a pattern? If so, explain the pattern.

Change the signs in the binomials so they are both the same, and multiply again. Show your steps. Does the pattern still hold? Explain why or why not.

4.2 Warm Up

Simplify.

1. $(5 - 4)7$

2. $-1(x - 7)$

3. $(3 + 4m)7$

4. $14r - 4r$

5. $6z^2 - 2z - 9z^2$

6. $6m - 3m - 4p - 5m$

4.2 Cumulative Review Warm Up

Find the value of c that makes the expression a perfect square trinomial. Then write the expression as the square of a binomial.

1. $x^2 + 5x + c$

2. $z^2 + 6z + c$

3. $w^2 - 12w + c$

4. $x^2 - 25x + c$

5. $x^2 - 8x + c$

6. $s^2 + 27x + c$

4.2 Practice A

In Exercises 1–3, find the sum.

1. $\left(-6x^2 + 3x - 7\right) + \left(10x^2 + 4x - 2\right)$

2. $\left(10x^4 + 3x^2 - 5x + 4\right) + \left(7x^5 - 5x^4 + 2x - 9\right)$

3. $\left(5x^4 + 3x^2 - 6x - 10\right) + \left(2x^3 - 7x^2 + 6x + 1\right)$

In Exercises 4–6, find the difference.

4. $\left(4x^3 + 6x^2 - 9x + 1\right) - \left(8x^3 + 2x^2 - 5x - 1\right)$

5. $\left(10x^4 - 4x^3 - 7x^2 + 5x + 9\right) - \left(2x^4 - 5x^3 - 4x^2 + 9x + 3\right)$

6. $\left(7x^5 + 4x^3 - 2x^2 + 12x + 5\right) - \left(6x^4 - 9x^3 + x^2 - 3\right)$

7. A city is planning a new sports park. The total area (in square feet) of the park is modeled by the expression $9x^2 + 4x - 5$. The area of the park designated for soccer fields is modeled by the expression $2x^2 - 5x + 3$. Write an expression that models the area of the park that is not designated for soccer fields.

In Exercises 8–11, find the product.

8. $5x^2\left(3x^2 + 7x + 6\right)$

9. $-2x^4\left(10x^3 - 9x^2 - 7x + 4\right)$

10. $\left(8x^2 - 3x + 1\right)(-3x + 2)$

11. $(-x - 6)\left(3x^2 + 2x + 9\right)$

12. Describe and correct the error in performing the operation.

$$\times \quad -3x^2\left(4x^2 - 5x + 7\right) = -12x^4 - 15x^3 + 21x^2$$

In Exercises 13–16, find the product of the binomials.

13. $(x - 1)(x + 4)(x - 3)$

14. $(x - 6)(x - 9)(x + 2)$

15. $(x + 3)(2x + 1)(2x - 3)$

16. $(3x + 5)(x - 4)(4x + 1)$

In Exercises 17–19, find the product.

17. $(x + 8)(x - 8)$

18. $(y + 4)^2$

19. $(2p - 3)^2$

4.2 Practice B

In Exercises 1 and 2, find the sum.

1. $\left(8x^7 - 6x^5 + 4x^3 - 6x\right) + \left(15x^6 + 4x^5 - 3x^3 + 2\right)$

2. $\left(8x^4 - 2x^3 + 9x^2 + 7x + 14\right) + \left(6x^4 - 5x^3 - 9x^2 - 11x - 9\right)$

In Exercises 3 and 4, find the difference.

3. $\left(9x^5 + 5x^4 - 9x^2 + 10x\right) - \left(12x^5 + 2x^4 - x^2 - 9\right)$

4. $\left(12x^4 - 6x^2 + 2x + 14\right) - \left(3x^4 - 5x^3 + 9x + 3\right)$

In Exercises 5–8, find the product.

5. $\left(x^2 - 7x - 2\right)\left(x^2 - 3x - 6\right)$

6. $\left(2x^2 + 3x - 1\right)\left(-5x^2 - 2x + 4\right)$

7. $\left(4x^2 - 3x + 6\right)\left(x^2 - 2x + 2\right)$

8. $\left(3x^2 - 6x - 5\right)\left(x^4 + 2x^2 + 5x\right)$

9. Describe and correct the error in performing the operation.

$$\times \quad 4x^2\left(3x^4 - 2x^3 + 7\right) = 12x^8 - 8x^6 + 28x^2$$

In Exercises 10–13, find the product of the binomials.

10. $(x - 3)(2x + 2)(3x - 1)$

11. $(2x + 3)(x - 5)(4x + 1)$

12. $(2x - 1)(3 - 2x)(4x + 5)$

13. $(5 - 2x)(2 - x)(4x + 3)$

In Exercises 14–16, find the product.

14. $(3x + 5)(3x - 5)$

15. $\left(6t + 7\right)^2$

16. $\left(pq + 2\right)^2$

17. A rectangular pool has a level floor. The length of the pool is $(3x - 1)$ feet, the width of the pool is $(x + 6)$ feet, and the depth of the pool is $(x + 6)$ feet.

   a. Write an expression for the volume of the pool as a product of binomials.

   b. Write an expression for the volume of the pool as a polynomial in standard form.

4.2 Enrichment and Extension

Adding, Subtracting, and Multiplying Polynomials

In Exercises 1–6, use the properties of adding, subtracting, and multiplying polynomials to solve for the variables.

1. When $ax^2 + bx - 1$ is added to $ax^3 + 2bx^2 - 2x - 1$, the result is $3x^3 + 11x^2 + 2x - c$. Find a, b, and c.

2. When $2bx^4 + x^2 - b$ is added to $3x^3 - dx^2 + cx + a$, the result is $6x^4 + bx^3 - 4x^2 + 2x - 2$. Find a, b, c, and d.

3. When $bx^4 - x^2 + 2x - 4$ is subtracted from $7x^4 + cx^2 + 5x + 6$, the result is $5x^4 + ax^3 - 3x^2 + 3x + d$. Find a, b, c, and d.

4. When $5x^3 - 3ax + 6$ is subtracted from $10x^3 + ax^2 - x + b$, the result is $cx^3 - 4x^2 + dx - 3$. Find a, b, c, and d.

5. The expression $35x^5 + 21x^4 + 7x^3$ is ax^3 times greater than $5x^2 + (3 + b)x + c$. Find a, b, and c.

6. The expression $ax^2 - bx + 25$ is $3x - c$ times greater than $3x - c$. Find a, b, and c.

7. Complete the missing values and bottom row of Pascal's Triangle.

$$
\begin{array}{ccccccc}
 & & & 1 & & & \\
 & & 1 & & 1 & & \\
 & & 1 & 2 & & \underline{} & \\
 & 1 & \underline{} & 3 & 1 & & \\
1 & & \underline{} & 6 & 4 & 1 & \\
1 & 5 & 10 & 10 & 5 & 1 & \\
\underline{} & \underline{} & \underline{} & \underline{} & \underline{} & \underline{} & \underline{}
\end{array}
$$

In Exercises 8–13, use Pascal's Triangle to expand $(a + b)^n$ with $n = 6$, for the a-b pair given

8. $a = x$ and $b = 1$

9. $a = 2y$ and $b = -2$

10. $a = 1$ and $b = -y$

11. $a = x^2$ and $b = 0$

12. $a = x^2$ and $b = -2$

13. $a = bc$ and $b = de$

Name _____ Date _____

 4.2 **Puzzle Time**

What Do You Get When You Cross A Centipede With A Parrot?

Write the letter of each answer in the box containing the exercise number.

Find the sum, difference, or product.

1. $(10x^2 + 5) - (6x^2 - x + 4)$

2. $(x^5 + 3x^4 - x + 7) + (3x^5 - 8x^4 - x^3 + 12)$

3. $(-3x^3 + 8x^2 - 4) - (-2x^3 - x^2)$

4. $-x^2(4x^3 - 2x^2 + 5x - 7)$

5. $(4x^3 - 2) - (3x^2 - 2)$

6. $(x - 4)(x + 3)$

7. $(5x^2 - x + 2)(-4x + 1)$

8. $(2 - x)(10x^2 - 7x + 9)$

9. $(-2x^2 - 5x + 1)(x^2 + 3x - 2)$

10. $(8x^3 - 2x^2 + 6x - 18) + (4x^3 - x^2 - 5x + 7)$

11. $(15x - 8) - (20x + 8)$

12. $(x - 2)(x + 4)(x - 10)$

13. $(2x - 1)(3 - x)(4 + 2x)$

Answers
A. $-x^3 + 9x^2 - 4$
A. $4x^2 + x + 1$
T. $-10x^3 + 27x^2 - 23x + 18$
W. $4x^5 - 5x^4 - x^3 - x + 19$
K. $-5x - 16$
K. $4x^3 - 3x^2$
I. $x^2 - x - 12$
E. $-20x^3 + 9x^2 - 9x + 2$
E. $-4x^3 + 6x^2 + 22x - 12$
A. $-2x^4 - 11x^3 - 10x^2 + 13x - 2$
L. $12x^3 - 3x^2 + x - 11$
L. $-4x^5 + 2x^4 - 5x^3 + 7x^2$
I. $x^3 - 8x^2 - 28x + 80$

1		2	3	4	5	6	7		8	9	10	11	12	13

4.3 Start Thinking

Factor the trinomial $x^2 + x - 2$ into the product of two binomials. Use your knowledge of inverse operations to explain why the equation $\dfrac{x^2 + x - 2}{x - 1} = x + 2$ must be true.

Using this example as evidence, can you conclude that factoring and division are the same? Explain why or why not.

4.3 Warm Up

Factor the expression completely.

1. $13t + 39y$

2. $3k^2 - 3k$

3. $5a^2b^2 - a^2b + 11ab^2$

4. $x^2 - 25$

5. $n^2 - 13n + 22$

6. $3x^2 + 30x + 63$

4.3 Cumulative Review Warm Up

Write a function g whose graph represents the indicated transformations of the graph of f.

1. $f(x) = x$; vertical stretch by a factor of 3, followed by a translation 2 units down

2. $f(x) = x$; vertical shrink by a factor of $\frac{1}{4}$, followed by a translation 1 unit up

3. $f(x) = |x|$; horizontal stretch by a factor of 3, followed by a translation 1 unit left

4.3 Practice A

In Exercises 1–4, divide using polynomial long division.

1. $\left(x^2 + x + 12\right) \div (x - 5)$

2. $\left(2x^2 - x - 1\right) \div (x - 2)$

3. $\left(x^3 + x^2 - 9x - 6\right) \div \left(x^2 - 9\right)$

4. $\left(6x^3 - x^2 + 12x\right) \div \left(x^2 + 2\right)$

In Exercises 5–10, divide using synthetic division.

5. $\left(x^2 + 6x + 1\right) \div (x - 3)$

6. $\left(3x^2 - 11x - 4\right) \div (x - 1)$

7. $\left(2x^2 - x + 5\right) \div (x + 2)$

8. $\left(x^3 - 2x + 6\right) \div (x + 3)$

9. $\left(x^2 + 25\right) \div (x - 5)$

10. $\left(5x^2 - 3x + 2\right) \div (x - 1)$

11. Describe and correct the error in using synthetic division to divide $x^3 + 2x^2 + 7$ by $x + 3$.

$$
\begin{array}{r|rrr}
\!\!\!\diagdown\ \ 3 & 1 & 2 & 0 & 7 \\
 & & 3 & 15 & 45 \\
\hline
 & 1 & 5 & 15 & 52
\end{array}
$$

$$\frac{x^3 + 2x^2 + 7}{x + 3} = x^2 + 5x + 15 + \frac{52}{x + 3}$$

In Exercises 12–15, use synthetic division to evaluate the function for the indicated value of x.

12. $f(x) = -x^2 - 7x + 18;\ x = -2$

13. $f(x) = 2x^2 - 3x + 6;\ x = 5$

14. $f(x) = x^3 + 2x^2 - 3x + 4;\ x = -1$

15. $f(x) = x^3 + 2x^2 - 5x + 12;\ x = -3$

16. You divide two polynomials and obtain the result $x^2 - 3 + \dfrac{6}{x + 1}$. What is the dividend? How did you find it?

4.3 Practice B

In Exercises 1–3, divide using polynomial long division.

1. $(x^3 + 3x^2 - 4x - 6) \div (x^2 - 4)$

2. $(4x^4 + 2x^3 - 9x^2 - 36) \div (x^2 + x - 4)$

3. $(2x^4 - 40x^2 - 28) \div (x^2 - 5x - 2)$

In Exercises 4–9, divide using synthetic division.

4. $(4x^2 - 15x + 7) \div (x - 2)$

5. $(x^3 - 9x + 12) \div (x + 3)$

6. $(x^2 + 16) \div (x - 4)$

7. $(2x^3 - 5x^2 + 3) \div (x + 1)$

8. $(x^4 + 5x^3 - 6x^2 - 11x + 14) \div (x + 4)$

9. $(x^4 + 2x^3 + 4x - 20) \div (x + 6)$

10. Describe and correct the error in using synthetic division to divide $x^3 + 2x^2 + 7$ by $x + 3$.

$$
\begin{array}{r|rrrr}
\diagdown \quad -3 & 1 & 2 & 0 & 7 \\
 & & -3 & 3 & -9 \\
\hline
 & 1 & -1 & 3 & -2
\end{array}
$$

$$\frac{x^3 + 2x^2 + 7}{x + 3} = x^3 - x^2 + 3x - 2$$

In Exercises 11–14, use synthetic division to evaluate the function for the indicated value of x.

11. $f(x) = x^3 + x^2 - 4x + 3;\ x = -1$

12. $f(x) = -x^3 - 6x^2 + 6;\ x = -2$

13. $f(x) = x^4 + 5x^2 - 8x + 1;\ x = 4$

14. $f(x) = -x^4 - x^2 - 5;\ x = 3$

15. What is the value of k such that $(x^3 + kx^2 - 9x - 36) \div (x + 4)$ has a remainder of zero?

4.3 Enrichment and Extension

Finding Oblique Asymptotes

A line is an *asymptote* when a graph approaches it more and more closely. An *oblique asymptote,* or *slant asymptote*, exists if the following statement is true.

A line $y = ax + b$ is a slant asymptote of the graph of f when
$f(x) - (ax + b)$ approaches 0 as x approaches positive or
negative infinity.

Example: Find the oblique asymptote of the graph of $f(x) = \dfrac{x^2 - 6}{x + 4}$.

Solution: Use synthetic or long division.

$f(x) = x - 4 + \dfrac{10}{x + 4}$, which can be rewritten as $f(x) - (x - 4) = \dfrac{10}{x + 4}$.

As x approaches positive or negative infinity, the remainder term $\dfrac{10}{x + 4}$ approaches 0.

So, the oblique asymptote is $y = x - 4$.

In Exercises 1–6, use synthetic or long division to find the oblique asymptote of the graph of the function.

1. $f(x) = \dfrac{-3x^2 + 2}{x - 1}$

2. $f(x) = \dfrac{x^2 + 3x + 2}{x - 2}$

3. $f(x) = \dfrac{6x^2 + 13x - 5}{3x + 5}$

4. $f(x) = \dfrac{x^2 + 8x + 15}{x + 2}$

5. $f(x) = \dfrac{2x^3 + 4x^2 - 9}{3 - x^2}$

6. $f(x) = \dfrac{ax^2 + bx + c}{x + d}$

4.3 Puzzle Time

Why Did The Other Vegetables Like The Corn?

A	B	C	D	E	F
G	H				

Complete each exercise. Find the answer in the answer column. Write the word under the answer in the box containing the exercise letter.

8 LEND	
3 WAS	
5 AN	
6 WILLING	

Divide using polynomial long division. Match the expression with the equivalent expression at the bottom.

A. $(x^2 + x - 10) \div (x - 2)$

B. $(x^3 + x^2 + x + 4) \div (x^2 + 2)$

C. $(8x^3 + 2x^2) \div (x^2 - 1)$

D. $(4x^4 - 36x^2 - 30x - 12) \div (x^2 - 3x)$

Divide using synthetic division. Match the expression with the equivalent expression at the bottom.

E. $(x^2 + 3x - 1) \div (x + 1)$ **F.** $(5x^2 - 2x + 8) \div (x - 4)$

G. $(x^3 - 2x^2 + x - 6) \div (x + 3)$

H. $(x^2 + 16) \div (x - 4)$

4 EAR	
2 HE	
1 ALWAYS	
7 TO	

Answers

1. $8x + 2 + \dfrac{8x + 2}{x^2 - 1}$

2. $x + 3 - \dfrac{4}{x - 2}$

3. $x + 1 + \dfrac{-x + 2}{x^2 + 2}$

4. $x + 4 + \dfrac{32}{x - 4}$

5. $x^2 - 5x + 16 + \dfrac{-54}{x + 3}$

6. $4x^2 + 12x + \dfrac{-30x - 12}{x^2 - 3x}$

7. $x + 2 + \dfrac{-3}{x + 1}$

8. $5x + 18 + \dfrac{80}{x - 4}$

Consider the polynomial $21xy + 3x + 40y - 5$. To factor a polynomial with four terms, consider each term separately, focusing first on the coefficients.

Is there any way you can group two of the terms together so that their coefficients have a common factor greater than 1? If so, what groups can you make? Can you group the polynomial together in such a way that it makes two groups, each with coefficients that have a common factor larger than 1? If so, state the groups.

Find the greatest common factor of the polynomial.

1. $9y + 3xy^3$

2. $6r^3s - 8rs$

3. $3x + 3xy - 3xz$

4. $4y^2z + 4yz - 5y^3z$

5. $5ab^3 - 5a^3b + 11a^3b$

6. $-x^2y + xy - xy$

Graph the function. Label the vertex and the axis of symmetry.

1. $y = 4x^2 + 4x - 5$

2. $y = -4x^2 + 5x$

3. $y = 5x^2 - 23x + 8$

4. $y = x^2 + 2x - 1$

5. $y = x^2 - x + 3$

6. $y = 2x^2 + 3x + 1$

Name_____ Date_____

4.4 Practice A

In Exercises 1–6, factor the polynomial completely.

1. $x^3 - x^2 - 12x$

2. $9p^7 - 36p^5$

3. $3n^6 - 33n^5 + 72n^4$

4. $2k^4 - 242k^2$

5. $2w^4 - 7w^3 - 15w^2$

6. $3q^6 - 17q^5 - 28q^4$

In Exercises 7–9, factor the polynomial completely.

7. $x^3 + 27$

8. $y^3 + 1000$

9. $w^3 - 125$

In Exercises 10–13, factor the polynomial completely.

10. $y^3 - 3y^2 + 4y - 12$

11. $q^3 - 2q^2 + 9q - 18$

12. $2d^3 + 10d^2 + 3d + 15$

13. $x^3 - 6x^2 - 9x + 54$

In Exercises 14–16, factor the polynomial completely.

14. $36p^4 - 25$

15. $n^4 + 11n^2 + 28$

16. $y^4 - 16$

In Exercises 17–20, determine whether the binomial is a factor of the polynomial function.

17. $f(x) = 3x^3 + 7x^2 - 8x - 5;\ x + 5$

18. $f(x) = 2x^3 + 15x^2 - 23x + 36;\ x + 9$

19. $f(x) = 6x^5 - 8x^4 - 6x^3 - 4x^2;\ x - 2$

20. $f(x) = 12x^3 - 69x^2 + 39x + 30;\ x - 6$

21. Fill in the blank of the divisor so that the remainder is 0. Justify your answer.

$f(x) = x^3 + 5x^2 - 6x;\ (x - \underline{\ \ })$

22. What is the value of k such that $x - 6$ is a factor of
$f(x) = 3x^3 - 17x^2 - kx + 18$? Justify your answer.

23. Factor each polynomial completely.

a. $5a^2c - 3a^2d + 5b^2c - 3b^2d$

b. $x^{2n} + 6x^n + 9$

Name _____ Date _____

In Exercises 1–6, factor the polynomial completely.

1. $5t^5 - 320t^3$

2. $2p^6 - 26p^5 + 84p^4$

3. $3x^4 - 432x^2$

4. $5a^6 - 16a^5 - 45a^4$

5. $12j^9 - 28j^8 + 15j^7$

6. $15q^{10} + 38q^9 + 24q^8$

In Exercises 7–9, factor the polynomial completely.

7. $2p^9 - 16p^6$

8. $25k^8 + 1600k^5$

9. $54w^7 - 16w^4$

In Exercises 10–13, factor the polynomial completely.

10. $x^3 - 7x^2 + 5x - 35$

11. $m^3 - 2m^2 - 16m + 32$

12. $9w^3 - 27w^2 - 4w + 12$

13. $25s^3 + 100s^2 - s - 4$

In Exercises 14–16, factor the polynomial completely.

14. $81g^4 - 625$

15. $2t^8 + 6t^5 - 20t^2$

16. $5v^{10} - 25v^6 + 30v^2$

In Exercises 17–20, determine whether the binomial is a factor of the polynomial function.

17. $f(x) = 4x^3 - 15x^2 - 30x + 25;\ x - 5$

18. $f(x) = 2x^3 + 16x^2 - 4x - 50;\ x + 7$

19. $f(x) = 8x^5 + 43x^4 - 58x^3 + 60x^2 - 70;\ x - 4$

20. $f(x) = 42x^4 + 143x^3 + 37x^2 - 27x + 45;\ x - 2$

21. Fill in the blank of the divisor so that the remainder is 0. Justify your answer.

$f(x) = 2x^3 + 7x^2 - 4x;\ (x + \underline{\ \ \ })$

22. The standard equation of a circle with radius r and center (h, k) is

$(x - h)^2 + (y - k)^2 = r^2$. Rewrite the equation of each circle in

standard form. Identify the center and radius of the circle. Then graph the circle.

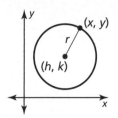

a. $x^2 + 8x + 16 + y^2 = 9$

b. $x^2 - 10x + 25 + y^2 = 4$

c. $x^2 - 4x + 4 + y^2 + 6y + 9 = 16$

4.4 Enrichment and Extension

Factoring Polynomials

In Exercises 1–6, use synthetic division or other methods to find the value of _k_ that makes the linear expression a factor of the nonlinear expression.

1. $x^3 - k; x - 3$

2. $x^3 + 3x^2 - x + k; x - 2$

3. $x^2 - kx + 2; x - 1$

4. $x^2 - kx + 4; x + 2$

5. $kx^3 - 2x^2 + x - 6; x + 3$

6. $x^5 + kx^3 - 5x^4 + 5x - 15; x - 3$

The pattern for the sum or difference of two cubes can be applied to the sum or difference of higher powers.

Recall:

$$\left(a^3 + b^3\right) = (a + b)\left(a^2 - ab + b^2\right)$$

$$\left(a^3 - b^3\right) = (a - b)\left(a^2 + ab + b^2\right)$$

When given $a^n \pm b^n$, where _n_ is a whole number ≥ 3:

- The first factor will be $a + b$, given an original sign of addition.

- The first factor will be $a - b$, given an original sign of subtraction.

- The first term of the second factor will be a^{n-1}, the following terms have alternating signs, and the last term will be b^{n-1}, given an original sign of addition.

- The first term of the second factor will be a^{n-1}, the following terms will be positive, and the last term will be b^{n-1}, given an original sign of subtraction.

- In the second factor, the exponents of _a_ will decrease by 1 and the exponents of _b_ will increase by 1 from left to right.

Example: Factor $x^9 + y^9$.

Solution:
$$x^9 + y^9 = (x + y)\left(x^8 - x^7y + x^6y^2 - x^5y^3 + x^4y^4 - x^3y^5 + x^2y^6 - xy^7 + y^8\right)$$

In Exercises 7–10, factor the expression.

7. $x^5 - y^5$

8. $a^7 + b^7$

9. $a^{14} - b^{14}$

10. $x^{10} - y^{10}$

4.4 Puzzle Time

What Type Of Player Gives Refunds?

Write the letter of each answer in the box containing the exercise number.

Factor the polynomial completely.

1. $x^3 + 125$

2. $1 - x^3$

3. $x^3 + 8$

4. $x^3 + x^2 - 6x$

5. $2x^4 - 162x^2$

6. $x^3 + 6x^2 + 3x + 18$

7. $x^3 - x^2 + 2x - 2$

8. $x^3 + 2x^2 - 4x - 8$

9. $9x^4 - 36$

10. $2x^4 + 4x^2$

11. $x^4 - 4x^2 - 5$

Answers

K. $(x^2 - 5)(x^2 + 1)$

A. $9(x^2 + 2)(x^2 - 2)$

A. $(x + 2)(x^2 - 2x + 4)$

R. $x(x - 2)(x + 3)$

T. $2x^2(x - 9)(x + 9)$

Q. $(x + 5)(x^2 - 5x + 25)$

E. $(x^2 + 3)(x + 6)$

R. $(x^2 + 2)(x - 1)$

U. $(1 - x)(1 + x + x^2)$

B. $(x + 2)^2(x - 2)$

C. $2x^2(x^2 + 2)$

1	2	3	4	5	6	7	8	9	10	11

4.5 Start Thinking

Using a graphing calculator, graph the function $f(x) = x^3 - 6x^2$. What are the two ordered pairs that represent where the graph of the function appears to cross the x-axis? Substitute the x- and y-values into the function (note that $f(x)$ and y are equivalent) and simplify.

Describe what happens when a point where the graph crosses the x-axis is inserted into the function.

4.5 Warm Up

Solve.

1. $4t - 6 = -7$

2. $8x - 28 = -68$

3. $-3 - \dfrac{r}{10} = 3$

4. $15 = \dfrac{5 - z}{-1}$

5. $-7m + 9 = 23$

6. $\dfrac{3b}{2} - 7 = 23$

4.5 Cumulative Review Warm Up

Solve the inequality algebraically.

1. $5x^2 > 25$

2. $x^2 + 12x \le -27$

3. $x^2 + 6x + 6 \ge 1$

4. $x^2 < 5$

5. $x^2 + 2x - 4 > -1$

6. $x^2 - 9x < -8$

4.5 Practice A

In Exercises 1–6, solve the equation.

1. $q^3 - q^2 - 30q = 0$

2. $k^3 + 6k^2 + 9k = 0$

3. $3y^4 - 6y^3 = -3y^2$

4. $n^3 + 2n^2 - 9n - 18 = 0$

5. $3p^3 = 21p$

6. $8u^6 = 16u^4$

In Exercises 7–10, find the zeros of the function. Then sketch a graph of the function.

7. $f(x) = x^4 + x^3 - 12x^2$

8. $g(x) = x^4 - 8x^2 + 16$

9. $h(x) = x^5 - 2x^4 - 15x^3$

10. $f(x) = -3x^3 - 15x^2 - 12x$

11. According to the Rational Root Theorem, which is *not* a possible solution of the equation $3x^4 - 6x^3 + 2x + 4 = 0$?

   A. 4   **B.** $\dfrac{1}{3}$ **C.** -3 **D.** $-\dfrac{2}{3}$

12. Describe and correct the error in listing the possible rational zeros of the function.

   $$\cancel{\hspace{1em}} \quad f(x) = x^3 + 3x^2 - 8x - 18$$
   $$\text{Possible zeros: } \pm 2, \pm 3, \pm 6, \pm 9$$

In Exercises 13 and 14, find all the real solutions of the equation.

13. $x^4 - 8x^2 - 9 = 0$

14. $x^3 + 2x^2 - 5x - 6 = 0$

15. Write a third or fourth degree polynomial function that has zeros at $\pm\dfrac{3}{2}$. Justify your answer.

16. Determine the value of k for each equation so that the given x-value is a solution.

   a. $x^3 + 2x^2 - 9x + k = 0;\ x = 3$

   b. $x^3 - 3x^2 + kx - 12 = 0;\ x = -4$

Name_____ Date _____

4.5 Practice B

In Exercises 1–6, solve the equation.

1. $4x^4 + 12x^3 + 9x^2 = 0$

2. $6h^5 = 12h^3$

3. $16q^4 - 8q^2 + 1 = 0$

4. $w^4 + 81 = 18w^2$

5. $p^3 - 25p = 50 - 2p^2$

6. $y^3 - 8y^2 = 9y - 72$

In Exercises 7–10, find the zeros of the function. Then sketch a graph of the function.

7. $f(x) = -5x^4 + 20x^3 + 60x^2$

8. $g(x) = -x^3 - x^2 + 30x$

9. $h(x) = x^3 + x^2 - 4x - 4$

10. $f(x) = x^3 - 4x^2 - 9x + 36$

11. According to the Rational Root Theorem, which is *not* a possible zero of the function $f(x) = 24x^4 - 16x^3 + 21x - 27$?

    A. $-\dfrac{3}{8}$

    B. -2

    C. $-\dfrac{1}{3}$

    D. $-\dfrac{9}{4}$

12. Describe and correct the error in listing the possible rational zeros of the function.

    $$\times \quad f(x) = 2x^3 + 5x^2 - 2x - 6$$
    Possible zeros: $\pm1, \pm2, \pm3, \pm6$

In Exercises 13 and 14, find all the real solutions of the equation.

13. $2x^3 - 3x^2 + 18x - 27 = 0$

14. $x^3 - 5x^2 - 2x + 24 = 0$

15. Write a third or fourth degree polynomial function that has zeros at $\pm\dfrac{7}{5}$. Justify your answer.

16. The sidewalk hazard marker is shaped like a pyramid, with a height 2 centimeters greater than the length of each side of its square base. The volume of the marker is 297 cubic centimeters. What are the dimensions of the sidewalk hazard marker?

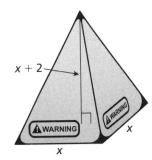

Name _____ Date _____

4.5 Enrichment and Extension

Solving Polynomial Equations

Given the zeros of a polynomial function, you can write the polynomial function.

Example: Write the simplest polynomial function for which -2 and $-3 + i$ are zeros and $P(0) = -40$.

Solution: Recall that if $a + bi$ is a zero of a polynomial function, then $a - bi$ is also a zero. So, the factors are $(x + 2)$, $\left[x - (-3 + i)\right]$, and $\left[x - (-3 - i)\right]$.

Allow for a stretch by a factor of a.

$$P(x) = a(x + 2)\left[(x + (3 - i)\right]\left[x + (3 + i)\right]$$

$$P(x) = a(x + 2)(x^2 + 6x + 10)$$

Because $P(0) = -40$, substitute 0 for x and -40 for $P(x)$.

$$-40 = a(0 + 2)(0^2 + 6(0) + 10)$$
$$-40 = 20a$$
$$a = -2$$

So, $P(x) = -2(x + 2)(x^2 + 6x + 10)$ or $P(x) = -2x^3 - 16x^2 - 44x - 40$.

In Exercises 1–5, write a polynomial function in standard form.

1. P is of degree 2; $P(0) = 14$; zeros: 1 and -2

2. P is of degree 3; $P(0) = 2$; zeros: -2 and 1 with a multiplicity of 2

3. P is of degree 4; $P(0) = 0$; zeros: -2, 3, and 0 with a multiplicity of 2

4. P is of degree 4; $P(0) = -60$; zeros: $-5, 1, -2i$, and $2i$

5. P is of degree 3; $P(0) = 45$; zeros: 3 and $-2 + i$

Name_____ Date_____

4.5 Puzzle Time

What Did The Weatherman Say About His Meteorology Test?

A	B	C	D	E	F
G	H	I	J		

Complete each exercise. Find the answer in the answer column. Write the word under the answer in the box containing the exercise letter.

$x = -14, 0, 2$
IT
$x = -1, 2,$
A
$x = -1, 0, 5$
FOGGY
$x = -2, 0, 2$
BREEZE
$x = -4, 0, 4$
WITH

Solve the equation.

A. $2x^3 + 24x^2 = 56x$

B. $2x^5 - 6x^4 = 56x^3$

C. $x^3 - x = 0$

D. $34x^3 - 48x = 22x^3$

E. $4x^4 - 64x^2 = 0$

F. $2x^3 - 4x^2 - 96x = -8x^2$

Find the real zeros of the function.

G. $f(x) = x^4 - x^3 + x^2 - 3x - 6$

H. $f(x) = 3x^3 - 5x^2 - 47x - 15$

I. $f(x) = x^3 - 4x^2 - 5x$

J. $f(x) = x^3 - 3x^2 - 4x + 12$

$x = -3, -\frac{1}{3}, 5$
FEW
$x = -4, 0, 7$
WAS
$x = -2, 2, 3$
PATCHES
$x = -8, 0, 6$
ONLY
$x = -1, 0, 1$
A

4.6 Start Thinking

Use a graphing calculator to complete the table.

Function	Number of *x*-intercepts
$f(x) = x + 4$	
$g(x) = x^2 - 5$	
$h(x) = x^3 + 3x^2 - x - 1$	
$j(x) = x^4 - x^3 - 4x^2 + 1$	

What is the pattern? Do you think the pattern will continue infinitely? Why or why not?

4.6 Warm Up

Identify the degree of the polynomial.

1. $8ab - 5b^3 + a^4$

2. $2x^3$

3. $4m^3 p^2 - 7$

4. $x^6 + 11 - 4x$

5. $3z + 3z + 6z^3$

6. $6x^3 y^2 - 3x$

4.6 Cumulative Review Warm Up

Graph the function and its parent function. Then describe the transformation, if any.

1. $g(x) = x - 5$

2. $f(x) = x^2$

3. $g(x) = |x + 6|$

4. $h(x) = -x$

Name_____ Date _____

4.6 Practice A

In Exercises 1–4, identify the number of solutions or zeros.

1. $x^4 + 3x^3 - 4x^2 + 2x = 0$

2. $3y^3 + y^2 - 3 = 0$

3. $8q^5 - 4q^3 + 7q = 0$

4. $6r^6 + 3r^4 - 7r^2 = 0$

In Exercises 5–8, find all zeros of the polynomial function.

5. $f(x) = x^4 - 5x^2 - 36$

6. $f(x) = x^4 + x^3 - 7x^2 - x + 6$

7. $g(x) = x^4 - x^3 + 9x^2 - 9x$

8. $h(x) = x^4 - 11x^2 + 18$

In Exercises 9 and 10, determine the number of imaginary zeros for the function with the given degree and graph. Explain your reasoning.

9. Degree: 5

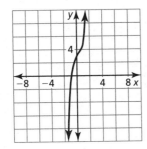

10. Degree: 4

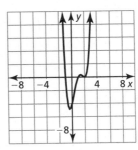

In Exercises 11–13, write a polynomial function f of least degree that has rational coefficients, a leading coefficient of 1, and the given zeros.

11. $-4, 1, 2$

12. $2, 3, -1$

13. $2, \sqrt{3}$

14. Write a polynomial function of degree 5 with zeros -1, 2, and i. Justify your answer.

In Exercises 15–17, determine the possible numbers of positive real zeros, negative real zeros, and imaginary zeros for the function.

15. $g(x) = x^3 - 2x^2 - 3x + 1$

16. $g(x) = x^4 + x^2 - 10$

17. $g(x) = x^5 - 2x^4 + x^2 - 3x - 2$

Name _____ Date _____

4.6 Practice B

In Exercises 1–4, identify the number of solutions or zeros.

1. $-x^4 + 4x^3 + 4x^2 - 3x = 0$

2. $3y^5 + 2y^3 - 5y = 0$

3. $8q^3 - 5q^2 + 7q = 0$

4. $9r^6 + 6r^5 - 7r^3 = 0$

In Exercises 5–8, find all zeros of the polynomial function.

5. $h(x) = x^4 - 4x^3 + 3x^2 + 4x - 4$

6. $f(x) = x^4 - 12x^3 + 54x^2 - 108x + 81$

7. $g(x) = x^5 + 4x^4 + x^3 - 14x^2 - 20x - 8$

8. $f(x) = x^5 + 2x^4 - 13x^3 - 26x^2 + 36x + 72$

In Exercises 9 and 10, determine the number of imaginary zeros for the function with the given degree and graph. Explain your reasoning.

9. Degree: 4

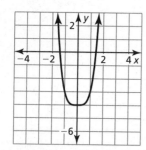

10. Degree: 3

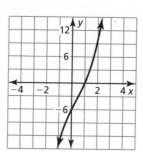

In Exercises 11–13, write a polynomial function f of least degree that has rational coefficients, a leading coefficient of 1, and the given zeros.

11. $2, 3 + i$

12. $2i, 1 - i$

13. $3, -\sqrt{7}$

14. Two zeros of $f(x) = x^3 - 2x^2 + 9x - 18$ are $3i$ and $-3i$. Explain why the third zero must be a real number.

15. Use Descartes' Rule of Signs to determine which function has no positive real zeros.

A. $f(x) = x^4 - 3x^2 + 6x - 7$

B. $f(x) = x^4 + 2x^2 + 4x - 3$

C. $f(x) = x^4 + x^2 + 10$

D. $f(x) = x^4 + 5x^3 - 9x - 7$

4.6 Enrichment and Extension

The Fundamental Theorem of Algebra

The Fundamental Theorem of Algebra states that an nth-degree polynomial function f has exactly n zeros. Given the zeros, factors can be written and ultimately simplified to represent the polynomial.

Represent a polynomial as a product of irreducible and linear factors, and state all zeros.

Example: $f(x) = x^4 - 19x^3 + 113x^2 - 163x - 296$

Solution: Use the Rational Root Theorem to find a zero, and continue factoring. $f(x)$ has possible zeros of ± 296, ± 148, ± 74, ± 37, ± 8, ± 4, ± 2, and ± 1. Synthetic division determines $x = 8$ is a rational zero. Continue dividing until factors are irreducible.

$f(x) = (x - 8)(x + 1)(x^2 - 12x + 37)$ 　　　Product of irreducible factors

$f(x) = (x - 8)(x + 1)\big[x - (6 + i)\big]\big[x - (6 - i)\big]$ 　　　Product of linear factors

The zeros are 8, -1, $6 - i$, and $6 + i$.

In Exercises 1–6, write the function as (a) the product of irreducible factors and (b) the product of linear factors. Then (c) list all zeros.

1. $f(x) = x^4 + 4x^3 - 19x^2 - 106x - 120$

2. $h(x) = x^4 - 5x^3 - 21x^2 + 119x - 130$

3. $g(x) = 4x^4 - 35x^3 + 140x^2 - 295x + 156$

4. $f(x) = x^4 - 3x^3 - 12x^2 + 8$

5. $g(x) = x^4 - 2x^3 - 17x^2 + 4x + 30$

6. $g(x) = 2x^5 + x^4 - 7x^3 + 21x^2 - 225x + 108$

Name_____ Date _____

4.6 Puzzle Time

What Do You Get When You Cross A Dog With Canvas?

Write the letter of each answer in the box containing the exercise number.

Write a polynomial function *f* of least degree that has rational coefficients, a leading coefficient of 1, and the given zeros.

1. $-4, 1, 2$

2. $0, 3, 5$

3. $-6, -1, 3$

4. $-4, 1, 12$

5. $-\sqrt{2}, 3$

6. $7, 1 + i$

7. $2i, 1 - i$

8. $2, 3 + 2i, \sqrt{5}$

Answers

E. $f(x) = x^3 - 9x^2 + 16x - 14$

N. $f(x) = x^4 - 2x^3 + 6x^2 - 8x + 8$

P. $f(x) = x^3 - 8x^2 + 15x$

A. $f(x) = x^3 + x^2 - 10x + 8$

U. $f(x) = x^3 + 4x^2 - 15x - 18$

T. $f(x) = x^3 - 3x^2 - 2x + 6$

P. $f(x) = x^3 - 9x^2 - 40x + 48$

T. $f(x) = x^5 - 8x^4 + 20x^3$
$+ 14x^2 - 125x + 130$

1		2	3	4		5	6	7	8

Use the graph of the function $g(x) = x^5$ to fill in the table.

Function	Transformation	Function	Transformation
$g(x) = (x - 2)^5$		$g(x) = -x^5$	
$g(x) = (x + 2)^5$		$g(x) = (2x)^5$	
$g(x) = x^5 - 2$		$g(x) = \left(\frac{1}{2}x\right)^5$	
$g(x) = x^5 + 2$		$g(x) = 2x^5$	

How are the transformations related to other parent functions?

4.7 **Warm Up**

Describe the transformation.

1. $g(x) = 5x$

2. $h(x) = -\frac{1}{3}x^2$

3. $g(x) = 2x$

4. $f(x) = -\frac{1}{2}|x|$

4.7 **Cumulative Review Warm Up**

Describe the transformation of $f(x) = x^2$ represented by g. Then graph each function.

1. $g(x) = x^2 + 5$

2. $g(x) = (x - 1)^2$

3. $g(x) = (x + 2)^2$

4. $g(x) = (x - 5)^2 + 3$

Name _____ Date _____

4.7 Practice A

In Exercises 1 and 2, describe the transformation of *f* represented by *g*. Then graph each function.

1. $f(x) = x^3$, $g(x) = x^3 - 2$

2. $f(x) = x^3$, $g(x) = (x + 3)^3$

In Exercises 3–6, describe the transformation of *f* represented by *g*. Then graph each function.

3. $f(x) = x^4$, $g(x) = -5x^4$

4. $f(x) = x^3$, $g(x) = 4x^3 - 3$

5. $f(x) = x^5$, $g(x) = \frac{2}{3}x^5 - 5$

6. $f(x) = x^4$, $g(x) = \frac{1}{2}(x - 2)^4$

In Exercises 7 and 8, write a rule for *g* and then graph each function. Describe the graph of *g* as a transformation of the graph of *f*.

7. $f(x) = x^3 + 2$, $g(x) = f(x - 1)$

8. $f(x) = x^4 - 3x + 1$, $g(x) = 2f(x)$

9. Describe and correct the error in graphing the function $g(x) = (x - 3)^2 + 2$.

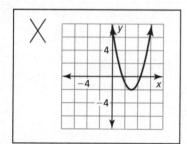

In Exercises 10 and 11, write a rule for *g* that represents the indicated transformations of the graph of *f*.

10. $f(x) = x^3 + 5$; translation 2 units right, followed by a reflection in the *y*-axis

11. $f(x) = x^4 - 3x + 1$; vertical shrink by a factor of $\frac{1}{3}$, followed by a translation 2 units down

12. The volume V (in cubic yards) of a rectangular box is given by $V = x^3 + 4x + 3$.

    a. The function $W(x) = V(3x)$ gives the volume (in cubic feet) of the box when *x* is measured in yards. Write a rule for W.

    b. The function $Z(x) = W(12x)$ gives the volume (in cubic inches) of the box when *x* is measured in yards. Write a rule for Z.

Name_____ Date_____

4.7 Practice B

In Exercises 1 and 2, describe the transformation of *f* represented by *g*. Then graph each function.

1. $f(x) = x^4$, $g(x) = (x - 3)^4 - 2$

2. $f(x) = x^5$, $g(x) = (x - 1)^5 + 4$

In Exercises 3–6, describe the transformation of *f* represented by *g*. Then graph each function.

3. $f(x) = x^5$, $g(x) = -3x^5$

4. $f(x) = x^4$, $g(x) = 3x^4 + 2$

5. $f(x) = x^4$, $g(x) = \frac{1}{3}x^4 - 3$

6. $f(x) = x^4$, $g(x) = \frac{2}{3}(x + 3)^4$

In Exercises 7 and 8, write a rule for *g* and then graph each function. Describe the graph of *g* as a transformation of the graph of *f*.

7. $f(x) = x^3 - 4x^2 + 2$, $g(x) = -\frac{1}{4}f(x)$

8. $f(x) = x^4 + x + 1$, $g(x) = f(-x) + 2$

9. Describe and correct the error in describing the transformation of the graph of $f(x) = x^4$ represented by the graph of $g(x) = 4x^4 + 3$.

$\times$ The graph of *g* is a vertical shrink by a factor of $\frac{1}{4}$, followed by a translation 3 units up of the graph of *f*.

In Exercises 10 and 11, write a rule for *g* that represents the indicated transformations of the graph of *f*.

10. $f(x) = x^3 - 3x^2 + 2$; horizontal stretch by a factor of 3 and a translation 3 units up, followed by a reflection in the *x*-axis

11. $f(x) = 3x^5 - x^3 + 5x^2 + 1$; reflection in the *y*-axis and a vertical shrink by a factor of $\frac{1}{2}$, followed by a translation 1 unit up

12. The volume *V* (in cubic inches) of a rectangular box is given by $V = 2x^3 + 9$.

    a. The function $W(x) = V\left(\frac{x}{12}\right)$ gives the volume (in cubic feet) of the box when *x* is measured in inches. Write a rule for *W*. Find and interpret $W(6)$.

    b. The function $Z(x) = W\left(\frac{x}{3}\right)$ gives the volume (in cubic yards) of the box when *x* is measured in inches. Write a rule for *Z*.

4.7 Enrichment and Extension

Transformations of Polynomial Functions

Displayed below are cubic functions.

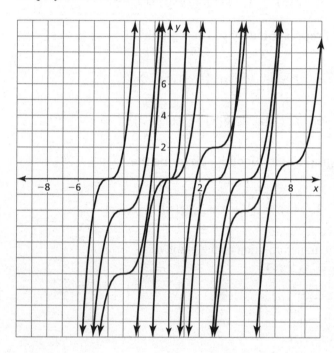

These are equations for three of the graphs:

$y = x^3$,

$y = 2(x + 4)^3$, and

$y = (x + 3)^3 - 2$.

Find the remaining equations.

Name_____ Date_____

4.7 Puzzle Time

What Day Does A Fish Hate The Most?

Write the letter of each answer in the box containing the exercise number.

Match the function with the correct transformation of the graph of $f(x) = x^4$.

1. $f(x) = (x - 2)^4 - 1$

2. $f(x) = (x + 1)^4 - 2$

3. $f(x) = (x - 1)^4 - 2$

4. $f(x) = (x + 2)^4 - 1$

5. $f(x) = (x - 2)^4 + 1$

6. $f(x) = (x + 2)^4 + 1$

Answers
Y. E
R. C
Y. F
D. B
A. D
F. A

A.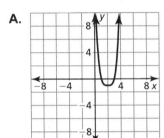

B.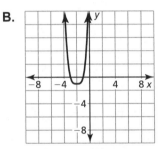

C.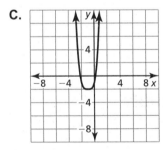

D.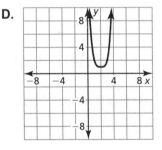

E.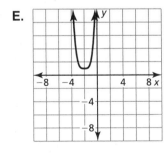

F.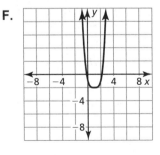

1	2	3	4	5	6

Use a graphing calculator to graph the function
$f(x) = 7x^3 + 4x^2 - 18x - 5$. Describe the shape of the
function. Use the *table* feature to look at the y-values where
the sign changes from positive to negative or vice versa.

What can you conclude from this data as it relates to the zeros
of the function? Does this view show the exact values that are
solutions? Explain.

4.8 **Warm Up**

Find the vertex of the function.

1. $y = x^2 - 10x - 8$

2. $y = -x^2 + 6x + 3$

3. $y = 3x^2 + 12x - 7$

4. $y = -3x^2 + 8x$

5. $y = -x^2 + 16x - 19$

6. $y = -x^2 + 4x + 6$

4.8 **Cumulative Review Warm Up**

**Write the quadratic function in vertex form. Then identify
the vertex.**

1. $f(x) = x^2 + 6x - 20$

2. $g(x) = x^2 + 4x + 2$

3. $g(x) = x^2 - 10x - 38$

4. $h(x) = x^2 - 20x - 91$

5. $h(x) = x^2 - 2x + 49$

6. $f(x) = x^2 - 6x + 3$

Name_____ Date_____

4.8 Practice A

In Exercises 1–4, graph the function.

1. $f(x) = (x + 2)^2(x - 3)$

2. $g(x) = (x - 1)^2(x + 1)(x + 3)$

3. $h(x) = 2(x - 1)(x - 2)(x + 2)$

4. $f(x) = 3(x - 1)^2(x + 1)^2$

5. Describe and correct the error in using factors to graph $f(x) = (x - 1)^2(x + 3)$.

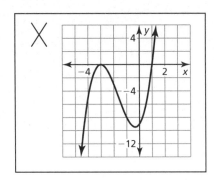

In Exercises 6–9, find all real zeros of the function.

6. $f(x) = x^3 + 3x^2 - 4x - 12$

7. $f(x) = x^3 + 7x^2 - x - 7$

8. $f(x) = x^3 - 5x^2 + x - 5$

9. $f(x) = 2x^3 - 3x^2 - 18x + 27$

In Exercises 10–13, graph the function. Identify the *x*-intercepts and the points where the local maximums and local minimums occur. Determine the intervals for which the function is increasing and decreasing.

10. $f(x) = 2x^3 - 5x^2 + 3$

11. $g(x) = -x^4 + 2x$

12. $h(x) = x^4 - 2x^2 + 3x$

13. $f(x) = x^4 - 4x^3 + 5x - 2$

In Exercises 14 and 15, estimate the coordinates of each turning point. State whether each is a local maximum or a local minimum. Then estimate the real zeros and find the least possible degree of the function.

14.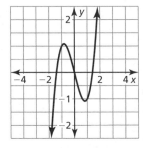

15.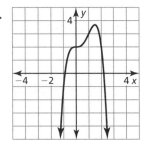

Name _____ Date _____

In Exercises 1–4, graph the function.

1. $f(x) = 4(x + 3)^2 (x - 2)^2$

2. $g(x) = \frac{1}{2}(x - 4)(x + 3)(x - 6)$

3. $h(x) = \frac{1}{5}(x - 3)(x - 4)(x + 8)$

4. $f(x) = (x - 2)(x^2 + x + 2)$

5. Describe and correct the error in using factors to graph $f(x) = x^2(x + 2)^3$.

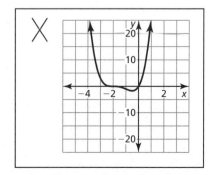

In Exercises 6–9, find all real zeros of the function.

6. $f(x) = 2x^3 - x^2 + 8x - 4$

7. $f(x) = 2x^3 + 7x^2 + x - 10$

8. $f(x) = 4x^3 - 3x^2 - 36x + 27$

9. $f(x) = 2x^3 + 3x^2 + 10x + 15$

In Exercises 10–13, graph the function. Identify the *x*-intercepts and the points where the local maximums and local minimums occur. Determine the intervals for which the function is increasing and decreasing.

10. $f(x) = 0.5x^3 - 3x^2 + 1.5$

11. $g(x) = 0.4x^3 - 3x$

12. $h(x) = x^5 - 3x^2 - 9x - 2$

13. $f(x) = x^4 - 3x^3 + 3x^2 + x - 2$

14. You are making a rectangular box out of a 12-inch by 8-inch piece of cardboard. The box will be formed by making the cuts shown in the diagram and folding up the sides. You want the box to have the greatest volume possible.

   a. How long should you make the cuts?

   b. What is the maximum volume?

   c. What are the dimensions of the finished box?

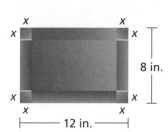

4.8 Enrichment and Extension

Analyzing Graphs of Polynomial Functions

The *bisection method*, also known as the *interval method*, is a root-finding method that repeatedly bisects an interval to obtain increasingly narrow subintervals in which a root must lie. This simple but slow method can be used to obtain a rough approximation of a zero of a polynomial function.

Suppose the bisection method is used to find the zero of the polynomial $f(x) = x^3 - 3$.

Two numbers a and b have to be found such that $f(a)$ and $f(b)$ have opposite signs. Because $f(1) = -2$ and $f(2) = 5$, $a = 1$ and $b = 2$ satisfy the condition.

The function is continuous, so the zero must lie within the interval $[1, 2]$. The average is taken and replaced into the function: $f(1.5) = 0.375$.

Because 1.5 produces a positive result, it replaces the positive result of 2. The interval is now $[1, 1.5]$. The pattern will continue until the outcome approaches 0.

The zero is about 1.44.

In Exercises 1–5, use the bisection method to approximate (to the nearest hundredth) the zero between the two values of x for the function.

1. $f(x) = x^2 - 10$, $f(3) = -1$, $f(4) = 6$

2. $f(x) = x^3 - x - 2$, $f(1) = -2$, $f(2) = 4$

3. $f(x) = 4x^3 - 3x + 5$, $f(-2) = -21$, $f(-1) = 4$

4. $f(x) = 3x^3 - 10x^2 - 20x + 110$, $f(-3) = -1$, $f(-2) = 86$

5. $f(x) = x^5 - 2x^3 - 12$, $f(1) = -13$, $f(2) = 4$

4.8 Puzzle Time

What Do You Call A Computer That Only Types In Uppercase?

Write the letter of each answer in the box containing the exercise number.

Match the function with its graph.

1. $f(x) = (x - 2)(x - 3)(x + 3)$

2. $f(x) = (x - 3)^2(x - 2)$

3. $f(x) = (x + 2)(x + 3)(x - 3)$

4. $f(x) = (x + 2)^2(x - 3)$

5. $f(x) = (x + 3)^2(x - 2)$

6. $f(x) = (x - 2)^2(x + 3)$

Answers	
H. A	**S.** B
Y. C	**F.** D
I. E	**T.** F

A.
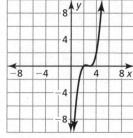

B.

C.

D.
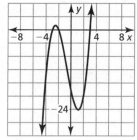

E.

F.
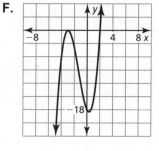

1	2	3	4	5	6

4.9 Start Thinking

Plot any two points in a coordinate plane. Connect them with a line. Plot a third point that is not on the line defined by the first two points. Connect them with a smooth curve, negating the need for the line connecting only the first two points.

What type of an equation could fit the three points? What familiar figure does the smooth curve represent? Plot a fourth point that is not on the line or smooth curve. Connect the four points with a smooth curve. What function does this curve represent?

4.9 Warm Up

Find the rate of change.

1.

x	4	6	8	10	12
y	−7	1	9	17	25

2.

x	−6	−3	0	3	6
y	4	3	2	1	0

3.

x	4	6	8	10	12
y	−7	1	9	17	25

4.

x	−5	−3	−1	1	3
y	−2	0	2	4	6

4.9 Cumulative Review Warm Up

Solve the system of linear equations using the substitution method.

1. $y = 5x + 1$
$y = -4x + 10$

2. $y = 3x - 2$
$-2x + y = -5$

Name _____ Date _____

4.9   Practice A

In Exercises 1 and 2, write a cubic function whose graph passes through the given points.

1.

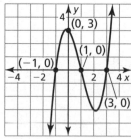

2.

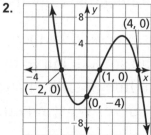

In Exercises 3–5, use finite differences to determine the degree of the polynomial function that fits the data. Then use technology to find the polynomial function.

3.

x	1	2	3	4	5	6	7
f(x)	1	3	7	14	25	41	63

4.

x	−4	−2	0	2	4	6
f(x)	−3	2	8	15	23	32

5.

x	1	2	3	4	5	6	7
f(x)	30	20	4	−16	−38	−60	−80

6. The data in the table show the cumulative number of customers during a 6-hour period.

x	1	2	3	4	5	6
f(x)	2	7	13	20	28	37

   a. Find a polynomial model for the data.

   b. The store is open 24 hours each day. Does this model seem reasonable for the next 6-hour period? Explain.

Name_____ Date_____

 4.9 **Practice B**

In Exercises 1 and 2, write a cubic function whose graph passes through the given points.

1.
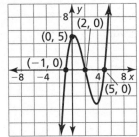

2.
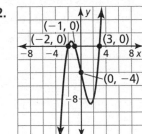

In Exercises 3–5, use finite differences to determine the degree of the polynomial function that fits the data. Then use technology to find the polynomial function.

3.

x	1	2	3	4	5	6
f(x)	−10	−14	−13	−7	4	20

4.

x	1	2	3	4	5	6	7	8
f(x)	24	12	6	9	24	54	102	171

5.

x	1	2	3	4	5	6	7
f(x)	20	4	0	4	16	40	84

6. The data in the table show the wave height (in inches) over a 7-second period.

x	1	2	3	4	5	6	7
f(x)	0.5	3	6.5	12	20.5	33	50.5

a. Find a polynomial model for the data.

b. Does this model seem reasonable for the next 7-second interval? Explain.

4.9 Enrichment and Extension

Modeling with Polynomial Functions

A *sequence* is an ordered list of numbers called terms. Sequences can be infinite (never ending) or finite. There are different types of sequences. *Arithmetic sequences* are sequences whose successive terms differ by the same number d, called the common difference. Most precisely, a sequence can be defined as a function.

An *explicit formula* is a function that represents each term of the sequence. For example, if given the infinite arithmetic sequence 3, 7, 11, 15, …

For the nth term, the common difference 4 is added $(n - 1)$ times.

So, the explicit formula is:

$t_n = t_1 + (n - 1)d$

$t_n = 3 + (n - 1)4$

$t_n = 4n - 1.$

In Exercises 1–6, state whether the sequence is arithmetic. If so, identify the common difference d.

1. 15, 18, 21, 24, …

2. 4, 6, 9, 13.5, …

3. 16, 7, −2, −11, …

4. 11, 8, 5, 3, …

5. $1, 1\frac{3}{5}, 2\frac{1}{5}, 2\frac{4}{5}, …$

6. 1, 2, 4, 6, …

In Exercises 7–12, write an explicit formula for the arithmetic sequence.

7. 4, 8, 12, 16, …

8. −3, −5, −7, −9, …

9. 18, 7, -4, −15, …

10. 12, 10, 8, 6, …

11. $1, 1\frac{2}{3}, 2\frac{1}{3}, 3, …$

12. 8.6, 7.3, 6, 4.7, …

Name_____ Date_____

 Puzzle Time

What Do You Throw Out When You Need It And Take In When You Don't Need It?

Write the letter of each answer in the box containing the exercise number.

Write a cubic function whose graph passes through the points.

1. $(-2, 0), (-1, 0), (0, -8), (2, 0)$

2. $(-1, 0), (1, 0), (2, 0), (3, 16)$

3. $(-10, 0), (-5, 0), (4, 0), (-8, -2)$

4. $(2, 0), (1, 0), (4, 0), (5, -3)$

Answers

R. $f(x) = \frac{3}{10}(x + 8)(x + 5)(x + 1)$

O. $f(x) = -\frac{5}{4}x(x + 3)(x - 2)$

A. $f(x) = 2x^3 + 2x^2 - 8x - 8$

N. $f(x) = 2(x - 1)(x + 1)(x - 2)$

H. $f(x) = -\frac{1}{4}(x - 2)(x - 1)(x - 4)$

C. $f(x) = -\frac{1}{36}(x + 10)(x + 5)(x - 4)$

5.

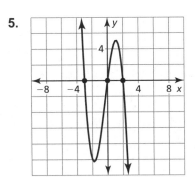

6.

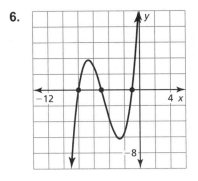

1	2	3	4	5	6

Chapter 4 Cumulative Review

In Exercises 1–12, simplify the expression.

1. $5j + 12j$

2. $-7p + 3p$

3. $3 - 4q + 9q$

4. $5m - 2m + 5$

5. $7 + 3b - 6b + 12$

6. $7x - 12 + 14 - 9x$

7. $4(c + 7)$

8. $-5(r - 3)$

9. $8(z - 3) - 20$

10. $-9(4 - a) - 2$

11. $12(3x - 5) + 43 + 2(x + 4)$

12. $8(2d + 4) - 27 - 3(5 - d)$

In Exercises 13–28, solve the equation.

13. $5x - 2x = 12$

14. $4y + 7y = 33$

15. $-7b + 13b - 11 = 1$

16. $4m - 9m + 3 = -22$

17. $3(a + 2) = 18$

18. $-4(p + 12) = -72$

19. $-2(4 - w) = 20$

20. $5(6 + x) = 40$

21. $-3(y + 2) + 12 = 21$

22. $7(s - 8) + 44 = 2$

23. $2(x - 6) + 44 = 50 + 11x$

24. $14x + 2(9 - x) - 12 = -5x + 40$

25. $42 - 3(6 - x) + 30 = 10x + 2(18 + x)$

26. $-31 + 4(x - 12) + 15 = 37 + 13x$

27. $6(4x + 3) - 20 + 2(x + 9) = 10(x - 2) + 12x$

28. $3(2x - 7) + 22 = 1 - (2x + 11) - 13$

29. An Internet music store charges $35 for monthly access, and you can download up to 56 songs every month. There is a $1.20 charge for every song downloaded after 56 songs per month.

  a. Write an equation for the Internet music store modeling the total cost y for x songs over the monthly 56-song limit.

  b. How much does it cost to download 50 songs?

  c. How much does it cost to download 64 songs?

  d. The Internet music company decides to omit the monthly access fee, but charge $0.75 per song. When is this a better deal, compared to the monthly access fee?

Chapter 4 Cumulative Review (continued)

In Exercises 30–37, write an expression for the given information.

30. a number x increased by 7

31. the difference of a number n and 5

32. 3 times a number m decreased by 9

33. $\frac{1}{5}$ of a number c plus 1

34. 17 plus the opposite of $4y$

35. the opposite of 5 plus 4 times a number p

36. 5 times a number j increased by the opposite of 14

37. $\frac{1}{2}$ a number t decreased by 4 times a number m

In Exercises 38–49, factor the expression.

38. $x^2 + 10x + 24$

39. $x^2 - 8x - 33$

40. $x^2 + 5x - 84$

41. $x^2 + 16x + 55$

42. $x^2 - 9x + 14$

43. $x^2 - 15x + 50$

44. $5x^2 + 47x + 56$

45. $9x^2 - 53x - 6$

46. $2x^2 + 3x - 20$

47. $3x^2 + 13x + 12$

48. $2x^2 - x - 3$

49. $2x^2 - x - 28$

50. Your family is purchasing new carpet for the living room. The length of the room is 14 feet and the width is 18 feet.

    a. How much carpet is needed?

    b. The carpet your family wants is \$3.29 per square foot. How much will the carpet for the living room cost?

51. The length (in feet) of a fence is $(x + 4)$, and the width (in feet) is $(2x - 23)$.

    a. Write an equation for the perimeter p of the fence.

    b. Write an equation for the area a of the fence.

    c. The perimeter of the fence is 76 feet. Find the dimensions of the length and the width.

    d. What is the area of the fence?

Chapter 4 **Cumulative Review** (continued)

In Exercises 52–61, solve the quadratic equation by factoring.

52. $x^2 - x - 6 = 0$

53. $x^2 - 8x - 9 = 0$

54. $x^2 + 12x + 35 = 0$

55. $x^2 - 6x + 9 = 0$

56. $x^2 + 7x - 44 = 0$

57. $x^2 - 8x + 7 = 0$

58. $6x^2 + 35x + 36 = 0$

59. $2x^2 + x - 21 = 0$

60. $5x^2 - 19x - 4 = 0$

61. $8x^2 - 14x - 9 = 0$

In Exercises 62–69, use the Quadratic Formula to solve the equation.

62. $x^2 - 7x + 8 = 0$

63. $x^2 + 13x - 1 = 0$

64. $x^2 - 14x = -2$

65. $x^2 + 9x = 4$

66. $3x^2 - 24x + 7 = 0$

67. $2x^2 + 9x - 3 = 0$

68. $4x^2 - 36x + 1 = 0$

69. $5x^2 - 42x - 4 = 0$

In Exercises 70–77, find all the zeros of the function.

70. $f(x) = x^2 - 9x + 21$

71. $g(x) = x^2 - x - 20$

72. $h(x) = x^2 - 3x - 1$

73. $f(x) = x^2 - 5x - 19$

74. $g(x) = 4x^2 - 5x + 10$

75. $h(x) = 3x^2 - 7x - 21$

76. $f(x) = 5x^2 - 11x + 8$

77. $g(x) = 2x^2 - 9x - 7$

78. Your class's midterm grades are modeled by the equation
$y = -0.0705x^2 + 10.460x - 384.21$, where x represents the midterm grade (percent) and y represents the number of students who earned the grade.

   a. Approximately how many students earned an 80%?

   b. Approximately how many students earned a 75%?

79. Your class's semester grades are modeled by the equation
$y = -0.0680x^2 + 11.845x - 511.86$, where x represents the semester grade (percent) and y represents the number of students who earned the grade.

   a. Approximately how many students earned an 85%?

   b. Approximately how many students earned a 93%?

Chapter 4 Cumulative Review (continued)

In Exercises 80–87, describe the transformation of $f(x) = x^2$ represented by g.

80. $g(x) = (x - 4)^2$

81. $g(x) = x^2 + 8$

82. $g(x) = (x - 3)^2 + 5$

83. $g(x) = (x + 1)^2 - 4$

84. $g(x) = -x^2 - 3$

85. $g(x) = -(x - 1)^2 + 5$

86. $g(x) = -5x^2 - 2$

87. $g(x) = \frac{1}{3}(x + 5)^2 - 3$

In Exercises 88–93, write a function whose graph represents the indicated transformation of the graph of f.

88. $f(x) = x - 1$; reflection in the y-axis and a translation 4 units up

89. $f(x) = |x + 3|$; vertical shrink by a factor of $\frac{1}{4}$ and a translation 1 unit up

90. $f(x) = \sqrt{x} + 4$; vertical stretch by a factor of 4, followed by a translation 2 units right

91. $f(x) = |x - 1| + 5$; translation of 3 units left and 4 units down

92. $f(x) = 2x - 7$; reflection in the x-axis, followed by a vertical shrink by a factor of $\frac{1}{2}$ and a translation 3 units up

93. $f(x) = x^2 - 3$; reflection in the x-axis, followed by a translation 2 units left and 5 units up

94. You are playing baseball. The ball follows a parabolic path modeled by the equation $y = -2x^2 + 19x + 2$, where x represents the time (in seconds) after the ball is hit and y represents the height of the ball (in feet) from the ground.

   a. How high is the ball after 3 seconds?

   b. How high is the ball after 6 seconds?

   c. What was the original starting height of the ball? What does this mean, according to the situation described?

   d. Does this function have a maximum or a minimum?

   e. What is the maximum or minimum, and when does this maximum or minimum occur?

Chapter 5

Name_____ Date_____

Dear Family,

In this chapter, you will solve equations to determine depreciation values of items. When an item depreciates, it loses value over time. You may have heard that when you buy a new car, the car loses value once you drive it off the lot. According to a certain website, the average depreciation rate for a new car is about 11%. That means, if you buy a brand new car for $30,000, the car is worth $26,700 once you drive away. The website also says that after 5 years, your car is only worth 37% of what you originally paid. Not all cars depreciate at the same rate, so these numbers are averages. Sources such as Kelley Blue Book give the market value prices for all new and used vehicles. When you use that website, you can give specific information about your vehicle, so you have an accurate value to use when pricing to sell or buying new.

Working together, choose three different cars to research.
Complete the table by finding the price of each car for five years.
For a fair comparison of each car, choose a constant annual mileage of 10,000 miles.

Car Values			
Year	Make/Model	Make/Model	Make/Model
	$	$	$
	$	$	$
	$	$	$
	$	$	$
	$	$	$

Use the completed table to answer the following questions.

- Which car has the lowest depreciation rate? the highest?

- Which car would you be most likely to buy? Explain.

- What factors contribute to a vehicle's depreciation rate?

When buying a new or a used car, you may also want to use the Internet to compare the reliability of each car. This may end up saving you time and money in the long run.

And remember to always buckle up!

Capítulo 5 — Exponentes racionales y funciones radicales

Estimada familia:

En este capítulo, resolverán ecuaciones para determinar los valores de depreciación de objetos. Cuando un objeto se deprecia, pierde su valor con el transcurso del tiempo. Tal vez hayan escuchado que cuando compran un carro nuevo, el carro pierde su valor cuando lo sacan del auto lote. De acuerdo con un sitio web, la tasa de depreciación promedio de un carro nuevo es de aproximadamente el 11%. Eso significa que si compran un carro nuevo por $30,000, el carro vale $26,700 cuando se lo llevan. El sitio web también dice que después de 5 años, su carro solo vale el 37% de lo que pagaron originalmente. No todos los carros se deprecian a la misma tasa, entonces estos números son un promedio. Fuentes tal como Kelley Blue Book dan los precios de valor de mercado de todos los vehículos nuevos y usados. Cuando usan ese sitio web, pueden dar información específica sobre su vehículo, así tienen un valor preciso cuando coticen para vender o para comprar un carro nuevo.

Trabajen juntos para elegir tres carros diferentes para investigar. Para completar la tabla, hallen el precio de cada carro durante cinco años. A fin de hacer una comparación equitativa de cada carro, elijan un millaje constante anual de 10,000 millas.

Valores de carros			
Año	Marca/Modelo	Marca/Modelo	Marca/Modelo
	$	$	$
	$	$	$
	$	$	$
	$	$	$
	$	$	$

Usen la tabla completada para responder las siguientes preguntas.

- ¿Cuál carro tiene la menor tasa de depreciación? ¿La mayor?

- ¿Cuál carro es más probable que compren? Expliquen.

- ¿Qué factores contribuyen a la tasa de depreciación de un vehículo?

Cuando compren un carro nuevo o usado, también pueden buscar en Internet para comparar la confiabilidad de cada carro. Esto puede ahorrarles tiempo y dinero a largo plazo.

¡Y recuerden siempre abrocharse el cinturón de seguridad!

5.1 Start Thinking

An exponent n, in the term x^n, indicates how many times x is a factor of the product. Any product in the form x^n may be written in expanded form. For example, $x^3 = x \bullet x \bullet x$.

Use expanded form to complete the table.

Example	Expanded Form	Simplest Form
$x^2 + x^2$		
$x^4 \bullet x^4$		
$\dfrac{x^8}{x^5}$		

Enter 2^{-2} into a scientific calculator. What is the answer in fraction form? How does this compare to 2^2?

5.1 Warm Up

Simplify.

1. $k(k^4)$

2. $(4u^5v)(6u^5v^2)$

3. $(5a^3b^{10}c)^2$

4. $(3x^3y)(3xy^2z)^4(3xyz)$

5. $(-g^2h)(-2gj^3)^3(-ghj)^4$

6. $(2xy^5)(-y)^4$

5.1 Cumulative Review Warm Up

Write an equation of the parabola in vertex form.

1. passes through: $(14, 7)$; vertex: $(4, 1)$

2. passes through: $(-6, -16)$; vertex: $(-4, 8)$

Name_____ Date _____

In Exercises 1–3, find the indicated real *n*th root(s) of *a*.

1. $n = 3, a = 125$

2. $n = 2, a = 49$

3. $n = 4, a = 81$

In Exercises 4–9, evaluate the expression without using a calculator.

4. $27^{1/3}$

5. $16^{1/4}$

6. $4^{3/2}$

7. $625^{3/4}$

8. $(-1000)^{2/3}$

9. $32^{1/5}$

In Exercises 10–15, evaluate the expression using a calculator. Round your answer to two decimal places when appropriate.

10. $\sqrt[5]{16,807}$

11. $\sqrt[6]{15,625}$

12. $12^{-1/3}$

13. $92^{1/5}$

14. $6561^{5/4}$

15. $113^{-3/4}$

In Exercises 16 and 17, find the radius of the figure with the given volume.

16. $V = 1726$ in.^{3}

17. $V = 734$ m^3

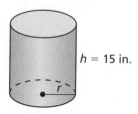
$h = 15$ in.

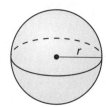

In Exercises 18–23, find the real solution(s) of the equation. Round your answer to two decimal places when appropriate.

18. $x^4 = 256$

19. $3x^3 = 375$

20. $(x - 6)^2 = 40$

21. $(x + 7)^3 = 1000$

22. $x^5 = -112$

23. $9x^4 = 54$

24. When the average price of an item increases from p_1 to p_2 over a period of *n* years, the price p_2 is given by $p_2 = p_1(r + 1)^n$, where *r* is the annual rate of inflation (in decimal form). Find the annual rate of inflation when the price of a loaf of bread was $1.19 in 1970 and $3.29 in 2010.

5.1 Practice B

In Exercises 1–3, find the indicated real nth root(s) of a.

1. $n = 3, a = 343$

2. $n = 6, a = -64$

3. $n = 5, a = -243$

In Exercises 4–9, evaluate the expression without using a calculator.

4. $36^{3/2}$

5. $16^{3/4}$

6. $(-32)^{2/5}$

7. $(-125)^{5/3}$

8. $256^{-5/4}$

9. $27^{-4/3}$

In Exercises 10–15, evaluate the expression using a calculator. Round your answer to two decimal places when appropriate.

10. $28^{-1/5}$

11. $150^{2/5}$

12. $40{,}351^{6/7}$

13. $750^{-2/5}$

14. $\left(\sqrt[5]{223}\right)^{3}$

15. $\left(\sqrt[7]{-34}\right)^{5}$

In Exercises 16 and 17, find the radius of the figure with the given volume.

16. $V = 425$ in.^{3}

17. $V = 1458$ m^3

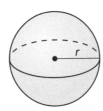

In Exercises 18–23, find the real solution(s) of the equation. Round your answer to two decimal places when appropriate.

18. $6x^4 = 60$

19. $x^5 = -233$

20. $x^4 + 19 = 100$

21. $x^3 + 17 = 57$

22. $\frac{1}{5}x^4 = 125$

23. $\frac{1}{7}x^3 = -49$

24. Kepler's third law states that the relationship between the mean distance d (in astronomical units) of a planet from the Sun and the time t (in years) it takes the planet to orbit the Sun can be given by $d^3 = t^2$.

    a. It takes Venus 0.616 year to orbit the Sun. Find the mean distance of Venus from the Sun (in astronomical units).

    b. The mean distance of Jupiter from the Sun is 5.24 astronomical units. How many years does it take Jupiter to orbit the Sun?

5.1 Enrichment and Extension

*n*th Roots and Rational Exponents

Recall the Properties of Exponents: Let a and b be nonzero real numbers. Let m and n be integers.

Product of Powers	$(a)^m (a)^n = a^{m+n}$
Quotient of Powers	$\dfrac{a^m}{a^n} = a^{m-n}$
Power of a Power	$\left(a^m\right)^n = a^{mn}$
Power of a Product	$(ab)^n = a^n b^n$
Power of a Quotient	$\left(\dfrac{a}{b}\right)^n = \dfrac{a^n}{b^n}$

Example: Find the value(s) of n for which the statement is true.

$$3^{2n-1} = 27$$
$$3^{2n-1} = 3^3$$
$$2n - 1 = 3$$
$$n = 2$$

In Exercises 1–14, find the value(s) of *n* for which the statement is true.

1. $2^n = 4^3$

2. $3^n = 9$

3. $9^{n-1} = 9^4$

4. $\left(5^n\right)\left(5^4\right) = 125$

5. $\left(2^n\right)^n = 4^8$

6. $3^{2n} = 9^8$

7. $\left(7^n\right)\left(7^4\right) = 49^{n+3}$

8. $2^n = -4$

9. $3^{2n} = 729$

10. $4^{n+1} = \dfrac{1}{64}$

11. $9^{n+4} = 3^{n-8}$

12. $8^{n-2} = \sqrt{8}$

13. $4^{2n^2 + 2n} = 8$

14. $3^{n^2 - 3n} = 81$

Challenge: Find a, b, and c such that $\left(x^{-2} y^3 z^2\right)\left(x^c y^a z^b\right) = x^{-3} y^4$ for all nonzero values of x, y, and z.

Name_____ Date _____

5.1 Puzzle Time

What Did The Waiter Say When The Customer Asked, "What Is This Insect In My Soup?"

A	B	C	D	E	F
G	H	I	J	K	L
M	N	O	P		

Complete each exercise. Find the answer in the answer column. Write the word under the answer in the box containing the exercise letter.

16 NOT
±5 WISH
±6 ME
−2 WOULD
3 I
$\frac{1}{16}$ ASK
−32 THAT
−16 YOU

Evaluate the expression. Round your answer to two decimal places when appropriate.

A. $27^{1/3}$

B. $\sqrt[4]{625}$

C. $-64^{2/3}$

D. $\sqrt[5]{-32}$

E. $(-1024)^{2/5}$

F. 2^{-4}

G. $-\sqrt[4]{1296}$

H. $\left(\sqrt[3]{-8}\right)^{5}$

I. $343^{4/3}$

J. $225^{3/2}$

K. $\left(\sqrt[7]{16{,}384}\right)^{1/2}$

L. $-4096^{1/4}$

M. $54^{1/3}$

N. $14^{-1/2}$

O. $\sqrt[5]{100}$

P. $\left(-\sqrt[3]{-18}\right)^{2}$

3.78 ONE
0.27 BUG
2 NOT
−8 KNOW
2401 I
3375 DO
2.51 FROM
6.87 ANOTHER

5.2 Start Thinking

Simplify $x^2 \cdot x^2$. What operation did you perform on the exponents?

Consider $\sqrt{x} \cdot \sqrt{x}$. Without simplifying, do you expect the answer to be greater than or less than x? Simplify the expression first by using rational number rules and then by using exponent rules. Is the answer greater than or less than x? Explain how the answer relates to the hypothesis you made before simplifying.

5.2 Warm Up

Simplify.

1. x^{-1}

2. $3x^{-6}$

3. $\dfrac{4}{b^{-7}}$

4. $\left(ab^4\right)^1$

5. $\dfrac{y^6}{y^4}$

6. $\dfrac{p^4}{p}$

5.2 Cumulative Review Warm Up

Find the discriminant of the quadratic equation. Then describe the number and type of solutions of the equation.

1. $x^2 - 13x - 35 = 0$

2. $5n^2 + 3n + 25 = 0$

3. $3x^2 = 6x + 9$

4. $25x = -49 + 4x^2$

5. $x^2 - 5x - 16 = 0$

6. $x^2 + 13x = -48$

5.2　Practice A

In Exercises 1–6, use the properties of rational exponents to simplify the expression.

1. $\left(7^2\right)^{1/4}$

2. $\left(14^3\right)^{1/2}$

3. $\dfrac{5^{1/5}}{5}$

4. $\dfrac{10}{10^{1/4}}$

5. $\left(\dfrac{6^5}{9^5}\right)^{-1/5}$

6. $\left(7^{-3/4} \cdot 7^{1/4}\right)^{-1}$

In Exercises 7–12, use the properties of radicals to simplify the expression.

7. $\sqrt{3} \cdot \sqrt{75}$

8. $\sqrt[3]{81} \cdot \sqrt[3]{9}$

9. $\sqrt[4]{12} \cdot \sqrt[4]{8}$

10. $\sqrt[4]{9} \cdot \sqrt[4]{9}$

11. $\dfrac{\sqrt[5]{128}}{\sqrt[5]{4}}$

12. $\dfrac{\sqrt{5}}{\sqrt{80}}$

In Exercises 13–18, write the expression in simplest form.

13. $\sqrt[4]{208}$

14. $\dfrac{\sqrt[3]{9}}{\sqrt[3]{4}}$

15. $\sqrt{\dfrac{5}{27}}$

16. $\dfrac{1}{2 + \sqrt{3}}$

17. $\dfrac{6}{4 - \sqrt{5}}$

18. $\dfrac{8}{\sqrt{2} + \sqrt{5}}$

In Exercises 19–24, simplify the expression.

19. $8\sqrt[4]{2} + 5\sqrt[4]{2}$

20. $7\sqrt[5]{13} - 17\sqrt[5]{13}$

21. $4\left(9^{1/4}\right) + 7\left(9^{1/4}\right)$

22. $4\sqrt{18} - 15\sqrt{2}$

23. $8\sqrt{7} + 12\sqrt{63}$

24. $\sqrt[4]{405} + 2\sqrt[4]{5}$

25. The volume of a cube is 80 cubic centimeters.

   a. Use exponents to solve the formula for the volume V of a cube with side length s, $V = s^3$, for s.

   b. Substitute the expression for s from part (a) into the formula for the surface area of a cube, $S = 6s^2$.

   c. Substitute the volume of the given cube into the formula found in part (b) to find the surface area, S. Simplify, if possible.

5.2 Practice B

In Exercises 1–6, use the properties of rational exponents to simplify the expression.

1. $\dfrac{2^{2/5}}{2}$

2. $\left(\dfrac{3^6}{12^6}\right)^{-1/6}$

3. $\left(11^{3/2} \bullet 11^{-5/2}\right)^{-1/3}$

4. $\left(9^{-3/5} \bullet 9^{1/5}\right)^{-1}$

5. $\dfrac{3^{3/4} \bullet 27^{3/4}}{9^{3/4}}$

6. $\dfrac{25^{5/9} \bullet 25^{7/9}}{5^{4/3}}$

In Exercises 7–12, use the properties of radicals to simplify the expression.

7. $\sqrt[3]{25} \bullet \sqrt[3]{625}$

8. $\sqrt[5]{6} \bullet \sqrt[5]{81}$

9. $\dfrac{\sqrt[4]{176}}{\sqrt[4]{11}}$

10. $\dfrac{\sqrt{7}}{\sqrt{700}}$

11. $\dfrac{\sqrt[3]{5} \bullet \sqrt[3]{50}}{\sqrt[3]{2}}$

12. $\dfrac{\sqrt[4]{4} \bullet \sqrt[4]{12}}{\sqrt[8]{3} \bullet \sqrt[8]{3}}$

In Exercises 13–18, write the expression in simplest form.

13. $\dfrac{\sqrt[3]{4}}{\sqrt[3]{9}}$

14. $\sqrt[3]{\dfrac{4}{25}}$

15. $\sqrt[4]{\dfrac{2401}{4}}$

16. $\dfrac{7}{5 - \sqrt{3}}$

17. $\dfrac{6}{\sqrt{2} + \sqrt{7}}$

18. $\dfrac{\sqrt{2}}{\sqrt{15} - \sqrt{3}}$

In Exercises 19–24, simplify the expression.

19. $10\left(25^{2/3}\right) - 6\left(25^{2/3}\right)$

20. $2\sqrt{54} - 11\sqrt{6}$

21. $13\sqrt[3]{3} - \sqrt[3]{375}$

22. $\sqrt[5]{486} + 10\sqrt[5]{2}$

23. $4\left(48^{1/4}\right) - 3\left(3^{1/4}\right)$

24. $\left(7^{1/3}\right) + 4\left(189^{1/3}\right)$

25. The volume of a right circular cylinder is $V = 9\pi r^2$, where r is the radius.

   a. Use radicals to solve $V = 9\pi r^2$ for r. Simplify, if possible.

   b. Substitute the expression for r from part (a) into the formula for the surface area of a right cylinder, $S = 18\pi r + \pi r^2$.

   c. Use the answer to part (b) to find the surface area of a right cylinder when the volume is 108 cubic meters.

Name_____ Date_____

5.2 Enrichment and Extension

Properties of Rational Exponents and Radicals

When the quantity $\left(a + \dfrac{b}{2a} \right)^2$ is simplified, it equals $a^2 + b + \dfrac{b^2}{4a^2}$.

The greater a is compared to b, the more the quantity $\dfrac{b^2}{4a^2}$ approaches zero.

So, if $a > b$, $a^2 + b + \dfrac{b^2}{4a^2} \approx a^2 + b$ and $\left(a + \dfrac{b}{2a} \right)^2 \approx a^2 + b$.

If you take the square root of each side, then $a + \dfrac{b}{2a} \approx \sqrt{a^2 + b}$.

The same process can be used to find the approximate value of $\left(a - \dfrac{b}{2a} \right)^2$.

Example:

Use the formula $\sqrt{a^2 \pm b} \approx a \pm \dfrac{b}{2a}$ to approximate each square root.

   a. $\sqrt{26} = \sqrt{25 + 1} = \sqrt{5^2 + 1} \approx 5 + \dfrac{1}{2(5)} \approx 5.1$

   b. $\sqrt{34} = \sqrt{36 - 2} = \sqrt{6^2 - 2} \approx 6 - \dfrac{2}{2(6)} \approx 5.83$

In Exercises 1–12, use the formula $\sqrt{a^2 \pm b} \approx a \pm \dfrac{b}{2a}$ to find an approximation for the square root to the nearest hundredth. Check your work with a calculator. Some of your answers may not be the same as those obtained with a calculator due to rounding.

   1. $\sqrt{10}$ **2.** $\sqrt{38}$

   3. $\sqrt{104}$ **4.** $\sqrt{126}$

   5. $\sqrt{83}$ **6.** $\sqrt{52}$

   7. $\sqrt{141}$ **8.** $\sqrt{164}$

   9. $\sqrt{13}$ **10.** $\sqrt{215}$

   11. $\sqrt{249}$ **12.** $\sqrt{395}$

Name _____ Date _____

Why Did The 25-Watt Bulb Flunk Out Of School?

Write the letter of each answer in the box containing the exercise number.

Simplify the expression.

1. $\left(8^2\right)^{1/3}$

2. $5^{3/4} \cdot 5^{1/2}$

3. $\left(\dfrac{64}{125}\right)^{1/3}$

4. $\left(2^4 \cdot 6^4\right)^{-1/4}$

5. $\left(3^{2/3} \cdot 5^{1/4}\right)^6$

6. $\dfrac{4}{4^{1/2}}$

7. $\sqrt[3]{27} \cdot \sqrt[3]{729}$

8. $\dfrac{\sqrt[4]{32}}{\sqrt[4]{256}}$

9. $\dfrac{\sqrt[3]{24} \cdot \sqrt[3]{12}}{\sqrt[3]{2}}$

10. $\dfrac{25^{1/6} \cdot 25^{1/3}}{5^{6/5}}$

11. $\dfrac{4}{8 - \sqrt{3}}$

12. $10\sqrt[4]{5} - 3\sqrt[4]{5}$

13. $12\left(4^{3/4}\right) + 5\left(4^{3/4}\right)$

14. $\sqrt[5]{3^5}$

15. $\left(3^{2/5}\right)^{1/2}$

16. $-3\left(2^{1/5}\right) - 2\left(2^{1/5}\right)$

Answers

E. $5^{5/4}$

W. $\dfrac{4}{5}$

H. 4

A. $\dfrac{1}{12}$

N. 2

S. $81 \cdot 5^{3/2}$

H. $3^{1/5}\, 3^{1/5}$

T. $\left(\dfrac{1}{8}\right)^{1/4}$

S. $2\sqrt[3]{18}$

O. 27

O. $\dfrac{1}{5^{1/5}}$

R. $7\sqrt[4]{5}$

G. 3

I. $17\left(4^{3/4}\right)$

T. $-5\left(2^{1/5}\right)$

B. $\dfrac{32 + 4\sqrt{3}}{61}$

1	2		3	4	5		6	7	8		9	10		11	12	13	14	15	16

5.3 Start Thinking

Create a function with a domain that consists of all real numbers, and a range that only consists of non-negative real numbers. Explain the thought process you went through when creating the function.

Consider the function $f(x) = \sqrt{x}$. What is its domain? What is its range?

5.3 Warm Up

Describe the transformation of $f(x) = x^2$ represented by g.

1. $g(x) = x^2 - 9$

2. $g(x) = \frac{1}{4}x^2 + 5$

3. $g(x) = \frac{1}{2}x^2$

4. $g(x) = x^2 - \frac{1}{2}$

5. $g(x) = x^2 + 3$

6. $g(x) = -2x^2 + 1$

5.3 Cumulative Review Warm Up

Determine whether the binomial is a factor of the polynomial function.

1. $g(x) = x^4 - 11x^2 + 21;\ x^2 - 3$

2. $t(x) = x^4 + 4x^3 + 8x - 46;\ x^3 + 2$

3. $f(x) = x^5 + 7x^4 + 7x + 49;\ x + 7$

4. $s(x) = x^3 - 5x^2 - 51x + 255;\ x^2 - 51$

5.3   Practice A

In Exercises 1–6, graph the function. Identify the domain and range of the function.

1. $g(x) = \sqrt{x} + 4$

2. $h(x) = \sqrt{x} - 2$

3. $f(x) = -\sqrt[3]{4x}$

4. $h(x) = \sqrt[3]{-2x}$

5. $f(x) = \frac{1}{3}\sqrt{x} - 2$

6. $g(x) = \frac{1}{4}\sqrt{x} + 5$

In Exercises 7–12, describe the transformation of *f* represented by *g*. Then graph each function.

7. $f(x) = \sqrt{x}; g(x) = \sqrt{x-1} + 4$

8. $f(x) = \sqrt{x}; g(x) = 3\sqrt{x+2}$

9. $f(x) = \sqrt[3]{x}; g(x) = -2\sqrt[3]{x}$

10. $f(x) = \sqrt[3]{x}; g(x) = \sqrt[3]{x-1} + 3$

11. $f(x) = x^{1/2}; g(x) = 3(-x)^{1/2}$

12. $f(x) = x^{1/3}; g(x) = -\frac{1}{3}x^{1/3}$

In Exercises 13–15, use a graphing calculator to graph the function. Then identify the domain and range of the function.

13. $f(x) = \sqrt{x^2 - x}$

14. $g(x) = \sqrt[3]{x^2 - x}$

15. $h(x) = \sqrt[3]{2x^2 + 3x}$

In Exercises 16 and 17, write a rule for *g* described by the transformations of the graph of *f*.

16. Let *g* be a vertical shrink by a factor of $\frac{1}{3}$, followed by a translation 3 units right of the graph of $f(x) = \sqrt{x+5}$.

17. Let *g* be a reflection in the *x*-axis, followed by a translation 2 units down of the graph of $f(x) = 5\sqrt{x} + 3$.

In Exercises 18 and 19, use a graphing calculator to graph the equation of the parabola. Identify the vertex and the direction that the parabola opens.

18. $\frac{1}{2}y^2 = x$

19. $-3y^2 = x + 6$

In Exercises 20 and 21, use a graphing calculator to graph the equation of the circle. Identify the radius and the intercepts.

20. $x^2 + y^2 = 16$

21. $25 - y^2 = x^2$

Name_____ Date_____

5.3 Practice B

In Exercises 1–6, graph the function. Identify the domain and range of the function.

1. $g(x) = -\sqrt{x} + 2$

2. $f(x) = \sqrt[3]{-4x}$

3. $f(x) = \frac{1}{4}\sqrt{x+5}$

4. $h(x) = (5x)^{1/2} - 2$

5. $g(x) = -2(x-3)^{1/3}$

6. $h(x) = -\sqrt[5]{x}$

In Exercises 7–12, describe the transformation of f represented by g. Then graph each function.

7. $f(x) = \sqrt{x}; g(x) = 4\sqrt{x-2}$

8. $f(x) = \sqrt[3]{x}; g(x) = \sqrt[3]{x-5} - 1$

9. $f(x) = x^{1/4}; g(x) = \frac{1}{3}(-x)^{1/4}$

10. $f(x) = x^{1/3}; g(x) = \frac{1}{2}x^{1/3} - 3$

11. $f(x) = \sqrt[4]{x}; g(x) = -\sqrt[4]{x-1} + 3$

12. $f(x) = \sqrt[5]{x}; g(x) = \sqrt[5]{-243x} - 2$

In Exercises 13–15, use a graphing calculator to graph the function. Then identify the domain and range of the function.

13. $g(x) = \sqrt[3]{2x^2 - 3x}$

14. $f(x) = \sqrt{\frac{1}{3}x^2 - x + 2}$

15. $h(x) = \sqrt[3]{3x^2 - 6x + 2}$

In Exercises 16 and 17, write a rule for g described by the transformations of the graph of f.

16. Let g be a horizontal stretch by a factor of 2, followed by a translation 2 units up of the graph of $f(x) = \sqrt{3x}$.

17. Let g be a translation 1 unit up and 4 units left, followed by a reflection in the y-axis of the graph of $f(x) = \sqrt{-x} - \frac{1}{2}$.

In Exercises 18 and 19, use a graphing calculator to graph the equation of the parabola. Identify the vertex and the direction that the parabola opens.

18. $3y^2 + 5 = x$

19. $x - 3 = -\frac{1}{2}y^2$

In Exercises 20 and 21, use a graphing calculator to graph the equation of the circle. Identify the radius and the intercepts.

20. $x^2 + y^2 = 81$

21. $-y^2 = x^2 - 49$

Name _____ Date _____

Polar Coordinates

All the graphs you have been using so far have been on a Cartesian coordinate plane. All coordinates have been Cartesian coordinates involving x and y. There are other coordinates that express the same location, and they are called *polar coordinates*.

For example, the Cartesian coordinates $(3, 4)$ are represented by moving 3 units right on the x-axis and 4 units up on the y-axis. The coordinates can also be expressed by the distance directly from the origin r and how many degrees it is from the x-axis.

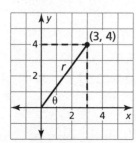

You can see that x, y, and r make a right triangle. So, you can solve for r using the Pythagorean Theorem.

$$x^2 + y^2 = r^2$$
$$3^2 + 4^2 = r^2$$
$$25 = r^2$$
$$5 = r$$

To find the number of degrees from the x-axis, or theta θ, recall trigonometric ratios.

$$\sin \theta = \frac{y}{r} \qquad \cos \theta = \frac{x}{r} \qquad \tan \theta = \frac{y}{x}$$

You could use all three, but the tangent trigonometric ratio deals with the x and y already given.

$$\tan \theta = \frac{y}{x} \qquad \tan \theta = \frac{4}{3} \qquad \tan^{-1}\left(\frac{4}{3}\right) = \theta \qquad \theta \approx 53.13°$$

So, the Cartesian coordinates $(3, 4)$ can also be approximated by the polar coordinates $(5, 53.13°)$.

In Exercises 1–6, convert the Cartesian coordinates into approximate polar coordinates. Graph the points in a coordinate plane, if needed, to help you understand. Round your answer to two decimal places when necessary.

  1. $(6, 8)$ **2.** $(1, 1)$

  3. $(8, 4)$ **4.** $(-10, 2)$

  5. $(-3, -4)$ **6.** $(-5, -7)$

 **Puzzle Time**

What Has Lots Of Eyes But Can't See?

Write the letter of each answer in the box containing the exercise number.

Match the graph with its function or equation.

1.

2.

3.

4.

Answers
O. $f(x) = \sqrt[3]{x-2}$
A. $f(x) = \sqrt{x-2} + 1$
T. $f(x) = x^{1/2} + 1$
A. $f(x) = \sqrt[4]{x-2} + 1$
O. $x^2 + y^2 = 4$
T. $f(x) = (x+1)^{1/4} - 2$
P. $f(x) = x^{1/3} - 2$

5.

6.

7.

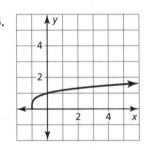

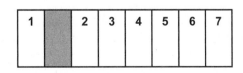

5.4 Start Thinking

Suppose the right triangle shown has hypotenuse length $c = 13$. Use the given information to write the Pythagorean Theorem in simplest form.

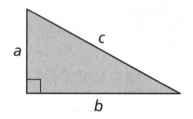

5.4 Warm Up

Determine if the given numbers could be the lengths of the sides of a right triangle.

1. $a = 9, b = 40, c = 41$

2. $a = \sqrt{6}, b = 6, c = 15$

3. $a = 18, b = 24, c = 30$

4. $a = 10, b = 20, c = 24$

5. $a = 8, b = 15, c = 17$

6. $a = 10, b = 28, c = 29$

5.4 Cumulative Review Warm Up

Use the graph to write an equation of the line and interpret the slope.

1.

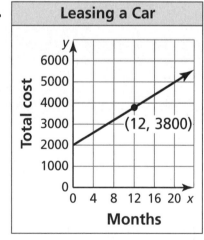

2.

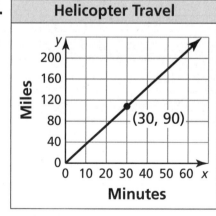

Name_____ Date _____

5.4 Practice A

In Exercises 1–6, solve the equation. Check your solution.

1. $\sqrt{3x - 2} = 5$

2. $\sqrt{6x + 1} = 9$

3. $\sqrt[3]{x + 10} = 4$

4. $\sqrt[3]{x} - 8 = -2$

5. $-3\sqrt{16x} + 14 = -10$

6. $6\sqrt[3]{25x} - 16 = 14$

7. Biologists have discovered that the shoulder height h (in centimeters) of a male Asian elephant can be modeled by $h = 62.5\sqrt[3]{t} + 75.8$, where t is the age (in years) of the elephant. Determine the age of an elephant with a shoulder height of 300 centimeters.

In Exercises 8–13, solve the equation. Check your solution(s).

8. $x - 8 = \sqrt{4x}$

9. $\sqrt{2x - 14} = x - 7$

10. $\sqrt{x + 22} = x + 2$

11. $\sqrt[3]{8x^3 + 27} = 2x + 3$

12. $\sqrt[4]{2 - 9x^2} = 3x$

13. $\sqrt{3x - 5} = \sqrt{x + 9}$

In Exercises 14–16, solve the equation. Check your solution(s).

14. $2x^{2/3} = 18$

15. $x^{3/4} + 10 = 0$

16. $(x + 12)^{1/2} = x$

17. Describe and correct the error in solving the equation.

$$\begin{aligned}
\sqrt[3]{2x + 1} &= 8 \\
2x + 1 &= 2 \\
2x &= 1 \\
x &= \frac{1}{2}
\end{aligned}$$

In Exercises 18–20, solve the inequality.

18. $3\sqrt{x} - 4 \geq 5$

19. $\sqrt{x - 3} \leq 7$

20. $5\sqrt{x - 1} > 10$

21. The length ℓ (in inches) of a standard nail can be modeled by $\ell = 54d^{3/2}$, where d is the diameter (in inches) of the nail.

   a. What is the diameter of a standard nail that is 2 inches long?

   b. What is the diameter of a standard nail that is 4 inches long?

   c. The nail in part (b) is twice as long as the nail in part (a). Is the diameter twice as long? Explain.

5.4 Practice B

In Exercises 1–6, solve the equation. Check your solution.

1. $\sqrt[3]{x - 14} = -2$

2. $-5\sqrt{16x} + 17 = -8$

3. $\frac{1}{4}\sqrt[3]{2x} + 8 = 6$

4. $\sqrt{3x} - \frac{3}{4} = 0$

5. $3\sqrt[5]{x} + 9 = 15$

6. $\sqrt[4]{8x} - 16 = -12$

In Exercises 7–12, solve the equation. Check your solution(s).

7. $\sqrt{10x + 24} = x + 12$

8. $x + 3 = \sqrt{\frac{22}{3}x + 9}$

9. $\sqrt[4]{2 - 25x^2} = 5x$

10. $\sqrt{4x - 4} - \sqrt{x + 8} = 0$

11. $\sqrt[3]{4x - 1} = \sqrt[3]{6x + 5}$

12. $\sqrt{4x - 10} = \sqrt{2x - 13} + 1$

In Exercises 13–15, solve the equation. Check your solution(s).

13. $3x^{2/3} - 30 = 18$

14. $(6x + 8)^{1/2} - 3x = 0$

15. $(2x^2 + 8)^{1/4} = x$

In Exercises 16–18, solve the inequality.

16. $4\sqrt{x} + 3 \le 23$

17. $\sqrt{x + 10} \ge 6$

18. $-3\sqrt{x + 2} < 15$

19. "Hang time" is the time you are suspended in the air during a jump. Your hang time t in seconds is given by the function $t = 0.5\sqrt{h}$, where h is the height (in feet) of the jump. A kite sailor has a hang time of 2.5 seconds. Find the height of the kite sailor's jump.

In Exercises 20–23, solve the nonlinear system. Justify your answer with a graph.

20. $y^2 = x + 2$
    $y = x + 2$

21. $y^2 = -x + 7$
    $y = x - 1$

22. $x^2 + y^2 = 9$
    $y = x - 3$

23. $x^2 + y^2 = 16$
    $y = x + 4$

24. The speed s (in miles per hour) of a car can be given by $s = \sqrt{30fd}$, where f is the coefficient of friction and d is the stopping distance (in feet). The coefficient of friction for a snowy road is 0.30. You are driving 20 miles per hour and approaching an intersection. How far away from the intersection must you begin to brake?

Name_____ Date_____

5.4 Enrichment and Extension

Solving Radical Equations and Inequalities

You can use a graphing calculator to solve radical equations and inequalities.

Example: $\sqrt{x + 1} = 5 - \sqrt{x + 6}$

$0 = \sqrt{x + 6} + \sqrt{x + 1} - 5$ Rewrite the equation to put all terms on one side.

$y = \sqrt{x + 6} + \sqrt{x + 1} - 5$ Write the corresponding function.

Graph the function. There is only one solution. To locate the intervals where the solution(s) lie, set up the starting value at 0. View the table. Y1 will either be 0, or there will be a change from negative to positive in the y-values, meaning there is a zero between the two x-values. To determine a zero between two numbers, graph the function and use the *zero* feature to determine the value of x.

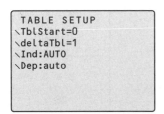 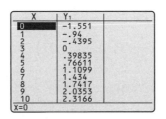 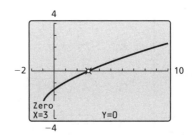

Example: $2\sqrt{x + 3} \geq 6$

Separate the original inequality into two functions: $y_1 = 2\sqrt{x + 3}$ and $y_2 = 6$.

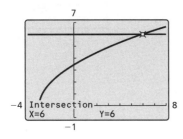

Graph each function. Use the *intersect* feature to approximate the intersection.

The screen shows the x-coordinate of the point where the graphs intersect. Find the region that satisfies the inequality.

In Exercises 1–6, use a graphing calculator to solve the radical equation or inequality. Round your answer to two decimal places when necessary.

    1. $\sqrt{x + 25} = 2$ **2.** $\sqrt{x + 1} = 5 - \sqrt{x + 6}$

    3. $\sqrt{2x + 5} = \sqrt{3x - 3} - 1$ **4.** $\sqrt[3]{x + 5} = 2\sqrt[3]{2x + 6}$

    5. $\sqrt{x - 3} \geq 4$ **6.** $\sqrt{x + 4} \geq 2\sqrt{x}$

Name _____ Date _____

5.4 **Puzzle Time**

What Did The Cucumber Say To The Vinegar?

A	B	C	D	E	F
G	H	I	J		

Complete each exercise. Find the answer in the answer column. Write the word under the answer in the box containing the exercise letter.

$x = 14$ WELL
$x = 16$ US
$x = 32$ FINE
$x = 128$ A
$x = 4$ YOU'VE

Solve the equation.

A. $\sqrt{2x - 3} = 5$

B. $\sqrt[3]{x - 4} = -2$

C. $3\sqrt{2x} + 10 = 22$

D. $\frac{1}{4}\sqrt[3]{4x} - 1 = 1$

E. $2\sqrt[5]{x} + 6 = 10$

F. $\left(\sqrt{x - 27}\right)^3 = 64$

G. $x = \sqrt{2x + 8}$

H. $\sqrt{5x - 3} = \sqrt{2x + 12}$

I. $\sqrt{x - 7} = 7 - \sqrt{x}$

J. $(x + 30)^{1/2} = x$

$x = 43$ PICKLE
$x = 6$ INTO
$x = 8$ IS
$x = -4$ THIS
$x = 5$ GOTTEN

The president of a company is calculating the company's yearly profit. The equation $f(x) = 3x - 750$ represents the company's earnings on bracelets when x is the number of bracelets sold. The equation $g(x) = 15x - 1300$ represents the company's earnings on designed T-shirts when x is the number of designed T-shirts sold.

In 2014, the company sold the same number of bracelets and T-shirts. Write the equations as a system. The company's president combines the equations to form $h(x) = 18x - 2050$. Is this equation logical? What does $h(x)$ represent?

5.5 **Warm Up**

Simplify.

1. $3x\left(x^3 + 2x\right)$

2. $\dfrac{14x}{-2x^7}$

3. $\dfrac{x^3}{x^2 - x}$

4. $(ab)^4$

5. $(a + b)(a - 6b)$

6. $(x - 7x + 6)(x)$

5.5 **Cumulative Review Warm Up**

Write an equation of the parabola in intercept form.

1. x-intercepts: 11 and -7; passes through: $(15, 3)$

2. x-intercepts: 10 and 0; passes through: $(1, -19)$

3. x-intercepts: -15 and -3; passes through: $(-17, 71)$

4. x-intercepts: -6 and -4; passes through: $(-1, -3)$

5.5 Practice A

In Exercises 1 and 2, find $(f + g)(x)$ and $(f - g)(x)$ and state the domain of each. Then evaluate $f + g$ and $f - g$ for the given value of x.

1. $f(x) = -3\sqrt[4]{x}$; $g(x) = 15\sqrt[4]{x}$; $x = 81$

2. $f(x) = 9x + 2x^2$; $g(x) = x^2 - 3x + 7$; $x = 1$

In Exercises 3–5, find $(fg)(x)$ and $\left(\dfrac{f}{g}\right)(x)$ and state the domain of each.

Then evaluate fg and $\dfrac{f}{g}$ for the given value of x.

3. $f(x) = x^2$; $g(x) = 2\sqrt{x}$; $x = 9$

4. $f(x) = 10x^3$; $g(x) = 4x^{5/3}$; $x = 8$

5. $f(x) = 4x^{2/3}$; $g(x) = 2x^{1/3}$; $x = -27$

In Exercises 6 and 7, use a graphing calculator to evaluate $(f + g)(x)$, $(f - g)(x)$, $(fg)(x)$, and $\left(\dfrac{f}{g}\right)(x)$ when $x = 5$. Round your answers to two decimal places.

6. $f(x) = 5x^3$; $g(x) = 20x^{1/4}$

7. $f(x) = 4x^{2/3}$; $g(x) = 16x^{4/3}$

8. Describe and correct the error in stating the domain.

$$\boxed{\quad X \quad \begin{array}{l} f(x) = 4x^{1/2} + 2 \text{ and } g(x) = -4x^{1/2} \\ \text{The domain of } (f + g)(x) \text{ is all real numbers.} \end{array}}$$

9. The growth of mold in Specimen A can be modeled by $A(t) = \frac{5}{6}t^{2/3}$. The growth of mold in Specimen B can be modeled by $B(t) = \frac{1}{3}t^{2/3}$.

   a. Find $(A - B)(t)$.

   b. Explain what the function $(A - B)(t)$ represents.

Name_____ Date_____

5.5 Practice B

In Exercises 1 and 2, find $(f + g)(x)$ and $(f - g)(x)$ and state the domain of each. Then evaluate $f + g$ and $f - g$ for the given value of x.

1. $f(x) = \sqrt[3]{4x}$; $g(x) = -9\sqrt[3]{4x}$; $x = -2$

2. $f(x) = 3x - 5x^2 - x^3$; $g(x) = 6x^2 - 4x$; $x = -1$

In Exercises 3–5, find $(fg)(x)$ and $\left(\dfrac{f}{g}\right)(x)$ and state the domain of each. Then evaluate fg and $\dfrac{f}{g}$ for the given value of x.

3. $f(x) = 3x^3$; $g(x) = \sqrt[3]{x^2}$; $x = -8$

4. $f(x) = 3x^2$; $g(x) = 5x^{1/4}$; $x = 16$

5. $f(x) = 10x^{5/6}$; $g(x) = 2x^{1/3}$; $x = 64$

In Exercises 6 and 7, use a graphing calculator to evaluate $(f + g)(x)$, $(f - g)(x)$, $(fg)(x)$, and $\left(\dfrac{f}{g}\right)(x)$ when $x = 5$. Round your answers to two decimal places.

6. $f(x) = -3x^{1/3}$; $g(x) = 4x^{1/2}$ **7.** $f(x) = 6x^{3/4}$; $g(x) = 3x^{1/2}$

8. Describe and correct the error in stating the domain.

$$\boxed{\begin{array}{l} \times \quad f(x) = 4x^{7/3} \text{ and } g(x) = 2x^{2/3} \\[2mm] \text{The domain of } \left(\dfrac{f}{g}\right)(x) \text{ is all real numbers.} \end{array}}$$

9. The table shows the outputs of the two functions f and g. Use the table to evaluate $(f + g)(5)$, $(f - g)(0)$, $(fg)(3)$, and $\left(\dfrac{f}{g}\right)(2)$.

x	0	1	2	3	4	5
f(x)	18	13	8	3	−2	−7
g(x)	64	32	16	8	4	2

Name_____ Date _____

5.5 Enrichment and Extension

Performing Function Operations

Recall the three trigonometric functions *sine*, *cosine*, and *tangent*. These trigonometric functions refer to the ratio of sides of a right triangle given an angle. The mnemonic used to remember these relationships is **SOH CAH TOA**.

$$\sin A = \frac{\text{opposite}}{\text{hypotenuse}} = \frac{a}{c}$$

$$\cos A = \frac{\text{adjacent}}{\text{hypotenuse}} = \frac{b}{c}$$

$$\tan A = \frac{\text{opposite}}{\text{adjacent}} = \frac{a}{b}$$

In Exercises 1–4, find $(f + g)(x)$, $(f - g)(x)$, $(fg)(x)$, and $\left(\dfrac{f}{g}\right)(x)$. Evaluate each for the given value of *x*. Use a calculator, in degree mode, to evaluate trigonometric ratios. Round your answers to two decimal places.

1. $f(x) = \sin x$, $g(x) = x$; $x = 1$

2. $f(x) = \cos x$, $g(x) = x^2$; $x = 2$

3. $f(x) = \tan x$, $g(x) = 2x$; $x = -1$

4. $f(x) = \sin x$, $g(x) = \cos x$; $x = 10$

Challenge:

Use the triangle above and the Pythagorean Theorem to prove the trigonometric identity $\sin^2 A + \cos^2 A = 1$.

Name_____ Date _____

 **Puzzle Time**

What Did One Plate Say To The Other?

Write the letter of each answer in the box containing the exercise number.

Find $(f + g)(x)$.

1. $f(x) = 3\sqrt{x}, g(x) = -8\sqrt{x}$

2. $f(x) = -\sqrt[3]{5x}, g(x) = -3\sqrt[3]{5x}$

3. $f(x) = 12\sqrt[4]{x-1}, g(x) = -3\sqrt[4]{x-1}$

4. $f(x) = 8x - 2x^2, g(x) = x^2 - 3x + 4$

Find $(f - g)(x)$.

5. $f(x) = 3\sqrt{x}, g(x) = -8\sqrt{x}$

6. $f(x) = -\sqrt[3]{5x}, g(x) = -3\sqrt[3]{5x}$

7. $f(x) = 12\sqrt[4]{x-1}, g(x) = -3\sqrt[4]{x-1}$

8. $f(x) = 8x - 2x^2, g(x) = x^2 - 3x + 4$

Find $(fg)(x)$.

9. $f(x) = 3x^2, g(x) = \sqrt{x}$

10. $f(x) = 2x^3, g(x) = 4x^{5/4}$

Find $\left(\dfrac{f}{g}\right)(x)$.

11. $f(x) = 9x^{5/4}, g(x) = 3x^{1/2}$

12. $f(x) = -2x^{2/3}, g(x) = 4x^2$

Answers

N. $8x^{17/4}$

N. $-x^2 + 5x + 4$

D. $-5\sqrt{x}$

N. $9\sqrt[4]{x-1}$

E. $11\sqrt{x}$

M. $3x^{3/4}, x \neq 0$

I. $15\sqrt[4]{x-1}$

I. $-4\sqrt[3]{5x}$

S. $-3x^2 + 11x - 4$

R. $2\sqrt[3]{5x}$

O. $3x^{5/2}$

E. $-\dfrac{1}{2x^{4/3}}$

1	2	3	4	5	6		7	8		9	10		11	12

5.6 **Start Thinking**

Consider the equation $y = -\frac{2}{3}x + 4$. Use a graphing calculator to graph the equation. Solve the equation for x. Then switch the x- and y-values in the new equation. This creates a system of equations. Graph the second equation in the same window of the graphing calculator and find the point of intersection. What does the point of intersection represent?

5.6 **Warm Up**

Solve the literal equation for y.

1. $3x - y = 4$
2. $3x - 2y = 10$
3. $5x + 6y = 9$
4. $4x + y - 6 = 1$
5. $x - 5y = 11$
6. $x - 6y = 9$

5.6 **Cumulative Review Warm Up**

Find the square root of the number.

1. $\sqrt{-25}$
2. $\sqrt{-20}$
3. $3\sqrt{-18}$
4. $-3\sqrt{-36}$
5. $\sqrt{-4}$
6. $\sqrt{-44}$

Name_____ Date_____

5.6 Practice A

In Exercises 1–3, solve $y = f(x)$ for x. Then find the input(s) when the output is -3.

1. $f(x) = 2x + 3$ 2. $f(x) = \frac{1}{3}x - 2$ 3. $f(x) = 8x^3$

In Exercises 4–6, find the inverse of the function. Then graph the function and its inverse.

4. $f(x) = 4x$ 5. $f(x) = 4x - 1$ 6. $f(x) = \frac{1}{2}x - 5$

7. Find the inverse of the function $f(x) = \frac{1}{5}x - 2$ by switching the roles of x and y and

   solving for y. Then find the inverse of the function f by using inverse operations in the reverse order. Which method do you prefer? Explain.

8. Determine whether each pair of functions f and g are inverses. Explain your reasoning.

a.

x	-2	-1	0	1	2
f(x)	-3	3	9	15	21

x	-3	3	0	15	21
g(x)	-2	-1	0	1	2

b.

x	1	2	3	4	5
f(x)	9	7	5	3	1

x	9	7	5	3	1
g(x)	1	2	3	4	5

In Exercises 9–11, find the inverse of the function. Then graph the function and its inverse.

9. $f(x) = 9x^2, x \geq 0$ 10. $f(x) = 16x^2, x \leq 0$ 11. $f(x) = (x + 2)^3$

In Exercises 12 and 13, use the graph to determine whether the inverse of f is a function. Explain your reasoning.

12.

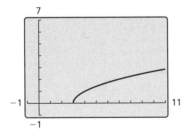

13.

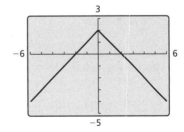

5.6 Practice B

In Exercises 1–3, solve $y = f(x)$ for x. Then find the input(s) when the output is -3.

1. $f(x) = -\frac{4}{3}x + 2$

2. $f(x) = 25x^4$

3. $f(x) = (x - 3)^2 - 4$

In Exercises 4–6, find the inverse of the function. Then graph the function and its inverse.

4. $f(x) = -3x + 4$

5. $f(x) = -\frac{1}{3}x + 1$

6. $f(x) = \frac{2}{5}x - \frac{1}{5}$

7. Describe and correct the error in finding the inverse function.

$$
\begin{array}{l}
f(x) = 3x - 8 \\
y = 3x - 8 \\
x = 3y - 8 \\
g(x) = 3x - 8
\end{array}
$$

In Exercises 8–10, find the inverse function. Then graph the function and its inverse.

8. $f(x) = -9x^2, x \le 0$

9. $f(x) = (x - 1)^3$

10. $f(x) = x^6, x \le 0$

11. Find the inverse of the function $f(x) = 8x^3$ by switching the roles of x and y and solving for y. Then find the inverse of the function f by using inverse operations in the reverse order. Which method do you prefer? Explain.

In Exercises 12–15, determine whether the functions are inverses.

12. $f(x) = 6x + 1; g(x) = 6x - 1$

13. $f(x) = \dfrac{\sqrt[3]{x - 6}}{2}; g(x) = 8x^3 + 6$

14. $f(x) = \dfrac{5 - x}{2}; g(x) = 5 - 2x$

15. $f(x) = 4x^2 + 3; g(x) = -\dfrac{x - 3}{4}$

16. The volume of a sphere is given by $V = \frac{4}{3}\pi r^3$, where r is the radius.

   a. Find the inverse function. Describe what it represents.

   b. Find the radius of a sphere with a volume of 146 cubic meters.

5.6 Enrichment and Extension

Inverse of a Function

Find the inverse of $f(x) = x^2 - 6x + 1, x \geq 3$.

$y = x^2 - 6x + 1$	Set y equal to $f(x)$.
$x = y^2 - 6y + 1$	Switch x and y.
$x - 1 = y^2 - 6y$	Subtract 1 from each side.

At this step, it is necessary to complete the square to solve for y.

$x - 1 + 9 = y^2 - 6y + 9$	To complete the square, $\left(\dfrac{b}{2}\right)^2$ is added to each side.
$x + 8 = (y - 3)^2$	Write right side as a binomial squared.
$\pm\sqrt{x + 8} = y - 3$	Take the square root of each side.
$3 \pm \sqrt{x + 8} = y$	Add 3 to each side.

The domain of f is restricted to values of $x \geq 3$. So, the range of the inverse must also be restricted to these values.

The inverse of f is $g(x) = 3 + \sqrt{x + 8}$.

In Exercises 1–12, find the inverse of the function by completing the square.

1. $f(x) = x^2 - 2x, x \geq 1$

2. $f(x) = x^2 + 8x, x \geq -4$

3. $f(x) = x^2 - 3x, x \geq \dfrac{3}{2}$

4. $f(x) = x^2 - 8x + 12, x \geq 4$

5. $f(x) = x^2 - 12x - 5, x \geq 6$

6. $f(x) = x^2 + 10x + 15, x \geq -5$

7. $f(x) = x^2 + 6x + 1, x \geq -\dfrac{3}{2}$

8. $f(x) = x^2 - 4x + 12, x \geq 2$

9. $f(x) = 4x^2 - 4x, x \geq \dfrac{1}{2}$

10. $f(x) = 6x^2 + 12x, x \geq -1$

11. $f(x) = 4x^2 - 16x - 15, x \geq 2$

12. $f(x) = 9x^2 - 18x + 5, x \geq 1$

5.6 Puzzle Time

What Do You Get When You Cross A SWAT Team With An Octopus?

Write the letter of each answer in the box containing the exercise number.

Find the inverse of the function.

1. $f(x) = 3x + 1$

2. $f(x) = -4x - 8$

3. $f(x) = \dfrac{x}{7} - 2$

4. $f(x) = \dfrac{2x}{3} - 4$

5. $f(x) = \dfrac{x-1}{5}$

6. $f(x) = -2x^2,\ x \geq 0$

7. $f(x) = 5x^4,\ x \geq 0$

8. $f(x) = (x + 1)^3$

9. $f(x) = \sqrt{8x - 3}$

10. $f(x) = (x - 21)^3$

Answers

A. $y = \dfrac{x - 1}{3}$

B. $y = 5x + 1$

B. $y = \dfrac{x + 8}{-4}$

O. $y = 7(x + 2)$

D. $y = \sqrt[3]{x} + 21$

S. $y = \sqrt{-\dfrac{x}{2}}$

Q. $y = \sqrt[4]{\dfrac{x}{5}}$

M. $y = \dfrac{3(x + 4)}{2}$

U. $y = \sqrt[3]{x} - 1$

I. $y = \dfrac{x^2 + 3}{8},\ x \geq 0$

1		2	3	4	5		6	7	8	9	10

Chapter 5 Cumulative Review

In Exercises 1–18, simplify the expression.

1. $w^9 \cdot w^2$

2. $b^2 \cdot b^{-1}$

3. $g^{-5} \cdot g^3$

4. $\dfrac{c^7}{c^2}$

5. $\dfrac{m^9}{m^2}$

6. $\dfrac{v^{12}}{v^6}$

7. $\dfrac{j^4}{j^3 \cdot j^1}$

8. $\dfrac{p^7}{p^3 \cdot p^9}$

9. $\dfrac{x^8}{x^2 \cdot x^4}$

10. $\dfrac{a^3}{a} \cdot 5a^6$

11. $\dfrac{y^8}{y^5} \cdot -4y^2$

12. $3n^3 \cdot \dfrac{n^7}{n^5}$

13. $\left(\dfrac{6m^3}{3n}\right)^5$

14. $\left(\dfrac{7y}{q^4}\right)^3$

15. $\left(\dfrac{8x^5}{2j^3}\right)^4$

16. $\left(\dfrac{x^3 \cdot x}{b^2 \cdot x^2}\right)^5$

17. $\left(\dfrac{3r^5 \cdot c^2}{r^3 \cdot r}\right)^4$

18. $\left(\dfrac{d^4 \cdot d^7}{d^6 \cdot w^2}\right)^3$

In Exercises 19–30, solve the literal equation for y.

19. $3x + y = 7$

20. $y - 8 = 1$

21. $-14x + 7y = 28$

22. $y - 3x = 4$

23. $2x - 10y = 40$

24. $x - \dfrac{1}{2}y = 6$

25. $4x - 2y = -12$

26. $-6x + 3y = -24$

27. $\dfrac{2}{3}x + \dfrac{1}{6}y = 1$

28. $4x - \dfrac{1}{4}y = -2$

29. $3xy + 9y = 12$

30. $4xy - 2y = 16$

31. You painted a picture that measures 18 inches by 24 inches.

   a. Find the perimeter of the picture.

   b. Find the area of the picture.

32. You are purchasing movies on Blu-ray that cost $18 each. You have $100 to spend.

   a. Write an expression that shows how much money you have left after purchasing m movies.

   b. Evaluate the expression when $m = 4$. What does this mean?

   c. Evaluate the expression when $m = 5$. What does this mean?

Chapter 5 Cumulative Review (continued)

In Exercises 33–48, simplify the expression. Write your answers using only positive exponents.

33. $4^2 \cdot 4$

34. $5^3 \cdot 5^2$

35. $6^5 \cdot 6^{-2}$

36. $3^{-4} \cdot 3^6$

37. $\dfrac{3^3}{3^4}$

38. $\dfrac{7^4}{7^6}$

39. $\dfrac{4^2}{4^{-2}}$

40. $\dfrac{9^5}{9^3}$

41. $\left(m^4\right)^{-3}$

42. $\left(p^{-2}\right)^5$

43. $\left(k^{-4}\right)^{-7}$

44. $\left(j^3\right)^8$

45. $\left(\dfrac{4y}{5}\right)^2$

46. $\left(\dfrac{2}{3z}\right)^3$

47. $\left(\dfrac{5w}{6}\right)^{-2}$

48. $\left(\dfrac{3}{4x}\right)^{-3}$

In Exercises 49–60, solve the equation. Check your solutions.

49. $\left|5x - 12\right| = 3$

50. $\left|3x + 6\right| = 24$

51. $\left|-7x + 12\right| = 40$

52. $\left|5x + 13\right| = 38$

53. $\left|6x - 17\right| = -21$

54. $\left|3x + 12\right| = -14$

55. $\left|4x - 12\right| = \left|x\right|$

56. $\left|x\right| = \left|3x + 16\right|$

57. $\left|4x - 24\right| = \left|2x\right|$

58. $\left|2x - 4\right| = \left|x + 9\right|$

59. $\left|4x - 13\right| = \left|5x + 16\right|$

60. $\left|6x - 12\right| = \left|4x - 6\right|$

In Exercises 61–68, determine whether the relation is a function.

61. $(3, -2), (-1, 2), (1, 7), (2, -7)$

62. $(4, -6), (-7, 1), (-7, 9), (-6, 7)$

63. $(6, -3), (8, -4), (-8, -4), (8, 1)$

64. $(2, 3), (-2, 5), (2, -3), (1, -4)$

65. $(3, 4), (9, -1), (6, -4), (-3, 6)$

66. $(5, -3), (5, -7), (-9, 3), (-6, -7)$

67. $(2, -1), (6, 5), (-2, 4), (4, 4)$

68. $(7, -8), (-5, 6), (5, 8), (6, -8)$

69. You want to buy either a Blu-ray or a DVD for 15 of your friends. Blu-rays cost $18 each and DVDs cost $15 each.

   a. Write an expression for the total amount you must spend.

   b. Evaluate the expression when six people get Blu-rays.

70. You decide to purchase a membership to a local art supply store in order to purchase acrylic paint at a discount. The monthly membership costs $5.85, and each tube of acrylic paint is $28.84.

   a. Write an expression for the total amount you spend on m months and t tubes of paint.

   b. Evaluate the expression for 5 months and 3 tubes of paint.

Chapter 5 **Cumulative Review** (continued)

In Exercises 71–77, write a function *g* whose graph represents the indicated transformation of the graph of *f*.

71. $f(x) = x + 7$; translation 5 units down

72. $f(x) = x - 1$; translation 3 units up

73. $f(x) = |2x - 1| + 3$; translation 4 units left

74. $f(x) = |3x + 4| - 1$; translation 6 units right

75. $f(x) = 3x + 4$; translation 1 unit left

76. $f(x) = -2x + 5$; reflection in the *x*-axis

77. $f(x) = -\frac{1}{4}x - 1$; translation 3 units left, followed by a translation 4 units up

In Exercises 78–86, solve the system. Check your solution, if possible.

78. $x - y + z = 9$
$2x - y + z = 12$
$-x + y + 3z = 11$

79. $x + y + z = 3$
$2x + y + 2z = 2$
$-2x - y + z = -11$

80. $x + y + z = 0$
$-x - y + z = 2$
$2x + 2y + z = -1$

81. $x - y - z = -10$
$2x - y + z = -5$
$-x + 2y - z = 5$

82. $2x - y + z = -11$
$-2x + y + z = 5$
$x + 2y + 3z = -3$

83. $2x - y + 2z = -15$
$x - y + 3z = -23$
$-x + y - z = 11$

84. $2x + 2y - 2z = 4$
$4x + 4y - 4z = 8$
$-3x - 3y + 3z = -6$

85. $2x + y + 2z = -5$
$-x + 2y - z = -4$
$-x - y + z = 9$

86. $x + y - z = -4$
$2x - 2y + 2z = 12$
$-x - y - z = -2$

87. A car salesperson's base salary is $28,000. She earns a 7% commission on total car sales. How much did she sell in car sales if she earns a total of $37,975 this year?

88. Your grocery bill came to a total of $61.29. The groceries cost $56.70. What percent sales tax did you pay? Round your answer to the nearest percent.

89. Your total bill for a new outfit is $131.25. There was 5% sales tax added. How much is the outfit without the sales tax?

90. Your total bill for a new pair of boots is $72.08. There was 6% sales tax added. How much are the boots without the sales tax?

91. You have to pay sales tax when you purchase a new vehicle. The cost of your new car is $32,560, and the cost after taxes are included is $34,513.60. What percent sales tax do you pay?

Chapter 5

Cumulative Review (continued)

In Exercises 92–106, solve the equation. Check your solutions.

92. $x^2 = 36$

93. $4x^2 = 256$

94. $5x^2 = 245$

95. $x^2 - 5 = 11$

96. $x^2 - 8 = 28$

97. $2x^2 - 4 = 124$

98. $x^2 - 3x - 10 = 0$

99. $x^2 - 2x - 3 = 0$

100. $x^2 - 7x + 6 = 0$

101. $x^2 - 11x + 28 = 0$

102. $x^2 - 9x + 8 = 0$

103. $x^2 + 10x + 21 = 0$

104. $2x^2 + 7x - 4 = 0$

105. $3x^2 + 10x - 8 = 0$

106. $5x^2 + 8x + 3 = 0$

In Exercises 107–116, add or subtract. Write the answer in standard form.

107. $(15 + 4i) + (10 - 13i)$

108. $(-7 + 2i) + (-14 + i)$

109. $(10 - 11i) + (-8 + 6i)$

110. $(-4 - i) + (-13 + 3i)$

111. $(-8 + 6i) + (4 - 3i)$

112. $(-6 + 14i) - (-13 + 6i)$

113. $(-15 + 4i) - (7 - 5i)$

114. $(11 + 8i) - (6 - 14i)$

115. $(11 + 7i) - (2 - 12i)$

116. $(-2 + 5i) - (13 + 7i)$

In Exercises 117–126, multiply. Write the answer in standard form.

117. $2i(5 + 3i)$

118. $-4i(4 - 2i)$

119. $(5 + 3i)(4 - i)$

120. $(2 + 7i)(3 + 4i)$

121. $(8 - 3i)(-5 + 9i)$

122. $(7 - 3i)(8 - 8i)$

123. $(-5 - 3i)(-8 - 7i)$

124. $(4 + 2i)(7 - 8i)$

125. $(6 + 2i)^2$

126. $(3 - 4i)^2$

127. You travel in a car at an average rate of 60 miles per hour on the highway and 40 miles per hour in the city.

   a. How long does it take you to travel 45 highway miles and 20 city miles?

   b. How long does it take you to travel 36 highway miles and 16 city miles?

128. You travel in a car at an average rate of 55 miles per hour on the highway and 35 miles per hour in the city.

   a. How long does it take you to travel 16.5 highway miles and 7 city miles?

   b. How long does it take you to travel 44 highway miles and 28 city miles?

Chapter 6

Chapter 6
Exponential and Logarithmic Functions

Dear Family,

What are some things you will need to save money for in the future? In the short term, you may be thinking about buying a car and what to do after high school. In the long term, things to think about are buying a house, starting a family, saving for retirement, or even a nice vacation.

The most important thing you can do with your money is set up a budget. You can see where your money goes each month. This also gives you a chance to see how you can start to save money each month. When you get into the habit of living within a budget instead of borrowing money through financing and credit cards, you end up saving a lot of money in the long run and are able to start investing money for the future. For example, if you do not have to finance a car, you may be able to negotiate a better deal and will not be spending money on interest. As a family, talk about your short- and long-term financial goals. How is your family's budget set up? Does your family use a financial advisor?

Choose one goal that you would like to be saving money toward.

- How much money will you need to meet your goal?

- When will you need the money?

- What type of investment options will meet your needs?

- Use the Internet to find the interest rate for your investment.

- Use an online financial calculator to find how much money you need to save each month to meet your goal.

- If you wait one year to start saving, how much additional money will you need to save each month to meet your goal?

Studies have shown that you are more likely to save money for retirement if you calculate different hypothetical situations than if you don't. When you get a job, see if your company has a retirement savings plan. Some companies even match what you invest up to a certain percentage. When the money is taken directly from your paycheck, you are less likely to miss it.

In this chapter, you will use exponential growth equations to determine the amount of money you have in your savings account. If you make it a habit to start saving money early in life, you are more likely to be prepared for the future.

The sooner you start saving, the better!

Capítulo 6 Funciones exponenciales y logarítmicas

Estimada familia:

¿Cuáles son algunas cosas para las que tendrán que ahorrar dinero en el futuro? A corto plazo, quizás piensen en comprar un carro y qué hacer después de la escuela secundaria. A largo plazo, cosas a considerar son comprar una casa, formar una familia, ahorrar para cuando se retiren o incluso unas lindas vacaciones.

Lo más importante que pueden hacer con su dinero es establecer un presupuesto. Pueden ver dónde va el dinero todos los meses. Además, les da una oportunidad para ver cómo pueden comenzar a ahorrar dinero todos los meses. Cuando adquieren el hábito de vivir de acuerdo a un presupuesto en lugar de pedir préstamos mediante financiación o tarjetas de crédito, terminan ahorrando mucho dinero a largo plazo y son capaces de comenzar a invertir dinero para el futuro. Por ejemplo, si no tienen que financiar un carro, quizás puedan negociar un precio mejor y no gastarán dinero en intereses. En familia, hablen sobre sus metas financieras a corto y largo plazo. ¿Cómo está establecido su presupuesto familiar? ¿Su familia tiene un asesor financiero?

Elijan una meta para la que les gustaría ahorrar dinero.

- ¿Cuánto dinero necesitarán para lograr su meta?

- ¿Cuándo necesitarán el dinero?

- ¿Qué clase de opciones de inversión cumplirán sus necesidades?

- Busquen en Internet la tasa de interés de su inversión.

- Usen una calculadora financiera en línea para hallar cuánto dinero necesitan ahorrar por mes para lograr su meta.

- Si esperan un año más para comenzar a ahorrar, ¿cuánto dinero adicional necesitarán ahorrar por mes para lograr su meta?

Los estudios han demostrado que tienen más probabilidades de ahorrar dinero para su jubilación si calculan diferentes situaciones hipotéticas que si no lo hacen. Cuando consigan un trabajo, fíjense si la compañía tiene un plan de ahorros para su retiro. Algunas compañías incluso igualan la cantidad que ustedes han invertido hasta cierto porcentaje. Cuando el dinero se saca directamente de su cheque de pago, tienen menos probabilidades de olvidarse.

En este capítulo, usarán ecuaciones de crecimiento exponencial para determinar la cantidad de dinero que tienen en su cuenta de ahorros. Si adquieren el hábito de comenzar a ahorrar dinero desde una temprana edad, tienen más probabilidades de estar preparados para el futuro.

¡Cuanto antes comiencen a ahorrar, mejor!

6.1 Start Thinking

In a linear growth model, y increases by the *same amount* for each change in x. In an exponential growth model, y increases by the *same percentage* for each change in x. Review the tables and determine which represent linear growth and which represent exponential growth. Then determine the slope for the linear models and the percent increase for the exponential models.

1.

x	y
0	1
1	1.1
2	1.21
3	1.331

2.

x	y
−3	−3.84
−1	−1.28
0	0
2	2.56

3.

x	y
−2	0.128
−1	0.16
0	0.2
1	0.25

6.1 Warm Up

Complete the table.

1. $y = 3x$

x	y
−1	
0	
1	
2	

2. $y = 2^x$

x	y
−1	
0	
1	
2	

3. $y = 2(3)^x$

x	y
−1	
0	
1	
2	

6.1 Cumulative Review Warm Up

Simplify the expression.

1. $2^3 2^4$

2. $\dfrac{x^5 x^2}{x^3}$

3. $\left(2b^5\right)^3$

4. $3^x 3^5$

5. $\dfrac{y^{4x} y^x}{y^{2x}}$

6. $\left(3a^x\right)^2$

Name_____ Date_____

In Exercises 1–3, evaluate the expression for (a) $x = -2$ and (b) $x = 3$.

1. 3^x

2. $5 \cdot 2^x$

3. $3 + 2^x$

In Exercises 4–9, tell whether the function represents _exponential growth_ or _exponential decay_. Then graph the function.

4. $y = 5^x$

5. $y = 3^x$

6. $y = \left(\frac{1}{5}\right)^x$

7. $y = \left(\frac{3}{2}\right)^x$

8. $y = (1.6)^x$

9. $y = (0.5)^x$

In Exercises 10 and 11, use the graph of $f(x) = b^x$ to identify the value of the base b.

10.

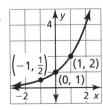

11.

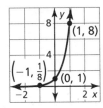

12. The value of a rare coin y (in dollars) can be approximated by the model $y = 0.25(1.06)^t$, where t is the number of years since the coin was minted.

   a. Tell whether the model represents exponential growth or exponential decay.

   b. Identify the annual percent increase or decrease in the value of the coin.

   c. What was the original value of the coin?

   d. Estimate when the value of the coin will be $0.60.

In Exercises 13–15, rewrite the function in the form $y = a(1 + r)^t$ or $y = a(1 - r)^t$.
Then state the growth or decay rate.

13. $y = a(3)^{t/2}$

14. $y = a(5)^{t/8}$

15. $y = a(0.4)^{3t}$

16. You deposit $3000 into a bank account that pays 1.25% annual interest, compounded semi-annually. How much interest does the account earn after 4 years?

Name _____ Date _____

In Exercises 1–3, evaluate the expression for (a) $x = -2$ and (b) $x = 3$.

1. 5^x

2. $10 \cdot 2^x$

3. $3^x - 3$

In Exercises 4–9, tell whether the function represents *exponential growth* or *exponential decay*. Then graph the function.

4. $y = 8^x$

5. $y = \left(\dfrac{5}{3}\right)^x$

6. $y = \left(\dfrac{2}{3}\right)^x$

7. $y = (2.5)^x$

8. $y = (0.4)^x$

9. $y = (0.1)^x$

In Exercises 10 and 11, use the graph of $f(x) = b^x$ to identify the value of the base b.

10.

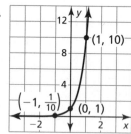

11.

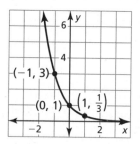

12. The value of a truck y (in dollars) can be approximated by the model $y = 54{,}000(0.80)^t$, where t is the number of years since the truck was new.

   a. Tell whether the model represents exponential growth or exponential decay.

   b. Identify the annual percent increase or decrease in the value of the truck.

   c. What was the original value of the truck?

   d. Estimate when the value of the truck will be $30,000.

In Exercises 13–15, rewrite the function in the form $y = a(1 + r)^t$ or $y = a(1 - r)^t$. Then state the growth or decay rate.

13. $y = a(0.75)^{t/6}$

14. $y = a\left(\dfrac{4}{3}\right)^{t/18}$

15. $y = a\left(\dfrac{1}{4}\right)^{4t}$

16. You deposit $3000 into a bank account that pays 1.25% annual interest, compounded monthly. How much interest does the account earn after 4 years?

6.1 Enrichment and Extension

Exponential Growth and Decay

In Exercises 1–4, match the function with its graph.

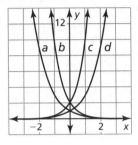

1. $y = 2(5)^x$

2. $y = 3^x$

3. $y = \left(\frac{1}{3}\right)^x$

4. $y = 2\left(\frac{1}{5}\right)^x$

5. When would the graph of $f(x) = ab^x$ be a horizontal line?

In Exercises 6–9, use the following functions to answer the question.

$$y = \left(\frac{1}{5}\right)^x \qquad y = 3^x \qquad y = 5^x \qquad y = \left(\frac{1}{3}\right)^x \qquad y = \left(\frac{1}{7}\right)^x$$

6. Which function exhibits the fastest growth?

7. Which function exhibits the slowest decay?

8. What is the y-intercept of each function?

9. What is the domain and range of each function?

In Exercises 10–13, use the function $f(x) = x^n$ to (a) graph the function with the given value of n, (b) classify the type of function, and (c) state the domain and range.

10. $n = \left(\frac{1}{2}\right)$

11. $n = 1$

12. $n = 2$

13. $n = 3$

6.1 **Puzzle Time**

What Happens When You Annoy A Clock?

Write the letter of each answer in the box containing the exercise number.

Evaluate the expression for $x = 3$.

1. 5^x

2. $\left(\frac{1}{2}\right)^x$

3. $(1.5)^x$

4. $(0.2)^x$

5. $\left(\frac{5}{2}\right)^x$

6. $2 \cdot 3^x$

7. $9 + 2^x$

8. $4^x - 1$

Tell whether the function represents *exponential growth* or *exponential decay*.

9. $y = \left(\frac{3}{2}\right)^x$

10. $y = \left(\frac{1}{4}\right)^x$

Match the graph with its function.

11.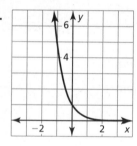

12.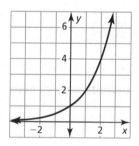

Answers
F. $y = (0.2)^x$
I. 15.625
Y. 125
T. exponential growth
O. $\frac{1}{8}$
F. $y = 2^x$
T. 0.008
C. 54
I. 63
U. 3.375
O. exponential decay
K. 17

1	2	3		4	5	6	7		8	9		10	11	12

6.2 Start Thinking

You deposit $7000 in an account that pays 2.25% annual interest. Compare what the balance will be after 5 years if the interest is compounded semi-annually, quarterly, monthly, and daily. What do you think will happen to the balance if the number of compoundings continues to increase?

6.2 Warm Up

Determine if the model represents *exponential growth* or *exponential decay*. Then identify the initial amount and the percent increase or decrease.

1. $y = 1.2^x$

2. $y = 0.78^x$

3. $y = \left(\frac{5}{8}\right)^x$

4. $y = 28(1.03)^x$

5. $y = 25{,}000(0.95)^x$

6. $y = 2^x$

6.2 Cumulative Review Warm Up

Find the inverse of the function. Then graph the function and its inverse in the same coordinate plane.

1. $y = \frac{1}{2}x - 5$

2. $y = -3x + 7$

3. $y = \dfrac{x - 9}{5}$

4. $y = (x + 2)^3$

5. $y = \dfrac{x^3 - 6}{2}$

6. $y = -2x^2,\ x \geq 0$

Name _____ Date _____

In Exercises 1–6, simplify the expression.

1. $e^2 \cdot e^5$

2. $e^{-3} \cdot e^8$

3. $\dfrac{12e^5}{36e^2}$

4. $\dfrac{15e^4}{3e^9}$

5. $\left(3e^{3x}\right)^2$

6. $\sqrt{16e^{10x}}$

7. Describe and correct the error in simplifying the expression.

$$\cancel{\times} \quad \left(2e^{3x}\right)^2 = (2)^2\left(e^{3x}\right)^2$$
$$= 4e^{9x^2}$$

In Exercises 8–10, tell whether the function represents *exponential growth* or *exponential decay*. Then graph the function.

8. $y = e^{4x}$

9. $y = e^{-x}$

10. $y = 4e^{-2x}$

In Exercises 11–13, use the properties of exponents to rewrite the function in the form $y = a(1 + r)^t$ or $y = a(1 - r)^t$. Then find the percent rate of change.

11. $y = e^{-0.5x}$

12. $y = 2e^{-0.2x}$

13. $y = 5e^{0.6x}$

In Exercises 14–16, use a table of values or a graphing calculator to graph the function. Then identify the domain and range.

14. $y = e^{x-1}$

15. $y = e^{x+2}$

16. $y = 3e^x + 2$

17. You invest $4000 in an account to save for college.

   a. Option 1 pays 5% annual interest compounded semi-annually. What would be the balance in the account after 2 years?

   b. Option 2 pays 4.5% annual interest compounded continuously. What would be the balance in the account after 2 years?

   c. At what time t (in years) would Option 1 give you $100 more than Option 2?

Name_____ Date _____

6.2 Practice B

In Exercises 1–6, simplify the expression.

1. $e^{-9} \cdot e^7$

2. $\dfrac{27e^4}{18e^7}$

3. $\left(5e^{-4x}\right)^3$

4. $\sqrt{20e^{8x}}$

5. $\sqrt[3]{64e^{9x}}$

6. $e^{2x} \cdot e^5 \cdot e^{x-2}$

7. Describe and correct the error in simplifying the expression.

$$\cancel{} \quad \left(2e^{-3x}\right)^4 = \frac{1}{16e^{12x}}$$

In Exercises 8–10, tell whether the function represents *exponential growth* or *exponential decay*. Then graph the function.

8. $y = 2e^{3x}$

9. $y = 0.5e^{-2x}$

10. $y = 0.4e^{0.5x}$

In Exercises 11–13, use the properties of exponents to rewrite the function in the form $y = a(1 + r)^t$ or $y = a(1 - r)^t$. Then find the percent rate of change.

11. $y = e^{0.25x}$

12. $y = 3e^{-0.65x}$

13. $y = 0.25e^{0.9x}$

In Exercises 14–16, use a table of values or a graphing calculator to graph the function. Then identify the domain and range.

14. $y = e^{x-4}$

15. $y = 4e^x - 1$

16. $y = 2e^x + 5$

17. You invest $5000 in an account to save for college.

   a. Option 1 pays 4% annual interest compounded monthly. What would be the balance in the account after 2 years?

   b. Option 2 pays 4% annual interest compounded continuously. What would be the balance in the account after 2 years?

   c. What is the difference between the two options after 10 years?

   d. How would your answer to part (c) change if you invested $50,000?

6.2 Enrichment and Extension

The Natural Base e

The natural base e is an irrational number like pi (π), so you cannot find its exact value. However, you have discovered how to approximate e by increasing the value of x in the expression $\left(1 + \dfrac{1}{x}\right)^x$. As x approaches infinity, $\left(1 + \dfrac{1}{x}\right)^x$ approaches $e \approx 2.71828182846$.

Another way to find e is to approximate the sum $1 + \dfrac{1}{1} + \dfrac{1}{1 \bullet 2} + \dfrac{1}{1 \bullet 2 \bullet 3} + \dfrac{1}{1 \bullet 2 \bullet 3 \bullet 4} + \ldots$.

The value of π can be approximated many ways as well. One way used is to approximate the sum $\sqrt{12}\left(1 - \dfrac{1}{3 \bullet 3} + \dfrac{1}{5 \bullet 3^2} - \dfrac{1}{7 \bullet 3^3} + \ldots\right)$. Use the table to approximate π.

Sum	Approximation
$\sqrt{12}\left(1 - \dfrac{1}{3 \bullet 3} + \dfrac{1}{5 \bullet 3^2} - \dfrac{1}{7 \bullet 3^3} + \ldots\right)$	
$\sqrt{12}\left(1 - \dfrac{1}{3 \bullet 3} + \dfrac{1}{5 \bullet 3^2} - \dfrac{1}{7 \bullet 3^3} + \dfrac{1}{9 \bullet 3^4} - \ldots\right)$	
$\sqrt{12}\left(1 - \dfrac{1}{3 \bullet 3} + \dfrac{1}{5 \bullet 3^2} - \dfrac{1}{7 \bullet 3^3} + \dfrac{1}{9 \bullet 3^4} - \dfrac{1}{11 \bullet 3^5} + \ldots\right)$	
$\sqrt{12}\left(1 - \dfrac{1}{3 \bullet 3} + \dfrac{1}{5 \bullet 3^2} - \dfrac{1}{7 \bullet 3^3} + \dfrac{1}{9 \bullet 3^4} - \dfrac{1}{11 \bullet 3^5} + \dfrac{1}{13 \bullet 3^6} \ldots\right)$	

In Exercises 1–5, use your textbook or another source to answer questions about π and e.

1. What is the definition of π?

2. State π up to 11 decimal places.

3. Because π is an irrational number, it cannot be written as a ratio of two integers. Why is π represented as $\frac{22}{7}$?

4. π is said to be a transcendental number. What does that mean? Is e transcendental as well?

5. An equation that relates π, e, and the imaginary number $i = \sqrt{-1}$ is $e^{i\pi} + 1 = 0$. What is this identity called?

6.2 Puzzle Time

What Does An Astronaut Use To Dust Those Hard-To-Reach Black Holes?

Write the letter of each answer in the box containing the exercise number.

Simplify the expression.

1. $e^{-2} \cdot e^8$

2. $e^7 \cdot e \cdot e^3$

3. $2e^4 \cdot 3e^2$

4. $\dfrac{12e^7}{8e^5}$

5. $\dfrac{5e^{11}}{10e^{14}}$

6. $\sqrt{64e^{10x}}$

7. $\sqrt[5]{32e^{10x}}$

8. $\left(3e^{2x}\right)^2$

9. $e^{-2x} \cdot e^x \cdot e^{6x+2}$

10. $\left(2e^{-5x}\right)^4$

Answers	
M. $8e^{5x}$	A. e^{11}
V. e^6	N. $y = e^{2x}$
C. $6e^6$	U. $\dfrac{3e^2}{2}$
C. $2e^{2x}$	L. $9e^{4x}$
R. $y = 2e^{0.5x}$	U. $\dfrac{1}{2e^3}$
E. e^{5x+2}	A. $\dfrac{16}{e^{20x}}$
E. $y = 4e^{-x}$	

Match the graph with its function.

11.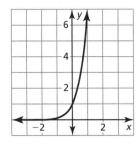

12.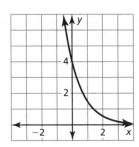

13.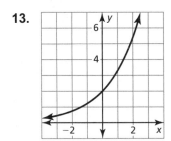

1	2	3	4	5	6		7	8	9	10	11	12	13

Start Thinking

A function and its inverse are sketched in the same coordinate plane. How are the two graphs related? How do the domain and range of $f(x)$ relate to the domain and range of $f^{-1}(x)$?

6.3 **Warm Up**

Determine the value of x in the expression.

1. $2^x = 4$ **2.** $8^x = 1$ **3.** $\left(\frac{2}{3}\right)^x = \frac{8}{27}$

4. $4^x = \frac{1}{4}$ **5.** $4^x = 2$ **6.** $4^x = \frac{1}{2}$

6.3 **Cumulative Review Warm Up**

Use the parent function to sketch the graph of each function.

1. Parent function: $y = x^2$

  a. $y = x^2 - 2$ **b.** $y = (x + 3)^2$ **c.** $y = -(x - 1)^2$

2. Parent function: $y = \sqrt{x}$

  a. $y = 2\sqrt{x}$ **b.** $y = \sqrt{-x}$ **c.** $y = -\sqrt{x - \frac{1}{2}} + 3$

Name_____ Date_____

In Exercises 1–3, rewrite the equation in exponential form.

1. $\log_2 8 = 3$
2. $\log_7 7 = 1$
3. $\log_5 25 = 2$

In Exercises 4–6, rewrite the equation in logarithmic form.

4. $4^2 = 16$
5. $5^0 = 1$
6. $6^{-1} = \dfrac{1}{6}$

In Exercises 7–12, evaluate the logarithm.

7. $\log_2 16$
8. $\log_5 125$
9. $\log_6 6$

10. $\log_5 \dfrac{1}{5}$
11. $\log_9 1$
12. $\log_2 \dfrac{1}{8}$

In Exercises 13–15, evaluate the logarithm using a calculator. Round your answer to three decimal places.

13. $\log 5$
14. $\ln 14$
15. $\log \dfrac{1}{4}$

16. The decibel level D of sound is given by the equation $D = 10 \log\left(\dfrac{I}{10^{-12}}\right)$, where

   I is the intensity of the sound. What is the decibel level when the intensity of the sound is 10^{-9}?

In Exercises 17–19, simply the expression.

17. $5^{\log_5 x}$
18. $8^{\log_8 2x}$
19. $\log_4 4^{3x}$

In Exercises 20–25, find the inverse of the function.

20. $y = 1.1^x$
21. $y = 3^x$
22. $y = \log_3 x$

23. $y = \log\left(\dfrac{1}{3}x\right)$
24. $y = \ln(3x)$
25. $y = e^{5x}$

26. The wind speed s (in miles per hour) near the center of a tornado can be modeled by $s = 93 \log d + 65$, where d is the distance (in miles) that the tornado travels.

   a. A tornado traveled 35 miles. Estimate the wind speed near the center of the tornado.

   b. The wind speed near the center of a tornado was 150 miles per hour. Find the distance that the tornado traveled.

Name _____ Date _____

6.3 Practice B

In Exercises 1–3, rewrite the equation in exponential form.

1. $\log_9 1 = 0$
2. $\log_6 216 = 3$
3. $\log_2 \frac{1}{4} = -2$

In Exercises 4–6, rewrite the equation in logarithmic form.

4. $13^{-2} = \frac{1}{169}$
5. $4^{3/2} = 8$
6. $81^{1/2} = 9$

In Exercises 7–12, evaluate the logarithm.

7. $\log_8 64$
8. $\log_2 32$
9. $\log_{10} 1$

10. $\log_3 \frac{1}{81}$
11. $\log_2 0.125$
12. $\log_{10} 0.01$

In Exercises 13–15, evaluate the logarithm using a calculator. Round your answer to three decimal places.

13. $\log\left(\frac{1}{5}\right)$
14. $2 \ln(1.4)$
15. $\ln(0.4) - 2$

16. The decibel level D of sound is given by the equation $D = 10 \log\left(\dfrac{I}{10^{-12}}\right)$, where

   I is the intensity of the sound. The pain threshold for sound is 125 decibels. Does a sound with an intensity of 10 exceed the pain threshold? Explain.

In Exercises 17–19, simply the expression.

17. $e^{\ln 7x}$
18. $10^{\log 18}$
19. $\log\left(10^{3x}\right)$

In Exercises 20–25, find the inverse of the function.

20. $y = 0.75^x$
21. $y = \log_{3/4} x$
22. $y = \log\left(\dfrac{x}{2}\right)$

23. $y = \ln(x + 2)$
24. $y = e^{x-3}$
25. $y = 6^x + 2$

26. The length ℓ (in inches) of an alligator and its weight w (in pounds) are related by the function $\ell = 27.1 \ln w - 32.8$.

   a. Estimate the length (in inches) of an alligator that weighs 250 pounds. What is its length in feet?

   b. Find the inverse of the given function. Use the inverse function to find the weight of a 14-foot alligator. (*Hint*: Convert to inches first.)

6.3 Enrichment and Extension

Logarithms and Logarithmic Functions

Rewriting a logarithmic function in exponential form allows you to find x.

Example: Find the value of x in each equation.

   a. $x = \log_4 64$ **b.** $\frac{1}{2} = \log_9 x$ **c.** $\frac{1}{3} = \log_x 4$

Solution:

	Logarithmic Form	*Exponential Form*	*Answer*
a.	$x = \log_4 64$	$4^x = 64$	$x = 3$
b.	$\frac{1}{2} = \log_9 x$	$9^{1/2} = x$	$x = 3$
c.	$\frac{1}{3} = \log_x 4$	$x^{1/3} = 4$	$x = 64$

In Exercises 1–24, find the value of x.

  1. $x = \log_2 32$ **2.** $\log_{10} 1000 = x$

  3. $x = \log_6 1296$ **4.** $\log_8 8 = x$

  5. $x = \log_{17} 289$ **6.** $x = \log_{125} 5$

  7. $x = \log_7 1$ **8.** $x = \log_3 \frac{1}{9}$

  9. $x = \log_{10} 0.01$ **10.** $3 = \log_7 x$

11. $\log_{11} x = 1$ **12.** $-3 = \log_6 x$

13. $6 = \log_3 x$ **14.** $\log_{13} x = 0$

15. $\log_8 x = \frac{1}{3}$ **16.** $-4 = \log_4 x$

17. $\log_8 x = -2$ **18.** $-1 = \log_3 x$

19. $3 = \log_x 27$ **20.** $2 = \log_x 16$

21. $\log_x 243 = 5$ **22.** $\frac{1}{3} = \log_x 8$

23. $\log_x \frac{1}{8} = -3$ **24.** $\frac{1}{2} = \log_x 49$

Name _____ Date _____

6.3 Puzzle Time

Where Do Spies Do Their Shopping?

Write the letter of each answer in the box containing the exercise number.

Rewrite the equation in exponential form.

1. $\log_3 9 = 2$

2. $\log_{25} 25 = 1$

3. $\log_2 32 = 5$

4. $\log_{1/8} 8 = -1$

Rewrite the equation in logarithmic form.

5. $7^2 = 49$

6. $3^{-1} = \frac{1}{3}$

7. $16^{3/4} = 8$

8. $7^{-3} = \frac{1}{343}$

Evaluate the logarithm.

9. $\log_2 64$

10. $\log_9 81$

11. $\log_8 2$

12. $\log_3 \frac{1}{27}$

13. $\log_{1/2} 16$

14. $\log_2 0.5$

15. $\log_{36} 6$

16. $\log_4 64$

Answers

A. $3^2 = 9$

A. $2^5 = 32$

N. $\log_7 49 = 2$

O. $\log_{16} 8 = \frac{3}{4}$

S. $\left(\frac{1}{8}\right)^{-1} = 8$

R. -4

O. $\log_3 \frac{1}{3} = -1$

P. $\log_7 \frac{1}{343} = -3$

R. 2

T. $25^1 = 25$

T. 3 M. $\frac{1}{3}$

A. -3 K. -1

E. $\frac{1}{2}$ E. 6

1	2		3		4	5	6	7	8	9	10		11	12	13	14	15	16

6.4 Start Thinking

A window manufacturing company trains new employees to assemble double-hung windows. The company has determined that the learning curve for the average employee is given by $W = 18 - 18e^{-0.08t}$, where W is the number of windows assembled in t days of training.

1. Use a graphing calculator to graph the function. What is an appropriate window setting to view the graph?

2. Approximate the number of windows a new employee should be able to assemble after 5 days of training, and then after 10 days of training.

3. What appears to be the maximum number of windows an employee would be able to assemble in a day? How many days of training does it take for the average employee to reach this maximum?

6.4 Warm Up

Describe the transformation of f represented by g.

1. $f(x) = x^2$, $g(x) = -x^2 + 3$
2. $f(x) = x^3$, $g(x) = \frac{1}{2}(x + 2)^3 - 5$

3. $f(x) = 2^x$, $g(x) = 2^{-3x}$
4. $f(x) = \left(\frac{2}{3}\right)^x$, $g(x) = 4\left(\frac{2}{3}\right)^{x-2}$

6.4 Cumulative Review Warm Up

Use the information to find an equation of the line.

1. slope: 3

   y-intercept: $(0, 5)$

2. slope: -5

   x-intercept: $\left(-\frac{2}{5}, 0\right)$

3. passes through $(1, 7)$ and $(0, 9)$
4. passes through $(-2, 8)$ and $(-7, -3)$

6.4 Practice A

In Exercises 1–8, describe the transformation of *f* represented by *g*. Then graph each function.

1. $f(x) = 2^x$, $g(x) = 2^x + 3$

2. $f(x) = e^x$, $g(x) = e^x - 2$

3. $f(x) = 3^x$, $g(x) = 3^{x-1}$

4. $f(x) = e^{-x}$, $g(x) = e^{-x} + 4$

5. $f(x) = e^x$, $g(x) = e^{3x}$

6. $f(x) = e^x$, $g(x) = \frac{3}{2}e^x$

7. $f(x) = 3^x$, $g(x) = -3^{x+2}$

8. $f(x) = e^{-x}$, $g(x) = 2e^{-5x}$

9. Describe and correct the error in graphing the function $f(x) = 2e^x$.

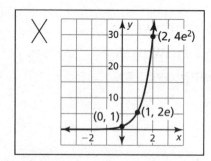

In Exercises 10 and 11, describe the transformation of *f* represented by *g*. Then graph each function.

10. $f(x) = \log_2 x$, $g(x) = 4\log_2 x - 1$

11. $f(x) = \log_{1/2} x$, $g(x) = -\log_{1/2} x + 3$

In Exercises 12–15, write a rule for *g* that represents the indicated transformation of the graph of *f*.

12. $f(x) = 3^x$; reflection in the *x*-axis, followed by a translation 3 units left and 1 unit down

13. $f(x) = e^x$; vertical shrink by a factor of $\frac{1}{4}$, followed by a translation 5 units up

14. $f(x) = \log_8 x$; reflection in the *y*-axis, followed by a translation 4 units left

15. $f(x) = \log_{1/6} x$; vertical stretch by a factor of 9, followed by translations 2 units right and 3 units down

Name_____ Date_____

6.4 Practice B

In Exercises 1–8, describe the transformation of *f* represented by *g*. Then graph each function.

1. $f(x) = e^x, g(x) = e^x - 4$

2. $f(x) = 4^x, g(x) = 4^{x+2}$

3. $f(x) = e^{-x}, g(x) = e^{-x} - 5$

4. $f(x) = \left(\frac{1}{3}\right)^x, g(x) = \left(\frac{1}{3}\right)^x + 2$

5. $f(x) = 3^x, g(x) = 3^{2x} - 1$

6. $f(x) = e^x, g(x) = -e^{x+2}$

7. $f(x) = e^{-x}, g(x) = e^{-4x+1}$

8. $f(x) = \left(\frac{1}{3}\right)^x, g(x) = \left(\frac{1}{3}\right)^{x-2} + 3$

9. Describe and correct the error in graphing the function $f(x) = 2^{x+3}$.

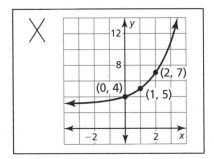

In Exercises 10 and 11, describe the transformation of *f* represented by *g*. Then graph each function.

10. $f(x) = \log_4 x, g(x) = \log_4(x - 2) + 4$

11. $f(x) = \log_{1/3} x, g(x) = -\log_{1/3}(-x)$

In Exercises 12–14, write a rule for *g* that represents the indicated transformation of the graph of *f*.

12. $f(x) = \left(\frac{2}{5}\right)^x$; reflection in the *y*-axis, followed by a horizontal shrink by a factor of 2 and a translation 4 units down

13. $f(x) = e^{-x}$; translation 2 units left and 3 units up, followed by a vertical stretch by a factor of 2

14. $f(x) = \log_{12} x$; translation 5 units right and 2 units down, followed by a reflection in the *x*-axis

6.4 Enrichment and Extension

Transformations of Exponential and Logarithmic Functions

In Exercises 1–14, match the function with its graph.

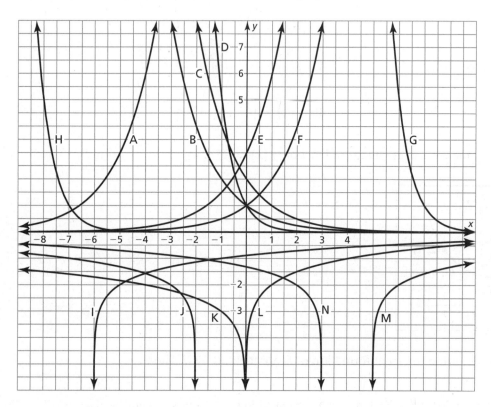

1. $y = \log_4(-x) - 3$

2. $y = \left(\frac{1}{5}\right)^x$

3. $y = 3(2)^x$

4. $y = \log_5(x - 5) - 2$

5. $y = \log_4 x - 2$

6. $y = \left(\frac{1}{5}\right)^{x-7}$

7. $y = \log_5(x + 6) - 2$

8. $y = \log_5(-x - 2) - 2$

9. $y = 2^x$

10. $y = 3(2)^{x+5}$

11. $y = \log_5(-x + 3) - 2$

12. $y = \left(\frac{1}{2}\right)^{x-1}$

13. $y = \left(\frac{1}{2}\right)^x$

14. $y = \left(\frac{1}{5}\right)^{x+7}$

6.4 **Puzzle Time**

What Do You Call A Mouse Who Hangs Out With A Bunch Of Pythons?

Write the letter of each answer in the box containing the exercise number.

Match the graph with its function.

1.
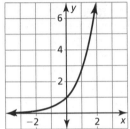

2.
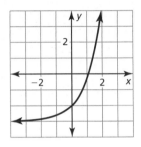

3.
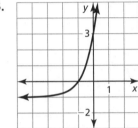

4.
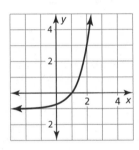

5.
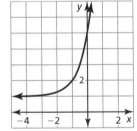

Answers
U. $f(x) = e^x - 3$
L. $f(x) = e^x$
H. $f(x) = 4^{x+1} + 1$
C. $f(x) = 4^{x-1} - 1$
N. $f(x) = 4^{x+1} - 1$

1	2	3	4	5

6.5 Start Thinking

Examine each group of logarithmic equations below. Try to identify any patterns that relate the three equations in each group. Then use your conclusion to make a prediction for the value of $\log_5 25x$ if you know $\log_5 x \approx 1.4$.

| $\log_2 3 \approx 1.6$ |
| $\log_2 4 = 2$ |
| $\log_2 12 \approx 3.6$ |

| $\log_3 15 \approx 2.5$ |
| $\log_3 \frac{1}{3} = -1$ |
| $\log_3 5 \approx 1.5$ |

| $\log_4 9 \approx 1.6$ |
| $\log_4 2 = 0.5$ |
| $\log_4 18 \approx 2.1$ |

6.5 Warm Up

Determine the value of n in the expression.

1. $\dfrac{3^n}{3^2} = 3^5$

2. $\dfrac{x^4}{x^n} = x^{-2}$

3. $x^2 x^n = x^{5/2}$

4. $\left(2^8\right)^n = 4$

5. $\dfrac{\left(y^n\right)^2}{y^3} = y$

6. $y^{2n} y = y^{-5}$

6.5 Cumulative Review Warm Up

Solve the equation. Write your answer in simplest form.

1. $2(x - 3)^2 = 8$

2. $6x^2 - 7x - 20 = 0$

3. $x^2 - 4x - 8 = 0$

4. $6x - 3x^2 = 15$

5. $x^2 = 6x - 9$

6. $-\frac{1}{2}(3x + 1)^2 = -5$

Name_____ Date_____

In Exercises 1–3, use $\log_5 3 \approx 0.683$ and $\log_5 6 \approx 1.113$ to evaluate the logarithm.

  1. $\log_5 2$ **2.** $\log_5 18$ **3.** $\log_5 9$

In Exercises 4–6, expand the logarithmic expression.

  4. $\log_2 5x$ **5.** $\log 7x^4$ **6.** $\log_6 \dfrac{2x}{y}$

  7. Describe and correct the error in expanding the logarithmic expression.

$$\bcancel{}\quad \log_4 3x = 3 \log_4 x$$

In Exercises 8–11, condense the logarithmic expression.

  8. $\log_7 3 - \log_7 5$ **9.** $\log 10 - \log 5$

  10. $3 \ln x + 9 \ln y$ **11.** $\log_2 9 + \dfrac{1}{2} \log_2 y$

In Exercises 12–14, use the change-of-base formula to evaluate the logarithm.

  12. $\log_5 3$ **13.** $\log_2 11$ **14.** $\log_6 10$

  15. Your friend claims that you can use the change-of-base formula to write the expression $\ln x$ as a common logarithm. Is your friend correct? Explain your reasoning.

  16. For a sound with intensity I (in watts per square meter), the loudness $L(I)$ of the sound (in decibels) is given by the function $L(I) = 10 \log \dfrac{I}{I_0}$, where I_0 is the intensity of a barely audible sound (about 10^{-12} watts per square meter). The sound of a coach's whistle is five times greater than the intensity of the referee's whistle. Find the difference in the decibel levels of the sounds made by the coach and the referee.

6.5 Practice B

In Exercises 1–3, use $\log_5 3 \approx 0.683$ and $\log_5 6 \approx 1.113$ to evaluate the logarithm.

1. $\log_5 81$

2. $\log_5 \frac{1}{6}$

3. $\log_5 \frac{1}{2}$

In Exercises 4–6, expand the logarithmic expression.

4. $\log_3 12x^7$

5. $\log_6 \frac{5x^2}{y^3}$

6. $\log_8 6\sqrt{xy}$

7. Describe and correct the error in expanding the logarithmic expression.

$$\times \quad \ln \sqrt[3]{xy} = \frac{1}{3} \ln x + \ln y$$

In Exercises 8–11, condense the logarithmic expression.

8. $5 \log_9 x - \log_9 4$

9. $\log_8 5 + \frac{1}{4} \log_8 x$

10. $2 \ln 4 + 5 \ln x + 3 \ln y$

11. $\log_6 9 + 2 \log_6 \frac{1}{3} - 3 \log_6 x$

In Exercises 12–14, use the change-of-base formula to evaluate the logarithm.

12. $\log_8 15$

13. $\log_3 30$

14. $\log_4 \frac{8}{17}$

15. Your friend claims you can use the change-of-base formula to write the expression $\frac{\ln y}{\ln 3}$ as a logarithm with base 3. Is your friend correct? Explain your reasoning.

16. For a sound with intensity I (in watts per square meter), the loudness $L(I)$ of the sound (in decibels) is given by the function $L(I) = 10 \log \frac{I}{I_0}$, where I_0 is the intensity of a barely audible sound $\left(\text{about } 10^{-12} \text{ watts per square meter}\right)$. The bass guitar player in a band turns up the volume of the speaker so that the intensity of the sound triples. By how many decibels does the loudness increase?

6.5 Enrichment and Extension

Properties of Logarithms

Recall the Exponential-Logarithmic Inverse Properties:

For $b > 0$ and $b \neq 1$:

$\log_b b^x = x$ and $b^{\log_b x} = x$ for $x > 0$.

Use these and other properties of logarithms to evaluate the expression.

Example: $\log_2 32 - 5^{\log_5 3}$

Solution: $\log_2 32 - 5^{\log_5 3} = 5 - 5^{\log_5 3} = 5 - 3 = 2$

In Exercises 1–16, evaluate the expression. Use the table to approximate the value of the logarithmic expression or use the change-of-base formula to simplify.

$\log_3 10 \approx 2.0959$	$\log_8 3 \approx 0.5283$	$\log_5 10 \approx 1.4307$
$\log_3 2 \approx 0.6309$	$\log_5 2 \approx 0.4307$	$\log_5 3 \approx 0.6826$

1. $4^{\log_4 8} + \log_2 2$

2. $5^{\log_5 5} + \log_5 45 - \log_5 9$

3. $\log_2 6 + \log_2 4 - \log_2 3$

4. $\log_3 30 - \log_4 4^5$

5. $2^{\log_2 3} - \log_8 64^7 + \log_8 24$

6. $\log_6 \frac{1}{36} + \log_6 36 + 5^{\log_6 1}$

7. $\log_5 2 + \log_5 20 - \log_5 4$

8. $9^{\log_3 20}$

9. $16^{\log_4 10} - 2^{\log_2 50}$

10. $\log_2 \frac{1}{8} + \log_2 4 + \log_6 \frac{1}{216}$

11. $\log_5 20 + \log_5 40 - \log_5 30$

12. $\log_5 50 + 2^{\log_5 1/5}$

13. $\log_3 162 + 27^{\log_3 4}$

14. $\log_4 6 + \log_4 3 - \log_4 9$

15. $25^{\log_5 10} - \log_4 64 + 1000^{\log_{10} 4}$

16. $81^{\log_3 10} - \log_{125} 5 - 81^{\log_9 4}$

6.5 Puzzle Time

What Type Of Lizard Loves To Tell Jokes?

Write the letter of each answer in the box containing the exercise number.

Match the expression with the logarithm that has the same value.

1. $\log_2 6 + \log_2 8$

2. $\log_3 10 - \log_3 5$

3. $4 \log_{1/2} 2$

4. $\log_2 2 - \log_2 3$

5. $\log_3 4 + \log_3 2$

6. $6 \log 8$

Condense the logarithmic expression.

7. $4 \log 2 - \log 5$

8. $\log 6 + \log 2 - \log 7$

9. $\frac{1}{2} \log 4 + \log 3$

10. $3 \log 2 - 2 \log 2$

11. $1 - \log 4$

12. $\ln 3 + 4 \ln x - \ln y$

Answers
I. $\log_{1/2} 16$
A. $\log_2 48$
M. $\log \frac{16}{5}$
Y. $\log(8^6)$
E. $\log \frac{5}{2}$
S. $\log_3 2$
N. $\log 6$
L. $\log_2 \frac{2}{3}$
L. $\log_3 8$
A. $\log \frac{12}{7}$
D. $\log 2$
R. $\ln \frac{3x^4}{y}$

1		2	3	4	5	6	7	8	9	10	11	12

6.6 Start Thinking

An investment account is created to provide funds for a student's college tuition. The balance B (in dollars) of the education fund after t years can be modeled by $B = 5000e^{0.0525t}$. What equation would you have to solve to determine how long it will take for the initial amount to double? Use a graphing calculator to solve the equation.

6.6 Warm Up

Rewrite the exponential equations in logarithmic form and the logarithmic equations in exponential form. Then solve for x and check your answer.

1. $2^{x-1} = 5$

2. $e^{-2x} = 11$

3. $3^{3-2x} = 4$

4. $\log_2(x + 5) = -1$

5. $\log(3 - x) = 2$

6. $\ln(2x) = \frac{1}{3}$

6.6 Cumulative Review Warm Up

Describe the end behavior of the graph of the polynomial function.

1. $f(x) = -3x^4 + 2x - 8$

2. $g(x) = 5x - x^2 - 9x^3$

3. $h(x) = x^5 - 5x^4 + 3x^2 - 15$

4. $p(x) = 1.8 - 2.5x^7 + 5.7x^{10}$

6.6 Practice A

In Exercises 1–6, solve the equation.

1. $6^{x-7} = 6^{2x+3}$

2. $e^{5x} = e^{3x+4}$

3. $3^{x+1} = 9^{x-3}$

4. $2^x = 5$

5. $8^x = 35$

6. $16^{3x-2} = \left(\frac{1}{4}\right)^{5-x}$

7. The length ℓ (in centimeters) of a scalloped hammerhead shark can be modeled by the function $\ell = 266 - 219e^{-0.05t}$, where t is the age (in years) of the shark.

   a. How old is a shark that is 200 centimeters long?

   b. How long is a shark that is twice as old as the shark in part (a)?

In Exercises 8–13, solve the equation.

8. $\ln(3x - 8) = \ln(x + 6)$

9. $\log_3(9x - 2) = \log_3(4x + 3)$

10. $\log(4x + 1) = \log 25$

11. $\log_6(5x + 4) = 2$

12. $\log(10x - 7) = 3$

13. $\log_3(4x + 2) = \log_3 6x$

In Exercises 14–17, solve the equation. Check for extraneous solutions.

14. $\log_2 x + \log_2(x - 3) = 2$

15. $\log_3 3x + \log_3(2x + 1) = 2$

16. $\ln x + \ln(x + 4) = 3$

17. $\log_6 2x^2 + \log_6 3 = 2$

18. You deposit \$400 in an account that pays 5% annual interest. How long will it take for the balance to double for each frequency of compounding?

   a. annually

   b. quarterly

   c. daily

   d. continuously

In Exercises 19–21, solve the inequality.

19. $7^x < 42$

20. $3^x \geq 24$

21. $\log_3 x > 2$

In Exercises 22 and 23, use a graphing calculator to solve the equation.

22. $\ln 3x = 4^{-x+5}$

23. $\log x = 9^{-2x}$

6.6 Practice B

In Exercises 1–6, solve the equation.

1. $9^{3x-5} = 81^{3x+2}$

2. $7^x = 32$

3. $9^{3x+6} = \left(\dfrac{1}{3}\right)^{8-x}$

4. $6^{4x} = 13$

5. $2e^{3x} + 6 = 10$

6. $4e^{2x} - 7 = 1$

7. Fifty grams of radium are stored in a container. The amount R (in grams) of radium present after t years can be modeled by $R = 50e^{-0.00043t}$.

   a. After how many years will only 20 grams of radium be present?

   b. Seventy-five grams of radium are stored in a different container. The amount R (in grams) of radium present after t years can be modeled by $R = 75e^{-0.00043t}$. Will it take *more years* or *fewer years* for only 20 grams of the radium in this container to be present, compared to the answer in part (a)? Explain.

In Exercises 8–13, solve the equation.

8. $\ln(5x - 2) = \ln(x + 6)$

9. $\log(3x + 5) = \log 6$

10. $\log_2(3x + 12) = 4$

11. $\log_3(3x + 7) = \log_3(10x)$

12. $\log_2(x^2 - 2x + 1) = 4$

13. $\log_3(x^2 + x + 7) = 3$

In Exercises 14–17, solve the equation. Check for extraneous solutions.

14. $\ln x + \ln(x - 2) = 5$

15. $\log_5 2x^2 + \log_5 8 = 2$

16. $\log_3(-x) + \log_3(x + 8) = 2$

17. $\log_2(x + 2) + \log_2(x + 5) = 4$

In Exercises 18–20, solve the inequality.

18. $e^{x-2} < 8$

19. $\ln x > 5$

20. $-2\log_3 x + 2 \le 10$

21. You deposit $2000 in Account A, which pays 2.25% annual interest compounded monthly. You deposit another $2000 in Account B, which pays 3% annual interest compounded monthly. When is the sum of the balance in both accounts at least $5000?

6.6 Enrichment and Extension

Solving Exponential and Logarithmic Equations

The natural base e is used to solve the equation that models Newton's Law of Cooling. The equation states that the difference in temperature between an object and its surroundings decreases exponentially as a function of time.

$$T(t) = T_s + (T_0 - T_s)e^{-kt}$$

where $T(t)$ = the temperature after t minutes, T_0 = the initial temperature, T_s = the surrounding temperature, t represents time, and $-k$ represents a constant rate of decrease in the temperature difference.

Example: When the constant surrounding temperature is $65°F$, an object will cool from $160°F$ to $120°F$ in 30 minutes. After how long will the object's temperature be $70°F$?

$120 = 65 + (160 - 65)e^{-k30}$ Substitute the given values into the function.

$\dfrac{55}{95} = e^{-k30}$ is the same as $\dfrac{95}{55} = e^{k30}$ Simplify to solve for k.

$\ln\left(\dfrac{95}{55}\right) = \ln(e)^{k30} \rightarrow 0.5465 = 30k \rightarrow k = 0.0182$

Use k to determine when the temperature is $70°F$.

$70 = 65 + (160 - 65)e^{-0.0182t}$

$\ln\left(\dfrac{5}{95}\right) = -0.0182t$

$\quad t \approx 2$ hours and 42 minutes

In Exercises 1 and 2, use $T(t) = T_s + (T_0 - T_s)e^{-kt}$.

1. At a local restaurant, the cook prepares enough soup at night so that there is plenty of soup for customers the next day. Refrigeration is necessary, but the soup is too hot at $220°F$ to put directly into the fridge. It needs to be no more than $70°F$. The cook cooled the soup by placing it in a sink of water constantly running at $40°F$. After 10 minutes, the soup had cooled down to $140°F$. After how long can the cook place the soup in the fridge?

2. Milk is taken out of the fridge and left on a table. Its temperature is $35°F$ and the house is a constant $70°F$. The temperature of the milk rose $5°F$ after 1 hour. However, milk is unsafe to consume at temperatures over $45°F$. How long can the milk be left out and still be safe to consume?

6.6 Puzzle Time

Why Do Elephants Have Big Trunks?

A	B	C	D	E	F
G	H	I	J	K	L

Complete each exercise. Find the answer in the answer column. Write the word under the answer in the box containing the exercise letter.

−2
THE
−6
SHOPPING
$-\dfrac{2}{3}$
HAVE
−1
GO
2
TO
−100
GROCERIES

Solve the equation.

A. $5^{3-2x} = 5^{-x}$

B. $3^{2x} = 3^{-x}$

C. $3^{-2x+1} \cdot 3^{-2x-3} = 3^{-x}$

D. $10^{1-x} = 10^4$

E. $3^{2x-1} = 27$

F. $4^{x+1} = \dfrac{1}{64}$

G. $\log_3(x + 3) = 0$

H. $\log(-x) + 2 = 4$

I. $\log_3(x - 3) = 4$

J. $2\log_7(-2x) = 0$

K. $\log(-2x + 9) = \log(7 - 4x)$

L. $\log_{12}(x^2 + 35) = \log_{12}(-12x - 1)$

0
THEY
$-\dfrac{1}{2}$
THEY
−4
PUT
−3
SOMEWHERE
84
WHEN
3
SO

Determine if the scatter plot is best modeled by a *linear*, a *quadratic*, or an *exponential* model. Then discuss a real-life situation that could be modeled by each plot.

1. 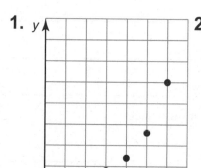   **2.** 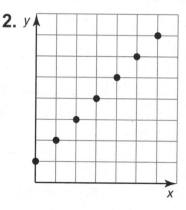   **3.**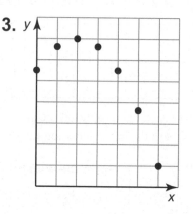

6.7 **Warm Up**

Use the *linear regression* feature on a graphing calculator to determine the line of best fit for the data set.

1.

x	0	2	4	6	8	10
y	−4	1	5	6	11	15

2.

x	2009	2010	2011	2012	2013	2014
y	122.8	124.2	123.7	120.5	118.3	115.6

6.7 **Cumulative Review Warm Up**

Solve the radical equation.

1. $\sqrt{2x - 1} = 4$

2. $4 + \sqrt{2x} = x$

3. $\sqrt{4 - 3x} - 2\sqrt{x} = 0$

4. $\sqrt{x + 3} - \sqrt{x - 1} = 1$

Name_____ Date_____

In Exercises 1 and 2, determine the type of function represented by the table. Explain your reasoning.

1.

x	1	3	5	7	9
y	81	27	9	3	1

2.

x	1	2	3	4	5
y	3	1	1	3	7

In Exercises 3–8, write an exponential function $y = ab^x$ whose graph passes through the given points.

3. $(1, 6), (2, 12)$

4. $(1, 20), (2, 80)$

5. $(2, 18), (3, 54)$

6. $(3, 250), (4, 1250)$

7. $(3, 56), (5, 224)$

8. $(2, 45), (4, 405)$

9. Describe and correct the error in determining the type of function represented by the data.

x	0	1	3	5	7
y	2	4	8	16	32

×2 ×2 ×2 ×2

The outputs have a common ratio of 2, so the data represent an exponential function.

In Exercises 10 and 11, determine whether the data show an exponential relationship. Then write a function that models the data.

10.

x	−4	−2	0	2	4
y	6	24	96	384	1536

11.

x	0	1	2	3	4
y	0	5	10	15	20

12. Use a graphing calculator to find an exponential model for the data in the table.

x	1	3	7	10	12
y	6	8.64	17.916	30.959	44.581

Name _____ Date _____

6.7 Practice B

In Exercises 1 and 2, determine the type of function represented by the table. Explain your reasoning.

1.

x	0	2	4	6	8
y	$\frac{1}{8}$	$\frac{1}{2}$	2	8	32

2.

x	0	1	2	3
y	8	12	18	27

In Exercises 3–8, write an exponential function $y = ab^x$ whose graph passes through the given points.

3. $(1, 10), (2, 20)$

4. $(1, 18), (3, 162)$

5. $(2, 36), (3, 72)$

6. $(3, 375), (4, 1875)$

7. $(2, 3.6), (5, 777.6)$

8. $(2, 8), (5, 512)$

9. Describe and correct the error in determining the type of function represented by the data.

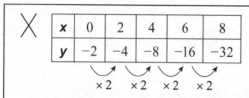

x	0	2	4	6	8
y	−2	−4	−8	−16	−32

×2   ×2   ×2   ×2

The outputs have a common ratio of 2, but the outputs are negative, so the data does not represent a recognizable function.

In Exercises 10 and 11, determine whether the data show an exponential relationship. Then write a function that models the data.

10.

x	1	3	5	7	9
y	64	32	16	8	4

11.

x	0	10	20	30	40
y	0	15	30	45	60

12. Use a graphing calculator to find an exponential model for the data in the table.

x	2	5	6	8	9
y	7.65	25.819	38.728	87.138	130.71

Name_____ Date_____

Modeling with Exponential and Logarithmic Functions

Alexander Graham Bell was a well-known scientist, inventor, engineer, and innovator who is credited with inventing the first practical telephone. The *bel*, a unit of measure for the intensity of sound, was named after him. Although the bel itself is rarely used, it is quite common to use the *decibel*, one-tenth of a bel.

- The function $y = 10 \log x$ models the relative intensities of sound.

- For example, the intensity of the faintest sound, called the *threshold of hearing*, is $10^{-12}\left(\dfrac{W}{m^2}\right)$.

To find the intensity level, or relative intensity, the formula $R = 10 \log \dfrac{I}{I_0}$ is used, where $\dfrac{I}{I_0}$ is the comparison of a sound to the threshold of hearing. Logarithms are used due to the range of intensities having a base of 10.

Use this formula to compare decibel levels and to find the relative intensity of a sound in decibels.

Example: The relative intensity for the threshold of pain is 130 decibels. How many times louder than the threshold of hearing is the threshold of pain?

$$130 = 10 \log \frac{I}{I_0} \rightarrow 13 = \log \frac{I}{I_0} \rightarrow 10^{13} = \frac{I}{I_0} \rightarrow 10^{13} \bullet I_0 = I$$

The threshold for pain is about 10^{13}, or 10,000,000,000,000 times as loud as the threshold of hearing.

In Exercises 1–4, use the formula $R = 10 \log \dfrac{I}{I_0}$ to compare decibel levels and find the relative intensity of a sound in decibels.

1. The alarm of a standard alarm clock is 80 decibels. Compare this intensity to the threshold of hearing.

2. The intensity of a rock concert is about 110 decibels. Compare the intensity of a concert to the threshold of hearing.

3. The television has been turned down to an intensity that is 1000 times as loud as the threshold of hearing. What is the relative intensity of the sound in decibels?

4. A normal conversation is one million times louder than the threshold of hearing. How many decibels is a normal conversation?

6.7 Puzzle Time

What Do You Call A Lamb Who Does Aerobics?

Write the letter of each answer in the box containing the exercise number.

Write an exponential function $y = ab^x$ whose graph passes through the given points.

1. $(0, 4), (2, 16)$

2. $(-1, 2), (2, 54)$

3. $(-2, 8), (-3, 16)$

4. $(1, 6), (3, 24)$

5. $(-2, 16), (-3, 32)$

6. $(0, 1), (1, 0.75)$

7. $(-2, 9), (-3, 27)$

8. $(0, 2), (1, 5)$

9.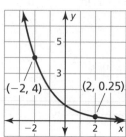

10.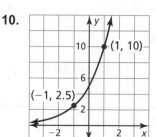

Answers
E. $y = 3 \cdot 2^x$
S. $y = 4 \cdot 2^x$
P. $y = \left(\frac{1}{2}\right)^x$
E. $y = 2 \cdot \left(\frac{1}{2}\right)^x$
A. $y = 2 \cdot \left(\frac{5}{2}\right)^x$
P. $y = 4 \cdot \left(\frac{1}{2}\right)^x$
H. $y = 6 \cdot 3^x$
S. $y = \left(\frac{3}{4}\right)^x$
H. $y = \left(\frac{1}{3}\right)^x$
E. $y = 5 \cdot 2^x$

1	2	3	4	5		6	7	8	9	10

Name_____ Date_____

In Exercises 1–18, evaluate the expression.

1. $5 \cdot 7^2$

2. $3 \cdot 4^2$

3. $6 \cdot 3^3$

4. $-4 \cdot 2^3$

5. $-7 \cdot 2^5$

6. $5 \cdot -4^3$

7. $(-2)^3$

8. $(-3)^2$

9. $(-2)^4$

10. $\left(\dfrac{2}{3}\right)^3$

11. $\left(\dfrac{4}{5}\right)^2$

12. $\left(\dfrac{1}{3}\right)^4$

13. $\left(-\dfrac{2}{5}\right)^3$

14. $\left(-\dfrac{1}{4}\right)^4$

15. $\left(-\dfrac{3}{4}\right)^3$

16. $-\left(\dfrac{1}{2}\right)^5$

17. $-\left(\dfrac{2}{3}\right)^4$

18. $-\left(\dfrac{3}{5}\right)^3$

In Exercises 19–36, write the number in scientific notation.

19. 0.0005

20. $382{,}000{,}000{,}000$

21. -0.0132

22. 0.0000057

23. $2{,}300{,}000$

24. -0.00000000092

25. -0.000359

26. $51{,}300$

27. 0.000041

28. 4500

29. $12{,}000{,}000$

30. $731{,}000$

31. -0.000000817

32. $417{,}000{,}000{,}000$

33. $-62{,}000$

34. $8{,}300{,}000{,}000{,}000$

35. 0.000000089

36. 0.002

37. Bowling Alley A charges \$5 admission and \$3.50 per game. Bowling Alley B charges \$25 admission, but offers unlimited games with no additional charge.

   a. How much does it cost to play four games at each bowling alley?

   b. How much does it cost to play five games at each bowling alley?

   c. When is it financially more beneficial to bowl at Bowling Alley B?

38. Admission to the local fair is \$15. Ride tickets are \$1.25 each.

   a. How much does it cost for admission and six ride tickets?

   b. How much does it cost for admission and eight ride tickets?

   c. You and three friends want to go to the fair and need eight ride tickets each. How much does that cost?

Chapter 6 Cumulative Review (continued)

In Exercises 39–56, write the number in standard form.

39. 1.85×10^{-3} **40.** -8.9×10^{4} **41.** 3.84×10^{-8}

42. 2.57×10^{-7} **43.** 4.6×10^{5} **44.** -3.34×10^{-3}

45. 3.05×10^{-8} **46.** 4.49×10^{4} **47.** 5.9×10^{5}

48. -2.25×10^{9} **49.** 3.08×10^{-1} **50.** -1.06×10^{-8}

51. 5.51×10^{7} **52.** 6.18×10^{8} **53.** 1.84×10^{-7}

54. 8.9×10^{5} **55.** 9.2×10^{-8} **56.** -7.32×10^{-5}

In Exercises 57–68, write an equation of the line that passes through the given point and has the given slope.

57. $(-5, -10); m = -\frac{2}{5}$ **58.** $(11, 1); m = \frac{5}{11}$

59. $(5, -6); m = \frac{3}{5}$ **60.** $(12, -1); m = \frac{1}{4}$

61. $(-8, 10); m = -\frac{7}{8}$ **62.** $(0, -12); m = \frac{3}{5}$

63. $(7, -7); m = -2$ **64.** $(8, 4); m = 3$

65. $(-2, -9); m = -\frac{1}{2}$ **66.** $(-3, 3); m = \frac{5}{6}$

67. $(7, -8); m = -3$ **68.** $(-6, 0); m = 4$

In Exercises 69–82, find the zero(s) of the function.

69. $f(x) = x^2 - 7x$ **70.** $h(x) = x^2 + 3x$

71. $g(x) = x^2 + 4x$ **72.** $h(x) = x^2 - 8x$

73. $g(x) = x^2 - 3x + 2$ **74.** $h(x) = x^2 + 6x - 27$

75. $f(x) = x^2 + 11x + 30$ **76.** $h(x) = x^2 - 6x - 16$

77. $g(x) = 2x^2 - 3x - 35$ **78.** $f(x) = 3x^2 + 14x - 5$

79. $h(x) = 2x^2 + x - 28$ **80.** $g(x) = 3x^2 - 20x - 7$

81. $f(x) = 5x^2 - 14x - 3$ **82.** $g(x) = 3x^2 - 34x + 63$

Chapter 6 Cumulative Review (continued)

In Exercises 83–96, add or subtract. Write the answer in standard form.

83. $(8 + i) + (-4 + 3i)$

84. $(-1 - i) + (5 - 2i)$

85. $(5 - 8i) + (6 - 4i)$

86. $(-3 + 2i) + (-9 - 3i)$

87. $(4 - i) + (6 + 7i)$

88. $(11 - 8i) + (-3 - 12i)$

89. $(4 + 7i) + (-3 - 10i)$

90. $(2 + 12i) - (4 - 2i)$

91. $(-9 + 2i) - (5 + 5i)$

92. $(12 - 2i) - (-9 + 3i)$

93. $(8 + 10i) - (3 + 2i)$

94. $(-11 - 2i) - (-1 - 8i)$

95. $(10 + 11i) - (-8 - 10i)$

96. $(-7 - 9i) - (10 - 4i)$

In Exercises 97–108, multiply. Write the answer in standard form.

97. $3i(4 + 2i)$

98. $5i(-1 + 2i)$

99. $-7i(3 - 4i)$

100. $-i(7 - 6i)$

101. $(12 + 3i)(-5 + 7i)$

102. $(6 - 3i)(-10 + 6i)$

103. $(-4 + 10i)(4 + 2i)$

104. $(-9 - 2i)(6 + 2i)$

105. $(-10 - 9i)(-4 - 9i)$

106. $(-1 + 8i)(7 + 3i)$

107. $(11 + 6i)(-5 + 4i)$

108. $(3 - 3i)(4 + 5i)$

In Exercises 109–116, find the zero(s) of the function.

109. $f(x) = 2x^2 + 6x + 5$

110. $f(x) = 3x^2 - x + 3$

111. $f(x) = 4x^2 + 3x + 6$

112. $f(x) = 6x^2 - 5x + 8$

113. $f(x) = -x^2 + 4x - 7$

114. $f(x) = 5x^2 - 6x + 3$

115. $f(x) = 4x^2 - 9x + 6$

116. $f(x) = -2x^2 + 5x - 4$

117. A rectangular swimming pool has a length of $4x - 10$ feet and a width of $x + 10$ feet.

    a. Write an equation for the perimeter of the swimming pool.

    b. Write an equation for the area of the swimming pool.

    c. You know that the total perimeter is 120 feet. What is the value of x?

    d. What is the area of the swimming pool?

Chapter 6 Cumulative Review (continued)

In Exercises 118–131, find the zero(s) of the function.

118. $x^2 + 5x - 4 = 0$

119. $2x^2 + 4x + 1 = 0$

120. $-x^2 + 8x + 5 = 0$

121. $x^2 - 3x + 2 = 0$

122. $2x^2 - 5x + 3 = 0$

123. $x^2 - 5x + 2 = 0$

124. $-3x^2 + 6x + 1 = 0$

125. $-5x^2 - 3x + 4 = 0$

126. $6x^2 - 5x + 1 = 0$

127. $-2x^2 + 7x + 3 = 0$

128. $x^2 + 7x + 3 = 0$

129. $-4x^2 + x + 8 = 0$

130. $3x^2 - 5x + 1 = 0$

131. $-2x^2 + 9x + 6 = 0$

132. A rectangular parking pad has a length of $2x$ feet and a width of $x + 4$ feet.

   a. Write an equation for the perimeter of the parking pad.

   b. Write an equation for the area of the parking pad.

   c. You know that the total perimeter is 56 feet. What is the value of x?

   d. What is the area of the parking pad?

133. You want to tile a bathroom. You know that the width of the room is 13.5 feet and the length is $3x$ feet.

   a. Write an equation for the area of the bathroom.

   b. You know the perimeter of the room is 63 feet. What is the value of x?

   c. What is the area of the bathroom?

   d. The tile you want to purchase is $2.49 per square foot. How much will it cost for the tile in the bathroom?

134. You want to put hardwood floor down in your living room. You know that the width of the room is 16 feet and the length is $2x$ feet.

   a. Write an equation for the area of the living room.

   b. You know the perimeter of the room is 76 feet. What is the value of x?

   c. What is the area of the room?

   d. The hardwood you want to purchase is $4.59 per square foot. How much will it cost for the hardwood in the living room?

Chapter 7

Name _____ Date _____

Chapter 7 Rational Functions

Dear Family,

Do you have a cell phone? If so, are you getting the most from your plan? Are you paying too much for your plan?

When choosing a service contract, you should compare different providers and their coverage areas and the different prices for talk, text, and data plans. You want to make sure your plan has what you need, so you don't end up paying fees for going over what your plan allows. The bigger cell phone companies offer a subsidized plan with a two-year contract in which you pay a smaller amount for a phone and then a monthly charge for service. Another option is an unlocked phone in which you buy the phone outright with a monthly fee for services and no fixed contract.

Use the Internet to compare two different plans for a two-year subsidized contract for the first 24 months of service. Then compare two cell phone plans for an unlocked phone for the first 24 months of service. Remember to include the initial cost of the phone in the total cost for the first month. Then find the average monthly cost for each plan. For a fair comparison of plans, choose the same cell phone for each plan. It may be helpful to use a spreadsheet to organize and calculate your data.

Month	Company A		Company B	
	Total cost (in dollars)	Cost per month (in dollars)	Total cost (in dollars)	Cost per month (in dollars)
1				
2				
⋮	⋮	⋮	⋮	⋮
24				

In this chapter, you will solve rational equations for situations in which you want to find the average monthly cost of service. Before you sign a contract with a cell phone provider, researching different plans may end up saving you time and money in the long run.

Have fun talking!

Nombre _____ Fecha_____

Estimada familia:

¿Tienen teléfono celular? Si lo tienen, ¿aprovechan su plan al máximo? ¿Pagan demasiado por su plan?

Cuando elijan un contrato de servicio, deberían comparar diferentes proveedores y sus áreas de cobertura y los diferentes precios de los planes de datos para hablar y mandar mensajes de texto. Les conviene asegurarse de que su plan tenga que lo necesitan, así no terminan pagando tarifas por pasarse del límite permitido por su plan. Las compañías de telefonía celular más grandes ofrecen un plan subvencionado con un contrato de dos años donde pagan una cantidad menor por un teléfono y luego, un cargo mensual por el servicio. Otra opción es un teléfono desbloqueado donde compran el teléfono en el acto con una tarifa mensual por los servicios sin contrato fijo.

Usen Internet para comparar dos planes diferentes con un contrato de dos años subvencionado para los primeros 24 meses del servicio. Luego, comparen dos planes de telefonía celular para un teléfono desbloqueado para los primeros 24 meses de servicio. Recuerden incluir el costo inicial del teléfono en el costo total del primer mes. Luego, hallen el costo mensual promedio de cada plan. Para hacer una comparación justa de los planes, elijan el mismo teléfono celular para cada plan. Quizás sea útil usar una hoja de cálculo para organizar y calcular sus datos.

Mes	Compañía A		Compañía B	
	Costo total (en dólares)	Costo por mes (en dólares)	Costo total (en dólares)	Costo por mes (en dólares)
1				
2				
⋮	⋮	⋮	⋮	⋮
24				

En este capítulo, resolverán ecuaciones racionales en situaciones donde quieran hallar el costo mensual promedio de un servicio. Antes de firmar un contrato con un proveedor de telefonía celular, investigar diferentes planes puede terminar ahorrándoles tiempo y dinero a largo plazo.

¡Diviértanse hablando!

Determine a relationship between x and y in the table. Then create a scatter plot for each set of points. What conclusions can you make about the graphs and the relationship you discovered between x and y?

1.

x	y
1	2
3	6
4	8
6	12

2.

x	y
1	2
2	1
4	$\frac{1}{2}$
6	$\frac{1}{3}$

3.

x	y
1	3
3	1
5	$\frac{3}{5}$
7	$\frac{3}{7}$

7.1 Warm Up

Use the given values of x and y to find the value of k in the equation.

1. $y = kx$

   $x = 4, y = -3$

2. $y = kx$

   $x = \dfrac{1}{2}, y = 5$

3. $y = kx$

   $x = -3.5, y = -2.8$

4. $y = \dfrac{k}{x}$

   $x = -2, y = 13$

5. $y = \dfrac{k}{x}$

   $x = 5.2, y = -5$

6. $y = \dfrac{k}{x}$

   $x = -\dfrac{3}{5}, y = \dfrac{5}{2}$

7.1 Cumulative Review Warm Up

Solve the system.

1. $-4x - 3y = -7$

   $6x + 2y = 3$

2. $y = -\dfrac{2}{3}x + 4$

   $-2y = 6$

3. $y = x^2$

   $y = 6 - x^2$

7.1 Practice A

In Exercises 1–6, tell whether _x_ and _y_ show _direct variation_, _inverse variation_, or _neither_.

1. $y = \dfrac{5}{x}$

2. $xy = 7$

3. $6x = y$

4. $\dfrac{y}{x} = 10$

5. $x + y = 8$

6. $2y = x$

In Exercises 7–10, tell whether _x_ and _y_ show _direct variation_, _inverse variation_, or _neither_.

7.

x	2	4	8	10
y	38	19	9.5	7.6

8.

x	3	5	8	10
y	15	9	6	5.5

9.

x	1.5	4	6.5	10
y	9	24	39	60

10.

x	1.5	4	6	12
y	84	31.5	21	10.5

In Exercises 11–13, the variables _x_ and _y_ vary inversely. Use the given values to write an equation relating _x_ and _y_. Then find _y_ when _x_ = 3.

11. $x = 6, y = -5$

12. $x = 1, y = 7$

13. $x = 3, y = \dfrac{2}{3}$

14. The variables x and y vary inversely. Describe and correct the error in writing an equation relating x and y.

$$
\begin{array}{l}
\times \quad x = 6, y = 5 \\[4pt]
\dfrac{y}{x} = a \\[6pt]
\dfrac{5}{6} = a \\[6pt]
\text{So, } y = \dfrac{5}{6x}.
\end{array}
$$

15. The number y of songs that can be stored on an MP3 player varies inversely with the average size x of a song. A certain MP3 player can store 3000 songs when the average size of a song is 5 megabytes. Find the number of songs that will fit on the MP3 player when the average size of a song is 4 megabytes.

Name _____ Date _____

7.1 Practice B

In Exercises 1–6, tell whether *x* and *y* show *direct variation*, *inverse variation*, or *neither*.

1. $y = \dfrac{12}{x}$

2. $xy = 15$

3. $9x = y$

4. $y = x - 3$

5. $\dfrac{y}{x} = 9$

6. $xy = \dfrac{1}{3}$

In Exercises 7–10, tell whether *x* and *y* show *direct variation*, *inverse variation*, or *neither*.

7.

x	2.5	4	7.5	9
y	30	48	90	108

8.

x	12	5	2.5	1.5
y	35	84	168	280

9.

x	2.5	3	6	10
y	8	9.6	1.6	6

10.

x	2.5	10	16	21
y	672	168	105	80

In Exercises 11–13, the variables *x* and *y* vary inversely. Use the given values to write an equation relating *x* and *y*. Then find *y* when *x* = 3.

11. $x = 4, y = -3$

12. $x = \dfrac{2}{3}, y = -5$

13. $x = -10, y = -\dfrac{1}{5}$

14. The variables *x* and *y* vary inversely. Describe and correct the error in writing an equation relating *x* and *y*.

> ✗ $x = \dfrac{1}{3}, y = 2$
>
> $xy = a$
>
> $\dfrac{1}{3} \cdot 2 = a$
>
> $a = \dfrac{2}{3}$
>
> So, $y = \dfrac{3x}{2}$.

15. The current *y* in a certain circuit varies inversely with the resistance *x* in the circuit. If the current is 8 amperes when the resistance is 20 ohms, what will the current be when the resistance increases to 25 ohms?

7.1 Enrichment and Extension

Inverse Variation

Combined variation involves a combination of direct and inverse variation. These equations are a little more complicated, so you will first want to substitute the given values to solve for the constant of variation. Then use the constant variation to find the missing value.

Example: Suppose y varies directly with x and w but varies inversely as the square of z. Find the equation of variation if $y = 100$ when $x = 2$, $w = 4$, and $z = 20$.

Solution:

$$y = \frac{axw}{z^2}$$ Given the direct variation with y, constant a, and x and w are in the numerators. Given the inverse variation with y, z^2 is in the denominator.

$$100 = \frac{a(2)(4)}{(20)^2}$$ Substitute.

$$a = 5000$$ Solve for a.

$$y = \frac{5000xw}{z^2}$$ Now you can solve for one of the variables when you are given the values of the other three variables.

In Exercises 1–4, solve the combined variation problems.

1. Suppose x varies directly with y and the square root of z. When $x = -18$ and $y = 2$, $z = 9$. Find y when $x = 10$ and $z = 4$.

2. Suppose w varies inversely with z and the cube root of v, but varies directly with y. When $w = 4$, $v = 27$, and $y = 2$, $z = 5$. Find w when $y = 3$, $v = 64$, and $z = 6$.

3. The volume V of wood in a tree varies directly with the height h and inversely with the square of the girth g. The volume of a tree is 144 cubic meters when the height is 20 meters and the girth is 1.5 meters. What is the height of a tree with a volume of 100 cubic meters and girth of 2 meters?

4. The pressure P of a gas varies directly with the number of moles n and temperature T of the gas and inversely with volume V. Given the equation of the situation described above, as the pressure of a gas increases, what happens to the volume of the gas? Now write the number of moles as a function of pressure, volume, and temperature.

Name_____ Date _____

 7.1 **Puzzle Time**

What Part Of A Computer Keyboard Do Astronauts Like The Best?

Write the letter of each answer in the box containing the exercise number.

Tell whether *x* and *y* show *direct variation*, *inverse variation*, or *neither*.

1. $xy = 3$

2. $x + y = 12$

3. $\dfrac{y}{x} = 6$

The variables *x* and *y* vary inversely. Use the given values to write an equation relating *x* and *y*.

4. $x = 5, y = -2$ 5. $x = 8, y = 2$

6. $x = \dfrac{1}{2}, y = 6$ 7. $x = -12, y = \dfrac{2}{3}$

8. $x = -\dfrac{1}{3}, y = -\dfrac{9}{2}$ 9. $x = 2, y = -\dfrac{3}{4}$

10. $x = -2.4, y = 8.6$

11. $x = -15, y = -\dfrac{2}{5}$

Answers

P. $y = \dfrac{16}{x}$

T. inverse variation

S. $y = -\dfrac{10}{x}$

R. $y = -\dfrac{6}{x}$

E. direct variation

A. $y = \dfrac{3}{x}$

A. $y = -\dfrac{20.64}{x}$

C. $y = -\dfrac{8}{x}$

E. $y = \dfrac{3}{2x}$

H. neither

B. $y = -\dfrac{3}{2x}$

1	2	3		4	5	6	7	8		9	10	11

Complete the table for the function $g(x) = \dfrac{1}{x}$. Review the values in the table to make conclusions about the nature of the graph of g as x-values approach zero and as x-values approach both positive and negative infinity.

1.

x	-1	$-\dfrac{1}{2}$	$-\dfrac{1}{10}$	$-\dfrac{1}{100}$	$\dfrac{1}{100}$	$\dfrac{1}{10}$	$\dfrac{1}{2}$	1
$g(x)$								

2.

x	-1000	-100	-10	10	100	1000
$g(x)$						

7.2 **Warm Up**

Use the graph of f to sketch the transformation.

1. $f(x) + 2$ **2.** $f(x - 2)$

3. $f(-x)$ **4.** $-f(x)$

5. $2f(x)$ **6.** $-f(x + 3) - 1$

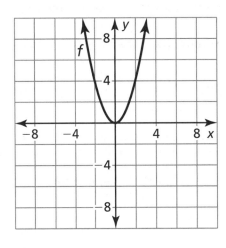

7.2 **Cumulative Review Warm Up**

Determine the maximum or minimum value of the function.

1. $y = -2x^2 + 5x$

2. $y = 3x^2 - 7x + 8$

3. $y = 4 - \dfrac{3}{2}x - \dfrac{1}{2}x^2$

Name _____ Date _____

In Exercises 1–3, graph the function. Compare the graph with the graph of
$f(x) = \dfrac{1}{x}$.

1. $h(x) = \dfrac{2}{x}$

2. $g(x) = \dfrac{9}{x}$

3. $h(x) = \dfrac{-4}{x}$

In Exercises 4–15, graph the function. State the domain and range.

4. $f(x) = \dfrac{3}{x} + 2$

5. $y = \dfrac{5}{x} - 1$

6. $g(x) = \dfrac{4}{x - 3}$

7. $y = \dfrac{1}{x + 4}$

8. $h(x) = \dfrac{-1}{x + 3}$

9. $y = \dfrac{-4}{x - 5}$

10. $f(x) = \dfrac{x + 3}{x - 2}$

11. $y = \dfrac{x - 5}{x + 3}$

12. $g(x) = \dfrac{x + 4}{2x - 6}$

13. $y = \dfrac{5x + 2}{3x - 9}$

14. $h(x) = \dfrac{-2x + 3}{3x + 4}$

15. $y = \dfrac{8x - 1}{5x - 1}$

In Exercises 16–21, rewrite the function in the form $g(x) = \dfrac{a}{x - h} + k$. **Graph the**

function. Describe the graph of g as a transformation of the graph of $f(x) = \dfrac{a}{x}$.

16. $g(x) = \dfrac{4x + 5}{x + 1}$

17. $g(x) = \dfrac{6x + 5}{x - 2}$

18. $g(x) = \dfrac{3x - 6}{x - 4}$

19. $g(x) = \dfrac{5x - 12}{x + 2}$

20. $g(x) = \dfrac{x + 15}{x - 5}$

21. $g(x) = \dfrac{x + 3}{x - 9}$

22. Your choir is taking a trip. The trip has an initial cost of $500, plus $150 for each student.

    a. Estimate how many students must go on the trip for the average cost per student to fall to $175.

    b. What happens to the average cost as more students go on the trip?

In Exercises 23–25, use a graphing calculator to graph the function. Then determine whether the function is *even*, *odd*, or *neither*.

23. $f(x) = \dfrac{5}{x^2 - 1}$

24. $g(x) = \dfrac{3x^2}{x^2 + 4}$

25. $h(x) = \dfrac{x^3}{2x^2 + x^4}$

Name_____ Date_____

7.2 Practice B

In Exercises 1–3, graph the function. Compare the graph with the graph of
$f(x) = \dfrac{1}{x}$.

1. $h(x) = \dfrac{12}{x}$

2. $g(x) = \dfrac{-8}{x}$

3. $h(x) = \dfrac{0.2}{x}$

In Exercises 4–15, graph the function. State the domain and range.

4. $f(x) = \dfrac{5}{x} - 2$

5. $g(x) = \dfrac{3}{x + 4}$

6. $y = \dfrac{-8}{x - 3}$

7. $h(x) = \dfrac{-1}{x + 5}$

8. $y = \dfrac{-2}{x + 1} + 3$

9. $y = \dfrac{9}{x - 4} - 2$

10. $f(x) = \dfrac{x + 5}{x - 4}$

11. $g(x) = \dfrac{x - 3}{2x + 8}$

12. $h(x) = \dfrac{-8x + 3}{5x + 2}$

13. $y = \dfrac{3x - 1}{5x - 1}$

14. $y = \dfrac{-3x}{-4x - 1}$

15. $y = \dfrac{-2x + 5}{-x + 8}$

In Exercises 16–21, rewrite the function in the form $g(x) = \dfrac{a}{x - h} + k$. **Graph the function. Describe the graph of g as a transformation of the graph of** $f(x) = \dfrac{a}{x}$.

16. $g(x) = \dfrac{3x + 7}{x + 2}$

17. $g(x) = \dfrac{4x - 2}{x - 3}$

18. $g(x) = \dfrac{4x - 10}{x + 5}$

19. $g(x) = \dfrac{x + 12}{x - 3}$

20. $g(x) = \dfrac{5x - 30}{x + 4}$

21. $g(x) = \dfrac{7x - 2}{x + 6}$

22. You are creating statues made of cement. The mold costs $300. The material for each statue costs $22.

    a. Estimate how many statues must be made for the average cost per statue to fall below $30.

    b. What happens to the average cost as more statues are created?

23. The concentration c of a certain drug in a patient's bloodstream t hours after an injection is given by $c(t) = \dfrac{t}{4t^2 + 1}$.

    a. Use a graphing calculator to graph the function. Describe a reasonable domain and range.

    b. Determine the time at which the concentration is the highest.

Name_____ Date _____

Graphing Rational Functions

It is important to take a look at the end behaviors of a function. You will investigate the values of y as the x-values approach a certain value. You will begin by looking at what value y approaches as x approaches $+\infty$ and $-\infty$.

Example: Use a graphing calculator to graph the function $f(x) = \dfrac{3x-4}{2x+1}$. Determine what value y approaches as x approaches $+\infty$ and $-\infty$.

Solution: As the x-values get larger and larger $(+\infty)$, the y-values approach $\dfrac{3}{2}$. As the x-values get smaller and smaller $(-\infty)$, the y-values also approach $\dfrac{3}{2}$. You can write:

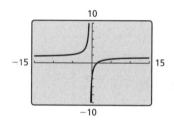

$$\text{As } x \to +\infty, y \to \frac{3}{2}. \text{ As } x \to -\infty, y \to \frac{3}{2}.$$

In Exercises 1–8 use a graphing calculator to graph the function. Determine the value y approaches as x approaches $+\infty$ and $-\infty$.

1. $h(x) = \dfrac{x^2 - 2x - 8}{x^2 - 9}$

2. $q(x) = \dfrac{7x^3 - 3}{2x^3 - 7x + 4}$

3. $g(x) = \dfrac{x}{x^2 - x - 2}$

4. $k(x) = \dfrac{3x^4 + 5x - 4}{6x^2 - 2x}$

5. $f(x) = \dfrac{-2x^2 + 4}{7x - 3}$

6. $j(x) = \dfrac{2x^3 - 4x}{x^4 + 6}$

7. $d(x) = \dfrac{-4x + 1}{x - 8}$

8. $k(x) = \dfrac{x^2 - 9}{-2x}$

7.2 Puzzle Time

What Has A Head And A Tail But No Body?

Write the letter of each answer in the box containing the exercise number.

Match the graph with its function .

1.

2.

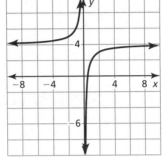

3.

4.

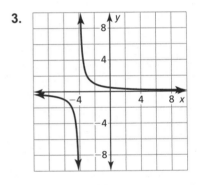

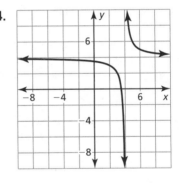

5.

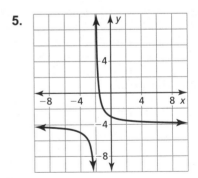

Answers

I. $y = \dfrac{2}{x-4} + 4$

A. $y = \dfrac{2}{x} + 4$

O. $y = \dfrac{2}{x+4}$

N. $y = \dfrac{4}{x+2} - 4$

C. $y = -\dfrac{2}{x} + 4$

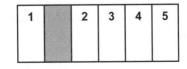

| 1 | | 2 | 3 | 4 | 5 |

In algebraic expressions, values that make a denominator zero are called *excluded values*. Determine the excluded values in the expression.

1. $\dfrac{1}{x+8}$

2. $\dfrac{1}{x^2-5x}$

3. $\dfrac{1}{6x^2-x-15}$

7.3 Warm Up

Perform the indicated operation. Simplify your answer and indicate any excluded values of x.

1. $\dfrac{2}{7} \cdot \dfrac{5}{3}$

2. $\dfrac{9}{10} \cdot \dfrac{8}{5}$

3. $\dfrac{4}{11} \div \dfrac{2}{3}$

4. $\dfrac{x-1}{5} \cdot \dfrac{2}{5}$

5. $\dfrac{x}{x-1} \cdot \dfrac{x}{x+1}$

6. $\dfrac{-3}{2x+1} \div \dfrac{x}{x+1}$

7.3 Cumulative Review Warm Up

You deposit $7000 in an account that pays annual interest. Find the balance in the account after 3 years if the interest is compounded as described below at the given rate.

1. quarterly; 1.26%

2. monthly; 3.25%

3. daily; 2.8%

4. continuously; 2.3%

5. annually; 4.125%

6. continuously; 1.86%

Name_____ Date_____

7.3 Practice A

In Exercises 1–6, simplify the expression, if possible.

1. $\dfrac{3x^2}{5x^2 + 2x}$

2. $\dfrac{6x^4 - x^3}{2x^4}$

3. $\dfrac{x^2 - 4x - 5}{x^2 - 7x + 10}$

4. $\dfrac{x^2 - 3x}{x^2 + 5x + 6}$

5. $\dfrac{x^2 - x - 2}{x^3 - 8}$

6. $\dfrac{x^2 - 3x - 4}{x^3 + 1}$

In Exercises 7–12, find the product.

7. $\dfrac{54x^4 y^2}{y^4} \cdot \dfrac{x^3 y^2}{9x^5 y^3}$

8. $\dfrac{x^3(x + 2)}{x - 1} \cdot \dfrac{(x - 1)(x - 3)}{x^4}$

9. $\dfrac{x^2(x - 5)}{x + 7} \cdot \dfrac{(x + 7)(x - 1)}{4x^2}$

10. $\dfrac{x^2 - 5x}{x + 3} \cdot \dfrac{x^2 + 4x + 3}{x}$

11. $\dfrac{x^2 + 3x}{x - 2} \cdot \dfrac{x^2 - 5x + 6}{4x}$

12. $\dfrac{x^2 - 4x - 5}{x^2 + 6x + 9} \cdot \dfrac{2x^2 + 6x}{x^2 + 3x + 2}$

13. Compare the function $f(x) = \dfrac{(4x + 1)(x - 5)}{(4x + 1)}$ to the function $g(x) = x - 5$.

In Exercises 14–17, find the quotient.

14. $\dfrac{28x^4 y}{y^7} \div \dfrac{y^9}{2x^5}$

15. $\dfrac{x^2 - x - 6}{3x^4 + 6x^3} \div \dfrac{x - 3}{6x^3}$

16. $\dfrac{4x^2 + 12x}{x^2 + 2x - 3} \div \dfrac{4x}{5x - 5}$

17. $\dfrac{x^2 + 5x - 14}{x + 3} \div \left(x^2 - 4x + 4\right)$

18. Manufacturers often package products in a way that uses the least amount of material. One measure of the efficiency of a package is the ratio of its surface area to its volume. The smaller the ratio, the more efficient the packaging. A company makes a cylindrical can to hold popcorn. The company is designing a new can with the same height h and twice the radius r of the old can.

  a. Write an expression for the efficiency ratio $\dfrac{S}{V}$, where S is the surface area

  of the can and V is the volume of the can.

  b. Find the efficiency ratio for each can.

  c. Did the company make a good decision by creating the new can? Explain.

Name_____ Date _____

In Exercises 1–6, simplify the expression, if possible.

1. $\dfrac{4x^3}{3x^3 + 7x}$

2. $\dfrac{x^2 + 5x + 6}{x^2 + 2x - 3}$

3. $\dfrac{2x^2 - 5x}{x^2 + 7x + 12}$

4. $\dfrac{x^2 - x - 20}{x^3 + 64}$

5. $\dfrac{x^4 - 16}{5x^3 - 3x^2 + 20x - 12}$

6. $\dfrac{6x^3 - 6x^2 + 5x - 5}{72x^4 - 50}$

In Exercises 7–12, find the product.

7. $\dfrac{x^4(x - 4)}{x + 3} \cdot \dfrac{(x + 3)(x - 2)}{x^5}$

8. $\dfrac{x^2 + 6x}{x - 4} \cdot \dfrac{x^2 - 2x - 8}{x}$

9. $\dfrac{x^2 - 2x}{x + 5} \cdot \dfrac{x^2 + 6x + 5}{3x}$

10. $\dfrac{x^2 - x - 6}{x^2 + 8x + 16} \cdot \dfrac{3x^2 + 12x}{x^2 - 2x - 3}$

11. $\dfrac{x^2 + 3x - 28}{x^2 - 25} \cdot \left(x^2 - 8x + 15\right)$

12. $\dfrac{x^2 + 2x - 15}{x^2 - 9} \cdot \left(x^2 - x - 12\right)$

In Exercises 13–16, find the quotient.

13. $\dfrac{2x^3 + 10x^2}{x^2 + x - 20} \div \dfrac{2x^2}{x - 4}$

14. $\dfrac{x^2 - 10x + 21}{x + 2} \div \left(x^2 - 14x + 49\right)$

15. $\dfrac{x^2 - 2x - 3}{x^2 + 2x - 8} \div \dfrac{x^2 + 4x + 3}{x^2 + 6x + 8}$

16. $\dfrac{x^2 + x - 6}{x^2 + 7x + 12} \div \dfrac{x^2 - 5x + 6}{x^2 + x - 12}$

17. Find the ratio of the perimeter to the area of the square shown.

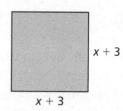

$x + 3$

$x + 3$

18. Find the expression that makes the following statement true.

$$\dfrac{x + 3}{x^2 - 8x + 12} \div \dfrac{\boxed{}}{x^2 + 3x - 10} = \dfrac{x + 5}{x - 6}$$

7.3 Enrichment and Extension

Multiplying and Dividing Rational Expressions

You can find the horizontal asymptote of a rational function by investigating the coefficients of the leading terms in the numerator and denominator.

$$f(x) = \frac{ax^n + \ldots}{bx^m + \ldots}, \text{ given } n\text{th and } m\text{th degree polynomials}$$

1. If $n < m$, then the x-axis is the horizontal asymptote.

2. If $n = m$, then the horizontal asymptote is the line $y = \dfrac{a}{b}$.

3. If $n > m$, then there is not a horizontal asymptote.

Remember that the function needs to be in the form shown above. In other words, the function must contain a polynomial in the numerator and a polynomial in the denominator. All terms must be combined. Also remember that the polynomial must be in standard form, meaning that the highest exponent should be in the first term of each polynomial. You also may need to factor the polynomials to divide out common factors. Then you will need to expand the remaining monomials or polynomials to analyze the leading term.

In Exercises 1–5, simplify the rational function. Then determine the horizontal asymptote.

1. $f(x) = \dfrac{x^2 - x - 2}{x^2 - 3x - 4} \bullet \dfrac{x^2 - x - 12}{x^2 - 2x - 35}$

2. $h(x) = \dfrac{x^2 + x - 2}{x^2 - 9} \div \dfrac{x^2 + 2x - 3}{x^3 - 3x^2 - 16x + 48}$

3. $k(x) = \dfrac{5x^2 - 4x^3 + 2}{5x + 2x^2 + 7x^3 - 9}$

4. $m(x) = \dfrac{2x^2 - 7x + 6}{2x^2 - 3x - 2} \bullet \dfrac{2x + 1}{3x^2 + 5x - 2}$

5. $t(x) = \dfrac{3x^2 + 5x - 2}{5x - 4} \div \dfrac{2x^2 + 7x + 6}{x - 7}$

7.3 Puzzle Time

What Is Black And White And Red All Over?

Write the letter of each answer in the box containing the exercise number.

Simplify the expression, if possible.

1. $\dfrac{45}{10x - 15}$

2. $\dfrac{x - 7}{x^2 - 3x - 28}$

3. $\dfrac{2x}{3x^2 + 8}$

Find the product or quotient.

4. $\dfrac{y}{x^2 - 1} \bullet \dfrac{x - 1}{2y}$

5. $\dfrac{3x}{x + 1} \bullet \left(x^2 + 2x + 1\right)$

6. $\dfrac{(x + 3)}{(x + 2)} \div \dfrac{(x - 1)(x + 3)}{(x - 1)^2}$

7. $\dfrac{1}{x + 9} \div \dfrac{6 - x}{3x - 18}$

8. $\dfrac{10x^2 yz^4}{5xy^3} \div 2x^5 y^2 z$

9. $\dfrac{x - 8}{x^2 - 2x - 48} \bullet \dfrac{4x^2 + 40x}{x + 10}$

10. $\dfrac{1}{5x^2} \div \dfrac{9x - 36}{5x^3 - 35x^2}$

Answers

E. $\dfrac{4x}{x + 6}, x \neq -10, x \neq 8$

S. $3x(x - 1), x \neq -1$

A. $\dfrac{9}{2x - 3}$

P. $\dfrac{z^3}{x^4 y^4}, z \neq 0$

N. $\dfrac{1}{x + 4}, x \neq 7$

W. $\dfrac{1}{2(x + 1)}, x \neq 1, y \neq 0$

P. $\dfrac{x - 1}{x + 2}, x \neq -3, x \neq 1$

R. $\dfrac{x - 7}{9(x - 4)}, x \neq 0, x \neq 7$

E. $\dfrac{2x}{3x^2 + 8}$

A. $-\dfrac{3}{x + 9}, x \neq 6$

1		2	3	4	5	6	7	8	9	10

To add or subtract rational numbers, you must first find a common denominator. The same is true for rational expressions in algebra. Determine the least common denominator (LCD) for the three rational expressions shown below. Then determine the values of x that make the LCD zero.

$$\frac{1}{3x^2 - 6x}, \quad \frac{4}{x + 3}, \quad \frac{5}{x^2 + x - 6}$$

7.4 **Warm Up**

Simplify the expression.

1. $\dfrac{3}{7} + \dfrac{2}{3}$

2. $\dfrac{7}{10} + \dfrac{8}{5}$

3. $\dfrac{3}{28} - \dfrac{1}{4}$

4. $\dfrac{\dfrac{2}{3} - \dfrac{1}{2}}{\dfrac{3}{5}}$

5. $\dfrac{-\dfrac{5}{8} - \dfrac{3}{4}}{2}$

6. $\dfrac{\dfrac{5}{2} - \dfrac{7}{5}}{-\dfrac{2}{3} + 4}$

7.4 **Cumulative Review Warm Up**

Given $f(x) = 2x - x^2$ and $g(x) = 4 - 3x$, determine the value of the expression.

1. $(f + g)(x)$

2. $f(x) \bullet g(x)$

3. $\left(\dfrac{g}{f}\right)(x)$

4. $f(g(x))$

5. $(f - g)(2)$

6. $g(f(3))$

7.4   Practice A

In Exercises 1–3, find the sum or difference.

1. $\dfrac{12}{5x} + \dfrac{3}{5x}$

2. $\dfrac{x}{9x^2} - \dfrac{3}{9x^2}$

3. $\dfrac{7}{x-2} - \dfrac{3x}{x-2}$

In Exercises 4–7, find the least common multiple of the expressions.

4. $3x^2,\ 6x - 18$

5. $5x,\ 5x(x+2)$

6. $x^2 - 9,\ x + 3$

7. $x^2 - 3x - 10,\ x + 2$

8. Describe and correct the error in finding the sum.

$$\cancel{\times}\quad \frac{x}{x+3} - \frac{2}{x-1} = \frac{x-2}{(x+3)(x-1)}$$

In Exercises 9–12, find the sum or difference.

9. $\dfrac{7}{2x^2} - \dfrac{4}{3x}$

10. $\dfrac{2}{x-1} + \dfrac{4}{x+2}$

11. $\dfrac{6}{x+4} - \dfrac{5x}{x-3}$

12. $\dfrac{14}{x^2 + 7x - 18} + \dfrac{6}{x+9}$

In Exercises 13 and 14, tell whether the statement is *always*, *sometimes*, or *never* true. Explain.

13. The LCD of two rational functions is the sum of the denominators.

14. The LCD of two rational functions is equal to one of the denominators.

In Exercises 15–18, rewrite the function g in the form $g(x) = \dfrac{a}{x-h} + k$.
Graph the function. Describe the graph of g as a transformation of the graph of $f(x) = \dfrac{a}{x}$.

15. $g(x) = \dfrac{4x-5}{x-2}$

16. $g(x) = \dfrac{5x+3}{x+4}$

17. $g(x) = \dfrac{10x}{x-3}$

18. $g(x) = \dfrac{3x+4}{x}$

Name_____ Date_____

7.4 Practice B

In Exercises 1–3, find the sum or difference.

1. $\dfrac{x}{25x^2} - \dfrac{5}{25x^2}$

2. $\dfrac{2x^2}{x+6} + \dfrac{8x}{x+6}$

3. $\dfrac{3x}{x-4} - \dfrac{12}{x-4}$

In Exercises 4–7, find the least common multiple of the expressions.

4. $36x^2, 9x^2 - 18x$

5. $x^2 - 100, x - 10$

6. $25x^2 - 4, 3x^2 - 10x - 8$

7. $x^2 + 7x - 18, x + 9$

8. Describe and correct the error in finding and simplifying the sum.

$$\times \quad \dfrac{4}{7x} + \dfrac{5}{x^3} = \dfrac{4(x^3)}{7x(x^3)} + \dfrac{5(7x)}{x^3(7x)} = \dfrac{4x^3 + 35x}{7x^4}$$

In Exercises 9–12, find the sum or difference.

9. $\dfrac{7}{x-5} + \dfrac{4x}{x+1}$

10. $\dfrac{7}{x^2 - 5x - 24} + \dfrac{3}{x-8}$

11. $\dfrac{x^2 - 3}{x^2 - 6x - 16} - \dfrac{x+5}{x+2}$

12. $\dfrac{x-2}{x-3} + \dfrac{3}{x} + \dfrac{6x}{2x+1}$

In Exercises 13 and 14, tell whether the statement is *always*, *sometimes*, or *never* true. Explain.

13. The LCD of two rational functions is one of the denominators when the other denominator is a factor.

14. The LCD of two rational functions will have a degree equal to that of the denominator with the higher degree.

In Exercises 15–18, rewrite the function g in the form $g(x) = \dfrac{a}{x-h} + k$.

Graph the function. Describe the graph of g as a transformation of the graph of $f(x) = \dfrac{a}{x}$.

15. $g(x) = \dfrac{5x+3}{x+4}$

16. $g(x) = \dfrac{9x}{x+12}$

17. $g(x) = \dfrac{5x-4}{x}$

18. $g(x) = \dfrac{8x+13}{x-6}$

7.4 Enrichment and Extension

Adding and Subtracting Rational Expressions

To add or subtract algebraic fractions, you have seen that you first find a common denominator.

$$\frac{3}{x+1} + \frac{2}{x-2} = \frac{3(x-2) + 2(x+1)}{(x+1)(x-2)} = \frac{3x - 6 + 2x + 2}{(x+1)(x-2)} = \frac{5x - 4}{x^2 - x - 2}$$

The decomposition of an algebraic fraction into partial fractions is the reverse of this process. The method shown in the example below can be used for fractions in which the degree of the numerator is less than the degree of the denominator, and in which the denominator can be factored into distinct linear factors.

Example: Decompose $\dfrac{5x - 4}{x^2 - x - 2}$ into partial fractions.

Solution: Factor the denominator. $\quad \dfrac{5x - 4}{x^2 - x - 2} = \dfrac{5x - 4}{(x+1)(x-2)}$

Express the fraction as the sum of two fractions, with the individual factors as denominators and the unknown numerators A and B.

$$\frac{5x - 4}{(x+1)(x-2)} = \frac{A}{x+1} + \frac{B}{x-2}$$

To clear fractions, multiply each side of the rational equation by the LCD, $(x+1)(x-2)$.

$$5x - 4 = A(x - 2) + B(x + 1)$$

To determine A and B, first eliminate B by letting $x = -1$.

$$5(-1) - 4 = A(-1 - 2) + B(-1 + 1)$$
$$-5 - 4 = -3A$$
$$A = 3$$

Then eliminate A by letting $x = 2$.

$$5(2) - 4 = A(2 - 2) + B(2 + 1)$$
$$10 - 4 = 3B$$
$$B = 2$$

Use the values of A and B to express the original fraction as the sum of two partial fractions.

$$\frac{5x - 4}{(x+1)(x-2)} = \frac{3}{x+1} + \frac{2}{x-2}$$

In Exercises 1–6, express the given fraction as the sum of partial fractions.

1. $\dfrac{3x + 18}{x^2 + 5x + 4}$

2. $\dfrac{6x^2 + 2x - 4}{x^3 - 4x}$

3. $\dfrac{6x^2 + 10x - 4}{x^3 + 2x^2 - 9x - 18}$

4. $\dfrac{2x + 12}{x^2 - 3x - 28}$

5. $\dfrac{2x^2 + 7x - 4}{x^3 - 9x}$

6. $\dfrac{7x^2 + 18x - 19}{x^3 + 2x^2 - 5x - 6}$

Name_____ Date _____

7.4 Puzzle Time

What Do You Get When You Cross Cinderella With A Barber?

Write the letter of each answer in the box containing the exercise number.

Find the sum or difference.

1. $\dfrac{10}{2x} - \dfrac{3}{2x}$

2. $\dfrac{5 - x}{x + 1} + \dfrac{2 + 3x}{x + 1}$

3. $\dfrac{x}{2x - 4} - \dfrac{5}{x + 1}$

4. $\dfrac{x - 2}{3x} + \dfrac{2x}{x}$

5. $\dfrac{7}{x + 8} - \dfrac{2}{x - 1}$

6. $\dfrac{3x}{x - 4} + \dfrac{8}{x - 3}$

7. $\dfrac{1}{x^2 + 3x - 10} - \dfrac{4}{x - 2}$

Simplify the complex fraction.

8. $\dfrac{\dfrac{x}{25}}{\dfrac{4}{x^2}}$

9. $\dfrac{\dfrac{x^2}{4}}{\dfrac{x}{x + 4}}$

10. $\dfrac{\dfrac{4}{3x} + \dfrac{2}{x^2}}{\dfrac{x}{x + 1} - \dfrac{4}{x + 1}}$

11. $\dfrac{\dfrac{x^2}{4} - \dfrac{4}{x}}{}$ $\dfrac{x^2}{\dfrac{4}{5} - \dfrac{4}{x}}$

12. $\dfrac{\dfrac{x^2}{9} + \dfrac{1}{4}}{6x}$

13. $\dfrac{\dfrac{1}{2} - \dfrac{x + 5}{4}}{\dfrac{x^2}{2} - \dfrac{5}{2}}$

Answers

R. $\dfrac{4x^2 + 9}{216x}$

L. $\dfrac{-4x - 19}{x^2 + 3x - 10}$

S. $\dfrac{5x - 23}{x^2 + 7x - 8}$

L. $\dfrac{2x + 7}{x + 1}$

P. $\dfrac{4x^2 + 10x + 6}{3x^3 - 12x^2}, x \neq -1$

S. $\dfrac{7x - 2}{3x}$

I. $\dfrac{x^3}{100}, x \neq 0$

G. $\dfrac{7}{2x}$

P. $\dfrac{x^2 + 4x}{4}, x \neq -4, x \neq 0$

C. $\dfrac{3x^2 - x - 32}{x^2 - 7x + 12}$

A. $\dfrac{x^2 - 9x + 20}{2x^2 - 2x - 4}$

E. $\dfrac{5x^3}{4x - 20}, x \neq 0$

S. $\dfrac{-x - 3}{2x^2 - 10}$

1	2	3	4	5		6	7	8	9	10	11	12	13

A racquetball club offers a $200 annual membership that includes unlimited free court rental. They also offer a $120 membership with a $10 fee for each court rental. Write a rational equation that represents the cost per court rental for each membership. Then use a graphing calculator to graph both rational functions and determine the point of intersection. What does this point of intersection represent in the context of the problem? Which membership is a better deal?

7.5 **Warm Up**

Solve the equation.

1. $-3(x - 1) = 4(x + 1)$

2. $2(x - 1) = x^2 - x$

3. $4\left(x + \dfrac{3}{2}\right) = (x - 2)3$

4. $-2(x + 1) = (x - 8)(x - 1)$

5. $3x(2x) = 8(x + 1)$

6. $x(x - 3) + 4x(x - 4) = 3x(x - 4)$

7.5 **Cumulative Review Warm Up**

Perform the indicated operation. Write your answer in standard form.

1. $(3 + 2i) - (5 + i)$

2. $-2i(11 + 7i)$

3. $(-5 + 3i)^2$

4. $(-4 + 9i)(5 + 6i)$

5. $3i^5(4i^2 - 5i + 8)$

6. $(5 - 3i^7) - (11 + 2i^6)$

Name_____ Date _____

In Exercises 1–3, solve the equation by cross multiplying. Check your solution(s).

1. $\dfrac{3}{4x} = \dfrac{1}{x-2}$

2. $\dfrac{4}{x+2} = \dfrac{6}{x-2}$

3. $\dfrac{-3}{x+1} = \dfrac{x-5}{x-5}$

4. So far in baseball practice, you have pitched 47 strikes out of 61 pitches. Solve the equation $\dfrac{80}{100} = \dfrac{47+x}{61+x}$ to find the number x of consecutive strikes you need to pitch to raise your strike percentage to 80%.

In Exercises 5 and 6, identify the least common denominator of the equation.

5. $\dfrac{x}{x-2} + \dfrac{2}{x} = \dfrac{5}{x}$

6. $\dfrac{3x}{x+5} - \dfrac{8}{x} = \dfrac{2}{x}$

In Exercises 7–12, solve the equation by using the LCD. Check your solution(s).

7. $\dfrac{4}{3} + \dfrac{2}{x} = 4$

8. $\dfrac{5}{2x} + \dfrac{1}{4} = \dfrac{9}{2x}$

9. $\dfrac{x-2}{x-3} + 3 = \dfrac{2x}{x}$

10. $\dfrac{4}{x-5} + \dfrac{1}{x} = \dfrac{x-1}{x-5}$

11. $\dfrac{8}{x} + 3 = \dfrac{x+8}{x-4}$

12. $\dfrac{12}{x^2-2x} - \dfrac{3}{x-2} = \dfrac{3}{x}$

13. Describe and correct the error in the first step of solving the equation.

$$\begin{array}{c} \times \qquad \dfrac{4}{x} + \dfrac{1}{2} = 1 \\[2mm] 2x \bullet \dfrac{4}{x} + 2x \bullet \dfrac{1}{2} = 1 \end{array}$$

14. You can clean the gutters of your house in 5 hours. Working together, you and your friend can clean the gutters in 3 hours. Let t be the time (in hours) your friend would take to clean the gutters when working alone. Write and solve an equation to find how long your friend would take to clean the gutters when working alone.

$\big($*Hint:* (Work done) $=$ (Work rate) $\times$ (Time)$\big)$

Name _____ Date _____

7.5 Practice B

In Exercises 1–3, solve the equation by cross multiplying. Check your solution(s).

1. $\dfrac{3}{x+2} = \dfrac{5}{x-2}$

2. $\dfrac{2}{x-4} = \dfrac{x-3}{x-1}$

3. $\dfrac{x-5}{4} = \dfrac{x^2-5}{x+4}$

4. So far in soccer practice, you have made 10 out of 32 goal attempts. Solve the equation $0.45 = \dfrac{10+x}{32+x}$ to find the number x of consecutive goals you need to make to raise your goal average to 0.45.

In Exercises 5 and 6, identify the least common denominator of the equation.

5. $\dfrac{6}{x+3} + \dfrac{x}{x+2} = \dfrac{4}{5}$

6. $\dfrac{6}{x-8} - \dfrac{2x}{3x-2} = \dfrac{9}{4}$

In Exercises 7–12, solve the equation by using the LCD. Check your solution(s).

7. $\dfrac{3}{4x} + \dfrac{1}{8} = \dfrac{7}{4x}$

8. $\dfrac{5}{x-6} + \dfrac{1}{x} = \dfrac{x-1}{x-6}$

9. $\dfrac{x-4}{x-5} + 5 = \dfrac{4x}{x}$

10. $\dfrac{16}{x^2-4x} - \dfrac{8}{x-4} = \dfrac{4}{x}$

11. $\dfrac{x+1}{x+2} + \dfrac{1}{x} = \dfrac{2x+1}{x+2}$

12. $\dfrac{4}{x} - 1 = \dfrac{4}{x+2}$

13. Describe and correct the error in the first step of solving the equation.

$$\times \qquad \dfrac{3}{x+2} + 5 = \dfrac{1}{x}$$
$$(x+2) \cdot \dfrac{3}{x+2} + (x+2) \cdot 5 = (x+2) \cdot \dfrac{1}{x}$$

14. You can kayak around a certain island in 3 hours. Kayaking together, you and your friend can kayak around the island in 1.4 hours. Let t be the time (in hours) your friend would take to kayak around the island when kayaking alone. Write and solve an equation to find how long your friend would take to kayak around the island when kayaking alone.

(Hint: (Work done) = (Work rate) × (Time))

248 Algebra 2
Resources by Chapter

Copyright © Big Ideas Learning, LLC
All rights reserved.

7.5 Enrichment and Extension

Solving Rational Equations

In Exercises 1–12, you are given the function $f(x) = \dfrac{2x + 9}{x + 2}$.

1. What are three points that lie on the graph of f^{-1}? Explain your reasoning.

2. Does the point $\left(\dfrac{11}{3}, 2\right)$ lie on the graph of f^{-1}? Explain your reasoning.

3. Algebraically find $f^{-1}(x)$.

4. Prove that they are inverse functions by algebraically showing that
$f\left(f^{-1}(x)\right) = f^{-1}\left(f(x)\right) = x.$

5. Graph both f and f^{-1} in the same coordinate plane.

6. Write the domain and range of f.

7. Write the domain and range of f^{-1}. How do the domain and range of f^{-1} compare with the domain and range of f?

8. What do you notice about the vertical asymptotes and horizontal asymptotes of the graphs of f and f^{-1}?

9. What is significant about where the graphs of f and f^{-1} intersect?

10. Is there a relationship between the asymptote of the graph of a function and the zero of its inverse? Explain.

11. Can you find the inverse of $g(x) = \dfrac{x - 7}{2x + 1}$? If so, find $g^{-1}(x)$.

12. Do all rational functions have an inverse? Explain.

7.5 Puzzle Time

What Is Green And Sings?

Write the letter of each answer in the box containing the exercise number.

Solve the equation by cross multiplying.

1. $\dfrac{x-5}{15} = \dfrac{4}{5}$

2. $\dfrac{x-6}{3} = \dfrac{-2x-2}{15}$

3. $\dfrac{x+3}{x+1} = \dfrac{15}{x+7}$

4. $\dfrac{5x}{x-1} = 4$

5. $\dfrac{x+2}{x-2} = \dfrac{2x+4}{x+1}$

6. $\dfrac{3}{x} = \dfrac{2}{5-x}$

Solve the equation by using the LCD.

7. $\dfrac{5}{x} + \dfrac{1}{3} = 1$

8. $\dfrac{2}{5x} + \dfrac{1}{3} = \dfrac{4}{15x}$

9. $\dfrac{1}{x} - 3 = \dfrac{4x}{x+2}$

10. $\dfrac{3}{x-1} + \dfrac{1}{x+1} = \dfrac{10}{x^2-1}$

11. $\dfrac{12}{x^2+4x} + \dfrac{3}{x} = \dfrac{1}{x+4}$

12. $\dfrac{8}{x+2} - \dfrac{2}{x} = \dfrac{x-2}{x^2+2x}$

Answers

L. $x = 2$

S. $x = -2,\ x = 5$

A. $x = \dfrac{15}{2}$

E. $x = 17$

P. $x = 3$

S. $x = \dfrac{2}{7},\ x = -1$

E. $x = -12$

I. $x = -4$

R. $x = -\dfrac{2}{5}$

Y. $x = \dfrac{2}{5}$

L. $x = 4$

V. $x = 3,\ x = 2$

1	2	3	4	5		6	7	8	9	10	11	12

Chapter 7 Cumulative Review

In Exercises 1–18, factor the polynomial.

1. $x^2 - 4x - 21$

2. $x^2 + 8x - 48$

3. $x^2 + 9x + 8$

4. $x^2 - 9x + 20$

5. $x^2 - 6x - 27$

6. $x^2 - 12x + 32$

7. $2x^2 + 5x - 3$

8. $2x^2 - 2x - 24$

9. $3x^2 + 23x - 36$

10. $5x^2 + 23x + 12$

11. $3x^2 - 25x + 42$

12. $4x^2 - 7x + 3$

13. $4x^2 + 30x + 56$

14. $6x^2 - 7x - 5$

15. $8x^2 - 2x - 3$

16. $5x^2 - 2x - 7$

17. $8x^2 + 22x - 6$

18. $12x^2 - 18x - 12$

In Exercises 19–34, write the prime factorization of the number. If the number is prime, then write *prime*.

19. 12

20. 201

21. 88

22. 56

23. 75

24. 300

25. 2

26. 99

27. 188

28. 199

29. 85

30. 41

31. 17

32. 169

33. 131

34. 65

In Exercises 35–46, solve the equation. Check your solution.

35. $\dfrac{1}{2}x + 6 = \dfrac{5}{2}x$

36. $\dfrac{3}{4}x - 7 = \dfrac{11}{4}x$

37. $\dfrac{5}{7}x - 4 = \dfrac{2}{5}$

38. $\dfrac{3}{5}x + 9 = \dfrac{2}{5}x - 7$

39. $\dfrac{1}{4}x + 5 = \dfrac{5}{4}x - 1$

40. $\dfrac{1}{2}x - 3 = 8x$

41. $\dfrac{1}{3}x + 5 = \dfrac{3}{5}x$

42. $\dfrac{2}{7}x - 3 = \dfrac{5}{8}x$

43. $\dfrac{7}{2}x - 3 = \dfrac{2}{5}x - \dfrac{3}{4}$

44. $\dfrac{4}{5}x - \dfrac{2}{7} = \dfrac{1}{4}x + \dfrac{2}{3}$

45. $\dfrac{5}{9}x - \dfrac{1}{4} = \dfrac{7}{8}x - \dfrac{2}{5}$

46. $\dfrac{3}{5}x + \dfrac{2}{7} = \dfrac{3}{4}x - \dfrac{7}{8}$

47. The expression for the area of a rectangle is $x^2 - 5x - 24$. What are the expressions for the length and the width?

48. The expression for the area of a rectangle is $2x^2 + 3x - 20$. What are the expressions for the length and the width?

49. The expression for the area of a rectangle is $6x^2 + x - 15$. What are the expressions for the length and the width?

Chapter 7 Cumulative Review (continued)

In Exercises 50–63, find the zero(s) of the function.

50. $f(x) = x^2 + 2x - 35$

51. $h(x) = x^2 + 3x - 18$

52. $f(x) = x^2 + 2x - 99$

53. $h(x) = x^2 - 2x - 48$

54. $h(x) = x^2 - 8x + 15$

55. $g(x) = x^2 - 4x - 45$

56. $g(x) = x^2 + 5x + 4$

57. $f(x) = x^2 - 25$

58. $h(x) = x^2 - 4x - 32$

59. $h(x) = x^2 + 3x$

60. $f(x) = 2x^2 + 17x + 8$

61. $g(x) = 3x^2 - 26x + 35$

62. $f(x) = 2x^2 + 7x - 15$

63. $f(x) = 4x^2 - 14x$

In Exercises 64–75, find the discriminant of the quadratic equation and describe the number and type of solutions of the equation.

64. $x^2 + 4x - 12 = 0$

65. $x^2 + 5x + 10 = 0$

66. $x^2 + 8x + 16 = 0$

67. $x^2 + 9x - 24 = 0$

68. $x^2 - 6x - 32 = 0$

69. $x^2 + 11x + 150 = 0$

70. $x^2 + 42 = 3x$

71. $x^2 + 14x = -49$

72. $2x^2 - 4x = 3$

73. $3x^2 = -6x + 8$

74. $4x^2 + 8 = -6x$

75. $x^2 + 25 = 10x$

In Exercises 76–87, solve the equation using the Quadratic Formula.

76. $2x^2 - 4x + 2 = 0$

77. $3x^2 - 5x + 2 = 0$

78. $5x^2 + 4x - 16 = 0$

79. $-3x^2 + 2x = 18$

80. $x^2 + 9x = 15$

81. $4x^2 + 5x = 2$

82. $6x^2 + 11 = 8x$

83. $-3x^2 - 24 = 7x$

84. $5x^2 + 36 = -2x$

85. $-4x^2 + 12x = -64$

86. $8x^2 - 7x = -5$

87. $x^2 = x - 4$

88. The expression for the area of a square is $x^2 + 16x + 64$. What is the expression for the length of one side?

89. The expression for the area of a square is $4x^2 + 20x + 25$. What is the expression for the length of one side?

90. The expression for the area of a square is $16x^2 - 8x + 1$. What is the expression for the length of one side?

Chapter 7 **Cumulative Review** (continued)

In Exercises 91–102, solve the system by substitution.

91. $y = x - 9$
$y = 12$

92. $y = x + 14$
$x = -3$

93. $y = x + 2x - 9$
$x = -4$

94. $y = 2x + 8$
$y = -6$

95. $y = 2x - 17$
$y = 13$

96. $y = 2x + 7$
$y = -11$

97. $y = 4x + 12$
$y = 6x$

98. $y = 4x + 5$
$y = 9x$

99. $y = 3x - 8$
$y = -5x$

100. $y = x^2 + 5x - 6$
$y = x - 1$

101. $y = x^2 - 2x - 15$
$y = x + 3$

102. $y = x^2 + 10x + 16$
$y = x + 2$

In Exercises 103–112, solve the system by elimination.

103. $2x - y = 8$
$-8x + y = 4$

104. $3x + 8y = 20$
$-3x - 4y = 8$

105. $3x - 4y = 15$
$-3x + 3y = -13$

106. $-2x + 6y - 14 = 0$
$5x - 6y = 10$

107. $2x - 4y = -13$
$-4x + 12y = 22$

108. $-3x + 4y = -7$
$2x - 8y = -10$

109. $6x^2 - 8x + 12 + y = 14$
$-5x^2 + 7x - 14 - y = -12$

110. $-3x^2 + 2y + 7x - 12 = -8$
$4x^2 - 5x + 8 - 2y = 14$

111. $3x^2 + 7x - 8 = 3y$
$x^2 + 3y + 5x + 9 = -2$

112. $9x^2 - 14 - 3x + 8x - 4y = 18$
$-6x^2 + 4y - 7x + 21 + 5x = 23$

113. Your friend has a swimming pool that is in the shape of a rectangular prism. It measures 18 feet by 34 feet, and is 4 feet deep. What is the volume of the swimming pool?

114. A cube has an edge length of 3 inches.

  a. Find the surface area of the cube.

  b. Find the volume of the cube.

115. A sphere has a radius of 7 centimeters.

  a. Find the surface area of the sphere.

  b. Find the volume of the sphere.

Chapter 7 **Cumulative Review** (continued)

In Exercises 116–122, evaluate the function for the given value of x.

116. $f(x) = -4x^3 + 2x^2 - 6x + 14; x = -3$

117. $h(x) = 4x^5 - 3x^3 + 7x^2 + x + 1; x = 4$

118. $g(x) = -3x^4 + 2x^3 - 11x + 36; x = -5$

119. $f(x) = 2x^6 - 7x^4 + 3x^3 - 12x^2 + 24x + 38; x = -2$

120. $g(x) = -6x^4 + 3x^3 - 2x^2 + 14x - 12; x = 3$

121. $h(x) = 3x^3 - 14x^2 + 21x - 37; x = \dfrac{1}{2}$

122. $g(x) = -2x^3 + 8x^2 - 12x + 52; x = -\dfrac{1}{4}$

In Exercises 123–129, find the sum.

123. $\left(5x^3 - 4x^2 + 7\right) + \left(-3x^3 + 12x^2 - 9\right)$

124. $\left(3x^4 - 7x^2 + 12x - 9\right) + \left(7x^4 - 5x^2 - 14x + 8\right)$

125. $\left(-6x^5 - 12x^2 + 7x - 5\right) + \left(-4x^4 + 2x^2 - 9x + 12\right)$

126. $\left(9x^4 - 7x^3 + 3x - 11\right) + \left(5x^3 - x^2 - 8x + 15\right)$

127. $\left(-4x^4 + 2x - 9\right) + \left(8x^4 - 3x^3 - 9x^2 + 7x + 10\right)$

128. $\left(8x^5 - 7x^4 + 5x^3 - 10x^2 - 3x + 1\right) + \left(3x^4 - 3x^2 - 5x + 9\right)$

129. $\left(7x^5 - 3x^3 + 4x^2 - 8x - 12\right) + \left(-4x^5 + 12x^4 + 8x^3 - 7x^2 + 13x + 10\right)$

In Exercises 130–135, find the difference.

130. $\left(-11x^3 + 10x - 1\right) - \left(-5x^3 - 8x + 9\right)$

131. $\left(12x^2 - 2x + 1\right) - \left(-7x^2 + 8x + 11\right)$

132. $\left(-12x^4 + 4x^3 + 6x - 9\right) - \left(12x^4 - 10x + 2\right)$

133. $\left(3x^4 - 3x^3 + 12x^2 + 7x - 3\right) - \left(-5x^3 + 9x + 10\right)$

134. $\left(-8x^5 + 4x^2 + 2x - 1\right) - \left(9x^5 - 2x^4 + 7x^3 + 4x^2 + 12x - 6\right)$

135. $\left(-6x^5 + x^2 - 4x + 5\right) - \left(8x^3 - 12x^2 - 10x - 5\right)$

Chapter 8

Name _____ Date _____

Dear Family,

In this chapter, you will be learning about ordered lists of numbers called sequences. You can usually determine the pattern of a sequence after the first few numbers are given. You will be using sequences to find the next numbers in the pattern, write a rule, and graph the numbers.

Here is a fun activity involving a sequence that you can do as a family. Using eight coins of the same size, determine the number of ways to arrange the coins in rows. Each coin in a row must be touching another coin in the same row (if there are any in the same row) and must be touching two coins below (if there are any below). So, each row has a smaller number of coins than the row below it and there are no spaces between the coins.

Examples:

1 coin = 1 arrangement

2 coins = 1 arrangement

3 coins = 2 arrangements

Coins	Number of arrangements
1	1
2	1
3	2
4	
5	
6	
7	
8	

Complete the table for all eight coins. What pattern do you notice about the sequence? Without using coins, what are the next two numbers in the pattern?

The pattern above is called the Fibonacci sequence, named after Leonardo Fibonacci, written in his book published in 1202. Use the Internet to check the terms of your sequence and learn more about the applications of the Fibonacci sequence in math, history, art, and music.

Enjoy finding patterns in your daily life!

Nombre _____ Fecha_____

Estimada familia:

En este capítulo, aprenderán sobre listas ordenadas de números llamadas secuencias. A menudo, se puede determinar el patrón de una secuencia después de que se den los primeros números. Usarán secuencias para hallar los próximos números en el patrón, escribir una regla y hacer la gráfica de los números.

He aquí una actividad divertida que incluye una secuencia que pueden hacer en familia. Con ocho monedas del mismo tamaño, determinen el número de maneras de colocar las monedas en filas. Cada moneda de una fila debe tocar otra moneda en la misma fila (si hay alguna en la misma fila) y debe tocar dos monedas en la fila inferior (si hay alguna fila inferior). Entonces, cada fila tiene un número más pequeño de monedas que la fila que está debajo y no hay espacios entre las monedas.

Ejemplos:

1 moneda = 1 distribución

2 monedas = 1 distribución

3 monedas = 2 distribuciones

Monedas	Número de distribuciones
1	1
2	
3	
4	
5	
6	
7	
8	

Completen la tabla para las ocho monedas. ¿Qué patrón observan sobre la secuencia? Sin usar monedas, ¿cuáles son los próximos dos números en el patrón?

El patrón que está arriba se llama secuencia de Fibonacci, que lleva el nombre de Leonardo Fibonacci, escrita en su libro publicado en 1202. Consulten en Internet para verificar los términos de su secuencia y aprender más sobre las aplicaciones de la secuencia de Fibonacci en matemáticas, historia, arte y música.

¡Disfruten al hallar patrones en su vida cotidiana!

8.1 Start Thinking

Review the list of numbers and then describe the pattern that relates the numbers in the list.

1. 5, 7, 9, 11, 13, …

2. $\dfrac{2}{3}, \dfrac{4}{7}, \dfrac{8}{11}, \dfrac{16}{15}, \dfrac{32}{19}, \ldots$

3. $8, \dfrac{13}{2}, 5, \dfrac{7}{2}, 2, \ldots$

4. 3, −6, 12, −24, 48, …

8.1 Warm Up

For the function, determine the value of $f(1)$, $f(2)$, $f(3)$, $f(4)$, and $f(5)$.

1. $f(x) = 2x - 2$

2. $f(x) = 2^x$

3. $f(x) = 2x - 1$

4. $f(x) = (-1)^x (5)$

5. $f(x) = \dfrac{2^{x-1}}{3}$

6. $f(x) = (-1)^{x-1} x^2$

8.1 Cumulative Review Warm Up

Solve the equation. Round to the nearest thousandth, if necessary.

1. $2^{x-1} + 5 = 13$

2. $3^{x+2} = 9^{x-1}$

3. $3e^{2x} - 4 = 8$

4. $3 + \log_2(4x) = 5$

5. $3\ln(2 - x) = -6$

6. $\log_3(x^2 - 3) = \log_3(2x)$

8.1 Practice A

In Exercises 1–6, write the first six terms of the sequence.

1. $a_n = n - 3$ 2. $a_n = 4 - n$ 3. $a_n = n^3$

4. $a_n = n^2 - 5$ 5. $a_n = 2^{2n}$ 6. $a_n = -n^2 + 1$

In Exercises 7–14, describe the pattern, write the next term, and write a rule for the nth term of the sequence.

7. $1, 4, 7, 10, \ldots$ 8. $1, 3, 9, 27, \ldots$

9. $1.5, 3, 4.5, 6, \ldots$ 10. $4.2, 5.8, 7.4, 9, \ldots$

11. $4.7, 3.4, 2.1, 0.8, \ldots$ 12. $-5, 10, -15, 20, \ldots$

13. $\dfrac{1}{6}, \dfrac{2}{6}, \dfrac{3}{6}, \dfrac{4}{6}, \ldots$ 14. $\dfrac{3}{2}, \dfrac{3}{4}, \dfrac{3}{6}, \dfrac{3}{8}, \ldots$

15. You agree to work for your uncle. You earn \$10 the first day, \$20 the second day, \$40 the third day, and \$80 the fourth day. Write a rule for the number of dollars that you will earn on the nth day. Then graph the sequence.

In Exercises 16–21, write the series using summation.

16. $4 + 8 + 12 + 16 + 20$ 17. $3 + 9 + 15 + 21 + 27$

18. $1 + 7 + 13 + 19 + \ldots$ 19. $-1 + 1 + 3 + 5 + \ldots$

20. $\dfrac{1}{5} + \dfrac{1}{25} + \dfrac{1}{125} + \dfrac{1}{625} + \ldots$ 21. $\dfrac{1}{7} + \dfrac{2}{8} + \dfrac{3}{9} + \dfrac{4}{10} + \ldots$

In Exercises 22–27, find the sum.

22. $\displaystyle\sum_{i=1}^{4} 3i$ 23. $\displaystyle\sum_{i=1}^{5} 6i$ 24. $\displaystyle\sum_{n=0}^{5} n^2$

25. $\displaystyle\sum_{n=2}^{7} (3n + 2)$ 26. $\displaystyle\sum_{k=1}^{6} (k^2 - 3)$ 27. $\displaystyle\sum_{i=3}^{7} \dfrac{5}{i}$

28. You are building a brick garden wall six rows high. The bottom row has 25 bricks. Each of the other rows has three fewer bricks than the one below it. How many bricks will you need to build the garden wall? Justify your answer.

8.1 Practice B

In Exercises 1–6, write the first six terms of the sequence.

1. $a_n = n^2 + 4$

2. $a_n = 3^{n-2}$

3. $a_n = (n-2)^2$

4. $a_n = -n^2 + 3$

5. $f(n) = \dfrac{-n}{n+5}$

6. $a_n = \dfrac{n}{3n-1}$

In Exercises 7–14, describe the pattern, write the next term, and write a rule for the nth term of the sequence.

7. $2, 7, 12, 17, \ldots$

8. $2.7, 6.2, 9.7, 13.2, \ldots$

9. $6.4, 3.5, 0.6, -2.3, \ldots$

10. $-\dfrac{1}{7}, -\dfrac{2}{7}, -\dfrac{3}{7}, -\dfrac{4}{7}, \ldots$

11. $\dfrac{5}{2}, \dfrac{5}{4}, \dfrac{5}{8}, \dfrac{5}{16}, \ldots$

12. $\dfrac{3}{1}, \dfrac{9}{2}, \dfrac{27}{3}, \dfrac{81}{4}, \ldots$

13. $\dfrac{2}{3}, \dfrac{4}{9}, \dfrac{8}{27}, \dfrac{16}{81}, \ldots$

14. $2, 20, 200, 2000, \ldots$

15. You are renting tables for a school event. There is a set-up and delivery fee of $100. The rental fee per table is $7. Write a rule for the cost of renting n tables. Then graph the sequence.

In Exercises 16–21, write the series using summation.

16. $6 + 13 + 20 + 27 + 34$

17. $10 + 13 + 16 + 19 + \ldots$

18. $-3 + 0 + 5 + 12 + \ldots$

19. $\dfrac{1}{4} + \dfrac{2}{16} + \dfrac{3}{64} + \dfrac{4}{256} + \ldots$

20. $\dfrac{2}{5} + \dfrac{2}{6} + \dfrac{2}{7} + \dfrac{2}{8} + \ldots$

21. $-1 + 3 - 5 + 7 - 9$

In Exercises 22–27, find the sum.

22. $\displaystyle\sum_{i=1}^{6} 9i$

23. $\displaystyle\sum_{i=0}^{5} 2i^3$

24. $\displaystyle\sum_{n=1}^{6} \left(n^2 + 2\right)$

25. $\displaystyle\sum_{k=3}^{5} \dfrac{1}{k+2}$

26. $\displaystyle\sum_{k=1}^{15} 3$

27. $\displaystyle\sum_{i=13}^{27} i$

28. You are making party favors. In the first hour you made 36 party favors. Each hour you make two more party favors than in the previous hour. How many party favors will you have made after 7 hours? Justify your answer.

8.1 Enrichment and Extension

Defining and Using Sequences and Series

A story told about the German mathematician Carl Friedrich Gauss (1777–1855) is that, as a child in third grade, he quickly solved the problem "Add the whole numbers from 1 to 100" when this task had been intended as a long punishment assignment for his class. Gauss recognized that to determine the sum of the first n terms of an arithmetic series, you simply multiply half the number of terms by the sum of the first and last terms, shown symbolically below.

$$S_n = \frac{n}{2}(a_1 + a_n)$$

To determine the sum of a given number of terms of a particular series, you need values for the first and last terms. When these are not given, you can write an expression for the nth term of the series.

To determine the sum of the first n even integers, write an expression for the nth term, as shown below. Because there is a constant difference of 2, the series of numbers is arithmetic. Apply the sum formula, using $a_1 = 2$ and $a_n = 2n$.

$$2 + 4 + 6 + \cdots + 2n$$

$$S_n = \frac{n}{2}(a_1 + a_n) = \frac{n}{2}(2 + 2n) = n(n + 1)$$

In Exercises 1–3, (a) verify that the given sequence of numbers is arithmetic by stating the constant difference, (b) write an expression for the nth term of the sequence, and (c) use your expression and the formula to determine the sum of the first n terms.

1. odd integers

2. positive multiples of 3

3. positive multiples of k, with $k > 0$

4. Explain how to use the result of Exercise 3 to predict the sum of the first n terms of the series $\log 10 + \log 100 + \log 1000 + \log 10{,}000 + \dots$. State the sum.

In Exercises 5 and 6, use the results of Exercises 3 and 4 to find the sum of the first n terms of the given series.

5. $\ln e + \ln e^2 + \ln e^3 + \ln e^4 + \dots$

6. $\log_b a + \log_b a^2 + \log_b a^3 + \log_b a^4 + \dots$

Name _____ Date _____

 8.1 **Puzzle Time**

What Do You Get When You Cross A Judge With Poison Ivy?

Write the letter of each answer in the box containing the exercise number.

Write the first four terms of the sequence.

1. $a_n = n^2 + 2$

2. $a_n = 2n - 4$

3. $a_n = 4 - n$

4. $a_n = \dfrac{n}{n+1}$

5. $f(n) = 2^{2n-2}$

6. $a_n = (n+2)^2$

Write the rule for the nth term of the sequence.

7. $-2, 4, -8, 16, \ldots$

8. $-1, 2, 5, 8, \ldots$

9. $1, \dfrac{1}{2}, \dfrac{1}{4}, \dfrac{1}{8}, \ldots$

10. $-0.2, 0.8, 1.8, 2.8, \ldots$

11. $1.5, 3, 4.5, 6, \ldots$

12. $5, -7, 17, -31, \ldots$

13. $-5, -6, -7, -8, \ldots$

Answers

S. $3, 2, 1, 0$

N. $f(n) = (-2)^{n+1} + 1$

R. $3, 6, 11, 18$

E. $9, 16, 25, 36$

O. $a_n = \dfrac{3n}{2}$

H. $\dfrac{1}{2}, \dfrac{2}{3}, \dfrac{3}{4}, \dfrac{4}{5}$

D. $1, 4, 16, 64$

C. $f(n) = (-2)^n$

I. $a_n = 3n - 4$

S. $a_n = -n - 4$

S. $f(n) = \left(\dfrac{1}{2}\right)^{n-1}$

A. $-2, 0, 2, 4$

I. $a_n = n - 1.2$

1	2	3	4		5	6	7	8	9	10	11	12	13

8.2 Start Thinking

List the five terms of the sequence shown in the graph. Then write a rule for the *n*th term of the sequence. Describe some of the common features of the graphs and the rules.

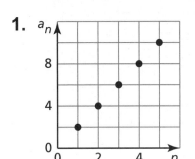

3. a_n

[graph]

8.2 Warm Up

Solve the system.

1. $x - 2y = 8$
$3x + y = -11$

2. $9 = 5x - 3y$
$16 = 2x + 5y$

3. $-12 = 5n + p$
$32 = -2n + 3p$

4. $8 = a + 5d$
$2 = a + 2d$

5. $-36 = a + 15d$
$-6 = a + 3d$

6. $6 = a + 36d$
$4 = a + 24d$

8.2 Cumulative Review Warm Up

Write a polynomial function *f* of least degree that has rational coefficients and the given zeros.

1. $-3, \sqrt{2}$

2. $1, -2 + \sqrt{3}$

3. $0, \dfrac{1}{2}, -\sqrt{6}$

4. $-\dfrac{3}{2}, -4, 4, 0$

5. $1 + \sqrt{2}, -3 - \sqrt{2}$

6. $0, \dfrac{5}{2}, -\dfrac{3}{5}, 5$

8.2 Practice A

In Exercises 1–4, tell whether the sequence is arithmetic. Explain your reasoning.

1. $5, 2, -1, -4, -7, \ldots$

2. $9, 7, 4, 0, -5, \ldots$

3. $\frac{1}{3}, \frac{2}{3}, \frac{3}{3}, \frac{4}{3}, \frac{5}{3}, \ldots$

4. $1, 3, 9, 27, 81, \ldots$

5. Write a rule for the arithmetic sequence with the given description.

  a. The first term is -5 and each term is 4 more than the previous term.

  b. The first term is 9 and each term is 3 less than the previous term.

In Exercises 6–9, write a rule for the nth term of the sequence. Then find a_{20}.

6. $15, 22, 29, 36, \ldots$

7. $62, 53, 44, 35, \ldots$

8. $-25, -10, 5, 20, \ldots$

9. $-3, -\frac{3}{2}, 0, \frac{3}{2}, \ldots$

10. Describe and correct the error in writing a rule for the nth term of the arithmetic sequence $-27, -12, 3, 18, 33, \ldots$.

$$\boxed{\begin{array}{l} \diagup\!\!\!\!\diagdown \quad \text{Use } a_1 = 27 \text{ and } d = 15. \\ a_n = 27 + (n-1)15 \\ a_n = 12 + 15n \end{array}}$$

In Exercises 11 and 12, write a rule for the nth term of the sequence. Then graph the first six terms of the sequence.

11. $a_9 = 35, d = 4$

12. $a_{15} = -32, d = -4$

In Exercises 13–16, write a rule for the nth term of the sequence.

13. $a_6 = 37, a_{10} = 53$

14. $a_8 = 66, a_{13} = 96$

15. $a_5 = 22, a_{12} = -48$

16. $a_{13} = -76, a_{16} = -97$

17. Find the sum of the positive even integers less than 250. Explain your reasoning.

8.2 Practice B

In Exercises 1–4, tell whether the sequence is arithmetic. Explain your reasoning.

1. 100, 50, 25, 12.5, 6.25, …

2. 0, −4, −8, −12, −16, …

3. $\frac{1}{6}, \frac{1}{3}, \frac{1}{2}, \frac{2}{3}, \frac{5}{6}, \ldots$

4. $\frac{3}{10}, \frac{3}{5}, \frac{9}{10}, \frac{6}{5}, \frac{3}{2}, \ldots$

5. Write a rule for the arithmetic sequence with the given description.

    a. The first term is 12 and each term is 7 less than the previous term.

    b. The first term is −8 and each term is 10 more than the previous term.

In Exercises 6–9, write a rule for the nth term of the sequence. Then find a_{20}.

6. 37, 29, 21, 13, …

7. $-4, -\frac{8}{3}, -\frac{4}{3}, 0, \ldots$

8. 0.2, 2.3, 4.4, 6.5, …

9. 2.2, 1.5, 0.8, 0.1, …

10. Describe and correct the error in writing a rule for the nth term of the arithmetic sequence −27, −12, 3, 18, 33, ….

$$\begin{aligned}
&\text{Use } a_1 = -27 \text{ and } d = 15. \\
&a_n = a_1 - (n - 1)d \\
&a_n = -27 - (n - 1)15 \\
&a_n = -12 - 15n
\end{aligned}$$

In Exercises 11 and 12, write a rule for the nth term of the sequence. Then graph the first six terms of the sequence.

11. $a_{23} = 107, d = 4$

12. $a_{13} = 12, d = \frac{1}{2}$

In Exercises 13–16, write a rule for the nth term of the sequence.

13. $a_4 = 44, a_9 = 69$

14. $a_9 = -73, a_{14} = -158$

15. $a_{15} = 63, a_{21} = 99$

16. $a_{15} = 28, a_{24} = 34$

17. Find the sum of the positive odd integers less than 500. Explain your reasoning.

8.2 Enrichment and Extension

Analyzing Arithmetic Sequences and Series

Remember the formula for the nth term of a general arithmetic sequence is

$$a_n = a_1 + (n - 1)d.$$

In Exercises 1–11, use the formula above.

1. How many terms are in the sequence 18, 24, …, 336?

2. How many terms are in the sequence 178, 170, …, 2?

3. How many terms are in the sequence 506, 500, …, −4?

4. Find the number of multiples of 7 between 30 and 300.

5. Find the number of multiples of 6 between 28 and 280.

6. Find the number of multiples of 11 between 999 and 1999.

7. How many 3-digit numbers are divisible by 4 and 6?

8. How many 4-digit numbers are not divisible by 11?

9. How many 4-digit numbers are not divisible by 2 and 8?

10. Find the formula for t_n, the nth term of the sequence
    $2a - 2b$, $3a - b$, $4a$, $5a + b$, ….

11. Find x and y if the sequence y, $2x + y$, $7y$, 20, …. is arithmetic.

Puzzle Time

What Do You Call A Haunted Chicken?

Write the letter of each answer in the box containing the exercise number.

Write a rule for the *n*th term of the arithmetic sequence.

1. $3, 7, 11, 15, \ldots$

2. $25, 16, 7, -2, \ldots$

3. $-10, -7, -4, -1, \ldots$

4. $-5, -9, -13, -17, \ldots$

5. $a_8 = 12, d = 7$

6. $a_{20} = -6, d = -3$

7. $a_{14} = 54, d = 8$

8. $a_{30} = -72, d = -15$

9. $a_2 = 11, a_{12} = 51$

10. $a_{15} = 73, a_{21} = 55$

11. $a_6 = -8, a_{20} = -50$

12. $a_{22} = 17, a_{30} = -23$

Answers

T. $a_n = -5n + 127$

P. $a_n = 4n - 1$

U. $a_n = 3n - 13$

T. $a_n = 7n - 44$

O. $a_n = -9n + 34$

I. $a_n = -3n + 118$

R. $a_n = -3n + 54$

L. $a_n = -4n - 1$

Y. $a_n = 8n - 58$

G. $a_n = -15n + 378$

E. $a_n = 4n + 3$

S. $a_n = -3n + 10$

1	2	3	4	5	6	7	8	9	10	11	12

8.3 Start Thinking

List the four terms of the sequence shown in the graph. Then write a rule for the *n*th term of the sequence. Describe some of the common features of the graphs and the rules.

1.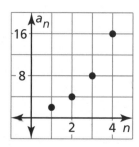

2.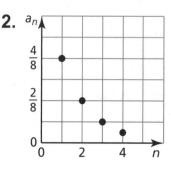

3.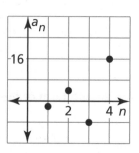

8.3 Warm Up

Find the sum.

1. $\displaystyle\sum_{i=1}^{4} 3i$

2. $\displaystyle\sum_{i=1}^{9} (2 - i)$

3. $\displaystyle\sum_{i=1}^{15} (i^2 + 2)$

4. $\displaystyle\sum_{k=5}^{7} (10 - 2k)$

5. $\displaystyle\sum_{i=1}^{4} 2^{i-1}$

6. $\displaystyle\sum_{i=1}^{5} 2\left(-\frac{1}{2}\right)^{i}$

8.3 Cumulative Review Warm Up

Sketch the graph of the function.

1. $f(x) = 2^{x-1}$

2. $f(x) = 2^x + 3$

3. $f(x) = 2^{-x}$

4. $f(x) = \log_2 x$

5. $f(x) = 3 + \log_2 x$

6. $f(x) = \log_2 (x + 1)$

8.3 Practice A

In Exercises 1–4, tell whether the sequence is geometric. Explain your reasoning.

1. 64, 32, 16, 8, 4, …

2. 88, 66, 44, 22, 0, …

3. 0.3, 1.2, 2.1, 3, 3.9, …

4. 0.8, 4.8, 28.8, 172.8, …

5. Write a rule for the geometric sequence with the given description.

   a. The first term is -5, and each term is 3 times the previous term.

   b. The first term is 54, and each term is $\frac{1}{6}$ times the previous term.

In Exercises 6–9, write a rule for the nth term of the sequence. Then find a_7.

6. 3, 6, 12, 24, …

7. 7, 21, 63, 189, …

8. 192, 96, 48, 24, …

9. 36, 24, 16, $\frac{32}{3}$, …

In Exercises 10–13, write a rule for the nth term. Then graph the first six terms of the sequence.

10. $a_3 = 9$, $r = 3$

11. $a_2 = 12$, $r = 4$

12. $a_4 = 5$, $r = \frac{1}{2}$

13. $a_5 = -208$, $r = 2$

14. Describe and correct the error in writing a rule for the nth term of the geometric sequence for which $a_3 = 147$, $r = 7$.

$$
\begin{aligned}
a_n &= r a_1^{\,n-1} \\
147 &= 7 a_1^2 \\
21 &= a_1^2 \\
\sqrt{21} &= a_1 \\
a_n &= 7\sqrt{21}^{\,n-1}
\end{aligned}
$$

15. You are buying a new car. You take out a 3-year loan for $10,000. The annual interest rate of the loan is 6%. You can calculate the monthly payment M (in dollars) for a loan using the formula $M = \dfrac{L}{\displaystyle\sum_{k=1}^{t}\left(\dfrac{1}{1+i}\right)^k}$, where L is the loan amount (in dollars), i is the monthly interest rate (in decimal form), and t is the term (in months). Calculate the monthly payment.

8.3 Practice B

In Exercises 1–4, tell whether the sequence is geometric. Explain your reasoning.

1. 3, 6, 18, 72, 360, ...

2. 162, 54, 18, 6, 2, ...

3. 0.7, 3.5, 17.5, 87.5, 437.5, ...

4. $\dfrac{5}{3}, \dfrac{10}{3}, \dfrac{20}{3}, \dfrac{40}{3}, \dfrac{80}{3}, \ldots$

5. Write a rule for the geometric sequence with the given description.

   a. The first term is −12, and each term is 7 times the previous term.

   b. The first term is 62, and each term is $\dfrac{1}{2}$ times the previous term.

In Exercises 6–9, write a rule for the *n*th term of the sequence. Then find a_7.

6. 9, 18, 36, 72, ...

7. 80, 20, 5, $\dfrac{5}{4}$, ...

8. 3, $\dfrac{6}{5}$, $\dfrac{12}{25}$, $\dfrac{24}{125}$, ...

9. 1.2, −2.4, 4.8, −9.6, ...

In Exercises 10–13, write a rule for the *n*th term. Then graph the first six terms of the sequence.

10. $a_3 = 50, r = 5$

11. $a_2 = 18, r = \dfrac{1}{3}$

12. $a_4 = -378, r = 3$

13. $a_5 = 1, r = -\dfrac{1}{4}$

14. Describe and correct the error in writing a rule for the *n*th term of the geometric sequence for which $a_3 = 147, r = 7$.

$$\begin{array}{l} \diagup\!\!\!\!\diagdown \quad a_n = a_1 r^{n-1} \\[4pt] \qquad a_n = 147(7)^{n-1} \end{array}$$

15. You are buying a new boat. You take out a 5-year loan for $20,000. The annual interest rate of the loan is 4%. You can calculate the monthly payment M (in dollars) for a loan using the formula $M = \dfrac{L}{\displaystyle\sum_{k=1}^{t}\left(\dfrac{1}{1+i}\right)^{k}}$, where L is the loan amount (in dollars), i is the monthly interest rate (in decimal form), and t is the term (in months). Calculate the monthly payment.

8.3 Enrichment and Extension

Analyzing Geometric Sequences and Series

The ideas of arithmetic and geometric sequences can be combined, as shown below.

Example: Three numbers form a geometric sequence whose constant ratio is 3. If the first is decreased by 1, the second is decreased by 3, and the third is reduced to 2 less than half its value, the resulting three numbers form an arithmetic sequence. Determine the original three numbers.

$x, 3x, 9x$ — Represent the three numbers that form a geometric sequence.

$x - 1, 3x - 3, \frac{9}{2}x - 2$ — Represent the three numbers that form an arithmetic sequence.

$(3x - 3) - (x - 1) = \left(\frac{9}{2}x - 2\right) - (3x - 3)$ — Apply the constant-difference property of an arithmetic sequence.

$x = 6$ — Solve for x.

Evaluate $x, 3x,$ and $9x$ when $x = 6$ to obtain the original numbers. The original numbers are 6, 18, and 54.

1. Three numbers form a geometric sequence whose constant ratio is $\frac{1}{2}$. If the first is reduced to 10 more than $\frac{1}{4}$ its value, the second is decreased by 10, and the third is increased by 10 more than twice its value, the resulting three numbers form an arithmetic sequence. Determine the original three numbers.

2. Three numbers form an arithmetic sequence whose constant difference is 3. If the first number is increased by 1, the second is increased by 6, and the third is increased by 19, the resulting three numbers form a geometric sequence. Determine the original three numbers.

3. Insert two real numbers between 2 and 9 so that the first three terms form an arithmetic sequence and the last three terms form a geometric sequence.

4. Determine the second term of an arithmetic sequence whose first term is 2 and whose first, third, and seventh terms form a geometric sequence.

5. Let a, b, and c represent real numbers that are not consecutive terms of an arithmetic sequence or of a geometric sequence. If $a < b < c$, determine a number that when added to a, b, and c yields consecutive terms of a geometric sequence.

6. Show that if a and b are real numbers, the arithmetic mean of a^2 and b^2 is greater than or equal to the absolute value of their geometric means.
   $\left(Hint: (a - b)^2 \geq 0 \text{ and } (a + b)^2 \geq 0\right)$

8.3 Puzzle Time

What Does The Cow Like To Do On Her Day Off?

Write the letter of each answer in the box containing the exercise number.

Write a rule for the *n*th term of the geometric sequence.

1. $3, 9, 27, 81, \ldots$

2. $7, 14, 28, 56, \ldots$

3. $100, -50, 25, -12.5, \ldots$

4. $125, 25, 5, 1, \ldots$

5. $a_3 = 12, r = 2$

6. $a_4 = 40, r = \dfrac{1}{2}$

7. $a_2 = -27, r = 3$

8. $a_5 = 240, r = -2$

9. $a_2 = 8, a_4 = 32$

10. $a_4 = 16, a_7 = 1024$

11. $a_3 = -24, a_5 = -6$

Answers

I. $a_n = \dfrac{1}{4}(4)^{n-1}$

V. $a_n = 4(2)^{n-1}$

S. $a_n = 3(3)^{n-1}$

E. $a_n = 7(2)^{n-1}$

A. $a_n = 125\left(\dfrac{1}{5}\right)^{n-1}$

O. $a_n = 320\left(\dfrac{1}{2}\right)^{n-1}$

E. $a_n = 100\left(-\dfrac{1}{2}\right)^{n-1}$

O. $a_n = -9(3)^{n-1}$

O. $a_n = 15(-2)^{n-1}$

M. $a_n = 3(2)^{n-1}$

E. $a_n = -96\left(-\dfrac{1}{2}\right)^{n-1}$

1	2	3		4		5	6	7	8	9	10	11

8.4 Start Thinking

List the first 10 terms of the geometric sequence $a_n = 0.1(0.1)^{n-1}$.

Then find the value of $\sum\limits_{n=1}^{10} 0.1(0.1)^{n-1}$ and make a conjecture about

the value of $\sum\limits_{n=1}^{\infty} 0.1(0.1)^{n-1}$.

8.4 Warm Up

Find the sum.

1. $\sum\limits_{n=1}^{5} 2^{n-1}$

2. $\sum\limits_{n=1}^{5} 2n - 1$

3. $\sum\limits_{n=1}^{8} 4\left(\dfrac{2}{3}\right)^{n-1}$

4. $\sum\limits_{n=1}^{12} -2(3)^{n-1}$

5. $\sum\limits_{n=1}^{200} 5 - \dfrac{1}{2}n$

6. $\sum\limits_{n=1}^{15} \dfrac{1}{2}(3)^{n-1}$

8.4 Cumulative Review Warm Up

Graph the function. State the domain and range.

1. $f(x) = \dfrac{1}{x-1} + 3$

2. $f(x) = \dfrac{-2}{x+3}$

3. $f(x) = \dfrac{3}{x-2} + 4$

4. $f(x) = \dfrac{x}{x+5}$

5. $f(x) = \dfrac{3x-1}{2x-1}$

6. $f(x) = \dfrac{-2x+5}{x-3}$

8.4　Practice A

In Exercises 1 and 2, consider the infinite geometric series. Find the partial sums S_n for $n = 1, 2, 3, 4,$ and 5. Then describe what happens to S_n as n increases.

1. $\dfrac{1}{3} + \dfrac{1}{6} + \dfrac{1}{12} + \dfrac{1}{24} + \dfrac{1}{48} + \ldots$

2. $5 + \dfrac{10}{3} + \dfrac{20}{9} + \dfrac{40}{27} + \dfrac{80}{81} + \ldots$

In Exercises 3–6, find the sum of the infinite geometric series, if it exists.

3. $\displaystyle\sum_{n=1}^{\infty} 7\left(\dfrac{1}{4}\right)^{n-1}$

4. $\displaystyle\sum_{n=1}^{\infty} 3\left(\dfrac{5}{4}\right)^{n-1}$

5. $3 + \dfrac{9}{5} + \dfrac{27}{25} + \dfrac{81}{125} + \ldots$

6. $-6 - 4 - \dfrac{8}{3} - \dfrac{16}{9} - \ldots$

7. Describe and correct the error in finding the sum of the infinite geometric series.

> $\times$ $\displaystyle\sum_{n=1}^{\infty} \dfrac{5}{2}\left(\dfrac{1}{3}\right)^{n-1}$
>
> For this series, $a_1 = \dfrac{5}{2}$ and $r = \dfrac{1}{3}$.
>
> Because $|a_1| \geq 1$, this series does not have a sum.

8. You push your younger sister on a swing one time and then allow your sister to swing freely. On the first swing, your sister travels a distance of 8 feet. On each successive swing, your sister travels 80% of the distance of the previous swing. What is the total distance your sister swings?

In Exercises 9–11, write the repeating decimal as a fraction in simplest form.

9. $0.18181818\ldots$

10. $0.5555\ldots$

11. $1.6666\ldots$

12. A company had a profit of $500,000 in its first year. Since then, the company's profit has decreased by 6% each year. Assuming this trend continues, what is the total profit the company can make over the course of its lifetime?

Name_____ Date_____

8.4 Practice B

In Exercises 1 and 2, consider the infinite geometric series. Find the partial sums S_n for $n = 1, 2, 3, 4,$ and 5. Then describe what happens to S_n as n increases.

1. $\dfrac{3}{4} + \dfrac{1}{4} + \dfrac{1}{12} + \dfrac{1}{36} + \dfrac{1}{108} + \dots$

2. $6 + 4 + \dfrac{8}{3} + \dfrac{16}{9} + \dfrac{32}{27} + \dots$

In Exercises 3–6, find the sum of the infinite geometric series, if it exists.

3. $\displaystyle\sum_{n=1}^{\infty} \dfrac{5}{3}\left(\dfrac{3}{4}\right)^{n-1}$

4. $\displaystyle\sum_{n=1}^{\infty} \dfrac{3}{7}\left(\dfrac{7}{2}\right)^{n-1}$

5. $8 - 10 + \dfrac{25}{2} - \dfrac{125}{4} + \dots$

6. $\dfrac{1}{5} + \dfrac{2}{15} + \dfrac{4}{45} + \dfrac{8}{135} + \dots$

7. Describe and correct the error in finding the sum of the infinite geometric series.

$$\cancel{\times}\quad \sum_{n=1}^{\infty} \dfrac{5}{2}\left(\dfrac{1}{3}\right)^{n-1}$$

For this series, $a_1 = \dfrac{5}{2}$ and $r = \dfrac{1}{3}$.

$$S = \dfrac{a_1}{1-r} = \dfrac{\dfrac{5}{2}}{\dfrac{1}{3}} = \dfrac{5}{2} \cdot \dfrac{3}{1} = \dfrac{15}{2}$$

8. You are going for a 4-mile run. You know that you can run half the distance, and you successfully run 2 miles. There are 2 miles to go, and you know that you can run half that distance. You successfully run that next mile. Now there is 1 mile to go, and you know that you can run half that distance. You successfully run that next half mile. This process continues. Will you cover the 4 miles over the course of your run? Explain your answer.

In Exercises 9–11, write the repeating decimal as a fraction in simplest form.

9. 0.45454545…

10. 0.05050505…

11. 1.4444…

12. A radio station has a daily contest in which a random listener is asked a trivia question. On the first day, the station gives $300 to the first listener who answers correctly. On each successive day, the winner receives 95% of the winnings from the previous day. What is the total amount of prize money the radio station gives away during the contest?

8.4 Enrichment and Extension

Finding Sums of Infinite Geometric Series

Example: For what values of x does the following infinite series converge?

$$1 + (x - 2) + (x - 2)^2 + (x - 2)^3 + \ldots$$

Solution: This is an infinite geometric series with $r = x - 2$. By the Sum of an Infinite Geometric Series Theorem, the series converges when $|r| < 1$; that is, when $|x - 2| < 1$, or $1 < x < 3$. This interval $1 < x < 3$ for which the series converges is called the interval of convergence for the series.

In Exercises 1–6, find (a) the interval of convergence and (b) the sum, expressed in terms of x.

1. $1 + x^2 + x^4 + x^6 + \ldots$

2. $1 + 3x + 9x^2 + \ldots$

3. $1 + (x - 3) + (x - 3)^2 + (x - 3)^3 + \ldots$

4. $1 - (x - 1) + (x - 1)^2 - (x - 1)^3 + \ldots$

5. $1 - \dfrac{2}{x} + \dfrac{4}{x^2} - \dfrac{8}{x^3} + \ldots$

6. $\dfrac{x^2}{3} - \dfrac{x^4}{6} + \dfrac{x^6}{12} - \ldots$

7. Show that the series $\sin^2 x + \sin^4 x + \sin^6 x + \ldots$ converges to $\tan^2 x$ if $x \neq \dfrac{\pi}{2} + n\pi$.

8. Show that the series $\tan^2 x - \tan^4 x + \tan^6 x - \ldots$ converges to $\sin^2 x$ if $-\dfrac{\pi}{4} < x < \dfrac{\pi}{4}$. Are there other values of x for which the series converges?

9. Explain why there is no infinite geometric series with first term 10 and sum 4.

 **8.4** **Puzzle Time**

What Kind Of Dog Does Dracula Have?

Write the letter of each answer in the box containing the exercise number.

Find the sum of the infinite geometric series, if it exists.

1. $1 + 0.5 + 0.25 + 0.125 + \ldots$

2. $3 - \dfrac{9}{4} + \dfrac{27}{16} - \dfrac{81}{64} + \ldots$

3. $1 - 0.6 + 0.36 - 0.216 + \ldots$

4. $\displaystyle\sum_{i=1}^{\infty} 5\left(-\dfrac{1}{5}\right)^{i-1}$

5. $\displaystyle\sum_{i=1}^{\infty} \left(\dfrac{1}{3}\right)^{i-1}$

6. $\displaystyle\sum_{i=1}^{\infty} -6\left(-\dfrac{1}{2}\right)^{i-1}$

7. $\displaystyle\sum_{i=1}^{\infty} 4^{i-1}$

8. $\displaystyle\sum_{i=1}^{\infty} 42\left(\dfrac{1}{2}\right)^{i-1}$

9. $\displaystyle\sum_{i=1}^{\infty} 8\left(-\dfrac{7}{9}\right)^{i-1}$

10. $\displaystyle\sum_{i=1}^{\infty} \dfrac{7}{6^i}$

Answers
H. -4
N. $\dfrac{9}{2}$
B. 2
O. $\dfrac{5}{8}$
D. $\dfrac{3}{2}$
O. $\dfrac{25}{6}$
O. no sum
U. 84
L. $\dfrac{12}{7}$
D. $\dfrac{7}{5}$

1	2	3	4	5	6	7	8	9	10

8.5 Start Thinking

Examine the sequence. Identify the pattern used to determine each consecutive term. Then find the missing term in the sequence.

1. 1, 2, 3, 5, 8, 13, ?

2. 1, 2, 2, 4, 8, 32, ?

3. 10, 5, 5, 0, 5, −5, ?

4. −2, −1, 2, −2, −4, 8, ?

8.5 Warm Up

Write the first six terms of the sequence.

1. $a_n = 4 - \dfrac{1}{2}n$

2. $f(n) = \dfrac{3n + 1}{n}$

3. $a_n = n^2 + n$

4. $f(n) = 2\left(\dfrac{3}{2}\right)^{n-1}$

5. $a_n = n^3 - 10$

6. $a_1 = 1,\ a_n = a_{n-1} + 3$

8.5 Cumulative Review Warm Up

Solve the quadratic equation.

1. $3x^2 - 2x - 2 = 0$

2. $-x^2 + 3x = -5x + 2$

3. $5 - 2x = x^2 - 5x + 7$

4. $7x^2 + 3 = x^2 + 15$

5. $\dfrac{1}{2}x^2 - 5x + 3 = 0$

6. $\dfrac{2}{3} - \dfrac{1}{2}x^2 = -\dfrac{1}{3}x - 2$

8.5 Practice A

In Exercises 1–6, write the first six terms of the sequence.

1. $a_1 = 1$

$a_n = a_{n-1} + 5$

2. $a_1 = 1$

$a_n = a_{n-1} - 4$

3. $f(0) = 3$

$f(n) = 4f(n-1)$

4. $f(0) = 12$

$f(n) = \frac{1}{3}f(n-1)$

5. $a_1 = 1$

$a_n = (a_{n-1})^2 + 2$

6. $a_1 = 2$

$a_n = \frac{1}{2}(a_{n-1})^2$

In Exercises 7–14, write a recursive rule for the sequence.

7. $32, 24, 16, 8, 0, \ldots$

8. $-47, -35, -23, -11, 1, \ldots$

9. $2, 6, 18, 54, 162, \ldots$

10. $5, -10, 20, -40, 80, \ldots$

11. $21, 7, \frac{7}{3}, \frac{7}{9}, \frac{7}{27}, \ldots$

12. $1, 7, 13, 19, 25, \ldots$

13. $2, 3, 5, 8, 13, \ldots$

14. $2, 3, 6, 18, 108, \ldots$

In Exercises 15–20, write a recursive rule for the sequence.

15. $a_n = 5 + 2n$

16. $a_n = -4 - 3n$

17. $a_n = 15 - 13n$

18. $a_n = 8(10)^{n-1}$

19. $a_n = -2(7)^{n-1}$

20. $a_n = 1.8 - 0.8n$

21. The basic fee for a sailboat rental is $75. There is an additional $20 fee for each additional hour over 2 hours. The explicit rule $a_n = 75 + 20n$ gives the amount of the rental for n hours over 2 hours. Write a recursive rule for the amount of the rental for n hours over 2 hours.

In Exercises 22–25, write an explicit rule for the sequence.

22. $a_1 = 5, a_n = a_{n-1} - 3$

23. $a_1 = 14, a_n = a_{n-1} + 5$

24. $a_1 = -3, a_n = 2a_{n-1}$

25. $a_1 = 20, a_n = \frac{1}{2}a_{n-1}$

8.5 Practice B

In Exercises 1–6, write the first six terms of the sequence.

1. $a_1 = 1$

$a_n = a_{n-1} + 9$

2. $f(0) = 32$

$f(n) = \frac{1}{4}f(n-1)$

3. $f(0) = 24$

$f(n) = \frac{3}{2}f(n-1)$

4. $a_1 = 1$

$a_n = (a_{n-1})^2 - 1$

5. $f(0) = 1,\ f(1) = 4$

$f(n) = f(n-2) - f(n-1)$

6. $f(1) = 256,\ f(2) = 2$

$f(n) = \dfrac{f(n-2)}{f(n-1)}$

In Exercises 7–14, write a recursive rule for the sequence.

7. $30, 21, 12, 3, -6, \ldots$

8. $3, -15, 75, -375, \ldots$

9. $28, 4, \frac{4}{7}, \frac{4}{49}, \frac{4}{343}, \ldots$

10. $1, 12, 23, 34, 45, \ldots$

11. $2, 6, 12, 72, 864, \ldots$

12. $1, 7, 8, 15, 23, \ldots$

13. $61, 39, 22, 17, 5, \ldots$

14. $-5, -3, 0, 4, 9, \ldots$

In Exercises 15–20, write a recursive rule for the sequence.

15. $a_n = -7 + 3n$

16. $a_n = 6(15)^{n-1}$

17. $a_n = -16(9)^{n-1}$

18. $a_n = -2.4 + 0.3n$

19. $a_n = -\frac{1}{3}\left(\frac{1}{5}\right)^{n-1}$

20. $a_n = \frac{1}{2}(7)^{n-1}$

21. The rate of growth of an organism is given by the explicit rule $a_n = 26(1.002)^{n-1}$, where n is the number of hours in an incubator. Write a recursive rule for the rate of growth of the organism.

In Exercises 22–25, write an explicit rule for the sequence.

22. $a_1 = -19,\ a_n = a_{n-1} + 7.2$

23. $a_1 = -7,\ a_n = 0.45a_{n-1}$

24. $a_1 = 4,\ a_n = a_{n-1} + \frac{1}{6}$

25. $a_1 = -9,\ a_n = \frac{1}{3}a_{n-1}$

8.5 Enrichment and Extension

Using Recursive Rules with Sequences

In Exercises 1 and 2, use the sequences defined recursively to solve the problem.

1. Give the first eight terms of the sequence defined recursively by $t_1 = 3$, $t_2 = 5$, and $t_n = t_{n-1} - t_{n-2}$. Observing the pattern you obtain, tell what the 100th term of the sequence will be.

2. Give the first 8 terms of the sequence defined recursively by $t_1 = 4$, $t_2 = 8$, and $t_n = \dfrac{t_{n-1}}{t_{n-2}}$. Observing the pattern you obtain, tell what the 100th term of the sequence will be.

3. Let d_n represent the number of diagonals that can be drawn in an n-sided polygon. The diagram below shows that a hexagon has nine diagonals, and so $d_6 = 9$.

 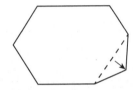

    a. Imagine pushing out one side of the hexagon so that a polygon of seven sides is formed. How many additional diagonals can be drawn?

    b. Imagine pushing out one side of a polygon with $n - 1$ sides so that an n-sided polygon is formed. Tell how many additional diagonals can be drawn. Then write a recursive equation for d_n.

4. Let S_n represent the number of dots in an n-by-n square array. Give a recursive equation that tells how S_{n+1} is related to S_n by reasoning how many extra dots are needed to form the $(n + 1)$ square from the previous nth square array. Illustrate your answer with a diagram.

Name_____ Date _____

 8.5 Puzzle Time

What Do You Call A Large Gorilla Who Likes To Dance?

Write the letter of each answer in the box containing the exercise number.

Write the first six terms of the sequence.

1. $a_1 = 2$
   $a_n = a_{n-1} + 4$

2. $a_1 = 2$
   $a_n = a_{n-1} - 3$

3. $a_1 = 2$
   $a_n = (a_{n-1})^2 - 1$

Write a recursive rule for the sequence.

4. 2, 4, 7, 11, 16, …

5. 15, 215, 415, 615, 815, …

6. 2, 3, 4.5, 6.75, 10.125, …

7. −6, 12, −24, 48, −96, …

8. 5, 15, 45, 135, …

9. 297, 99, 33, 11, …

Answers

C. $a_1 = 15$
$a_n = u_{n-1} + 200$

K. 2, 6, 10, 14, 18, 22

N. 2; 3; 8; 63; 3968; 15,745,023

O. $a_1 = 2$
$a_n = \dfrac{3}{2}a_{n-1}$

G. $a_1 = 2$
$a_n = a_{n-1} + n$

N. $a_1 = -6$
$a_n = -2 \bullet a_{n-1}$

I. 2, −1, −4, −7, −10, −13

G. $a_1 = 5$
$a_n = 3 \bullet a_{n-1}$

A. $a_1 = 297$
$a_n = \dfrac{1}{3}a_{n-1}$

1	2	3	4		5	6	7	8	9

Name_____ Date_____

In Exercises 1–9, copy and complete the table to evaluate the function.

1. $y = -11x + 26$

x	y
4	
8	
12	
16	

2. $y = 18x - 34$

x	y
2	
4	
6	
8	

3. $y = 6x + 13$

x	y
6	
12	
18	
24	

4. $y = 5x^2 - 8$

x	y
2	
3	
4	
5	

5. $y = -3x^2 + 4$

x	y
2	
3	
4	
5	

6. $y = 4x^2 - 19$

x	y
2	
3	
4	
5	

7. $y = 2^x - 3$

x	y
0	
1	
2	
3	

8. $y = 5 - 2^x$

x	y
0	
1	
2	
3	

9. $y = 3^x - 12$

x	y
0	
1	
2	
3	

In Exercises 10–21, solve the equation. Check your solution.

10. $8x + 17 = 73$

11. $-17x + 8 = -43$

12. $-7x + 2 = 79$

13. $\frac{1}{3}x - 6 = 14$

14. $-\frac{1}{2}x + 8 = -16$

15. $\frac{2}{3}x - 11 = 15$

16. $2x - 10 = 4x + 8$

17. $13x - 8 = 19x + 16$

18. $11x - 2 = -20x + 60$

19. $2^x - 3 = 61$

20. $3^x - 31 = 50$

21. $4 + 4^x = 68$

22. At 9:00 A.M. the temperature is 51°F. The temperature increases 3°F each hour for the next 6 hours. Write a function to model the temperature T at h hours after 9:00 A.M.

23. At 6:00 P.M. the temperature is 44°F. The temperature decreases 2°F each hour for the next 8 hours. Write a function to model the temperature T at h hours after 6:00 P.M.

Chapter 8 Cumulative Review (continued)

In Exercises 24–29, evaluate the function for the given value of *x*.

24. $g(x) = 8x^4 - 9x^3 + x^2 + 4x - 14; x = -7$

25. $h(x) = -9x^4 + 12x^3 + 2x^2 - 3x - 1; x = 5$

26. $f(x) = 6x^4 + 10x^3 - 3x^2 - 8x + 7; x = 9$

27. $h(x) = 7x^5 - 15x^4 - 14x^3 + 14x^2 + 12x - 12; x = -5$

28. $p(x) = -x^5 - 8x^4 + 4x^3 + 14x^2 - 2x + 10; x = 8$

29. $g(x) = 2x^5 - 12x^4 - 8x^3 + 2x^2 - 9x + 5; x = 3$

In Exercises 30–33, find the sum.

30. $\left(6x^2 + 5x + 15\right) + \left(-8x^2 - x + 9\right)$

31. $\left(2x^3 - 6x^2 + 14x - 4\right) + \left(x^3 + 13x^2 - 11x + 9\right)$

32. $\left(9x^4 - 9x^5 + x^2 - x + 2\right) + \left(4x^3 - 2x^5 + x^4 + 7x - 6\right)$

33. $\left(8x^3 - 12x + 6x^4 + 13x^5 + 1\right) + \left(-6x^5 + x^4 - 6x^3 - 2x + 7x^2 - 7\right)$

In Exercises 34–37, find the difference.

34. $\left(10x^3 - 11x^2 + 9x - 8\right) - \left(8x^3 - 6x^2 - 6x + 1\right)$

35. $\left(3x^4 + 7x^3 - 3x^2 - 4x + 3\right) - \left(-3x^4 - 8x^3 + 5x^2 - 15x + 13\right)$

36. $\left(4x^4 - 13x^3 + 9x^2 - 11x - 6\right) - \left(10x^4 + 3x^2 - 14x + 2\right)$

37. $\left(5x^5 + 10x^4 - 10x^3 - 3x^2 + 12x - 3\right) - \left(10x^5 - 12x^4 + 10x^3 - 15x - 12\right)$

In Exercises 38–43, find the product.

38. $7x^2\left(3x^2 - 5x + 3\right)$

39. $8x\left(7x^5 - 15x^4 + 11x^3 + 3x^2 - 7x - 9\right)$

40. $(15x + 7)\left(-2x^2 + 3x + 2\right)$

41. $\left(11x^2 + x\right)\left(4x^2 + 13x - 7\right)$

42. $(7x - 1)\left(8x^3 - 2x^2 + 13x - 3\right)$

43. $\left(x^2 + x - 12\right)\left(2x^2 - 8x + 1\right)$

In Exercises 44–49, find the product of the binomials.

44. $(x + 5)(x + 2)(x - 4)$

45. $(x + 5)(x - 1)(x - 2)$

46. $(x + 4)(x - 4)(x + 4)$

47. $(x - 2)(x - 4)(x - 5)$

48. $(4x + 3)(x + 1)(5x - 2)$

49. $(3x - 1)(4x + 1)(2x + 5)$

In Exercises 50–55, find the product of the binomials.

50. $(x + 6)^2$

51. $(x - 7)(x + 7)$

52. $(x - 8)^2$

53. $(2x + 11)^2$

54. $(6x - 11)^2$

55. $(9x + 10)^2$

In Exercises 56–61, divide the polynomials.

56. $(2x^2 - 3x + 7) \div (x + 4)$

57. $(5x^2 + 6x - 7) \div (x + 7)$

58. $(9x^2 - x - 2) \div (x - 2)$

59. $(4x^3 + 5x^2 - 6x + 6) \div (x - 7)$

60. $(5x^4 - 3x^3 - 5x^2 + 2x - 8) \div (x + 4)$

61. $(3x^4 - 5x^3 + 4x - 5) \div (x + 5)$

62. A rectangle has an area expressed by $2x^2 + 10x + 12$ and a length expressed by $x + 3$.

    a. Write the expression for the width of the rectangle.

    b. The value of x is 2. Determine the area of the rectangle using the value of x.

63. A rectangle has an area expressed by $4x^2 + 29x + 30$ and a width expressed by $x + 6$.

    a. Write the expression for the length of the rectangle.

    b. The value of x is 3. Determine the area of the rectangle using the value of x.

    c. Determine the width of the rectangle using the value of x given in part (b).

    d. Determine the length of the rectangle using the expression from part (a) and the value of x given in part (b).

Chapter 8 **Cumulative Review** (continued)

In Exercises 64–79, factor the polynomial completely.

64. $x^3 + 5x^2 - 24x$

65. $c^3 + 8c^2 - 9c$

66. $m^3 - 13m^2 + 40m$

67. $a^3 + 2a^2 - 3a$

68. $d^3 + 512$

69. $g^3 - 27$

70. $y^3 - 125$

71. $n^3 + 343$

72. $8b^3 + 125$

73. $27w^3 - 343$

74. $f^3 - 7f^2 + 3f - 21$

75. $3r^3 + 5r^2 - 6r - 10$

76. $5h^3 - 8h^2 - 5h + 8$

77. $3s^3 - 7s^2 + 12s - 28$

78. $4v^4 - v^3 + 28v - 7$

79. $7p^4 + 2p^3 - 63p - 18$

In Exercises 80–85, solve the equation.

80. $z^3 + 4z^2 - 12z = 0$

81. $x^4 = 8x^3 + 33x^2$

82. $m^3 = 7m^2 + 44m$

83. $h^3 + 13h^2 = -30h$

84. $-3v^3 = 42v^2 + 135v$

85. $5f^3 + 160f = 60f^2$

In Exercises 86–91, find the zeros of the function.

86. $f(x) = x^4 - 3x^3 - 28x^2$

87. $g(x) = x^4 + 5x^3 - 24x^2$

88. $h(x) = x^5 - 22x^4 + 120x^3$

89. $g(x) = x^3 - 7x^2 + 10x$

90. $h(x) = x^5 - 12x^4 + 20x^3$

91. $f(x) = x^4 - 8x^3 - 33x^2$

92. The area of a square picture is represented by the expression $9x^2 + 30x + 25$.

    a. Write an expression for the side length of the square.

    b. The value of x is 1. Determine the area of the square, using the value of x.

93. The area of a square picture is represented by the expression $36x^2 + 132x + 121$.

    a. Write an expression for the side length of the square.

    b. The value of x is 1.5. Determine the area of the square using the value of x.

    c. Determine the side length of the square using the value of x given in part (b) and the expression found in part (a).

Chapter 9

Chapter 9 Trigonometric Ratios and Functions

Dear Family,

Do you have a local coffee shop, diner, or café that you like to visit? What times of the day do you usually go? What hours are they open? Is the menu the same all day? Many restaurants collect data throughout the day to meet the needs of their customers, which makes their business more efficient and profitable.

The graph below shows the number of people in a café during a normal business day.

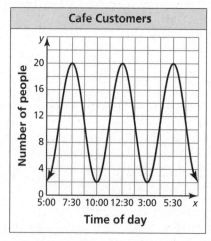

As a family, pretend you are the owners of the café. Use the graph to answer the following questions.

- When would you open and close the café?

- What hours would your employees work?

- At what times of the day would you need the most employees working for you?

- When would your employees change shifts?

- What type of menu would you have?

- What types of food would you serve at the busiest times of the day?

- What different types of music would you play throughout the day?

- How else could you use the graph above to help your business meet the needs of your customers?

The graph above is an example of a trigonometric function. What do you notice about the graph? Use the Internet to research other applications of trigonometric functions.

Enjoy your next experience at your favorite local coffee shop, diner, or café!

Nombre _____ Fecha _____

Estimada familia:

¿Hay alguna cafetería, restaurante o café local donde les gusta ir? ¿En qué horario suelen ir? ¿En qué horario están abiertos? ¿El menú es el mismo todo el día? Muchos restaurantes recopilan datos durante el día para satisfacer las necesidades de sus clientes, que hace que su negocio sea más eficiente y rentable.

En la siguiente gráfica, se muestra el número de personas en un café durante un día hábil normal.

En familia, imaginen ser los dueños del café. Usen la gráfica para responder las siguientes preguntas:

- ¿Cuándo abrirían y cerrarían el café?
- ¿En qué horario trabajarían sus empleados?
- ¿A qué horas del día necesitarían que trabajen más empleados?
- ¿Cuándo sería el cambio de turno de sus empleados?
- ¿Qué tipo de menú tendrían?
- ¿Qué clase de comida servirían en los horarios más atareados?
- ¿Qué clases de música diferente podrían durante el día?
- ¿De qué otras maneras podrían usar la gráfica de arriba para ayudar a que su negocio satisfaga las necesidades de sus clientes?

La gráfica de arriba es un ejemplo de una función trigonométrica. ¿Qué observan sobre la gráfica? Investiguen en Internet otros usos de las funciones trigonométricas.

¡Disfruten su próxima visita a su cafetería, restaurante o café local favorito!

9.1 Start Thinking

Use a ruler and a protractor to draw two right triangles, as shown below. Make one hypotenuse exactly 3 inches long and the other exactly 4 inches long. Use a ruler to find the measure of the remaining sides of each triangle. Determine the value of each of the ratios below. Round to the nearest hundredth, when necessary. Compare the ratios and make a conjecture about them in general, for any 30°-60°-90° triangle.

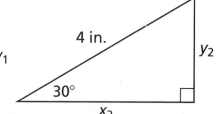

1. $\dfrac{y_1}{3}$

2. $\dfrac{x_1}{3}$

3. $\dfrac{y_1}{x_1}$

4. $\dfrac{y_2}{4}$

5. $\dfrac{x_2}{4}$

6. $\dfrac{y_2}{x_2}$

9.1 Warm Up

Use the Pythagorean Theorem to find the missing sides.

1.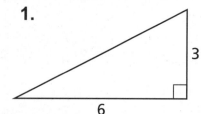

2.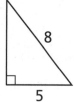

3.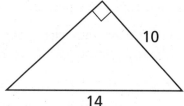

9.1 Cumulative Review Warm Up

Write a rule for the *n*th term of the sequence.

1. 11, 5, −1, −7, −13, ...

2. 4, −8, 16, −32, 64, ...

3. 0, 8, 16, 24, 32, ...

4. −1, 3, −5, 7, −9, ...

5. $\dfrac{2}{1}, \dfrac{3}{4}, \dfrac{4}{9}, \dfrac{5}{16}, \dfrac{6}{25}, \ldots$

6. $\dfrac{1}{2}, \dfrac{3}{5}, \dfrac{9}{8}, \dfrac{27}{11}, \dfrac{81}{14}, \ldots$

Name_____ Date_____

9.1 **Practice A**

In Exercises 1 and 2, evaluate the six trigonometric functions of the angle θ.

1.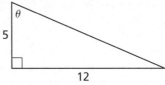

2.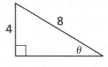

3. Let θ be an acute angle of a right triangle. Use the two trigonometric functions
$\sin \theta = \frac{3}{7}$ and $\cot \theta = \frac{2\sqrt{10}}{3}$ to sketch and label the triangle. Then evaluate
the other four trigonometric functions of θ.

In Exercises 4–6, let θ be an acute angle of a right triangle. Evaluate the other five trigonometric functions of θ.

4. $\sin \theta = \frac{4}{11}$

5. $\cos \theta = \frac{5}{6}$

6. $\tan \theta = \frac{3}{4}$

7. Describe and correct the error in finding $\tan \theta$ of the triangle below.

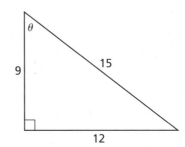

$$ \cancel{\times} \quad \tan \theta = \frac{\text{adj.}}{\text{opp.}} = \frac{9}{12} = \frac{3}{4} $$

In Exercises 8 and 9, find the value of x for the right triangle.

8.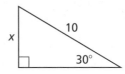

9.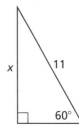

10. A parasailor is attached to a boat with a rope 80 feet long. The angle of elevation
from the boat to the parasailor is 36°. Estimate the parasailor's height above the
boat. Round your answer to the nearest tenth.

Name _____ Date _____

9.1 Practice B

In Exercises 1 and 2, evaluate the six trigonometric functions of the angle θ.

1.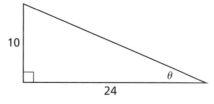

2.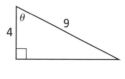

3. Evaluate the six trigonometric functions of the $90° - \theta$ angle in Exercise 1. Describe the relationships you notice.

In Exercises 4–6, let θ be an acute angle of a right triangle. Evaluate the other five trigonometric functions of θ.

4. $\cos \theta = \dfrac{5}{11}$

5. $\cot \theta = \dfrac{7}{8}$

6. $\sec \theta = \dfrac{11}{9}$

7. Describe and correct the error in finding $\csc \theta$ of the triangle below.

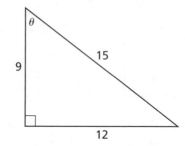

$$ \sout{\quad} \quad \sec \theta = \frac{\text{adj.}}{\text{hyp.}} = \frac{9}{15} = \frac{3}{5} $$

In Exercises 8 and 9, find the value of x for the right triangle.

8.

9.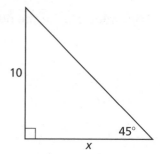

10. A cable is attached to the top of a pole and mounted to the ground 3 feet from the base of the pole. The angle of elevation from the mounting to the top of the pole is $78°$. Estimate the height of the pole. Round your answer to the nearest tenth.

Name _____ Date _____

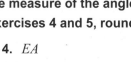

9.1 Enrichment and Extension

Right Triangle Trigonometry

Trigonometry can be used to solve problems involving one or more right triangles. Different triangles can share common parts.

Example: As shown in the diagram, a pole, $\overline{TF}$, is on the roof of a shed, $\overline{FB}$. From a point, P, on the ground 27 feet from the foot of the shed, the measure of the angle of elevation to the top of the pole, T, is $38°$, and the measure of the angle of elevation to the foot of the pole, F, is $32°$. Determine the height of the pole, to the nearest tenth of a foot. Because $\overline{TF}$ is not the side of a triangle, first determine TB in $\triangle TBP$ and FB in $\triangle FBP$, and then subtract to determine TF.

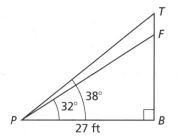

In $\triangle TBP$:

$$\tan 38° = \frac{\text{opp.}}{\text{adj.}} = \frac{TB}{27}$$

$$TB = 27 \tan 38° \approx 21.09$$

In $\triangle FBP$:

$$\tan 32° = \frac{\text{opp.}}{\text{adj.}} = \frac{FB}{27}$$

$$FB = 27 \tan 32° \approx 16.87$$

So, $TF = TB - FB \approx 21.09 - 16.87 \approx 4.2$ feet.

A ship is headed directly toward a coastline formed by a vertical cliff $\left(\overline{BC}\right)$ that is 80 meters high. At point A, from the ship, the measure of the angle of elevation to the top of the cliff (B) is $10°$. A few minutes later, at point D, the measure of the angle of elevation to the top of the cliff has increased to $20°$. In Exercises 1–3, round your answer to the nearest meter.

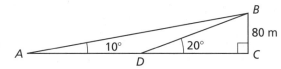

1. DC

2. AC

3. the distance between the two sightings

The heights $\left(\text{shown by } \overline{AB} \text{ and } \overline{CD}\right)$ of buildings on opposite sides of a 90-foot-wide avenue are 100 feet and 50 feet, respectively. From a point E on the avenue, the measure of the angle of elevation to B is $55°$. In Exercises 4 and 5, round your answer to the nearest foot.

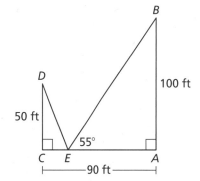

4. EA

5. ED

Puzzle Time

What's A Chrysler's Favorite Game?

Write the letter of each answer in the box containing the exercise number.

Let θ be an acute angle of a right triangle. Evaluate $\csc \theta$.

1. $\sin \theta = \dfrac{2}{3}$

2. $\cos \theta = \dfrac{4}{7}$

3. $\tan \theta = \dfrac{10}{3}$

Let θ be an acute angle of a right triangle. Evaluate $\sin \theta$.

4. $\sec \theta = \dfrac{5}{2}$

5. $\cot \theta = \dfrac{2}{9}$

6. $\csc \theta = \dfrac{6}{5}$

Let θ be an acute angle of a right triangle. Evaluate $\sec \theta$.

7. $\cos \theta = \dfrac{3}{14}$

8. $\sin \theta = \dfrac{4}{11}$

9. $\tan \theta = \dfrac{1}{2}$

Answers

A. $\dfrac{14}{3}$

O. $\dfrac{7\sqrt{33}}{33}$

L. $\dfrac{11\sqrt{105}}{105}$

D. $\dfrac{\sqrt{109}}{10}$

D. $\dfrac{3}{2}$

E. $\dfrac{9\sqrt{85}}{85}$

B. $\dfrac{5}{6}$

G. $\dfrac{\sqrt{21}}{5}$

L. $\dfrac{\sqrt{5}}{2}$

1	2	3	4	5	6	7	8	9

9.2 Start Thinking

Use a compass and a ruler to draw three circles, one with a radius of 1 inch, one with a radius of 2 inches, and one with a radius of 4 inches. Use a piece of string to measure a 1-inch long arc length on the 1-inch circle. Then use a protractor to measure the central angle that would create this arc length. Repeat the process with the other two circles using a 2-inch string and a 4-inch string. What conclusion can you make about the central angle that is needed to create an arc length that is equal to the radius of a circle?

9.2 Warm Up

Use a protractor and a straightedge to draw the angle in the *x-y* coordinate plane according to the description given. One ray should align with the positive *x*-axis.

1. $45°$ **2.** $210°$ **3.** $300°$

9.2 Cumulative Review Warm Up

Solve the system.

1. $y = 2x + 5$

$$y = -\frac{1}{2}x - 5$$

2. $x - y = 4$

$$2x + 3y = 3$$

3. $-3x + 4y = 6$

$$x - \frac{4}{3}y = -2$$

4. $x^2 + y^2 = 9$

$$2x - y = -6$$

5. $x^2 - x - y = 0$

$$x - y = -3$$

6. $2x^2 - x - y = -1$

$$3x + y = 5$$

9.2 Practice A

In Exercises 1–6, draw an angle with the given measure in standard position.

1. $170°$

2. $540°$

3. $-80°$

4. 5π

5. $\dfrac{2\pi}{3}$

6. $-\dfrac{3\pi}{4}$

In Exercises 7–9, match the angle measure with the angle.

7. $500°$

8. $\dfrac{7\pi}{3}$

9. $-130°$

A.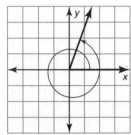

B.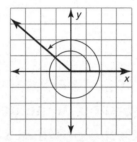

C.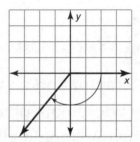

In Exercises 10–12, find one positive angle and one negative angle that are coterminal with the given angle.

10. $75°$

11. $-40°$

12. $\dfrac{7\pi}{3}$

In Exercises 13–18, convert the degree measure to radians or the radian measure to degrees.

13. $225°$

14. $50°$

15. $-160°$

16. $\dfrac{\pi}{12}$

17. $\dfrac{5\pi}{9}$

18. $-\dfrac{\pi}{8}$

19. You work every Saturday in the yard from 8:00 A.M. to 11:30 A.M. Draw a diagram that shows the rotation completed by the hour hand of a clock during this time. Find the measure of the angle generated by the hour hand in both degrees and radians. Compare this angle with the angle generated by the minute hand from 8:00 A.M. to 11:30 A.M.

Name_____ Date_____

9.2 Practice B

In Exercises 1–6, draw an angle with the given measure in standard position.

1. $260°$

2. $400°$

3. $-200°$

4. $\dfrac{5\pi}{2}$

5. $\dfrac{7\pi}{6}$

6. -4π

In Exercises 7–9, match the angle measure with the angle.

7. $-300°$

8. $\dfrac{5\pi}{3}$

9. $-\dfrac{11\pi}{6}$

A.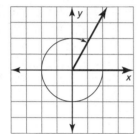

B.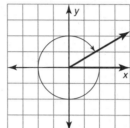

C.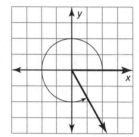

In Exercises 10–12, find one positive angle and one negative angle that are coterminal with the given angle.

10. $\dfrac{5\pi}{4}$

11. $-420°$

12. $-\dfrac{11\pi}{2}$

In Exercises 13–18, convert the degree measure to radians or the radian measure to degrees.

13. $200°$

14. $1°$

15. $-475°$

16. $\dfrac{3\pi}{10}$

17. $-\dfrac{5\pi}{12}$

18. 6

19. There are 60 minutes in 1 degree of arc, and 60 seconds in 1 minute of arc. The notation $50°30'10"$ represents an angle with a measure of $50°$, 30 minutes, and 10 seconds.

 a. Write the angle measure $160.44°$ using the notation above.

 b. Write the angle measure $98°15'45"$ to the nearest hundredth of a degree.

9.2 Enrichment and Extension

Angles and Radian Measures

In Exercises 1–12, without using a calculator or table, complete the statement with <, >, or =.

1. $\sin 40°$ ____ $\sin 30°$

2. $\cos 40°$ ____ $\cos 30°$

3. $\sin 172°$ ____ $\sin 8°$

4. $\sin 310°$ ____ $\sin 230°$

5. $\sin 130°$ ____ $\sin 50°$

6. $\cos 50°$ ____ $\cos(-50°)$

7. $\sin 214°$ ____ $\cos 213°$

8. $\sin 169°$ ____ $\sin 168°$

9. $\sin \dfrac{5\pi}{4}$ ____ $\cos\left(\dfrac{-3\pi}{4}\right)$

10. $\sin \dfrac{\pi}{4}$ ____ $\cos \dfrac{5\pi}{6}$

11. $\sin \dfrac{5\pi}{3}$ ____ $\cos \dfrac{3\pi}{4}$

12. $\sin 5$ ____ $\cos 6$

In Exercises 13 and 14, list the values in order from least to greatest.

13. $\sin 1,\ \sin 2,\ \sin 3,\ \sin 4$

14. $\cos 1,\ \cos 2,\ \cos 3,\ \cos 4$

In Exercises 15 and 16, solve using the arc length and area of a sector formulas.

15. A sector of a circle has a perimeter of 7 centimeters and an area of 3 square centimeters. Find all possible radii.

16. A sector of a circle has a perimeter of 12 centimeters and an area of 8 square centimeters. Find all possible radii.

17. The sector shown has a perimeter of 20 centimeters.

    a. Show that $\theta = \dfrac{20}{r} - 2$, and that the area of the sector is $K = 10r - r^2$.

    b. What value of r gives the maximum possible area of a sector of perimeter 20 centimeters?

    c. What is the measure of the central angle of the sector of maximum area?

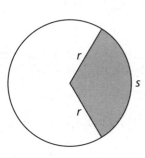

Name_____ Date_____

9.2 Puzzle Time

Why Did The Kangaroo Lose The Basketball Game?

Write the letter of each answer in the box containing the exercise number.

Find one positive angle and one negative angle that are coterminal with the given angle.

1. $80°$

2. $-124°$

3. $112°$

4. $-31°$

5. $\dfrac{3\pi}{2}$

6. $-\dfrac{5\pi}{3}$

7. $-\dfrac{\pi}{4}$

8. $\dfrac{12\pi}{7}$

Convert the degree measure to radians or the radian measure to degrees.

9. $-425°$

10. $\dfrac{7\pi}{2}$

11. $135°$

12. $\dfrac{34\pi}{5}$

13. $74°$

14. $-\dfrac{\pi}{4}$

15. $-18°$

16. $-\dfrac{2\pi}{3}$

Answers

E. $236°; -484°$ A. $329°; -391°$

H. $440°; -280°$ F. $630°$

O. $1224°$ O. $\dfrac{\pi}{3}; -\dfrac{11\pi}{3}$

R. $472°; -248°$ D. $-\dfrac{\pi}{10}$

U. $\dfrac{7\pi}{4}; -\dfrac{9\pi}{4}$ T. $\dfrac{26\pi}{7}; -\dfrac{2\pi}{7}$

O. $-\dfrac{85\pi}{36}$ S. $-120°$

B. $\dfrac{3\pi}{4}$ U. $\dfrac{37\pi}{90}$

N. $\dfrac{7\pi}{2}; -\dfrac{\pi}{2}$ N. $-45°$

1	2		3	4	5		6	7	8		9	10		11	12	13	14	15	16

9.3 Start Thinking

Diagram A shows a unit circle with five labeled points. Use the diagram to find the coordinates of the point (x, y). How could you define sin 45°, cos 45°, and tan 45°

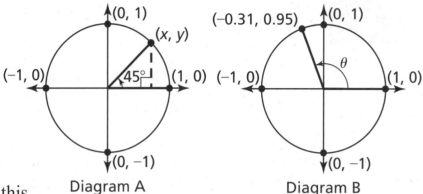

Diagram A   Diagram B

according to x and y? Use this definition to find the values of sin θ, cos θ, and tan θ shown in Diagram B. Round to the nearest hundredth, when necessary. If this definition was applied to angles in the third and fourth quadrant, what conclusions could you make?

9.3 Warm Up

Find the measure of the hypotenuse of the triangle.

1.

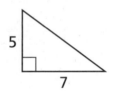

2.

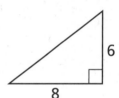

3.

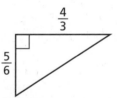

4.

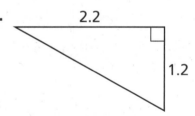

9.3 Cumulative Review Warm Up

Perform the indicated operation.

1. $\left(x^2 - 3x + 8\right) - \left(3x^2 - 5x\right)$

2. $\left(2x^2 + x - 5\right)(x - 7)$

3. $(2x - 1)^2$

4. $(3 - 5x)(3 + 5x)$

5. $\left(3 - x^2\right)^2$

6. $(3x - 2)^3$

Name_____ Date _____

In Exercises 1–4, evaluate the six trigonometric functions of θ.

1.
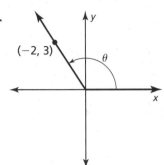

2.
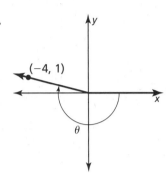

3.
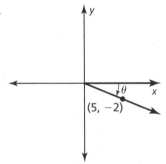

4.
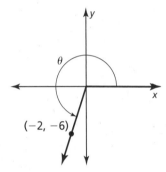

In Exercises 5–7, use the unit circle to evaluate the six trigonometric functions of θ.

5. $180°$

6. $450°$

7. $\dfrac{3\pi}{2}$

In Exercises 8–13, find the angle's reference angle.

8. $-170°$

9. $130°$

10. $220°$

11. $\dfrac{17\pi}{6}$

12. $\dfrac{15\pi}{4}$

13. $-\dfrac{7\pi}{3}$

In Exercises 14–16, evaluate the function without using a calculator.

14. $\csc 150°$

15. $\tan \dfrac{5\pi}{4}$

16. $\cos(-210°)$

17. The horizontal distance d (in feet) traveled by a projectile launched at an angle θ and with an initial speed v (in feet per second) is given by $d = \dfrac{v^2}{32} \sin 2\theta$. Estimate the horizontal distance (in feet) traveled by a football that is kicked at an angle of $60°$ with initial speed of $v = 80$ feet per second. What is the horizontal distance in yards? Round your answers to the nearest tenth.

Name _____ Date _____

9.3 Practice B

In Exercises 1–4, evaluate the six trigonometric functions of θ.

1.

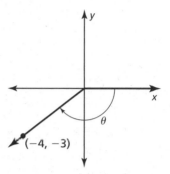

2.

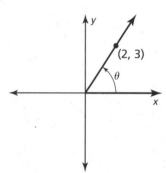

3.

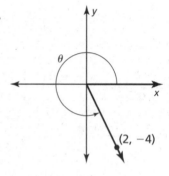

4.

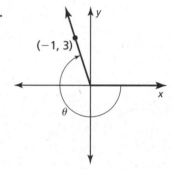

In Exercises 5–7, use the unit circle to evaluate the six trigonometric functions of θ.

5. 5π

6. $-720°$

7. $-\dfrac{5\pi}{2}$

In Exercises 8–13, find the angle's reference angle.

8. $-250°$

9. $110°$

10. $-310°$

11. $\dfrac{13\pi}{4}$

12. $\dfrac{11\pi}{6}$

13. $-\dfrac{13\pi}{3}$

In Exercises 14–16, evaluate the function without using a calculator.

14. $\cot 240°$

15. $\sin 315°$

16. $\sec\left(-\dfrac{5\pi}{6}\right)$

17. The horizontal distance d (in feet) traveled by a projectile launched at an angle θ and with an initial speed v (in feet per second) is given by $d = \dfrac{v^2}{32} \sin 2\theta$. To win a shot-put competition, your last throw must travel a horizontal distance of at least 15 feet. You release the shot put at a $45°$ angle with an initial speed of 22 feet per second. Do you win the competition? Justify your answer.

Name_____ Date_____

Trigonometric Functions of Any Angle

1. When a light ray passes from one medium, such as air, into another medium, such as glass, the light ray is bent, or *refracted*, at the boundary between the two media. The *index of refraction*, n, of a particular medium is given by the equation below.

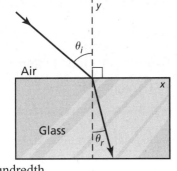

$$n = \frac{\sin \theta_i}{\sin \theta_r} \begin{cases} \theta_i \text{ is the incoming } \textit{angle of incidence} \text{ of the light ray.} \\ \theta_r \text{ is the outgoing } \textit{angle of refraction.} \end{cases}$$

Measurements taken using a piece of crown glass gave an angle of incidence of 43.7° and an angle of refraction of 27.1°. Determine the index of refraction of crown glass. Round your answer to the nearest hundredth.

2. The Dutch physicist Willebrond Snell (1580–1626) discovered that the sine of the angle of incidence is proportional to the sine of the angle of refraction for any given interface between two media. As shown below, Snell's Law may be stated in terms of the indices of refraction of the media.

$$n_1 \sin \theta_i = n_2 \sin \theta_r \begin{cases} n_1 \text{ is the index of refraction of the first medium.} \\ n_2 \text{ is the index of refraction of the second medium.} \end{cases}$$

The measure of θ_i is 30° and the measure of θ_r for crown glass is 19.2°. Use the index of refraction of crown glass that you determined in Exercise 1 to find the index of refraction of air. Round your answer to the nearest tenth.

3. Snell's Law may also be stated in terms of the velocity of light in the two media.

$$\frac{\sin \theta_i}{\sin \theta_r} = \frac{v_1}{v_2} \begin{cases} v_1 \text{ is the speed of light in the first medium.} \\ v_2 \text{ is the speed of light in the second medium.} \end{cases}$$

The measure of the angle of incidence with which a ray of light strikes crown glass is 30° and the measure of the angle of refraction is 19.2°. The speed of light in air is 3.0×10^8 meters per second. Find the approximate speed of light in crown glass. Give your answer in scientific notation to two decimal places.

4. When light crosses a boundary and its speed increases in the second medium, the measure of the angle of refraction is greater than the measure of the angle of incidence. There is an angle of incidence, called the *critical angle* (θ_c), for which the corresponding angle of refraction is 90°, and the ray of light emerges parallel to the boundary. You can determine the measure of a critical angle when light passes from some medium into air by using the formula below.

$$\sin \theta_c = \frac{1}{n}, \text{ where } n \text{ is the index of refraction of the first medium.}$$

When light passes from diamond to air, the measure of the critical angle is 24.4°. Find the index of refraction of diamond. Round your answer to the nearest hundredth.

Name _____ Date _____

9.3 Puzzle Time

What Kind Of Match Doesn't Light On Fire?

Write the letter of each answer in the box containing the exercise number.

Use the unit circle to find sin θ, cos θ, and tan θ.

1. −90°

2. 180°

3. −360°

4. $\dfrac{\pi}{2}$

Find the angle's reference angle.

5. −230°

6. 120°

7. $\dfrac{3\pi}{5}$

8. $-\dfrac{11\pi}{4}$

Evaluate the function without using a calculator.

9. sin 120°

10. tan(−105°)

11. cos $\dfrac{4\pi}{3}$

12. cot $\dfrac{2\pi}{3}$

Answers

C. $-\dfrac{1}{2}$

T. sin θ = 0; cos θ = −1;
   tan θ = 0

A. $\dfrac{\sqrt{3}}{2}$

E. sin θ = 0; cos θ = 1;
   tan θ = 0

N. 50°

A. sin θ = −1; cos θ = 0;
   tan θ = undefined

I. 60°

H. $-\dfrac{\sqrt{3}}{3}$ S. $\dfrac{2\pi}{5}$

N. sin θ = 1; cos θ = 0;
   tan θ = undefined

M. $\dfrac{\pi}{4}$ T. $2 + \sqrt{3}$

1		2	3	4	5	6	7		8	9	10	11	12

9.4 Start Thinking

In section 9.3, you learned to define the six trigonometric functions using the unit circle. Consider the function $f(\theta) = \sin \theta$. Use the unit circle to fill in the table of values. What is the highest value of $f(\theta)$? What is the lowest value of $f(\theta)$? How often do the high and low values repeat? What conclusions can you make about the graph of $f(\theta) = \sin \theta$?

θ		0	$\dfrac{\pi}{2}$	π	$\dfrac{3\pi}{2}$	2π	$\dfrac{5\pi}{2}$	3π	$\dfrac{7\pi}{2}$	4π
$f(\theta) = \sin \theta$										

9.4 Warm Up

Describe the transformation of f represented by g.

1. $f(x) = x^2,\ g(x) = 4x^2$

2. $f(x) = x^3,\ g(x) = -\frac{1}{2}x^3$

3. $f(x) = 2^x,\ g(x) = 2^{3x}$

4. $f(x) = \left(\frac{4}{5}\right)^x,\ g(x) = 7\left(\frac{4}{5}\right)^{x-2}$

5. $f(x) = \sin x,\ g(x) = 3 \sin x$

6. $f(x) = \cos x,\ g(x) = \cos\left(x + \frac{\pi}{2}\right)$

9.4 Cumulative Review Warm Up

Write a rule for the nth term of the sequence.

1. $0,\ \dfrac{1}{2},\ 1,\ \dfrac{3}{2},\ 2,\ \dfrac{5}{2},\ \ldots$

2. $7,\ -2,\ -11,\ -20,\ -29,\ \ldots$

3. $\dfrac{5}{2},\ \dfrac{7}{4},\ \dfrac{9}{8},\ \dfrac{11}{16},\ \dfrac{13}{32},\ \ldots$

4. $-3,\ 2,\ -\dfrac{4}{3},\ \dfrac{8}{9},\ -\dfrac{16}{27},\ \ldots$

Name _____ Date _____

In Exercises 1 and 2, identify the amplitude and period of the graph of the function.

1.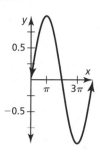

2.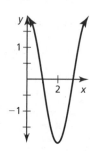

In Exercises 3–6, identify the amplitude and period of the function. Then graph the function and describe the graph of *g* as a transformation of the graph of its parent function.

3. $g(x) = 2 \sin x$

4. $g(x) = 4 \cos x$

5. $g(x) = \sin 2x$

6. $g(x) = 3 \cos \pi x$

7. Which functions have an amplitude of 2 and a period of π?

    A. $y = 2 \sin 2x$ **B.** $y = -2 \cos \pi x$

    C. $y = 4 \sin 2x$ **D.** $y = -2 \cos 2x$

8. The motion of a pendulum can be modeled by the function $d = 3 \cos 6\pi t$, where *d* is the horizontal displacement (in inches) of the pendulum relative to its position at rest and *t* is the time (in seconds). Find and interpret the period and amplitude in the context of this situation. Then graph the function.

In Exercises 9–12, graph the function.

9. $g(x) = \sin x - 3$

10. $g(x) = \cos\left(x + \frac{\pi}{2}\right)$

11. $g(x) = 2 \sin x + 1$

12. $g(x) = \cos 2(x + \pi)$

In Exercises 13 and 14, write a rule for *g* that represents the indicated transformations of the graph of *f*.

13. $f(x) = 2 \cos x$; translation 4 units down and π units left

14. $f(x) = \sin 4x$; translation 1 unit up and 2 units right

Name_____ Date _____

9.4 **Practice B**

In Exercises 1 and 2, identify the amplitude and period of the graph of the function.

1.
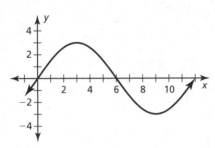

2.
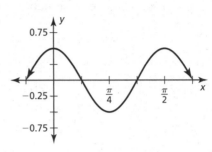

In Exercises 3–6, identify the amplitude and period of the function. Then graph the function and describe the graph of g as a transformation of the graph of its parent function.

3. $g(x) = 4 \sin x$

4. $g(x) = \cos \pi x$

5. $g(x) = 5 \sin 4x$

6. $g(x) = \frac{1}{4} \cos 2x$

7. Write an equation of the form $y = a \cos bx$, where $a > 0$ and $b > 0$, so that the graph has the given amplitude and period.

   a. amplitude: 1
      period: 3

   b. amplitude: 3
      period: 4

   c. amplitude: 12
      period: 2π

   d. amplitude: $\frac{1}{3}$
      period: π

In Exercises 8–11, graph the function.

8. $g(x) = \cos x + 3$

9. $g(x) = 2 \sin x - 1$

10. $g(x) = \sin \frac{1}{2}(x - \pi) - 2$

11. $g(x) = \cos \frac{1}{2}(x + \pi) - 4$

In Exercises 12 and 13, write a rule for g that represents the indicated transformations of the graph of f.

12. $f(x) = \frac{1}{2} \cos 3x$; translation 2 units up, followed by a reflection in the line $y = 2$

13. $f(x) = \frac{1}{3} \sin \pi x$; translation 3 units down, followed by a reflection in the line $y = -3$

9.4 Enrichment and Extension

Graphing Sine and Cosine Functions

In Exercises 1 and 2, a half-cycle of a sinusoid is shown. Find the particular equation for the sinusoid.

1.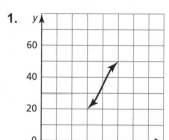

2.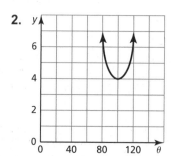

In Exercises 3 and 4, a quarter-cycle of a sinusoid is shown. Find the particular equation for the sinusoid.

3.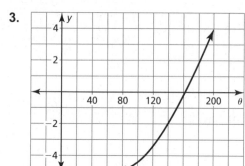

4.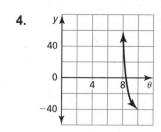

5. If the sinusoid in Exercise 3 is extended to $\theta = 300°$, what is the value of y? If the sinusoid is extended to $\theta = 5678°$, is the point on the graph above or below the sinusoidal axis? How far? Round your answers to the nearest hundredth, if necessary.

6. If the sinusoid in Exercise 4 is extended to the left to $\theta = 2.5°$, what is the value of y? If the sinusoid is extended to $\theta = 328°$, is the point on the graph above or below the sinusoidal axis? How far? Round your answers to the nearest hundredth, if necessary.

Name_____ Date _____

9.4 Puzzle Time

What Goes Best With Toast When You're In A Car?

Write the letter of each answer in the box containing the exercise number.

Identify the amplitude and period of the function.

1. $g(x) = 2 \sin 3x$

2. $g(x) = \dfrac{1}{2} \sin 4x$

3. $g(x) = \cos \pi x$

4. $g(x) = 3 \cos 4x$

5. $g(x) = \sin x$

6. $g(x) = -\dfrac{1}{2} \cos 6x$

7. $g(x) = 2 \sin \pi x$

8. $g(x) = -2 \cos 2\pi x$

Match the graph with the correct function.

9.

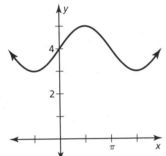

10.

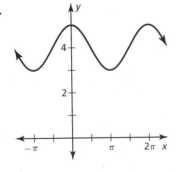

Answers

A. $a = 1$; period $= 2$

I. $a = \dfrac{1}{2}$; period $= \dfrac{\pi}{3}$

T. $a = 2$; period $= \dfrac{2\pi}{3}$

M. $g(x) = \cos x + 4$

J. $a = 2$; period $= 1$

F. $a = 3$; period $= \dfrac{\pi}{2}$

C. $a = 2$; period $= 2$

R. $a = \dfrac{1}{2}$; period $= \dfrac{\pi}{2}$

F. $a = 1$; period $= 2\pi$

A. $g(x) = \sin x + 4$

1	2	3	4	5	6	7		8	9	10

Consider the portion of the unit circle shown in the diagram. What angles are represented as you move from $(1, 0)$ to $(0, 1)$ in a counterclockwise direction? What angles are represented as you move from $(1, 0)$ to $(0, -1)$ in a clockwise direction? Describe what is happening to the values of x and y in both cases. Now consider the function $f(\theta) = \tan \theta$. How is this function defined using the unit circle? Describe the values of $f(\theta)$ as θ moves according to the descriptions above. What conclusions can you make about the graph of $f(\theta) = \tan \theta$?

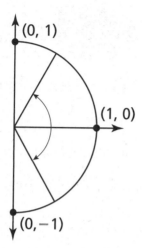

9.5 **Warm Up**

Graph the function.

1. $f(x) = 3 - \sin x$

2. $f(x) = 2 \cos 4x$

3. $f(x) = \dfrac{2}{3} \cos\left(x + \dfrac{\pi}{2}\right) - 3$

4. $f(x) = 2 - \dfrac{5}{2} \sin\left(x - \dfrac{\pi}{4}\right)$

9.5 **Cumulative Review Warm Up**

Expand the expression.

1. $\log_2 3x^2$

2. $\log \dfrac{2 - x}{x^3}$

3. $\ln \dfrac{\sqrt{2x^3}}{5}$

Condense the expression.

4. $\ln 8 - 2 \ln x$

5. $\dfrac{1}{2} \log(x - 1) + \log 7$

6. $-2 \log_3 x + 3 \log_3 (x - 2)$

Name_____ Date_____

In Exercises 1–4, graph one period of the function. Describe the graph of g as a transformation of the graph of its parent function.

1. $g(x) = 4 \tan x$

2. $g(x) = 3 \cot x$

3. $g(x) = \tan 2x$

4. $g(x) = \cot 4x$

5. Describe and correct the error in finding the period of the function $f(x) = \tan 2\pi x$.

$$\boxed{\quad \times \quad \text{Period: } \frac{\pi}{|b|} = \frac{\pi}{|2|} = \frac{\pi}{2} \quad}$$

6. Use the given graph to graph each function.

   a. $f(x) = 2 \sec 3x$

   b. $f(x) = 3 \csc 2x$

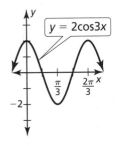

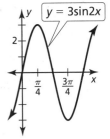

In Exercises 7–10, graph one period of the function. Describe the graph of g as a transformation of the graph of its parent function.

7. $g(x) = 4 \csc x$

8. $g(x) = \sec 2x$

9. $g(x) = \frac{1}{3} \sec 2\pi x$

10. $g(x) = 4 \csc \pi x$

Name_____ Date_____

9.5 Practice B

In Exercises 1–4, graph one period of the function. Describe the graph of _g_ as a transformation of the graph of its parent function.

1. $g(x) = 2 \tan 4x$

2. $g(x) = 3 \cot \frac{1}{2}x$

3. $g(x) = \frac{1}{4} \tan 2\pi x$

4. $g(x) = \frac{1}{3} \cot \pi x$

5. Describe and correct the error in describing the transformation of $f(x) = \tan x$ represented by $g(x) = 4 \tan \frac{1}{2}x$.

> ✗ A vertical stretch by a factor of 4 and a horizontal shrink by a factor of $\frac{1}{2}$

6. Use the given graph to graph each function.

a. $f(x) = 4 \sec \frac{1}{2}x$

b. $f(x) = \frac{1}{2} \csc \pi x$

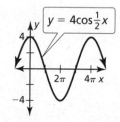

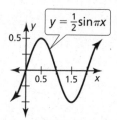

In Exercises 7–10, graph one period of the function. Describe the graph of _g_ as a transformation of the graph of its parent function.

7. $g(x) = \frac{1}{3} \csc \pi x$

8. $g(x) = \frac{1}{2} \sec 6x$

9. $g(x) = \sec \frac{\pi}{2}x$

10. $g(x) = \csc \frac{\pi}{3}x$

Name_____ Date_____

9.5 Enrichment and Extension

Graphing Other Trigonometric Functions

Consider the graph at the right. It looks like a tangent graph with some transformations. The graph of $y = \tan x$ has the center point of one period passing through the origin. The center of the middle period of this graph passes through the point $(1, -2)$. This indicates that both a vertical translation and a phase shift are included in the equation of the function. The period is 2π and indicates a horizontal stretch in the period of the graph of the parent function, $y = \tan x$ by a factor of 2. Using these observations, an equation for the function is $y = \tan(0.5(x - 1)) - 2$. Due to the periodic nature of the tangent function, other equations are possible.

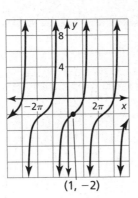

$(1, -2)$

In Exercises 1–6, write an equation for the graph.

1.
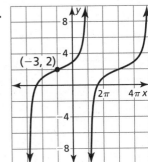

$(-3, 2)$

2.
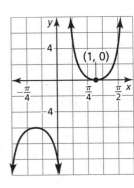

$(1, 0)$

3.
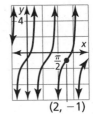

$(2, -1)$

4.
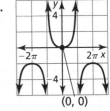

$(-1, 3)$

5.
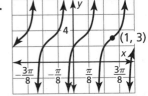

$(1, 3)$

6.
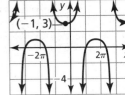

$(0, 0)$

9.5 Puzzle Time

What's An Elephant's Favorite Card Game?

Write the letter of each answer in the box containing the exercise number.

Match the graph with the correct equation.

1.
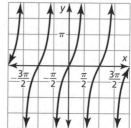

2.
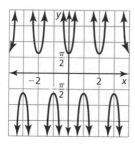

3.
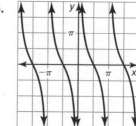

4.
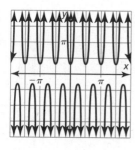

5.
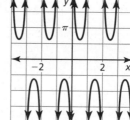

6.
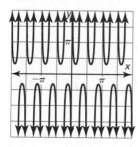

Answers

O. $g(x) = \sec 4x$

Y. $g(x) = \csc 4x$

M. $g(x) = 2 \tan x$

M. $g(x) = 2 \cot x$

E. $g(x) = 2 \sec \pi x$

R. $g(x) = 2 \csc \pi x$

1	2	3	4	5	6

You are riding a Ferris wheel. The graph to the right represents your height h (in feet) above the ground atany time t (in seconds). What are the x-intercepts of the graph and what do they represent in relationship to your ride? Approximately how tall is the Ferris wheel? If one ride includes four complete revolutions, how long is your ride? Describe the function in terms of translations of the graph of $h = \cos t$.

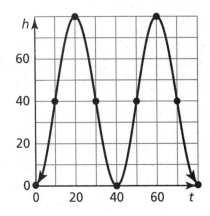

9.6 **Warm Up**

Identify the amplitude and the period of the function.

1. $y = -2\cos(x - \pi)$

2. $y = \dfrac{2}{3} \sin(2\pi x)$

3. $y = 4 - \sin\left(3x + \dfrac{\pi}{2}\right)$

4. $y = \dfrac{\sqrt{3}}{2} \cos(2x)$

5. $y = 1.4 \sin(x - 0.3)$

6. $y = -2.4 \cos(1.8x + 3)$

9.6 **Cumulative Review Warm Up**

Describe the domain and range of the function.

1. $f(x) = x^2 + 2x - 1$

2. $g(x) = 3 - \log_2(x - 2)$

3. $h(x) = \sqrt{x + 8} - 4$

4. $f(x) = 2x^3 - 5x^2 + x - 7$

5. $g(x) = -4 + 2 \sin x$

6. $h(x) = 3 \cos 2\pi x$

Name _____ Date _____

In Exercises 1–4, find the frequency of the function.

1. $y = \sin 2x$

2. $y = \cos 3x - 1$

3. $y = -\sin 4x$

4. $y = \cos 5\pi x$

5. A middle-C tuning fork vibrates with a frequency f of 262 hertz (cycles per second). You strike a middle-C tuning fork with a force that produces a maximum pressure of 5 Pascals. Write and graph a sine model that gives the pressure P as a function of the time t (in seconds).

In Exercises 6 and 7, write a function for the sinusoid.

6.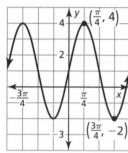

7.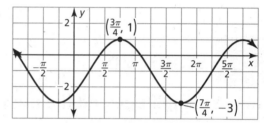

8. The table shows the depth d (in feet) of the water at the end of an inland dock that is located in a saltwater river that is affected by ocean tides. The time t is measured in hours, with $t = 0$ representing midnight.

t	Midnight	2 A.M.	4 A.M.	6 A.M.	8 A.M.	10 A.M.	Noon
d	2.55	3.80	4.40	3.80	2.55	1.80	2.27

a. Use sinusoidal regression to find a model that gives d as a function of t.

b. Predict the depth of the water at the end of the dock at 5 P.M.

Name_____ Date_____

9.6   Practice B

In Exercises 1–4, find the frequency of the function.

1. $y = \cos 3x$

2. $y = -\cos 4x - 3$

3. $y = \sin \dfrac{\pi x}{2}$

4. $y = 4 \cos 0.4x - 3$

5. A sub-contra-octave A tuning fork (corresponds to the lowest note on a piano keyboard) vibrates with a frequency f of 27.5 hertz (cycles per second). You strike a sub-contra-octave A tuning fork with a force that produces a maximum pressure of 4 Pascals. Write and graph a sine model that gives the pressure P as a function of the time t (in seconds).

In Exercises 6 and 7, write a function for the sinusoid.

6.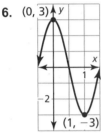

7.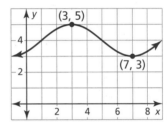

8. When you ride a Ferris wheel, your distance from the ground will vary with respect to the number of seconds that have elapsed since the wheel started. The table shows your height h (in meters) above the ground at time t as you ride the Ferris wheel.

t	0	1	2	3	4	5	6	7	8	9	10	11	12	15	20
h	1	2.3	5.8	10.2	13.7	15	13.7	10.2	5.8	2.3	1	2.3	5.8	15	1

a. Use sinusoidal regression to find a model that gives h as a function of t.

b. Predict your height above the ground after 42 seconds have elapsed.

9.6 Enrichment and Extension

Modeling with Trigonometric Functions

The monthly values of carbon dioxide below are expressed in parts per million (ppm). They are estimated values based on real-life data collected over a 40-year period.

Year	Jan	Feb	Mar	Apr	May	June	July	Aug	Sept	Oct	Nov	Dec
1965	319	320	320	322	321	321	320	318	317	318	319	320
1985	344	346	347	347	348	346	344	343	342	344	345	345
2005	376	377	378	380	379	379	377	375	374	374	375	377

1. Create an appropriate model for the amount of carbon dioxide in the atmosphere each month in the year 1965.

2. Create an appropriate model for the amount of carbon dioxide in the atmosphere each month in the year 1985.

3. Create an appropriate model for the amount of carbon dioxide in the atmosphere each month in the year 2005.

4. You noticed that a trigonometric model can be used to model this data. This is because most of the world's plant life is above the equator. When the northern hemisphere is facing the sun, there is more carbon dioxide being taken in by the plants. When the northern hemisphere faces away from the sun, there is less carbon dioxide. This creates a cyclical pattern. What do you notice when you compare the graphs from the 3 years? What implications does this have for our environment?

9.6 Puzzle Time

What Do You Get When You Cross A Monster With A Cat?

Write the letter of each answer in the box containing the exercise number.

Find the frequency of the function.

1. $y = \sin 3x$

2. $y = 4 \cos 3\pi x$

3. $y = 2 \sin \dfrac{x}{3}$

4. $y = 3 \cos \dfrac{x}{2}$

5. $y = 2 \cos 4x$

6. $y = \sin 4\pi x$

7. $y = 2 \sin 0.2x$

8. $y = \cos x - 4$

9. $y = -\cos 5x$

10. $y = -4 \sin \pi x$

Answers
O. $\dfrac{5}{2\pi}$
T. $\dfrac{1}{10\pi}$
A. $\dfrac{3}{2\pi}$
M. $\dfrac{3}{2}$
T. $\dfrac{2}{\pi}$
W. $\dfrac{1}{4\pi}$
N. $\dfrac{1}{2}$
A. 2
E. $\dfrac{1}{6\pi}$
I. $\dfrac{1}{2\pi}$

1		2	3	4	5	6	7	8	9	10

Consider the graphs of $y = \sin x$ and $y = \cos x$ shown below. Describe how you can use a single transformation of the cosine curve to obtain the sine curve. Then describe how you can use two transformations of the cosine curve to obtain the sine curve. Write a formula for each of your transformations and check your answers using a graphing calculator.

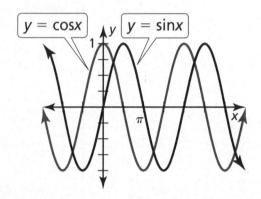

9.7 **Warm Up**

Evaluate the six trigonometric functions for the angle θ.

1.
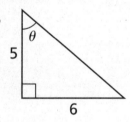

2.
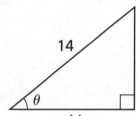

3.
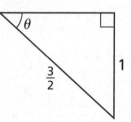

9.7 **Cumulative Review Warm Up**

Find the sum or difference.

1. $\dfrac{2x}{x + 4} - \dfrac{x - 1}{x + 4}$

2. $\dfrac{x - 1}{x^2 - x - 12} + \dfrac{3}{x - 4}$

3. $\dfrac{-3x}{x^2 + 5x} + \dfrac{1 - x}{x^2 - 25}$

4. $\dfrac{7}{2x^2} - \dfrac{3x + 4}{4x - 2}$

9.7 Practice A

In Exercises 1–6, find the values of the other five trigonometric functions of θ.

1. $\sin \theta = \dfrac{2}{3}, \ 0 < \theta < \dfrac{\pi}{2}$

2. $\cos \theta = -\dfrac{3}{5}, \ \dfrac{\pi}{2} < \theta < \pi$

3. $\tan \theta = \dfrac{4}{7}, \ \pi < \theta < \dfrac{3\pi}{2}$

4. $\cot \theta = -\dfrac{5}{4}, \ \dfrac{\pi}{2} < \theta < \pi$

5. $\sec \theta = \dfrac{7}{3}, \ \dfrac{3\pi}{2} < \theta < 2\pi$

6. $\csc \theta = -\dfrac{6}{5}, \ \pi < \theta < \dfrac{3\pi}{2}$

In Exercises 7–12, simplify the expression.

7. $\cos x \tan x$

8. $\sin x \left(\csc^2 x - 1 \right)$

9. $\dfrac{\tan(-\theta)}{\sin(-\theta)}$

10. $\dfrac{\sin^2 \theta}{\tan^2 \theta}$

11. $\dfrac{\tan\left(\dfrac{\pi}{2} - x \right)}{\csc x}$

12. $\dfrac{1 - \sin^2 x}{\sec x}$

13. Describe and correct the error in simplifying the expression.

$$\times \quad \tan^2 x + \sec^2 x = \tan^2 x + \left(\tan^2 x - 1 \right)$$
$$= \tan^2 x + \tan^2 x - 1$$
$$= 2 \tan^2 x - 1$$

In Exercises 14–17, verify the identity.

14. $\tan x \cot x = 1$

15. $\sin\left(\dfrac{\pi}{2} - x \right) \sec x = 1$

16. $\dfrac{\sin^2 x + \left(1 - \cos^2 x \right)}{\tan x \cos x} = 2 \sin x$

17. $\dfrac{\cos^2(-x) \csc x}{\cot x} = \cos x$

18. As the value of $\sin \theta$ decreases, what happens to the value of $\csc \theta$? Explain your reasoning.

9.7 **Practice B**

In Exercises 1–6, find the values of the other five trigonometric functions of θ.

1. $\sin \theta = \dfrac{3}{8}, \dfrac{\pi}{2} < \theta < \pi$

2. $\cos \theta = -\dfrac{1}{3}, \pi < \theta < \dfrac{3\pi}{2}$

3. $\tan \theta = 3, 0 < \theta < \dfrac{\pi}{2}$

4. $\cot \theta = \dfrac{10}{3}, \pi < \theta < \dfrac{3\pi}{2}$

5. $\sec \theta = -\dfrac{9}{5}, \dfrac{\pi}{2} < \theta < \pi$

6. $\csc \theta = -\dfrac{7}{2}, \dfrac{3\pi}{2} < \theta < 2\pi$

In Exercises 7–12, simplify the expression.

7. $\sin x \left(\cot^2 x + 1 \right)$

8. $\dfrac{\cot(-\theta)}{\cos(-\theta)}$

9. $\cos \left(\dfrac{\pi}{2} - \theta \right) \cot \theta$

10. $\dfrac{\tan^2 \theta - \sec^2 \theta}{\cos \left(\dfrac{\pi}{2} - \theta \right) \sec \theta}$

11. $\dfrac{\sin(-x)}{\tan(-x) \sec x} + \sin^2 x$

12. $\dfrac{\csc^2 x - \tan x \cot x}{\csc x - 1}$

13. Describe and correct the error in simplifying the expression.

$$\boxed{\begin{array}{l} \diagdown\!\!\!\!\diagup \quad \csc \theta \, \cot \theta \, \cos \theta = \dfrac{1}{\cos \theta} \cdot \dfrac{\cos \theta}{\sin \theta} \cdot \cos \theta \\[2mm] \qquad\qquad\qquad\quad = \dfrac{\cos \theta}{\sin \theta} \\[2mm] \qquad\qquad\qquad\quad = \cot \theta \end{array}}$$

In Exercises 14–17, verify the identity.

14. $\tan \left(\dfrac{\pi}{2} - x \right) \cos^2 \left(\dfrac{\pi}{2} - x \right) = \cos x \sin x$

15. $\dfrac{1 + \sin(-x)}{\cos x \tan x - 1} = -1$

16. $\dfrac{1 - \cos x}{\sin x} = \csc x - \cot x$

17. $\dfrac{1 + \sin \theta}{\cos \theta} + \dfrac{\cos \theta}{1 - \sin \theta} = 2 \sec \theta + 2 \tan \theta$

18. Use the sine and cosine functions to verify the identity $\tan x \cot x = 1$.

Name_____ Date_____

9.7 Enrichment and Extension

Using Trigonometric Identities

As you learned, equations that are true for all values of the variables for which they are defined are called *identities*. There are three groups of basic trigonometric identities. You can use the reciprocal, ratio, and Pythagorean identities and build upon them. You can use these identities to express one trigonometric function in terms of another.

Example: Express $\tan\theta$ in terms of $\sin\theta$.

$$\tan\theta = \frac{\sin\theta}{\cos\theta}$$

To express $\tan\theta$ in terms of $\sin\theta$, begin with the ratio identity for $\tan\theta$.

$$\sin^2\theta + \cos^2\theta = 1$$

Now find $\cos\theta$ in terms of $\sin\theta$.

$$\cos^2\theta = 1 - \sin^2\theta$$

$$\cos\theta = \pm\sqrt{1 - \sin^2\theta}$$

Use the appropriate Pythagorean identity to solve for $\cos\theta$.

$$\tan\theta = \frac{\sin\theta}{\pm\sqrt{1 - \sin^2\theta}}$$

Return to the ratio identity and substitute for $\cos\theta$.

In Exercises 1–3, express the given function in terms of $\cos\theta$.

1. $\tan\theta$ 2. $\cot\theta$ 3. $\csc\theta$

In Exercises 4–6, express the given function in terms of $\tan\theta$.

4. $\cot\theta$ 5. $\sin\theta$ 6. $\cos\theta$

In Exercises 7–8, express the given function in terms of $\csc\theta$.

7. $\cos\theta$ 8. $\tan\theta$ 9. $\sec\theta$

In Exercises 10–12, express the given function in terms of $\sec\theta$.

10. $\tan\theta$ 11. $\sin\theta$ 12. $\cot\theta$

Name _____ Date _____

9.7 **Puzzle Time**

What Do You Call A Little Blue Man Who Lives On The West Coast?

Write the letter of each answer in the box containing the exercise number.

Find the value of cos θ.

1. $\sin \theta = \dfrac{1}{4}, 0 < \theta < \dfrac{\pi}{2}$

2. $\tan \theta = -\dfrac{4}{5}, \dfrac{\pi}{2} < \theta < \pi$

Find the value of sin θ.

3. $\csc \theta = \dfrac{5}{4}, \dfrac{\pi}{2} < \theta < \pi$

4. $\cos \theta = -\dfrac{2}{3}, \pi < \theta < \dfrac{3\pi}{2}$

Find the value of tan θ.

5. $\sin \theta = -\dfrac{2}{3}, \dfrac{3\pi}{2} < \theta < 2\pi$

6. $\cot \theta = 4, 0 < \theta < \dfrac{\pi}{2}$

Find the value of csc θ.

7. $\sec \theta = -\dfrac{7}{3}, \dfrac{\pi}{2} < \theta < \pi$

8. $\tan \theta = -\dfrac{8}{5}, \dfrac{3\pi}{2} < \theta < 2\pi$

Answers

A. $-\dfrac{5\sqrt{41}}{41}$

U. $\dfrac{1}{4}$

P. $\dfrac{\sqrt{15}}{4}$

P. $\dfrac{4}{5}$

F. $-\dfrac{\sqrt{89}}{8}$

A. $-\dfrac{\sqrt{5}}{3}$

S. $-\dfrac{2\sqrt{5}}{5}$

R. $\dfrac{7\sqrt{10}}{20}$

1	2	3	4		5	6	7	8

9.8 Start Thinking

The formulas given below can be used to find the sine of angles that would normally require the use of a calculator. For each value of θ, determine two familiar angles whose sum or difference is equal to θ. Then use the appropriate formula to determine the value of $\sin \theta$.

$$\sin(a + b) = \sin a \cos b + \cos a \sin b$$

$$\sin(a - b) = \sin a \cos b - \cos a \sin b$$

1. $\theta = 75°$ **2.** $\theta = \dfrac{\pi}{12}$ **3.** $\theta = \dfrac{19\pi}{12}$

9.8 Warm Up

Evaluate the expression given that $\sin a = -\dfrac{3}{7}$ **with** $\pi < a < \dfrac{3\pi}{2}$ **and** $\cos b = \dfrac{5}{8}$ **with** $\dfrac{3\pi}{2} < b < 2\pi$.

1. $\sin b$ **2.** $\cos a$ **3.** $\tan b$

4. $\tan a$ **5.** $\csc b$ **6.** $\sec a$

9.8 Cumulative Review Warm Up

Use the given annual interest rate and method of compounding to find the amount A in an account earning compound interest after 8 years when the principal is $5000.

1. $r = 2.25\%$, daily   **2.** $r = 1.125\%$, quarterly

3. $r = 1.84\%$, monthly   **4.** $r = 2.16\%$, continuously

9.8 Practice A

In Exercises 1–6, find the exact value of the expression.

1. $\tan 105°$

2. $\tan(-75°)$

3. $\sin \dfrac{\pi}{12}$

4. $\sin 255°$

5. $\cos(-165°)$

6. $\cos \dfrac{7\pi}{12}$

In Exercises 7–12, evaluate the expression given that $\sin a = \dfrac{3}{5}$ with $0 < a < \dfrac{\pi}{2}$ and $\cos b = -\dfrac{5}{13}$ with $\pi < b < \dfrac{3\pi}{2}$.

7. $\sin(a + b)$

8. $\sin(a - b)$

9. $\cos(a - b)$

10. $\cos(a + b)$

11. $\tan(a + b)$

12. $\tan(a - b)$

In Exercises 13–15, simplify the expression.

13. $\sin\left(x + \dfrac{\pi}{2}\right)$

14. $\tan(x - \pi)$

15. $\cos(x + \pi)$

16. Describe and correct the error in simplifying the expression.

$$\cancel{\times} \quad \cos\left(x + \dfrac{3\pi}{2}\right) = \cos x \cos \dfrac{3\pi}{2} + \sin x \sin \dfrac{3\pi}{2}$$
$$= (0)\cos x + (-1)\sin x$$
$$= -\sin x$$

In Exercises 17–20, solve the equation for $0 \le x < 2\pi$.

17. $\cos\left(x - \dfrac{\pi}{2}\right) = 0$

18. $\tan(x + \pi) = 1$

19. $\cos\left(x + \dfrac{\pi}{4}\right) + \cos\left(x - \dfrac{\pi}{4}\right) = 1$

20. $\sin\left(x + \dfrac{\pi}{6}\right) - \sin\left(x - \dfrac{\pi}{6}\right) = 0$

21. Verify that the tangent function has a period of π by deriving the identity $\tan(x - \pi) = \tan x$ using the difference formula for tangent.

9.8 Practice B

In Exercises 1–6, find the exact value of the expression.

1. $\tan 165°$

2. $\sin \dfrac{13\pi}{12}$

3. $\sin(-105°)$

4. $\cos 75°$

5. $\cos\left(-\dfrac{5\pi}{12}\right)$

6. $\tan \dfrac{25\pi}{12}$

In Exercises 7–12, evaluate the expression given that $\sin a = \dfrac{12}{13}$ with $0 < a < \dfrac{\pi}{2}$
and $\cos b = -\dfrac{8}{17}$ with $\pi < b < \dfrac{3\pi}{2}$.

7. $\sin(a + b)$

8. $\sin(a - b)$

9. $\cos(a - b)$

10. $\cos(a + b)$

11. $\tan(a + b)$

12. $\tan(a - b)$

In Exercises 13–15, simplify the expression.

13. $\tan(x + 3\pi)$

14. $\cos\left(x + \dfrac{3\pi}{2}\right)$

15. $\sin(x - \pi)$

16. Describe and correct the error in simplifying the expression.

$$\times \quad \sin\left(x + \dfrac{\pi}{2}\right) = \sin x \sin \dfrac{\pi}{2} + \cos x \cos \dfrac{\pi}{2}$$
$$= (1) \sin x + (0) \cos x$$
$$= \sin x$$

In Exercises 17–20, solve the equation for $0 \le x < 2\pi$.

17. $\cos\left(x - \dfrac{3\pi}{2}\right) = \dfrac{1}{2}$

18. $\cos\left(x + \dfrac{\pi}{3}\right) + \cos\left(x - \dfrac{\pi}{3}\right) = 0$

19. $\tan\left(x + \dfrac{\pi}{4}\right) - \tan\left(\dfrac{\pi}{4} - x\right) = 0$

20. $\sin(x - \pi) - \cos(x + \pi) = 0$

21. Verify the identity $\tan(a + b) = \dfrac{\sin(a + b)}{\cos(a + b)}$ by using the angle sum formula for tangent.

9.8 Enrichment and Extension

Sum and Difference Formulas

In Exercises 1–4, use your knowledge of the sum and difference formulas for sine, cosine, and tangent to decide whether the statement is true or false. Give an explanation to support your decision.

1. $\sin\left(x - \dfrac{11\pi}{2}\right) = \cos x$

2. $\cos(n\pi + \theta) = (-1)^n \cos \theta, n = \text{integer}$

3. $\sin(n\pi + \theta) = (-1)^{n+1} \sin \theta, n = \text{integer}$

4. $\sin(n\pi - \theta) = (-1)^n \sin \theta$

In Exercises 5 and 6, apply the sum and difference formulas to create the formula.

5. $\cos(u + v + w)$

6. $\sin(u + v + w)$

In Exercises 7–10, use the sum and difference formulas to prove the even/odd identity.

7. $\sin(-u) = -\sin u$

8. $\cos(-u) = \cos u$

9. $\tan(-u) = -\tan u$

10. $\sec(-u) = \sec u$

Use the tangent sum formula.

11. Simplify $\tan(x + \pi)$ and interpret your answer graphically. What does your answer illustrate about the period of the tangent function?

9.8 Puzzle Time

What Do You Get When You Cross A Secretary With A CD Player?

Write the letter of each answer in the box containing the exercise number.

Find the exact value of the expression.

1. $\sin 195°$

2. $\cos 165°$

3. $\tan(-15°)$

4. $\cos 75°$

5. $\sin 105°$

6. $\tan \dfrac{13\pi}{12}$

Simplify the expression.

7. $\sin\left(x + \dfrac{\pi}{2}\right)$

8. $\cos(x - \pi)$

9. $\tan(x - \pi)$

10. $\sin(x - 2\pi)$

Answers
Y. $-\cos x$
R. $\dfrac{\sqrt{6} - \sqrt{2}}{4}$
T. $\dfrac{-\sqrt{6} - \sqrt{2}}{4}$
S. $\dfrac{\sqrt{2} - \sqrt{6}}{4}$
E. $\sqrt{3} - 2$
O. $2 - \sqrt{3}$
E. $\sin x$
T. $\cos x$
E. $\dfrac{\sqrt{6} + \sqrt{2}}{4}$
P. $\tan x$

1	2	3	4	5	6	7	8	9	10

Chapter 9 Cumulative Review

In Exercises 1–8, order the expression by value from least to greatest.

1. $-|4|, |-6|, |7 - 8|, |-1 + 6|$

2. $|-4 + 3|, -|4 + 1|, |-8 + 3|, |9|$

3. $|2|, |-2 + 5|, |-6|, \dfrac{|-6|}{|8|}$

4. $|4 - 9|, |-5 + 5|, \dfrac{|5|}{|-7|}, |-8|$

5. $|8| + |-4|, |9 - 9|, |-6| - |4|, |-7 \bullet -6|$

6. $|9 + 6|, |4 \bullet -4|, |-8| + |4|, |-4 + 6|$

7. $|7 - 5|, |3^2|, |9| + |-4|, |-2 \bullet -9|$

8. $|-6 \bullet -6|, |7 \bullet 3|, |-8|, |-7|, |-4^2|$

In Exercises 9–18, find the midpoint between the two points.

9. $(17, -20), (3, 14)$

10. $(2, -14), (-20, -12)$

11. $(-11, 13), (11, -1)$

12. $(13, -10), (7, -2)$

13. $(-16, -11), (10, 7)$

14. $(-4, -9), (4, 9)$

15. $(-4, -20), (18, -12)$

16. $(-18, 7), (-10, 5)$

17. $(-19, 21), (19, -11)$

18. $(9, -7), (-13, 5)$

In Exercises 19–28, find the distance between the two points.

19. $(17, 14), (3, -6)$

20. $(7, -19), (1, 8)$

21. $(-8, 8), (13, 14)$

22. $(-16, 9), (9, 14)$

23. $(2, -15), (1, -18)$

24. $(11, 2), (8, 11)$

25. $(3, 2), (-18, -16)$

26. $(-3, -12), (17, -15)$

27. $(-2, 9), (-7, -1)$

28. $(18, 3), (0, -17)$

29. A sandbox is in the shape of a right triangular prism. Both side lengths are 4 feet, and it is 1.5 feet tall.

   a. What is the length of the third side of the sandbox, or hypotenuse of the triangle? Round your answer to the nearest tenth of a foot.

   b. What is the volume of the sandbox?

   c. You want to put sand in the sandbox, but you only want the sand to be one foot deep. How much sand do you need?

   d. Sand costs $1.19 per cubic foot. Use your answer from part (c) to determine how much it will cost to fill the sandbox 1 foot deep. Round your answer to the nearest cent.

Chapter 9 **Cumulative Review** (continued)

In Exercises 30–35, find the missing side length of the triangle.

30.

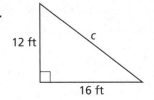

12 ft
c
16 ft

31.

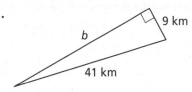

9 km
b
41 km

32.

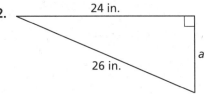

24 in.
26 in.
a

33.

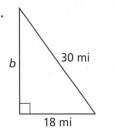

30 mi
b
18 mi

34.

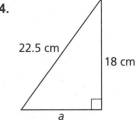

22.5 cm
18 cm
a

35.

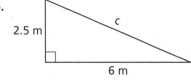

2.5 m
c
6 m

36. A mirror is in the shape of a right triangle and has side lengths of 6.5 inches and 7.5 inches. What is the area of the mirror? Round your answer to the nearest tenth.

37. A flower box is in the shape of a right triangular prism. Both side lengths are 3 feet, and it is 1 foot tall.

   a. What is the length of the third side of the flower box, or hypotenuse of the triangle? Round your answer to the nearest tenth of a foot.

   b. What is the volume of the flower box?

   c. You want to put potting soil in the sandbox, but you only want the soil to be 0.75 foot deep. How much soil do you need? Round your answer to the nearest tenth.

   d. Potting soil costs $2.49 per cubic foot. Use your answer from part (c) to determine how much it will cost to fill the sandbox 0.75 foot deep. Round your answer to the nearest cent.

Chapter 9 **Cumulative Review** (continued)

In Exercises 38–46, find the circumference of the circle with the given radius or diameter. Leave your answers in terms of π.

38. $r = 22$ inches

39. $r = 17$ kilometers

40. $d = 2$ miles

41. $d = 20$ centimeters

42. $r = 3$ feet

43. $d = 14$ millimeters

44. $r = 16$ yards

45. $d = 24$ meters

46. $r = 12$ centimeters

In Exercises 47–55, find the area of the circle with the given radius or diameter. Leave your answer in terms of π.

47. $d = 12$ miles

48. $r = 3$ inches

49. $d = 8$ kilometers

50. $r = 22$ yards

51. $r = 15$ feet

52. $r = 7$ centimeters

53. $d = 4$ meters

54. $d = 18$ miles

55. $r = 2$ yards

In Exercises 56–64, evaluate the expression for (a) $x = -3$ and (b) $x = 2$.

56. 3^x

57. 5^x

58. $2 \bullet 3^x$

59. $4 \bullet 2^x$

60. $3 \bullet 5^x$

61. $3 + 4^x$

62. $2 + 2^x$

63. $3^x - 4$

64. $2^x - 7$

In Exercises 65–79, simplify the expression.

65. $e^{-6} \bullet e^{-5}$

66. $e^9 \bullet e^5$

67. $e^6 \bullet e^{-3}$

68. $\dfrac{15e^2}{5e^{-3}}$

69. $\dfrac{-4e^7}{8e^5}$

70. $\dfrac{18e^9}{3e^2}$

71. $\left(2e^{-8x}\right)^3$

72. $\left(3e^{-9x}\right)^3$

73. $\left(-3e^{6x}\right)^2$

74. $\sqrt{16e^{12x}}$

75. $\sqrt{36e^{4x}}$

76. $\sqrt[3]{27e^{15x}}$

77. $e^x \bullet e^5 \bullet e^{6x}$

78. $e^7 \bullet e^{-3x} \bullet e^{x+2}$

79. $e^{2x} \bullet e^2 \bullet e^{x+2}$

80. The value of a pair of rollerblades y (in dollars) can be approximated by the model $y = 150(0.8)^t$, where t is the number of years since the pair of rollerblades was new.

   a. Tell whether the model represents exponential growth or exponential decay.

   b. Identify the annual percent increase or decrease in the value of the rollerblades.

   c. Estimate when the value of the rollerblades will be $60.

Chapter 9 Cumulative Review (continued)

In Exercises 81–92, evaluate the logarithm.

81. $\log_4 1024$

82. $\log_2 64$

83. $\log_3 81$

84. $\log_5 5$

85. $\log_6 36$

86. $\log_{1/4} 1$

87. $\log_3 \dfrac{1}{243}$

88. $\log_7 \dfrac{1}{343}$

89. $\log_9 \dfrac{1}{729}$

90. $\log_5 0.04$

91. $\log_2 0.25$

92. $\log_4 0.0625$

In Exercises 93–104, expand the logarithmic expression.

93. $\log_2 5x$

94. $\log_7 8x$

95. $\log_9 5x$

96. $\log_4 8x^3$

97. $\log_2 4x^5$

98. $\log_2 3x^4$

99. $\ln \dfrac{2x}{y}$

100. $\ln \dfrac{x}{5y}$

101. $\ln \dfrac{4x}{3y}$

102. $\log_9 3\sqrt{x}$

103. $\log_8 \sqrt[3]{xy^4}$

104. $\log_4 2\sqrt{x^3}$

In Exercises 105–116, condense the logarithmic expression.

105. $\log_7 6 + \log_7 11$

106. $\ln 6 - \ln 3$

107. $\ln 7 + \ln 6$

108. $3 \log_8 x - 2 \log_8 y$

109. $9 \log_5 y + 4 \log_5 z$

110. $10 \log_9 w + 8 \log_9 x$

111. $7 \ln 5 + 6 \ln 4$

112. $7 \log 4 - 4 \log 5$

113. $2 \ln 7 + 7 \ln x + 9 \ln y$

114. $\log_4 5 + \log_4 x$

115. $3 \ln z - 4 \ln y$

116. $6 \log_3 x + 4 \log_3 y + 2 \log_3 5$

In Exercises 117–126 simplify the expression, if possible.

117. $\dfrac{4x}{3x^3 - x}$

118. $\dfrac{2x^2}{6x^4 + 8x}$

119. $\dfrac{3x^3}{9x - 21}$

120. $\dfrac{x^2 + 4x + 3}{x^2 + x - 6}$

121. $\dfrac{x^2 - 3x - 28}{x^2 - 12x + 35}$

122. $\dfrac{x^2 - 4x + 3}{x^2 + x - 12}$

123. $\dfrac{x^2 + 2x - 3}{x^2 - 9x + 8}$

124. $\dfrac{x^2 + 7x + 10}{x^2 + 9x + 20}$

125. $\dfrac{x^3 + 9x^2 + 27x + 27}{x^2 + 9x + 18}$

126. $\dfrac{x^3 - 6x^2 + 12x - 8}{x^2 + 6x - 16}$

Chapter 10

Chapter 10 — Probability

Dear Family,

What is your favorite game to play as a family? Is this game based on chance, strategy, or both? Some board games use dice, cards, or a spinner to determine how a player must move around the board. Other games involve drawing tiles out of a bag or drawing from a deck of cards. When you play these games, you hope to draw, spin, or roll outcomes that are in your favor. You then use these outcomes and some strategy to try and win the game. In this chapter, you will be using dice, coins, cards, and spinners to study probability. It can be frustrating to play a game when you seem to always draw, spin, or roll outcomes that are not in your favor. Which game involving probabilities do you find to be the most frustrating? Which game do you find to be the most fair?

As a family, complete the table using examples of games you have played.

	Die or Dice (with numbers)	Die or Dice (with letters)	Drawing from a deck of cards	Drawing from a bag	Spinner
Name of game					
Total number of outcomes					
Is the probability of each outcome equally likely?					
Does the game involve chance, strategy, or both?					

The best outcome of game night is having fun together!

Capítulo 10 Probabilidad

Estimada familia:

¿Cuál su juego favorito para jugar en familia? ¿Es un juego basado en posibilidad, estrategia o ambas? En algunos juegos de mesa, se usan dados, tarjetas o una rueda giratoria para determinar cómo debe moverse un jugador por el tablero. En otros juegos, se sacan fichas de una bolsa o se saca una tarjeta de un mazo de tarjetas. Cuando juegan a estos juegos, esperan sacar, girar o lanzar resultados que estén a su favor. Luego, usan estos resultados y alguna estrategia para tratar de ganar el juego. En este capítulo, usarán dados, monedas, tarjetas y ruedas giratorias para estudiar la probabilidad. Puede ser frustrante jugar a un juego cuando siempre parecen sacar, girar o lanzar resultados que no los favorecen. ¿Cuál juego donde se usan las probabilidades les parece más frustrante? ¿Cuál juego les parece más justo?

En familia, completen la tabla con ejemplos de juegos que hayan jugado.

	Dado o dados (con números)	Dado o dados (con letras)	Sacar de un mazo de tarjetas	Sacar de una bolsa	Rueda giratoria
Nombre del juego					
Número total de resultados					
¿La probabilidad de cada resultado es igualmente probable?					
¿El juego implica posibilidad, estrategia o ambas?					

¡El mejor resultado de una noche de juego es divertirse juntos!

10.1 Start Thinking

Last season's basketball uniforms were stored in two boxes. One box contains 15 numbered jerseys; the other contains the matching numbered shorts. Your coach tells you to grab a jersey from one box and a pair of shorts from the other box. All 15 players grab a jersey from the first box.

1. You are the first one to reach into the box of shorts. You grab the first pair of shorts you touch. How likely is it that you will grab the number that matches your jersey?

2. Assuming the 15 uniforms are numbered 1 to 15, list all the possible outcomes for your uniform if your jersey is number 11.

10.1 Warm Up

List the possible outcomes for the situation.

1. tossing a coin three times

2. spinning a spinner twice that contains four equally likely colors—blue, red, yellow, and green

3. spinning the spinner mentioned in Exercise 2 followed by tossing a coin

10.1 Cumulative Review Warm Up

Let θ be an acute angle of a right triangle. Evaluate the other five trigonometric functions of θ.

1. $\sin \theta = \dfrac{4}{7}$

2. $\cos \theta = \dfrac{8}{9}$

3. $\tan \theta = \dfrac{5}{4}$

4. $\csc \theta = \dfrac{8}{3}$

5. $\cot \theta = \dfrac{3}{4}$

6. $\sec \theta = \dfrac{9}{5}$

10.1 Practice A

In Exercises 1 and 2, find the number of possible outcomes in the sample space. Then list the possible outcomes.

1. You roll three dice.

2. A clown has three purple balloons labeled a, b, and c, three yellow balloons labeled a, b, and c, and three turquoise balloons labeled a, b, and c. The clown chooses a balloon at random.

3. Your friend has eight sweatshirts. Three sweatshirts are green, one is white, and four are blue. You forgot your sweatshirt, so your friend is going to bring one for you as well as one for himself. What is the probability that your friend will bring two blue sweatshirts?

4. The estimated percentage student GPA distribution is shown. Find the probability of each event.

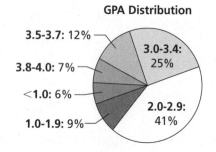

GPA Distribution

3.5-3.7: 12%

3.8-4.0: 7%

<1.0: 6%

1.0-1.9: 9%

3.0-3.4: 25%

2.0-2.9: 41%

   a. A student chosen at random has GPA of at least 3.0.

   b. A student chosen at random has GPA between 1.0 and 2.9, inclusive.

5. A bag contains the same number of each of four different colors of marbles. A marble is drawn, its color is recorded, and then the marble is placed back in the bag. This process is repeated until 40 marbles have been drawn. The table shows the results. For which marble is the experimental probability of drawing the marble the same as the theoretical probability?

Drawing Results			
yellow	red	blue	black
12	10	7	11

Name_____ Date_____

In Exercises 1 and 2, find the number of possible outcomes in the sample space. Then list the possible outcomes.

1. You roll a die and draw a token at random from a bag containing three pink tokens and one red token.

2. You draw 3 marbles without replacement from a bag containing two brown marbles and three yellow marbles.

3. When two six-sided dice are rolled, there are 36 possible outcomes.

   a. Find the probability that the sum is 5.

   b. Find the probability that the sum is not 5.

   c. Find the probability that the sum is less than or equal to 5.

   d. Find the probability that the sum is less than 5.

4. A tire is hung from a tree. The outside diameter is 34 inches and the inside diameter is 14 inches. You throw a baseball toward the opening of the tire. Your baseball is equally likely to hit any point on the tire or in the opening of the tire. What is the probability that you will throw the baseball through the opening in the tire?

In Exercises 5–7, tell whether the statement is *always*, *sometimes*, or *never* true. Explain your reasoning.

5. If there are exactly five possible outcomes and all outcomes are equally likely, then the theoretical probability of any of the five outcomes occurring is 0.20.

6. The experimental probability of an event occurring is equal to the theoretical probability of an event occurring.

7. The probability of an event added to the probability of the complement of the event is equal to 1.

8. A manufacturer tests 900 dishwashers and finds that 24 of them are defective. Find the probability that a dishwasher chosen at random has a defect. An apartment building orders 40 of the dishwashers. Predict the number of dishwashers in the apartment with defects.

Name_____ Date _____

Sample Spaces and Probability

The diagram at right shows a method of graphically recording the results of 12 coin tosses that occur in one-second intervals. The horizontal axis shows time t and the vertical axis shows position s. Beginning at the origin, the graph moves one unit up to record "heads" and one unit down to record "tails."

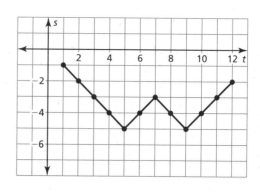

This type of graph is called a *random walk*. Random walks are mathematical formalizations of paths that consist of successions of random steps. Other examples include tracing the path of a molecule as it travels in a liquid or gas, or the price of a fluctuating stock.

1. Using H for "heads" and T for "tails," write the sequence for the random walk shown above.

Graph the random walk for the given coin sequences A, B, and C.

2. A: H, H, H, H, T, T, T, H, T, H, T, T, T, T, H

3. B: T, T, H, T, T, H, H, T, H, T, T, H, H, H, H

4. C: H, H, H, H, T, T, H, T, T, H, H, H, T, T, T

Refer to the graphs of sequences A, B, and C. For each sequence, give the time, if it exists, at which the random walk first returns to position $s = 0$. Then give the amount of time that the random walk spends in the first quadrant.

5. Sequence A 6. Sequence B 7. Sequence C

8. With a partner, toss a coin 20 times to generate a random walk. Generate 5 such walks.

   a. In what percent of your walks do you return to position $s = 0$ during the walk?

   b. What is the average number of tosses to return to position $s = 0$?

9. Give an example of a real-life situation for which a random walk would be an appropriate model. How are these models helpful when analyzing data?

10.1 Puzzle Time

What Happens When You Throw A Clock In The Air?

Write the letter of each answer in the box containing the exercise number.

Find the number of possible outcomes in the sample space.

1. You roll a die and flip two coins.

2. You draw two marbles without replacement from a bag containing four red marbles, two yellow marbles, and five blue marbles.

3. You flip six coins.

4. A bag contains eight black cards numbered 1 through 8 and six red cards numbered 1 through 6. You choose a card at random.

Find the probability.

5. You draw a number card from a standard deck of cards.

6. When two six-sided dice are rolled, there are 36 possible outcomes. Find the probability that the sum is less than 5.

7. In a classroom of 20 students, 12 students have brown hair, 4 students have blonde hair, 3 students have red hair, and one student has black hair. Find the probability of randomly selecting a blonde haired student from the classroom.

Answers
P. $\dfrac{1}{5}$
T. 24
E. 14
S. $\dfrac{9}{13}$
I. 40
M. 64
U. $\dfrac{1}{6}$

1	2	3	4	5		6	7

10.2 Start Thinking

Abbey has applied for admittance to her favorite college. Abbey's softball team is playing for the district championship. If they win, they will play for the state championship. Which of the three events (being accepted at her favorite college, winning the district championship, and winning the state championship) are dependent? Which are independent? Explain.

10.2 Warm Up

A group of 128 students was asked to select their favorite high school sport: basketball, football, lacrosse, or baseball. The table shows the results. Use the results to find the probabilities that a student chosen at random from this group would prefer the following.

Survey Results			
basketball	football	lacrosse	baseball
48	35	20	25

1. lacrosse

2. football

3. baseball or basketball

4. football or lacrosse

5. one of the four sports

6. none of the four sports

10.2 Cumulative Review Warm Up

Factor the polynomial completely.

1. $2x^2 - 8$

2. $18x^2 - 3x - 36$

3. $8 - 27x^3$

4. $x^4 - 7x^2 - 18$

5. $5x^7 + 5x^4$

6. $x^4 - 5x^3 - 9x^2 + 45x$

Name_____ Date_____

10.2 Practice A

In Exercises 1 and 2, tell whether the events are *independent* or *dependent*. Explain your reasoning.

1. A box contains an assortment of tool items on clearance. You randomly choose a sale item, look at it, and then put it back in the box. Then you randomly choose another sale item.

   Event *A*: You choose a hammer first.

   Event *B*: You choose a pair of pliers second.

2. A cooler contains an assortment of juice boxes. You randomly choose a juice box and drink it. Then you randomly choose another juice box.

   Event *A*: You choose an orange juice box first.

   Event *B*: You choose a grape juice box second.

In Exercises 3 and 4, determine whether the events are independent.

3. You are playing a game that requires rolling a die twice. Use a sample space to determine whether rolling a 2 and then a 6 are independent events.

4. A game show host picks contestants for the next game, from an audience of 150. The host randomly chooses a thirty year old, and then randomly chooses a nineteen year old. Use a sample space to determine whether randomly choosing a thirty year old first and randomly selecting a nineteen year old second are independent events.

5. A hat contains 10 pieces of paper numbered from 1 to 10. Find the probability of each pair of events occurring as described.

   a. You randomly choose the number 1, you replace the number, and then you randomly choose the number 10.

   b. You randomly choose the number 5, you do not replace the number, and then you randomly choose the number 6.

6. The probability that a stock increases in value on a Monday is 60%. When the stock increases in value on Monday, the probability that the stock increases in value on Tuesday is 80%. What is the probability that the stock increases in value on both Monday and Tuesday of a given week?

10.2 Practice B

In Exercises 1 and 2, tell whether the events are *independent* or *dependent*. Explain your reasoning.

1. You and a friend are picking teams for a softball game. You randomly choose a player. Then your friend randomly chooses a player.

    Event *A*: You choose a pitcher.

    Event *B*: Your friend chooses a first baseman.

2. You are making bracelets for party favors. You randomly choose a charm and a piece of leather.

    Event *A*: You choose heart-shaped charm first.

    Event *B*: You choose a brown piece of leather second.

In Exercises 3 and 4, determine whether the events are independent.

3. You are playing a game that requires flipping a coin twice. Use a sample space to determine whether flipping heads and then tails are independent events.

4. A game show host picks contestants for the next game from an audience of 5 females and 4 males. The host randomly chooses a male, and then randomly chooses a male. Use a sample space to determine whether randomly choosing a male first and randomly choosing a male second are independent events.

5. A sack contains the 26 letters of the alphabet, each printed on a separate wooden tile. You randomly draw one letter, and then you randomly draw a second letter. Find the probability of each pair of events.

    a. You replace the first letter before drawing the second letter.

    Event *A*: The first letter drawn is T.

    Event *B*: The second letter drawn is A.

    b. You do not replace the first letter tile before drawing the second letter tile.

    Event *A*: The first letter drawn is P.

    Event *B*: The second letter drawn is S.

6. At a high school football game, 80% of the spectators buy a beverage at the concession stand. Only 20% of the spectators buy both a beverage and a food item. What is the probability that a spectator who buys a beverage also buys a food item?

10.2 Enrichment and Extension

Independent and Dependent Events

	25 to 34	35 to 54	55 and over	Total
Did not complete high school	5325	9152	16,035	30,512
Completed high school	14,061	24,070	18,320	56,451
1 to 3 years of college	11,659	19,926	9662	41,247
4 or more years of college	10,342	19,878	8005	38,225
Total	41,387	73,026	52,022	166,435

In Exercises 1–4, use your knowledge of probability to analyze the table about years of education completed by age. If a person is chosen at random from this population:

1. What is the probability that the person is in the 25 to 34 age range and in the 55 and over age range?

2. What is the probability that a person is between 25 and 34 years of age and they have completed 1 to 3 years of college?

3. If the person is in the 55 and over age range, what is the probability that they completed 1 to 3 years of college?

4. If the person has completed high school, what is the probability that they are 35 to 54 years old?

5. If a person is vaccinated properly, the probability of his/her getting a certain disease is 0.05. Without a vaccination, the probability of getting the disease is 0.35. Assume that $\frac{1}{3}$ of the population is properly vaccinated.

   a. If a person is selected at random from the population, what is the probability of that person's getting the disease?

   b. If a person gets the disease, what is the probability that he/she was vaccinated?

6. Suppose a test for diagnosing a certain serious disease is successful in detecting the disease in 95% of all persons infected, but that it incorrectly diagnoses 4% of all healthy people as having the serious disease. If it is known that 2% of the population has the serious disease, find the probability that a person selected at random has the serious disease if the test indicates that he or she does.

7. The probability that a football player weighs more than 230 pounds is 0.69, that he is at least 75 inches tall is 0.55, and that he weighs more than 230 pounds and is at least 75 inches tall is 0.43. Find the probability that he is at least 75 inches tall if he weighs more than 230 pounds.

Name _____ Date _____

10.2 Puzzle Time

What Do You Put In A Barrel To Make It Lighter?

Write the letter of each answer in the box containing the exercise number.

Tell whether the events are dependent or independent.

1. You roll number cube and select a card from a standard deck of cards.

   Event *A*: You roll a 3.

   Event *B*: You select a face card.

2. A bag of marbles contains 3 red marbles, 2 yellow marbles, and 4 blue marbles. You randomly choose a marble, and without replacing it, you randomly choose another marble.

   Event *A*: You choose a red marble first.

   Event *B*: You choose a blue marble second.

Find the probability.

3. A container contains 13 almonds, 8 walnuts, and 19 peanuts. You randomly choose one nut and eat it. Then you randomly choose another nut. Find the probability that you choose a walnut on your first pick and an almond on your second pick.

4. The letters M, A, R, B, L, and E are each written on a card and placed into a hat. You randomly choose a card, return it, and then choose another card. Find the probability that you choose a vowel on your first pick and a consonant on your second pick.

5. A bag contains 3 red chips, 4 blue chips, 5 yellow chips, and 3 green chips. You randomly choose a chip, and without replacing it, you randomly choose another chip. Find the probability that you choose a yellow chip on your first pick and a blue chip on your second pick.

Answers
L. $\dfrac{2}{9}$
H. dependent
E. $\dfrac{2}{21}$
O. $\dfrac{1}{15}$
A. independent

1		2	3	4	5

10.3 Start Thinking

In a survey, 50 students were asked: Do you own a dog or a cat? The Venn diagram shows the results. Use the information in the Venn diagram to complete the two-way table. Discuss which format you prefer for displaying the survey results and why.

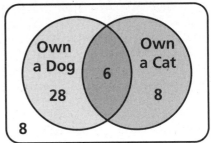

Survey of 50 Students

		Owns a Dog		
		Yes	No	Total
Owns a Cat	Yes			
	No			
	Total			

10.3 Warm Up

1. Complete the two-way table.

		Age Started Driving		
		≤ 16	> 16	Total
Gender	Male	28		33
	Female		8	22
	Total			

10.3 Cumulative Review Warm Up

Graph the function.

1. $y = \left(\frac{1}{2}\right)^{x-3}$

2. $y = \log_2(x + 1)$

3. $y = -\frac{2}{3}(3)^x$

4. $y = 2 - \log_3 x$

5. $y = 2^{x+4} - 5$

6. $y = -2 + \frac{1}{2}\log_4(x - 3)$

10.3 Practice A

In Exercises 1 and 2, complete the two-way table.

1.

		Ran a Half Marathon		
		Yes	No	Total
Role	Student	12		124
	Teacher	7		
	Total		263	

2.

		Owns Dog		
		Yes	No	Total
Owns Cat	Yes	24	61	
	No	107		
	Total			226

3. In a survey, 112 people feel that the amount of fresh water allowed to empty into the salt water river should be reduced, and 87 people did not feel that the amount of fresh water allowed to empty into the salt water river should be reduced. Of those who feel that the amount of fresh water released should be reduced, 98 people fish the salt water river. Of those that do not feel that the amount of fresh water released should be reduced, 12 people fish the salt water river.

   a. Organize these results in a two-way table. Then find and interpret the marginal frequencies.

   b. Make a two-way table that shows the joint and marginal relative frequencies.

   c. Make a two-way table that shows the conditional relative frequencies for each fish category.

10.3 Practice B

In Exercises 1 and 2, use the two-way table to create another two-way table that shows the joint and marginal relative frequencies.

1.

		Surfing Style		
		Regular	Advanced	Total
Gender	Male	86	24	110
	Female	77	18	95
	Total	163	42	205

2.

		Fishing License		
		Yes	No	Total
Hunting License	Yes	65	37	102
	No	177	341	518
	Total	242	378	620

3. In a survey, 5 people exercise regularly and 21 people do not. Of those who exercise regularly, 1 person felt tired. Of those that did not exercise regularly, 1 person felt tired.

   a. Organize these results in a two-way table. Then find and interpret the marginal frequencies.

   b. Make a two-way table that shows the joint and marginal relative frequencies.

   c. Make a two-way table that shows the conditional relative frequencies for each exercise category.

Name _____ Date _____

10.3 Enrichment and Extension

Two-Way Tables and Probability

The table shows the joint relative frequencies for how many adults and students attended a concert at the local park on Friday night, and whether or not each bought a program for the concert at the concession stand.

Use the table to complete the exercises.

	Yes	No
Adults	0.42	0.31
Students	0.21	0.06

1. Find the marginal relative frequencies for the data. Round your answers to the nearest hundredth, if necessary.

	Yes	No	Total
Adults	0.42	0.31	
Students	0.21	0.06	
Total			

2. Based on this data, use a percentage to express how likely it is that a student at a football game next Friday will not buy a program at the concession stand. Round your answer to the nearest whole percent, if necessary.

3. Based on this data, use a percentage to express how likely it is that an adult at a football game next Friday will buy a program at the concession stand. Round your answer to the nearest whole percent, if necessary.

4. Based on this data, use a percentage to express how likely it is an adult or student at a football game next Friday will buy a program at the concession stand. Round your answer to the nearest whole percent, if necessary.

5. If 35 students did not buy a program at the concession stand, then how many adults and students altogether do the data represent?

Puzzle Time

How Is A Basketball Player Like A Baby?

Write the letter of each answer in the box containing the exercise number.

Complete the two-way table.

	Response		
	Yes	**No**	**Total**
Male	15	**1.**	**2.**
Female	**3.**	**4.**	37
Total	**5.**	42	84

	Choice		
	AWD	**4WD**	**Total**
SUV	**6.**	10	**7.**
Van	5	**8.**	12
Total	16	**9.**	**10.**

	Highest Level of Education		
	High School	**College**	**Total**
Male	58	**11.**	113
Female	**12.**	94	**13.**
Total	**14.**	**15.**	362

Answers

B. 42

B. 249

Y. 10

L. 213

O. 11

T. 32

T. 21

I. 55

E. 149

H. 7

D. 17

H. 47

R. 33

E. 27

B. 155

1	2	3	4		5	6	7	8	.	9	10	11	12	13	14	15	16

10.4 Start Thinking

Use the spinner shown to complete the exercises.

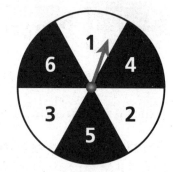

1. What is the sample space if the spinner is spun one time?

2. What is the probability of the spinner stopping on 3?

3. What is the probability of the spinner stopping on a white space?

4. What is the probability of the spinner stopping on a black space or an even number?

5. What is the probability of the spinner stopping on 6 or a white space?

10.4 Warm Up

There are three different colors of gumballs in a package, but not the same number of each color. Use the given probabilities of randomly selecting red and blue to find the missing probability if you know there are 24 gumballs in the package.

1. $P(\text{red}) = \frac{5}{24}$, $P(\text{blue}) = \frac{1}{3}$, $P(\text{green}) =$

2. $P(\text{red}) = \frac{1}{6}$, $P(\text{blue}) = \frac{1}{2}$, $P(\text{green or blue}) =$

10.4 Cumulative Review Warm Up

Write a rule for the nth term of the sequence.

1. 0, 3, 6, 9, 12, ...

2. $\frac{1}{4}, \frac{2}{6}, \frac{3}{8}, \frac{4}{10}, \frac{5}{12}, ...$

3. $-2, 4, -8, 16, -32, ...$

10.4 Practice A

In Exercises 1 and 2, events *A* and *B* are disjoint. Find *P*(*A* or *B*).

1. $P(A) = 0.4,\ P(B) = 0.2$

2. $P(A) = \frac{1}{3},\ P(B) = \frac{1}{2}$

3. At the high school swim meet, you and your friend are competing in the 50 Freestyle event. You estimate that there is a 40% chance you will win and a 35% chance your friend will win. What is the probability that you or your friend will win the 50 Freestyle event?

In Exercises 4 and 5, you roll a die. Find *P*(*A* or *B*).

4. **Event *A*:** Roll a 2.

   Event *B*: Roll an odd number.

5. **Event *A*:** Roll an even number.

   Event *B*: Roll a number greater than 3.

6. You bring your cat to the veterinarian for her yearly check-up. The veterinarian tells you that there is a 75% probability that your cat has a kidney disorder or is diabetic, with a 40% chance it has a kidney disorder and a 50% chance it is diabetic. What is the probability that your cat has both a kidney disorder and is diabetic?

7. A game show has three doors. A Grand Prize is behind one of the doors, a Nice Prize is behind one of the doors, and a Dummy Prize is behind one of the doors. You have been watching the show for a while and the table gives your estimates of the probabilities for the given scenarios.

	Door 1	Door 2	Door 3
Grand Prize	0.25	0.45	0.3
Nice Prize	0.4	0.25	0.35
Dummy Prize	0.35	0.3	0.35

   a. Find the probability that you win either the Grand Prize or a Nice Prize if you choose Door 1.

   b. Find the probability that you win either the Grand Prize or a Nice Prize if you choose Door 2.

   c. Find the probability that you win either the Grand Prize or a Nice Prize if you choose Door 3.

   d. Which door should you choose? Explain.

10.4 Practice B

In Exercises 1 and 2, events *A* and *B* are disjoint. Find *P(A or B)*.

1. $P(A) = 0.375,\ P(B) = 0.2$

2. $P(A) = \frac{1}{4},\ P(B) = \frac{1}{5}$

3. You are performing an experiment to determine how well pineapple plants grow in different soils. Out of the 40 pineapple plants, 16 are planted in sandy soil, 18 are planted in potting soil, and 7 are planted in a mixture of sandy soil and potting soil. What is the probability that a pineapple plant in the experiment is planted in sandy soil or potting soil?

In Exercises 4 and 5, you roll a die. Find *P(A or B)*.

4. **Event *A*:** Roll a prime number.

    Event *B*: Roll a number greater than 2.

5. **Event *A*:** Roll an even number.

    Event *B*: Roll an odd number.

6. An Educational Advisor estimates that there is a 90% probability that a freshman college student will take either a mathematics class or an English class, with an 80% probability that the student will take a mathematics class and a 75% probability that the student will take an English class. What is the probability that a freshman college student will take both a mathematics class and an English class?

7. A test diagnoses a disease correctly 92% of the time when a person has the disease and 80% of the time when the person does not have the disease. Approximately 4% of people in the United States have the disease. Fill in the probabilities along the branches of the probability tree diagram and then determine the probability that a randomly selected person is correctly diagnosed by the test.

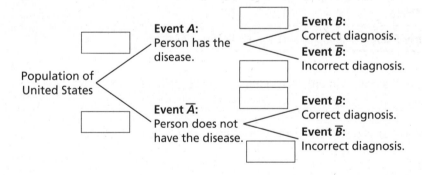

10.4 Enrichment and Extension

Probability of Disjoint and Overlapping Events

Use the formula for overlapping events to complete the exercises.

1. A certain drug causes a skin rash or hair loss in 35% of patients. Twenty-five percent of patients experience only a skin rash, and 5% experience both a skin rash and hair loss. A doctor wants to know the probability that a patient will experience hair loss only.

   a. Using A to represent "experiences a skin rash" and B to represent "experiences hair loss," write a symbolic representation of the problem.

   b. Using the symbolic representation from part (a), find the probability that a patient will experience hair loss only.

2. You and your friend recorded a compact disc together. The CD contained solos and duets. Your friend recorded twice as many duets as solos, and you recorded six more solos than duets. When a CD player selects one of these songs at random, the probability that it will select a duet is 25%. Let s represent the number of solos that your friend recorded.

   a. Write a rational equation to express the probability of randomly selecting a duet in terms of s.

   b. Solve the equation. Then determine the total number of songs recorded.

   c. Find the probability of selecting one of your solos or a duet when a CD player selects one song at random.

3. Police report that 78% of drivers stopped on suspicion of driving under the influence are given a breath test, 36% a blood test, and 22% both tests. What is the probability that a randomly selected driver suspected of driving under the influence is given a blood test or a breath test, but not both?

4. A bag contains 36 marbles, some of which are red and the rest are black. The black and red marbles are either clear or opaque. When a marble is randomly selected from the bag, the probability that it is red is $\frac{1}{4}$, that is is opaque is $\frac{7}{9}$, and that it is red or opaque is $\frac{11}{12}$.

   a. How many marbles are black?

   b. How many marbles are black and opaque?

10.4 Puzzle Time

What Are A Plumber's Favorite Shoes?

Write the letter of each answer in the box containing the exercise number.

Find the probability.

1. In a group of 25 students at lunch, 10 prefer ketchup on their hamburger, 10 prefer mustard on their hamburger, and 5 like both ketchup and mustard on their hamburger. The rest of the students in the group prefer neither. What is the probability that a student selected from this group will prefer ketchup or mustard on their hamburger?

2. A card is randomly selected from a standard deck of 52 cards. What is the probability that it is a 2 or an 8?

3. In a class of 50 high school juniors, 32 students either play a sport or are in the marching band. There are 22 juniors who play a sport and 16 who are in the marching band. What is the probability that a randomly selected junior plays a sport and is in the marching band?

4. You roll a die. What is the probability that you roll an even number or a 5?

5. You roll a die. What is the probability that you roll an odd number or a factor of 6?

Answers
O. $\dfrac{3}{25}$
L. $\dfrac{2}{13}$
G. $\dfrac{2}{3}$
C. $\dfrac{3}{5}$
S. $\dfrac{5}{6}$

1	2	3	4	5

10.5 Start Thinking

A die is rolled and then two coins are tossed. The possible outcomes are shown in the tree diagram below. How many outcomes are possible? What does each row in the tree diagram represent? What does each branch in the tree diagram represent? Describe two ways of determining the total number of outcomes from the tree diagram.

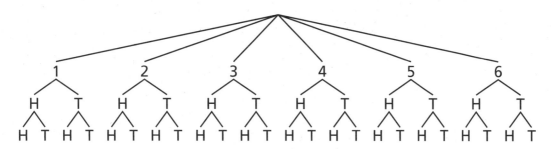

10.5 Warm Up

Count the number of different ways the letters can be arranged.

1. POP   **2.** TAP   **3.** NOON   **4.** KEEP

10.5 Cumulative Review Warm Up

Solve △*ABC*. Round your answers to four decimal places.

1.

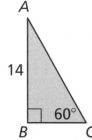

2.

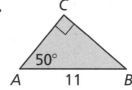

3.

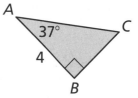

10.5   Practice A

In Exercises 1–3, find the number of ways that you can arrange (a) all of the letters and (b) 2 of the letters in the given word.

1. HAT
2. PORT
3. CHURN

In Exercises 4–9, evaluate the expression.

4. $_4P_3$
5. $_6P_2$
6. $_8P_1$

7. $_5P_4$
8. $_9P_5$
9. $_{11}P_0$

10. Fifteen sailboats are racing in a regatta. In how many different ways can three sailboats finish first, second, and third?

11. Your bowling team and your friend's bowling team are in a league with 6 other teams. In tonight's competition, find the probability that your friend's team finishes first and your team finishes second.

In Exercises 12 and 13, count the possible combinations of _r_ letters chosen from the given list.

12. H, I, J, K, L; $r = 3$
13. U, V, W, X, Y; $r = 2$

In Exercises 14–19, evaluate the expression.

14. $_6C_1$
15. $_7C_5$
16. $_8C_8$

17. $_9C_7$
18. $_{11}C_5$
19. $_{12}C_2$

20. You and your friends are ordering a 3-topping pizza. The pizzeria offers 8 different pizza toppings. How many combinations of 3 pizza toppings are possible?

In Exercises 21 and 22, tell whether the question can be answered using _permutations_ or _combinations_. Explain your reasoning. Then answer the question.

21. On a biology lab exam, there are 8 stations available. You must complete the labs at 6 of the 8 stations. In how many ways can you complete the exam?

22. Your committee is voting on their logo. There are 7 possible logos and you are to rank your top 3 logos. In how many ways can you rank your top 3 logos?

10.5 Practice B

In Exercises 1–3, find the number of ways that you can arrange (a) all of the letters and (b) 2 of the letters in the given word.

1. SMILE
2. POLITE
3. WONDERFUL

In Exercises 4–9, evaluate the expression.

4. $_6P_4$
5. $_{12}P_1$
6. $_{10}P_7$

7. $_{11}P_0$
8. $_{25}P_2$
9. $_{20}P_6$

10. You have textbooks for 7 different classes. In how many different ways can you arrange them together on your bookshelf?

11. You make wristbands for Team Spirit Week. Each wristband has a bead containing a letter of the word COLTS. You randomly draw one of the 8 beads from a cup. Find the probability that COLTS is spelled correctly when you draw the beads.

In Exercises 12 and 13, count the possible combinations of *r* letters chosen from the given list.

12. P, Q, R, S, T, U; $r = 2$
13. G, H, I, J, K, L; $r = 4$

In Exercises 14–19, evaluate the expression.

14. $_9C_1$
15. $_7C_7$
16. $_{10}C_4$

17. $_{13}C_7$
18. $_{14}C_8$
19. $_{25}C_5$

In Exercises 20 and 21, tell whether the question can be answered using *permutations* or *combinations*. Explain your reasoning. Then answer the question.

20. Ninety-five tri-athletes are competing in a triathlon. In how many ways can 3 tri-athletes finish in first, second, and third place?

21. Your band director is choosing 6 seniors to represent your band at the Band Convention. There are 44 seniors in the band. In how many groupings can the band director choose 6 seniors?

In Exercises 22–24, use the Binomial Theorem to write the binomial expansion.

22. $(x + 3)^4$
23. $(2m - 5)^3$
24. $(3s + t)^5$

10.5 Enrichment and Extension

Permutations and Combinations

As you learned, a *permutation* is an arrangement of objects in a specific order. Sometimes there are also other conditions that must be satisfied. In such cases, you should deal with the special conditions first.

Example: Using the letters in the word *square*, how many 6-letter arrangements with no repetitions are possible if vowels and consonants alternate, beginning with a vowel?

Of the 6 letters in the word, 3 are vowels (u, a, e) and 3 are consonants (s, q, r).

Beginning with a vowel, every other slot is to be filled by a vowel. There are 3 such slots and 3 vowels to be arranged in them.

$$\underline{3} \times \underline{} \times \underline{2} \times \underline{} \times \underline{1} \times \underline{}$$

The remaining 3 slots have 3 consonants to be arranged in them.

$$\underline{3} \times \underline{3} \times \underline{2} \times \underline{2} \times \underline{1} \times \underline{1}$$

Multiply to determine the total number of arrangements.

There are 36 possible arrangements.

The girls Amy, Ann, and Doris and the boys Al, Aaron, Bob, and Roy are in a nursery group. Determine the number of ways the children can be arranged in a line with the following conditions.

1. A girl is always at the head of the line.

2. Roy is always at the head of the line.

3. A child whose name begins with A is always at the head of the line.

4. A child whose name begins with A is always at the head and the rear of the line.

The diamond suit from a standard deck of 52 playing cards is removed from the deck, shuffled, and laid out in a row. Determine the number of possible arrangements.

5. The first card is the ace.

6. The first card is a face card.

Use the digits 0, 1, 2, 3, 4 without repetition. Determine the number of ways to form each arrangement.

7. 3-digit numerals whose values are at least 100.

8. 4-digit numerals whose values are at least 1000 and less than 4000.

9. 4-digit numerals whose values are at least 2000 and less than 3000.

10.5 Puzzle Time

Why Was The Pantry So Good At Telling The Future?

Write the letter of each answer in the box containing the exercise number.

Evaluate the expression.

1. $_3P_1$

2. $_7P_3$

3. $_{10}P_4$

4. $_{21}P_4$

5. $_9P_6$

6. $_{11}P_8$

7. $_{15}P_3$

8. $_6P_6$

9. $_5C_2$

10. $_{30}C_{28}$

11. $_{15}C_9$

12. $_8C_4$

13. $_{19}C_{14}$

14. $_8C_8$

15. $_{44}C_{41}$

16. $_9C_4$

17. $_{28}C_{25}$

18. $_{20}C_{15}$

19. A row contains five empty desks. How many different ways could five students sit in the desks in the row?

20. Sixteen students are competing in the 100-yard dash. In how many different ways can the students finish first, second, and third?

Answers	
E. 60,480	**T.** 435
I. 3	**K.** 5040
W. 6,652,800	**O.** 15,504
H. 720	**A.** 10
W. 5005	**A.** 70
R. 120	**T.** 210
S. 11,628	**I.** 1
T. 3276	**N.** 143,640
N. 13,244	**S.** 126
W. 2730	**E.** 3360

1	2		3	4	5	6		7	8	9	10		11	12	13	

14	15		16	17	18	19	20

10.6 Start Thinking

The spinner in the diagram is spun twice. An outcome is identified as the sum of the two spins, so there are seven possible outcomes. Complete the chart to determine the frequency of each outcome. Do you notice a pattern in the chart?

$$
\begin{array}{c}
\quad 2+1 \\
1+1\quad 1+2 \\
\hline
2\quad3\quad4\quad5\quad6\quad7\quad8
\end{array}
$$

Sum of the two spins

Frequency

10.6 Warm Up

Evaluate the expression without the use of a calculator.

1. $_4C_2$ **2.** $_7C_1$ **3.** $_5C_0$ **4.** $_9C_4$

5. $_8C_8$ **6.** $_{11}C_{10}$ **7.** $_6C_3$ **8.** $_{10}C_2$

10.6 Cumulative Review Warm Up

Identify the amplitude and the period of the function.

1. $y = 2\cos(3x)$ **2.** $y = 3 - \sin\left(\dfrac{\pi x}{4}\right)$

3. $y = \dfrac{4}{3}\sin(3x - \pi)$ **4.** $y = \cos(x) + 8$

5. $y = \dfrac{1}{2}\sin(x - 4)$ **6.** $y = 3.8\cos(1.5x + 7)$

Name_____ Date_____

In Exercises 1 and 2, make a table and draw a histogram showing the probability distribution for the random variable.

1. X = the letter that is spun on a wheel that contains 2 sections labeled "A," five sections labeled "B," and 1 section labeled "C."

2. F = the type of fruit randomly chosen from a bowl that contains three apples, four pears, and four oranges.

In Exercises 3 and 4, use the probability distribution to determine (a) the number that is most likely to be spun on a spinner, and (b) the probability of spinning an even number.

3.
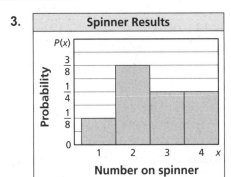

4.
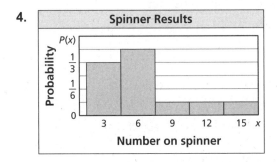

In Exercises 5–7, calculate the probability of flipping a coin 20 times and getting the given number of heads.

5. 2   6. 7   7. 14

8. Describe and correct the error in calculating the probability of rolling a five exactly four times in six rolls of a six-sided number cube.

$$\times \quad P(k = 4) = {}_6C_4\left(\frac{1}{6}\right)^4\left(\frac{5}{6}\right)^6 \approx 0.0039$$

10.6 Practice B

In Exercises 1 and 2, make a table and draw a histogram showing the probability distribution for the random variable.

1. $V = 1$ if a randomly chosen letter consists only of line segments (i.e. A, E, F, …) and 2 otherwise (i.e. B, C, D, G, …).

2. $X =$ the number of digits in a random perfect square from 1 to 1225.

In Exercises 3–5, calculate the probability of flipping a coin 20 times and getting the given number of heads.

3. 3

4. 15

5. 18

6. According to a survey, 22% of high school students watch at most five movies a month. You ask seven randomly chosen high school students whether they watch at most five movies a month.

   a. Draw a histogram of the binomial distribution for your survey.

   b. What is the most likely outcome of your survey?

   c. What is the probability that at most three people watch at most five movies a month.

7. Describe and correct the error in calculating the probability of rolling a four exactly five times in six rolls of a six-sided number cube.

$$ \text{✗} \quad P(k = 4) = {}_6C_4\left(\frac{1}{6}\right)^4\left(\frac{5}{6}\right)^{6-4} \approx 0.008 $$

8. A cereal company claims that there is a prize in one out of five boxes of cereal.

   a. You purchase 5 boxes of the cereal. You open four of the boxes and do not get a prize. Evaluate the validity of this statement: "The first four boxes did not have a prize, so the next one will probably have a prize."

   b. What is the probability of opening four boxes without a prize and then a box with a prize?

   c. What is the probability of opening all five boxes and not getting a prize?

   d. What is the probability of opening all five boxes and getting five prizes?

10.6 Enrichment and Extension

Binomial Distributions

You can find the mean and standard deviation of a binomial distribution using the following formulas: Mean: $\mu = np$ and Standard Deviation: $\sigma = \sqrt{np(1 - p)}$.
Sometimes the mean is referred to as the average or expected value when referenced in problems.

Example: Ninety percent of the people who open a checking account at a particular bank keep the account open at least one year. A random sample of 20 new accounts is taken and the bank looks at how many will be kept open for at least one year. What are the expected value and standard deviation of the distribution?

Mean (expected value): $\mu = np = 20 \bullet 0.90 = 18$

Standard Deviation: $\sigma = \sqrt{np(1 - p)} = \sqrt{20 \bullet 0.90 \bullet 0.10} \approx 1.34$

Complete the exercises using your knowledge of the binomial distribution.

1. An Olympic archer is able to hit the bull's-eye 80% of the time. Assume that each shot is independent of the others. If she shoots six arrows, find the following.

   a. The mean and standard deviation of the number of bull's-eyes she may get.

   b. The probability she gets at most four bull's-eyes.

   c. The probability she gets at least four bull's-eyes.

   d. The probability she misses the bull's-eye at least once.

2. It is generally believed that nearsightedness affects about 12% of all children. A school district tests the vision of 169 incoming kindergarten children. How many would you expect to be nearsighted? What is the standard deviation?

3. At a certain college, 6% of all students come from outside the United States. Incoming students are assigned at random to freshman dorms, where students live in residential clusters of 40 freshmen sharing a common lounge area. How many international students would you expect to find in a typical cluster? What is the standard deviation?

4. The degree to which democratic and non-democratic countries attempt to control the news media was examined in the *Journal of Peace Research* (Nov. 1997). Between 1948 and 1996, 80% of all democratic regimes allowed a free press. In contrast, over the same time period, 10% of all non-democratic regimes allowed a free press. In a random sample of 50 democratic regimes, how many would you expect to allow a free press? What is the standard deviation?

10.6 Puzzle Time

What Did The Police Do With The Hamburger?

Write the letter of each answer in the box containing the exercise number.

Use the probability distribution to determine the probability.

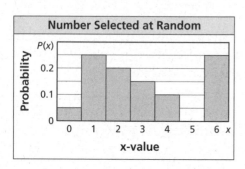

Answers	
L.	80%
M.	100%
I.	1.5%
G.	1 or 6
I.	40%
L.	5
E.	25%
R.	60%
D.	75%
H.	0%

1. What is the most likely number to be selected?

2. What is the probability of selecting an even number?

3. What is the probability of selecting a multiple of three?

4. What is the least likely number to be selected?

5. What is the probability of selecting a number other than two?

6. What is the probability of selecting a three or four?

7. What is the probability of selecting a number that is no greater than four?

8. What is the probability of selecting a five?

9. What is the probability of selecting a three, replacing it, then selecting a four?

10. What is the probability of selecting a number that is not less than zero?

1	2	3	4	5	6	7		8	9	10

Chapter 10 Cumulative Review

In Exercises 1–10, write and solve a proportion to answer the question.

1. What percent of 80 is 14?

2. What number is 74% of 78?

3. 25.2 is what percent of 35?

4. What percent of 48 is 9?

5. What number is 45% of 63?

6. 15.68 is what percent of 98?

7. What percent of 120 is 45?

8. What number is 32% of 230?

9. 12.1 is what percent of 55?

10. What percent of 68 is 57.8?

Draw a Venn diagram of the set described.

11. Of the positive numbers less than or equal to 9, set A consists of the factors of 9 and set B consists of all odd numbers.

12. Of the positive numbers less than or equal to 13, set A consists of all odd numbers and set B consists of all prime numbers.

13. Of the positive numbers less than or equal to 36, set A consists of all the multiples of 2 and set B consists of all the multiples of 3.

14. Of all positive numbers less than or equal to 24, set A consists of the factors of 24 and set B consists of all even numbers.

15. Of all positive numbers less than or equal to 36, set A consists of all the multiples of 3 and set B consists of all factors of 36.

16. Of all positive numbers less than or equal to 14, set A consists of all even numbers and set B consists of all factors of 14.

17. Your history test has 55 questions. You get 48 questions correct. What is the percent of correct answers? Round your answer to the nearest tenth of a percent.

18. Your English test has 25 questions. You get 23 questions correct. What is the percent of incorrect answers? Round your answer to the nearest tenth of a percent.

19. Your biology test has 35 questions.

   a. You get 29 questions correct. What is the percent of correct answers? Round your answer to the nearest tenth of a percent.

   b. Your friend gets 31 questions correct. What is the percent of correct answers for your friend? Round your answer to the nearest tenth of a percent.

   c. How much better did your friend do on the test?

Chapter 10 Cumulative Review (continued)

In Exercises 20–33, describe the transformation of $f(x) = x^2$ represented by g.
Then graph the function.

20. $g(x) = x^2 - 1$

21. $g(x) = x^2 + 9$

22. $g(x) = x^2 - 5$

23. $g(x) = (x - 3)^2$

24. $g(x) = (x + 6)^2$

25. $g(x) = (x - 4)^2$

26. $g(x) = (x + 9)^2 - 3$

27. $g(x) = (x - 2)^2 - 6$

28. $g(x) = (x + 5)^2 + 8$

29. $g(x) = -x^2$

30. $g(x) = 4x^2$

31. $g(x) = -3x^2$

32. $g(x) = \frac{1}{4}x^2$

33. $g(x) = -\frac{1}{2}x^2$

In Exercises 34–43, determine the vertex and axis of symmetry.

34. $f(x) = (x + 5)^2$

35. $g(x) = (x - 9)^2$

36. $h(x) = x^2 + 4$

37. $f(x) = x^2 - 5$

38. $h(x) = (x + 8)^2 + 1$

39. $g(x) = (x - 3)^2 + 8$

40. $f(x) = -2x^2 + 7$

41. $g(x) = 3(x + 1)^2 - 1$

42. $h(x) = \frac{1}{2}(x - 6)^2 - 7$

43. $g(x) = -2(x - 8)^2 - 6$

In Exercises 44–47, find the value of x.

44. Area of square = 49

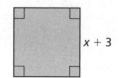

$x + 3$

45. Area of rectangle = 32

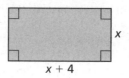

x

$x + 4$

46. Area of circle = 36π

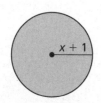

$x + 1$

47. Area of square = 81

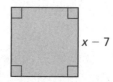

$x - 7$

Chapter 10 **Cumulative Review** (continued)

In Exercises 48–53, simplify the radical expression.

48. $\sqrt{-144}$

49. $\sqrt{-49}$

50. $5\sqrt{-100}$

51. $-12\sqrt{-121}$

52. $4\sqrt{-500}$

53. $-3\sqrt{-128}$

In Exercises 54–59, add or subtract. Write the answer in standard form.

54. $(8 - 14i) - (9 - 5i)$

55. $(-6 + 6i) + (-3 - 14i)$

56. $(3 + 8i) + (3 + 2i)$

57. $(3 - 14i) - (-5 + 9i)$

58. $(-5 + 6i) + (5 - 8i)$

59. $10 + (18 + 5i) - 11$

In Exercises 60–65, multiply. Write the answer in standard form.

60. $15i(1 + 10i)$

61. $-6i(5 + 8i)$

62. $(6 - 14i)(7 - 6i)$

63. $(2 + 15i)(-11 - 12i)$

64. $(17 - 17i)^2$

65. $(10 + 12i)^2$

In Exercises 66–71, evaluate the expression without using a calculator.

66. $81^{1/4}$

67. $256^{1/4}$

68. $125^{1/3}$

69. $36^{3/2}$

70. $216^{2/3}$

71. $81^{3/4}$

In Exercises 72–77, evaluate the expression using a calculator. Round your answer to two decimal places when appropriate.

72. $9^{1/3}$

73. $28^{-1/4}$

74. $6561^{1/4}$

75. $18^{2/3}$

76. $32,768^{1/5}$

77. $27^{5/3}$

In Exercises 78–83, simplify the expression.

78. $e^4 \cdot e^6$

79. $e^{-2} \cdot e^{10}$

80. $\dfrac{12e^7}{2e^{-2}}$

81. $\dfrac{9e^8}{3e^{-10}}$

82. $\left(4e^{12x}\right)^3$

83. $\left(3e^{-2x}\right)^6$

Chapter 10 Cumulative Review (continued)

In Exercises 84–91, write the first six terms of the sequence.

84. $a_n = n + 7$ **85.** $f(n) = 4 - n$

86. $a_n = -8 + n$ **87.** $f(n) = n^3$

88. $a_n = n^3 - 2$ **89.** $a_n = n^2 - 3$

90. $f(n) = (n - 7)^2$ **91.** $f(n) = (n + 1)^2$

In Exercises 92–100, find the sum.

92. $\displaystyle\sum_{i=1}^{4} 4i$ **93.** $\displaystyle\sum_{m=0}^{9} m^2$ **94.** $\displaystyle\sum_{h=1}^{5} 2h^2$

95. $\displaystyle\sum_{k=4}^{9} (3k + 1)$ **96.** $\displaystyle\sum_{n=2}^{7} (-4n + 5)$ **97.** $\displaystyle\sum_{d=3}^{5} \frac{d}{d + 2}$

98. $\displaystyle\sum_{z=7}^{9} \frac{z - 2}{z}$ **99.** $\displaystyle\sum_{f=8}^{13} 2$ **100.** $\displaystyle\sum_{f=6}^{12} 3f^2$

101. You want to save $300 for a new bicycle. You begin by saving one penny on the first day. You save an additional penny each day after that. For example, you will save two pennies on the second day, three pennies on the third day, and so on.

     a. How much money will you have saved after 50 days?

     b. Use a series to determine how many days it takes you to save $350.

102. A dance team is arranged in rows on a stage. The first row has three dancers, and each row after the first has one more dancer than the row before it.

     a. Write a rule for the number of dancers in the nth row.

     b. How many dancers are on the stage with six rows?

     c. How many dancers are on the stage with seven rows?

     d. How many more dancers are on stage where there are seven rows, compared to when there are six rows?

Chapter 11

Chapter 11 Data Analysis and Statistics

Dear Family,

What types of surveys have you participated in? Did you volunteer for the survey or did the surveyor contact you? The Internet has changed the way we do business with each other. Examples include buying and selling merchandise, researching contractors to hire, and restaurants to eat at. Within an online community, there is a reputation system in place such that the consumer can rate a product, service, packaging, and more. Other consumers use this information to decide whether or not to trust a store, buy a product, or make a purchase. Most places use a five-star rating system such that five is the best and one is the worst.

As a family, discuss the following questions:

- What are the benefits of the reputation system?

- What are the drawbacks of the reputation system?

- What stores have you rated?

- What products have you rated?

- Does the rating system help you when you are making a decision?

- What are some things to consider when comparing the ratings of different products or stores?

- What are some strategies business owners can do to boost their ratings?

People who leave feedback are a self-selected sample, so the ratings may be biased. In this chapter, you will learn about the different ways to conduct an experiment by choosing a sample of the population, collecting the data, and analyzing the data. From the data, you can make predictions about the population.

The next time you buy something online, remember to leave feedback for other consumers!

Capítulo 11 · Análisis de datos y estadística

Estimada familia:

¿En qué tipos de encuestas han participado? ¿Se ofrecieron a responder la encuesta o el encuestador los contactó? Internet ha cambiado la manera en que hacemos negocios con los demás. Entre los ejemplos, se incluyen comprar y vender mercadería, investigar contratistas para contratar o restaurantes donde comer. Dentro de una comunidad en línea, hay un sistema de reputación para que el comprador pueda calificar un producto, servicio, embalaje y más. Otros compradores usan esta información para decidir si confían o no en una tienda, compran un producto o hacen una compra. La mayoría de los lugares usan un sistema de calificación de cinco estrellas, donde cinco es el mejor y uno es el peor.

En familia, comenten las siguientes preguntas:

- ¿Cuáles son los beneficios de un sistema de reputación?

- ¿Cuáles son las desventajas de un sistema de reputación?

- ¿Qué tiendas ustedes han calificado?

- ¿Qué productos ustedes han calificado?

- ¿El sistema de calificación los ayuda cuando están por tomar una decisión?

- ¿Cuáles son algunas cosas a considerar cuando comparan las calificaciones de diferentes productos o tiendas?

- ¿Cuáles son algunas estrategias que pueden implementar los dueños de los negocios para aumentar sus calificaciones?

Las personas que dejan comentarios son una muestra autoseleccionada, entonces las calificaciones pueden ser tendenciosas. En este capítulo, aprenderán sobre las diferentes maneras de llevar a cabo un experimento eligiendo una muestra de población, recopilando datos y analizando los datos. A partir de los datos, pueden hacer predicciones sobre la población.

La próxima vez que compren algo en línea, ¡recuerden dejar un comentario para otros compradores!

11.1 Start Thinking

The scores for a recent calculus test are shown in the table. Find the mean of the data set and complete the frequency table using the described intervals. Use your frequency table to create a histogram. Does your histogram appear to have a symmetric distribution?

Calculus Test Scores

54	70	78	84
56	72	79	84
60	72	79	87
62	75	80	90
68	76	83	91

Score	Frequency
50–59	
60–69	
70–79	
80–89	
90–99	

11.1 Warm Up

Find the mean and the median of the data set. Round to the nearest hundredth, when necessary.

1. 18, 22, 15, 12, 25, 13, 21, 16, 22, 17

2. 120, 140, 108, 115, 116, 135, 121

3. 1.8, 4.5, 3.2, 6.1, 4.7, 5.1, 4.3, 5.7

11.1 Cumulative Review Warm Up

Write a function $g(x)$ whose graph represents the transformation of the graph of $f(x) = |x|$.

1.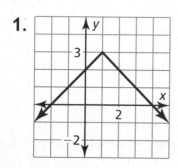

2.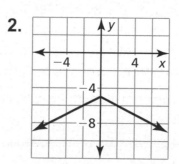

Name_____ Date_____

In Exercises 1 and 2, give the percent of the area under the normal curve represented by the shaded region.

1.

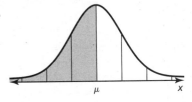

2.

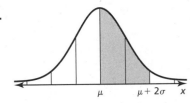

In Exercises 3–5, a normal distribution has mean μ and standard deviation σ. Find the indicated probability for a randomly selected x-value from the distribution.

3. $P(x \geq \mu + 3\sigma)$ 4. $P(x \geq \mu - 3\sigma)$ 5. $P(\mu - 2\sigma \leq x \leq \mu)$

In Exercises 6–8, a normal distribution has a mean of 28 and a standard deviation of 3. Find the probability that a randomly selected x-value from the distribution is in the given interval.

6. between 25 and 31   7. between 22 and 28   8. at least 31

9. The scores on an entrance mathematics exam are normally distributed with a mean of 76 and a standard deviation of 9.

   a. About what percent of students have scores between 67 and 94?

   b. About what percent of students have scores above 85?

10. A normal distribution has a mean of 18 and a standard deviation of 3. Describe and correct the error in finding the probability that a randomly selected x-value is in the given interval.

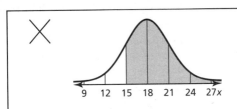

The probability that x is at least 15 is 0.8385.

11.1 Practice B

In Exercises 1 and 2, give the percent of the area under the normal curve represented by the shaded region.

1.

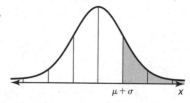

2.

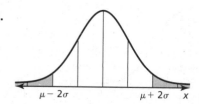

In Exercises 3–5, a normal distribution has mean μ and standard deviation σ. Find the indicated probability for a randomly selected x-value from the distribution.

3. $P(x \geq \mu - 2\sigma)$

4. $P(\mu - \sigma \leq x \leq \mu + 3\sigma)$

5. $P(\mu + \sigma \leq x \leq \mu + 2\sigma)$

In Exercises 6–8, a normal distribution has a mean of 28 and a standard deviation of 3. Find the probability that a randomly selected x-value from the distribution is in the given interval.

6. between 19 and 34

7. at most 31

8. at least 34

9. The times a restaurant takes to prepare its "quick lunch" specials are normally distributed with a mean of 3 minutes and a standard deviation of 0.5 minute.

   a. About what percent of customers have their "quick lunch" between 2 minutes and 4 minutes?

   b. About what percent of customers have their "quick lunch" in fewer than 2 minutes?

10. A normal distribution has a mean of 18 and a standard deviation of 3. Describe and correct the error in finding the probability that a randomly selected x-value is in the given interval.

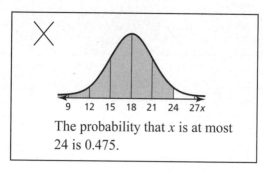

The probability that x is at most 24 is 0.475.

Name_____ Date_____

11.1 Enrichment and Extension

Using Normal Distributions

Pearson's Coefficient of Skewness is a measure drawn from a frequency distribution to measure the direction of variation. It is a measure of how far positively skewed (below the mean) or negatively skewed (above the mean) the majority of the data lies. It is useful when conducting a study using histograms.

Pearson first came up with the formula $P = \dfrac{3(\overline{X} - \text{mode})}{s}$, where $\overline{X}$ is the mean and s is the standard deviation.

Then he also created the formula $P = \dfrac{3(\overline{X} - \text{median})}{s}$.

If the index is between -1 and 1, then the distribution is approximately symmetric. If the index is less than -1 then it is skewed to the left, and if it is more than 1, then it is skewed to the right.

Use the formula containing the median to show the skewness of the data.

1. the price (in cents per pound) of bananas reported from 14 markets surveyed by the U.S. Department of Agriculture:

51	52	45	48	53	52	50
49	52	48	43	46	45	42

2. the change in score (Friday–Monday) of 25 students who were given a vocabulary test on Friday and then retested when they returned to school on Monday:

6	0	−1	10	4
5	4	4	9	2
13	3	3	0	7
3	−2	4	9	9
9	6	−5	11	1

3. the number of pieces of mail received at a school office for 36 days:

112	70	90	551	115	97	80	78	72
100	128	130	52	103	138	66	135	76
112	92	93	143	900	88	218	118	106
110	75	60	95	131	559	710	405	685

Name_____ Date _____

11.1 Puzzle Time

What is Moby Dick's Favorite Dinner?

Write the letter of each answer in the box containing the exercise number.

**A normal distribution has mean μ and standard deviation σ.
Find the indicated probability for a randomy selected x-value
from the distribution.**

1. $P(x \geq \mu + \sigma)$

2. $P(x \geq \mu - 2\sigma)$

3. $P(x \leq \mu - 2\sigma)$

4. $P(\mu - 2\sigma \leq x \leq \mu + 2\sigma)$

5. $P(x \leq \mu + 3\sigma)$

**A normal distribution has a mean of 24 and a standard deviation
of 3. Find the probability that a randomly selected x-value from
the distribution is in the given interval.**

6. between 18 and 27

7. between 21 and 33

8. between 24 and 33

9. at least 27

10. at most 15

11. not greater than 24

12. not less than 18

Answers
S. 2.5%
A. 99.85%
F. 16%
H. 95%
S. 97.5%
N. 81.5%
S. 49.85%
I. 97.5%
I. 0.15%
H. 16%
D. 83.85%
P. 50%

1	2	3	4		5	6	7		8	9	10	11	12

11.2 Start Thinking

When three coins are tossed, what is the theoretical probability that all three will land heads up? Conduct an experiment to verify your answer. How many times did you have to toss the three coins before you got all heads? Compare your results with your classmates and discuss how the experimental probability relates to the theoretical probability. What would you expect to be the relationship between the two probabilities as you increase the number of times you toss the coins?

11.2 Warm Up

Describe the sample space for the experiment.

1. A card is drawn from a regular deck of 52 cards.

2. A spinner that contains four colors, red, blue, yellow and green, is spun twice.

3. Each member of your class is asked if they want to participate in a mud run.

4. For one full day, patients at a clinic are asked if the wait time is acceptable.

11.2 Cumulative Review Warm Up

Solve the system of linear equations.

1. $2x - y = 8$
   $x + 3y = 4$

2. $x - y = 8$
   $-2x + 2y = -16$

3. $3x + 5y = -1$
   $-2x + 3y = 7$

4. $\dfrac{1}{2}x - \dfrac{2}{3}y = \dfrac{5}{2}$
   $\dfrac{1}{4}x + \dfrac{4}{3}y = 0$

5. $y = -\dfrac{1}{2}x + 5$
   $y = \dfrac{7}{2}x - 11$

6. $y = x$
   $y = -x$

11.2 Practice A

In Exercises 1 and 2, determine whether the data is collected from a population or a sample. Explain your reasoning.

1. the number of popcorn kernels in 25 bags of popcorn

2. the college degrees of every employee at the hospital

In Exercises 3 and 4, identify the population and sample. Describe the sample.

3. In a university, a survey of 1641 students found that 479 of them do not know the name of their college's mascot.

4. In the United States, a survey of 1000 households with at least one child found that 874 of them have at least two computers.

In Exercises 5 and 6, determine whether the numerical value is a parameter or a statistic. Explain your reasoning.

5. On a high school football team, 2% of the players are vegetarians.

6. The average amount of the surveyed utility bills is $176.42.

7. You roll a six-sided die 5 times and get all ones. The probability of this happening is, $\left(\frac{1}{6}\right)^5 \approx 0.0001286$, so you suspect this die favors ones. The die maker claims the die does not favor ones. You simulate rolling the die 30 times by repeatedly drawing 100 samples of size 30. The histogram shows the results.

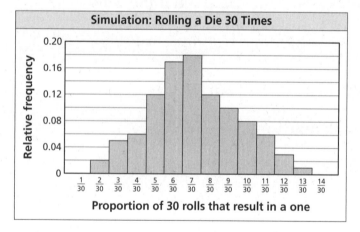

a. What should you conclude when you roll the actual die 30 times and get 6 ones?

b. What should you conclude when you roll the actual die 30 times and get 12 ones?

Name_____ Date_____

In Exercises 1 and 2, determine whether the data is collected from a population or a sample. Explain your reasoning.

1. the address of every student in the school

2. a survey of 80 people who access a website

In Exercises 3 and 4, identify the population and sample. Describe the sample.

3. In an office building, a survey of 648 employees found that 147 of them ride the subway to work each day.

4. In Florida, a survey of 2500 homeowners found that 1145 of them have switched their homeowner's insurance policy to a different company within the last 3 years.

In Exercises 5 and 6, determine whether the numerical value is a parameter or a statistic. Explain your reasoning.

5. Thirty-four percent of the surveyed hockey players first played hockey before their 10th birthday.

6. Eighty-two percent of all the tickets sold were for the Saturday matinee.

7. You roll a six-sided die 8 times and get either threes or fours. The probability of this happening is $\left(\dfrac{2}{6}\right)^8 \approx 0.0001524$, so you suspect this die favors threes and fours.

   The die maker claims the die does not favor threes or fours. You simulate rolling the die 30 times by repeatedly drawing 200 samples of size 30. The histogram shows the results.

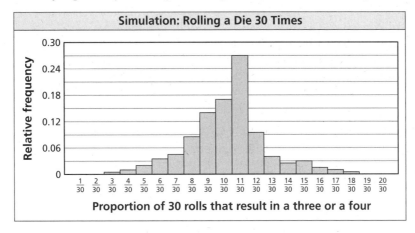

   a. What should you conclude when you roll the actual die 30 times and get 5 threes and fours?

   b. What should you conclude when you roll the actual die 30 times and get 10 threes and fours?

11.2 Enrichment and Extension

Populations, Samples, and Hypotheses

If you decide that a hypothesis is false when the hypothesis is true, this is called a Type I error. If you decide that a hypothesis is true when the hypothesis is false, this is called a Type II error. In experiments, the researcher often has to decide which error is worse.

For each of the following (a) state the Type I and Type II errors, (b) state the consequences of each error, and (c) decide which one is more serious. Explain.

Example: Researchers tested a new drug for migraine headaches against a placebo in a cross-over design. Can you conclude that the majority of the patients had better pain relief with the new drug? The hypothesis is that the new drug is not better.

Solution: a and b. Type I: Decide the new drug is better when it really is not; Consequence: Migraine patients use a pain medication that is not better than the current one on the market and do not get the necessary pain relief; Type II: Decide the new drug is not better when it really is better; Consequence: Migraine patients do not get to use a better pain medication.

c. Either could be argued, but probably Type I is more serious because people are not getting relief.

1. A recent study considered whether daily consumption of 1200 milligrams of garlic could reduce tick bites. This was tested against a placebo in a cross-over design. The hypothesis is that garlic is not effective in reducing tick bites.

2. Production managers on an assembly line must monitor the output to be sure that the level of defective products remains small. They periodically inspect a random sample of the items produced. If they find a significant increase in the proportion of items that must be rejected, they will halt the assembly process until the problem can be identified and repaired. The hypothesis is that there are not too many defects.

3. A clean air standard requires that vehicle exhaust emissions not exceed specified limits for various pollutants. Many states require that cars be tested annually to be sure they meet these standards. Suppose state regulators double-check a random sample of cars that a suspect repair shop has certified as okay. The hypothesis is that the shop is meeting car standards.

4. A statistics professor has observed that for several years about 13% of students who initially enroll in his Introductory Statistics course withdraw before the end of the semester. A salesperson suggests that he try a statistic software package that gets students more involved with computers, predicting that it will cut the dropout rate. The software is expensive, and the salesperson offers to let the professor use it for a semester to see if the dropout rate goes down significantly. The hypothesis is that the dropout rate does not decrease.

Name_____ Date _____

11.2 Puzzle Time

Where Do You Find Canada?

Write the letter of each answer in the box containing the exercise number.

Determine whether the data are collected from a population or a sample.

1. a survey of 400 high school sophomores at a school with 842 sophomores

2. the number of people 65 or older in the United States

Identify the population and sample.

3. In the United States, a survey of 5000 high school seniors found that 3284 of them plan on attending a 4-year university following graduation.

4. In the United States, a survey of 2500 homeowners with a monthly mortgage payment found that 1280 of them have refinanced their mortgage within the last five years.

5. In a school district, a survey of 1000 middle school students found that 894 of them participate in an extracurricular activity.

6. A survey of 5000 elementary students found that 1974 of them have cell phones.

Answers

P. Population: All elementary students; Sample: 5000 elementary students in the survey

M. Population: All homeowners with mortgage payments in the United States; Sample: 2500 homeowners in the survey

O. sample

A. Population: All high school seniors in the United States; Sample: 5000 high school seniors in the survey

N. population

A. population: All middle school students in the school district; Sample: 1000 middle school students in the survey

1	2		3		4	5	6

The purpose of a statistical study is to collect data so that an informed and reliable decision can be made. In each of the scenerios described below, determine if a random survey of 50 students from your school would provide good information for making a realiable decision.

1. The school board wants to make a decision about allocating funds for a robotics team at your school.

2. The Student Government Association at your school wants to know if families would be interested in participating in a school carnival.

11.3 Warm Up

Explain why the sample might be biased.

1. Twenty pet owners are surveyed at a veterinary clinic to determine if pets should be permitted in hotel rooms.

2. One hundred shoppers are asked if the mall hours should be extended.

3. Fifty high school students are surveyed to determine if the amount of homework should be decreased.

4. Twenty members of an athletic club were surveyed to determine how many times the average American exercises each week.

11.3 Cumulative Review Warm Up

Graph the function.

1. $y = \dfrac{2}{x - 5}$ 2. $y = \dfrac{3}{x + 2} - 1$ 3. $y = \dfrac{2x - 1}{x + 4}$

11.3 Practice A

In Exercises 1 and 2, identify the type of sample described.

1. A bank wants to know whether its drive-thru customers are satisfied with the service. Customers receive a code on their receipt that allows them to go online and fill out a survey.

2. A school wants to know whether high school teachers prefer before-school or after-school faculty meetings. Ten teachers with classrooms near the front office are surveyed.

In Exercises 3 and 4, identify the type of sample and explain why the sample is biased.

3. Every fifth customer who walks into a locally owned hardware store answers a survey that asks for opinions about lowering taxes for locally owned businesses to increase the likelihood that they can stay open for business.

4. A fitness center wants to find out whether its members would sign up for an afternoon yoga class. It surveys the first twenty members on the alphabetized membership list.

In Exercises 5 and 6, determine whether the sample is biased. Explain your reasoning.

5. Every fourth passenger who boards an airplane is asked whether they like the new method of seat assignment.

6. Your teacher is choosing 4 students to participate in a pizza-eating contest. The names of all 30 students are put in a hat and four names are randomly drawn from the hat.

In Exercises 7 and 8, explain why the survey question may be biased or otherwise introduce bias into the survey. Then describe a way to correct the flaw.

7. A guidance counselor asks high school students, "Do you miss school often?"

8. "The fish being caught in our lake are found to have lesions, which could be toxic when eaten. Do you think the city should address this health problem?"

11.3 Practice B

In Exercises 1 and 2, identify the type of sample described.

1. An amphitheater wants to know if Saturday morning concerts would be attended. The amphitheater is divided into 30 different seating areas. It surveys all the members in five randomly selected seating areas.

2. The manager of an orange juice plant wants to test the quality of the plant's new extra-pulp orange juice. She does a taste test of every twentieth container of extra-pulp orange juice.

In Exercises 3 and 4, identify the type of sample and explain why the sample is biased.

3. A town council wants to know whether residents support lower taxes for those who own waterfront property. Thirty-four owners of waterfront property are surveyed.

4. A local radio station is considering switching from country music to classical music. Randomly throughout the day it announces the phone number and website where listeners can go to place their vote for either country music or classical music.

In Exercises 5 and 6, determine whether the sample is biased. Explain your reasoning.

5. A local senator is proposing a bill to lower the limit on the number of lobster that can be caught each day. Participants in a local fishing tournament are asked to complete a survey.

6. A triathlon organizer wants to know if a Saturday morning triathlon is preferred over a Sunday morning triathlon. The organizer randomly surveys five triathletes in one of the age groups.

In Exercises 7 and 8, explain why the survey question may be biased or otherwise introduce bias into the survey. Then describe a way to correct the flaw.

7. "Our plant has not been making a profit. Do you agree that the company should close this plant?"

8. "Do you agree that the mayor is receiving a salary that is far beyond what is reasonable?"

11.3 Enrichment and Extension

Collecting Data

1. A researcher is considering three methods of evaluating two different types of fertilizer for corn. Classify each method as a survey, an experiment, or an observational study. Then identify which method would be most reliable.

Method 1	Method 2	Method 3
Randomly divide the rows of corn in the same test field into two groups. Put fertilizer on one group of rows, and record the yield for those rows and for the rows without the fertilizer. Draw conclusions based on your findings.	Choose some of the rows of corn at random from a field. Determine which type of fertilizer has been applied in the past, and what the yield is for each row. Extrapolate the findings to the whole field.	Monitor the yield of all rows of corn in various test fields being fertilized with a product chosen by the farmer. Record the yield for those rows.

2. A researcher is considering three methods of evaluating the expected charge-length of two new batteries that can be used in electric cars. Classify each method as a survey, an experiment, or an observational study. Then identify which method would be most reliable.

Method 1	Method 2	Method 3
Randomly divide some electric cars into two groups. Have each group use a different battery, and record how long the batteries last in each group before they need to be recharged. Confirm or reject your hypothesis.	Monitor the batteries in a large number of electric cars. Record how long the batteries last before they need to be recharged.	Choose a group of owners of electric cars at random. Ask which types of batteries they have used in the past, and how quickly the batteries need to be recharged. Estimate parameters for the entire population based on your data.

Puzzle Time

Why Did The Watch Go On Vacation?

Write the letter of each answer in the box containing the exercise number.

Identify the type of sample described.

1. You list all the counties in Pennsylvania and choose every third county.

2. You distribute questionnaires in the cafeteria and use only the questionnaires that are returned.

3. You ask all of the players on your baseball team.

4. You randomly select four students from each table in the cafeteria.

5. You divide all the students at a university into commuting students and campus-dwelling students, and then you randomly select all the students from the commuting group.

Identify the method of data collection each situation describes.

6. A student researcher records whether people at a restaurant leave a tip for their server.

7. A scientist provides natural light to 50 plants and fluorescent light to 50 plants in a study.

8. A teacher asks the students in her fifth-period class how many siblings they have in their immediate family so that she can draw conclusions about all her students.

Answers
N. experiment
I. observational
U. convenience
T. systematic
O. self-selected
N. stratified
W. cluster
D. survey

1	2		3	4	5	6	7	8

11.4 Start Thinking

Discuss how you might determine if a spinner or a coin are "fair" (equally likely to come up with each possibility).

11.4 Warm Up

Identify the method of data collection the situation describes.

1. A researcher places 20 plants in natural sunlight and 20 plants in artificial light. The researcher then compares the growth of the plants after 10 weeks and determines which light is better.

2. A researcher records whether people at a gym clean the machines after they use them.

11.4 Cumulative Review Warm Up

Simplify the expression.

1. $\dfrac{48^{1/3}}{16^{1/3}}$

2. $\left(3^{1/2} \bullet 6^{1/2}\right)^4$

3. $\sqrt{27}\,\sqrt[3]{27}$

4. $\dfrac{\sqrt{12}}{\sqrt[3]{12}}$

5. $\dfrac{\sqrt[5]{64}\,\sqrt[5]{4}}{\sqrt[5]{8}}$

6. $\dfrac{25^{3/2}25^{-1}}{5^{1/2}}$

11.4 Practice A

In Exercises 1 and 2, determine whether the study is a randomized comparative experiment. If it is, describe the treatment, the treatment group, and the control group. If it is not, explain why not and discuss whether the conclusions drawn from the study are valid.

1. To test the effect of using a computer for testing, 300 students are randomly divided into two groups. One group is tested using paper and pencil, and one group is tested using the computer. After analyzing the test results, it was found that the average test scores in both groups were not significantly different.

2. At a health fair, people can choose to enroll in a six-month healthy eating plan. Sixty people who chose the "eat six vegetables a day" plan were monitored for 6 months, as were 60 people who chose the "drink 12 glasses of water a day" plan. At the end of the 6 months, people who chose the "drink 12 glasses of water a day" plan had 20% lower cholesterol than people in the other group.

In Exercises 3 and 4, explain whether the research topic is best investigated through an experiment or an observational study. Then describe the design of the experiment or observational study.

3. A cycling team wants to know whether incorporating yoga into the workout routine improves racing times.

4. A researcher wants to compare the effects of a new experimental cancer drug with a cancer drug that has been used for at least 10 years.

5. A researcher wants to test whether stretching after exercising decreases the number of injuries due to muscle damage. Identify a potential problem, if any, with each experimental design. Then describe how you can improve it.

   a. The researcher selects 400 people who exercise on a regular basis. The people are divided into two groups based on age. Within each age group, the people are randomly assigned to stretch after exercising or to not stretch. The people's occurrence of injuries due to muscle damage is monitored. The stretching after exercise significantly decreases the number of injuries due to muscle damage.

   b. The researcher randomly selects 150 people who exercise on a regular basis. Half the people stretch after exercising, and the number of their injuries due to muscle damage is monitored. The other half do not stretch after exercising, and the number of their injuries due to muscle damage is monitored. The number of injuries due to muscle damage significantly decreases for those who stretch after exercising.

11.4 Practice B

In Exercises 1 and 2, determine whether the study is a randomized comparative experiment. If it is, describe the treatment, the treatment group, and the control group. If it is not, explain why not and discuss whether the conclusions drawn from the study are valid.

1. A pool cleaning service is offering a new chlorine solution to its customers. Of 90 customers, the 45 customers who chose to switch to the new chlorine solution were monitored for a year, as were the 45 customers who did not switch. At the end of the year, the customers who switched to the new chlorine solution were 30% more satisfied with the condition of their pools while those who did not switch experienced no significant change.

2. A recycling company is testing the use of recyclables containers rather than recyclables bins, in the hopes of increasing the amount of recycling. It randomly divided 150 customers into two groups. One group received the new recyclables containers, and the other group continued using their recyclables bins. After 6 months, the customers with the new recyclables containers recycled 25% more pounds of recyclables than customers with the recyclables bins.

In Exercises 3 and 4, explain whether the research topic is best investigated through an experiment or an observational study. Then describe the design of the experiment or observational study.

3. An organization wants to know whether donating 20% of one's income to charities affects one's satisfaction with his or her job.

4. A rancher wants to know whether a new feed affects the quality of the milk produced by cows.

5. A researcher wants to test whether drinking diet soda increases sugar cravings. Identify a potential problem, if any, with each experimental design. Then describe how you can improve it.

   a. The researcher randomly selects 200 people. Half of the people drink diet soda, and the occurrence of sugar cravings is monitored. The other half of the people do not drink diet soda, and their occurrence of sugar cravings is monitored. The occurrence of sugar cravings for the people who drink diet soda is significantly higher than the occurrence of cravings for those who do not.

   b. The researcher selects 300 people. The people are divided into two groups based on exercise habits. Within each group, the people are randomly assigned to drink diet soda or to not drink diet soda. The people's sugar cravings are monitored. There is no significant difference in the occurrence of sugar cravings between the two groups.

11.4 Enrichment and Extension

Experimental Design

The *response variable* is the variable that is being measured after the treatment is applied in an experiment. A *blind or blinded experiment* is a test or experiment in which information about the test that might lead to bias in the results is concealed from the tester, the subject, or both until after the test. Bias may be intentional or unconscious. If both tester and subject are blinded, the trial is a *double-blind trial*.

In Exercises 1–4, (a) find the treatment, (b) find the response variable, (c) find the number of treatment groups, and (d) decide if the experiment could be blind or double blind. Explain.

1. A mathematics education researcher was interested in determining the effects of class size (small, medium, and large) and the use of a traditional statistics textbook versus a new pilot textbook. The researcher conducted her own experiment, assigning each combination of class size and type of textbook to two classes at each of five chosen schools. The average final grade for each class was then recorded at the end of the year.

2. A botanist was interested in determining the effects of scheduled watering (three days a week or daily) and the use of fertilizer (traditional, and organic) in hopes of increasing the heat rating of jalapeño peppers. The botanist conducted his own experiment, assigning each combination of watering schedule and type of fertilizer to plots that had similar soil and full sun. The average final heat rating for the plot was then recorded at the end of the growing season.

3. A new dog food, specially designed for dogs with kidney problems, has been developed. A veterinarian wants to test this new food against another dog food currently on the market to see if it improves a dog's health. Thirty dogs with kidney problems were recruited to participate in the study. They were fed either the "new" or "old" food for 6 months and the improvement in kidney health was rated.

4. Does talking while walking slow you down? In a study reported in the journal Physical Therapy, the cadence was measured for subjects who were walking (using no device, a standard walker, or a rolling walker) and who were required (or not required) to respond to a signal while walking.

5. Researchers have developed a new insulin inhaler to replace daily insulin shots needed by patients with diabetes. Design an experiment to test the effects of this new insulin treatment on a volunteer group of 100 diabetes patients.

11.4 Puzzle Time

What Kind Of Hair Does The Ocean Have?

Write the letter of each answer in the box containing the exercise number.

Identify a potental problem with the experimental design.

1. A school district's administrators want to identify whether their current after-school tutoring program is worth implementing for the following school year. A student participant from the tutoring program is given a benchmark test. A student who does not attend the program is given the same benchmark test. After grading each student's benchmark test, it is determined that the student who attends the tutoring program did not perform better than the student who does not participate in the tutoring program, so the tutoring program should not be implemented the following year.

2. The local humane society wants to test the effectiveness of a name-brand flea control medicine. The subjects are divided into a group for cats and a group for dogs, with both receiving the same medicine in proper dosages. After one week, a significantly larger number of cats have no fleas.

Answers
V. observational study
W. sample size is not large enough
Y. experiment
A. groups are not similar

Explain whether the research topic is best investigated through an experiment or an observational study.

3. The manager of a grocery store produce department wants to know which type of apple more customers prefer.

4. A pet storeowner wants to know whether distilled water or natural spring water leads to longer life in the fish he sells.

1	2	3	4

You conduct a sample survey to determine what percent of high school students in your town have a part-time job. Based on the students that you know, you predict that 25% of high school students have a part-time job. You survey 40 randomly chosen students and find that 14 of them have a part-time job. Based on your sample survey, what percent of the students have a part-time job? Do you think that you should change your prediction based on your sample survey? Explain your reasoning.

11.5 **Warm Up**

Sample surveys are conducted to determine the monthly cell phone bill and the number of sick or personal days taken in a calendar year. Calculate the mean, $\overline{x}$, of the data shown in the table. Round your answer to the nearest tenth, when necessary.

1. **Monthly cell phone bill**

148	210	160	190	124
165	189	194	280	215
210	160	115	220	240
228	140	169	187	218
240	215	192	115	122

2. **Sick or personal days taken annually**

2	4	1	0	8
3	12	6	7	5
7	4	15	4	2
1	2	9	5	7
0	3	6	5	2

11.5 **Cumulative Review Warm Up**

Use the Binomial Theorem to write the binomial expansion.

1. $(x - 3)^5$

2. $(2x + 5)^4$

3. $(1 - 2x)^7$

4. $(x + y^2)^4$

5. $(2a - 3b)^6$

6. $(x^3 - y^4)^8$

11.5 Practice A

1. The numbers of words per text message in a random sample of 30 text messages are shown in the table.

Number of Words Per Text Message									
3	10	9	12	21	17	4	6	18	2
10	3	9	12	5	24	19	4	1	7
5	11	14	6	2	4	14	6	9	12

   a. Estimate the population mean μ.

   b. Estimate the population proportion ρ of text messages that contain more than 12 words.

   c. Estimate the population proportion ρ of text messages that contain less than five words.

2. A survey asks a random sample of U.S. college students how many hours they spend surfing the Internet each day. The survey reveals that the sample mean is 2.7 hours per day. How confident are you that the average time spent surfing the Internet each day of all U. S. college students is exactly 2.7 hours per day? Explain your reasoning.

3. The number of households with pets is increasing. A national polling company claims that 43% of U.S. households have at least one pet. You survey a random sample of 50 households.

   a. What can you conclude about the accuracy of the claim that the population proportion is 0.43 when 29 households have at least one pet?

   b. What can you conclude about the accuracy of the claim that the population proportion is 0.43 when 22 households have at least one pet?

   c. Assume that the true proportion is 0.43. Estimate the variation among sample proportions for samples of size 50.

11.5 Practice B

1. The numbers of bait fish caught in a random sample of 40 cast net throws are shown in the table.

Number of Bait Fish Per Cast Net Throw									
4	8	6	15	1	6	8	0	1	14
9	6	8	7	3	10	4	11	2	4
15	2	0	5	1	2	7	5	6	6
9	11	8	9	5	1	4	7	2	1

   a. Estimate the population mean μ.

   b. Estimate the population proportion ρ of cast net throws that produce at least eight bait fish.

   c. Estimate the population proportion ρ of cast net throws that produce fewer than three bait fish.

2. A survey asks a random sample of U.S. voters how many times they have gone to the polls unknowledgeable about who they are voting for. The survey reveals that the sample mean is 5.8 times. How confident are you that the average number of times all U. S. voters have gone to the polls unknowledgeable is exactly 5.8 times? Explain your reasoning.

3. A national polling company claims that 45% of U.S. drivers do not adhere to the speed limits in construction areas. You survey a random sample of 50 households.

   a. What can you conclude about the accuracy of the claim that the population proportion is 0.45 when 15 drivers do not adhere to the speed limits in construction areas?

   b. What can you conclude about the accuracy of the claim that the population proportion is 0.45 when 23 drivers do not adhere to the speed limits in construction areas?

   c. Assume that the true proportion is 0.45. Estimate the variation among sample proportions for samples of size 50.

11.5 Enrichment and Extension

Making Inferences from Sample Surveys

Suppose you want to determine if you should start a new club at your school. Fill in the blanks to help you design an unbiased survey.

√	Characteristic
	1. Write the survey question.
	2. Is the survey question clear? Explain.
	3. Describe the population you will sample.
	4. Describe the method you will use to sample the population.
	5. Is your sample biased? Explain how you know.
	6. Is the sample representative of the entire population? Explain.
	7. Do a trial run of the survey with several students in your class. Re-evaluate your survey question. Does the question need modifying? Explain.
	8. Conduct the survey. Find the margin of error of your sample to help you predict the opinion of the entire school. Based on the results of the survey, make a prediction about the opinion of the entire population of the school. Did your results become more accurate the more people you surveyed?

Name_____ Date _____

11.5 Puzzle Time

What Do You Call A Bird That's Been Eaten By A Cat?

Write the letter of each answer in the box containing the exercise number.

1. The table shows the daily number of lunch-hour customers to a local fish market for 16 days. Estimate the population mean μ.

Number of Customers			
15	16	27	8
12	21	26	24
18	32	38	34
24	14	42	25

2. The table shows the total number of free throws made by a high school basketball team for eight consecutive games. Estimate the population mean μ.

Total Number of Free Throws Made			
24	19	7	14
13	11	12	4

Find the margin of error for a survey that has the given sample size. Round your answer to the nearest tenth of a percent.

3. 100	**4.** 2400	**5.** 32
6. 289	**7.** 750	**8.** 170

Answers
L. ±0.06
W. ±0.1
O. ±0.04
W. ±0.08
A. ±0.02
A. 23.5
L. ±0.18
S. 13.25

1		2	3	4	5	6	7	8

11.6 Start Thinking

A marketing expert is consulted to help a company increase sales of their new sports drink. The expert advises them to consider repackaging the sports drink by changing the size of the bottle as well as the label. Because of the cost of such changes, the company wants to test the marketing expert's hypothesis before making a large investment in the change. How could the hypothesis be tested?

11.6 Warm Up

The table shows results of two different randomized comparative experiments. Find the mean value of the control group, the mean value of the treatment group, and the difference between the two means.

1.

Height (inches)										
Control Group	14	15.2	14.2	15	15.5	15	14.8	15.5	14.1	14.6
Treatment Group	14.3	15.3	14.8	15	15.4	15.4	14.8	15.8	14.5	14.9

2.

Weight (pounds)										
Control Group	58	60	61	65	57	55	62	61	60	57
Treatment Group	51	58	55	61	50	55	60	58	55	51

11.6 Cumulative Review Warm Up

Simplify the expression.

1. $\sin x \csc x$

2. $\dfrac{1 - \cos^2(-x)}{\cos^2 x}$

3. $\dfrac{\sin x}{1 + \cos x} + \dfrac{1 + \cos x}{\sin x}$

4. $\dfrac{\cos\left(\dfrac{\pi}{2} - x\right)}{\tan x}$

5. $\cos x\left(1 + \tan^2 x\right)$

6. $\dfrac{\sin x \cos x - \cos\left(\dfrac{\pi}{2} - x\right)}{\sin x}$

11.6 Practice A

1. A randomized comparative experiment tests whether pet therapy affects the mood scores of hospital patients. The mood scores range from 1 to 10, with scores close to 10 indicating a good mood. The control group has eight patients and the treatment group, which receives the pet therapy, has eight patients. The table shows the results.

	Mood Score							
Control Group	1	4	2	3	8	5	4	2
Treatment Group	3	9	4	7	3	6	2	9

   a. Find the mean score of the control group.

   b. Find the mean score of the treatment group.

   c. Find the experimental difference of the means.

   d. Display the data in a double dot plot.

   e. What can you conclude?

   f. Resample the data using a simulation.

   g. Find the mean score of the new control group.

   h. Find the mean score of the new treatment group.

   i. Find the experimental difference of the new means.

Name_____ Date _____

1. A randomized comparative experiment tests whether photo therapy affects the size of the area of skin irritations. The control group has eight patients and the treatment group, which receives the photo therapy, has eight patients. The table shows the results.

	Area of Skin Irritation (square centimeters)							
Control Group	4.2	1.3	5.1	3.4	2.7	4.1	3.6	2.4
Treatment Group	1.2	2.5	4.1	3.7	2.1	1.5	2.4	1.9

   a. Find the mean area of the control group.

   b. Find the mean area of the treatment group.

   c. Find the experimental difference of the means.

   d. Display the data in a double dot plot.

   e. What can you conclude?

   f. Resample the data using a simulation.

   g. Find the mean score of the new control group.

   h. Find the mean score of the new treatment group.

   i. Find the experimental difference of the new means.

Name _____ Date _____

11.6 Enrichment and Extension

Making Inferences from Experiments

In statistics, a confidence interval (CI) is a type of interval estimate of a population parameter and is used to indicate the reliability of an estimate. It is an observed interval (it is calculated from observations), in principle different from sample to sample, that frequently includes the parameter of interest if the experiment is repeated. The CI formed for two sample means (which was studied in Section 11.6) looks at whether or not zero is located in the interval. If zero is located in the interval, then there is insufficient evidence that the means vary. If zero is not located in the interval, then there is sufficient evidence to suggest a difference between the means.

Example: An experimenter constructed the appropriate CI on batteries $\left(\mu_{\text{generic}} - \mu_{\text{brand name}}\right)$ and found 95% of the time the interval 2.1 minutes to 35.1 minutes captures the mean amount of time by which generic batteries outlast brand-name batteries. What can the experimenter conclude from the experiment and the calculations?

Solution: Because zero is not in the interval, there is enough evidence that generic batteries do last longer than brand-name batteries. If it is cheaper and easy to get generic batteries, then there is no reason not to use them over brand-name batteries.

Decide the conclusion of the experiment based on the given confidence interval.

1. An experimenter was curious about the fat content (in grams) of two kinds of hotdogs: meat (usually a mixture of pork, turkey, and chicken) and all beef. The CI on hotdogs $\left(\mu_{\text{meat}} - \mu_{\text{beef}}\right)$ found 95% of the time the interval −6.5 grams to −1.4 grams captures the mean amount of fat content between meat and beef hotdogs.

2. A man commuting to work finds two routes he could take to work. The man decides to experiment. Each day he flips a coin to determine which way to go, driving each route 20 days. He calculates the appropriate confidence interval $\left(\mu_{\text{route A}} - \mu_{\text{route B}}\right)$ and finds the interval to be −1.4 minutes to 4.65 minutes.

3. An experimenter examined top-loading and front-loading washing machines, testing several different brands of each type. One of the variables was "cycle time", the number of minutes it took each machine to wash a load of clothes. Among the machines rated good to excellent, the corresponding CI for the difference in mean cycle time $\left(\mu_{\text{top}} - \mu_{\text{front}}\right)$ is $(-40$ minutes, -22 minutes$)$.

4. A father decided to see if children's cereal has a higher sugar content (as percentage of weight) than adults' cereal. He constructed the corresponding CI for the difference in sugar content $\left(\mu_{\text{children's}} - \mu_{\text{adult's}}\right)$ and found the interval to be 32.5% to 40.8%.

11.6 Puzzle Time

How Do You Get An Astronaut's Baby To Fall Asleep?

Write the letter of each answer in the box containing the exercise number.

Complete the exercises.

A randomized comparative experiment tests whether time spent outdoors affects the calculus exam scores of college students during finals week. The control group has five students and the treatment group, which receives time outdoors, has five students. The table shows the results.

	Calculus Exam Score				
Control Group	80	64	95	92	71
Treatment Group	83	98	88	79	94

1. Find the mean score of the control group.

2. Find the mean score of the treatment group.

3. Find the experimental difference of the means.

A randomized comparative experiment tests whether tire tread thickness affects the gas mileage of a vehicle. The control group, which receives tires that are 1 year old, has 10 vehicles and the treatment group, which receives brand new tires, has 10 vehicles. All vehicles are identical except for their tires. The table shows the results.

	Vehicle Gas Mileage (mi/gal)									
Control Group	18	15	19	21	20	17	20	21	17	20
Treatment Group	19	24	21	22	18	23	20	25	21	23

4. Find the mean mileage of the control group.

5. Find the mean mileage of the treatment group.

6. Find the experimental difference of the means.

Answers

K. 18.8

R. 80.4

T. 2.8

C. 8

O. 88.4

E. 21.6

1	2	3	4	5	6

Chapter 11 Cumulative Review

In Exercises 1–8, find the mean, median, and mode of the data set. Round your answer to the nearest tenth, when necessary.

1. 14, 1, 14, 10, 15, 18

2. 46, 47, 37, 49, 45, 46

3. 64, 73, 80, 63, 68, 80, 60

4. 40, 43, 45, 47, 47, 44, 43

5. 3, 17, 20, 8, 10, 19, 16

6. 15, 19, 20, 15, 14, 14, 11

7. 65, 57, 58, 61, 63, 60, 59, 54

8. 10, 1, 11, 7, 12, 11, 3, 10

In Exercises 9–14, find and interpret the standard deviation of the data set. Round your answer to the nearest tenth, when necessary.

9. 30, 29, 30, 20, 26, 22

10. 6, 7, 2, 9, 6, 3

11. 69, 53, 50, 51, 60, 54, 54

12. 18, 16, 17, 19, 14, 18, 17

13. 85, 82, 81, 87, 86, 85, 89, 85

14. 63, 62, 60, 60, 69, 70, 62, 65

In Exercises 15–20, tell whether x and y show *direct variation*, *inverse variation*, or *neither*.

15. $xy = 4$

16. $\dfrac{y}{7} = x$

17. $y = x + 4$

18. $x = y - 3$

19. $\dfrac{x}{3} = y$

20. $y = -4x$

In Exercises 21–28, the variables x and y vary inversely. Use the given value to write an equation relating x and y. Then find y when $x = 3$.

21. $x = -1, y = -7$

22. $x = -10, y = 4$

23. $x = -7, y = 1$

24. $x = 5, y = -2$

25. $x = \dfrac{8}{9}, y = 7$

26. $x = 2, y = \dfrac{3}{4}$

27. $x = 4, y = \dfrac{1}{5}$

28. $x = \dfrac{2}{3}, y = 4$

29. The results for your test scores are as follows: 73, 95, 76, 99, 85, 92, 78, 72, 71, 87, 98, 81, 88, 92, 93, 79, 75, 95, 77, 71, 90, 77, 100, 75, 94, 89, 84. What is the mean, median, and mode of the test scores? Round your answers to the nearest tenth, where necessary.

Chapter 11 Cumulative Review (continued)

In Exercises 30–35, simplify the expression.

30. $\dfrac{3x}{6x^2 - 27x^5}$

31. $\dfrac{6x + 2x^4}{3x}$

32. $\dfrac{x^2 - 3x - 4}{x^2 + 6x + 5}$

33. $\dfrac{x^2 + 8x - 9}{x^2 + 3x - 4}$

34. $\dfrac{x^2 - 16x + 63}{x^2 - x - 42}$

35. $\dfrac{x^2 - 13x + 40}{x^2 - 5x - 24}$

In Exercises 36–41, find the product.

36. $\dfrac{2xy^4}{x^3 y} \cdot \dfrac{y}{6x^2}$

37. $\dfrac{5x^3 y}{xy^2} \cdot \dfrac{y^4}{30x^2 y}$

38. $\dfrac{x(x - 4)}{x + 8} \cdot \dfrac{(x + 8)(x - 2)}{x^2}$

39. $\dfrac{x^2 - x - 6}{x^2 - 16x + 60} \cdot \dfrac{x^2 - 7x + 6}{x^2 - 4x + 3}$

40. $\dfrac{x^2 - 10x + 16}{x^2 + x - 72} \cdot \dfrac{x^2 + 17x + 72}{x^2 + 15x + 56}$

41. $\dfrac{x^2 + 16x + 55}{x^2 - 3x - 40} \cdot \dfrac{x^2 - 5x - 24}{x^2 + x - 110}$

In Exercises 42–51, find the sum or difference.

42. $\dfrac{12}{7x} + \dfrac{8}{7x}$

43. $\dfrac{x}{2x^2} - \dfrac{3}{2x^2}$

44. $\dfrac{8}{x - 2} + \dfrac{3x}{x - 2}$

45. $\dfrac{3x^2}{x + 5} - \dfrac{1}{x + 5}$

46. $\dfrac{x}{3x + 4} - \dfrac{8x}{3x + 4}$

47. $\dfrac{x^3}{x^2 + 1} + \dfrac{x^2}{x^2 + 1}$

48. $\dfrac{x + 8}{x^2 + 3x - 40} - \dfrac{x + 2}{x + 8}$

49. $\dfrac{x + 6}{x - 7} + \dfrac{x - 8}{x^2 - 12x + 35}$

50. $\dfrac{3x + 7}{x - 1} - \dfrac{x - 9}{x^2 - 12x + 11}$

51. $\dfrac{x + 11}{x^2 - 11x - 12} + \dfrac{x + 3}{x - 12} - \dfrac{4}{x + 1}$

52. The sides of a rectangle are $(2x + 7)$ inches and $(3x + 9)$ inches.

 a. Write an equation for the perimeter P of the rectangle.

 b. Write an equation for the area A of the rectangle.

 c. The value of x is 2. What is the perimeter and area of the rectangle?

Chapter 11 **Cumulative Review** (continued)

In Exercises 53–56, evaluate the six trigonometric functions of the angle θ.

53.

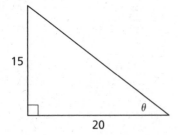

54.

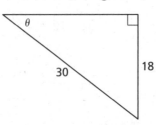

55.

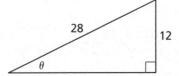

56.

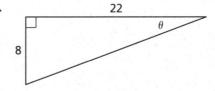

In Exercises 57–60, find the value of *x* for the right triangle.

57.

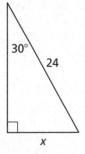

58.

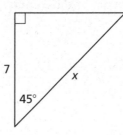

59.

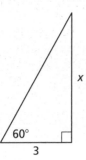

60.

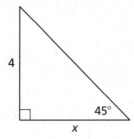

Chapter 11 **Cumulative Review** (continued)

In Exercises 61–66, find one positive angle and one negative angle that are coterminal with the given angle.

61. $88°$

62. $-305°$

63. $-\dfrac{3\pi}{4}$

64. $\dfrac{5\pi}{6}$

65. $420°$

66. $-\dfrac{4\pi}{3}$

In Exercises 67–72, convert the degree measure to radians or the radian measure to degrees.

67. $110°$

68. $310°$

69. $-\dfrac{4\pi}{3}$

70. $\dfrac{5\pi}{6}$

71. $-60°$

72. $-\dfrac{3\pi}{4}$

In Exercises 73–78, use the unit circle to evaluate the six trigonometric functions of θ.

73. $180°$

74. $495°$

75. $-\dfrac{\pi}{3}$

76. $\dfrac{\pi}{6}$

77. $-120°$

78. $\dfrac{7\pi}{4}$

In Exercises 79–90, graph the function.

79. $g(x) = 5 \sin x$

80. $g(x) = 2 \cos x$

81. $g(x) = \cos 3x$

82. $g(x) = \sin 4x$

83. $g(x) = \dfrac{1}{2} \sin 2x$

84. $g(x) = \dfrac{1}{4} \cos 2x$

85. $g(x) = \dfrac{1}{2} \sin 4\pi x$

86. $g(x) = 3 \cos 2\pi x$

87. $g(x) = \sin x - 1$

88. $g(x) = \cos x + 3$

89. $g(x) = 3 \sin 2x + 1$

90. $g(x) = \dfrac{1}{2} \cos x - 5$

Credits

Puzzle Time jokes are excerpted from: Jokelopedia, 3rd
Edition. Copyright ©2000 by Somerville House, 2006 by Key
Porter and Workman Publishing, 2013 by Workman
Publishing, Inc. Used by permission of Workman Publishing
Co., New York. All Rights Reserved.

Answers

Chapter 1

1.1 Start Thinking

As the string V gets wider, the points on the string move closer to the *x*-axis. This activity mimics a vertical shrink of a parabola.

1.1 Warm Up

1.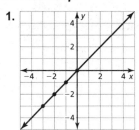

2.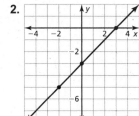

3.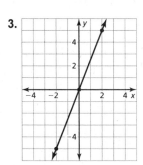

4.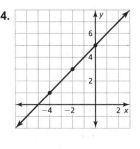

1.1 Cumulative Review Warm Up

1. $-\frac{1}{2}$ **2.** 1   **3.** $\frac{1}{2}$ **4.** 25

1.1 Practice A

1. quadratic; The graph of *f* is a vertical shrink by a factor of $\frac{1}{3}$ followed by a translation 1 unit down of the graph of the parent quadratic function.

2. constant; The graph of *f* is a translation 1 unit up of the graph of the parent constant function.

3. a linear function

4.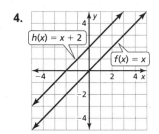

Sample answer: The graph of *h* is a translation 2 units up of the graph of the parent linear function.

5.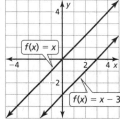

Sample answer: The graph of *f* is a translation 3 units right of the parent linear function.

6.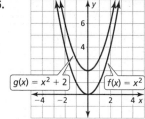

The graph of *g* is a translation 2 units up of the parent quadratic function.

7.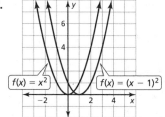

The graph of *f* is a translation 1 unit right of the graph of the parent quadratic function.

8.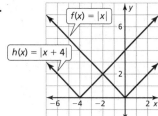

The graph of *h* is a translation 4 units left of the graph of the parent function.

9.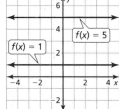

The graph of *f* is a translation 4 units up of the graph of the parent constant function.

Answers

10.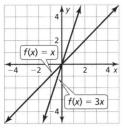

Sample answer: The graph of *f* is a vertical stretch by a factor of 3 of the graph of the parent linear function.

11.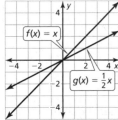

Sample answer: The graph of *g* is a vertical shrink by a factor of $\frac{1}{2}$ of the parent linear function.

12.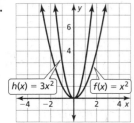

The graph of *h* is a vertical stretch by a factor of 3 of the graph of the parent quadratic function.

13.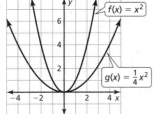

Sample answer: The graph of *g* is a vertical shrink by a factor of $\frac{1}{4}$ of the graph of the parent quadratic function.

14.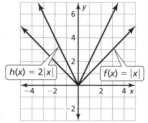

The graph of *h* is a vertical stretch by a factor of 2 of the graph of the parent absolute value function.

15.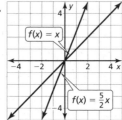

Sample answer: The graph of *f* is a vertical stretch by a factor of $\frac{5}{2}$ of the graph of the parent linear function.

16.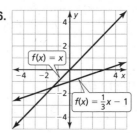

The graph of *f* is a vertical shrink by a factor of $\frac{1}{3}$ followed by a translation 1 unit down of the graph of the parent linear function.

17.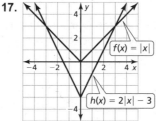

The graph of *h* is a vertical stretch by a factor of 2 followed by a translation 3 units down of the graph of the parent absolute value function.

Answers

18.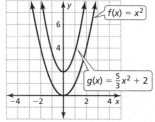

The graph of g is a vertical stretch by a factor of $\frac{5}{3}$ followed by a translation 2 units up of the graph of the parent quadratic function.

19. *Sample answer:*

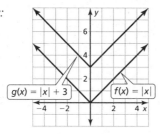

The graph of g is a translation 3 units up of the graph of the parent absolute value function.

1.1 Practice B

1. absolute value; The graph of f is a vertical shrink by a factor of $\frac{2}{5}$ followed by a translation 3 units right of the graph of the parent absolute value function.

2. linear; The graph of f is a vertical stretch by a factor of 2 followed by a translation 1 unit up of the graph of the parent linear function.

3.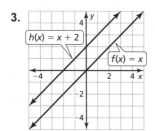

Sample answer: The graph of h is a translation 2 units up of the graph of the parent linear function.

4.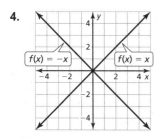

Sample answer: The graph of f is a reflection in the x-axis of the graph of the parent linear function.

5.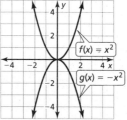

The graph of g is a reflection in the x-axis of the graph of the parent quadratic function.

6.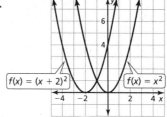

The graph of f is a translation 2 units left of the graph of the parent quadratic function.

7.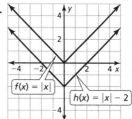

The graph of h is a translation 2 units down of the graph of the parent absolute value function.

8.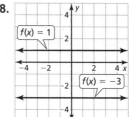

The graph of f is a translation 4 units down of the parent constant function.

Answers

9.

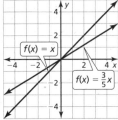

Sample answer: The graph of *f* is a vertical shrink by a factor of $\frac{3}{5}$ of the graph of the parent linear function.

10.

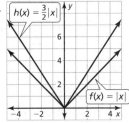

Sample answer: The graph of *h* is a vertical stretch by a factor of $\frac{3}{2}$ of the graph of the parent absolute value function.

11.

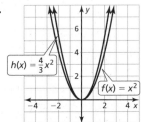

The graph of *h* is a vertical stretch by a factor of $\frac{4}{3}$ of the graph of the parent quadratic function.

12.

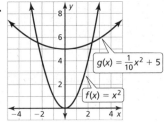

The graph of *g* is a vertical shrink by a factor of $\frac{1}{10}$ followed by a translation 5 units up of the graph of the parent quadratic function.

13.

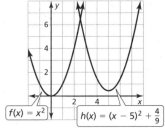

The graph of *h* is a translation 5 units right and $\frac{4}{9}$ units up of the graph of the parent quadratic function.

14.

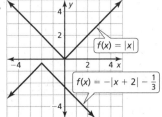

The graph of *f* is a reflection in the *x*-axis, followed by a translation 2 units left and $\frac{1}{3}$ units down of the graph of the parent absolute value function.

15. absolute value; domain: all real numbers, range: $y \geq 3$

16. linear; domain: all real numbers, range: all real numbers

17. quadratic; domain: all real numbers, range: $y \geq -3$

18. a. quadratic function

    b. 0; *t* is the number of seconds after the ball is thrown, so when the ball is thrown $t = 0$.

    c. 6 ft; $f(0) = 6$

1.1 Enrichment and Extension

1.

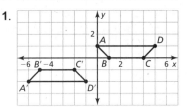

Sample answer: Trapezoid $A'B'C'D'$ a reflection in the *x*-axis, followed by translation 1 unit down and 6 units left of trapezoid *ABCD*.

Answers

2. a. quadratic function

b. after $5\sqrt{2} \approx 7.07$ years

c. domain: $x \geq 0$, range: $0 \leq y \leq 15{,}000$

3. *Sample answer:* domain: all real numbers; range: all real numbers; vertical shrink by a factor of $\frac{1}{2}$; reflection in y-axis; translation 5 units up

4. *Sample answer:* domain: all real numbers; range: $y \leq -3$; vertical stretch by a factor of 4; reflection in x-axis; translation 3 units down

5. *Sample answer:* domain: all real numbers; range: $y \geq 5$; horizontal stretch by a factor of 3; reflection in y-axis; translation 5 units up and 3 units to the left

1.1 Puzzle Time

BECAUSE PEOPLE ALWAYS SAY IF IT IS NOT BROKEN DO NOT FIX IT

1.2 Start Thinking

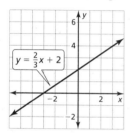

The equation becomes $y = \frac{2}{3}x + 3$; The equation becomes $y = \frac{2}{3}x + 1$; When 1 is added, by definition, the y-intercept moves up one unit. The slope is the same, so each point is moved up one unit. When -1 is added, the y-intercept moves down one unit, along with every other point on the line.

1.2 Warm Up

1.
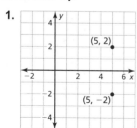

2.
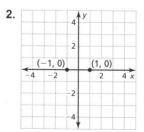

3.
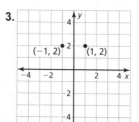

4.
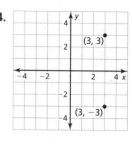

5.
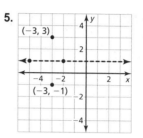

6.
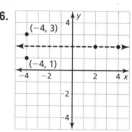

1.2 Cumulative Review Warm Up

1. one   **2.** one   **3.** zero

T   -E-

4. one   **5.** two   **6.** zero

W   -H-

1.2 Practice A

1. $g(x) = x + 3$

2. $g(x) = x - 3$

3. $g(x) = |3x + 2| + 1$

4. $g(x) = 4x - 2$

5. $g(x) = 3x - 7$

6. $g(x) = -\frac{1}{3}x + 2$

7. $g(x) = |-4x| - 6$

8. $g(x) = |-3x - 5| + 3$

9. $g(x) = 4x + 12$

10. $g(x) = \frac{4}{3}x + 1$

11. $g(x) = |9x| + 2$

12. $g(x) = \left|\frac{1}{3}x + 1\right|$

13. $g(x) = \frac{1}{3}x - 4$

14. $g(x) = |2x + 3|$

1.2 Practice B

1. $g(x) = 5x - 27$

2. $g(x) = 3x + 10$

3. $g(x) = 3 - |x|$

4. $g(x) = |2x| + 1$

5. $g(x) = x + 3$

6. $g(x) = -\frac{2}{3}x + 4$

Answers

7. $g(x) = -5 + |-x + 8|$ **8.** $g(x) = |-4x - 1| + 2$

9. $g(x) = 3 - \frac{1}{2}x$ **10.** $g(x) = x + \frac{5}{3}$

11. $g(x) = |9x| + 2$ **12.** $g(x) = -4|x - 2| + 8$

13. $g(x) = \frac{1}{4}x + \frac{5}{4}$ **14.** $g(x) = -|x + 2|$

1.2 Enrichment and Extension

1. $g(x) = 2x - 8; x = 4$

2. $g(x) = -2x - 1; x = -\frac{1}{2}$

3. $g(x) = 6x - 6; x = 1$

4. $g(x) = 6x + 4; x = -\frac{2}{3}$

5. $g(x) = 4x - 14; x = \frac{7}{2}$

6. $g(x) = -2x - 6; x = -3$

7. $g(x) = |x - 1| - 2; x = 3, x = -1$

8. $g(x) = |x + 3| + 1;$ no solution, does not intersect x-axis

9. $g(x) = -|x + 5|; x = -5$

10. $g(x) = 2|x + 1| - 6; x = 2, x = -4$

11. $g(x) = -|4x - 38|; x = \frac{19}{2}$

12. $g(x) = -\frac{1}{2}|x - 3| + 2; x = 7, -1$

1.2 Puzzle time

JAMES MONROE

1.3 Start Thinking

You can model this situation with the equation $y = 14.99x - 8.50x$, where x represents the number of units sold and y represents the total profit. You are looking for the point that has a y-value of 150,000. By substituting 150,000 for y in the equation and solving for x, you obtain $x = 23,113$.

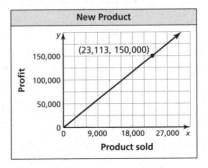

1.3 Warm Up

1. $D = \{0 \le x \le 82\}$
$R = \{0 \le y \le 12,300,000\}$

2. $D = \{0 \le x \le 5\}$
$R = \{0 \le y \le 4220\}$

3. $D = \{0 \le x \le 2500\}$
$R = \{0 \le y \le 13,125\}$

1.3 Cumulative Review Warm Up

1. 5.1 **2.** 9.3

3. 10.3 **4.** $130,533.30

1.3 Practice A

1. $y = \frac{3}{50}x;$ The sales tax rate is $\frac{3}{50} = 6\%$.

2. $y = -\frac{1}{2}x + 10;$ An amount of $\frac{1}{2}$ ounce of soap is used each day.

3. Soapy Car Wash; 6 extras

4. not linear

5. yes; $y = \frac{1}{2}x; y = 7.5;$ This means 7.5 cars are washed in 15 minutes.

6. yes; A correlation coefficient close to -1 is a strong, negative correlation.

Answers

1.3 Practice B

1. $y = 5x + 15$; A child gains about 5 pounds per year.

2. $y = -\frac{11}{4}x + 20$; One loaf of bread uses $\frac{11}{4}$ cups of flour.

3. yes; $y = 22x + 10$; $y = 340$; After 15 days, 340 tickets were sold.

4. not linear

5. $y = 0.42x + 2.67$; $r = 0.65$; The points lie somewhat close to the line.

6. $y = -x + 6$; $r = -0.85$; The points lie close to the line.

1.3 Enrichment and Extension

1. $y = 4$ **2.** $y = \frac{2}{3}x - 2$ **3.** $y = 7$

4. $y = \frac{1}{2}x - 3$ **5.** -9 **6.** 14

7. $-\frac{3}{2}$ **8.** -18 **9.** 3   **10.** $-\frac{4}{3}$

11. $y = \frac{5}{4}x - 2488$; \$30,750

12. $y = \frac{7}{4}x - 3490$; \$36,250; \$5500

1.3 Puzzle Time

ROADTRIP

1.4 Start Thinking

The point of intersection of the three models would be when all three models create the same profit for the same cost.

1.4 Warm Up

1. $y = \frac{3}{2}x - \frac{3}{2}$ **2.** $y = -\frac{1}{3}x + \frac{7}{2}$

3. $y = -\frac{3}{2}x$ **4.** $y = -\frac{7}{2}x + \frac{13}{2}$

5. $y = \frac{1}{4}x - \frac{5}{4}$ **6.** $y = \frac{7}{8}x - \frac{19}{8}$

1.4 Cumulative Review Warm Up

1. yes   **2.** no   **3.** no

4. yes   **5.** no   **6.** yes

1.4 Practice A

1. $(1, -3, -7)$ **2.** $(2, 1, 5)$

3. Each term of the second equation should be multiplied by 5.

$$5x + 3y - z = 15$$
$$\underline{-5x + 10y + 15z = 50}$$
$$13y + 14z = 65$$

4. no solution

5. Any ordered triple of the form $(x, 0, x - 2)$ is a solution of the system.

6. Roses cost \$3 each, carnations cost \$1 each, and tulips cost \$3 each.

7. $(4, -3, -4)$ **8.** $(7, 2, 1)$

9. a. $\ell + m + n = 90$
$$m = 5n - 5$$
$$\ell = \frac{5}{4}m - n$$
$$\ell = 41, m = 40, n = 9$$

b. yes; $9^2 + 40^2 = 41^2$

1.4 Practice B

1. $(-1, 1, 3)$ **2.** $(2, 1, 4)$

3. Each term of the first equation should be multiplied by 3.

$$15x + 9y - 3z = 45$$
$$\underline{3x - 4y + 3z = 8}$$
$$18x + 5y = 53$$

4. no solution

5. Any ordered triple of the form $(x, 2 + 2x, -x + 1)$ is a solution.

6. $(5, 4, -3)$ **7.** no solution

8. no; The solution of the system is 16.4 nickels, 8.2 dimes, and 5.4 quarters. You cannot have part of a coin.

9. a. $\left(\frac{1}{5}, -\frac{7}{5}\right)$

b. yes; There is one solution, so the lines intersect at a point.

Answers

1.4 Enrichment and Extension

1. $(3, -2, 2, 1)$ **2.** $(0, -3, -1, 4)$ **3.** $(5, -2, 3, 4)$

1.4 Puzzle Time

THE TALLEST LIVING HORSE WHO MEASURED SIX FEET TEN INCHES

Cumulative Review

1. solution

2. solution

3. not a solution

4. solution

5. not a solution

6. solution

7. not a solution

8. solution

9. not a solution

10. solution

11. solution

12. solution

13. $10.5 \leq t \leq 12$

14. a. $21 \leq m \leq 25$ **b.** 1.5 gal   **c.** 4 gal

15. $z = 1$ **16.** $c = 4$ **17.** $y = -6$

18. $h = -10$ **19.** $p = 9$ **20.** $b = -49$

21. $r = -\frac{1}{8}$ **22.** $s = 7$

23. $f = -5$ and $f = 13$ **24.** $k = -3$ and $k = \frac{25}{3}$

25. $g = -\frac{9}{2}$ and $g = \frac{5}{2}$ **26.** $v = -\frac{3}{4}$ and $v = \frac{5}{4}$

27. $w = 1$ and $w = 9$ **28.** $d = -\frac{1}{3}$ and $d = 1$

29. $y = -3x + 2$ **30.** $y = 9x - 8$

31. $y = 2x - 1$ **32.** $y = -\frac{1}{2}x + \frac{5}{2}$

33. $y = -6x + 12$ **34.** $y = 5x - 30$

35. $y = \frac{4}{3}x + \frac{5}{3}$ **36.** $y = 2x + 8$

37. $y = \dfrac{7 - x}{5x}$ or $y = \dfrac{7}{5x} - \dfrac{1}{5}$

38. $\dfrac{108}{x}$ **39.** $55 - x$

40. $32 + x$ **41.** $40x$

42. a. $2.50 + 2.25m$ **b.** \$22.75   **c.** \$27.25   **d.** \$34.75

43. a. $2.12p$ **b.** \$10.60   **c.** \$7.28
    d. 9.43 lbs, or about 9 lbs

44. 26 min   **45.** 3 gigabytes

46. Distributive Property

47. Additive Inverse Property

48. Commutative Property of Multiplication

49. Associative Property of Multiplication

50. Commutative Property of Addition

51. Associative Property of Addition

52. Additive Identity Property

53. Multiplicative Identity Property

54.

55.

56.

57.

Answers

58. $(7, -3)$ **59.** $(4, 9)$ **60.** $(-1, -7)$

61. no solution **62.** $(-2, 7)$ **63.** no solution

64. no solution **65.** $(7, -2)$

66. infinitely many solutions

67. $(1, 7)$

68. infinitely many solutions

69. $(-2, -9)$ **70.** $9a^2 + 12a + 4$

71. $b^2 - 14b + 49$ **72.** $25c^2 + 90c + 81$

73. $9d^2 - 48d + 64$ **74.** $16m^2 - 32m + 16$

75. $4n^2 + 4n + 1$ **76.** $25p^2 - 60p + 36$

77. $q^2 - 4q + 4$

78. x-intercept: 3, y-intercept: 2

79. x-intercept: -8, y-intercept: $\frac{8}{5}$

80. x-intercept: 7, y-intercept: $-\frac{7}{6}$

81. x-intercept: $\frac{5}{2}$, y-intercept: $\frac{5}{3}$

82. x-intercept: 4, y-intercept: $\frac{1}{2}$

83. x-intercept: 9, y-intercept: $-\frac{1}{2}$

84. $y = 2x + 3$ **85.** $y = x - 4$

86. $y = -\frac{1}{4}x + 1$ **87.** $y = -\frac{3}{4}x - 5$

88. $y = 4x$ **89.** $y = \frac{4}{5}$

90. $y = -\frac{2}{7}x - \frac{1}{2}$ **91.** $y = \frac{2}{3}x + 2$

92. $g(x) = |x + 2| - 3$ **93.** $g(x) = |x + 5| - 5$

94. $g(x) = 3|x + 2| - 15$

95. $g(x) = |x + 2| - 6$

96. infinitely many solutions

97. $(2, 4, 7)$

98. infinitely many solutions

99. no solution **100.** $(-3, -4, 2)$

101. $(1, -4, 7)$ **102.** 3 in. by 6 in.

103. **a.** You need 7.5 pounds of peanuts, 3.5 pounds of raisins, 4.5 pounds of pretzels, and 3 pounds of chocolate candy pieces.
  b. Recipe B **c.** 3 lbs

104. your friend; $6.50

Chapter 2

2.1 Start Thinking

Sample answer:

$f(x) = x^2$

x	-2	-1	0	1	2
$f(x)$	4	1	0	1	4

$f(x) = (x - 1)^2$

x	-2	-1	0	1	2
$f(x)$	9	4	1	0	1

$f(x) = 2x^2$

x	-2	-1	0	1	2
$f(x)$	8	2	0	2	8

$f(x) = x^2 + 1$

x	-2	-1	0	1	2
$f(x)$	5	2	1	2	5

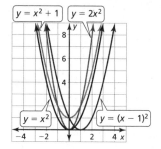

The function $f(x) = (x - 1)^2$ is a horizontal translation 1 unit right $(h = 1)$. The function $f(x) = 2x^2$ is a vertical stretch by a factor of 2 $(a = 2)$. The function $f(x) = x^2 + 1$ is a vertical translation 1 unit up $(k = 1)$.

Answers

2.1 Warm Up

1. $6x^2 - 16x + 8$

2. $20x^2 + 13x + 2$

3. $8x^2 - 10xy - 3y^2$

4. $12a^2 + 3a$

5. $20x^2 - 3x - 2$

6. $15y^2 + 22y + 8$

2.1 Cumulative Review Warm Up

1. $g(x) = x + 3$

2. $g(x) = x - 2$

3. $g(x) = |5x - 2| - 4$

2.1 Practice A

1. The graph of g is a translation 2 units down of the graph of f.

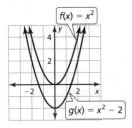

2. The graph of g is a translation 1 unit up of the graph of f.

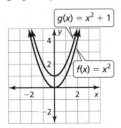

3. The graph of g is a translation 1 unit left of the graph of f.

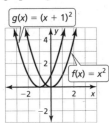

4. The graph of g is a translation 2 units right of the graph of f.

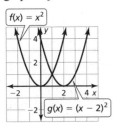

5. The graph of g is a translation 5 units right of the graph of f.

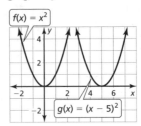

6. The graph of g is a translation 2 units left and 1 unit down of the graph of f.

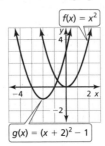

7. The graph of g is a reflection in the x-axis followed by a vertical stretch by a factor of 2 of the graph of f.

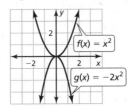

8. The graph of g is a reflection in the y-axis followed by a horizontal shrink of the graph of f by a factor of $\frac{1}{2}$.

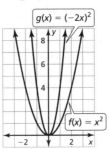

9. The graph of g is a vertical shrink by a factor of $\frac{1}{4}$ of the graph of f.

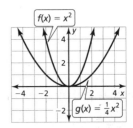

Answers

10. When $0 < a < 1$ in the function $g(x) = a \cdot f(x)$, the transformation is a vertical shrink, not stretch; The graph of g is a reflection in the x-axis followed by a vertical shrink by a factor of $\frac{1}{3}$ of the graph of the parent quadratic function.

11. The graph is a vertical stretch by a factor of 2, followed by a translation 3 units left and 2 units up of the parent quadratic function; $(-3, 2)$

12. The graph is a reflection in the x-axis, followed by a vertical stretch by a factor of 5 and a translation 1 unit down of the parent quadratic function; $(0, -1)$

13. $g(x) = -3x^2 - 3$; $(0, -3)$

14. $g(x) = -x^2 - 7$; $(0, -7)$

15. a. $a = 2, h = 3, k = -4$; $g(x) = (2x - 3)^2 - 4$

  b. $a = 4, h = 3, k = -4$; $g(x) = 4(x - 3)^2 - 4$

2.1 Practice B

1. The graph of g is a translation 3 units up of the graph of f.

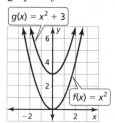

2. The graph of g is a translation 5 units left of the graph of f.

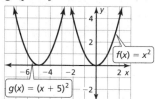

3. The graph of g is a translation 6 units left and 4 units down of the graph of f.

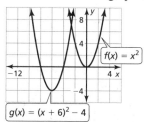

4. The graph of g is a translation 1 unit right and 5 units up of the graph of f.

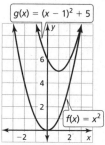

5. The graph of g is a translation 4 units right and 3 units up of the graph of f.

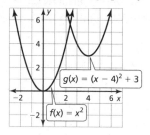

6. The graph of g is a translation 8 units left and 2 units down of the graph of f.

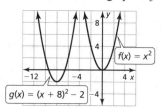

7. The graph of g is a reflection in the x-axis, followed by a horizontal stretch by a factor of 2 of the graph of f.

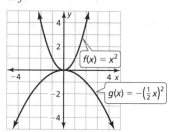

8. The graph of g is a vertical shrink by a factor of $\frac{1}{3}$, followed by a translation 2 units up of the graph of f.

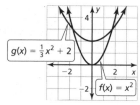

Answers

9. The graph of g is a vertical shrink by a factor of $\frac{1}{3}$, followed by a translation 1 unit left of the graph of f.

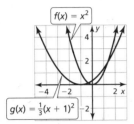

10. The graph is a reflection in the x-axis, followed by a vertical stretch by a factor of 3 and a translation 6 units left and 4 units down of the parent quadratic function; $(-6, -4)$

11. The graph is a vertical shrink by a factor of $\frac{1}{3}$, followed by a translation 2 units right and 1 unit up of the parent quadratic function; $(2, 1)$

12. $g(x) = \dfrac{(x + 2)^2}{2}; (-2, 0)$

13. $g(x) = -(3x + 4)^2 - 4; \left(-\frac{4}{3}, -4\right)$

14.

$h(x) = f(x) + 3$	Add 3 to the output.
$= 4x^2 - 3x + 3$	Substitute $f(x)$ and simplify.
$g(x) = h(-x)$	Multiply the input by -1.
$= 4x^2 + 3x + 3$	Substitute $-x$ into $h(x)$ and simplify.

2.1 Enrichment and Extension

$y = -3x^2; y = 3(x + 1)^2 + 1; y = 3(x - 1)^2 + 1;$
$y = -3(x + 1)^2 - 1; y = 3(x - 4)^2 - 2;$
$y = -3(x - 2)^2 + 2; y = -3(x + 2)^2 + 2$

2.1 Puzzle Time

EL SALVADOR

2.2 Start Thinking

x	-2	-1	0	1	2
$f(x)$	2	1	0	1	2

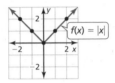

V shape; yes; yes; The line of symmetry is the y-axis.

2.2 Warm Up

1. $P'(5, 3)$ **2.** $P'(-5, -3)$

3. $P'(-5, -15)$ **4.** $P'(3, 3)$

2.2 Cumulative Review Warm Up

1. linear; $y = 11x$; $y = 220$; After jogging for 20 minutes, 220 calories were burned.

2. not linear

2.2 Practice A

1.

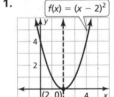

2.

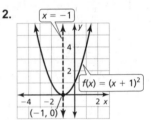

3.

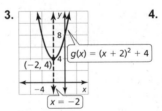

4.

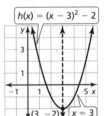

5.

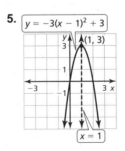

Answers

6.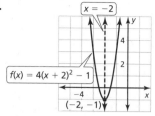

7.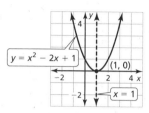

8.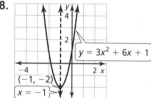

9.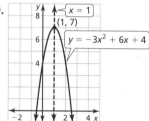

10.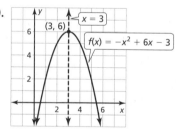

11.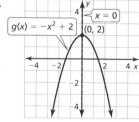

12.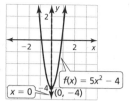

13. Both graphs have the same axis of symmetry, $x = -2$.

14. C; It has the largest leading coefficient, $a = 3$.

15. minimum: 2; domain: all real numbers, range: $y \geq 2$; increasing to the right of $x = 0$; decreasing to the left of $x = 0$

16. minimum: -3; domain: all real numbers, range: $y \geq -3$; increasing to the right of $x = 0$; decreasing to the left of $x = 0$

17. maximum: 3; domain: all real numbers, range: $y \leq 3$; increasing to the left of $x = 2$; decreasing to the right of $x = 2$

18. maximum: 11; domain: all real numbers, range: $y \leq 11$; increasing to the left of $x = 1$; decreasing to the right of $x = 1$

19. a. noon   **b.** 75 customers

2.2 Practice B

1.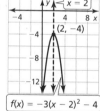

2.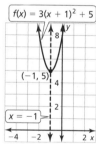

3.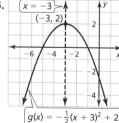

4.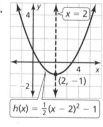

Answers

5.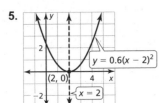

6.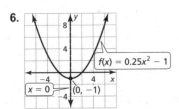

7. 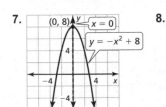 **8.**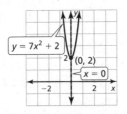

9. 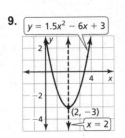 **10.**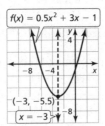

11. 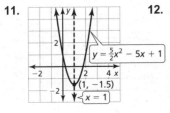 **12.**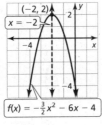

13. lowest; The y-values on either side of $x = 3$ are greater than 3.

14. A; Both have an axis of symmetry of $x = 2$.

15. minimum: 12; domain: all real numbers, range: $y \geq 12$; increasing to the right of $x = 0$; decreasing to the left of $x = 0$

16. maximum: 9; domain: all real numbers, range: $y \leq 9$; increasing to the left of $x = -3$; decreasing to the right of $x = -3$

17. maximum: 6; domain: all real numbers, range: $y \leq 6$; increasing to the left of $x = -3$; decreasing to the right of $x = -3$

18. minimum: 2.5; domain: all real numbers, range: $y \geq 2.5$; increasing to the right of $x = -3$; decreasing to the left of $x = -3$

19. a. The maximum height occurs $\frac{1}{6}$ mile from the base of the bridge.

  b. The maximum height is $\frac{1}{12}$ mile.

2.2 Enrichment and Extension

1. $y = 3x^2 - 6x + 1$ **2.** $y = x^2 + 2x - 1$

3. $y = -2x^2 - 8x + 1$ **4.** $y = -3x^2 - 6x - 3$

5. $y = -x^2 + 2x + 5$ **6.** $y = \frac{1}{2}x^2 + 2x + 2$

7. no; The definition of a quadratic function says $a \neq 0$, but for the axis of symmetry to be undefined, a would have to be 0.

8. *Sample answer:* $(-1, 10)$; The x-value 7 is 4 units away from the vertex x-value 3. Because the x-value -1 is also 4 units away from 3, it has the same output value 10.

2.2 Puzzle Time

THIS BRITISH ROWER WAS THE FIRST WOMAN TO ROW ACROSS THREE OCEANS.

2.3 Start Thinking

Sample answer:

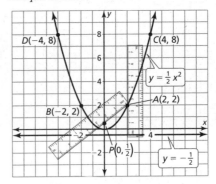

yes; Point P is the same distance from the parabola as the line $y = -\frac{1}{2}$ is to the parabola. So, it will always yield the same distance as long as the measurement is taken from a point on the graph of the parabola.

Answers

2.3 Warm Up

1. 11.7   **2.** 3.2   **3.** 18

4. 7.3   **5.** 12.6   **6.** 14.3

2.3 Cumulative Review Warm Up

1. $x = 0.75$
$y = -2$
$z = 0.5$

2. $x = 8.125$
$y = 8.5$
$z = -2.625$

2.3 Practice A

1. $y = \frac{1}{8}x^2$ **2.** $y = -\frac{1}{12}x^2$ **3.** $y = -\frac{1}{24}x^2$

4. $y = -\frac{1}{16}x^2$ **5.** $y = -\frac{1}{4}x^2$ **6.** $y = -\frac{1}{8}x^2$

7. A; The directrix is below the focus.

8. focus: $(0, 3)$, directrix: $y = -3$,
axis of symmetry: $x = 0$

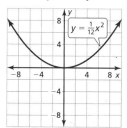

9. focus: $(0, -4)$, directrix: $y = 4$,
axis of symmetry: $x = 0$

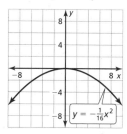

10. focus: $(2, 0)$, directrix: $x = -2$,
axis of symmetry: $y = 0$

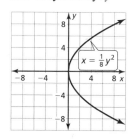

11. 12 in.; The receiver is at the focus.

12. $x = \frac{1}{8}y^2$ **13.** $x = -\frac{1}{16}y^2$ **14.** $y = \frac{1}{3}x^2$

15. $x = \frac{1}{24}y^2$ **16.** $y = \frac{1}{8}x^2$ **17.** $x = -\frac{1}{4}y^2$

18. vertex: $(1, 3)$, focus: $(1, 6)$, directrix: $y = 0$, axis of symmetry: $x = 1$; The graph is a vertical shrink by a factor of $\frac{1}{3}$, followed by a translation 1 unit right and 3 units up.

19. vertex: $(-5, -2)$, focus: $(-5, -4)$, directrix: $y = 0$, axis of symmetry: $x = -5$; The graph is a vertical shrink by a factor of $\frac{1}{2}$, followed by a reflection in the x-axis and a translation 5 units left and 2 units down.

20. vertex: $(2, -4)$, focus: $(3, -4)$, directrix: $x = 1$, axis of symmetry: $y = -4$; The graph is a translation 2 units right and 4 units down.

21. vertex: $(-6, 10)$, focus: $(-6, 3)$, directrix: $y = 17$, axis of symmetry: $x = -6$; The graph is a vertical shrink by a factor of $\frac{1}{7}$, followed by a reflection in the x-axis and a translation 6 units left and 10 units up.

2.3 Practice B

1. $y = \frac{1}{20}x^2$ **2.** $y = -\frac{1}{24}x^2$ **3.** $y = \frac{1}{16}x^2$

4. $y = -\frac{1}{32}x^2$ **5.** $y = -\frac{1}{28}x^2$ **6.** $y = \frac{1}{8}x^2$

7. focus: $(0, -8)$, directrix: $y = 8$,
axis of symmetry: $x = 0$

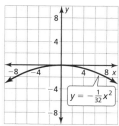

Answers

8. focus: $(1, 0)$, directrix: $x = -1$,
axis of symmetry: $y = 0$

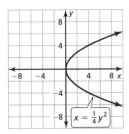

9. focus: $(3, 0)$, directrix: $x = -3$,
axis of symmetry: $y = 0$

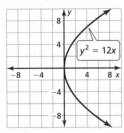

10. focus: $(0, -9)$, directrix: $y = 9$,
axis of symmetry: $x = 0$

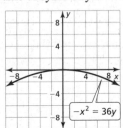

11. focus: $\left(0, -\frac{1}{16}\right)$, directrix: $y = \frac{1}{16}$,
axis of symmetry: $x = 0$

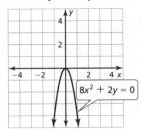

12. focus: $\left(0, \frac{1}{8}\right)$, directrix: $y = -\frac{1}{8}$,
axis of symmetry: $x = 0$

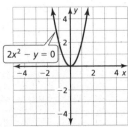

13. $y = \frac{1}{12}x^2$ **14.** $y = -\frac{1}{8}x^2$ **15.** $y = -x^2$

16. $x = -\frac{1}{48}y^2$ **17.** $x = \frac{5}{12}y^2$ **18.** $y = -\frac{3}{8}x^2$

19. $x = -\frac{1}{3}y^2$ **20.** $x = \frac{3}{4}y^2$

21. vertex: $(-3, 2)$, focus: $(-7, 2)$, directrix: $x = 1$,
axis of symmetry: $y = 2$; The graph is a shrink
towards the y-axis by a factor of $\frac{1}{4}$, followed by a
reflection in the y-axis and a translation 3 units left
and 2 units up.

22. vertex: $(-2, -1)$, focus: $\left(-2, -\frac{31}{32}\right)$,
directrix: $y = -\frac{33}{32}$, axis of symmetry: $x = -2$;
The graph is a vertical stretch by a factor of
32, followed by a translation 2 units left and 1 unit
down.

23. vertex: $(6, -3)$, focus: $\left(\frac{121}{20}, -3\right)$, directrix: $x = \frac{119}{120}$,
axis of symmetry: $y = -3$; The graph is a stretch
away from the y-axis by a factor of 20, followed by
a translation 6 units right and 3 units down.

24. vertex: $(-1, 9)$, focus: $(-1, 1)$, directrix: $y = 17$,
axis of symmetry: $x = -1$; The graph is a vertical
shrink by a factor of $\frac{1}{8}$, followed by a reflection
in the x-axis and a translation 1 unit left and 9 units
up.

2.3 Enrichment and Extension

1. $x = \frac{a^2}{4}y^2$ **2.** $y = \frac{n}{8}x^2$

3. $y = \frac{b}{12}x^2$ **4.** $x = \frac{3n}{2}y^2$

5. $\overline{RS}$ has a slope of
$$\frac{s^2 - r^2}{s - r} = \frac{(s - r)(s + r)}{s - r} = s + r = r + s.$$

$\overline{OT}$ has a slope of $\dfrac{t^2 - 0}{t - 0} = \dfrac{t^2}{t} = t.$

Because $\overrightarrow{RS}$ and $\overrightarrow{OT}$ are parallel lines, their slopes
are equal.
So, $r + s = t$.

Answers

6. To find the midpoint of a line segment, find the average of the x-values and y-values of the endpoints.

The x-value of the midpoint of $\overline{RS}$ would be $\dfrac{r+s}{2}$.

The x-value of the midpoint $\overline{OT}$ would be $\dfrac{t}{2}$.

The x-value of the midpoint $\overline{UV}$ would be $\dfrac{u+v}{2}$.

$\overline{UV}$ has as slope of

$$\dfrac{v^2 - u^2}{v - u} = \dfrac{(v - u)(v + u)}{v - u} = v + u = u + v.$$

Because $\overline{UV}$ is parallel to both $\overline{RS}$ and $\overline{OT}$, all slopes are equal and $u + v = r + s = t$.

So, the x-values of their midpoints are all the same and lie on the same line, $x = \dfrac{t}{2}$ or $x = \dfrac{r+s}{2}$ or $x = \dfrac{u+v}{2}$.

2.3 Puzzle Time

YELLOWSTONE PARK

2.4 Start Thinking

Sample answer:

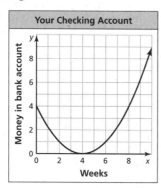

$y = 110.25$; After 25 weeks, you have \$110.25 in your bank account.

2.4 Warm Up

1. $y = -\frac{1}{6}(x - 6)$ **2.** $y - 3 = \frac{1}{2}(x - 1)$

3. $y + 1 = -2(x - 4)$ **4.** $y + 3 = 3(x - 3)$

5. $y + 18 = -\frac{1}{4}(x - 4)$ **6.** $y + 1 = -3(x - 6)$

2.4 Cumulative Review Warm Up

1.

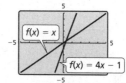

The graph is a vertical stretch by a factor of 4, followed by a translation 1 unit down of its parent function.

2.

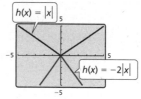

The graph is a vertical stretch by a factor of 2, followed by a reflection in the x-axis of its parent function.

3.

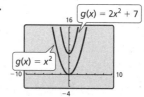

The graph is a vertical stretch by a factor of 2, followed by a translation 7 units up of its parent function.

4.

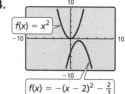

The graph is a reflection in the x-axis, followed by a translation 2 units right and $\frac{2}{3}$ unit down.

2.4 Practice A

1. $y = \frac{7}{16}(x - 2)^2 - 3$ **2.** $y = -\frac{1}{18}(x - 3)^2 - 8$

3. $y = -9(x + 1)^2 + 4$ **4.** $y = \frac{8}{5}(x - 10)(x - 6)$

5. $y = \frac{3}{16}(x - 2)(x - 8)$

6. $y = -\frac{2}{7}(x + 14)(x + 2)$

Answers

7. a. $y = -\frac{5}{9}(x - 1)^2 + 5$

b. $y = -\frac{5}{9}x^2 + \frac{10}{9}x + \frac{40}{9}$

c. $y = -\frac{5}{9}(x + 2)(x - 4)$

d. $y = -\frac{5}{9}x^2 + \frac{10}{9}x + \frac{40}{9}$

e. yes; intercept form; Two intercepts were given.

8. 9.21 ft

2.4 Practice B

1. $y = -\frac{1}{9}(x - 1)^2 - 6$ **2.** $-\frac{9}{49}(x + 2)^2 + 5$

3. $y = \frac{1}{3}(x + 1)^2 - 1$

4. $y = -\frac{5}{3}(x - 12)(x - 8)$

5. $y = \frac{1}{16}(x + 7)(x + 1)$

6. $y = -\frac{4}{81}(x + 9)(x - 9)$

7. The two given sets of coordinates were not substituted into the correct places.

$y = a(x - h)^2 + k$

$-7 = a(1 - 3)^2 - 5$

$-7 = 4a - 5$

$-2 = 4a$

$-\frac{1}{2} = a$

The equation is $y = -\frac{1}{2}(x - 3) - 5$.

8. a. The maximum area of 2500 square feet occurs when the length is 50 feet.

b. $A(x) = -x^2 + 100x$; $A(2) = 196 \text{ ft}^2$

c. 0 to 50 ft: $50\frac{\text{ft}^2}{\text{ft}}$; 50 to 100 ft: $-50\frac{\text{ft}^2}{\text{ft}}$

2.4 Enrichment and Extension

1. linear; $y = -1.8x + 212.10$

2. quadratic

a. $y = -4.9x^2 + 19.6x + 58.8$

b. $y = -4.9(x - 2)^2 + 78.4$

c. The graph of the function is a reflection in the x-axis, followed by a vertical stretch by a factor of 4.9 and a translation 2 units right and 78.4 units up of its parent function.

3. quadratic

a. $y = -3x^2 + 30x + 12$

b. $y = -3(x - 5)^2 + 87$

c. The graph of the function is a reflection in the x-axis, followed by a vertical stretch by a factor of 3 and a translation 5 units right and 87 units up of its parent function.

4. linear; $y = 0.433x + 14.7$

5. quadratic

a. $y = -5x^2 + 14x + 3$

b. $y = -5(x - 1.4)^2 + 12.8$

c. The graph of the function is a reflection in the x-axis, followed by a vertical stretch by a factor of 5 and a translation 1.4 units right and 12.8 units up of its parent function.

2.4 Puzzle Time

PINK FLAMINGO

Cumulative Review

1. $x = -18$ **2.** $x = -15$ **3.** $x = -12$

4. $x = -26$ **5.** $x = 75$ **6.** $x = -2$

7. $x = 3$ **8.** $x = 12$ **9.** $x = 21$

10. $x = 9$ **11.** $x = 8$ **12.** $x = 6$

13. $x = 26$ **14.** $x = -7$ **15.** $x = 8$

16. $x = -45$

17. a. 89%

b. 95%

c. 55 correct answers

d. 60 correct answers

18. a. 89%

b. 75%

c. 24 correct answers

d. 26 correct answers

e. 22 correct answers

19. 3 cups   **20.** 4 tablespoons

21. 5.83 **22.** 7.07 **23.** 2.83

24. 10.44 **25.** 18.87 **26.** 7.07

27. 12.37 **28.** 7.21 **29.** 10.44

Answers

30. 19.24   **31.** 10.00   **32.** 10.00   **33.** 12.08

34. 17.03   **35.** 12.04   **36.** $\frac{35}{3}$ **37.** $-\frac{9}{4}$

38. $5\frac{4}{7}$ or $\frac{39}{7}$ **39.** -2 **40.** -10

41. 8   **42.** 5   **43.** -3 **44.** 2

45. $x = \frac{1}{8}y - 3$ **46.** $x = 2y - 6$

47. $x = -\frac{1}{5}y + 7$ **48.** $x = 4y + 7$

49. $x = 2y + \frac{8}{3}$ **50.** $x = \frac{3}{2}y - \frac{5}{4}$

51. $x = 2y + 10$ **52.** $x = -\frac{1}{4}y - 5$

53. $x = 3y - 8$ **54.** $x = \frac{1}{4}$

55. no solution   **56.** no solution

57. no solution   **58.** $x = \frac{28}{9}$

59. $x = 6$ **60.** $x = \frac{81}{2}$

61. $x = \frac{100}{3}$ **62.** $x = 1$

63. $x = \frac{100}{9}$ **64.** $x = 8$

65. no solution   **66.** 5 h

67. 2.25 h   **68.** about 52.5 h

69. $y = -\frac{1}{8}x - \frac{5}{8}$ **70.** $y = 4x - 41$

71. $y = \frac{1}{2}x + 4$ **72.** $y = -\frac{7}{2}x - \frac{19}{2}$

73. $y = -\frac{13}{10}x + \frac{22}{5}$ **74.** $y = -\frac{3}{7}x + \frac{20}{7}$

75. $y = \frac{3}{5}x + \frac{37}{5}$ **76.** $y = \frac{19}{8}x - \frac{21}{4}$

77. $y = -4x + 17$ **78.** $y = -\frac{5}{4}x - 2$

79. $y = \frac{11}{8}x - \frac{23}{2}$ **80.** $y = -\frac{3}{4}x + \frac{21}{4}$

81. $y = -\frac{3}{14}x + \frac{41}{14}$ **82.** $y = \frac{1}{7}x - \frac{27}{7}$

83. $y = -\frac{5}{4}x + \frac{21}{4}$ **84.** $(x + 3)(x - 2)$

85. $(x + 6)(x - 7)$ **86.** $(x - 4)(x + 12)$

87. $(x - 11)(x + 7)$ **88.** $(x + 1)(x + 12)$

89. $(x + 8)(x - 2)$ **90.** $(x - 6)(x + 4)$

91. $(x + 5)(x - 1)$ **92.** $(x - 3)(x - 1)$

93. $(x + 6)(x + 5)$ **94.** $(x - 12)(x - 8)$

95. $(x + 5)(x + 8)$ **96.** $(2x + 7)(x - 5)$

97. $(3x + 10)(x - 4)$ **98.** $(2x - 1)(x + 10)$

99. $(3x - 2)(x - 10)$ **100.** $(4x - 12)(x + 12)$

101. $(5x - 3)(x + 2)$ **102.** $(2x - 4)(3x + 11)$

103. $(x + 9)(4x - 9)$

104. $(2x + 10)(x - 4)$ or $(2x - 8)(x + 5)$

105. $y = -x^2 - 4x + 32$

106. $y = 4x^2 + 4x - 48$

107. $y = -2x^2 - 2x + 4$

108. $y = -6x^2 + 6x + 72$

109. $y = -5x^2 + 55x - 120$

110. $y = 3x^2 - 9x - 84$

111. $y = 6x^2 - 36x + 54$

112. $y = -7x^2 - 14x - 7$

113. $y = 2x^2 - 16x + 32$

114. $y = x^2 - 8x + 17$

115. $y = x^2 + 10x + 18$

116. $y = x^2 - 16x + 73$

117. $y = 3x^2 + 6x + 7$

118. $y = -7x^2 - 70x - 178$

119. $y = -9x^2 + 54x - 74$

120. $y = -4x^2 - 64x - 261$

121. $y = 2x^2 - 20x + 51$

122. $y = 3x^2 + 6x + 2$

Answers

123. 6 in.   **124.** 42 ft^2 **125.** 18 in.

126. 5184 in.^{2} **127.** $x = 2 \pm 3i\sqrt{6}$

128. $x = -1 \pm \sqrt{15}$

129. $x = \dfrac{-3 \pm \sqrt{73}}{2}$

130. $x = \dfrac{5 \pm i\sqrt{47}}{2}$

131. $x = -3 \pm \sqrt{30}$ **132.** $x = 4 \pm \sqrt{34}$

133. $x = \dfrac{-7 \pm \sqrt{139}}{2}$ **134.** $x = \dfrac{5 \pm i\sqrt{47}}{6}$

135. $x = \dfrac{7 \pm \sqrt{129}}{-8}$ **136.** $x = \dfrac{2 \pm 2i\sqrt{39}}{5}$

137. $x = \dfrac{7 \pm i\sqrt{47}}{12}$ **138.** $x = \dfrac{-13 \pm i\sqrt{167}}{-8}$

139. $x = \dfrac{-3 \pm i\sqrt{55}}{4}$ **140.** $x = \dfrac{-5 \pm i\sqrt{119}}{-4}$

141. $x = \dfrac{-8 \pm i\sqrt{38}}{-3}$ **142.** $x = \dfrac{15 \pm i\sqrt{223}}{-8}$

143. $x = 3 \pm \sqrt{6}$ **144.** $x = \dfrac{-3 \pm i\sqrt{23}}{4}$

145. $x = \dfrac{9 \pm \sqrt{103}}{2}$ **146.** $x = \dfrac{3 \pm i\sqrt{111}}{12}$

147.

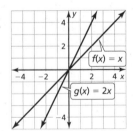

The graph of $g(x)$ is a vertical stretch by a factor of 2 of the graph of $f(x)$.

148.

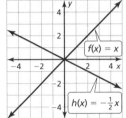

The graph of $h(x)$ is a vertical shrink by a factor of $\frac{1}{2}$ and a reflection in the y-axis of the graph of $f(x)$.

149.

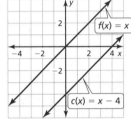

The graph of $c(x)$ is a vertical translation 4 units down of the graph of $f(x)$.

150.

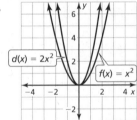

The graph of $d(x)$ is a vertical stretch by a factor of 2 of the graph of $f(x)$.

151.

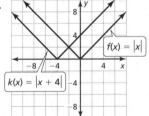

The graph of $k(x)$ is a horizontal translation 4 units left of the graph of $f(x)$.

152. The graph of $m(x)$ is a translation 3 units right and 2 units up of the graph of $f(x)$.

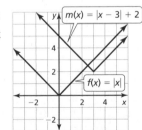

Answers

153. $g(x) = -2x - 3$ **154.** $g(x) = \frac{4}{7}x + 1$

155. $g(x) = |x + 2| + 4$

156. $g(x) = \frac{1}{2}|x - 6| - 7$

157. $g(x) = -|x - 3| - 5$

158. $g(x) = -|x + 1| + 2$

159. $g(x) = -3x - 1$

160. $g(x) = -\frac{3}{4}x + 5$

Chapter 3

3.1 Start Thinking

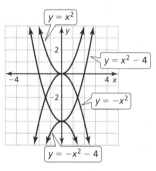

Equation	Number of x-intercepts	Point(s)
$y = x^2$	1	$(0, 0)$
$y = -x^2$	1	$(0, 0)$
$y = x^2 - 4$	2	$(-2, 0), (2, 0)$
$y = -x^2 - 4$	0	N/A

Yes, there are patterns; *Sample answer:* A quadratic equation has one x-intercept when the vertex is on the x-axis. If the quadratic equation opens down, the graph has two x-intercepts if the constant is positive and none if the constant is negative. If the quadratic equation opens up, the graph has two x-intercepts if the constant is negative and none if the constant is positive; The vertex is a minimum if the x^2 term is positive; The vertex is a maximum if the x^2 term is negative.

3.1 Warm Up

1. $(4, -2)$ **2.** $(-3, 4)$

3. infinitely many solutions

4. no solution

5. $\left(\frac{3}{11}, -\frac{21}{11}\right)$ or about $(0.27, -1.91)$

6. $(-1, -2)$

3.1 Cumulative Review Warm Up

1.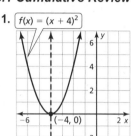

2.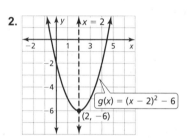

3.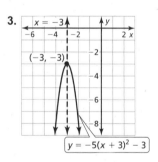

4.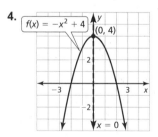

3.1 Practice A

1. $x = 5$ and $x = 1$ **2.** $x = 3$

3. $x = 5$ and $x = -5$ **4.** $x = -2$ and $x = 6$

5. $x = 4$ and $x = -4$ **6.** $x = 3$ and $x = -\frac{1}{2}$

Answers

7. $t = 10$ and $t = -10$ **8.** $g = 8$ and $g = -8$

9. $y = 2$ and $y = -6$

10. took the square root of each side before subtracting 16, and then incorrectly added the square roots of the terms on the left side; $(x - 2)^2 + 16 = 25$; $(x - 2)^2 = 9$; $x - 2 = \pm 3$; $x = 2 \pm 3$; $x = -1$ and $x = 5$

11. $x = 2$ and $x = -2$ **12.** $x = 2$ and $x = -3$

13. $m = 0$ and $m = -4$ **14.** 9

15. 1 or 7

16. $c = 2\sqrt{10}$ and $c = -2\sqrt{10}$; *Sample answer:* square root property; There is no linear term.

17. $v = 0$ and $v = 7$; *Sample answer:* factoring and zero product property; The binomial is factorable.

18. no solution; left side always negative, right side positive

19. $x = 8$ and $x = -3$; *Sample answer:* factoring and zero product property; The trinomial is factorable.

20. *Sample answer:* $x^2 + 10x - 24 = 0$

3.1 Practice B

1. $x = 1$ and $x = -1$ **2.** $x = 1$ and $x = -\dfrac{1}{3}$

3. $x = -7$ and $x = 2$ **4.** $x = \dfrac{3}{4}$ and $x = -3$

5. $x = -2$ and $x = 6$ **6.** $x = -3$ and $x = -6$

7. $k = 14$ and $k = -8$

8. $x = -1 + \sqrt{3}$ and $x = -1 - \sqrt{3}$

9. $x = 3$ and $x = -3$

10. *Sample answer:*

   a. $(x - 2)^2 + 4 = 20$

   b. $(x - 3)^2 + 4 = 10$

   c. $(x - 2)^2 + 10 = 4$

11. $x = 11$ and $x = -11$ **12.** $k = 9$ and $k = 0$

13. $w = 5$ and $w = -2$ **14.** $y = 0$ and $y = 3$

15. $x = \dfrac{2}{5}$ and $x = \dfrac{3}{5}$; *Sample answer:* Quadratic Formula; The trinomial contains fractions.

16. $n = 1.3$ and $n = -1.3$; *Sample answer:* square root property; There is no linear term.

17. 2 and -9 **18.** 4 and -4

19. 0 and 13   **20.** $\dfrac{4}{3}$

21. \$30 per rental; \$720

22. $h(t) = -16t^2 + 15$; $t \approx 0.968$ sec

3.1 Enrichment and Extension

1. 12 units   **2.** 16 in.

3. -3 or 2   **4.** 7 units by 15 units

5. 16 and 14 or -14 and -16

6. 8 and 9 or -9 and -8

7. -24 and -22 or 22 and 24

8. 16 and 9   **9.** 15 years old

10. 15 units by 17 units   **11.** 1 ft

12. 6 ft by 12 ft   **13.** 25 in.

14. 10 cm

3.1 Puzzle Time

BUY A DECK OF CARDS

3.2 Start Thinking

Most calculators will show an error screen instead of answering the keystrokes entered; There is no real number answer to the expression. Most calculators are not set up to consider the imaginary number set.

3.2 Warm Up

1. $10x + 32$ **2.** $10y + 58$

3. $12x + 18$ **4.** $12x + 64$

5. $7x + 10$ **6.** $12x - 82$

Answers

3.2 Cumulative Review Warm Up

1. vertex: $(-4, -1)$, focus: $\left(-4, \frac{3}{4}\right)$, directrix:

$y = -\frac{11}{4}$, axis of symmetry: $x = -4$

2. vertex: $(-4, 0)$, focus: $\left(-4, \frac{15}{4}\right)$, directrix:

$y = -\frac{15}{4}$, axis of symmetry: $x = -4$

3. vertex: $(3, 0)$, focus: $(3, -2)$, directrix: $y = 2$, axis of symmetry: $x = 3$

4. vertex: $(4, 4)$, focus: $(4, 5)$, directrix: $y = 3$, axis of symmetry: $x = 4$

3.2 Practice A

1. $5i$

2. $9i$

3. $4i\sqrt{2}$

4. $x = 3$ and $y = 3$

5. $x = -2$ and $y = 5$

6. $x = 13$ and $y = 4$

7. $x = 6$ and $y = -10$

8. $8 + 9i$

9. $13 - i$

10. $2 + 2i$

11. $-3 - i$

12. a. $0 + 11i$

b. $0 + \left(3\sqrt{3} - 1\right)i$

13. $-10 - 20i$

14. $9 + 24i$

15. $7 - i$

16. $48 + 46i$

17.

$[(14 + 5) - 3i] - 4i$	Definition of complex addition
$(19 - 3i) - 4i$	Simplify.
$19 + (-3i - 4i)$	Definition of complex addition
$19 - 7i$	Write in standard form.

18. $i\sqrt{3}$ and $-i\sqrt{3}$

19. $i\sqrt{7}$ and $-i\sqrt{7}$

20. $x = 6i$ and $x = -6i$

21. $x = 2i\sqrt{5}$ and $x = -2i\sqrt{5}$

3.2 Practice B

1. $15i$

2. $4i\sqrt{10}$

3. $12i\sqrt{6}$

4. $x = 7$ and $y = -4$

5. $x = 24$ and $y = 2$

6. $x = 11$ and $y = -10$

7. $x = 1$ and $y = \frac{10}{3}$

8. $-6 + 13i$

9. $8 + 6i$

10. $-3 + 15i$

11. $5 + i$

12. a. $-2 - 3i$

b. $-4 + 4i$

c. $5 - 2i$

13. $6 + 43i$

14. $34 + 0i$

15. $149 + 0i$

16. $20 - 48i$

17.

$48 - 18i - 16i + 6i^2$	Multiply using FOIL.
$48 - 34i + 6i^2$	Simplify and use $i^2 = -1$.
$48 - 34i + 6(-1)$	Simplify.
$42 - 34i$	Write in standard form.

18. $4i\sqrt{3}$ and $-4i\sqrt{3}$

19. $2i\sqrt{13}$ and $-2i\sqrt{13}$

20. $x = 2i\sqrt{11}$ and $x = -2i\sqrt{11}$

21. $x = 3i\sqrt{5}$ and $x = -3i\sqrt{5}$

3.2 Enrichment and Extension

1. $\frac{3}{5} - \frac{6}{5}i$

2. $\frac{1}{2} + \frac{1}{2}i$

3. $-1 + 0i$

4. $-\frac{1}{3} - \frac{4}{3}i$

5. $-\frac{2}{25} - \frac{14}{25}i$

6. $\frac{132}{25} - \frac{24}{25}i$

Answers

7–18.

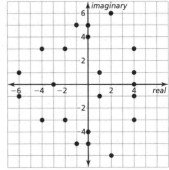

19. Complex numbers and their conjugates are the reflection of one another in the real axis.

20. $a = 0$, so $a + bi$ is a pure imaginary number.

3.2 Puzzle Time

YOU'D KNOW THE DIFFERENCE IF YOU EVER LET A PTERODACTYL SIT ON YOUR SHOULDER

3.3 Start Thinking

$x^2 + 8x + 16$; To find the middle term, multiply the terms inside the parentheses and then multiply the result by 2. To find the last term, square the second term inside the parentheses; $a^2 + 6a + 9 = (a + 3)^2$, $b^2 + 14b + 49 = (b + 7)^2$; You could take the coefficient of the middle term, divide it by 2, and then square the result.

3.3 Warm Up

1. $(5z + y)(5z - y)$ **2.** $(5x + 1)(5x - 1)$

3. $(7x + 2y)^2$ **4.** $\left(\dfrac{1}{x} + 1\right)\left(\dfrac{1}{x} - 1\right)$

5. $2(2y + 1)(2y - 1)$ **6.** $r(2s - 1)^2$

3.3 Cumulative Review Warm Up

1. absolute value, domain: all real numbers, range: $y \geq 0$

2. linear, domain: all real numbers, range: all real numbers

3. quadratic, domain: all real numbers, range: $y \geq 1$

4. absolute value, domain: all real numbers, range: $y \geq -1$

5. linear, domain: all real numbers, range: all real numbers

6. quadratic, domain: all real numbers, range: $y \leq -5$

3.3 Practice A

1. $x = 5$ and $x = -1$ **2.** $y = 13$ and $y = -1$

3. $n = 10 + 2\sqrt{10}$ and $n = 10 - 2\sqrt{10}$

4. $p = -7 + \sqrt{2}$ and $p = -7 - \sqrt{2}$

5. $c = 16; (x + 4)^2$ **6.** $c = 49; (x + 7)^2$

7. $c = 81; (y - 9)^2$

8. $c = 169; (y + 13)^2$

9. $x = -4 + \sqrt{11}$ and $x = 4 - \sqrt{11}$

10. $h = 5 + \sqrt{29}$ and $h = 5 - \sqrt{29}$

11. $t = 6 + \sqrt{26}$ and $t = 6 - \sqrt{26}$

12. $s = -7 + \sqrt{58}$ and $s = -7 - \sqrt{58}$

13. $y = -3 + \sqrt{11}$ and $y = -3 - \sqrt{11}$

14. $g = -5 + \sqrt{19}$ and $g = -5 - \sqrt{19}$

15. square roots; Both sides are perfect squares; $x = 8$ and $x = -2$

16. factoring; factorable; $x = -4$ and $x = -1$

17. *Sample answer:* factoring and square roots; factorable, both sides are perfect squares; $x = 3$

18. completing the square; even middle term; $x = 5 + \sqrt{33}$ and $x = 5 - \sqrt{33}$

19. 4   **20.** $-2 + 2\sqrt{6}$

21. $f(x) = (x + 5)^2 + 7; (-5, 7)$

22. $g(x) = (x - 3)^2 - 11; (3, -11)$

3.3 Practice B

1. $w = 20$ and $w = 2$

2. $k = 8 + 2i\sqrt{2}$ and $k = 8 - 2i\sqrt{2}$

3. $t = 15 + 2i\sqrt{6}$ and $t = 15 - 2i\sqrt{6}$

Answers

4. $p = \dfrac{-1 + 2\sqrt{3}}{3}$ and $p = \dfrac{-1 - 2\sqrt{3}}{3}$

5. $c = 64; (x + 8)^2$ **6.** $c = \dfrac{49}{4}; \left(x + \dfrac{7}{2}\right)^2$

7. $c = \dfrac{9}{4}; \left(y - \dfrac{3}{2}\right)^2$ **8.** $c = 100; (y + 10)^2$

9. $q = -3 + \sqrt{10}$ and $q = -3 - \sqrt{10}$

10. $h = \dfrac{1}{2} + \dfrac{\sqrt{13}}{2}$ and $h = \dfrac{1}{2} - \dfrac{\sqrt{13}}{2}$

11. $x = -4 + \sqrt{11}$ and $x = -4 - \sqrt{11}$

12. $y = 6$ and $y = 2$

13. $t = 2 + \sqrt{6}$ and $t = 2 - \sqrt{6}$

14. $s = -\dfrac{5}{2} + \dfrac{\sqrt{31}}{2}$ and $s = -\dfrac{5}{2} - \dfrac{\sqrt{31}}{2}$

15. square roots; Both sides are perfect squares;
$x = -16$ and $x = -2$

16. completing the square; not factorable;
$x = -1 + \dfrac{\sqrt{21}}{3}$ and $x = -1 - \dfrac{\sqrt{21}}{3}$

17. *Sample answer:* factoring; factorable; $x = 12$ and
$x = -12$

18. factoring; factorable; $x = 3$ and $x = -3$

19. $f(x) = (x + 9)^2 + 19; (-9, 19)$

20. $g(x) = (x - 1)^2 - 27; (1, -27)$

21. $h(x) = (x + 11)^2 - 25; (-11, -25)$

22. $f(x) = \left(x - \dfrac{1}{2}\right)^2 + \dfrac{7}{4}; \left(\dfrac{1}{2}, \dfrac{7}{4}\right)$

23. a. 18 ft

     b. $t = 1 + \dfrac{\sqrt{11}}{4}$ sec or $t \approx 1.8$ sec

3.3 Enrichment and Extension

1. $f(x) = 4(x - 0)^2 + 0; (0, 0); x = 0$

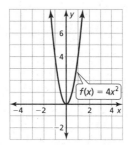

The graph is a vertical stretch by a factor of 4 of the graph of the parent quadratic function.

2. $f(x) = -(x - 0)^2 + 3; (0, 3); x = -\sqrt{3} \approx -1.73$
and $x = \sqrt{3} \approx 1.73$

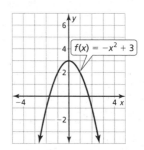

The graph is a reflection in the x-axis followed by a vertical translation 3 units up of the graph of the parent quadratic function.

3. $f(x) = \left(x - \dfrac{5}{2}\right)^2 - \dfrac{25}{4}; \left(\dfrac{5}{2}, -\dfrac{25}{4}\right); x = 0$ and
$x = 5$

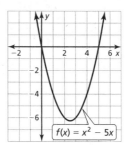

The graph is a horizontal translation $\dfrac{5}{2}$ units right
followed by a vertical translation $\dfrac{25}{4}$ units down of
the graph of the parent quadratic function.

Answers

4. $f(x) = (x + 4)^2 - 5; (-4, -5);$

$x = -4 - \sqrt{5} \approx -6.24$ and

$x = -4 + \sqrt{5} \approx -1.76$

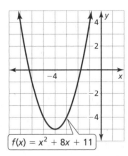

$f(x) = x^2 + 8x + 11$

The graph is a horizontal translation 4 units left followed by a vertical translation 5 units down of the graph of the parent quadratic function.

5. $f(x) = -3(x - 1)^2 - 6; (1, -6);$ no x-intercepts

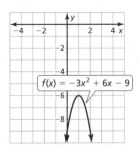

$f(x) = -3x^2 + 6x - 9$

The graph is a reflection in the x-axis followed by a vertical stretch by a factor of 3, and a horizontal translation 1 unit right and vertical translation 6 units down of the graph of the parent quadratic function.

6. $f(x) = 2(x + 3)^2 - 5; (-3, -5);$

$x = -3 - \dfrac{\sqrt{10}}{2} \approx -4.58$ and

$x = -3 + \dfrac{\sqrt{10}}{2} \approx -1.42$

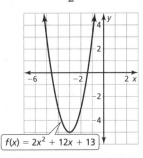

$f(x) = 2x^2 + 12x + 13$

The graph is a vertical stretch by a factor of 2 followed by horizontal translation 3 units left and vertical translation 5 units down of the graph of the parent quadratic function.

A26 **Algebra 2**
Answers

3.3 Puzzle Time

ONLINE SKATER

3.4 Start Thinking

Sample answer: completing the square: Use when $a = 1$ and b is even. Also, use when there is no c term; factoring: Use when the function is easily factorable; graphing: Use when the equation includes decimals or when approximated answers are accepted; using square roots: Use when the algebraic expression is a perfect square; graphing, using square roots, factoring, completing the square

3.4 Warm Up

1. $\dfrac{3}{2}$ **2.** -1 **3.** -4

4. 4   **5.** 16   **6.** $-\dfrac{6}{5}$

3.4 Cumulative Review Warm Up

1. $g(x) = 6x - 3$ **2.** $g(x) = -\dfrac{1}{3}x + 5$

3.4 Practice A

1. $x = \dfrac{-9 \pm \sqrt{65}}{2}$ **2.** $x = -1$ and $x = 2$

3. $x = -3$ **4.** $x = \dfrac{1}{4}$ and $x = -1$

5. $x = \dfrac{5}{6} \pm \dfrac{\sqrt{23}}{6}i$ **6.** $x = 12$

7. $x = \dfrac{-7}{4} \pm \dfrac{\sqrt{23}}{4}i$ **8.** $x = \dfrac{1}{3} \pm \dfrac{5\sqrt{2}}{6}i$

9. 12; two real solutions   **10.** 0; one real solution

11. -207; two imaginary solutions

12. 16; two real solutions   **13.** B

14. *Sample answer:*
$a = 1; c = 16; x^2 + 8x + 16 = 0$

15. *Sample answer:*
$a = 2; c = 10; 2x^2 - 5x + 10 = 0$

16. $4x^2 - 9x + 10 = 0$ **17.** $-3x^2 + 11x - 2 = 0$

18. $x = \dfrac{2}{3}$; square root; perfect square

Answers

19. $x = 3$ and $x = \dfrac{1}{4}$; Quadratic Formula; difficult to factor

20. $x = 6 \pm 3\sqrt{3}$; complete the square; even middle term and leading coefficient of 1

21. $x = -2$ and $x = 6$; factoring; easy to factor

22. $b^2 - 4ac > 0$

$1 - 4c > 0$

$c < \dfrac{1}{4}$

3.4 Practice B

1. $x = -4$ and $x = 1$ **2.** $x = -1$

3. $x = -\dfrac{5}{2} \pm \dfrac{\sqrt{55}}{2}i$ **4.** $x = \dfrac{3 \pm \sqrt{89}}{8}$

5. $x = -6 \pm \sqrt{51}$ **6.** $x = 1 \pm \dfrac{\sqrt{66}}{3}i$

7. $v = 5 \pm \sqrt{21}$ **8.** $t = \dfrac{4}{3} \pm \dfrac{\sqrt{2}}{3}i$

9. -24; two imaginary solutions

10. 0; one real solution **11.** 132; two real solutions

12. -23; two imaginary solutions

13. C

14. *Sample answer:* $a = 1; c = -7; x^2 - 3x - 7 = 0$

15. *Sample answer:*
$a = 4; c = 12; 4x^2 + 10x + 12 = 0$

16. $7x^2 - 10x + 6 = 0$ **17.** $4x^2 + 3x - 1 = 0$

18. $x = 1$; square root; perfect square after factoring out 7

19. $x = -10 \pm 6\sqrt{3}$; complete the square; even middle term and leading coefficient of 1

20. $x = -\dfrac{1}{2} \pm \dfrac{\sqrt{7}}{2}i$; Quadratic Formula; odd middle term

21. $x = 2$ and $x = 4$; factoring; easy to factor

22. $b^2 - 4ac < 0$

$1 - 4c < 0$

$c > \dfrac{1}{4}$

3.4 Enrichment and Extension

1. $x = 1$ and $x = -\dfrac{1}{8}$; yes

2. $x = -\dfrac{5}{2}$ and $x = \dfrac{4}{3}$; yes

3. $x = -1$ and $x = 7$; yes

4. $x = -\dfrac{2}{3}$ and $x = \dfrac{4}{5}$; yes

5. $x = -2.25$ and $x = 14$; yes

6. $x = 2$ and $x = -\dfrac{20}{7}$; yes

7. one real solution; $x = 0$

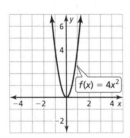

8. two real solutions; $x = -\sqrt{3}$ and $x = \sqrt{3}$

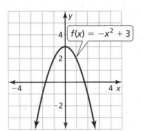

9. two real solutions; $x = 0$ and $x = 5$

Answers

10. The average of the *x*-intercepts is the *x*-value of the vertex.

3.4 Puzzle Time

SOFA SO GOOD

3.5 Start Thinking

Sample answer:

system with one linear equation and one quadratic equation, two points of intersection:

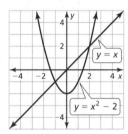

system with two quadratic equations, one point of intersection:

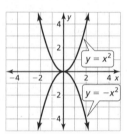

system with two quadratic equations, two points of intersection:

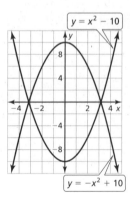

3.5 Warm Up

1. $(3.4, -1.4)$ **2.** $(0, 0)$ **3.** $(2, -1)$

4. infinitely many solutions

3.5 Cumulative Review Warm Up

1.

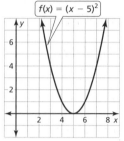

2.

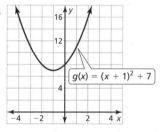

3.

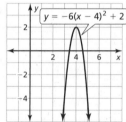

4.

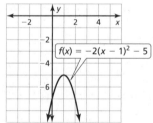

3.5 Practice A

1. $(-6, 0)$ and $(-4, 2)$ **2.** $(-2, -3)$

3. $(0, 3)$ and $(1, 2)$ **4.** $(1, -1)$ and $(4, 5)$

5. $(1, 2)$ **6.** no solution

7. $(1, -3)$ and $(4, 0)$ **8.** $(0, 5)$ and $(5, 0)$

9. $(1, 0)$ **10.** $(1, 7)$ and $\left(-\dfrac{1}{4}, 7\right)$

11. $(3, -8)$

Answers

12. $(-0.25, -7.5)$ and $(1, -10)$

13. no solution   **14.** $(3, 3)$ and $(1, 3)$

15. The horizontal line cuts through the circle, intersecting in two places.

3.5 Practice B

1. no solution   **2.** $(1, 3)$ and $(-2, -6)$

3. $(0, -9)$ and $(-3, 0)$ **4.** $(1, 2)$

5. $(0.27, 0)$ and $(3.7, 0)$ **6.** $(0, 6)$ and $(-2, 2)$

7. $(1, -2)$ and $(-1, -2)$ **8.** $(1, 0)$

9. no solution   **10.** $(-3, -2)$ and $(2, 3)$

11. no solution   **12.** $(-8, 32)$ and $(2, 2)$

13. $(-4, 24)$ and $(-2, 12)$ **14.** $(3, -8)$ and $\left(\dfrac{7}{3}, -8\right)$

15. The horizontal line is tangent to the circle either at the top or the bottom.

3.5 Enrichment and Extension

1. parabola; $y = \dfrac{9}{4}(x - 1)^2 - 3$

2. circle; $(x - 1)^2 + (y - 1)^2 = 8$

3. hyperbola; $\dfrac{(x + 2)^2}{5} - \dfrac{(y + 3)^2}{20} = 1$

4. parabola; $y = (x + 3)^2 - 4$

5. circle; $(x + 1)^2 + (y + 3)^2 = 25$

6. hyperbola: $\dfrac{(x + 1)^2}{9} - \dfrac{(y - 2)^2}{4} = 1$

3.5 Puzzle Time

SPUDNIK

3.6 Start Thinking

Sample answer:

Graph the <u>parabola</u> with $y = x^2 + bx + c$. Make the <u>parabola</u> *dashed* for inequalities with $<$ or $>$ and *solid* for inequalities with $\leq$ or $\geq$.

Test a point (x, y) <u>inside</u> the <u>parabola</u> to determine whether the point is a solution to the inequality.

Shade the region <u>inside</u> the <u>parabola</u> if the point is a solution. Shade the region <u>outside</u> the <u>parabola</u> if the point is not a solution.

3.6 Warm Up

1. 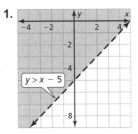   **2.**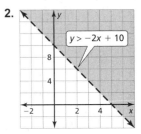

3. 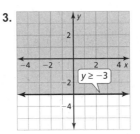   **4.**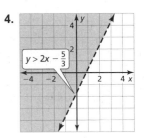

3.6 Cumulative Review Warm Up

1. $x = 8$
     $y = -1$
     $z = 6$

2. $x = -2$
     $y = -4$
     $z = 7$

3.6 Practice A

1. 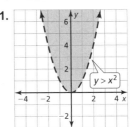   **2.**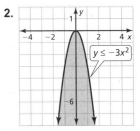

Answers

3.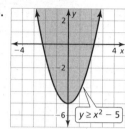
$y \geq x^2 - 5$

4.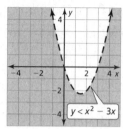
$y < x^2 - 3x$

5. $y \geq f(x)$

6. $y \leq f(x)$

7.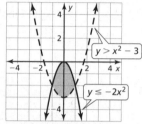
$y > x^2 - 3$
$y \leq -2x^2$

8.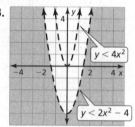
$y < 4x^2$
$y < 2x^2 - 4$

9. $x < -\dfrac{4}{3}$ or $x > \dfrac{4}{3}$

10. $x \leq 1$ or $x \geq 7$

11. $-7 \leq x \leq -3$

12. $1 < x < \dfrac{9}{2}$

13. all real numbers

14. $-5.54 \leq x \leq 0.54$

15. $-5 \leq x \leq -1$

16. $x < -3.73$ or $x > -0.27$

17. a. $125w - w^2 \geq 2500$

  b. $25 \leq w \leq 100$

3.6 Practice B

1.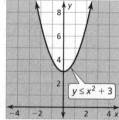
$y \leq x^2 + 3$

2.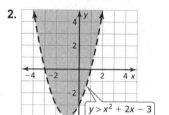
$y > x^2 + 2x - 3$

3.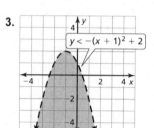
$y < -(x + 1)^2 + 2$

4.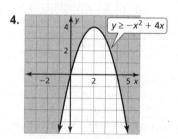
$y \geq -x^2 + 4x$

5. wrong side was shaded
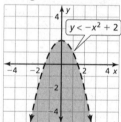
$y < -x^2 + 2$

6.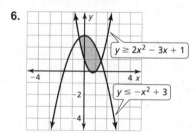
$y \geq 2x^2 - 3x + 1$
$y \leq -x^2 + 3$

7.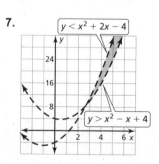
$y < x^2 + 2x - 4$
$y > x^2 - x + 4$

Answers

8. $x > \dfrac{1}{2}$ or $x < -6$ **9.** $\dfrac{1}{2} \le x \le 2$

10. $x \le -3 - \sqrt{13}$ or $x \ge -3 + \sqrt{13}$

11. $-3 < x < 9$ **12.** $x < -2.64$ or $x > 1.14$

13. $-1.66 \le x \le 0.91$ **14.** $-3.24 \le x \le 1.24$

15. $x < -4.37$ or $x > 1.37$

16. a. 25 ft; $h(t) = 25$ when $t = 0$.

    b. $-16t^2 - 28t + 25 > 0$

    c. $0 < t < 0.65$

3.6 Enrichment and Extension

Number of handbags purchased	Price per handbag (dollars)	Revenue per order (dollars)
1	368	368
2	366	732
3	364	1092
4	362	1448
5	360	1800
6	358	2148
$\vdots$	$\vdots$	$\vdots$
x	$370 - 2x$	$x(370 - 2x)$

    a. $R(x) = -2x^2 + 370x$

    b. \$17,112

    c. 92 or 93

    d. $C(x) = 30x + 312$

    e. $P(x) = -2x^2 + 340x - 312 > 0$

    f. between 1 and 169, including 1 and 169

    g. \$14,138; 85 handbags

3.6 Puzzle Time

BAGELS

Cumulative Review

1. $5\sqrt{2}$ **2.** $3\sqrt{5}$ **3.** $4\sqrt{6}$

4. $8\sqrt{3}$ **5.** $10\sqrt{3}$ **6.** $-3\sqrt{6}$

7. $-5\sqrt{7}$ **8.** $-6\sqrt{2}$ **9.** $\dfrac{\sqrt{5}}{6}$

10. $\dfrac{\sqrt{6}}{7}$ **11.** $\dfrac{\sqrt{3}}{2}$ **12.** $\dfrac{\sqrt{7}}{3}$

13. $\dfrac{1}{4}$ **14.** $-\dfrac{2}{5}$ **15.** $-\dfrac{\sqrt{7}}{9}$

16. $-\dfrac{\sqrt{5}}{8}$ **17.** 3   **18.** 0

19. 2   **20.** 3   **21.** $\sqrt{11}$

22. $\sqrt{10}$ **23.** $\sqrt{67}$ **24.** 1

25. $-46x + 5$ **26.** $28x + 22$

27. $7x^2 + 12x - 8$ **28.** $x^2 + 20x - 15$

29. $33x - 24$ **30.** $-x^2 + 25x - 35$

31. $27x^3 - 7x^2 + 41x + 9$

32. $-x^5 + 4x^4 - 16x^2 - 7x - 6$

33. $8x^3 + 10x^2 + 22x + 19$

34. $-10x^4 + 35x^3 - 19x^2 + 8x - 20$

35. a. 20.4 min   **b.** 21 min   **c.** 1.1 min

36. $4x^2 - 40x + 44$ **37.** $-10x^2 + 5x + 15$

38. $x^2 + 6x + 8$ **39.** $x^2 - 3x + 2$

40. $-20x^2 + 5x + 90$

41. $6x^3 - 21x^2 - 22x + 77$

42. $12x^3 - 142x^2 + 60x + 14$

43. $30x^4 - 40x^3 + 21x^2 - 8x + 3$

44. $-84x^3 - 164x^2 - 79x - 9$

45. $x^4 - 4x^3 - 30x^2 + 116x - 99$

46. $-2x^5 + 12x^4 - 5x^3 + 58x^2 - 129x - 11$

47. $6x^4 + 65x^3 + 53x^2 - 156x + 60$

Answers

48. $4x^2 + 28x + 12$ **49.** $-10x^2 - 25x + 50$

50. $x^2 + 16x + 48$ **51.** $-8x^2 + 160x - 792$

52. $3x^2 + 6x - 9$ **53.** $16x^2 - 12x - 28$

54. $-96x^2 - 444x + 462$ **55.** $2x^2 + 20x - 10$

56. $7x^2 + 23x - 17$ **57.** $54x^2 + 9x + 31$

58. $-6x^2 - 47x - 28$ **59.** $4x^2 + 21x - 87$

60. a. 95 items
   b. 22 items

61. brother $= 7$ min, sister $= 12$ min

62. a. width $= 14$ ft, length $= 19$ ft
   b. \$1056
   c. 266 ft^2

63. $x = -4, x = 7$ **64.** $x = 2, x = 3$

65. $x = -7, x = 9$ **66.** $x = -1, x = \dfrac{5}{2}$

67. $x = -3, x = -\dfrac{9}{4}$ **68.** $x = -3, x = \dfrac{2}{5}$

69. $x = -\dfrac{2}{3}, x = \dfrac{7}{5}$ **70.** $x = \dfrac{5}{4}, x = \dfrac{7}{2}$

71. $x = -\dfrac{1}{4}, x = \dfrac{1}{6}$ **72.** $x = -\dfrac{3}{7}, x = \dfrac{1}{12}$

73. $x = -\dfrac{4}{7}, x = \dfrac{1}{4}$ **74.** $x = -\dfrac{1}{5}, x = \dfrac{9}{8}$

75. $x = -12, x = \dfrac{5}{6}$ **76.** $x = -\dfrac{5}{2}, x = \dfrac{10}{11}$

77. $x = -\dfrac{4}{3}, x = \dfrac{6}{11}$ **78.** $y = x + 9$

79. $y = \dfrac{1}{2}x + 5$ **80.** $y = 3x - 17$

81. $y = 2x - 4$ **82.** $y = 11x - 23$

83. $y = -\dfrac{3}{4}x + \dfrac{5}{4}$ **84.** $y = 6x + 3$

85. $y = 5x + 9$ **86.** $y = -14x + 21$

87. $y = 6x - 24$ **88.** $y = -2x + 28$

89. $y = 45x - 20$ **90.** -108

91. -524 **92.** 448 **93.** 368

94. 57 **95.** 53 **96.** -20

97. -28 **98.** -279 **99.** -116

100. 73 **101.** -4

102. a. $(b) + (b + 4) = 18$
   b. 11 baskets
   c. 7 baskets

103. a. 55 mi/h
   b. 2.75 h

104. $x = -8, x = 10$ **105.** $x = -34, x = 22$

106. $x = 0, x = 4$ **107.** $x = -14, x = 6$

108. $x = -13, x = 3$ **109.** $x = -9, x = 25$

110. $x = \dfrac{11}{3}, x = \dfrac{13}{3}$ **111.** $x = -18, x = 12$

112. no solution   **113.** $(7, -3)$

114. $(-4, -2)$ **115.** no solution

116. $(6, -6)$

117. infinitely many solutions

118. $(5, -7)$ **119.** $(3, -4, 6)$

120. $(9, 8, -2)$ **121.** $(-6, -2, 1)$

122. infinitely many solutions

123. $(2, -1, -4)$ **124.** no solution

125. $6 + 15i$ **126.** $-12 + 10i$

127. $-5 - 5i$ **128.** $7 - 18i$

129. $9 + 7i$ **130.** $-12 - 8i$

131. $2 + 2i$ **132.** $2i$

133. $26 - 3i$ **134.** $11 + 22i$

Answers

135. $16 + 72i$ **136.** $-60 - 24i$

137. $-39 - 4i$ **138.** $79 + 16i$

139. $47 - i$ **140.** $27 - 36i$

141. $-23 + 264i$ **142.** $80 + 18i$

143. a. 23 lb

  b. $0.45

  c. about $0.91

Chapter 4

4.1 Start Thinking

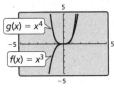

The graph of $f(x) = x^3$ is a curvy line that is moving upward from left to right as x increases. The graph of $g(x) = x^4$ is similar to a parabola that opens up with its vertex at the origin. Both graphs have positive y-values when x is positive. When x is negative, the y-values of $f(x)$ are negative, and the y-values of $g(x)$ are positive; The exponent is even; yes; $(0, 0)$ and $(1, 1)$

4.1 Warm Up

1. -20 **2.** 39 **3.** 10

4. 40 **5.** -45.8 **6.** 33.96

4.1 Cumulative Review Warm Up

1. down **2.** up **3.** down **4.** up

4.1 Practice A

1. polynomial function;
 $f(x) = 5x^3 + 4x^2 - 3x - 7$, degree is 3, cubic, leading coefficient is 5

2. not a polynomial function

3. polynomial function;
 $g(x) = x^4 - 4x^3 - \dfrac{1}{3}x^2 + 2x + 10$, degree is 4, quartic, leading coefficient is 1

4. polynomial function; $f(x) = 8x^2 - \sqrt{3}x + 2$, degree is 2, quadratic, leading coefficient is 8

5. -2 **6.** 6848 **7.** 15,651

8. $g(x) \to +\infty$ as $x \to +\infty$ and $g(x) \to +\infty$ as $x \to -\infty$.

9. $h(x) \to -\infty$ as $x \to +\infty$ and $h(x) \to +\infty$ as $x \to -\infty$.

10. 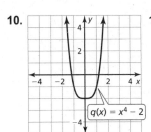 **11.**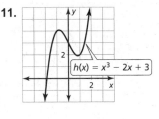

12. 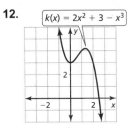 **13.**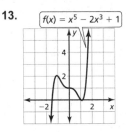

14. f is increasing when $x > 3$. f is decreasing when $x < 3$. f is positive when $x < 2$ and $x > 4$. f is negative when $2 < x < 4$.

15. f is increasing when $x < -1.2$ and $x > 1.2$. f is decreasing when $-1.2 < x < 1.2$. f is positive when $-2 < x < 0$ and $x > 2$. f is negative when $x < -2$ and $0 < x < 2$.

16. The degree is even and the leading coefficient is negative.

4.1 Practice B

1. not a polynomial function

2. polynomial function; $f(x) = 11x^2 + 12x - \sqrt{7}$, degree is 2, quadratic, leading coefficient is 11

3. polynomial function;
 $g(x) = 2x^4 - \sqrt{14}x^3 - \dfrac{1}{3}x^2 + 2x - \dfrac{5}{3}$, degree is 4, quartic, leading coefficient is 2

4. not a polynomial function

5. 1841 **6.** $-\dfrac{47}{9}$ **7.** $-\dfrac{5}{8}$

Answers

8. $g(x) \to -\infty$ as $x \to +\infty$ and $g(x) \to -\infty$ as $x \to -\infty$.

9. $h(x) \to +\infty$ as $x \to +\infty$ and $h(x) \to -\infty$ as $x \to -\infty$.

10.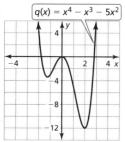

$q(x) = x^4 - x^3 - 5x^2$

11.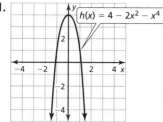

$h(x) = 4 - 2x^2 - x^4$

12.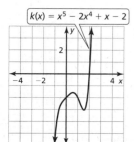

$k(x) = x^5 - 2x^4 + x - 2$

13.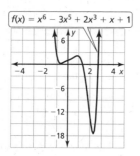

$f(x) = x^6 - 3x^5 + 2x^3 + x + 1$

14.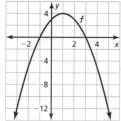

The degree is even and the leading coefficient is negative.

15.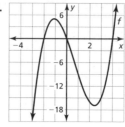

The degree is odd and the leading coefficient is positive.

16. *Sample answer*: $-2 \le x \le 8$; $-5 \le y \le 50$

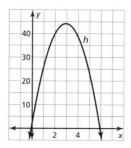

4.1 Enrichment and Extension

1. $y \approx 1.17x^4 - 14.33x^3 + 60.83x^2 - 102.67x + 56$

2. $y \approx 0.12x^4 - 2.89x^3 + 23.51x^2 - 76.96x + 84$

3. $y \approx -0.29x^4 + 1.07x^3 + 1.96x^2 - 5.93x - 0.60$

4. $y \approx 1.39 \times 10^{-4}x^4 - 0.03x^3 + 2.78x^2 - 88.57x + 969.47$

4.1 Puzzle Time

COBWEBS

4.2 Start Thinking

Sample answer:

$$(x + 1)(x - 1) = x^2 - x + x - 1 = x^2 - 1;$$
$$(x + 3)(x - 3) = x^2 - 3x + 3x - 9 = x^2 - 9;$$

yes; In each example, the middle terms cancel out, leaving only two terms. The first term is the square of the first term in each binomial. The second term is the square of the second term in each binomial;

$$(x + 1)(x + 1) = x^2 + x + x + 1 = x^2 + 2x + 1;$$
$$(x - 3)(x - 3) = x^2 - 3x - 3x + 9 = x^2 - 6x + 9;$$

no; The signs are the same inside the binomials, so the middle terms no longer cancel.

Answers

1. 7 **2.** $-x + 7$ **3.** $28m + 21$

4. $10r$ **5.** $-3z^2 - 2z$ **6.** $-2m - 4p$

4.2 Cumulative Review Warm Up

1. $\dfrac{25}{4}; \left(x + \dfrac{5}{2}\right)^2$ **2.** $9; (z + 3)^2$

3. $36; (w - 6)^2$ **4.** $\dfrac{625}{4}; \left(x - \dfrac{25}{2}\right)^2$

5. $16; (x - 4)^2$ **6.** $\dfrac{729}{4}; \left(s + \dfrac{27}{2}\right)^2$

4.2 Practice A

1. $4x^2 + 7x - 9$

2. $7x^5 + 5x^4 + 3x^2 - 3x - 5$

3. $5x^4 + 2x^3 - 4x^2 - 9$

4. $-4x^3 + 4x^2 - 4x + 2$

5. $8x^4 + x^3 - 3x^2 - 4x + 6$

6. $7x^5 - 6x^4 + 13x^3 - 3x^2 + 12x + 8$

7. $7x^2 + 9x - 8$

8. $15x^4 + 35x^3 + 30x^2$

9. $-20x^7 + 18x^6 + 14x^5 - 8x^4$

10. $-24x^3 + 25x^2 - 9x + 2$

11. $-3x^3 - 20x^2 - 21x - 54$

12. The negative was distributed incorrectly;
$-3x^2\left(4x^2 - 5x + 7\right) = -12x^4 + 15x^3 - 21x^2$

13. $x^3 - 13x + 12$

14. $x^3 - 13x^2 + 24x + 108$

15. $4x^3 + 8x^2 - 15x - 9$

16. $12x^3 - 25x^2 - 87x - 20$

17. $x^2 - 64$ **18.** $y^2 + 8y + 16$

19. $4p^2 - 12p + 9$

4.2 Practice B

1. $8x^7 + 15x^6 - 2x^5 + x^3 - 6x + 2$

2. $14x^4 - 7x^3 - 4x + 5$

3. $-3x^5 + 3x^4 - 8x^2 + 10x + 9$

4. $9x^4 + 5x^3 - 6x^2 - 7x + 11$

5. $x^4 - 10x^3 + 13x^2 + 48x + 12$

6. $-10x^4 - 19x^3 + 7x^2 + 14x - 4$

7. $4x^4 - 11x^3 + 20x^2 - 18x + 12$

8. $3x^6 - 6x^5 + x^4 + 3x^3 - 40x^2 - 25x$

9. The exponents were multiplied instead of added;
$4x^2\left(3x^4 - 2x^3 + 7\right) = 12x^6 - 8x^5 + 28x^2$

10. $6x^3 - 14x^2 - 14x + 6$

11. $8x^3 - 26x^2 - 67x - 15$

12. $-16x^3 + 12x^2 + 28x - 15$

13. $8x^3 - 30x^2 + 13x + 30$

14. $9x^2 - 25$

15. $36t^2 + 84t + 49$

16. $p^2q^2 + 4pq + 4$

17. a. *Sample answer:* $(3x - 1)(x + 6)^2$

  b. $3x^3 + 35x^2 + 96x - 36$

4.2 Enrichment and Extension

1. $a = 3, b = 4, c = 2$

2. $a = 1, b = 3, c = 2, d = 5$

3. $a = 0, b = 2, c = -4, d = 10$

4. $a = -4, b = 3, c = 5, d = -13$

5. $a = 7, b = 0, c = 1$

6. $a = 9, b = -30, c = -5$ or $a = 9, b = 30,$
  $c = 5$

Answers

7.

```
                1
             1     1
          1     2     1
       1     3     3     1
    1     4     6     4     1
 1     5    10    10     5     1
1   6    15    20    15    6    1
```

8. $(x + 1)^6 = x^6 + 6x^5 + 15x^4 + 20x^3 + 15x^2 + 6x + 1$

9. $(2y - 2)^6 = 64y^6 - 384y^5 + 960y^4 - 1280y^3 + 960y^2 - 384y + 64$

10. $(1 - y)^6 = 1 - 6y + 15y^2 - 20y^3 + 15y^4 - 6y^5 + y^6$

11. x^{12}

12. $(x^2 - 2)^6 = x^{12} - 12x^{10} + 60x^8 - 160x^6 + 240x^4 - 192x^2 + 64$

13. $(bc + de)^6 = b^6c^6 + 6b^5c^5de + 15b^4c^4d^2e^2 + 20b^3c^3d^3e^3 + 15b^2c^2d^4e^4 + 6bcd^5e^5 + d^6e^6$

4.2 Puzzle Time
A WALKIE TALKIE

4.3 Start Thinking

$(x + 2)(x - 1)$; Inverse operations undo one another, so if two binomials are multiplied to make a product, you can divide the product by one binomial to obtain the other binomial; no; Factoring will only work as division if there is no remainder. It is possible to divide polynomials that are not factorable.

4.3 Warm Up

1. $13(t + 3y)$ **2.** $3k(k - 1)$

3. $ab(5ab - a + 11b)$ **4.** $(x + 5)(x - 5)$

5. $(n - 11)(n - 2)$ **6.** $3(x + 7)(x + 3)$

4.3 Cumulative Review Warm Up

1. $g(x) = 3x - 2$ **2.** $g(x) = \frac{1}{4}x + 1$

3. $g(x) = \left| \frac{x}{3} + \frac{1}{3} \right|$

4.3 Practice A

1. $x + 6 + \dfrac{42}{x - 5}$ **2.** $2x + 3 + \dfrac{5}{x - 2}$

3. $x + 1 + \dfrac{3}{x^2 - 9}$ **4.** $6x - 1 + \dfrac{2}{x^2 + 2}$

5. $x + 9 + \dfrac{28}{x - 3}$ **6.** $3x - 8 - \dfrac{12}{x - 1}$

7. $2x - 5 + \dfrac{15}{x + 2}$ **8.** $x^2 - 3x + 7 - \dfrac{15}{x + 3}$

9. $x + 5 + \dfrac{50}{x - 5}$ **10.** $5x + 2 + \dfrac{4}{x - 1}$

11. $k = -3$;

```
-3 | 1    2    0    7
   |     -3    3   -9
   ------------------
     1   -1    3   -2
```

$\dfrac{x^3 + 2x^2 + 7}{x + 3} = x^2 - x + 3 - \dfrac{2}{x + 3}$

12. 28 **13.** 41 **14.** 8 **15.** 18

16. $x^3 + x^2 - 3x + 3$; Multiply the result by $x + 1$.

4.3 Practice B

1. $x + 3 + \dfrac{6}{x^2 - 4}$

2. $4x^2 - 2x + 9 - \dfrac{17x}{x^2 + x - 4}$

3. $2x^2 + 10x + 14 + \dfrac{90x}{x^2 - 5x - 2}$

4. $4x - 7 - \dfrac{7}{x - 2}$

5. $x^2 - 3x + \dfrac{12}{x + 3}$

6. $x + 4 + \dfrac{32}{x - 4}$

7. $2x^2 - 7x + 7 - \dfrac{4}{x + 1}$

8. $x^3 + x^2 - 10x + 29 - \dfrac{102}{x + 4}$

Answers

9. $x^3 - 4x^2 + 24x - 140 + \dfrac{820}{x + 6}$

10. The powers in the quotient are too large by 1. The remainder (-2) was not divided by $(x + 3)$;

$$\begin{array}{r|rrrr} -3 & 1 & 2 & 0 & 7 \\ & & -3 & 3 & -9 \\ \hline & 1 & -1 & 3 & -2 \end{array}$$

$$\dfrac{x^3 + 2x^2 + 7}{x + 3} = x^2 - x + 3 - \dfrac{2}{x + 3}$$

11. 7   **12.** -10 **13.** 305

14. -95 **15.** $k = 4$

4.3 Enrichment and Extension

1. $y = -3x - 3$ **2.** $y = x + 5$

3. $y = 2x + 1$ **4.** $y = x + 6$

5. $y = -2x - 4$ **6.** $y = ax + b - ad$

4.3 Puzzle Time

HE WAS ALWAYS WILLING TO LEND AN EAR

4.4 Start Thinking

yes; You can group the terms with coefficients of 3 and 21 together, or you can group the terms with coefficients of -5 and 40 together; yes; You can group $3x$ and $21xy$ together, and you can group -5 and $40y$ together.

4.4 Warm Up

1. $3y$ **2.** $2rs$ **3.** $3x$

4. yz **5.** ab **6.** xy

4.4 Cumulative Review Warm Up

1.

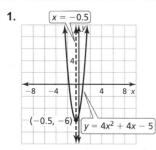

2.

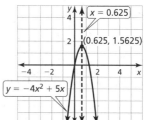

3.

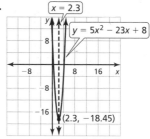

4.

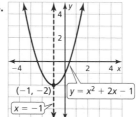

5.

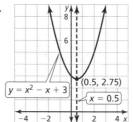

6.

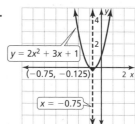

4.4 Practice A

1. $x(x - 4)(x + 3)$ **2.** $9p^5(p + 2)(p - 2)$

3. $3n^4(n - 8)(n - 3)$ **4.** $2k^2(k + 11)(k - 11)$

5. $w^2(2w + 3)(w - 5)$ **6.** $q^4(3q + 4)(q - 7)$

Answers

7. $(x + 3)(x^2 - 3x + 9)$

8. $(y + 10)(y^2 - 10y + 100)$

9. $(w - 5)(w^2 + 5w + 25)$

10. $(y - 3)(y^2 + 4)$ **11.** $(q - 2)(q^2 + 9)$

12. $(d + 5)(2d^2 + 3)$ **13.** $(x - 6)(x - 3)(x + 3)$

14. $(6p^2 - 5)(6p^2 + 5)$ **15.** $(n^2 + 4)(n^2 + 7)$

16. $(y^2 + 4)(y + 2)(y - 2)$

17. no   **18.** yes   **19.** yes   **20.** no

21. *Sample answer:* $f(x) = x^3 + 5x^2 - 6x$; $(x - 1)$;
$x(x - 1)(x + 6) = x^3 + 5x^2 - 6x$

22. $k = 9$; $f(x) = 3x^3 - 17x^2 - 9x + 18$;
$3x^3 - 17x^2 - 9x + 18 = (x - 6)(3x^2 + x - 3)$

23. a. $(a^2 + b^2)(5c - 3d)$

   b. $(x^n + 3)^2$

4.4 Practice B

1. $5t^3(t + 8)(t - 8)$ **2.** $2p^4(p - 7)(p - 6)$

3. $3x^2(x + 12)(x - 12)$ **4.** $a^4(5a + 9)(a - 5)$

5. $j^7(2j - 3)(6j - 5)$ **6.** $q^8(3q + 4)(5q + 6)$

7. $2p^6(p - 2)(p^2 + 2p + 4)$

8. $25k^5(k + 4)(k^2 - 4k + 16)$

9. $2w^4(3w - 2)(9w^2 + 6w + 4)$

10. $(x - 7)(x^2 + 5)$

11. $(m - 2)(m + 4)(m - 4)$

12. $(w - 3)(3w + 2)(3w - 2)$

13. $(s + 4)(5s + 1)(5s - 1)$

14. $(9g^2 + 25)(3g + 5)(3g - 5)$

15. $2t^2(t^3 + 5)(t^3 - 2)$ **16.** $5v^2(v^4 - 3)(v^4 - 2)$

17. yes   **18.** no

19. no   **20.** no

21. *Sample answer:* $f(x) = 2x^3 + 7x^2 - 4x$;
$(x + 4)$; $x(x + 4)(2x - 1) = 2x^3 + 7x^2 - 4x$

22. a. $(x - (-4))^2 + y^2 = 3^2$; $(h, k) = (-4, 0)$,
   $r = 3$

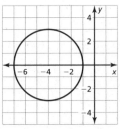

   b. $(x - 5)^2 + y^2 = 2^2$; $(h, k) = (5, 0)$, $r = 2$

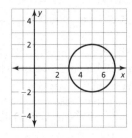

   c. $(x - 2)^2 + (y - (-3))^2 = 4^2$;
   $(h, k) = (2, -3)$, $r = 4$

4.4 Enrichment and Extension

1. 27   **2.** -18 **3.** 3

4. -4 **5.** -1 **6.** 6

7. $(x^5 - y^5) = (x - y)(x^4 + x^3y + x^2y^2 + xy^3 + y^4)$

Answers

8. $(a^7 + b^7) = (a + b)(a^6 - a^5b + a^4b^2 - a^3b^3 + a^2b^4 - ab^5 + b^6)$

9. $(a^{14} - b^{14}) = (a^7 + b^7)(a^7 - b^7) = (a + b)(a - b)(a^6 - a^5b + a^4b^2 - a^3b^3 + a^2b^4 - ab^5 + b^6)(a^6 + a^5b + a^4b^2 + a^3b^3 + a^2b^4 + ab^5 + b^6)$

10. $(x^{10} - y^{10}) = (x^5 + y^5)(x^5 - y^5) = (x + y)(x - y)(x^4 - x^3y + x^2y^2 - xy^3 + y^4)(x^4 + x^3y + x^2y^2 + xy^3 + y^4)$

4.4 Puzzle Time

QUARTERBACK

4.5 Start Thinking

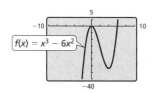

$(0, 0)$ and $(6, 0)$; The function simplifies to $0 = 0$; These points have x-values which yield a y-value of zero, meaning the graph crosses the x-axis. These are the only points that can be inserted into the function $f(x) = x^3 - 6x^2$ to get this result.

4.5 Warm Up

1. $t = -\dfrac{1}{4}$ **2.** $x = -5$

3. $r = -60$ **4.** $z = 20$

5. $m = -2$ **6.** $b = 20$

4.5 Cumulative Review Warm Up

1. $x < -\sqrt{5}$ or $x > \sqrt{5}$

2. $-9 \le x \le -3$ **3.** $x < -5$ or $x > -1$

4. $-\sqrt{5} < x < \sqrt{5}$ **5.** $x < -3$ or $x > 1$

6. $1 < x < 8$

4.5 Practice A

1. $q = -5, q = 0, q = 6$

2. $k = -3, k = 0$ **3.** $y = 0, y = 1$

4. $n = -3, n = -2, n = 3$

5. $p = 0, p = \pm\sqrt{7}$ **6.** $u = 0, u = \pm\sqrt{2}$

7. $x = -4, x = 0, x = 3$

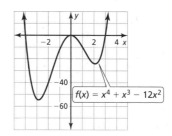

8. $x = -2, x = 2$

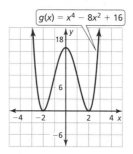

9. $x = -3, x = 0, x = 5$

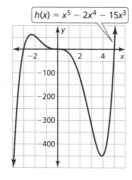

10. $x = -4, x = -1, x = 0$

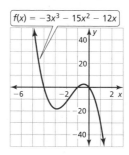

11. C

Answers

12. The factors of 18 include ± 1 and ± 18;

$f(x) = x^3 + 3x^2 - 8x - 18$;

Possible zeros: $\pm 1, \ \pm 2, \ \pm 3, \ \pm 6, \ \pm 9, \ \pm 18$

13. $x = 3, x = -3$

14. $x = -1, x = 2, x = -3$

15. *Sample answer:* $f(x) = 4x^3 + 4x^2 - 9x - 9$;

$f\left(\dfrac{3}{2}\right) = 0; \ f\left(-\dfrac{3}{2}\right) = 0$

16. a. $k = -18$ **b.** $k = -31$

4.5 Practice B

1. $x = -\dfrac{3}{2}, \ x = 0$ **2.** $h = 0, h = \pm\sqrt{2}$

3. $q = \pm\dfrac{1}{2}$ **4.** $w = \pm 3$

5. $p = -2, p = \pm 5$ **6.** $y = \pm 3, y = 8$

7. $x = -2, x = 0, x = 6$

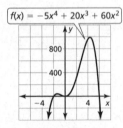

8. $x = -6, x = 0, x = 5$

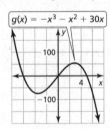

9. $x = -2, x = -1, x = 2$

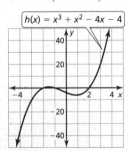

10. $x = -3, x = 3, x = 4$

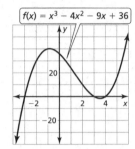

11. B

12. The factors of 2 include ± 2;

$f(x) = 2x^3 + 5x^2 - 2x - 6$;

Possible zeros: $\pm 1, \ \pm 2, \ \pm 3, \ \pm 6, \ \pm\dfrac{1}{2}, \ \pm\dfrac{3}{2}$

13. $x = \dfrac{3}{2}$

14. $x = -2, x = 3, x = 4$

15. *Sample answer:*
$f(x) = 25x^3 - 50x^2 - 49x + 98$;

$f\left(\dfrac{7}{5}\right) = 0; \ f\left(-\dfrac{7}{5}\right) = 0$

16. height is 11 cm, side length is 9 cm

4.5 Enrichment and Extension

1. $P(x) = -7x^2 - 7x + 14$

2. $P(x) = x^3 - 3x + 2$

3. $P(x) = a(x^4 - x^3 - 6x^2)$, a can be any real number

4. $P(x) = 3x^4 + 12x^3 - 3x^2 + 48x - 60$

5. $P(x) = -3x^3 - 3x^2 + 21x + 45$

4.5 Puzzle Time

IT WAS A BREEZE WITH ONLY A FEW FOGGY PATCHES

Answers

4.6 Start Thinking

Sample answer:

Function	Number of x-intercepts
$f(x) = x + 4$	1
$g(x) = x^2 - 5$	2
$h(x) = x^3 + 3x^2 - x - 1$	3
$j(x) = x^4 - x^3 - 4x^2 + 1$	4

The degree of the function and the number of x-intercepts are the same; no; Sometimes, there are solutions to polynomial functions that are imaginary numbers, which are not shown on the graph of the function.

4.6 Warm Up

1. 4   **2.** 3   **3.** 5

4. 6   **5.** 3   **6.** 5

4.6 Cumulative Review Warm Up

1.

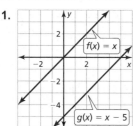

The graph of $g(x) = x - 5$ is a vertical translation 5 units down of the parent linear function.

2.

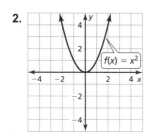

The graph of $f(x) = x^2$ is the parent quadratic function, so there was no transformation.

3.

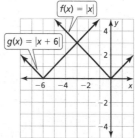

The graph of $g(x) = |x + 6|$ is a horizontal translation 6 units left of the parent absolute value function.

4.

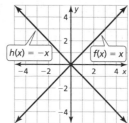

Sample answer: The graph of $h(x) = -x$ is a reflection in the x-axis of the parent linear function.

4.6 Practice A

1. 4   **2.** 3   **3.** 5   **4.** 6

5. $-3, -2i, 2i, 3$ **6.** $-3, -1, 1, 2$

7. $0, 1, -3i, 3i$ **8.** $-3, -\sqrt{2}, \sqrt{2}, 3$

9. 4; The graph shows 1 real zero, so the remaining zeros must be imaginary.

10. 0; There are 4 zeros for this function. The graph crosses the x-axis twice and touches the x-axis once at the repeated zero, leaving 0 imaginary zeros.

11. $f(x) = x^3 + x^2 - 10x + 8$

12. $f(x) = x^3 - 4x^2 + x + 6$

13. $f(x) = x^3 - 2x^2 - 3x + 6$

14. *Sample answer:*
$f(x) = x^5 - 2x^3 - 2x^2 - 3x - 2$; Because i is a zero, $-i$ is also a zero. The graph touches the x-axis at -1 (has a multiplicity of 2) and the graph crosses the x-axis at 2.

Answers

15.

Positive real zeros	Negative real zeros	Imaginary zeros	Total zeros
2	1	0	3
0	1	2	3

16.

Positive real zeros	Negative real zeros	Imaginary zeros	Total zeros
1	1	2	4

17.

Positive real zeros	Negative real zeros	Imaginary zeros	Total zeros
3	2	0	5
3	0	2	5
1	2	2	5
1	0	4	5

4.6 Practice B

1. 4   **2.** 5   **3.** 3   **4.** 6

5. $-1, 1, 2, 2$ **6.** $3, 3, 3, 3$

7. $-2, -2, -1, -1, 2$ **8.** $-3, -2, -2, 2, 3$

9. 2; *Sample answer*: There are four zeros for this function. The graph crosses the x-axis twice, leaving two imaginary zeros.

10. 2; *Sample answer*: There are three zeros for this function. The graph crosses the x-axis only once, leaving two imaginary zeros.

11. $f(x) = x^3 - 8x^2 + 22x - 20$

12. $f(x) = x^4 - 2x^3 + 6x^2 - 8x + 8$

13. $f(x) = x^3 - 3x^2 - 7x + 21$

14. Complex zeros come in pairs, so the remaining zero cannot be complex.

15. C

4.6 Enrichment and Extension

1. a and b. $f(x) = (x + 2)(x + 4)(x + 3)(x - 5)$

    c. $-4, -3, -2, 5$

2. a. $f(x) = (x + 5)(x - 2)(x^2 - 8x + 13)$

    b. $f(x) = (x + 5)(x - 2)\left[x - \left(4 - \sqrt{3}\right)\right]$
$\left[x - \left(4 + \sqrt{3}\right)\right]$

    c. $-5, 2, 4 - \sqrt{3}, 4 + \sqrt{3}$

3. a. $f(x) = (x - 4)(4x - 3)(x^2 - 4x + 13)$

    b. $f(x) = (x - 4)(4x - 3)\left[x - (2 + 3i)\right]$
$\left[x - (2 - 3i)\right]$

    c. $\dfrac{3}{4}, 4, 2 - 3i, 2 + 3i$

4. a. $f(x) = (x + 2)(x + 1)(x^2 - 6x + 4)$

    b. $f(x) = (x + 2)(x + 1)\left[x - \left(3 + \sqrt{5}\right)\right]$
$\left[x - \left(3 - \sqrt{5}\right)\right]$

    c. $-2, -1, 3 - \sqrt{5}, 3 + \sqrt{5}$

5. a. $f(x) = (x + 3)(x - 5)(x^2 - 2)$

    b. $f(x) = (x + 3)(x - 5)\left(x + \sqrt{2}\right)\left(x - \sqrt{2}\right)$

    c. $-3, -\sqrt{2}, 5, \sqrt{2}$

6. a. $f(x) = (x - 3)(x + 4)(2x - 1)(x^2 + 9)$

    b. $f(x) = (x - 3)(x + 4)(2x - 1)(x + 3i)$
$(x - 3i)$

    c. $-4, -3i, \dfrac{1}{2}, 3$

4.6 Puzzle Time

A PUP TENT

Answers

4.7 Start Thinking

Function	Transformation	Function	Transformation
$g(x) = (x-2)^5$	Translation 2 units right	$g(x) = -x^5$	Reflection in the x-axis
$g(x) = (x+2)^5$	Translation 2 units left	$g(x) = (2x)^5$	Horizontal shrink by a factor of $\frac{1}{2}$
$g(x) = x^5 - 2$	Translation 2 units down	$g(x) = \left(\frac{1}{2}x\right)^5$	Horizontal stretch by a factor of 2
$g(x) = x^5 + 2$	Translation 2 units up	$g(x) = 2x^5$	Vertical stretch by a factor of 2

The transformations of $g(x) = x^5$ behave in the same manner as other parent function transformations. Numbers added or subtracted inside parentheses translate the graph left or right, and numbers added or subtracted outside the parentheses translate the graph up or down. Numbers multiplied inside the parentheses horizontally stretch or shrink the graph, and numbers multiplied outside the parentheses vertically stretch or shrink the graph.

4.7 Warm Up

1. *Sample answer:* The graph of g is a vertical stretch by a factor of 5 of the graph of the parent function.

2. The graph of h is a reflection in the x-axis, followed by a vertical shrink by a factor of $\frac{1}{3}$ of the graph of the parent function.

3. *Sample answer:* The graph of g is a vertical stretch by a factor of 2 of the graph of the parent function.

4. The graph of f is a reflection in the x-axis, followed by a vertical shrink by a factor of $\frac{1}{2}$ of the graph of the parent function.

4.7 Cumulative Review Warm Up

1. The graph of $g(x) = x^2 + 5$ is a vertical translation 5 units up of the graph of the parent quadratic function.

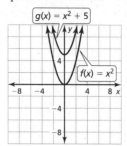

2. The graph of $g(x) = (x-1)^2$ is a horizontal translation 1 unit right of the graph of the parent quadratic function.

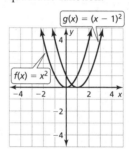

3. The graph of $g(x) = (x+2)^2$ is a horizontal translation 2 units left of the graph of the parent quadratic function.

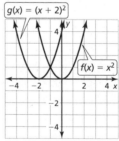

4. The graph of $g(x) = (x-5)^2 + 3$ is a horizontal translation 5 units right, followed by a vertical translation 3 units up of the graph of the parent quadratic function.

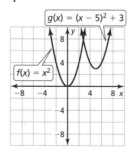

Answers

1. The graph of g is a vertical translation 2 units down of the graph of the parent function f.

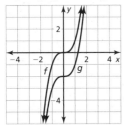

2. The graph of g is a horizontal translation 3 units left of the graph of the parent function f.

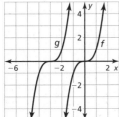

3. The graph of g is a reflection in x-axis, followed by a vertical stretch by a factor of 5 of the graph of the parent function f.

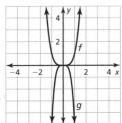

4. The graph of g is a vertical stretch by a factor of 4, followed by a vertical translation 3 units down of the graph of the parent function f.

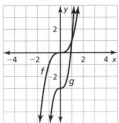

5. The graph of g is a vertical shrink by a factor of $\frac{2}{3}$, followed by a vertical translation 5 units down of the graph of the parent function f.

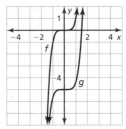

6. The graph of g is a vertical shrink by a factor of $\frac{1}{2}$, followed by a horizontal translation 2 units right of the graph of the parent function f.

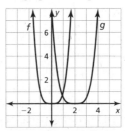

7. $g(x) = (x - 1)^3 + 2$

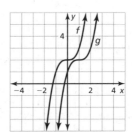

The graph of g is a horizontal translation 1 unit right of the graph of the parent function f.

8. $g(x) = 2x^4 - 6x + 2$

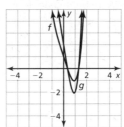

The graph of g is a vertical stretch by a factor of 2 of the graph of the parent function f.

Answers

9. The parent function was translated 2 units down instead of 2 units up.

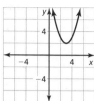

10. $g(x) = (-x - 2)^3 + 5$

11. $g(x) = \dfrac{1}{3}x^4 - x - \dfrac{5}{3}$

12. a. $W(x) = 27x^3 + 12x + 3$

   b. $Z(x) = 46{,}656x^3 + 144x + 3$

4.7 Practice B

1. The graph of g is a horizontal translation 3 units right, followed by a vertical translation 2 units down of the graph of the parent function f.

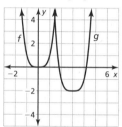

2. The graph of g is a horizontal translation 1 unit right, followed by a vertical translation 4 units up of the graph of the parent function f.

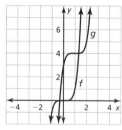

3. The graph of g is a reflection in the x-axis, followed by a vertical stretch by a factor of 3 of the graph of the parent function f.

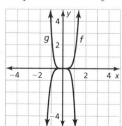

4. The graph of g is a vertical stretch by a factor of 3, followed by a vertical translation 2 units up of the graph of the parent function f.

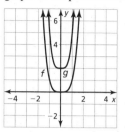

5. The graph of g is a vertical shrink by a factor of $\frac{1}{3}$, followed by a vertical translation 3 units down of the graph of the parent function f.

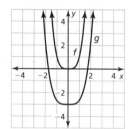

6. The graph of g is a vertical shrink by a factor of $\frac{2}{3}$, followed by a horizontal translation 3 units left of the graph of the parent function f.

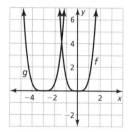

7. $g(x) = -\dfrac{1}{4}x^3 + x^2 - \dfrac{1}{2}$

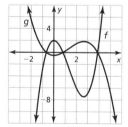

The graph of g is a reflection in the x-axis, followed by a vertical shrink by a factor of $\dfrac{1}{4}$ of the graph of the parent function f.

Answers

8. $g(x) = x^4 - x + 3$

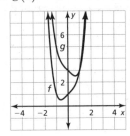

The graph of g is a reflection in the y-axis, followed by a vertical translation 2 units up of the graph of the parent function f.

9. The graph of g is a vertical stretch by a factor of 4, not a vertical shrink by a factor of $\frac{1}{4}$, of the graph of the parent function $f(x) = x^4$; The graph of g is a vertical stretch by a factor of 4, followed by a translation 3 units up of the graph of f.

10. $g(x) = -\frac{1}{27}x^3 + \frac{1}{3}x^2 - 5$

11. $g(x) = -\frac{3}{2}x^5 + \frac{1}{2}x^3 + \frac{5}{2}x^2 + \frac{3}{2}$

12. a. $W(x) = \frac{1}{864}x^3 + 9; W(6) = 9.25;$ When $x = 6$ inches, the volume of the box is 9.25 cubic feet.

b. $Z(x) = \frac{1}{23,328}x^3 + 9$

4.7 Enrichment and Extension

$y = 2(x + 4)^3; y = (x + 3)^3 - 2;$
$y = (x + 3)^3 - 6; y = x^3; y = (2x)^3;$
$y = (x - 3)^3 + 2; y = 2(x - 3)^3; y = (x - 5)^3;$
$y = (x - 5)^3 - 2; y = (x - 8)^3 + 1$

4.7 Puzzle Time

FRYDAY

4.8 Start Thinking

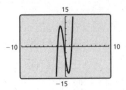

The shape of the graph of the function is a rounded "N"; There is one zero where $-2 < x < -1$, another zero where $-1 < x < 0$, and a third zero where $1 < x < 2$; no; The y-values are changing signs, but the table does not show an x-value when $y = 0$.

4.8 Warm Up

1. $(5, -33)$ **2.** $(3, 12)$ **3.** $(-2, -19)$

4. $\left(\frac{4}{3}, 5\frac{1}{3}\right)$ **5.** $(8, 45)$ **6.** $(2, 10)$

4.8 Cumulative Review Warm Up

1. $f(x) = (x + 3)^2 - 29; (-3, -29)$

2. $g(x) = (x + 2)^2 - 2; (-2, -2)$

3. $g(x) = (x - 5)^2 - 63; (5, -63)$

4. $h(x) = (x - 10)^2 - 191; (10, -191)$

5. $h(x) = (x - 1)^2 + 48; (1, 48)$

6. $f(x) = (x - 3)^2 - 6; (3, -6)$

4.8 Practice A

1.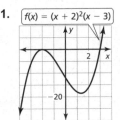
$f(x) = (x + 2)^2(x - 3)$

2.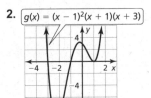
$g(x) = (x - 1)^2(x + 1)(x + 3)$

3.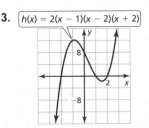
$h(x) = 2(x - 1)(x - 2)(x + 2)$

Answers

4.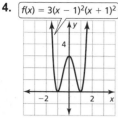
$f(x) = 3(x - 1)^2(x + 1)^2$

5. The function was graphed as if the zero $x = -3$ had a multiplicity of 2 instead of the zero $x = 1$.

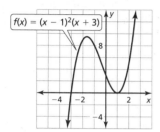
$f(x) = (x - 1)^2(x + 3)$

6. $-3, -2, 2$

7. $-7, -1, 1$

8. 5

9. $-3, \frac{3}{2}, 3$

10.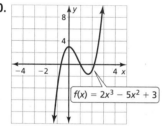
$f(x) = 2x^3 - 5x^2 + 3$

x-intercepts: $-0.69, 1, 2.19$; local maximum: $(0, 3)$; local minimum: $(1.67, -1.63)$; increasing: $x < 0, x > 1.67$; decreasing: $0 < x < 1.67$

11.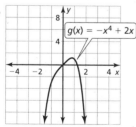
$g(x) = -x^4 + 2x$

x-intercepts: $0, 1.26$; local maximum: $(0.790, 1.19)$; local minimum: none; increasing: $x < 0.79$; decreasing: $x > 0.79$

12.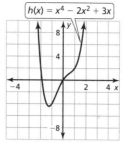
$h(x) = x^4 - 2x^2 + 3x$

x-intercepts: $-1.89, 0$; local maximum: none; local minimum: $(-1.26, -4.43)$; increasing: $x > -1.26$; decreasing: $x < -1.26$

13.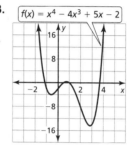
$f(x) = x^4 - 4x^3 + 5x - 2$

x-intercepts: $-1.15, 0.48, 1, 3.67$; local maximum: $(0.74, 0.38)$; local minimum: $(-0.59, 4.01)$, $(2.85, -14.37)$; increasing: $-0.59 < x < 0.74$, $x > 2.85$; decreasing: $x < -0.59$, $0.74 < x < 2.85$

14. $(-0.82, 1.09), (0.82, -1.09)$; The point $(-0.82, 1.09)$ is a local maximum. The point $(0.82, -1.09)$ is a local minimum; The real zeros are $-1.41, 0$, and 1.41; The minimum degree is 3.

15. $(1.50, 3.69)$; The point $(1.50, 3.69)$ is a local maximum; The real zeros are -0.89 and 2.19; The minimum degree is 4.

4.8 Practice B

1.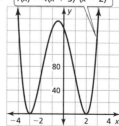
$f(x) = 4(x + 3)^2(x - 2)^2$

2.
$g(x) = \frac{1}{2}(x - 4)(x + 3)(x - 6)$

Answers

3.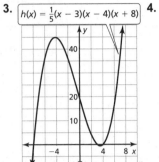

4.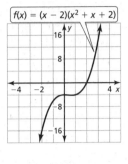

5. The function was graphed as if the zero $x = 0$ had a multiplicity of 1 instead of a multiplicity of 2.

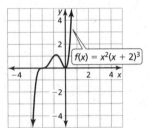

6. $\dfrac{1}{2}$

7. $-\dfrac{5}{2}, -2, 1$

8. $-3, \dfrac{3}{4}, 3$

9. $-\dfrac{3}{2}$

10.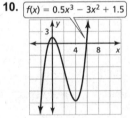

x-intercepts: $-0.67, 0.76, 5.91$; local maximum: $(0, 1.5)$; local minimum: $(4, -14.5)$; increasing: $x < 0, x > 4$; decreasing: $0 < x < 4$

11.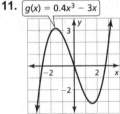

x-intercepts: $-2.74, 0, 2.74$; local maximum: $(-1.58, 3.16)$; local minimum: $(1.58, -3.16)$; increasing: $x < -1.58, x > 1.58$; decreasing: $-1.58 < x < 1.58$

12.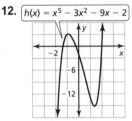

x-intercepts: $-1.36, -0.24, 2$; local maximum: $(-0.92, 3.08)$; local minimum: $(1.36, -15.14)$; increasing: $x < -0.92, 1.36 < x$; decreasing: $-0.92 < x < 1.36$

13.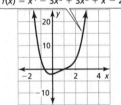

x-intercepts: $-0.7, 1$; local maximum: none; local minimum: $(-0.14, -2.07)$; increasing: $-0.14 < x$; decreasing: $x < -0.14$

14. a. about 1.6 in.
   b. about 67.6 in.[3]
   c. length $\approx$ 8.8 in., width $\approx$ 4.8 in., height $\approx$ 1.6 in.

4.8 Enrichment and Extension

1. $x = 3.16$ **2.** $x = 1.52$ **3.** $x = -1.31$

4. $x = -2.99$ **5.** $x = 1.92$

4.8 Puzzle Time

SHIFTY

4.9 Start Thinking

Sample answer:

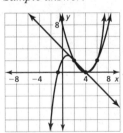

quadratic; parabola; cubic

Answers

4.9 Warm Up

1. 4   **2.** $-\dfrac{1}{3}$ **3.** 4   **4.** 1

4.9 Cumulative Review Warm Up

1. $(1, 6)$ **2.** $(-3, -11)$

4.9 Practice A

1. $f(x) = x^3 - 3x^2 - x + 3$

2. $f(x) = -\dfrac{1}{2}x^3 + \dfrac{3}{2}x^2 + 3x - 4$

3. $3; f(x) = \dfrac{1}{6}x^3 + \dfrac{5}{6}x$

4. $2; f(x) = \dfrac{1}{8}x^2 + \dfrac{13}{4}x + 8$

5. $3; f(x) = \dfrac{1}{3}x^3 - 5x^2 + \dfrac{8}{3}x + 32$

6. a. $f(x) = \dfrac{1}{2}x^2 + \dfrac{7}{2}x - 2$

b. yes; The cumulative number of customers will continue to increase.

4.9 Practice B

1. $f(x) = \dfrac{1}{2}x^3 - 3x^2 + \dfrac{3}{2}x + 5$

2. $f(x) = \dfrac{2}{3}x^3 - \dfrac{14}{3}x - 4$

3. $2; f(x) = \dfrac{5}{2}x^2 - \dfrac{23}{2}x - 1$

4. $3; f(x) = \dfrac{1}{2}x^3 - \dfrac{31}{2}x + 39$

5. $4; f(x) = \dfrac{1}{6}x^4 - \dfrac{7}{3}x^3 + \dfrac{95}{6}x^2 - \dfrac{149}{3}x + 56$

6. a. $f(x) = \dfrac{1}{6}x^3 - \dfrac{1}{2}x^2 + \dfrac{17}{6}x - 2$

b. no; The wave height will decrease eventually. After 14 seconds, the height of the wave will not be 397 inches.

4.9 Enrichment and Extension

1. arithmetic; $d = 3$ **2.** not arithmetic

3. arithmetic; $d = -9$ **4.** not arithmetic

5. arithmetic; $d = \dfrac{3}{5}$ **6.** not arithmetic

7. $t_n = 4n$ **8.** $t_n = -2n - 1$

9. $t_n = -11n + 29$ **10.** $t_n = -2n + 14$

11. $t_n = \dfrac{2}{3}n + \dfrac{1}{3}$ **12.** $t_n = -1.3n + 9.9$

4.9 Puzzle Time

ANCHOR

Cumulative Review

1. $17j$ **2.** $-4p$

3. $5q + 3$ **4.** $3m + 5$

5. $-3b + 19$ **6.** $-2x + 2$

7. $4c + 28$ **8.** $-5r + 15$

9. $8z - 44$ **10.** $9a - 38$

11. $38x - 9$ **12.** $19d - 10$

13. $x = 4$ **14.** $y = 3$

15. $b = 2$ **16.** $m = 5$

17. $a = 4$ **18.** $p = 6$

19. $w = 14$ **20.** $x = 2$

21. $y = -5$ **22.** $s = 2$

23. $x = -2$ **24.** $x = 2$

25. $x = 2$ **26.** $x = -11\dfrac{2}{9}$

27. $x = -9$ **28.** $x = -3$

29. a. $y = 35 + 1.20x$

b. $35

c. $44.60

d. when you are downloading 46 songs or fewer or when you are downloading 72 songs or more

30. $x + 7$ **31.** $n - 5$

32. $3m - 9$ **33.** $\dfrac{1}{5}c + 1$

Answers

34. $17 - 4y$

35. $-5 + 4p$

36. $5j - 14$

37. $\dfrac{1}{2}t - 4m$

38. $(x + 6)(x + 4)$

39. $(x - 11)(x + 3)$

40. $(x + 12)(x - 7)$

41. $(x + 11)(x + 5)$

42. $(x - 7)(x - 2)$

43. $(x - 10)(x - 5)$

44. $(5x + 7)(x + 8)$

45. $(x - 6)(9x + 1)$

46. $(2x - 5)(x + 4)$

47. $(3x + 4)(x + 3)$

48. $(2x - 3)(x + 1)$

49. $(2x + 7)(x - 4)$

50. a. $252\ \text{ft}^2$
   b. \$829.08

51. a. $p = 2(x + 4) + 2(2x - 23)$ or $p = 6x - 38$
   b. $a = (x + 4)(2x - 23)$ or $a = 2x^2 - 15x - 92$
   c. length $= 23$ ft, width $= 15$ ft
   d. $345\ \text{ft}^2$

52. $x = -2$ and $x = 3$

53. $x = -1$ and $x = 9$

54. $x = -7$ and $x = -5$

55. $x = 3$

56. $x = -11$ and $x = 4$

57. $x = 1$ and $x = 7$

58. $x = -\dfrac{9}{2}$ and $x = -\dfrac{4}{3}$

59. $x = -\dfrac{7}{2}$ and $x = 3$

60. $x = -\dfrac{1}{5}$ and $x = 4$

61. $x = -\dfrac{1}{2}$ and $x = \dfrac{9}{4}$

62. $x = \dfrac{7 \pm \sqrt{17}}{2}$

63. $x = \dfrac{-13 \pm \sqrt{173}}{2}$

64. $x = 7 \pm \sqrt{47}$

65. $x = \dfrac{-9 \pm \sqrt{97}}{2}$

66. $x = \dfrac{12 \pm \sqrt{123}}{3}$

67. $x = \dfrac{-9 \pm \sqrt{105}}{4}$

68. $x = \dfrac{9 \pm 4\sqrt{5}}{2}$

69. $x = \dfrac{21 \pm \sqrt{461}}{5}$

70. $\dfrac{9 + i\sqrt{3}}{2}$ and $\dfrac{9 - i\sqrt{3}}{2}$

71. -4 and 5

72. $\dfrac{3 + \sqrt{13}}{2}$ and $\dfrac{3 - \sqrt{13}}{2}$

73. $\dfrac{5 + \sqrt{101}}{2}$ and $\dfrac{5 - \sqrt{101}}{2}$

74. $\dfrac{5 + 3i\sqrt{15}}{8}$ and $\dfrac{5 - 3i\sqrt{15}}{8}$

75. $\dfrac{7 + \sqrt{301}}{6}$ and $\dfrac{7 - \sqrt{301}}{6}$

76. $\dfrac{11 + i\sqrt{39}}{10}$ and $\dfrac{11 - i\sqrt{39}}{10}$

77. $\dfrac{9 + \sqrt{137}}{4}$ and $\dfrac{9 - \sqrt{137}}{4}$

78. a. 1 student
   b. 4 students

79. a. 4 students
   b. 2 students

80. The graph of g is a translation 4 units right of the graph of f.

81. The graph of g is a translation 8 units up of the graph of f.

82. The graph of g is a translation 3 units right and 5 units up of the graph of f.

83. The graph of g is a translation 1 unit left and 4 units down of the graph of f.

84. The graph of g is a reflection in the x-axis, followed by a translation 3 units down of the graph of f.

Answers

85. The graph of g is a reflection in the x-axis, followed by a translation 1 unit right and 5 units up of the graph of f.

86. The graph of g is a reflection in the x-axis, followed by a vertical stretch by a factor of 5 and a translation 2 units down of the graph of f.

87. The graph of g is a vertical shrink by a factor of $\dfrac{1}{3}$, followed by a translation 5 units left and 3 units down of the graph of f.

88. $g(x) = -x + 3$

89. $g(x) = \dfrac{1}{4}|x + 3| + 1$

90. $g(x) = 4\sqrt{x - 2} + 16$

91. $g(x) = |x + 2| + 1$

92. $g(x) = -x + \dfrac{13}{2}$

93. $g(x) = -(x + 2)^2 + 8$

94. a. 41 ft
   b. 44 ft
   c. 2 ft; The ball was initially hit from 2 feet above the ground.
   d. maximum
   e. $(4.75, 47.125)$; 4.75 sec

Chapter 5

5.1 Start Thinking

Example	Expanded Form	Simplest Form
$x^2 + x^2$	$x \bullet x + x \bullet x$	$2x^2$
$x^4 \bullet x^4$	$(x \bullet x \bullet x \bullet x) \bullet (x \bullet x \bullet x \bullet x)$	x^8
$\dfrac{x^8}{x^5}$	$\dfrac{x \bullet x \bullet x \bullet x \bullet x \bullet x \bullet x \bullet x}{x \bullet x \bullet x \bullet x \bullet x}$	x^3

$2^{-2} = \dfrac{1}{4}$; Because $2^2 = 4$, they are reciprocals.

5.1 Warm Up

1. k^5 **2.** $24u^{10}v^3$ **3.** $25a^6 b^{20} c^2$

4. $729x^8 y^{10} z^5$ **5.** $8g^9 h^5 j^{13}$ **6.** $2xy^9$

5.1 Cumulative Review Warm Up

1. $y = 0.06(x - 4)^2 + 1$

2. $y = -6(x + 4)^2 + 8$

5.1 Practice A

1. 5   **2.** ± 7 **3.** ± 3

4. 3   **5.** 2   **6.** 8

7. 125   **8.** 100   **9.** 2

10. 7   **11.** 5   **12.** 0.44

13. 2.47   **14.** 59,049   **15.** 0.03

16. 6.05 in.   **17.** 5.6 m   **18.** $x = \pm 4$

19. $x = 5$ **20.** $x = 12.32, -0.32$

21. $x = 3$ **22.** $x = -2.57$

23. $x = \pm 1.57$ **24.** 2.57%

5.1 Practice B

1. 7   **2.** no real roots   **3.** -3

4. 216   **5.** 8   **6.** 4   **7.** -3125

8. $\dfrac{1}{1024}$ **9.** $\dfrac{1}{81}$ **10.** 0.51   **11.** 7.42

12. 8,869.01   **13.** 0.07   **14.** 25.64

15. -12.41 **16.** 7.6 in.   **17.** 7 m

18. $x = \pm 1.78$ **19.** $x = -2.97$ **20.** $x = \pm 3$

21. $x = 3.42$ **22.** $x = \pm 5$ **23.** $x = -7$

24. a. about 0.72 au
   b. 12 years

5.1 Enrichment and Extension

1. $n = 6$ **2.** $n = 2$

3. $n = 5$ **4.** $n = -1$

5. $n = -4$ or $n = 4$ **6.** $n = 8$

Answers

7. $n = -2$ **8.** no solution

9. $n = 3$ **10.** $n = -4$

11. $n = -16$ **12.** $n = \frac{5}{2}$

13. $n = \frac{1}{2}, n = -\frac{3}{2}$ **14.** $n = 4, n = -1$

Challenge: $a = 1, b = -2,$ and $c = -1$

5.1 Puzzle Time

I WISH YOU WOULD NOT ASK ME THAT I DO NOT KNOW ONE BUG FROM ANOTHER

5.2 Start Thinking

$x^2 \cdot x^2 = x^4$

When multiplying numbers with exponents, the exponents are added. Most students will probably expect $\sqrt{x} \cdot \sqrt{x}$ to yield an answer less than the value of x.

$$\sqrt{x} \cdot \sqrt{x} = x^{1/2} \cdot x^{1/2}$$
$$= x^{1/2 + 1/2}$$
$$= x^1$$
$$= x$$

The answer is not greater than or less than x; It is equal to x. This answer may surprise some students whose intuition is to think of multiplying fractions.

5.2 Warm Up

1. $\frac{1}{x}$ **2.** $\frac{3}{x^6}$ **3.** $4b^7$

4. ab^4 **5.** y^2 **6.** p^3

5.2 Cumulative Review Warm Up

1. $b^2 - 4ac = 309;$ two real solutions

2. $b^2 - 4ac = -491;$ two imaginary solutions

3. $b^2 - 4ac = 144;$ two real solutions

4. $b^2 - 4ac = 1409;$ two real solutions

5. $b^2 - 4ac = 89;$ two real solutions

6. $b^2 - 4ac = -23;$ two imaginary solutions

5.2 Practice A

1. $7^{1/2}$ **2.** $14^{3/2}$ **3.** $\frac{1}{5^{4/5}}$ **4.** $10^{3/4}$

5. $\frac{3}{2}$ **6.** $7^{1/2}$ **7.** 15   **8.** 9

9. $2\sqrt[4]{6}$ **10.** 3   **11.** 2   **12.** $\frac{1}{4}$

13. $2\sqrt[4]{13}$ **14.** $\frac{\sqrt[3]{18}}{2}$ **15.** $\frac{\sqrt{15}}{9}$ **16.** $2 - \sqrt{3}$

17. $\frac{24 + 6\sqrt{5}}{11}$ **18.** $\frac{-8\sqrt{2} + 8\sqrt{5}}{3}$

19. $13\sqrt[4]{2}$ **20.** $-10\sqrt[5]{13}$ **21.** $11\left(9^{1/4}\right)$

22. $-3\sqrt{2}$ **23.** $44\sqrt{7}$ **24.** $5\sqrt[4]{5}$

25. a. $s = V^{1/3}$

b. $S = 6V^{2/3}$

c. $24\left(10^{2/3}\right) \, \text{cm}^2$

5.2 Practice B

1. $\frac{1}{2^{3/5}}$ **2.** 4   **3.** $11^{1/3}$

4. $9^{2/5}$ **5.** $9^{3/4}$ or $3^{3/2}$ **6.** $5^{4/3}$

7. 25   **8.** $3\sqrt[5]{2}$ **9.** 2

10. $\frac{1}{10}$ **11.** 5   **12.** 2   **13.** $\frac{\sqrt[3]{12}}{3}$

14. $\frac{\sqrt[3]{20}}{5}$ **15.** $\frac{7\sqrt[4]{4}}{2}$ **16.** $\frac{35 + 7\sqrt{3}}{22}$

17. $\frac{-6\sqrt{2} + 6\sqrt{7}}{5}$ **18.** $\frac{\sqrt{30} + \sqrt{6}}{12}$

19. $4\left(25^{2/3}\right)$ **20.** $-5\sqrt{6}$ **21.** $8\sqrt[3]{3}$

22. $13\sqrt[5]{2}$ **23.** $5\left(3^{1/4}\right)$ **24.** $13\left(7^{1/3}\right)$

25. a. $r = \frac{\sqrt{\pi V}}{3\pi}$

b. $S = 6\sqrt{\pi V} + \frac{V}{9}$

c. $\left(36\sqrt{3\pi} + 12\right) \text{m}^2$

5.2 Enrichment and Extension

1. 3.17   **2.** 6.17   **3.** 10.20

Answers

4. 11.23 **5.** 9.11 **6.** 7.21

7. 11.88 **8.** 12.81 **9.** 3.63

10. 14.67 **11.** 15.78 **12.** 19.88

5.2 Puzzle Time

HE WAS NOT SO BRIGHT

5.3 Start Thinking

Sample answer:

$f(x) = |x|$ is a function with a domain of all real numbers, but because the values of $f(x)$ will be non-negative, the range is non-negative. When constructing this function, it is necessary to consider operations that make numbers positive and can include zero.

The function $f(x) = \sqrt{x}$ has a domain of all real non-negative numbers because you cannot get a real number value of $f(x)$ if $x < 0$. Its range is also all real non-negative numbers.

5.3 Warm Up

1. translation 9 units down

2. vertical shrink by a factor of $\frac{1}{4}$ and a translation 5 units up

3. vertical shrink by a factor of $\frac{1}{2}$

4. translation 0.5 unit down

5. translation 3 units up

6. reflection in the *x*-axis, a vertical stretch by a factor of 2, and a translation 1 unit up

5.3 Cumulative Review Warm Up

1. no **2.** no **3.** yes **4.** yes

5.3 Practice A

1.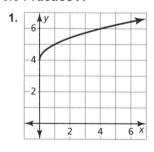

$x \geq 0; y \geq 4$

2.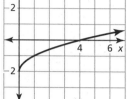

$x \geq 0; y \geq -2$

3.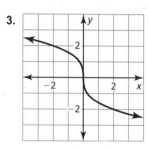

$-\infty < x < \infty; -\infty < y < \infty$

4.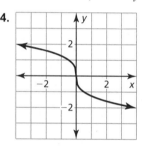

$-\infty < x < \infty; -\infty < y < \infty$

5.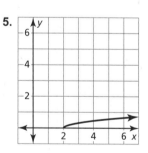

$x \geq 2; y \geq 0$

6.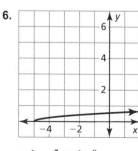

$x \geq -5; y \geq 0$

Answers

7. translation 1 unit right and 4 units up

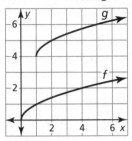

8. translation 2 units left and a vertical stretch by a factor of 3

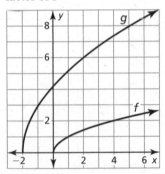

9. vertical stretch by a factor of 2 and a reflection in the *x*-axis

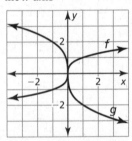

10. translation 1 unit right and 3 units up

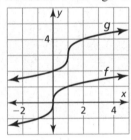

11. reflection in the *y*-axis and a vertical stretch by a factor of 3

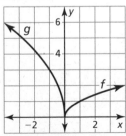

12. reflection in the *x*-axis and a vertical shrink by a factor of $\frac{1}{3}$

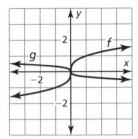

13.

$x \le 0, x \ge 1; y \ge 0$

14.

$-\infty < x < \infty; y \ge -0.63$

15.

$-\infty < x < \infty; y \ge -1.04$

16. $g(x) = \frac{1}{3}\sqrt{x} + 2$ **17.** $g(x) = -5\sqrt{x} - 5$

18. vertex: $(0, 0)$; opens right

19. vertex: $(-6, 0)$; opens left

20. $r = 4$; *x*-intercepts: ± 4; *y*-intercepts: ± 4

21. $r = 5$; *x*-intercepts: ± 5; *y*-intercepts: ± 5

Answers

1.

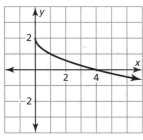

$x \geq 0; y \leq 2$

2.

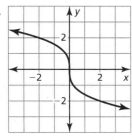

$-\infty < x < \infty; -\infty < y < \infty$

3.

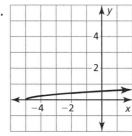

$x \geq -5; y \geq 0$

4.

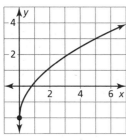

$x \geq 0; y \geq -2$

5.

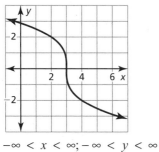

$-\infty < x < \infty; -\infty < y < \infty$

6.

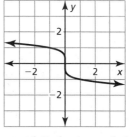

$-\infty < x < \infty; -\infty < y < \infty$

7. translation 2 units right and a vertical stretch by a factor of 4

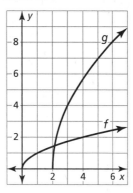

8. translation 5 units right and 1 unit down

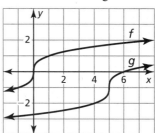

9. vertical shrink by a factor of $\frac{1}{3}$ and a reflection in the y-axis

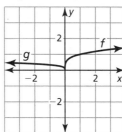

Answers

10. vertical shrink by a factor of $\frac{1}{2}$ and a translation 3 units down

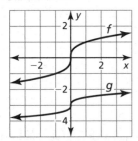

11. reflection in the x-axis and a translation 1 unit right and 3 units up

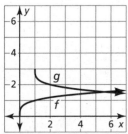

12. reflection in the y-axis, a horizontal shrink by a factor of $\frac{1}{243}$, and a translation 2 units down

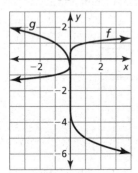

13.

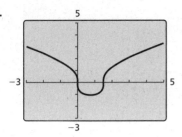

$-\infty < x < \infty; \ y \geq -1.04$

14.

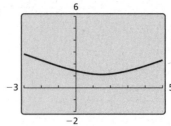

$-\infty < x < \infty; \ y \geq 1.12$

15.

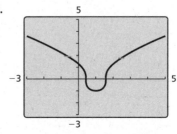

$-\infty < x < \infty; \ y \geq -1$

16. $g(x) = \sqrt{\frac{3}{2}x} + 2$

17. $g(x) = \sqrt{x - 4} + \frac{1}{2}$

18. vertex: $(5, 0)$; opens right

19. vertex: $(3, 0)$; opens left

20. $r = 9$; x-intercepts: ± 9; y-intercepts: ± 9

21. $r = 7$; x-intercepts: ± 7; y-intercepts: ± 7

5.3 Enrichment and Extension

1. $(10, 53.13°)$ **2.** $(1.41, 45°)$

3. $(8.94, 26.57°)$ **4.** $(10.20, 168.69°)$

5. $(5, 233.13°)$ **6.** $(8.60, 234.46°)$

5.3 Puzzle Time

A POTATO

5.4 Start Thinking

You can manipulate the Pythagorean Theorem to show the following.

$$a^2 + b^2 = c^2$$
$$a^2 + b^2 = 13^2$$
$$\sqrt{a^2 + b^2} = \sqrt{13^2}$$
$$\sqrt{a^2 + b^2} = 13$$

Answers

5.4 Warm Up

1. yes **2.** no **3.** yes

4. no **5.** yes **6.** no

5.4 Cumulative Review Warm Up

1. $y = 150x + 2000$; The slope indicates the car costs $150 per month to lease.

2. $y = 3x$; The slope indicates the helicopter is traveling at a rate of speed of 3 miles per minute.

5.4 Practice A

1. $x = 9$ **2.** $x = \frac{40}{3}$ **3.** $x = 54$

4. $x = 216$ **5.** $x = 4$ **6.** $x = 5$

7. about 46 years **8.** $x = 16$ **9.** $x = 7, 9$

10. $x = 3$ **11.** $x = 0, -\frac{3}{2}$ **12.** $x = \frac{1}{3}$

13. $x = 7$ **14.** $x = 27$ **15.** no solution

16. $x = 4$

17. The cube root, instead of the cube, of the right side of the equation was found.

$$\sqrt[3]{2x + 1} = 8$$
$$\left(\sqrt[3]{2x + 1}\right)^3 = (8)^3$$
$$2x + 1 = 512$$
$$2x = 511$$
$$x = \frac{511}{2}$$

18. $x \geq 9$ **19.** $3 \leq x \leq 52$

20. $x > 5$

21. a. about 0.11 in.
  b. about 0.18 in.
  c. no; It is about 1.59 times as long.

5.4 Practice B

1. $x = 6$ **2.** $x = \frac{25}{16}$ **3.** $x = -256$

4. $x = \frac{3}{16}$ **5.** $x = 32$ **6.** $x = 32$

7. no solution **8.** $x = 0, x = \frac{4}{3}$

9. $x = \frac{1}{5}$ **10.** $x = 4$ **11.** $x = -3$

12. no solution **13.** $x = 64$ **14.** $x = \frac{4}{3}$

15. $x = 2$ **16.** $0 \leq x \leq 25$

17. $x \geq 26$ **18.** $x > -2$ **19.** 25 ft

20. $(-2, 0), (-1, 1)$ **21.** $(3, 2), (-2, -3)$

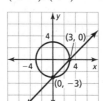

22. $(0, -3), (3, 0)$ **23.** $(-4, 0), (0, 4)$

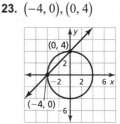

24. about 44.4 ft

5.4 Enrichment and Extension

1. $x = -21$ **2.** $x = 3$

3. $x \approx 23.39$ **4.** $x \approx -2.87$

5. $x \geq 19$ **6.** $0 \leq x \leq 1.33$

5.4 Puzzle Time

WELL THIS IS A FINE PICKLE YOU'VE GOTTEN US INTO

5.5 Start Thinking

The equations as a system are
$$f(x) = 3x - 750$$
$$g(x) = 15x - 1300$$

The equation is only logical because the company sold the same number of bracelets and T-shirts. If the numbers were different, the new equation would not work. The combined equation $h(x) = 18x - 2050$ represents the total amount of earnings, $h(x)$, on bracelets and T-shirts, where x is the number of bracelets sold or the number of T-shirts sold, but not the combined number of bracelets and T-shirts.

5.5 Warm Up

1. $3x^4 + 6x^2$ **2.** $-\dfrac{7}{x^6}$

3. $\dfrac{x^2}{x - 1}$ **4.** a^4b^4

5. $a^2 - 5ab - 6b^2$ **6.** $-6x^2 + 6x$

Answers

5.5 Cumulative Review Warm Up

1. $y = \frac{3}{88}(x + 7)(x - 11)$

2. $y = \frac{19}{9}(x - 10)(x)$

3. $y = \frac{71}{28}(x + 15)(x + 3)$

4. $y = -\frac{1}{5}(x + 6)(x + 4)$

5.5 Practice A

1. $(f + g)(x) = 12\sqrt[4]{x};\ x \ge 0;$

$(f - g)(x) = -18\sqrt[4]{x};\ x \ge 0;$

$(f + g)(81) = 36;\ (f - g)(81) = -54$

2. $(f + g)(x) = 3x^2 + 6x + 7;\ -\infty < x < \infty;$

$(f - g)(x) = x^2 + 12x - 7;\ -\infty < x < \infty;$

$(f + g)(1) = 16;\ (f - g)(1) = 6$

3. $(fg)(x) = 2x^2\sqrt{x};\ x \ge 0;\ \left(\dfrac{f}{g}\right)(x) = \dfrac{x^2}{2\sqrt{x}};$

$x > 0;\ (fg)(9) = 486;\ \left(\dfrac{f}{g}\right)(9) = \dfrac{27}{2}$

4. $(fg)(x) = 40x^{14/3};\ -\infty < x < \infty;$

$\left(\dfrac{f}{g}\right)(x) = \dfrac{5}{2}x^{4/3};\ -\infty < x < 0,\ 0 < x < \infty;$

$(fg)(8) = 655{,}360;\ \left(\dfrac{f}{g}\right)(8) = 40$

5. $(fg)(x) = 8x;\ -\infty < x < \infty;\ \left(\dfrac{f}{g}\right)(x) = 2x^{1/3};$

$-\infty < x < 0,\ 0 < x < \infty;\ (fg)(-27) = -216;$

$\left(\dfrac{f}{g}\right)(-27) = -6$

6. $(f + g)(5) = 654.91;\ (f - g)(5) = 595.09;$

$(fg)(5) = 18{,}691.86;\ \left(\dfrac{f}{g}\right)(5) = 20.90$

7. $(f + g)(5) = 148.49;\ (f - g)(5) = -125.10;$

$(fg)(5) = 1600.00;\ \left(\dfrac{f}{g}\right)(5) = 0.09$

8. Raising a number to the power $\frac{1}{2}$ is the same as taking the square root of a number, and you cannot take the square root of a negative number.

$$f(x) = 4x^{1/2} + 2 \text{ and } g(x) = -4x^{1/2}$$

The domain of $(f + g)(x)$ is $x \ge 0$.

9. a. $(A - B)(t) = \frac{1}{2}t^{2/3}$

b. the difference in the amount of mold in the two specimens

5.5 Practice B

1. $(f + g)(x) = -8\sqrt[3]{4x};\ -\infty < x < \infty;$

$(f - g)(x) = 10\sqrt[3]{4x};\ -\infty < x < \infty;$

$(f + g)(-2) = 16;\ (f - g)(-2) = -20$

2. $(f + g)(x) = -x^3 + x^2 - x;\ -\infty < x < \infty;$

$(f - g)(x) = -x^3 - 11x^2 + 7x;\ -\infty < x < \infty;$

$(f + g)(-1) = 3;\ (f - g)(-1) = -17$

3. $(fg)(x) = 3x^3\sqrt[3]{x^2};\ -\infty < x < \infty;$

$\left(\dfrac{f}{g}\right)(x) = 3x^2\sqrt[3]{x};\ -\infty < x < 0,\ 0 < x < \infty;$

$(fg)(-8) = -6144;\ \left(\dfrac{f}{g}\right)(-8) = -384$

4. $(fg)(x) = 15x^{9/4};\ x \ge 0;\ \left(\dfrac{f}{g}\right)(x) = \dfrac{3}{5}x^{7/4};$

$x > 0;\ (fg)(16) = 7680;\ \left(\dfrac{f}{g}\right)(16) = \dfrac{384}{5}$

5. $(fg)(x) = 20x^{7/6};\ x \ge 0;\ \left(\dfrac{f}{g}\right)(x) = 5x^{1/2};$

$x > 0;\ (fg)(64) = 2560;\ \left(\dfrac{f}{g}\right)(64) = 40$

6. $(f + g)(5) = 3.81;\ (f - g)(5) = -14.07;$

$(fg)(5) = -45.88;\ \left(\dfrac{f}{g}\right)(5) = -0.57$

7. $(f + g)(5) = 26.77;\ (f - g)(5) = 13.35;$

$(fg)(5) = 134.58;\ \left(\dfrac{f}{g}\right)(5) = 2.99$

Answers

8. $g(0)$ is equal to 0, and 0 cannot be in the denominator of a fraction.

$f(x) = 4x^{7/3}$ and $g(x) = 2x^{2/3}$

The domain of $\left(\dfrac{f}{g}\right)(x)$ is all real numbers except $x = 0$.

9. $(f + g)(5) = -5$, $(f - g)(0) = -46$,

$(fg)(3) = 24$, and $\left(\dfrac{f}{g}\right)(2) = \dfrac{1}{2}$

5.5 Enrichment and Extension

1. $(f + g)(x) = \sin x + x$;

$(f - g)(x) = \sin x - x$; $(fg)(x) = x \sin x$;

$\left(\dfrac{f}{g}\right)(x) = \dfrac{\sin x}{x}$; $x \neq 0$; $(f + g)(1) \approx 1.02$;

$(f - g)(1) \approx -0.98$; $(fg)(1) \approx 0.02$;

$\left(\dfrac{f}{g}\right)(1) \approx 0.02$

2. $(f + g)(x) = \cos x + x^2$;

$(f - g)(x) = \cos x - x^2$; $(fg)(x) = x^2 \cos x$;

$\left(\dfrac{f}{g}\right)(x) = \dfrac{\cos x}{x^2}$; $x \neq 0$; $(f + g)(2) \approx 5.00$;

$(f - g)(2) \approx -3.00$; $(fg)(2) \approx 4.00$;

$\left(\dfrac{f}{g}\right)(2) \approx 0.25$

3. $(f + g)(x) = \tan x + 2x$;

$(f - g)(x) = \tan x - 2x$; $(fg)(x) = 2x\tan x$;

$\left(\dfrac{f}{g}\right)(x) = \dfrac{\tan x}{2x}$; $x \neq 0$; $(f + g)(-1) \approx -2.02$;

$(f - g)(-1) \approx 1.98$; $(fg)(-1) \approx 0.03$;

$\left(\dfrac{f}{g}\right)(-1) \approx 0.01$

4. $(f + g)(x) = \sin x + \cos x$;

$(f - g)(x) = \sin x - \cos x$;

$(fg)(x) = \cos x \sin x$; $\left(\dfrac{f}{g}\right)(x) = \dfrac{\sin x}{\cos x}$;

$x \neq 90$; $(f + g)(10) \approx 1.16$;

$(f - g)(10) \approx -0.81$; $(fg)(10) \approx 0.17$;

$\left(\dfrac{f}{g}\right)(10) \approx 0.18$

Challenge:

$\sin^2 A + \cos^2 A = 1$

$(\sin A)^2 + (\cos A)^2 = 1$

$\left(\dfrac{a}{c}\right)^2 + \left(\dfrac{b}{c}\right)^2 = 1$

$\dfrac{a^2}{c^2} + \dfrac{b^2}{c^2} = 1$

$\dfrac{a^2 + b^2}{c^2} = 1$

$a^2 + b^2 = c^2$

5.5 Puzzle Time

DINNER IS ON ME

5.6 Start Thinking

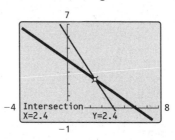

When solved for x, the equation is $x = -\dfrac{3}{2}y + 6$.

Switching x and y, it is $y = -\dfrac{3}{2}x + 6$, and the system is $y = -\dfrac{2}{3}x + 4$.

$y = -\dfrac{3}{2}x + 6$

The point of intersection is $(2.4, 2.4)$. The point of intersection represents the only x-value that, when substituted into the original equation, yields the same y-value.

5.6 Warm Up

1. $y = 3x - 4$ **2.** $y = \dfrac{3}{2}x - 5$

3. $y = -\dfrac{5}{6}x + \dfrac{3}{2}$ **4.** $y = -4x + 7$

5. $y = \dfrac{1}{5}x - \dfrac{11}{5}$ **6.** $y = \dfrac{1}{6}x - \dfrac{3}{2}$

5.6 Cumulative Review Warm Up

1. $5i$ **2.** $2i\sqrt{5}$ **3.** $9i\sqrt{2}$

4. $-18i$ **5.** $2i$ **6.** $2i\sqrt{11}$

Answers

5.6 Practice A

1. $x = \dfrac{y - 3}{2}; x = -3$

2. $x = 3y + 6; x = -3$

3. $x = \dfrac{1}{2}\sqrt[3]{y}; x = -\dfrac{1}{2}\sqrt[3]{3}$

4. $g(x) = \dfrac{x}{4}$

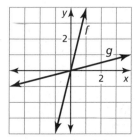

5. $g(x) = \dfrac{1}{4}x + \dfrac{1}{4}$

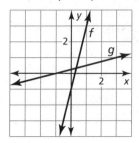

6. $g(x) = 2x + 10$

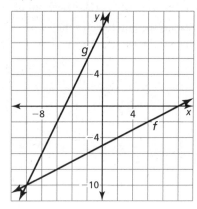

7. $g(x) = 5x + 10;$ *Sample answer:* switching the positions of x and y and solving for y; less mental math

8. a. no; The coordinates of $(0, 9)$ cannot be switched to obtain $(0, 0)$.

b. yes; The coordinates of the corresponding points are switched.

9. $g(x) = \dfrac{\sqrt{x}}{3}$

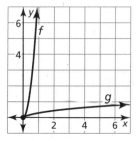

10. $g(x) = -\dfrac{\sqrt{x}}{4}$

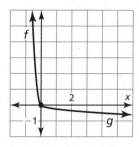

11. $g(x) = \sqrt[3]{x} - 2$

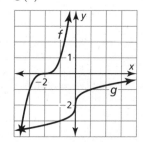

12. yes; passes the horizontal line test

13. no; does not pass the horizontal line test

5.6 Practice B

1. $x = -\dfrac{3}{4}y + \dfrac{3}{2}; x = \dfrac{15}{4}$

2. $x = \dfrac{\sqrt[4]{25y}}{5};$ The output cannot be -3.

3. $x = \pm\sqrt{y + 4} + 3; x = 2, x = 4$

Answers

4. $g(x) = \dfrac{-x + 4}{3}$

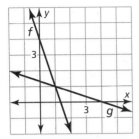

5. $g(x) = -3x + 3$

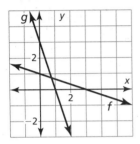

6. $g(x) = \dfrac{5}{2}x + \dfrac{1}{2}$

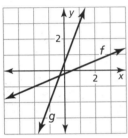

7. After switching the positions of x and y, y was not solved for.

$f(x) = 3x - 8$

$y = 3x - 8$

$x = 3y - 8$

$x + 8 = 3y$

$y = \dfrac{x + 8}{3}$

$g(x) = \dfrac{x + 8}{3}$

8. $g(x) = -\dfrac{\sqrt{-x}}{3}$

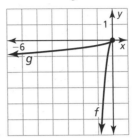

9. $g(x) = \sqrt[3]{x} + 1$

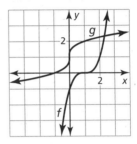

10. $g(x) = -\sqrt[6]{x}$

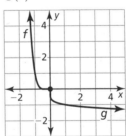

11. $g(x) = \dfrac{\sqrt[3]{x}}{2}$; *Sample answer:* switching the positions of x and y and solving for y; less mental math

12. no   **13.** yes   **14.** yes   **15.** no

16. a. $r = \sqrt[3]{\dfrac{3V}{4\pi}}$; The new equation represents the radius in terms of the volume.

b. $r = 3.27\,\text{m}$

5.6 Enrichment and Extension

1. $g(x) = 1 + \sqrt{x + 1}$

2. $g(x) = -4 + \sqrt{x + 16}$

3. $g(x) = \dfrac{3}{2} + \sqrt{x + \dfrac{9}{4}}$

Answers

4. $g(x) = 4 + \sqrt{x+4}$

5. $g(x) = 6 + \sqrt{x+41}$

6. $g(x) = -5 + \sqrt{x+10}$

7. $g(x) = -3 + \sqrt{x+8}$

8. $g(x) = 2 + \sqrt{x-8}$

9. $g(x) = \dfrac{1}{2} + \sqrt{\dfrac{x+1}{4}}$

10. $g(x) = -1 + \sqrt{\dfrac{x+6}{6}}$

11. $g(x) = 2 + \sqrt{\dfrac{x+31}{4}}$

12. $g(x) = 1 + \sqrt{\dfrac{x+4}{9}}$

5.6 Puzzle Time

A BOMB SQUID

Cumulative Review

1. w^{11} **2.** b **3.** $\dfrac{1}{g^2}$

4. c^5 **5.** m^7 **6.** v^6

7. 1 **8.** $\dfrac{1}{p^5}$ **9.** x^2

10. $5a^8$ **11.** $-4y^5$ **12.** $3n^5$

13. $\dfrac{32m^{15}}{n^5}$ **14.** $\dfrac{343y^3}{q^{12}}$ **15.** $\dfrac{256x^{20}}{j^{12}}$

16. $\dfrac{x^{10}}{b^{10}}$ **17.** $81r^4c^8$ **18.** $\dfrac{d^{15}}{w^6}$

19. $y = -3x + 7$ **20.** $y = 9$

21. $y = 2x + 4$ **22.** $y = 3x + 4$

23. $y = \frac{1}{5}x - 4$ **24.** $y = 2x - 12$

25. $y = 2x + 6$ **26.** $y = 2x - 8$

27. $y = -4x + 6$ **28.** $y = 16x + 8$

29. $y = \dfrac{4}{x+3}$ **30.** $y = \dfrac{8}{2x-1}$

31. a. 84 in.   **b.** 432 in.²

32. a. $100 - 18m$

     b. \$28; You have \$28 left over after purchasing 4 movies.

     c. \$10; You have \$10 left over after purchasing 5 movies.

33. 64   **34.** 3125   **35.** 216

36. 9   **37.** $\dfrac{1}{3}$ **38.** $\dfrac{1}{49}$

39. 256   **40.** 81   **41.** $\dfrac{1}{m^{12}}$

42. $\dfrac{1}{p^{10}}$ **43.** k^{28} **44.** j^{24}

45. $\dfrac{16y^2}{25}$ **46.** $\dfrac{8}{27z^3}$ **47.** $\dfrac{36}{25w^2}$

48. $\dfrac{64x^3}{27}$ **49.** $x = \dfrac{9}{5}$ and $x = 3$

50. $x = -10$ and $x = 6$ **51.** $x = -4$ and $x = \dfrac{52}{7}$

52. $x = -\dfrac{51}{5}$ and $x = 5$ **53.** no solution

54. no solution   **55.** $x = \dfrac{12}{5}$ and $x = 4$

56. $x = -8$ and $x = -4$

57. $x = 4$ and $x = 12$ **58.** $x = -\dfrac{5}{3}$ and $x = 13$

59. $x = -29$ and $x = -\dfrac{1}{3}$

60. $x = \dfrac{9}{5}$ and $x = 3$ **61.** function

62. not a function   **63.** not a function

64. not a function   **65.** function

Answers

66. not a function   **67.** function

68. function

69. **a.** $3x + 225$ **b.** $243

70. **a.** $5.85m + 28.84t$ **b.** $115.77

71. $g(x) = x + 2$ **72.** $g(x) = x + 2$

73. $g(x) = |2x + 7| + 3$

74. $g(x) = |3x - 14| - 1$

75. $g(x) = 3(x + 1) + 4$

76. $g(x) = 2x - 5$

77. $g(x) = -\dfrac{1}{4}(x + 3) + 3$

78. $(3, -1, 5)$ **79.** $(2, 4, -3)$

80. There are an infinite number of solutions.

81. $(-3, 3, 4)$ **82.** $(-2, 4, -3)$ **83.** $(2, 7, -6)$

84. There are an infinite number of solutions.

85. $(-3.8, -2.6, 2.6)$ **86.** $(1, -2, 3)$

87. $142,500   **88.** 8%   **89.** $125

90. $68   **91.** 6%

92. $x = -6$ and $x = 6$

93. $x = -8$ and $x = 8$

94. $x = -7$ and $x = 7$

95. $x = -4$ and $x = 4$

96. $x = -6$ and $x = 6$

97. $x = -8$ and $x = 8$

98. $x = -2$ and $x = 5$

99. $x = -1$ and $x = 3$

100. $x = 1$ and $x = 6$

101. $x = 4$ and $x = 7$

102. $x = 1$ and $x = 8$

103. $x = -7$ and $x = -3$

104. $x = -4$ and $x = \dfrac{1}{2}$

105. $x = -4$ and $x = \dfrac{2}{3}$

106. $x = -1$ and $x = -\dfrac{3}{5}$

107. $25 - 9i$ **108.** $-21 + 3i$

109. $2 - 5i$ **110.** $-17 + 2i$

111. $-4 + 3i$ **112.** $7 + 8i$

113. $-22 + 9i$ **114.** $5 + 22i$

115. $9 + 19i$ **116.** $-15 - 2i$

117. $-6 + 10i$ **118.** $-8 - 16i$

119. $23 + 7i$ **120.** $-22 + 29i$

121. $-13 + 87i$ **122.** $32 - 80i$

123. $19 + 59i$ **124.** $44 - 18i$

125. $32 + 24i$ **126.** $-7 - 24i$

127. **a.** 1.25 h   **b.** 1 h

128. **a.** 0.5 h   **b.** 1.6 h

Chapter 6

6.1 Start Thinking

1. exponential growth; 10% increase

2. linear growth; slope: 1.28

3. exponential growth; 25% increase

6.1 Warm Up

1.

x	y
-1	-3
0	0
1	3
2	6

2.

x	y
-1	0.5
0	1
1	2
2	4

3.

x	y
-1	$\dfrac{2}{3}$
0	2
1	6
2	18

Answers

6.1 Cumulative Review Warm Up

1. 2^7 **2.** x^4 **3.** $8b^{15}$

4. 3^{x+5} **5.** y^{3x} **6.** $9a^{2x}$

6.1 Practice A

1. a. $\dfrac{1}{9}$ **b.** 27   **2. a.** $\dfrac{5}{4}$ **b.** 40

3. a. $\dfrac{13}{4}$ **b.** 11

4. exponential growth

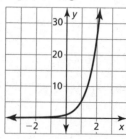

5. exponential growth

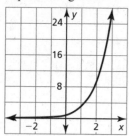

6. exponential decay

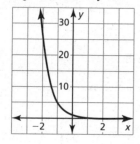

7. exponential growth

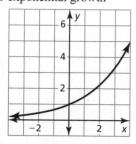

8. exponential growth

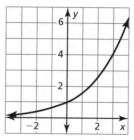

9. exponential decay

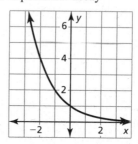

10. $b = 2$ **11.** $b = 8$

12. a. exponential growth
    b. 6% increase
    c. $0.25
    d. 15 years

13. $y = a(1 + 0.732)^t$; growth rate = 73.2%

14. $y = a(1 + 0.223)^t$; growth rate = 22.3%

15. $y = a(1 - 0.936)^t$; decay rate = 93.6%

16. $153.32

6.1 Practice B

1. a. $\dfrac{1}{25}$ **b.** 125   **2. a.** $\dfrac{5}{2}$ **b.** 80

3. a. $-\dfrac{26}{9}$ **b.** 24

4. exponential growth

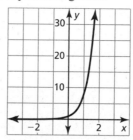

Answers

5. exponential growth

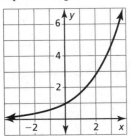

6. exponential decay

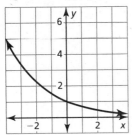

7. exponential growth

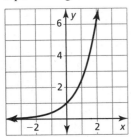

8. exponential decay

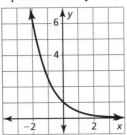

9. exponential decay

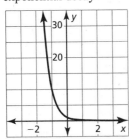

10. $b = 10$

11. $b = \dfrac{1}{3}$

12. a. exponential decay

 b. 20% decrease

 c. \$54,000

 d. 2.6 yr

13. $y = a(1 - 0.0468)^t$; decay rate $= 4.68\%$

14. $y = a(1 + 0.016)^6$; growth rate $= 1.6\%$

15. $y = a(1 - 0.996)^t$; decay rate $= 99.6\%$

16. \$153.73

6.1 Enrichment and Extension

1. c **2.** d **3.** a **4.** b

5. if $a = 0$ or $b = 1$

6. $y = 5^x$ **7.** $y = \left(\dfrac{1}{3}\right)^x$

8. All five functions have a y-intercept of $(0, 1)$.

9. All five functions have the same domain and range; domain: all real numbers, range: $y > 0$.

10. a.

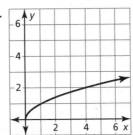

 b. $y = \sqrt{x}$, radical function

 c. domain: $x \geq 0$

  range: $y \geq 0$

11. a.

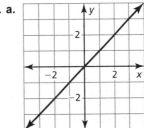

 b. $y = x$, linear function

 c. domain: all real numbers

  range: all real numbers

Answers

12. a.

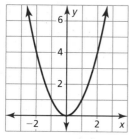

b. $y = x^2$, quadratic function

c. domain: all real numbers

range: $y \geq 0$

13. a.

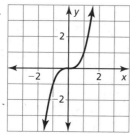

b. $y = x^3$, cubic function

c. domain: all real numbers

range: all real numbers

6.1 Puzzle Time

YOU TICK IT OFF

6.2 Start Thinking

semi-annual balance = $7828.59, quarterly balance = $7831.04, monthly balance = $7832.68, daily balance = $7833.48

Sample answer: The balance after 5 years will increase by a small amount as the number of compoundings increases. However, it seems there is a limit as to how high the balance will increase. The balance only increased by $0.80 when the number of compoundings jumped from 12 to 365.

6.2 Warm Up

1. growth; initial value 1; percent increase 20%

2. decay; initial value 1; percent decrease 22%

3. decay; initial value 1; percent decrease 37.5%

4. growth; initial value 28; percent increase 3%

5. decay; initial value 25,000; percent decrease 5%

6. growth; initial value 1; percent increase 100%

6.2 Cumulative Review Warm Up

1. $y = 2x + 10$

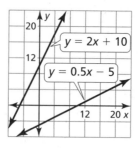

2. $y = -\dfrac{1}{3}x + \dfrac{7}{3}$

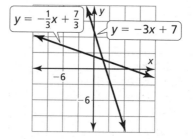

3. $y = 5x + 9$

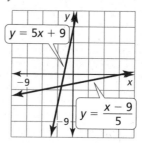

4. $y = \sqrt[3]{x} - 2$

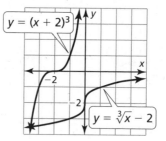

5. $y = \sqrt[3]{2x + 6}$

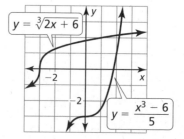

Answers

6. $y = \sqrt{-\dfrac{1}{2}x}$, $x \le 0$

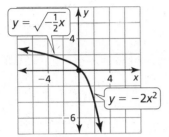

6.2 Practice A

1. e^7

2. e^5

3. $\dfrac{e^3}{3}$

4. $\dfrac{5}{e^5}$

5. $9e^{6x}$

6. $4e^{5x}$

7. incorrectly squared the exponent $3x$, instead of multiplying by 2

$$\left(2x^{3x}\right)^2 = (2)^2\left(e^{3x}\right)^2$$
$$= 4e^{6x}$$

8. exponential growth

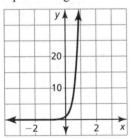

9. exponential decay

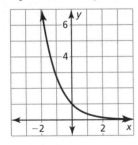

10. exponential decay

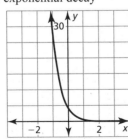

11. $y = (1 - 0.393)^x$; 39.3%

12. $y = 2(1 - 0.181)^x$; 18.1%

13. $y = 5(1 + 0.822)^x$; 82.2%

14.

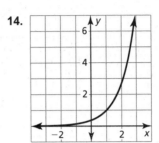

domain: $-\infty < x < \infty$; range: $y > 0$

15.

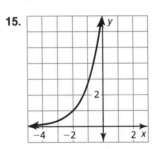

domain: $-\infty < x < \infty$; range: $y > 0$

16.

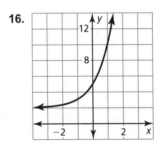

domain: $-\infty < x < \infty$; range: $y > 2$

17. a. $4415.25   **b.** $4376.70   **c.** 4.6 years

6.2 Practice B

1. $\dfrac{1}{e^2}$

2. $\dfrac{3}{2e^3}$

3. $\dfrac{125}{e^{12x}}$

4. $2\sqrt{5}e^{4x}$

5. $4e^{3x}$

6. e^{3x+3}

7. incorrectly placed 2^4 in the denominator, although the exponent is not negative

$$\left(2e^{-3x}\right)^4 = \dfrac{16}{e^{12x}}$$

Answers

8. exponential growth

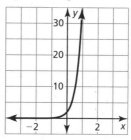

9. exponential decay

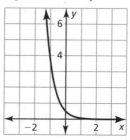

10. exponential growth

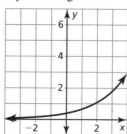

11. $y = (1 + 0.284)^x$; 28.4%

12. $y = 3(1 - 0.478)^x$; 47.8%

13. $y = 0.25(1 + 1.4596)^x$; 145.96%

14.

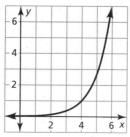

domain: $-\infty < x < \infty$; range: $y > 0$

15.

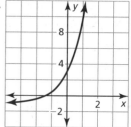

domain: $-\infty < x < \infty$; range: $y > -1$

16.

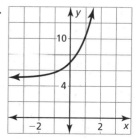

domain: $-\infty < x < \infty$; range: $y > 5$

17. a. $5415.71   **b.** $5416.44

    c. $4.96   **d.** $49.60; 10 times more

6.2 Enrichment and Extension

Sum	Approximation
$\sqrt{12}\left(1 - \dfrac{1}{3 \cdot 3} + \dfrac{1}{5 \cdot 3^2} - \dfrac{1}{7 \cdot 3^3} + \cdots\right)$	≈ 3.137852892
$\sqrt{12}\left(1 - \dfrac{1}{3 \cdot 3} + \dfrac{1}{5 \cdot 3^2} - \dfrac{1}{7 \cdot 3^3} + \dfrac{1}{9 \cdot 3^4} - \cdots\right)$	≈ 3.142604746
$\sqrt{12}\left(1 - \dfrac{1}{3 \cdot 3} + \dfrac{1}{5 \cdot 3^2} - \dfrac{1}{7 \cdot 3^3} + \dfrac{1}{9 \cdot 3^4} - \dfrac{1}{11 \cdot 3^5} + \cdots\right)$	≈ 3.141308785
$\sqrt{12}\left(1 - \dfrac{1}{3 \cdot 3} + \dfrac{1}{5 \cdot 3^2} - \dfrac{1}{7 \cdot 3^3} + \dfrac{1}{9 \cdot 3^4} - \dfrac{1}{11 \cdot 3^5} + \dfrac{1}{13 \cdot 3^6} \cdots\right)$	≈ 3.141674313

Answers

1. The number π is a mathematical constant that is the ratio of a circle's circumference to its diameter.

2. 3.14159265359

3. The fraction $\dfrac{22}{7} \approx 3.142857$ is only an approximation, just like 3.14.

4. In mathematics, a transcendental number is a number that is *not* the root of any nonzero polynomial. π and e are both transcendental numbers. Note that all transcendental numbers are irrational, but not all irrational numbers are transcendental. For example, the irrational number $\sqrt{2}$ is a root of the polynomial $x^2 - 2$, so it is not transcendental.

5. Euler's Identity

6.2 Puzzle Time

VACUUM CLEANER

6.3 Start Thinking

The graph of $f^{-1}(x)$ is a reflection of $f(x)$ in the line $y = x$. The domain of $f(x)$ is the range of $f^{-1}(x)$ and the range of $f(x)$ is the domain of $f^{-1}(x)$.

6.3 Warm Up

1. 2   2. 0   3. 3

4. −1   5. $\dfrac{1}{2}$ 6. $-\dfrac{1}{2}$

6.3 Cumulative Review Warm Up

1. a.
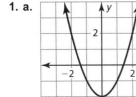

b.
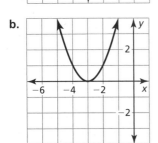

c.
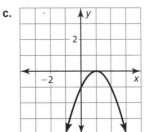

2. a.
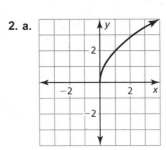

b.
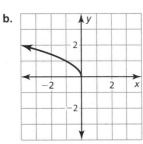

c.
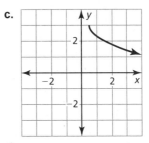

6.3 Practice A

1. $2^3 = 8$ 2. $7^1 = 7$ 3. $5^2 = 25$

4. $\log_4 16 = 2$ 5. $\log_5 1 = 0$ 6. $\log_6 \dfrac{1}{6} = -1$

7. 4   8. 3   9. 1

10. −1   11. 0   12. −3

13. 0.699   14. 2.639   15. −0.602

16. 30 decibels   17. x 18. $2x$

19. $3x$ 20. $y = \log_{1.1} x$ 21. $y = \log_3 x$

22. $y = 3^x$ 23. $y = 3\left(10^x\right)$

Answers

24. $y = \frac{1}{3}e^x$ **25.** $y = \frac{1}{5}\ln x$

26. a. 208.6 mi/h   **b.** 8.2 mi

6.3 Practice B

1. $9^0 = 1$ **2.** $6^3 = 216$

3. $2^{-2} = \frac{1}{4}$ **4.** $\log_{13}\frac{1}{169} = -2$

5. $\log_4 8 = \frac{3}{2}$ **6.** $\log_{81} 9 = \frac{1}{2}$

7. 2   **8.** 5   **9.** 0

10. -4 **11.** -3 **12.** -2

13. -0.699 **14.** 0.673 **15.** -2.916

16. yes; The sound is 130 decibels.

17. $7x$ **18.** 18   **19.** $3x$

20. $y = \log_{0.75} x$ **21.** $y = \left(\frac{3}{4}\right)^x$

22. $y = 2\left(10^x\right)$ **23.** $y = e^x - 2$

24. $y = \ln x + 3$ **25.** $y = \log_6(x - 2)$

26. a. 116.83 in.; 9.74 ft
    b. 1651.8 lb

6.3 Enrichment and Extension

1. 5   **2.** 3   **3.** 4

4. 1   **5.** 2   **6.** $\frac{1}{3}$

7. 0   **8.** -2 **9.** -2

10. 343   **11.** 11   **12.** $\frac{1}{216}$

13. 729   **14.** 1   **15.** 2

16. $\frac{1}{256}$ **17.** $\frac{1}{64}$ **18.** $\frac{1}{3}$

19. 3   **20.** 4   **21.** 3

22. 512   **23.** 2   **24.** 2401

6.3 Puzzle Time

AT A SNOOPER MARKET

6.4 Start Thinking

1.

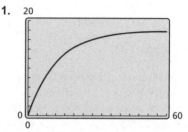

Sample answer: $x\text{min} = 0,\ x\text{max} = 60,$
$x\text{scl} = 4,\ y\text{min} = 0,\ y\text{max} = 20,\ y\text{scl} = 2$

2. approximately 6 windows after 5 days;
approximately 10 windows after 10 days

3. approximately 17 windows in approximately
36 days; Note that the graph asymptotically
approaches 18 from below, but never reaches it.

6.4 Warm Up

1. reflection in x-axis, followed by a translation
3 units up

2. vertical shrink by a factor of $\frac{1}{2}$, followed by a
translation 2 units left and 5 units down

3. reflection in y-axis, and a horizontal shrink by a
factor of $\frac{1}{3}$

4. translation 2 units right, and a vertical stretch by a
factor of 4

6.4 Cumulative Review Warm Up

1. $y = 3x + 5$ **2.** $y = -5x - 2$

3. $y = -2x + 9$ **4.** $y = \frac{11}{5}x + \frac{62}{5}$

6.4 Practice A

1. translation 3 units up

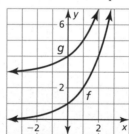

Answers

2. translation 2 units down

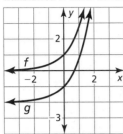

3. translation 1 unit right

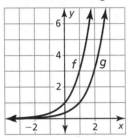

4. translation 4 units up

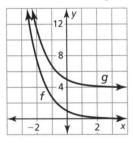

5. horizontal shrink by a factor of $\dfrac{1}{3}$

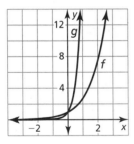

6. vertical stretch by a factor of $\dfrac{3}{2}$

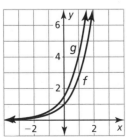

7. reflection in the *x*-axis, followed by a horizontal translation 2 units left

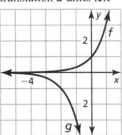

8. horizontal shrink by a factor of $\dfrac{1}{5}$ and a vertical stretch by a factor of 2

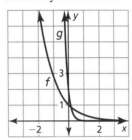

9. incorrectly evaluates as $(2e)^x$, but in $f(x) = 2e^x$, the 2 is the leading coefficient and not part of the base

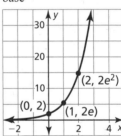

10. vertical stretch by a factor of 4, followed by a translation 1 unit down

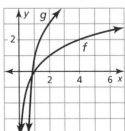

Answers

11. reflection in the *x*-axis, followed by a translation 3 units up

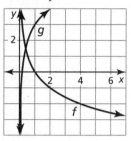

12. $g(x) = -3^{x+3} - 1$ **13.** $g(x) = \dfrac{1}{4}e^x + 5$

14. $g(x) = \log_8\left(-(x + 4)\right)$

15. $g(x) = 9\log_{1/6}(x - 2) - 3$

6.4 Practice B

1. translation 4 units down

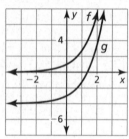

2. translation 2 units left

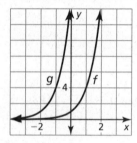

3. translation 5 units down

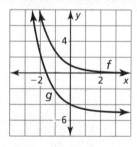

4. translation 2 units up

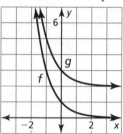

5. horizontal shrink by a factor of $\dfrac{1}{2}$, followed by a translation 1 unit down

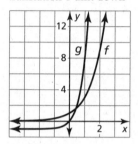

6. reflection in the *x*-axis, followed by a translation 2 units left

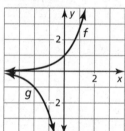

7. translation 1 unit right, followed by a horizontal shrink by a factor of $\dfrac{1}{4}$

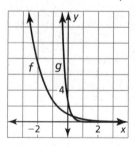

Answers

8. translation 2 units right and 3 units up

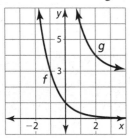

9. incorrectly evaluated as $2^x + 3$, but in $f(x) = 2^{x+3}$, the 3 is in the exponent and is added to x first

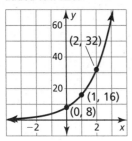

10. translation 2 units right and 4 units up

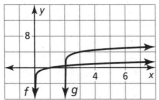

11. reflection in the y-axis, followed by a reflection in the x-axis

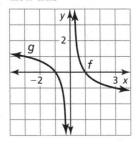

12. $g(x) = \left(\dfrac{2}{5}\right)^{-x/2} - 4$

13. $g(x) = 2\left(e^{-(x+2)} + 3\right) = 2e^{-x-2} + 6$

14. $g(x) = -\log_{12}(x - 5) + 2$

6.4 Enrichment and Extension

1. K **2.** D **3.** E **4.** M

5. L **6.** G **7.** I **8.** J

---

9. F **10.** A **11.** N **12.** C

13. B **14.** H

6.4 Puzzle Time

LUNCH

6.5 Start Thinking

Sample answer: In each group, the right side of the third equation is the sum of the previous two, whereas the left side of the third equation involves a product inside the log.

$$\log_2(3 \bullet 4) = \log_2(3) + \log_2(4)$$

$$\log_3\left(15 \bullet \frac{1}{3}\right) = \log_3(15) + \log_3\left(\frac{1}{3}\right)$$

$$\log_4(9 \bullet 2) = \log_4(9) + \log_4(2)$$

Following this pattern:

$$\log_5(25 \bullet x) = \log_5 25 + \log_5 x$$
$$= 2 + \log_5 x$$
$$\approx 2 + 1.4$$
$$= 3.4$$

6.5 Warm Up

1. $n = 7$ **2.** $n = 6$ **3.** $n = \dfrac{1}{2}$

4. $n = \dfrac{1}{4}$ **5.** $n = 2$ **6.** $n = -3$

6.5 Cumulative Review Warm Up

1. $5, 1$ **2.** $-\dfrac{4}{3}, \dfrac{5}{2}$ **3.** $2 \pm 2\sqrt{3}$

4. $1 \pm 2i$ **5.** 3 **6.** $\dfrac{-1 \pm \sqrt{10}}{3}$

6.5 Practice A

1. 0.43 **2.** 1.796 **3.** 1.366

4. $\log_2 5 + \log_2 x$ **5.** $\log 7 + 4 \log x$

6. $\log_6 2 + \log_6 x - \log_6 y$

7. confuses logarithm rules for products and powers; The log of a product is the sum of the logs, not another product.

$$\log_4 3x = \log_4 3 + \log_4 x$$

8. $\log_7 \dfrac{3}{5}$ **9.** $\log 2$ **10.** $\ln\left(x^3 y^9\right)$

Answers

11. $\log_2\left(9y^{1/2}\right)$ **12.** 0.683 **13.** 3.459

14. 1.285 **15.** yes; $\ln x = \dfrac{\log x}{\log e}$

16. about 7 decibel levels

6.5 Practice B

1. 2.732 **2.** -1.113 **3.** -0.43

4. $\log_3 12 + 7 \log_3 x$

5. $\log_6 5 + 2 \log_6 x - 3 \log_6 y$

6. $\log_8 6 + \dfrac{1}{2}\log_8 x + \dfrac{1}{2}\log_8 y$

7. does not distribute the $\dfrac{1}{3}$ power to y as well as x

$\ln \sqrt[3]{xy} = \dfrac{1}{3}\ln x + \dfrac{1}{3}\ln y$

8. $\log_9\left(\dfrac{x^5}{4}\right)$ **9.** $\log_8\left(5\sqrt[4]{x}\right)$

10. $\ln\left(16x^5 y^3\right)$ **11.** $\log_6\left(\dfrac{1}{x^3}\right)$

12. 1.302 **13.** 3.096 **14.** -0.544

15. yes; $\dfrac{\ln y}{\ln 3} = \log_3 y$

16. about 4.77 decibel levels

6.5 Enrichment and Extension

1. 9 **2.** 6 **3.** 3

4. -1.9041 **5.** -9.4717 **6.** 1

7. 1.4307 **8.** 400 **9.** 50

10. -4 **11.** 2.0402 **12.** 2.9307

13. 68.6309 **14.** 0.5 **15.** 161

16. 9983.6667

6.5 Puzzle Time

A SILLYMANDER

6.6 Start Thinking

$10{,}000 = 5000 e^{0.0525t}$; $t \approx 13.2$ years

6.6 Warm Up

1. $\log_2 5 = x - 1$; $x = 1 + \log_2 5$

2. $\ln 11 = -2x$; $x = -\dfrac{1}{2}\ln 11$

3. $\log_3 4 = 3 - 2x$; $x = \dfrac{3}{2} - \dfrac{1}{2}\log_3 4$

4. $2^{-1} = x + 5$; $x = -\dfrac{9}{2}$

5. $10^2 = 3 - x$; $x = -97$

6. $e^{1/3} = 2x$; $x = \dfrac{1}{2}\sqrt[3]{e}$

6.6 Cumulative Review Warm Up

1. $f(x) \to -\infty$ as $x \to -\infty$ and $f(x) \to -\infty$ as $x \to +\infty$

2. $g(x) \to +\infty$ as $x \to -\infty$ and $g(x) \to -\infty$ as $x \to +\infty$

3. $h(x) \to -\infty$ as $x \to -\infty$ and $h(x) \to +\infty$ as $x \to +\infty$

4. $p(x) \to +\infty$ as $x \to -\infty$ and $p(x) \to +\infty$ as $x \to +\infty$

6.6 Practice A

1. $x = -10$ **2.** $x = 2$

3. $x = 7$ **4.** $x = \log_2 5 \approx 2.322$

5. $x = \log_8 35 \approx 1.71$ **6.** $x = -\dfrac{1}{5}$

7. a. 24 years **b.** 246.1 cm

8. $x = 7$ **9.** $x = 1$

10. $x = 6$ **11.** $x = \dfrac{32}{5}$

12. $x = 100.7$ **13.** $x = 1$

14. $x = 4$; extraneous solution: $x = -1$

15. $x = 1$; extraneous solution: $x = -\dfrac{3}{2}$

16. $x = 2.91$; extraneous solution: $x = -6.91$

Answers

17. $x = \pm\sqrt{6}$

18. a. 14.2 years

    b. 13.95 years

    c. 13.864 years

    d. 13.863 years

19. $x < 1.92$ **20.** $x \geq 2.89$ **21.** $x > 9$

22. $x \approx 4.32$ **23.** $x \approx 1.03$

6.6 Practice B

1. $x = -3$

2. $x = \log_7 32 \approx 1.781$

3. $x = -4$

4. $x = \dfrac{1}{4}\log_6 13 \approx 0.358$

5. $x = \dfrac{1}{3}\ln 2 \approx 0.231$

6. $x = \dfrac{1}{2}\ln 2 \approx 0.347$

7. a. 2130.9 years

    b. more years; 942.95 more years

8. $x = 2$ **9.** $x = \dfrac{1}{3}$ **10.** $x = \dfrac{4}{3}$

11. $x = 1$ **12.** $x = 5, -3$ **13.** $x = -5, 4$

14. $x = 13.22$; extraneous solution: $x = -11.22$

15. $x = \pm\dfrac{5}{4}$ **16.** $x = -1.35, -6.65$

17. $x = 0.772$; extraneous solution: $x = -7.772$

18. $x < 2 + 3\ln 3 \approx 4.08$

19. $x > e^5 \approx 148.4$

20. $x \geq \dfrac{1}{81} \approx 0.012$ **21.** 8.5 years

6.6 Enrichment and Extension

1. after about 30 min

2. about 2 h and 11 min

6.6 Puzzle Time

SO THEY HAVE SOMEWHERE TO PUT THE
GROCERIES WHEN THEY GO SHOPPING

6.7 Start Thinking

1. exponential; *Sample answer*: An account balance increases over time.

2. linear; *Sample answer*: A scientist introduces a specific amount of chemical to a solution each hour.

3. quadratic; *Sample answer*: A model rocket is shot from a platform.

6.7 Warm Up

1. $y = 1.8x - 3.333$

2. $y = -1.626x + 3390.974$

6.7 Cumulative Review Warm Up

1. $x = \dfrac{17}{2}$ **2.** $x = 8$

3. $x = \dfrac{4}{7}$ **4.** $x = \dfrac{13}{4}$

6.7 Practice A

1. exponential; common ratio $= \dfrac{1}{3}$

2. quadratic; common second difference

3. $y = 3(2)^x$ **4.** $y = 5(4)^x$ **5.** $y = 2(3)^x$

6. $y = 2(5)^x$ **7.** $y = 7(2)^x$ **8.** $y = 5(3)^x$

9. The x-values must have a common difference before a common ratio in the y-values can be used.

x	0	1	3	5	7
y	2	4	8	16	32

$\times 2$ $\times 2$ $\times 2$ $\times 2$

The outputs have a common ratio of 2, but the inputs do not have a common difference, so the data do not represent a recognizable function.

10. exponential relationship; $y = 96(2)^x$

11. linear relationship; For every increase of x by 1, y increases by 5.

Answers

12. $y = 5(1.2)^x$

6.7 Practice B

1. exponential; common ratio = 4

2. exponential; common ratio = $\dfrac{3}{2}$

3. $y = 5(2)^x$ **4.** $y = 6(3)^x$ **5.** $y = 9(2)^x$

6. $y = 3(5)^x$ **7.** $y = \dfrac{1}{10}(6)^x$ **8.** $y = \dfrac{1}{2}(4)^x$

9. assumed that the output of any exponential function is always positive, because b^x is always positive, but forgot that the coefficient a can be negative

x	0	2	4	6	8
y	-2	-4	-8	-16	-32

$\times 2 \quad \times 2 \quad \times 2 \quad \times 2$

The outputs have a common ratio of 2, so the data represent an exponential function.

10. exponential relationship; $y = 64\left(\dfrac{\sqrt{2}}{2}\right)^{x-1}$

11. linear relationship; For every increase of x by 10, y increases by 15.

12. $y = 3.4(1.5)^x$

6.7 Enrichment and Extension

1. 10^8, or 100,000,000 times louder

2. 10^{11}, or 100,000,000,000 times louder

3. 30 decibels   **4.** 60 decibels

6.7 Puzzle Time

SHEEP SHAPE

Cumulative Review

1. 245   **2.** 48   **3.** 162

4. -32 **5.** -224 **6.** -320

7. -8 **8.** 9   **9.** 16

10. $\dfrac{8}{27}$ **11.** $\dfrac{16}{25}$ **12.** $\dfrac{1}{81}$

13. $-\dfrac{8}{125}$ **14.** $\dfrac{1}{256}$ **15.** $-\dfrac{27}{64}$

16. $-\dfrac{1}{32}$ **17.** $-\dfrac{16}{81}$ **18.** $-\dfrac{27}{125}$

19. 5×10^{-4} **20.** 3.82×10^{11}

21. -1.32×10^{-2} **22.** 5.7×10^{-6}

23. 2.3×10^{6} **24.** -9.2×10^{-10}

25. -3.59×10^{-4} **26.** 5.13×10^{4}

27. 4.1×10^{-5} **28.** 4.5×10^{3}

29. 1.2×10^{7} **30.** 7.31×10^{5}

31. -8.17×10^{-7} **32.** 4.17×10^{11}

33. -6.2×10^{4} **34.** 8.3×10^{12}

35. 8.9×10^{-8} **36.** 2×10^{-3}

37. a. Bowling Alley A: \$19, Bowling Alley B: \$25

   b. Bowling Alley A: \$22.50, Bowling Alley B: \$25

   c. 6 games or more

38. a. \$22.50   **b.** \$25   **c.** \$100

39. 0.00185   **40.** $-89,000$

41. 0.0000000384   **42.** 0.000000257

43. 460,000   **44.** -0.00334

45. 0.0000000305   **46.** 44,900

47. 590,000   **48.** $-2,250,000,000$

49. 0.308   **50.** -0.0000000106

51. 55,100,000   **52.** 618,000,000

53. 0.000000184   **54.** 890,000

55. 0.000000092   **56.** -0.0000732

57. $y = -\dfrac{2}{5}x - 12$ **58.** $y = \dfrac{5}{11}x - 4$

59. $y = \dfrac{3}{5}x - 9$ **60.** $y = \dfrac{1}{4}x - 4$

Answers

61. $y = -\frac{7}{8}x + 3$ **62.** $y = \frac{3}{5}x - 12$

63. $y = -2x + 7$ **64.** $y = 3x - 20$

65. $y = -\frac{1}{2}x - 10$ **66.** $y = \frac{5}{6}x + 5\frac{1}{2}$

67. $y = -3x + 13$ **68.** $y = 4x + 24$

69. $x = 0$ and $x = 7$ **70.** $x = -3$ and $x = 0$

71. $x = -4$ and $x = 0$

72. $x = 0$ and $x = 8$

73. $x = 1$ and $x = 2$

74. $x = -9$ and $x = 3$

75. $x = -6$ and $x = -5$

76. $x = -2$ and $x = 8$

77. $x = -\frac{7}{2}$ and $x = 5$

78. $x = -5$ and $x = \frac{1}{3}$

79. $x = -4$ and $x = \frac{7}{2}$

80. $x = -\frac{1}{3}$ and $x = 7$

81. $x = -\frac{1}{5}$ and $x = 3$

82. $x = \frac{7}{3}$ and $x = 9$

83. $4 + 4i$ **84.** $4 - 3i$

85. $11 - 12i$ **86.** $-12 - i$

87. $10 + 6i$ **88.** $8 - 20i$

89. $1 - 3i$ **90.** $-2 + 14i$

91. $-14 - 3i$ **92.** $21 - 5i$

93. $5 + 8i$ **94.** $-10 + 6i$

95. $18 + 21i$ **96.** $-17 - 5i$

97. $-6 + 12i$ **98.** $-10 - 5i$

99. $-28 - 21i$ **100.** $-6 - 7i$

101. $-81 + 69i$ **102.** $-42 + 66i$

103. $-36 + 32i$ **104.** $-50 - 30i$

105. $-41 + 126i$ **106.** $-31 + 53i$

107. $-79 + 14i$ **108.** $27 + 3i$

109. $x = \dfrac{-3 \pm i}{2}$ **110.** $x = \dfrac{1 \pm i\sqrt{35}}{6}$

111. $x = \dfrac{-3 \pm i\sqrt{87}}{8}$ **112.** $x = \dfrac{5 \pm i\sqrt{167}}{12}$

113. $x = 2 \pm i\sqrt{3}$ **114.** $x = \dfrac{3 \pm i\sqrt{6}}{5}$

115. $x = \dfrac{9 \pm i\sqrt{15}}{8}$ **116.** $x = \dfrac{5 \pm i\sqrt{7}}{4}$

117. a. $P = 10x$

    b. $A = 4x^2 + 30x - 100$

    c. $x = 12$

    d. 836 ft^2

118. $x = \dfrac{-5 \pm \sqrt{41}}{2}$ **119.** $x = \dfrac{-2 \pm \sqrt{2}}{2}$

120. $x = 4 \pm \sqrt{21}$ **121.** $x = 1$ and $x = 2$

122. $x = 1$ and $x = \frac{3}{2}$

123. $x = \dfrac{5 \pm \sqrt{17}}{2}$ **124.** $x = \dfrac{3 \pm 2\sqrt{3}}{3}$

125. $x = \dfrac{-3 \pm \sqrt{89}}{10}$ **126.** $x = \frac{1}{3}$ and $x = \frac{1}{2}$

127. $x = \dfrac{7 \pm \sqrt{73}}{4}$ **128.** $x = \dfrac{-7 \pm \sqrt{37}}{2}$

129. $x = \dfrac{1 \pm \sqrt{129}}{8}$ **130.** $x = \dfrac{5 \pm \sqrt{13}}{6}$

131. $x = \dfrac{9 \pm \sqrt{129}}{4}$

Answers

132. a. $P = 6x + 8$

b. $A = 2x^2 + 8x$

c. $x = 8$

d. 192 ft^2

133. a. $A = 40.5x$

b. $x = 6$

c. 243 ft^2

d. $605.07

134. a. $A = 32x$

b. $x = 11$

c. 352 ft^2

d. $1615.68

Chapter 7

7.1 Start Thinking

1. The quotient of x and y is the same for each point, $\dfrac{x}{y} = \dfrac{1}{2}$. The graph is the line $y = 2x$.

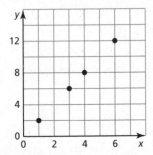

2. The product of x and y is the same for each point, $xy = 2$. The graph is not a line but curved.

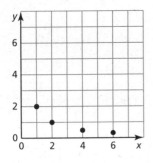

3. The product of x and y is the same for each point, $xy = 3$. The graph is not a line but curved.

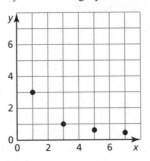

7.1 Warm Up

1. $-\dfrac{3}{4}$ **2.** 10 **3.** 0.8

4. -26 **5.** -26 **6.** $-\dfrac{3}{2}$

7.1 Cumulative Review Warm Up

1. $\left(-\dfrac{1}{2}, 3\right)$ **2.** $\left(\dfrac{21}{2}, -3\right)$

3. $\left(\sqrt{3}, 3\right), \left(-\sqrt{3}, 3\right)$

7.1 Practice A

1. inverse variation   **2.** inverse variation

3. direct variation   **4.** direct variation

5. neither   **6.** direct variation

7. inverse variation   **8.** neither

9. direct variation   **10.** inverse variation

11. $y = -\dfrac{30}{x};\ y = -10$ **12.** $y = \dfrac{7}{x};\ y = \dfrac{7}{3}$

13. $y = \dfrac{2}{x};\ y = \dfrac{2}{3}$

14. incorrectly used the equation $\dfrac{y}{x} = a$, which implied a direct variation between x and y, not inverse variation;

$xy = a$

$(5)(6) = a$

$a = 30$

So, $y = \dfrac{30}{x}$.

15. 3750 songs

Answers

7.1 Practice B

1. inverse variation
2. inverse variation
3. direct variation
4. neither
5. direct variation
6. inverse variation
7. direct variation
8. inverse variation
9. neither
10. inverse variation

11. $y = -\dfrac{12}{x}$; $y = -4$ 12. $y = -\dfrac{10}{3x}$; $y = -\dfrac{10}{9}$

13. $y = \dfrac{2}{x}$; $y = \dfrac{2}{3}$

14. The final equation given is a direct variation, not an inverse variation;

$xy = a$

$\dfrac{1}{3} \bullet 2 = a$

$a = \dfrac{2}{3}$

So, $y = \dfrac{2}{3x}$.

15. 6.4 amperes

7.1 Enrichment and Extension

1. $y = -\dfrac{5}{3}$ 2. $w = \dfrac{15}{4}$

3. $h \approx 24.7$ m

4. As pressure increases, volume decreases; $n = \dfrac{PV}{RT}$

7.1 Puzzle Time

THE SPACE BAR

7.2 Start Thinking

1.

x	-1	$-\frac{1}{2}$	$-\frac{1}{10}$	$-\frac{1}{100}$	$\frac{1}{100}$	$\frac{1}{10}$	$\frac{1}{2}$	1
$g(x)$	-1	-2	-10	-100	100	10	2	1

$g(x)$ approaches $-\infty$ as x approaches 0 from the left and $g(x)$ approaches $+\infty$ as x approaches 0 from the right.

2.

x	-1000	-100	-10	10	100	1000
$g(x)$	$-\frac{1}{1000}$	$-\frac{1}{100}$	$-\frac{1}{10}$	$\frac{1}{10}$	$\frac{1}{100}$	$\frac{1}{1000}$

$g(x)$ approaches 0 as x approaches both $+\infty$ and $-\infty$.

7.2 Warm Up

1.

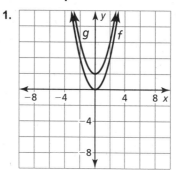

2.

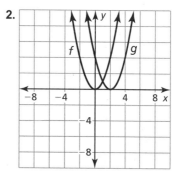

3.

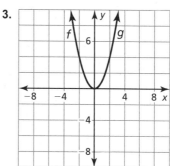

4.

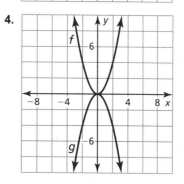

Answers

5.

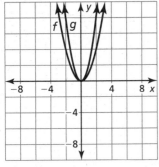

6.

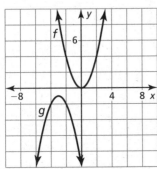

7.2 Cumulative Review Warm Up

1. maximum: $\dfrac{25}{8}$ **2.** minimum: $\dfrac{47}{12}$

3. maximum: $\dfrac{41}{8}$

7.2 Practice A

1.

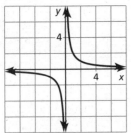

The graph of h lies farther from the axes than the graph of f. Both graphs lie in the first and third quadrants and have the same asymptotes, domain, and range.

2.

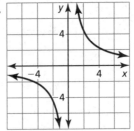

The graph of g lies farther from the axes than the graph of f. Both graphs lie in the first and third quadrants and have the same asymptotes, domain, and range.

3.

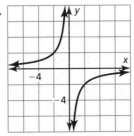

The graph of h is a reflection in the x-axis of the graph of f, and lies farther from the axes than the graph of f. The graphs have the same asymptotes, domain, and range.

4.

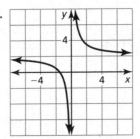

domain: all real numbers except 0, range: all real numbers except 2

5.

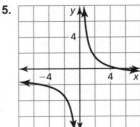

domain: all real numbers except 0, range: all real numbers except -1

Answers

6.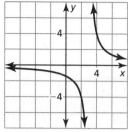

domain: all real numbers except 3, range: all real numbers except 0

7.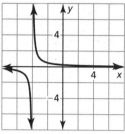

domain: all real numbers except −4, range: all real numbers except 0

8.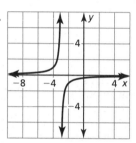

domain: all real numbers except −3, range: all real numbers except 0

9.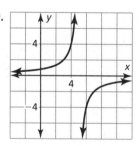

domain: all real numbers except 5, range: all real numbers except 0

10.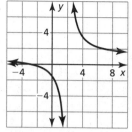

domain: all real numbers except 2, range: all real numbers except 1

11.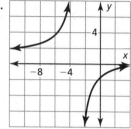

domain: all real numbers except −3, range: all real numbers except 1

12.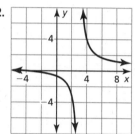

domain: all real numbers except 3, range: all real numbers except $\frac{1}{2}$

13.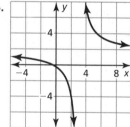

domain: all real numbers except 3, range: all real numbers except $\frac{5}{3}$

Answers

14.

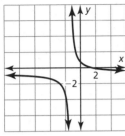

domain: all real numbers except $-\dfrac{4}{3}$, range: all real

numbers except $-\dfrac{2}{3}$

15.

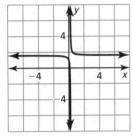

domain: all real numbers except $\dfrac{1}{5}$, range: all real

numbers except $\dfrac{8}{5}$

16. $g(x) = \dfrac{1}{x+1} + 4$

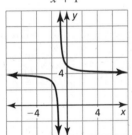

translation 1 unit left and 4 units up

17. $g(x) = \dfrac{17}{x-2} + 6$

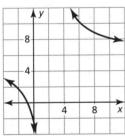

translation 2 units right and 6 units up

18. $g(x) = \dfrac{6}{x-4} + 3$

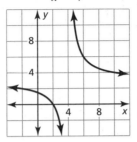

translation 4 units right and 3 units up

19. $g(x) = \dfrac{-22}{x+2} + 5$

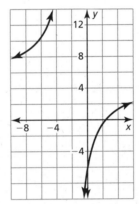

translation 2 units left and 5 units up

20. $g(x) = \dfrac{20}{x-5} + 1$

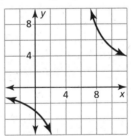

translation 5 units right and 1 unit up

21. $g(x) = \dfrac{12}{x-9} + 1$

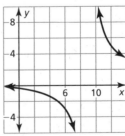

translation 9 units right and 1 unit up

Answers

22. a. 20 students

b. The average cost approaches $150.

23.

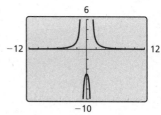

even

24.

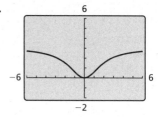

even

25.

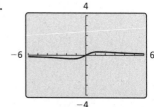

odd

7.2 Practice B

1.

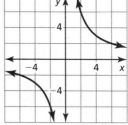

The graph of g lies farther from the axes than the graph of f. Both graphs lie in the first and third quadrants and have the same asymptotes, domain, and range.

2.

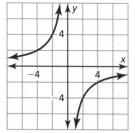

The graph of h is a reflection in the x-axis of the graph of f, and lies farther from the axes than the graph of f. The graphs have the same asymptotes, domain, and range.

3.

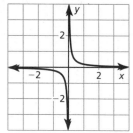

The graph of g lies closer to the axes than the graph of f. Both graphs lie in the first and third quadrants and have the same asymptotes, domain, and range.

4.

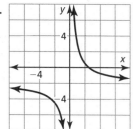

domain: all real numbers except 0, range: all real numbers except -2

5.

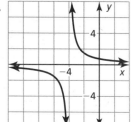

domain: all real numbers except -4, range: all real numbers except 0

Answers

6.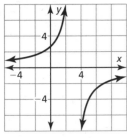

domain: all real numbers except 3, range: all real numbers except 0

7.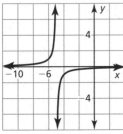

domain: all real numbers except -5, range: all real numbers except 0

8.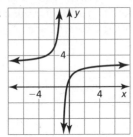

domain: all real numbers except -1, range: all real numbers except 3

9.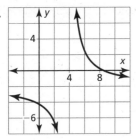

domain: all real numbers except 4, range: all real numbers except -2

10.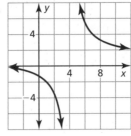

domain: all real numbers except 4, range: all real numbers except 1

11.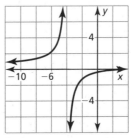

domain: all real numbers except -4, range: all real numbers except $\dfrac{1}{2}$

12.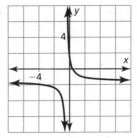

domain: all real numbers except $-\dfrac{2}{5}$, range: all real numbers except $-\dfrac{8}{5}$

13.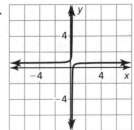

domain: all real numbers except $\dfrac{1}{5}$, range: all real numbers except $\dfrac{3}{5}$

Answers

14.

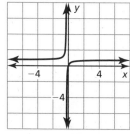

domain: all real numbers except $-\dfrac{1}{4}$, range: all real

numbers except $\dfrac{3}{4}$

15.

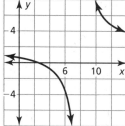

domain: all real numbers except 8, range: all real numbers except 2

16. $g(x) = \dfrac{1}{x + 2} + 3$

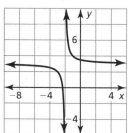

translation 2 units left and 3 units up

17. $g(x) = \dfrac{10}{x - 3} + 4$

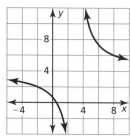

translation 3 units right and 4 units up

18. $g(x) = \dfrac{-30}{x + 5} + 4$

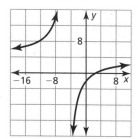

translation 5 units left and 4 units up

19. $g(x) = \dfrac{15}{x - 3} + 1$

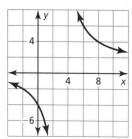

translation 3 units right and 1 unit up

20. $g(x) = \dfrac{-50}{x + 4} + 5$

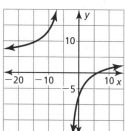

translation 4 units left and 5 units up

21. $g(x) = \dfrac{-44}{x + 6} + 7$

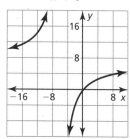

translation 2 units left and 7 units up

22. a. 38 statues

b. The average cost decreases, approaching $22.

Answers

23. a.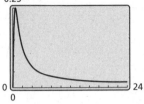

Sample answer: $0 < x \le 24$; $0 < y \le 0.25$

b. $t = \dfrac{1}{2}\,\text{h}$

7.2 Enrichment and Extension

1.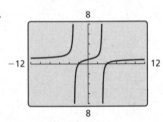

As $x \to +\infty$, $y \to 1$. As $x \to -\infty$, $y \to 1$.

2.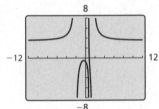

As $x \to +\infty$, $y \to \dfrac{7}{2}$. As $x \to -\infty$, $y \to \dfrac{7}{2}$.

3.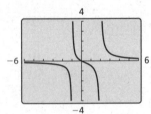

As $x \to +\infty$, $y \to 0$. As $x \to -\infty$, $y \to 0$.

4.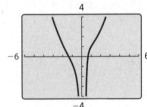

As $x \to +\infty$, $y \to +\infty$. As $x \to -\infty$, $y \to +\infty$.

5.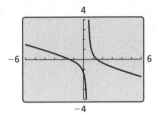

As $x \to +\infty$, $y \to -\infty$. As $x \to -\infty$, $y \to +\infty$.

6.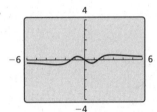

As $x \to +\infty$, $y \to 0$. As $x \to -\infty$, $y \to 0$.

7.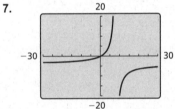

As $x \to +\infty$, $y \to -4$. As $x \to -\infty$, $y \to -4$.

8.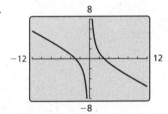

As $x \to +\infty$, $y \to -\infty$. As $x \to -\infty$, $y \to +\infty$.

7.2 Puzzle Time

A COIN

7.3 Start Thinking

1. -8　　　**2.** $0, 5$　　　**3.** $-\dfrac{3}{2}, \dfrac{5}{3}$

7.3 Warm Up

1. $\dfrac{10}{21}$　　　**2.** $\dfrac{36}{25}$　　　**3.** $\dfrac{6}{11}$

4. $\dfrac{2x - 2}{25}$　　　　　**5.** $\dfrac{x^2}{x^2 - 1}$, $x \ne \pm 1$

Answers

6. $\dfrac{-3x - 3}{2x^2 + x}, x \neq -1, -\dfrac{1}{2}, 0$

7.3 Cumulative Review Warm Up

1. \$7269.23   **2.** \$7715.86

3. \$7613.38   **4.** \$7500.05

5. \$7902.47   **6.** \$7401.70

7.3 Pratice A

1. $\dfrac{3x}{5x + 2}, x \neq 0$ **2.** $\dfrac{6x - 1}{2x}$

3. $\dfrac{x + 1}{x - 2}, x \neq 5$ **4.** cannot be simplified

5. $\dfrac{x + 1}{x^2 + 2x + 4}, x \neq 2$ **6.** $\dfrac{x - 4}{x^2 - x + 1}, x \neq -1$

7. $\dfrac{6x^2}{y^3}, x \neq 0$ **8.** $\dfrac{(x + 2)(x - 3)}{x}, x \neq 1$

9. $\dfrac{(x - 5)(x - 1)}{4}, x \neq 0, x \neq -7$

10. $(x - 5)(x + 1), x \neq 0, x \neq -3$

11. $\dfrac{(x + 3)(x - 3)}{4}, x \neq 0, x \neq 2$

12. $\dfrac{2x(x - 5)}{(x + 3)(x + 2)}, x \neq -1$

13. The only difference between the two functions is the domain. The domain of f is all real numbers except $-\dfrac{1}{4}$. The domain of g is all real numbers.

14. $\dfrac{56x^9}{y^{15}}, x \neq 0$

15. $2, x \neq 0, x \neq -2, x \neq 3$

16. $5, x \neq 0, x \neq 1, x \neq -3$

17. $\dfrac{x + 7}{(x + 3)(x - 2)}$

18. a. $\dfrac{2h + 2r}{rh}$

b. old: $\dfrac{2h + 2r}{rh}$; new: $\dfrac{h + 2r}{rh}$

c. yes; $h + 2r < 2h + 2r$

7.3 Practice B

1. $\dfrac{4x^2}{3x^2 + 7}, x \neq 0$ **2.** $\dfrac{x + 2}{x - 1}, x \neq -3$

3. cannot be simplified

4. $\dfrac{x - 5}{x^2 - 4x + 16}, x \neq -4$

5. $\dfrac{x^2 - 4}{5x - 3}$ **6.** $\dfrac{x - 1}{12x^2 - 10}$

7. $\dfrac{(x - 4)(x - 2)}{x}, x \neq -3$

8. $(x + 6)(x + 2), x \neq 0, x \neq 4$

9. $\dfrac{(x - 2)(x + 1)}{3}, x \neq 0, x \neq -5$

10. $\dfrac{3x(x + 2)}{(x + 1)(x + 4)}, x \neq 3$

11. $\dfrac{(x + 7)(x - 4)(x - 3)}{x + 5}, x \neq 5$

12. $(x + 5)(x - 4), x \neq 3, x \neq -3$

13. $1, x \neq 0, x \neq -5, x \neq 4$

14. $\dfrac{x - 3}{(x + 2)(x - 7)}$

15. $\dfrac{(x - 3)(x + 2)}{(x - 2)(x + 3)}, x \neq -1, x \neq -4, x \neq -2$

16. $1, x \neq 3, x \neq -3, x \neq -4, x \neq 2$

17. $\dfrac{4}{x + 3}$ **18.** $x + 3$

7.3 Enrichment and Extension

1. $f(x) = \dfrac{x^2 + x - 6}{x^2 - 2x - 35}; y = 1$

Answers

2. $h(x) = \dfrac{x^3 + 2x^2 - 16x - 32}{x^2 + 6x + 9}$; There is no horizontal asymptote.

3. $k(x) = \dfrac{-4x^3 + 5x^2 + 2}{7x^3 + 2x^2 + 5x - 9}$; $y = -\dfrac{4}{7}$

4. $m(x) = \dfrac{2x - 3}{3x^2 + 5x - 2}$; $y = 0$

5. $t(x) = \dfrac{3x^2 - 22x + 7}{10x^2 + 7x - 12}$; $y = \dfrac{3}{10}$

7.3 Puzzle Time

A NEWSPAPER

7.4 Start Thinking

LCD: $3x(x - 2)(x + 3)$, $x = 0$, $x = 2$, $x = -3$

7.4 Warm Up

1. $\dfrac{23}{21}$ **2.** $\dfrac{23}{10}$ **3.** $-\dfrac{1}{7}$

4. $\dfrac{5}{8}$ **5.** $-\dfrac{11}{16}$ **6.** $\dfrac{33}{100}$

7.4 Cumulative Review Warm Up

1. $-x^2 - x + 4$ **2.** $3x^3 - 10x^2 + 8x$

3. $\dfrac{4 - 3x}{2x - x^2}$ **4.** $-9x^2 + 18x - 8$

5. 2 **6.** 13

7.4 Practice A

1. $\dfrac{3}{x}$ **2.** $\dfrac{x - 3}{9x^2}$ **3.** $\dfrac{7 - 3x}{x - 2}$

4. $x^2(6x - 18)$ **5.** $5x(x + 2)$

6. $x^2 - 9$ **7.** $x^2 - 3x - 10$

8. The calculation shown simply subtracts the numerators of the two rational expressions, without first rewriting each rational expression with a common denominator.

$$\frac{x}{x + 3} - \frac{2}{x - 1} = \frac{x(x - 1)}{(x + 3)(x - 1)} - \frac{2(x + 3)}{(x + 3)(x - 1)}$$

$$= \frac{(x^2 - x) - (2x + 6)}{(x + 3)(x - 1)}$$

$$= \frac{x^2 - 3x - 6}{(x + 3)(x - 1)}$$

9. $\dfrac{21 - 8x}{6x^2}$ **10.** $\dfrac{6x}{(x - 1)(x + 2)}$

11. $\dfrac{-5x^2 - 14x - 18}{(x + 4)(x - 3)}$ **12.** $\dfrac{6x + 2}{(x + 9)(x - 2)}$

13. never; The LCD is a multiple of each denominator, not a sum.

14. sometimes; This happens if one denominator divides into the other; For example, the LCD of $\dfrac{1}{x(x - 1)}$ and $\dfrac{1}{x - 1}$ is $x(x - 1)$.

15. $g(x) = \dfrac{3}{x - 2} + 4$

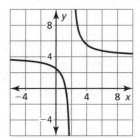

translation 2 units right and 4 units up

16. $g(x) = \dfrac{-17}{x + 4} + 5$

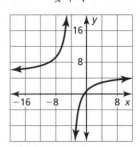

translation 4 units left and 5 units up

Answers

17. $g(x) = \dfrac{30}{x-3} + 10$

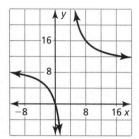

translation 3 units right and 10 units up

18. $g(x) = \dfrac{4}{x} + 3$

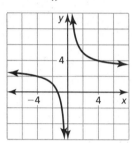

translation 3 units up

7.4 Practice B

1. $\dfrac{x-5}{25x^2}$

2. $\dfrac{2x^2 + 8x}{x+6}$

3. 3

4. $36x^2(x-2)$

5. $x^2 - 100$

6. $(25x^2 - 4)(3x^2 - 10x - 8)$

7. $x^2 + 7x - 18$

8. By not using the least common denominator, the resulting rational expression is not in simplest form. The numerator and denominator still share a common factor of x.

$$\dfrac{4}{7x} + \dfrac{5}{x^3} = \dfrac{4(x^2)}{7x(x^2)} + \dfrac{5(7)}{x^3(7)} = \dfrac{4x^2 + 35}{7x^3}$$

9. $\dfrac{4x^2 - 13x + 7}{(x-5)(x+1)}$

10. $\dfrac{3x + 16}{(x-8)(x+3)}$

11. $\dfrac{3x + 37}{(x+2)(x-8)}$

12. $\dfrac{8x^3 - 15x^2 - 17x - 9}{x(x-3)(2x+1)}$

13. always; If one denominator divides the other, then any multiple of the larger one is also a multiple of the smaller one.

14. sometimes; This happens if one denominator divides the other.

15. $g(x) = \dfrac{-17}{x+4} + 5$

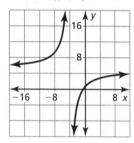

translation 4 units left and 5 units up

16. $g(x) = \dfrac{-108}{x+12} + 9$

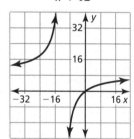

translation 12 units left and 9 units up

17. $g(x) = \dfrac{-4}{x} + 5$

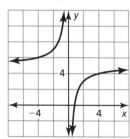

translation 5 units up

Answers

18. $g(x) = \dfrac{61}{x - 6} + 8$

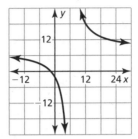

translation 6 units right and 8 units up

7.4 Enrichment and Extension

1. $\dfrac{5}{x + 1} - \dfrac{2}{x + 4}$

2. $\dfrac{1}{x} + \dfrac{2}{x + 2} + \dfrac{3}{x - 2}$

3. $\dfrac{\frac{8}{3}}{x - 3} + \dfrac{\frac{10}{3}}{x + 3}$

4. $\dfrac{\frac{26}{11}}{x - 7} - \dfrac{\frac{4}{11}}{x + 4}$

5. $\dfrac{\frac{4}{9}}{x} + \dfrac{\frac{35}{18}}{x - 3} - \dfrac{\frac{7}{18}}{x + 3}$

6. $\dfrac{5}{x + 1} + \dfrac{3}{x - 2} - \dfrac{1}{x + 3}$

7.4 Puzzle Time

GLASS CLIPPERS

7.5 Start Thinking

$200 membership: $y = \dfrac{200}{x}$, $120 membership:

$y = \dfrac{120 + 10x}{x}$

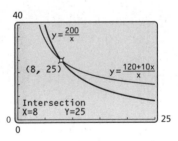

The point of intersection (8, 25) indicates that with 8 court rentals, both memberships will have the same cost per rental, $25.

If more than 8 rentals per year are expected, the $200 membership is a better deal. You can see the graph that represents the cost per rental for the $200 membership lies below the $120 membership graph for values of x greater than 8.

7.5 Warm Up

1. $-\dfrac{1}{7}$ **2.** 1, 2 **3.** -12

4. 2, 5 **5.** $-\dfrac{2}{3}$, 2 **6.** 0, $\dfrac{7}{2}$

7.5 Cumulative Review Warm Up

1. $-2 + i$ **2.** $14 - 22i$ **3.** $16 + 30i$

4. $-74 + 21i$ **5.** $15 + 12i$ **6.** $-4 + 3i$

7.5 Practice A

1. $x = -6$ **2.** $x = -10$

3. $x = -4$ **4.** $x = 9$

5. $x(x - 2)$ **6.** $x(x + 5)$

7. $x = \dfrac{3}{4}$ **8.** $x = 8$

9. $x = \dfrac{5}{2}$ **10.** $x = 1$

11. $x = 8, -2$ **12.** $x = 3$

13. did not multiply the right side of the equation by the LCD, $2x$

$$\dfrac{4}{x} + \dfrac{1}{2} = 1$$

$$2x \cdot \dfrac{4}{x} + 2x \cdot \dfrac{1}{2} = 2x \cdot 1$$

14. $\dfrac{3}{5} + \dfrac{3}{t} = 1; t = 7.5 \text{ h}$

7.5 Practice B

1. $x = -8$ **2.** $x = 2, 7$

3. $x = 0, -\dfrac{1}{3}$ **4.** $x = 8$

5. $5(x + 3)(x + 2)$ **6.** $4(x - 8)(3x - 2)$

7. $x = 8$ **8.** $x = 1$

9. $x = \dfrac{9}{2}$ **10.** $x = \dfrac{8}{3}$

11. $x = 2, -1$ **12.** $x = 2, -4$

Answers

13. incorrectly multiplied by $(x + 2)$, which is not the common denominator $x(x + 2)$

$$\frac{3}{x + 2} + 5 = \frac{1}{x}$$

$$x(x + 2) \cdot \frac{3}{x + 2} + x(x + 2) \cdot 5 = x(x + 2) \cdot \frac{1}{x}$$

14. $\dfrac{1.4}{3} + \dfrac{1.4}{t} = 1; t = 2.625$ h

7.5 Enrichment and Extension

1. *Sample answer:* $\left(\dfrac{11}{3}, 1\right), (7, -1), \left(\dfrac{9}{2}, 0\right)$. If point (x, y) lies on the graph of f, then point (y, x) lies on the graph of f^{-1}.

2. no; Because $f(1) = \dfrac{11}{3}$ and $f(2) = \dfrac{13}{4}$, the points $\left(\dfrac{11}{3}, 1\right)$ and $\left(\dfrac{13}{4}, 2\right)$ lie on the graph of f^{-1}, but the given point $\left(\dfrac{11}{3}, 2\right)$ does not.

3. $f^{-1}(x) = \dfrac{9 - 2x}{x - 2}$

4. $f\left(f^{-1}(x)\right) = \dfrac{2\left(\dfrac{9 - 2x}{x - 2}\right) + 9}{\left(\dfrac{9 - 2x}{x - 2}\right) + 2} = x$ and

$f^{-1}\left(f(x)\right) = \dfrac{9 - 2\left(\dfrac{2x + 9}{x + 2}\right)}{\left(\dfrac{2x + 9}{x + 2}\right) - 2} = x$

5.

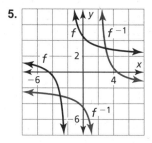

6. domain: all real numbers, $x \neq -2$; range: all real numbers, $x \neq 2$

7. domain: all real numbers, $x \neq 2$; range: all real numbers, $x \neq -2$; The domain of f is the range of f^{-1} and the range of f is the domain of f^{-1}.

8. The vertical asymptote of the graph of f is the horizontal asymptote of the graph of f^{-1}. The horizontal asymptote of the graph of f is the vertical asymptote of the graph of f^{-1}.

9. The graph of f and f^{-1} intersect at points on the line $y = x$.

10. no; The zero of f^{-1} is the x-value where $f^{-1}(x) = 0$, or equivalently $f(0) = x$. This is the y-intercept of the graph of f, not the asymptotes.

11. yes; $g^{-1}(x) = \dfrac{-x - 7}{2x - 1}$

12. no; Rational functions of the form $f(x) = \dfrac{ax + b}{cx + d}$ will have an inverse, but not all rational functions will have an inverse. To have an inverse, the function must pass the horizontal line test, and not all rational functions pass the horizontal line test.

7.5 Puzzle Time

ELVIS PARSLEY

Cumulative Review

1. $(x + 3)(x - 7)$ **2.** $(x - 4)(x + 12)$

3. $(x + 1)(x + 8)$ **4.** $(x - 4)(x - 5)$

5. $(x + 3)(x - 9)$ **6.** $(x - 4)(x - 8)$

7. $(2x - 1)(x + 3)$ **8.** $2(x - 4)(x + 3)$

9. $(3x - 4)(x + 9)$ **10.** $(5x + 3)(x + 4)$

11. $(3x - 7)(x - 6)$ **12.** $(4x - 3)(x - 1)$

13. $2(2x + 7)(x + 4)$ **14.** $(3x - 5)(2x + 1)$

15. $(2x + 1)(4x - 3)$ **16.** $(5x - 7)(x + 1)$

17. $2(4x - 1)(x + 3)$ **18.** $6(x - 2)(2x + 1)$

Answers

19. $2^2 \cdot 3$ **20.** $3 \cdot 67$

21. $2^3 \cdot 11$ **22.** $2^3 \cdot 7$

23. $5^2 \cdot 3$ **24.** $5^2 \cdot 2^2 \cdot 3$

25. prime   **26.** $3^2 \cdot 11$

27. $2^2 \cdot 47$ **28.** prime

29. $5 \cdot 17$ **30.** prime

31. prime   **32.** 13^2

33. prime   **34.** $13 \cdot 5$

35. $x = 3$ **36.** $x = -\dfrac{7}{2}$

37. $x = \dfrac{154}{25}$ **38.** $x = -80$

39. $x = 6$ **40.** $x = -\dfrac{2}{5}$

41. $x = \dfrac{75}{4}$ **42.** $x = -\dfrac{168}{19}$

43. $x = \dfrac{45}{62}$ **44.** $x = \dfrac{400}{231}$

45. $x = \dfrac{54}{115}$ **46.** $x = \dfrac{325}{42}$

47. $x + 3$ and $x - 8$ **48.** $2x - 5$ and $x + 4$

49. $3x + 5$ and $2x - 3$ **50.** $x = -7$ and $x = 5$

51. $x = -6$ and $x = 3$ **52.** $x = -11$ and $x = 9$

53. $x = -6$ and $x = 8$ **54.** $x = 3$ and $x = 5$

55. $x = -5$ and $x = 9$ **56.** $x = -4$ and $x = -1$

57. $x = -5$ and $x = 5$ **58.** $x = -4$ and $x = 8$

59. $x = -3$ and $x = 0$

60. $x = -8$ and $x = -\dfrac{1}{2}$

61. $x = \dfrac{5}{3}$ and $x = 7$

62. $x = -5$ and $x = \dfrac{3}{2}$

63. $x = 0$ and $x = \dfrac{7}{2}$

64. 64; two real solutions

65. −15; two imaginary solutions

66. 0; one real solution   **67.** 177; two real solutions

68. 164; two real solutions

69. −479; two imaginary solutions

70. −159; two imaginary solutions

71. 0; one real solution

72. 40; two real solutions

73. 132; two real solutions

74. −92; two imaginary solutions

75. 0; one real solution

76. $x = 1$ **77.** $x = \dfrac{5 \pm 1}{6} = \dfrac{2}{3}, 1$

78. $x = \dfrac{-2 \pm 2\sqrt{21}}{5}$ **79.** $x = \dfrac{1 \pm i\sqrt{53}}{3}$

80. $x = \dfrac{-9 \pm \sqrt{141}}{2}$ **81.** $x = \dfrac{-5 \pm \sqrt{57}}{8}$

82. $x = \dfrac{4 \pm 5i\sqrt{2}}{6}$ **83.** $x = \dfrac{7 \pm i\sqrt{239}}{-6}$

84. $x = \dfrac{-1 \pm i\sqrt{179}}{5}$ **85.** $x = \dfrac{3 \pm \sqrt{73}}{2}$

86. $x = \dfrac{-7 \pm i\sqrt{111}}{16}$ **87.** $x = \dfrac{1 \pm i\sqrt{15}}{2}$

88. $x + 8$ **89.** $2x + 5$

90. $4x - 1$ **91.** $(21, 12)$

92. $(-3, 11)$ **93.** $(-4, -21)$

94. $(-7, -6)$ **95.** $(15, 13)$

96. $(-9, -11)$ **97.** $(6, 36)$

98. $(1, 9)$ **99.** $(1, -5)$

Answers

100. $(-5, -6)$ and $(1, 0)$

101. $(-3, 0)$ and $(6, 9)$

102. $(-7, -5)$ and $(-2, 0)$

103. $(-2, -12)$ **104.** $(-12, 7)$

105. $\left(\dfrac{7}{3}, -2\right)$ **106.** $(8, 5)$

107. $\left(-\dfrac{17}{2}, -1\right)$ **108.** $\left(6, \dfrac{11}{4}\right)$

109. $\left(\dfrac{1 + \sqrt{17}}{2}, -21 + \sqrt{17}\right)$ and
$\left(\dfrac{1 - \sqrt{17}}{2}, -21 - \sqrt{17}\right)$

110. $\left(-1 + \sqrt{11}, \dfrac{47 - 13\sqrt{11}}{2}\right)$ and
$\left(-1 - \sqrt{11}, \dfrac{47 + 13\sqrt{11}}{2}\right)$

111. $\left(-3 + \sqrt{6}, \dfrac{16 - 11\sqrt{6}}{3}\right)$ and
$\left(-3 - \sqrt{6}, \dfrac{16 + 11\sqrt{6}}{3}\right)$

112. $\left(\dfrac{-3 + \sqrt{417}}{6}, \dfrac{108 - \sqrt{417}}{6}\right)$ and
$\left(\dfrac{-3 - \sqrt{417}}{6}, \dfrac{108 + \sqrt{417}}{6}\right)$

113. 2448 ft^3

114. a. 54 in.^2 **b.** 27 in.^3

115. a. $196\pi \text{ cm}^2$ **b.** $\dfrac{1372}{3}\pi \text{ cm}^3$

116. 158 **117.** 4021

118. -2034 **119.** -66

120. -393 **121.** $-\dfrac{237}{8}$

122. $\dfrac{1777}{32}$ **123.** $2x^3 + 8x^2 - 2$

124. $10x^4 - 12x^2 - 2x - 1$

125. $-6x^5 - 4x^4 - 10x^2 - 2x + 7$

126. $9x^4 - 2x^3 - x^2 - 5x + 4$

127. $4x^4 - 3x^3 - 9x^2 + 9x + 1$

128. $8x^5 - 4x^4 + 5x^3 - 13x^2 - 8x + 10$

129. $3x^5 + 12x^4 + 5x^3 - 3x^2 + 5x - 2$

130. $-6x^3 + 18x - 10$

131. $19x^2 - 10x - 10$

132. $-24x^4 + 4x^3 + 16x - 11$

133. $3x^4 + 2x^3 + 12x^2 - 2x - 13$

134. $-17x^5 + 2x^4 - 7x^3 - 10x + 5$

135. $-6x^5 - 8x^3 + 13x^2 + 6x + 10$

Chapter 8

8.1 Start Thinking

1. Start with 5, then add 2 to the prior term to find each consecutive term.

2. Start with $\dfrac{2}{3}$, then take the prior term and multiply the numerator by 2 and add 4 to the denominator to find each consecutive term.

3. Start with 8, then subtract $\dfrac{3}{2}$ from the prior term to find each consecutive term.

4. Start with 3, then multiply the prior term by -2 to find each consecutive term.

8.1 Warm Up

1. $f(1) = 0, f(2) = 2, f(3) = 4, f(4) = 6,$
$f(5) = 8$

2. $f(1) = 2, f(2) = 4, f(3) = 8, f(4) = 16,$
$f(5) = 32$

3. $f(1) = 1, f(2) = 3, f(3) = 5, f(4) = 7,$
$f(5) = 9$

Answers

4. $f(1) = -5, f(2) = 5, f(3) = -5, f(4) = 5,$
$f(5) = -5$

5. $f(1) = \dfrac{1}{3}, f(2) = \dfrac{2}{3}, f(3) = \dfrac{4}{3}, f(4) = \dfrac{8}{3},$
$f(5) = \dfrac{16}{3}$

6. $f(1) = 1, f(2) = -4, f(3) = 9, f(4) = -16,$
$f(5) = 25$

8.1 Cumulative Review Warm Up

1. $x = 4$ **2.** $x = 4$

3. $x = \dfrac{1}{2} \ln 4 = \ln 2$ **4.** $x = 1$

5. $x = 2 - \dfrac{1}{e^2} \approx 1.865$ **6.** $x = 3$

8.1 Practice A

1. $-2, -1, 0, 1, 2, 3$ **2.** $3, 2, 1, 0, -1, -2$

3. $1, 8, 27, 64, 125, 216$ **4.** $-4, -1, 4, 11, 20, 31$

5. $4, 16, 64, 256, 1024, 4096$

6. $0, -3, -8, -15, -24, -35$

7. Start with 1, then each consecutive term is 3 more than the previous term: 13, $a_n = 3n - 2$.

8. Start with 1, then each consecutive term is 3 raised to a power 1 more than the power 3 is raised to in the previous term: 81, $a_n = 3^{n-1}$.

9. Start with 1.5, then each consecutive term is 1.5 more than the previous term: 7.5, $a_n = 1.5n$.

10. Start with 4.2, then each consecutive term is 1.6 more than the previous term: 10.6, $a_n = 2.6 + 1.6n$.

11. Start with 4.7, then each consecutive term is 1.3 less than the previous term: -0.5, $a_n = 6 - 1.3n$.

12. Start with -5, then the absolute value of each consecutive term is 5 more than the absolute value of the previous term, and the signs alternate: $-25, a_n = (-1)^n 5n$.

13. Start with $\dfrac{1}{6}$, then the numerator of each consecutive term is 1 more than the numerator of the previous term: $\dfrac{5}{6}$, $a_n = \dfrac{n}{6}$.

14. Start with $\dfrac{3}{2}$, then the denominator of each consecutive term is 2 more than the denominator of the previous term: $\dfrac{3}{10}$, $a_n = \dfrac{3}{2n}$.

15. $a_n = 10\left(2^{n-1}\right)$

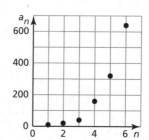

16. $\displaystyle\sum_{n=1}^{5} 4n$ **17.** $\displaystyle\sum_{n=1}^{5}(6n - 3)$ **18.** $\displaystyle\sum_{n=1}^{\infty}(6n - 5)$

19. $\displaystyle\sum_{n=1}^{\infty}(2n - 3)$ **20.** $\displaystyle\sum_{n=1}^{\infty}\dfrac{1}{5^n}$ **21.** $\displaystyle\sum_{n=1}^{\infty}\dfrac{n}{n + 6}$

22. 30   **23.** 90   **24.** 55

25. 93   **26.** 73   **27.** $\dfrac{153}{28}$

28. $105; \displaystyle\sum_{n=1}^{6}(28 - 3n)$

8.1 Practice B

1. $5, 8, 13, 20, 29, 40$ **2.** $\dfrac{1}{3}, 1, 3, 9, 27, 81$

3. $1, 0, 1, 4, 9, 16$

4. $2, -1, -6, -13, -22, -33$

5. $-\dfrac{1}{6}, -\dfrac{2}{7}, -\dfrac{3}{8}, -\dfrac{4}{9}, -\dfrac{1}{2}, -\dfrac{6}{11}$

6. $\dfrac{1}{2}, \dfrac{2}{5}, \dfrac{3}{8}, \dfrac{4}{11}, \dfrac{5}{14}, \dfrac{6}{17}$

7. Start with 2, then each consecutive term is 5 more than the previous term: 22, $a_n = 5n - 3$.

Answers

8. Start with 2.7, then each consecutive term is 3.5 more than the previous term: 16.7, $a_n = 3.5n - 0.8$.

9. Start with 6.4, then each consecutive term is 2.9 less than the previous term: -5.2, $a_n = 9.3 - 2.9n$.

10. Start with $-\dfrac{1}{7}$, then each consecutive term is $\dfrac{1}{7}$ less than the previous term: $-\dfrac{5}{7}$, $a_n = -\dfrac{n}{7}$.

11. Start with $\dfrac{5}{2}$, then the denominator of each consecutive term is twice the denominator of the previous term: $\dfrac{5}{32}$, $a_n = \dfrac{5}{2^n}$.

12. Start with $\dfrac{3}{1}$, then the numerator of each consecutive term is 3 times the numerator of the previous term, and the denominator of each term is 1 more than the denominator of the previous term: $\dfrac{243}{5}$, $a_n = \dfrac{3^n}{n}$.

13. Start with $\dfrac{2}{3}$, then each consecutive term is $\dfrac{2}{3}$ times the previous term: $\dfrac{32}{243}$, $a_n = \left(\dfrac{2}{3}\right)^n$.

14. Start with 2, then each consecutive term is 10 times the previous term: 20,000, $a_n = 2\left(10^{n-1}\right)$.

15. $a_n = 100 + 7n$

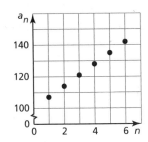

16. $\displaystyle\sum_{n=1}^{5}(7n - 1)$ **17.** $\displaystyle\sum_{n=1}^{\infty}(3n + 7)$

18. $\displaystyle\sum_{n=1}^{\infty}\left(n^2 - 4\right)$ **19.** $\displaystyle\sum_{n=1}^{\infty}\dfrac{n}{4^n}$

20. $\displaystyle\sum_{n=1}^{\infty}\dfrac{2}{n+4}$ **21.** $\displaystyle\sum_{n=1}^{5}(-1)^n(2n - 1)$

22. 189   **23.** 450   **24.** 103

25. $\dfrac{107}{210}$ **26.** 45   **27.** 300

28. $294;\ \displaystyle\sum_{i=1}^{7}(34 + 2i)$

8.1 Enrichment and Extension

1. a. 2   **b.** $2n - 1$ **c.** n^2

2. a. 3   **b.** $3n$ **c.** $\dfrac{3}{2}n(n + 1)$

3. a. k **b.** nk **c.** $\dfrac{k}{2}n(n + 1)$

4. The series is equivalent to
$\log 10 + \log 10^2 \log 10^3 + \ldots + \log 10^n$ which by the Power Property of Logarithms, is equivalent to $\log 10 + 2 \log 10 + 3 \log 10 + \ldots + n \log 10$.

By Exercise 3, the sum is $\dfrac{\log 10}{2}n(n + 1)$. Because

$\log 10 = 1$, this reduces to $\dfrac{n}{2}(n + 1)$.

5. $\dfrac{\ln e}{2}n(n + 1)$ or $\dfrac{n}{2}(n + 1)$

6. $\dfrac{\log_b a}{2}n(n + 1)$

8.1 Puzzle Time

RASH DECISIONS

8.2 Start Thinking

1. 2, 4, 6, 8, 10; $a_n = 2n$

2. 9.5, 9, 8.5, 8, 7.5; $a_n = 10 - \dfrac{1}{2}n$

3. 2.5, 4, 5.5, 7, 8.5; $a_n = 1 + \dfrac{3}{2}n$

Sample answer: All the graphs appear to be linear and the rules are linear equations.

8.2 Warm Up

1. $(-2, -5)$ **2.** $(3, 2)$ **3.** $(-4, 8)$

4. $(-2, 2)$ **5.** $\left(\dfrac{3}{2}, -\dfrac{5}{2}\right)$ **6.** $\left(0, \dfrac{1}{6}\right)$

Answers

1. $f(x) = x^3 + 3x^2 - 2x - 6$

2. $f(x) = x^3 + 3x^2 - 3x - 1$

3. $f(x) = 2x^4 - x^3 - 12x^2 + 6x$

4. $f(x) = 2x^4 + 3x^3 - 32x^2 - 48x$

5. $f(x) = x^4 + 4x^3 - 6x^2 - 20x - 7$

6. $f(x) = 10x^4 - 69x^3 + 80x^2 + 75x$

8.2 Practice A

1. yes; $d = -3$

2. no; no common difference

3. yes; $d = \dfrac{1}{3}$

4. no; no common difference

5. a. $a_n = 4n - 9$ **b.** $a_n = 12 - 3n$

6. $a_n = 7n + 8; a_{20} = 148$

7. $a_n = 71 - 9n; a_{20} = -109$

8. $a_n = 15n - 40; a_{20} = 260$

9. $a_n = \dfrac{3}{2}n - \dfrac{9}{2}; a_{20} = \dfrac{51}{2}$

10. The number 27 was used as the first term in the formula instead of -27.

Use $a_1 = -27$ and $d = 15$.

$a_n = -27 + (n - 1)15$

$a_n = -42 + 15n$

11. $a_n = 4n - 1$

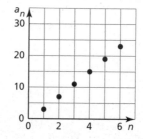

12. $a_n = 28 - 4n$

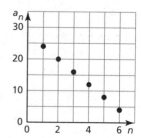

13. $a_n = 4n + 13$ **14.** $a_n = 6n + 18$

15. $a_n = 72 - 10n$ **16.** $a_n = 15 - 7n$

17. $15{,}500; a_n = 2n; a_{124} = 248; \displaystyle\sum_{n=1}^{124} 2n = 15{,}500$

8.2 Practice B

1. no; no common difference

2. yes; $d = -4$ **3.** yes; $d = \dfrac{1}{6}$ **4.** yes; $d = \dfrac{3}{10}$

5. a. $a_n = 19 - 7n$ **b.** $a_n = 10n - 18$

6. $a_n = 45 - 8n; a_{20} = -115$

7. $a_n = \dfrac{4}{3}n - \dfrac{16}{3}; a_{20} = \dfrac{64}{3}$

8. $a_n = 2.1n - 1.9; a_{20} = 40.1$

9. $a_n = 2.9 - 0.7n; a_{20} = -11.1$

10. The formula $a_n = n_1 - (n - 1)d$ was used instead of the formula $a_n = n_1 + (n - 1)d$.

Use $a_1 = -27$ and $d = 15$.

$a_n = -27 + (n - 1)15$

$a_n = -42 + 15n$

11. $a_n = 4n + 15$

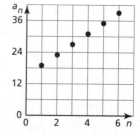

Answers

12. $a_n = \dfrac{1}{2}n + \dfrac{11}{2}$

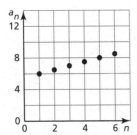

13. $a_n = 5n + 24$ **14.** $a_n = 80 - 17n$

15. $a_n = 6n - 27$ **16.** $a_n = \dfrac{2}{3}n + 18$

17. $62{,}500; a_n = 2n - 1; a_{250} = 499;$

$$\sum_{n=1}^{250}(2n - 1) = 62{,}500$$

8.2 Enrichment and Extension

1. 54 **2.** 23 **3.** 85

4. 38 **5.** 42 **6.** 91

7. 75 **8.** 8181 **9.** 7876

10. $t_n = (a - 3b) + n(a + b)$

11. $x = 3, y = 2$

8.2 Puzzle Time

POULTRYGEIST

8.3 Start Thinking

1. $2, 4, 8, 16; a_n = 2^n$

2. $\dfrac{1}{2}, \dfrac{1}{4}, \dfrac{1}{8}, \dfrac{1}{16}; a_n = \left(\dfrac{1}{2}\right)^n$

3. $-2, 4, -8, 16; a_n = (-1)^n(2)^n = (-2)^n$

Sample answer: The first two graphs appear to be exponential growth and decay. The third graph oscillates between negative and positive values. All the equations involve exponential expressions.

8.3 Warm Up

1. 30 **2.** -27 **3.** 1270

4. -6 **5.** 15 **6.** $-\dfrac{11}{16}$

8.3 Cumulative Review Warm Up

1.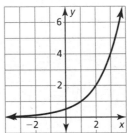

2.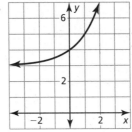

3.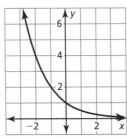

4.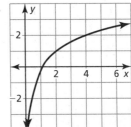

5.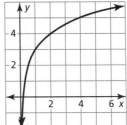

6.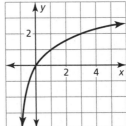

Answers

1. yes; $r = \dfrac{1}{2}$ **2.** no; no common ratio

3. no; no common ratio   **4.** yes; $r = 6$

5. a. $a_n = -5(3)^{n-1}$ **b.** $a_n = 54\left(\dfrac{1}{6}\right)^{n-1}$

6. $a_n = 3(2)^{n-1}$; $a_7 = 192$

7. $a_n = 7(3)^{n-1}$; $a_7 = 5103$

8. $a_n = 192\left(\dfrac{1}{2}\right)^{n-1}$; $a_7 = 3$

9. $a_n = 36\left(\dfrac{2}{3}\right)^{n-1}$; $a_7 = \dfrac{256}{81}$

10. $a_n = 3^{n-1}$

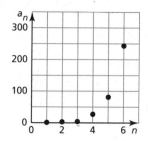

11. $a_n = 3(4)^{n-1}$

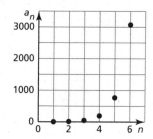

12. $a_n = 40\left(\dfrac{1}{2}\right)^{n-1}$

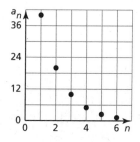

13. $a_n = -13(2)^{n-1}$

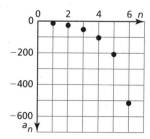

14. r, not a_1, should be raised to the $(n-1)$ power.

$a_n = a_1 r^{n-1}$

$147 = a_1 7^2$

$3 = a_1$

$a_n = 3(7)^{n-1}$

15. $304.22

1. no; no common ratio

2. yes; $r = \dfrac{1}{3}$ **3.** yes; $r = 5$ **4.** yes; $r = 2$

5. a. $a_n = -12(7)^{n-1}$ **b.** $a_n = 62\left(\dfrac{1}{2}\right)^{n-1}$

6. $a_n = 9(2)^{n-1}$; $a_7 = 576$

7. $a_n = 80\left(\dfrac{1}{4}\right)^{n-1}$; $a_7 = \dfrac{5}{256}$

8. $a_n = 3\left(\dfrac{2}{5}\right)^{n-1}$; $a_7 = \dfrac{192}{15,625}$

9. $a_n = 1.2(-2)^{n-1}$; $a_7 = 76.8$

10. $a_n = 2(5)^{n-1}$

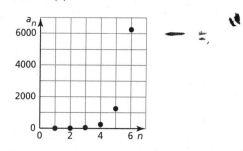

Answers

11. $a_n = 54\left(\dfrac{1}{3}\right)^{n-1}$

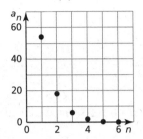

12. $a_n = -14(3)^{n-1}$

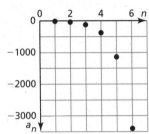

13. $a_n = 256\left(-\dfrac{1}{4}\right)^{n-1}$

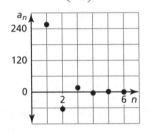

14. The number 147 is the third term of the sequence, not the first term.

$a_n = a_1 r^{n-1}$

$147 = a_1 7^2$

$3 = a_1$

$a_n = 3(7)^{n-1}$

15. \$368.33

8.3 Enrichment and Extension

1. 160, 80, 40

2. 7, 10, 13

3. 2, 4, 6, 9 or $2, \dfrac{1}{4}, -\dfrac{3}{2}, 9$

4. When $d = 0, a_2 = 2$; When $d = 1, a_2 = 3$.

---

5. $x = \dfrac{ac - b^2}{2b - c - a}$

6. *Sample answer*: Arithmetic mean is $\dfrac{a^2 + b^2}{2}$.

Geometric mean is ab or $-ab$.

Show: $\dfrac{a^2 + b^2}{2} \geq ab$ and $\dfrac{a^2 + b^2}{2} \geq -ab$

Because all squares are nonnegative,

$(a - b)^2 \geq 0$; So $a^2 - 2ab + b^2 \geq 0$ and

$\dfrac{a^2 + b^2}{2} \geq -ab$. Because all squares are

nonnegative, $(a + b)^2 \geq 0$; So

$a^2 + 2ab + b^2 \geq 0$ and $\dfrac{a^2 + b^2}{2} \geq -ab$.

8.3 Puzzle Time

SEE A MOOOVIE

8.4 Start Thinking

0.1, 0.01, 0.001, 0.0001, 0.00001, 0.000001, 0.0000001, 0.00000001, 0.000000001, 0.0000000001;

0.1111111111; $0.\bar{1} = \dfrac{1}{9}$

8.4 Warm Up

1. 31

2. 25

3. $\dfrac{25,220}{2187} \approx 11.53$

4. $-531,440$

5. -9050

6. 3,587,226.5

8.4 Cumulative Review Warm Up

1.

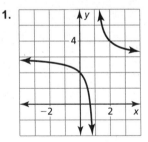

domain: all real numbers except 1, range: all real numbers except 3

Answers

2.

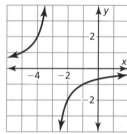

domain: all real numbers except -3, range: all real numbers except 0

3.

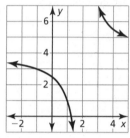

domain: all real numbers except 2, range: all real numbers except 4

4.

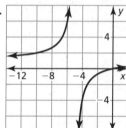

domain: all real numbers except -5, range: all real numbers except 1

5.

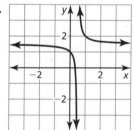

domain: all real numbers except $\dfrac{1}{2}$, range: all real numbers except $\dfrac{3}{2}$

6.

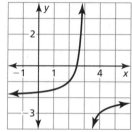

domain: all real numbers except 3, range: all real numbers except -2

8.4 Practice A

1. $S_1 = \dfrac{1}{3}, S_2 = \dfrac{1}{2}, S_3 = \dfrac{7}{12}, S_4 = \dfrac{5}{8}, S_5 = \dfrac{31}{48}$

As n increases, $S \approx \dfrac{2}{3}$.

2. $S_1 = 5, S_2 = \dfrac{25}{3}, S_3 = \dfrac{95}{9}, S_4 = \dfrac{325}{27},$

$S_5 = \dfrac{1055}{81}$

As n increases, $S \approx 15$.

3. $S = \dfrac{28}{3}$ 　　　　　　　**4.** does not exist

5. $S = \dfrac{15}{2}$ 　　　　　　　**6.** $S = -18$

7. a can be any value, but the absolute value of r must be less than 1.

For this series, $a_1 = \dfrac{5}{2}$ and $r = \dfrac{1}{3}$.

$$S = \frac{a_1}{1-r} = \frac{\dfrac{5}{2}}{1-\dfrac{1}{3}} = \frac{\dfrac{5}{2}}{\dfrac{2}{3}} = \frac{5}{2} \bullet \frac{3}{2} = \frac{15}{4}$$

8. 40 ft 　　**9.** $\dfrac{2}{11}$ 　　**10.** $\dfrac{5}{9}$ 　　**11.** $\dfrac{5}{3}$

12. about \$8,333,333

8.4 Practice B

1. $S_1 = \dfrac{3}{4}, S_2 = 1, S_3 = \dfrac{13}{12}, S_4 = \dfrac{10}{9}, S_5 = \dfrac{121}{108}$

As n increases, $S \approx \dfrac{9}{8}$.

Answers

2. $S_1 = 6, S_2 = 10, S_3 = \dfrac{38}{3}, S_4 = \dfrac{130}{9}, S_5 = \dfrac{422}{27}$

As n increases, $S \approx 18$.

3. $S = \dfrac{20}{3}$ **4.** does not exist

5. does not exist **6.** $S = \dfrac{3}{5}$

7. $1 - r$ is equal to $\dfrac{2}{3}$, not $\dfrac{1}{3}$.

For this series, $a_1 = \dfrac{5}{2}$ and $r = \dfrac{1}{3}$.

$$S = \frac{a_1}{1 - r} = \frac{\dfrac{5}{2}}{1 - \dfrac{1}{3}} = \frac{\dfrac{5}{2}}{\dfrac{2}{3}} = \frac{5}{2} \bullet \frac{3}{2} = \frac{15}{4}$$

8. yes; $a_1 = 2, r = \dfrac{1}{2}, S = \dfrac{2}{\dfrac{1}{2}} = 4$

9. $\dfrac{5}{11}$ **10.** $\dfrac{5}{99}$ **11.** $\dfrac{13}{9}$ **12.** \$6000

8.4 Enrichment and Extension

1. $-1 < x < 1; \dfrac{1}{1 - x^2}$ **2.** $-\dfrac{1}{3} < x < \dfrac{1}{3}; \dfrac{1}{1 - 3x}$

3. $2 < x < 4; \dfrac{1}{4 - x}$ **4.** $0 < x < 2; \dfrac{1}{x}$

5. $x < -2$ or $x > 2; \dfrac{x}{x + 2}$

6. $-\sqrt{2} < x < \sqrt{2}; \dfrac{2x^2}{6 + 3x^2}$

7. $\left| \sin^2 x \right| < 1$ is true when $x \neq \dfrac{\pi}{2} + n\pi$, so

$$S = \frac{\sin^2 x}{1 - \sin^2 x} = \frac{\sin^2 x}{\cos^2 x} = \tan^2 x.$$

8. $\left| -\tan^2 x \right| < 1$ simplifies to $\tan^2 x < 1$, which

is true when $\dfrac{-\pi}{4} < x < \dfrac{\pi}{4}$. So

$$S = \frac{\tan^2 x}{1 - \left(-\tan^2 x \right)} = \frac{\tan^2 x}{\sec^2 x} = \frac{\sin^2 x \cos^2 x}{\cos^2 x}$$

$$= \sin^2 x.$$

This is also true when $\dfrac{3\pi}{4} < x < \dfrac{5\pi}{4}$.

9. When the values are substituted into the sum formula, r will be greater than 1.

8.4 Puzzle Time

BLOODHOUND

8.5 Start Thinking

1. To determine each term in the sequence, you add the two terms that come before it. For example, $a_3 = a_1 + a_2$, or $3 = 1 + 2$. Then to find a_7, you find the sum of a_5 and a_6, or $8 + 13 = 21$.

2. To determine each term in the sequence, you multiply the two terms that come before it. For example, $a_3 = a_1 \cdot a_2$, or $2 = 1 \cdot 2$. Then to find a_7, you find the product of a_5 and a_6, or $8 \bullet 32 = 256$.

3. To determine each term in the sequence, you find the difference of the two terms that come before it. For example, $a_3 = a_1 - a_2$, or $5 = 10 - 5$. Then to find a_7, you find the difference a_5 and a_6, or $5 - (-5) = 10$.

4. To determine each term in the sequence, you multiply the two terms that come before it. For example, $a_3 = a_1 \bullet a_2$ or $2 = (-2)(-1)$. Then to find a_7, you find the product of a_5 and a_6, or $(-4)(8) = -32$.

8.5 Warm Up

1. $\dfrac{7}{2}, 3, \dfrac{5}{2}, 2, \dfrac{3}{2}, 1$ **2.** $4, \dfrac{7}{2}, \dfrac{10}{3}, \dfrac{13}{4}, \dfrac{16}{5}, \dfrac{19}{6}$

3. $2, 6, 12, 20, 30, 42$ **4.** $2, 3, \dfrac{9}{2}, \dfrac{27}{4}, \dfrac{81}{8}, \dfrac{243}{16}$

5. $-9, -2, 17, 54, 115, 206$

6. $1, 4, 7, 10, 13, 16$

Answers

8.5 Cumulative Review Warm Up

1. $x = \dfrac{1 \pm \sqrt{7}}{3}$ **2.** $x = 4 \pm \sqrt{14}$

3. $x = 2, 1$ **4.** $x = \pm\sqrt{2}$

5. $x = 5 \pm \sqrt{19}$ **6.** $x = \dfrac{8}{3}, -2$

8.5 Practice A

1. $1, 6, 11, 16, 21, 26$

2. $1, -3, -7, -11, -15, -19$

3. $3, 12, 48, 192, 768, 3072$

4. $12, 4, \dfrac{4}{3}, \dfrac{4}{9}, \dfrac{4}{27}, \dfrac{4}{81}$

5. $1; 3; 11; 123; 15{,}131; 228{,}947{,}163$

6. $2, 2, 2, 2, 2, 2$

7. $a_1 = 32, a_n = a_{n-1} - 8$

8. $a_1 = -47, a_n = a_{n-1} + 12$

9. $a_1 = 2, a_n = 3a_{n-1}$

10. $a_1 = 5, a_n = -2a_{n-1}$

11. $a_1 = 21, a_n = \dfrac{1}{3}a_{n-1}$

12. $a_1 = 1, a_n = a_{n-1} + 6$

13. $a_1 = 2, a_2 = 3, a_n = a_{n-2} + a_{n-1}$

14. $a_1 = 2, a_2 = 3, a_n = (a_{n-2})(a_{n-1})$

15. $a_1 = 7, a_n = a_{n-1} + 2$

16. $a_1 = -7, a_n = a_{n-1} - 3$

17. $a_1 = 2, a_n = a_{n-1} - 13$

18. $a_1 = 8, a_n = 10a_{n-1}$

19. $a_1 = -2, a_n = 7a_{n-1}$

20. $a_1 = 1, a_n = a_{n-1} - 0.8$

21. $a_1 = 95, a_n = a_{n-1} + 20$

22. $a_n = 8 - 3n$ **23.** $a_n = 9 + 5n$

24. $a_n = -3(2)^{n-1}$ **25.** $a_n = 20\left(\dfrac{1}{2}\right)^{n-1}$

8.5 Practice B

1. $1, 10, 19, 28, 37, 46$ **2.** $32, 8, 2, \dfrac{1}{2}, \dfrac{1}{8}, \dfrac{1}{32}$

3. $24, 36, 54, 81, 121.5, 182.25$

4. $1, 0, -1, 0, -1, 0$ **5.** $1, 4, -3, 7, -10, 17$

6. $256, 2, 128, \dfrac{1}{64}, 8192, \dfrac{1}{524{,}288}$

7. $a_1 = 30, a_n = a_{n-1} - 9$

8. $a_1 = 3, a_n = -5a_{n-1}$ **9.** $a_1 = 28, a_n = \dfrac{1}{7}a_{n-1}$

10. $a_1 = 1, a_n = a_{n-1} + 11$

11. $a_1 = 2, a_2 = 6, a_n = (a_{n-2})(a_{n-1})$

12. $a_1 = 1, a_2 = 7, a_n = a_{n-2} + a_{n-1}$

13. $a_1 = 61, a_2 = 39, a_n = a_{n-2} - a_{n-1}$

14. $a_1 = -5, a_n = a_{n-1} + n$

15. $a_1 = -4, a_n = a_{n-1} + 3$

16. $a_1 = 6, a_n = 15a_{n-1}$

17. $a_1 = -16, a_n = 9a_{n-1}$

18. $a_1 = -2.1, a_n = a_{n-1} + 0.3$

19. $a_1 = -\dfrac{1}{3}, a_n = \dfrac{1}{5}a_{n-1}$

20. $a_1 = \dfrac{1}{2}, a_n = 7a_{n-1}$

21. $a_1 = 26, a_n = 1.002a_{n-1}$

22. $a_n = -26.2 + 7.2n$ **23.** $a_n = -7(0.45)^{n-1}$

24. $a_n = \dfrac{23}{6} + \dfrac{1}{6}n$ **25.** $a_n = -9\left(\dfrac{1}{3}\right)^{n-1}$

8.5 Enrichment and Extension

1. a. $3, 5, 2, -3, -5, -2, 3, 5, \ldots$ **b.** -3

2. a. $4, 8, 2, \dfrac{1}{4}, \dfrac{1}{8}, \dfrac{1}{2}, 4, 8, \ldots$ **b.** $\dfrac{1}{4}$

Answers

3. a. 5

   b. $n - 2$ additional diagonals; $d_4 = 2$,
     $d_n = d_{n-1} + n - 2$

4. $S_{n+1} = S_n + 2n + 1$;

8.5 Puzzle Time

KING CONGA

Cumulative Review

1.

x	y
4	−18
8	−62
12	−106
16	−150

2.

x	y
2	2
4	38
6	74
8	110

3.

x	y
6	49
12	85
18	121
24	157

4.

x	y
2	12
3	37
4	72
5	117

5.

x	y
2	−8
3	−23
4	−44
5	−71

6.

x	y
2	−3
3	17
4	45
5	81

7.

x	y
0	−2
1	−1
2	1
3	5

8.

x	y
0	4
1	3
2	1
3	−3

9.

x	y
0	−11
1	−9
2	−3
3	15

10. $x = 7$ **11.** $x = 3$ **12.** $x = -11$

13. $x = 60$ **14.** $x = 48$ **15.** $x = 39$

16. $x = -9$ **17.** $x = -4$ **18.** $x = 2$

19. $x = 6$ **20.** $x = 4$ **21.** $x = 3$

22. $T = 51 + 3h$ **23.** $T = 44 - 2h$

24. 22,302   **25.** −4091   **26.** 46,348

27. −29,222   **28.** −62,598   **29.** −706

30. $-2x^2 + 4x + 24$ **31.** $3x^3 + 7x^2 + 3x + 5$

32. $-11x^5 + 10x^4 + 4x^3 + x^2 + 6x - 4$

33. $7x^5 + 7x^4 + 2x^3 + 7x^2 - 14x - 6$

34. $2x^3 - 5x^2 + 15x - 9$

35. $6x^4 + 15x^3 - 8x^2 + 11x - 10$

36. $-6x^4 - 13x^3 + 6x^2 + 3x - 8$

37. $-5x^5 + 22x^4 - 20x^3 - 3x^2 + 27x + 9$

38. $21x^4 - 35x^3 + 21x^2$

39. $56x^6 - 120x^5 + 88x^4 + 24x^3 - 56x^2 - 72x$

40. $-30x^3 + 31x^2 + 51x + 14$

41. $44x^4 + 147x^3 - 64x^2 - 7x$

42. $56x^4 - 22x^3 + 93x^2 - 34x + 3$

43. $2x^4 - 6x^3 - 31x^2 + 97x - 12$

44. $x^3 + 3x^2 - 18x - 40$

45. $x^3 + 2x^2 - 13x + 10$

46. $x^3 + 4x^2 - 16x - 64$

47. $x^3 - 11x^2 + 38x - 40$

Answers

48. $20x^3 + 27x^2 + x - 6$

49. $24x^3 + 58x^2 - 7x - 5$

50. $x^2 + 12x + 36$ **51.** $x^2 - 49$

52. $x^2 - 16x + 64$ **53.** $4x^2 + 44x + 121$

54. $36x^2 - 132x + 121$ **55.** $81x^2 + 180x + 100$

56. $2x - 11 + \dfrac{51}{x + 4}$ **57.** $5x - 29 + \dfrac{196}{x + 7}$

58. $9x + 17 + \dfrac{32}{x - 2}$

59. $4x^2 + 33x + 225 + \dfrac{1581}{x - 7}$

60. $5x^3 - 23x^2 + 87x - 346 + \dfrac{1376}{x + 4}$

61. $3x^3 - 20x^2 + 100x - 496 + \dfrac{2475}{x + 5}$

62. a. $(2x + 4)$ ft   **b.** 40 ft^2

63. a. $(4x + 5)$ ft   **b.** 153 ft^2 **c.** 9 ft   **d.** 17 ft

64. $x(x + 8)(x - 3)$ **65.** $c(c + 9)(c - 1)$

66. $m(m - 5)(m - 8)$ **67.** $a(a - 1)(a + 3)$

68. $(d + 8)(d^2 - 8d + 64)$

69. $(g - 3)(g^2 + 3g + 9)$

70. $(y - 5)(y^2 + 5y + 25)$

71. $(n + 7)(n^2 - 7n + 49)$

72. $(2b + 5)(4b^2 - 10b + 25)$

73. $(3w - 7)(9w^2 + 21w + 49)$

74. $(f^2 + 3)(f - 7)$ **75.** $(r^2 - 2)(3r + 5)$

76. $(h + 1)(h - 1)(5h - 8)$

77. $(s^2 + 4)(3s - 7)$ **78.** $(v^3 + 7)(4v - 1)$

79. $(p^3 - 9)(7p + 2)$

80. $z = -6, z = 0,$ and $z = 2$

81. $x = -3, x = 0,$ and $x = 11$

82. $m = -4, m = 0,$ and $m = 11$

83. $h = -10, h = -3,$ and $h = 0$

84. $v = -9, v = -5,$ and $v = 0$

85. $f = 0, f = 4,$ and $f = 8$

86. $x = -4, x = 0,$ and $x = 7$

87. $x = -8, x = 0,$ and $x = 3$

88. $x = 0, x = 10,$ and $x = 12$

89. $x = 0, x = 2,$ and $x = 5$

90. $x = 0, x = 2,$ and $x = 10$

91. $x = -3, x = 0,$ and $x = 11$

92. a. $(3x + 5)$ in.   **b.** 64 in.^{2}

93. a. $(6x + 11)$ in.   **b.** 400 in.^{2} **c.** 20 in.

Chapter 9

9.1 Start Thinking

Sample answer:

$$x_1 \approx 2\frac{5}{8} \text{ in., } y_1 \approx 1\frac{1}{2} \text{ in., } x_2 \approx 3\frac{7}{16} \text{ in., } y_2 \approx 2 \text{ in.}$$

1. $\dfrac{y_1}{3} = \dfrac{1}{2} = 0.5$ **2.** $\dfrac{x_1}{3} = \dfrac{7}{8} \approx 0.88$

3. $\dfrac{y_1}{x_1} = \dfrac{4}{7} \approx 0.57$ **4.** $\dfrac{y_2}{4} = \dfrac{1}{2} = 0.5$

5. $\dfrac{x_2}{4} = \dfrac{55}{64} \approx 0.86$ **6.** $\dfrac{y_2}{x_2} = \dfrac{32}{55} \approx 0.58$

It appears that regardless of the size of the 30°-60°-90° triangle, the ratios of corresponding sides are equal or approximately equal.

9.1 Warm Up

1. $3\sqrt{5}$ **2.** $\sqrt{39}$ **3.** $4\sqrt{6}$

Answers

1. $a_n = -6n + 17$ **2.** $a_n = 4(-2)^{n-1}$

3. $a_n = 8n - 8$ **4.** $a_n = (-1)^n (2n - 1)$

5. $a_n = \dfrac{n + 1}{n^2}$ **6.** $a_n = \dfrac{3^{n-1}}{3n - 1}$

9.1 Practice A

1. $\sin \theta = \dfrac{12}{13}$, $\cos \theta = \dfrac{5}{13}$, $\tan \theta = \dfrac{12}{5}$,

$\csc \theta = \dfrac{13}{12}$, $\sec \theta = \dfrac{13}{5}$, $\cot \theta = \dfrac{5}{12}$

2. $\sin \theta = \dfrac{1}{2}$, $\cos \theta = \dfrac{\sqrt{3}}{2}$, $\tan \theta = \dfrac{\sqrt{3}}{3}$,

$\csc \theta = 2$, $\sec \theta = \dfrac{2\sqrt{3}}{3}$, $\cot \theta = \sqrt{3}$

3. $\cos \theta = \dfrac{2\sqrt{10}}{7}$, $\tan \theta = \dfrac{3\sqrt{10}}{20}$, $\csc \theta = \dfrac{7}{3}$,

$\sec \theta = \dfrac{7\sqrt{10}}{20}$

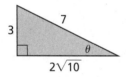

4. $\cos \theta = \dfrac{\sqrt{105}}{11}$, $\tan \theta = \dfrac{4\sqrt{105}}{105}$, $\csc \theta = \dfrac{11}{4}$,

$\sec \theta = \dfrac{11\sqrt{105}}{105}$, $\cot \theta = \dfrac{\sqrt{105}}{4}$

5. $\sin \theta = \dfrac{\sqrt{11}}{6}$, $\tan \theta = \dfrac{\sqrt{11}}{5}$, $\csc \theta = \dfrac{6\sqrt{11}}{11}$,

$\sec \theta = \dfrac{6}{5}$, $\cot \theta = \dfrac{5\sqrt{11}}{11}$

6. $\sin \theta = \dfrac{3}{5}$, $\cos \theta = \dfrac{4}{5}$, $\csc \theta = \dfrac{5}{3}$,

$\sec \theta = \dfrac{5}{4}$, $\cot \theta = \dfrac{4}{3}$

7. tangent is opposite over adjacent, not adjacent over

opposite: $\tan \theta = \dfrac{\text{opp.}}{\text{adj.}} = \dfrac{12}{9} = \dfrac{4}{3}$

8. $x = 5$ **9.** $x = 5.5$ **10.** $h \approx 47.0\,\text{ft}$

9.1 Practice B

1. $\sin \theta = \dfrac{5}{13}$, $\cos \theta = \dfrac{12}{13}$, $\tan \theta = \dfrac{5}{12}$,

$\csc \theta = \dfrac{13}{5}$, $\sec \theta = \dfrac{13}{12}$, $\cot \theta = \dfrac{12}{5}$

2. $\sin \theta = \dfrac{\sqrt{65}}{9}$, $\cos \theta = \dfrac{4}{9}$, $\tan \theta = \dfrac{\sqrt{65}}{4}$,

$\csc \theta = \dfrac{9\sqrt{65}}{65}$, $\sec \theta = \dfrac{9}{4}$, $\cot \theta = \dfrac{4\sqrt{65}}{65}$

3. $\sin \theta = \dfrac{12}{13}$, $\cos \theta = \dfrac{5}{13}$, $\tan \theta = \dfrac{12}{5}$,

$\csc \theta = \dfrac{13}{12}$, $\sec \theta = \dfrac{13}{5}$, $\cot \theta = \dfrac{5}{12}$;

Sine and cosine switch values; Tangent and cotangent switch values; Secant and cosecant switch values.

4. $\sin \theta = \dfrac{4\sqrt{6}}{11}$, $\tan \theta = \dfrac{4\sqrt{6}}{5}$, $\csc \theta = \dfrac{11\sqrt{6}}{24}$,

$\sec \theta = \dfrac{11}{5}$, $\cot \theta = \dfrac{5\sqrt{6}}{24}$

5. $\sin \theta = \dfrac{8\sqrt{113}}{113}$, $\cos \theta = \dfrac{7\sqrt{113}}{113}$, $\tan \theta = \dfrac{8}{7}$,

$\csc \theta = \dfrac{\sqrt{113}}{8}$, $\sec \theta = \dfrac{\sqrt{113}}{7}$

6. $\sin \theta = \dfrac{2\sqrt{10}}{11}$, $\cos \theta = \dfrac{9}{11}$, $\tan \theta = \dfrac{2\sqrt{10}}{9}$,

$\csc \theta = \dfrac{11\sqrt{10}}{20}$, $\cot \theta = \dfrac{9\sqrt{10}}{20}$

7. secant is hypotenuse over adjacent, not adjacent over hypotenuse; $\sec \theta = \dfrac{\text{hyp.}}{\text{adj.}} = \dfrac{15}{9} = \dfrac{5}{3}$

8. $x = 8$ **9.** $x = 10$ **10.** $h \approx 14.1\,\text{ft}$

9.1 Enrichment and Extension

1. 220 m **2.** 454 m **3.** 234 m

4. 70 ft **5.** 54 ft

9.1 Puzzle Time

DODGEBALL

Answers

9.2 Start Thinking

Sample answer:

In each case, the central angle is approximately 57°. It seems that regardless of the size of the radius, this angle is the same.

9.2 Warm Up

1.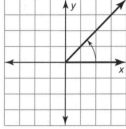

2.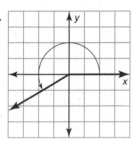

3.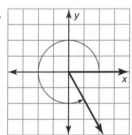

9.2 Cumulative Review Warm Up

1. $(-4, -3)$ **2.** $(3, -1)$

3. infinitely many solutions

4. $(-3, 0)$ and $\left(-\dfrac{9}{5}, \dfrac{12}{5}\right)$ **5.** $(-1, 2)$ and $(3, 6)$

6. $(1, 2)$ and $(-2, 11)$

9.2 Practice A

1.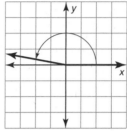

2.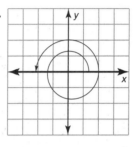

3.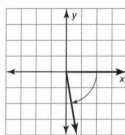

4.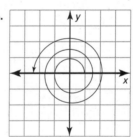

5.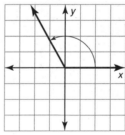

Answers

6.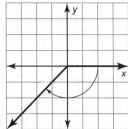

7. B   **8.** A   **9.** C

10. $435°, -285°$ **11.** $320°, -400°$

12. $\dfrac{13\pi}{3}, -\dfrac{5\pi}{3}$ **13.** $\dfrac{5\pi}{4}$

14. $\dfrac{5\pi}{18}$ **15.** $-\dfrac{8\pi}{9}$

16. $15°$ **17.** $100°$ **18.** $-22.5°$

19. hour hand: $105° = \dfrac{7\pi}{12}$ radians

minute hand: $1260° = 7\pi$ radians

The minute degrees and radians are 12 times the hour degrees and radians.

9.2 Practice B

1.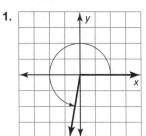

2.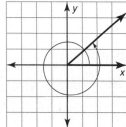

3.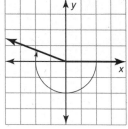

4.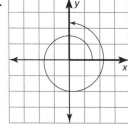

5.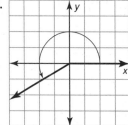

6.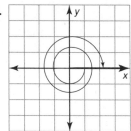

7. A   **8.** C   **9.** B

10. $\dfrac{13\pi}{4}, -\dfrac{3\pi}{4}$ **11.** $300°, -60°$

12. $\dfrac{\pi}{2}, -\dfrac{3\pi}{2}$ **13.** $\dfrac{10\pi}{9}$

Answers

14. $\dfrac{\pi}{180}$

15. $-\dfrac{95\pi}{36}$

16. $54°$

17. $-75°$

18. $\left(\dfrac{1080}{\pi}\right)° \approx 343.8°$

19. a. $160°\,26'\,24''$

    b. $98.26°$

9.2 Enrichment and Extension

1. $>$ **2.** $<$ **3.** $=$ **4.** $=$

5. $=$ **6.** $=$ **7.** $>$ **8.** $<$

9. $=$ **10.** $>$ **11.** $<$ **12.** $<$

13. $\sin 4$, $\sin 3$, $\sin 1$, $\sin 2$

14. $\cos 3$, $\cos 4$, $\cos 2$, $\cos 1$

15. 1.5 cm or 2 cm   **16.** 2 cm or 4 cm

17. a. $20 = 2r + s = 2r + r\theta;\ \theta = \dfrac{20 - 2r}{r}$

$$K = \frac{1}{2}r^2\theta = \frac{1}{2}r^2\left(\frac{20}{r} - 2\right) = 10r - r^2$$

    b. 5 cm

    c. 2 radians

9.2 Puzzle Time

HE RAN OUT OF BOUNDS

9.3 Start Thinking

Sample answer:

$$(x, y) = \left(\frac{\sqrt{2}}{2}, \frac{\sqrt{2}}{2}\right),\ \sin 45° = \frac{y}{1} = y,$$

$$\cos 45° = \frac{x}{1} = x,\ \tan 45° = \frac{y}{x}$$

$$\sin \theta = 0.95,\ \cos \theta = -0.31,\ \tan \theta = \frac{0.95}{-0.31} \approx -3.06$$

For angles in the third quadrant, because both x-values and y-values are negative, the sine and cosine would be negative and the tangent would be positive. For angles in the fourth quadrant, because x-values are positive and y-values are negative, both the sine and the tangent will be negative and the cosine will be positive.

9.3 Warm Up

1. $\sqrt{74}$ **2.** 10   **3.** $\dfrac{\sqrt{89}}{6}$ **4.** $\sqrt{6.28}$

9.3 Cumulative Review Warm Up

1. $-2x^2 + 2x + 8$

2. $2x^3 - 13x^2 - 12x + 35$

3. $4x^2 - 4x + 1$ **4.** $9 - 25x^2$

5. $9 - 6x^2 + x^4$

6. $27x^3 - 54x^2 + 36x - 8$

9.3 Practice A

1. $\sin \theta = \dfrac{3\sqrt{13}}{13}$, $\cos \theta = -\dfrac{2\sqrt{13}}{13}$, $\tan \theta = -\dfrac{3}{2}$,

   $\csc \theta = \dfrac{\sqrt{13}}{3}$, $\sec \theta = -\dfrac{\sqrt{13}}{2}$, $\cot \theta = -\dfrac{2}{3}$

2. $\sin \theta = \dfrac{\sqrt{17}}{17}$, $\cos \theta = -\dfrac{4\sqrt{17}}{17}$, $\tan \theta = -\dfrac{1}{4}$,

   $\csc \theta = \sqrt{17}$, $\sec \theta = -\dfrac{\sqrt{17}}{4}$, $\cot \theta = -4$

3. $\sin \theta = -\dfrac{2\sqrt{29}}{29}$, $\cos \theta = \dfrac{5\sqrt{29}}{29}$, $\tan \theta = -\dfrac{2}{5}$,

   $\csc \theta = -\dfrac{\sqrt{29}}{2}$, $\sec \theta = \dfrac{\sqrt{29}}{5}$, $\cot \theta = -\dfrac{5}{2}$

4. $\sin \theta = -\dfrac{3\sqrt{10}}{10}$, $\cos \theta = -\dfrac{\sqrt{10}}{10}$, $\tan \theta = 3$,

   $\csc \theta = -\dfrac{\sqrt{10}}{3}$, $\sec \theta = -\sqrt{10}$, $\cot \theta = \dfrac{1}{3}$

5. $\sin \theta = 0$, $\cos \theta = -1$, $\tan \theta = 0$,

   $\csc \theta =$ undefined, $\sec \theta = -1$,

   $\cot \theta =$ undefined

6. $\sin \theta = 1$, $\cos \theta = 0$, $\tan \theta =$ undefined,

   $\csc \theta = 1$, $\sec \theta =$ undefined, $\cot \theta = 0$

7. $\sin \theta = -1$, $\cos \theta = 0$, $\tan \theta =$ undefined,

   $\csc \theta = -1$, $\sec \theta =$ undefined, $\cot \theta = 0$

8. $10°$ **9.** $50°$ **10.** $40°$

Answers

11. $\dfrac{\pi}{6}$ **12.** $\dfrac{\pi}{4}$ **13.** $\dfrac{\pi}{3}$

14. 2 **15.** 1 **16.** $-\dfrac{\sqrt{3}}{2}$

17. 173.2 ft; 57.7 yd

9.3 Practice B

1. $\sin \theta = -\dfrac{3}{5}$, $\cos \theta = -\dfrac{4}{5}$, $\tan \theta = \dfrac{3}{4}$,

$\csc \theta = -\dfrac{5}{3}$, $\sec \theta = -\dfrac{5}{4}$, $\cot \theta = \dfrac{4}{3}$

2. $\sin \theta = \dfrac{3\sqrt{13}}{13}$, $\cos \theta = \dfrac{2\sqrt{13}}{13}$, $\tan \theta = \dfrac{3}{2}$,

$\csc \theta = \dfrac{\sqrt{13}}{3}$, $\sec \theta = \dfrac{\sqrt{13}}{2}$, $\cot \theta = \dfrac{2}{3}$

3. $\sin \theta = -\dfrac{2\sqrt{5}}{5}$, $\cos \theta = \dfrac{\sqrt{5}}{5}$, $\tan \theta = -2$,

$\csc \theta = -\dfrac{\sqrt{5}}{2}$, $\sec \theta = \sqrt{5}$, $\cot \theta = -\dfrac{1}{2}$

4. $\sin \theta = \dfrac{3\sqrt{10}}{10}$, $\cos \theta = -\dfrac{\sqrt{10}}{10}$, $\tan \theta = -3$,

$\csc \theta = \dfrac{\sqrt{10}}{3}$, $\sec \theta = -\sqrt{10}$, $\cot \theta = -\dfrac{1}{3}$

5. $\sin \theta = 0$, $\cos \theta = -1$, $\tan \theta = 0$,

$\csc \theta =$ undefined, $\sec \theta = -1$,

$\cot \theta =$ undefined

6. $\sin \theta = 0$, $\cos \theta = 1$, $\tan \theta = 0$,

$\csc \theta =$ undefined, $\sec \theta = 1$,

$\cot \theta =$ undefined

7. $\sin \theta = -1$, $\cos \theta = 0$, $\tan \theta =$ undefined,

$\csc \theta = -1$, $\sec \theta =$ undefined, $\cot \theta = 0$

8. 70° **9.** 70° **10.** 50°

11. $\dfrac{\pi}{4}$ **12.** $\dfrac{\pi}{6}$ **13.** $\dfrac{\pi}{3}$

14. $\dfrac{\sqrt{3}}{3}$ **15.** $-\dfrac{\sqrt{2}}{2}$ **16.** $-\dfrac{2\sqrt{3}}{3}$

17. yes; $d = \dfrac{22^2}{32}\sin(2 \bullet 45°) = 15.125$ ft

9.3 Enrichment and Extension

1. about 1.52 **2.** 1.0

3. 1.97×10^8 m/sec **4.** 2.42

9.3 Puzzle Time

A TENNIS MATCH

9.4 Start Thinking

θ	0	$\dfrac{\pi}{2}$	π	$\dfrac{3\pi}{2}$	2π
$f(\theta) = \sin \theta$	0	1	0	-1	0

θ	$\dfrac{5\pi}{2}$	3π	$\dfrac{7\pi}{2}$	4π
$f(\theta) = \sin \theta$	1	0	-1	0

The highest value of $f(\theta)$ is 1. The lowest value of $f(\theta)$ is -1. The high and low value repeat every 2π units.

Sample answer:

The graph of $f(\theta) = \sin\theta$ on the interval $0 \le \theta \le 4\pi$ starts at $(0,0)$ then moves up to the point $\left(\dfrac{\pi}{2}, 1\right)$, then down to $(\pi, 0)$, then down further to $\left(\dfrac{3\pi}{2}, -1\right)$, and then up to $(2\pi, 0)$. This same cycle repeats on the interval $2\pi \le \theta \le 4\pi$.

9.4 Warm Up

1. vertical stretch by a factor of 4

2. vertical shrink by a factor of $\dfrac{1}{2}$, reflection in x-axis

3. horizontal shrink by a factor of $\dfrac{1}{3}$

4. vertical stretch by a factor of 7, translation 2 units right

5. vertical stretch by a factor of 3

6. translation $\dfrac{\pi}{2}$ units left

Answers

9.4 Cumulative Review Warm Up

1. $a_n = \dfrac{1}{2}n - \dfrac{1}{2}$

2. $a_n = -9n + 16$

3. $a_n = \dfrac{2n + 3}{2^n}$

4. $a_n = -3\left(-\dfrac{2}{3}\right)^{n-1}$

9.4 Practice A

1. amplitude $= 1$, period $= 4\pi$

2. amplitude $= 2$, period $= 4$

3. amplitude $= 2$, period $= 2\pi$

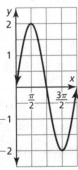

vertical stretch by a factor of 2

4. amplitude $= 4$, period $= 2\pi$

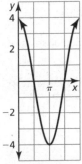

vertical stretch by a factor of 4

5. amplitude $= 1$, period $= \pi$

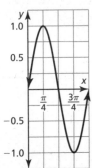

horizontal shrink by a factor of $\dfrac{1}{2}$

6. amplitude $= 3$, period $= 2$

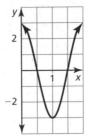

vertical stretch by a factor of 3 and a horizontal

shrink by a factor of $\dfrac{1}{\pi}$

7. A, D

8. The amplitude is 3, so the pendulum swings 3 inches to the left and 3 inches to the right. The period is $\frac{1}{3}$, so it takes one-third of a second to go left, right, and back to a position of rest.

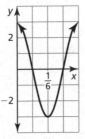

9.

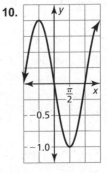

10.

11.

12.

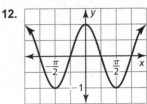

13. $f(x) = 2\cos(x + \pi) - 4$

Answers

14. $f(x) = \sin(4x - 8) + 1$

9.4 Practice B

1. amplitude $= 3$, period $= 12$

2. amplitude $= 0.5$, period $= \dfrac{\pi}{2}$

3. amplitude $= 4$, period $= 2\pi$

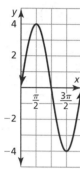

vertical stretch by a factor of 4

4. amplitude $= 1$, period $= 2$

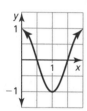

horizontal shrink by a factor of $\dfrac{1}{\pi}$

5. amplitude $= 5$, period $= \dfrac{\pi}{2}$

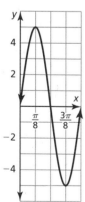

vertical stretch by a factor of 5 and a horizontal
shrink by a factor of $\dfrac{1}{4}$

6. amplitude $= \dfrac{1}{4}$, period $= \pi$

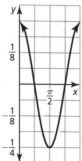

vertical shrink by a factor of $\dfrac{1}{4}$ and a horizontal

shrink by a factor of $\dfrac{1}{2}$

7. a. $y = \cos\dfrac{2\pi}{3}x$

   b. $y = 3\cos\dfrac{\pi}{2}x$

   c. $y = 12\cos x$

   d. $y = \dfrac{1}{3}\cos 2x$

8. 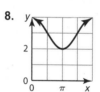   **9.**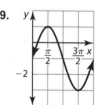

10. 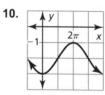   **11.**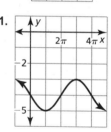

12. $f(x) = -\dfrac{1}{2}\cos 3x + 2$

13. $f(x) = -\dfrac{1}{3}\sin \pi x - 3$

9.4 Enrichment and Extension

1. $y = 35 + 15 \sin 90\vartheta$ **2.** $y = 7 - 3 \sin 4.5\vartheta$

3. $y = 4 - 9 \sin \dfrac{9}{13}(\vartheta + 60°)$

Answers

4. $y = 60 - 100 \sin 45\vartheta$

5. $y = 12.42$ at $\vartheta = 300°$; $y = 2.06$ at $\vartheta = 5678°$, which is 1.94 below the sinusoidal axis.

6. $y = -32.39...$ at $\vartheta = 2.5°$; $y = 60$, on the sinusoidal axis, at $\vartheta = 328°$

9.4 Puzzle Time

TRAFFIC JAM

9.5 Start Thinking

$0 \le \theta \le \dfrac{\pi}{2}$ or $0° \le \theta \le 90°$; $-\dfrac{\pi}{2} \le \theta \le 0$ or $-90° \le \theta \le 0$; As the angles move from 0 to $\dfrac{\pi}{2}$, the x-values decrease from 1 to 0. The x-values do the same thing as the angles move from 0 to $-\dfrac{\pi}{2}$. As the angles move from 0 to $\dfrac{\pi}{2}$, the y-values increase from 0 to 1. The y-values decrease from 0 to -1 as the angles move from 0 to $-\dfrac{\pi}{2}$;

$\tan\theta = \dfrac{y}{x}$;

Sample answer: As the angles move from 0 to $\dfrac{\pi}{2}$, the value of $\tan\theta = \dfrac{y}{x}$ is going to increase because the denominator (x-value) is approaching zero and y is positive. As the angles move from 0 to $-\dfrac{\pi}{2}$, the value of $\tan\theta = \dfrac{y}{x}$ is going to decrease because the denominator (x-value) is approaching zero and y is negative; The graph of $f(\theta) = \tan\theta$ will cross the x-axis (have an x-intercept) every time $y = 0$, which occurs when the angle is 0 and when the angle is any multiple of π added to 0. That is $0 + n\pi = n\pi$, where n is any integer. The graph of $f(\theta) = \tan\theta$ will have a vertical asymptote every time $x = 0$, which occurs when the angle is $\dfrac{\pi}{2}$ and when the angle is any multiple of π added to $\dfrac{\pi}{2}$. That is $\dfrac{\pi}{2} + n\pi$, where n is any integer.

9.5 Warm Up

1.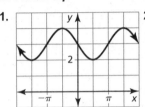

2.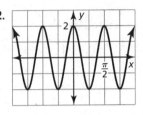

3.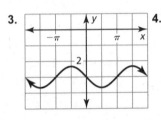

4.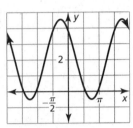

9.5 Cumulative Review Warm Up

1. $\log_2 3 + 2 \log_2 x$

2. $\log(2 - x) + 3 \log x$

3. $\dfrac{1}{2} \ln 2 + \dfrac{3}{2} \ln x - \ln 5$

4. $\ln \dfrac{8}{x^2}$

5. $\log 7\sqrt{x - 1}$

6. $\log_3 \dfrac{(x - 2)^3}{x^2}$

9.5 Practice A

1.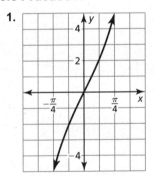

vertical stretch by a factor of 4

2.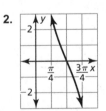

vertical stretch by a factor of 3

Answers

3.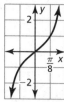

horizontal shrink by a factor of $\dfrac{1}{2}$

4.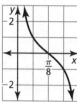

horizontal shrink by a factor of $\dfrac{1}{4}$

5. The value of b is 2π and not 2;

Period: $\dfrac{\pi}{|b|} = \dfrac{\pi}{|2\pi|} = \dfrac{\pi}{2\pi} = \dfrac{1}{2}$

6. a. 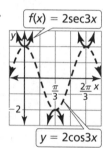 **b.**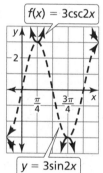

7.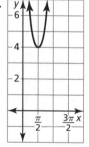

vertical stretch by a factor of 4

8.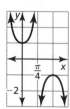

horizontal shrink by a factor of $\dfrac{1}{2}$

9.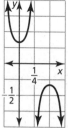

vertical shrink by a factor of $\dfrac{1}{3}$ and a horizontal

shrink by a factor of $\dfrac{1}{2\pi}$

10.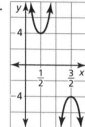

vertical stretch by a factor of 4 and a horizontal

shrink by a factor of $\dfrac{1}{\pi}$

9.5 Practice B

1.

vertical stretch by a factor of 2 and a horizontal

shrink by a factor of $\dfrac{1}{4}$

2.

vertical stretch by a factor of 3 and a horizontal
stretch by a factor of 2

Answers

3.

vertical shrink by a factor of $\frac{1}{4}$ and a horizontal

shrink by a factor of $\frac{1}{2\pi}$

4.

vertical shrink by a factor of $\frac{1}{3}$ and a horizontal

shrink by a factor of $\frac{1}{\pi}$

5. There is a horizontal stretch instead of a horizontal
shrink; a vertical stretch by a factor of 4 and a
horizontal stretch by a factor of 2

6. a. 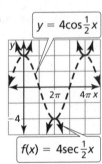 **b.**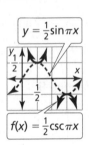

7.

vertical shrink by a factor of $\frac{1}{3}$ and a horizontal

shrink by a factor of $\frac{1}{\pi}$

8.

vertical shrink by a factor of $\frac{1}{2}$ and a horizontal

shrink by a factor of $\frac{1}{6}$

9.

horizontal shrink by a factor of $\frac{2}{\pi}$

10.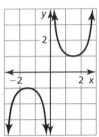

horizontal shrink by a factor of $\frac{3}{\pi}$

9.5 Enrichment and Extension

1. $y = \cot\big(0.25(x + 3)\big) + 2$

2. $y = 3\sec\big(2(x - 1)\big) - 3$

3. $y = \tan\big(3(x - 2)\big) - 1$

4. $y = \csc\big(0.5(x + 1)\big) + 2$

5. $y = \cot\big(4(x - 1)\big) + 3$

6. $y = \sec\big(0.5x\big) - 1$

9.5 Puzzle Time

MEMORY

9.6 Start Thinking

The *x*-intercepts occur at $(0, 0)$, $(40, 0)$, and $(80, 0)$.
They represent the time you load the Ferris wheel car
and then each time when the car is at ground level.
The Ferris wheel is approximately 80 feet tall. The ride
takes 160 seconds or 2 minutes and 40 seconds. The
graph of $h = \cos t$ has been reflected in the *t*-axis,
shifted 40 units up, vertically stretched by a factor of
40, and horizontally stretched so that the period is
now 40.

9.6 Warm Up

1. amplitude: 2, period: 2π

Answers

2. amplitude: $\dfrac{2}{3}$, period: 1

3. amplitude: 1, period: $\dfrac{2\pi}{3}$

4. amplitude: $\dfrac{\sqrt{3}}{2}$, period: π

5. amplitude: 1.4, period: 2π

6. amplitude: 2.4, period: $\dfrac{2\pi}{1.8} = \dfrac{10\pi}{9}$

9.6 Cumulative Review Warm Up

1. domain: all real numbers, range: $f(x) \geq -2$

2. domain: $x > 2$, range: all real numbers

3. domain: $x \geq -8$, range: $h(x) \geq -4$

4. domain: all real numbers, range: all real numbers

5. domain: all real numbers, range: $-6 \leq g(x) \leq -2$

6. domain: all real numbers, range: $-3 \leq h(x) \leq 3$

9.6 Practice A

1. $f = \dfrac{1}{\pi}$ **2.** $f = \dfrac{3}{2\pi}$

3. $f = \dfrac{2}{\pi}$ **4.** $f = \dfrac{5}{2}$

5. $P = 4 \sin 524\pi t$

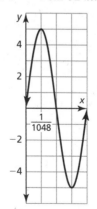

6. $y = 3 \sin 2x + 1$

7. $y = 2 \sin\left(x - \dfrac{\pi}{4}\right) - 1$

8. a. $y = 1.3 \sin(0.5x - 0.437) + 3.1$

    b. 4.37 ft

9.6 Practice B

1. $f = \dfrac{3}{2\pi}$ **2.** $f = \dfrac{2}{\pi}$

3. $f = \dfrac{1}{4}$ **4.** $f = \dfrac{0.2}{\pi}$

5. $P = 4 \sin 55\pi t$

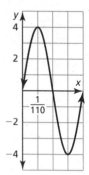

6. $y = 3 \sin \pi\left(x + \dfrac{1}{2}\right)$

7. $y = \sin \dfrac{\pi}{4}(x - 1) + 4$

8. a. $y = 7 \sin(0.628x - 1.57) + 7.998$

    b. 5.8 m

9.6 Enrichment and Extension

1. *Sample answer:* $y = 2.5 \cos \dfrac{\pi}{6}(x - 4) + 319.5$

2. *Sample answer:* $y = 3 \cos \dfrac{\pi}{6}(x - 5) + 345$

3. *Sample answer:* $y = 3 \cos \dfrac{\pi}{6}(x - 4) + 377$

4. The axis of the wave increases over the years. That is, there is more carbon dioxide in the atmosphere; People could be harming the environment.

9.6 Puzzle Time

A MEWTATION

Answers

9.7 Start Thinking

Sample answer: Transform the cosine curve into the sine curve by moving it $\dfrac{\pi}{2}$ units to the right. Transform the cosine curve into the sine curve by reflecting it in the x-axis and then moving it $\dfrac{\pi}{2}$ units to the left;

$$\sin x = \cos\left(x - \dfrac{\pi}{2}\right), \quad \sin x = -\cos\left(x + \dfrac{\pi}{2}\right)$$

9.7 Warm Up

1. $\sin \theta = \dfrac{6\sqrt{61}}{61}$, $\cos \theta = \dfrac{5\sqrt{61}}{61}$, $\tan \theta = \dfrac{6}{5}$,

$\csc \theta = \dfrac{\sqrt{61}}{6}$, $\sec \theta = \dfrac{\sqrt{61}}{5}$, $\cot \theta = \dfrac{5}{6}$

2. $\sin \theta = \dfrac{5\sqrt{3}}{14}$, $\cos \theta = \dfrac{11}{14}$, $\tan \theta = \dfrac{5\sqrt{3}}{11}$,

$\csc \theta = \dfrac{14\sqrt{3}}{15}$, $\sec \theta = \dfrac{14}{11}$, $\cot \theta = \dfrac{11\sqrt{3}}{15}$

3. $\sin \theta = \dfrac{2}{3}$, $\cos \theta = \dfrac{\sqrt{5}}{3}$, $\tan \theta = \dfrac{2\sqrt{5}}{5}$,

$\csc \theta = \dfrac{3}{2}$, $\sec \theta = \dfrac{3\sqrt{5}}{5}$, $\cot \theta = \dfrac{\sqrt{5}}{2}$

9.7 Cumulative Review Warm Up

1. $\dfrac{x + 1}{x + 4}$

2. $\dfrac{4(x + 2)}{(x - 4)(x + 3)}$

3. $\dfrac{-4x(x - 4)}{x(x + 5)(x - 5)}$

4. $\dfrac{-3x^3 - 4x^2 + 14x - 7}{2x^2(2x - 1)}$

9.7 Practice A

1. $\cos \theta = \dfrac{\sqrt{5}}{3}$, $\tan \theta = \dfrac{2\sqrt{5}}{5}$, $\csc \theta = \dfrac{3}{2}$,

$\sec \theta = \dfrac{3\sqrt{5}}{5}$, $\cot \theta = \dfrac{\sqrt{5}}{2}$

2. $\sin \theta = \dfrac{4}{5}$, $\tan \theta = -\dfrac{4}{3}$, $\csc \theta = \dfrac{5}{4}$,

$\sec \theta = -\dfrac{5}{3}$, $\cot \theta = -\dfrac{3}{4}$

3. $\sin \theta = -\dfrac{4\sqrt{65}}{65}$, $\cos \theta = -\dfrac{7\sqrt{65}}{65}$,

$\csc \theta = -\dfrac{\sqrt{65}}{4}$, $\sec \theta = -\dfrac{\sqrt{65}}{7}$, $\cot \theta = \dfrac{7}{4}$

4. $\sin \theta = \dfrac{4\sqrt{41}}{41}$, $\cos \theta = -\dfrac{5\sqrt{41}}{41}$, $\tan \theta = -\dfrac{4}{5}$,

$\csc \theta = \dfrac{\sqrt{41}}{4}$, $\sec \theta = -\dfrac{\sqrt{41}}{5}$

5. $\sin \theta = -\dfrac{2\sqrt{10}}{7}$, $\cos \theta = \dfrac{3}{7}$, $\tan \theta = -\dfrac{2\sqrt{10}}{3}$,

$\csc \theta = -\dfrac{7\sqrt{10}}{20}$, $\cot \theta = -\dfrac{3\sqrt{10}}{20}$

6. $\sin \theta = -\dfrac{5}{6}$, $\cos \theta = -\dfrac{\sqrt{11}}{6}$, $\tan \theta = \dfrac{5\sqrt{11}}{11}$,

$\sec \theta = -\dfrac{6\sqrt{11}}{11}$, $\cot \theta = \dfrac{\sqrt{11}}{5}$

7. $\sin x$

8. $\cot x \cos x$

9. $\sec \theta$

10. $\cos^2 \theta$

11. $\cos x$

12. $\cos^3 x$

13. $\sec^2 x$ is equal to $\tan^2 x + 1$ and not $\tan^2 x - 1$;

$$\tan^2 x + \sec^2 x = \tan^2 x + \left(\tan^2 x + 1\right)$$
$$= \tan^2 x + \tan^2 x + 1$$
$$= 2\tan^2 x + 1$$

14. $\tan x \cot x = \tan x \cdot \dfrac{1}{\tan x}$
$$= 1$$

15. $\sin\left(\dfrac{\pi}{2} - x\right)\sec x = \cos x \cdot \dfrac{1}{\cos x}$
$$= 1$$

16. $\dfrac{\sin^2 x + \left(1 - \cos^2 x\right)}{\tan x \cos x} = \dfrac{\sin^2 x + \sin^2 x}{\dfrac{\sin x}{\cos x} \cdot \cos x}$

$$= \dfrac{2\sin^2 x}{\sin x}$$
$$= 2\sin x$$

Answers

17. $\dfrac{\cos^2(-x)\,\csc x}{\cot x} = \dfrac{\cos^2 x \cdot \dfrac{1}{\sin x}}{\dfrac{\cos x}{\sin x}}$

$= \dfrac{\dfrac{\cos^2 x}{\sin x}}{\dfrac{\cos x}{\sin x}}$

$= \dfrac{\cos^2 x}{\sin x} \cdot \dfrac{\sin x}{\cos x}$

$= \cos x$

18. increases; $\sin\theta$ and $\csc\theta$ are reciprocals of each other, so as one decreases, the other increases.

9.7 Practice B

1. $\cos\theta = -\dfrac{\sqrt{55}}{8}$, $\tan\theta = -\dfrac{3\sqrt{55}}{55}$, $\csc\theta = \dfrac{8}{3}$,

$\sec\theta = -\dfrac{8\sqrt{55}}{55}$, $\cot\theta = -\dfrac{\sqrt{55}}{3}$

2. $\sin\theta = -\dfrac{2\sqrt{2}}{3}$, $\tan\theta = 2\sqrt{2}$, $\csc\theta = -\dfrac{3\sqrt{2}}{4}$,

$\sec\theta = -3$, $\cot\theta = \dfrac{\sqrt{2}}{4}$

3. $\sin\theta = \dfrac{3\sqrt{10}}{10}$, $\cos\theta = \dfrac{\sqrt{10}}{10}$, $\csc\theta = \dfrac{\sqrt{10}}{3}$,

$\sec\theta = \sqrt{10}$, $\cot\theta = \dfrac{1}{3}$

4. $\sin\theta = -\dfrac{3\sqrt{109}}{109}$, $\cos\theta = -\dfrac{10\sqrt{109}}{109}$,

$\tan\theta = \dfrac{3}{10}$, $\csc\theta = -\dfrac{\sqrt{109}}{3}$, $\sec\theta = -\dfrac{\sqrt{109}}{10}$

5. $\sin\theta = \dfrac{2\sqrt{14}}{9}$, $\cos\theta = -\dfrac{5}{9}$, $\tan\theta = -\dfrac{2\sqrt{14}}{5}$,

$\csc\theta = \dfrac{9\sqrt{14}}{28}$, $\cot\theta = -\dfrac{5\sqrt{14}}{28}$

6. $\sin\theta = -\dfrac{2}{7}$, $\cos\theta = \dfrac{3\sqrt{5}}{7}$, $\tan\theta = -\dfrac{2\sqrt{5}}{15}$,

$\sec\theta = \dfrac{7\sqrt{5}}{15}$, $\cot\theta = -\dfrac{3\sqrt{5}}{2}$

7. $\csc x$

8. $-\csc\theta$

9. $\cos\theta$

10. $-\cot\theta$

11. 1

12. $\csc x + 1$

13. $\csc\theta$ is equal to $\dfrac{1}{\sin\theta}$ and not $\dfrac{1}{\cos\theta}$;

$\csc\theta\,\cot\theta\,\cos\theta = \dfrac{1}{\sin\theta} \cdot \dfrac{\cos\theta}{\sin\theta} \cdot \cos\theta$

$= \dfrac{\cos^2\theta}{\sin^2\theta}$

$= \cot^2\theta$

14. $\tan\left(\dfrac{\pi}{2} - x\right)\cos^2\left(\dfrac{\pi}{2} - x\right) = \cot x\,\sin^2 x$

$= \dfrac{\cos x}{\sin x} \cdot \sin^2 x$

$= \cos x\,\sin x$

15. $\dfrac{1 + \sin(-x)}{\cos x\,\tan x - 1} = \dfrac{1 - \sin x}{\cos x \cdot \dfrac{\sin x}{\cos x} - 1}$

$= \dfrac{1 - \sin x}{\sin x - 1}$

$= -1$

16. $\dfrac{1 - \cos x}{\sin x} = \dfrac{1}{\sin x} - \dfrac{\cos x}{\sin x}$

$= \csc x - \cot x$

Answers

17. $\dfrac{1 + \sin\theta}{\cos\theta} + \dfrac{\cos\theta}{1 - \sin\theta}$

$$= \dfrac{1 + \sin\theta}{\cos\theta} \cdot \dfrac{1 - \sin\theta}{1 - \sin\theta} + \dfrac{\cos\theta}{1 - \sin\theta} \cdot \dfrac{\cos\theta}{\cos\theta}$$

$$= \dfrac{1 - \sin^2\theta}{\cos\theta(1 - \sin\theta)} + \dfrac{\cos^2\theta}{\cos\theta(1 - \sin\theta)}$$

$$= \dfrac{\cos^2\theta}{\cos\theta(1 - \sin\theta)} + \dfrac{\cos^2\theta}{\cos\theta(1 - \sin\theta)}$$

$$= \dfrac{2\cos^2\theta}{\cos\theta(1 - \sin\theta)}$$

$$= \dfrac{2\cos\theta}{1 - \sin\theta}$$

$$= \dfrac{2\cos\theta}{1 - \sin\theta} \cdot \dfrac{1 + \sin\theta}{1 + \sin\theta}$$

$$= \dfrac{2\cos\theta(1 + \sin\theta)}{1 - \sin^2\theta}$$

$$= \dfrac{2\cos\theta(1 + \sin\theta)}{\cos^2\theta}$$

$$= \dfrac{2(1 + \sin\theta)}{\cos\theta}$$

$$= \dfrac{2 + 2\sin\theta}{\cos\theta}$$

$$= \dfrac{2}{\cos\theta} + \dfrac{2\sin\theta}{\cos\theta}$$

$$= 2\sec\theta + 2\tan\theta$$

18. $\tan x \cot x = \dfrac{\sin x}{\cos x} \cdot \dfrac{\cos x}{\sin x}$

$$= \dfrac{\sin x \cos x}{\cos x \sin x}$$

$$= 1$$

9.7 Enrichment and Extension

1. $\dfrac{\pm\sqrt{1 - \cos^2\theta}}{\cos\theta}$

2. $\dfrac{\cos\theta}{\pm\sqrt{1 - \cos^2\theta}}$

3. $\dfrac{1}{\pm\sqrt{1 - \cos^2\theta}}$

4. $\dfrac{1}{\tan\theta}$

5. $\dfrac{\tan\theta}{\pm\sqrt{1 + \tan^2\theta}}$

6. $\dfrac{1}{\pm\sqrt{1 + \tan^2\theta}}$

7. $\dfrac{\pm\sqrt{\csc^2\theta - 1}}{\csc\theta}$

8. $\dfrac{1}{\pm\sqrt{\csc^2\theta - 1}}$

9. $\dfrac{\csc\theta}{\pm\sqrt{\csc^2\theta - 1}}$

10. $\pm\sqrt{\sec^2\theta - 1}$

11. $\dfrac{\pm\sqrt{\sec^2\theta - 1}}{\sec\theta}$

12. $\dfrac{1}{\pm\sqrt{\sec^2\theta - 1}}$

9.7 Puzzle Time

PAPA SURF

9.8 Start Thinking

1. *Sample answer:* $75° = 30° + 45°$;

$$\sin 75° = \sin(30° + 45°)$$

$$= \sin 30° \cos 45° + \cos 30° \sin 45°$$

$$= \dfrac{1}{2}\left(\dfrac{\sqrt{2}}{2}\right) + \dfrac{\sqrt{3}}{2}\left(\dfrac{\sqrt{2}}{2}\right)$$

$$= \dfrac{\sqrt{2} + \sqrt{6}}{4}$$

2. *Sample answer:* $\dfrac{\pi}{12} = \dfrac{\pi}{3} - \dfrac{\pi}{4}$;

$$\sin\dfrac{\pi}{12} = \sin\left(\dfrac{\pi}{3} - \dfrac{\pi}{4}\right)$$

$$= \sin\dfrac{\pi}{3}\cos\dfrac{\pi}{4} - \cos\dfrac{\pi}{3}\sin\dfrac{\pi}{4}$$

$$= \dfrac{\sqrt{3}}{2}\left(\dfrac{\sqrt{2}}{2}\right) - \dfrac{1}{2}\left(\dfrac{\sqrt{2}}{2}\right)$$

$$= \dfrac{\sqrt{6} - \sqrt{2}}{4}$$

3. *Sample answer:* $\dfrac{19\pi}{12} = \dfrac{11\pi}{6} - \dfrac{\pi}{4}$;

$$\sin\dfrac{19\pi}{12} = \sin\left(\dfrac{11\pi}{6} - \dfrac{\pi}{4}\right)$$

$$= \sin\dfrac{11\pi}{6}\cos\dfrac{\pi}{4} - \cos\dfrac{11\pi}{6}\sin\dfrac{\pi}{4}$$

$$= \dfrac{-1}{2}\left(\dfrac{\sqrt{2}}{2}\right) - \dfrac{\sqrt{3}}{2}\left(\dfrac{\sqrt{2}}{2}\right)$$

$$= \dfrac{-\sqrt{2} - \sqrt{6}}{4}$$

9.8 Warm Up

1. $\sin b = -\dfrac{\sqrt{39}}{8}$

2. $\cos a = -\dfrac{2\sqrt{10}}{7}$

Answers

3. $\tan b = -\dfrac{\sqrt{39}}{5}$ **4.** $\tan a = \dfrac{3\sqrt{10}}{20}$

5. $\csc b = -\dfrac{8\sqrt{39}}{39}$ **6.** $\sec a = -\dfrac{7\sqrt{10}}{20}$

9.8 Cumulative Review Warm Up

1. $A = \$5986.05$ **2.** $A = \$5470.18$

3. $A = \$5792.28$ **4.** $A = \$5943.14$

9.8 Practice A

1. $-2 - \sqrt{3}$ **2.** $-2 - \sqrt{3}$ **3.** $\dfrac{\sqrt{6} - \sqrt{2}}{4}$

4. $\dfrac{-\sqrt{2} - \sqrt{6}}{4}$ **5.** $\dfrac{-\sqrt{2} - \sqrt{6}}{4}$ **6.** $\dfrac{\sqrt{2} - \sqrt{6}}{4}$

7. $-\dfrac{63}{65}$ **8.** $\dfrac{33}{65}$ **9.** $-\dfrac{56}{65}$

10. $\dfrac{16}{65}$ **11.** $-\dfrac{63}{16}$ **12.** $-\dfrac{33}{56}$

13. $\cos x$ **14.** $\tan x$ **15.** $-\cos x$

16. The cosine of a sum is the difference of the products, not the sum;

$$\cos\left(x + \frac{3\pi}{2}\right) = \cos x \cos \frac{3\pi}{2} - \sin x \sin \frac{3\pi}{2}$$
$$= (0)\cos x - (-1)\sin x$$
$$= \sin x$$

17. $x = 0, \pi$ **18.** $x = \dfrac{\pi}{4}, \dfrac{5\pi}{4}$

19. $x = \dfrac{\pi}{4}, \dfrac{7\pi}{4}$ **20.** $x = \dfrac{\pi}{2}, \dfrac{3\pi}{2}$

21. $\tan(x - \pi) = \dfrac{\tan x - \tan \pi}{1 + \tan x \tan \pi}$

$$= \dfrac{\tan x - 0}{1 + \tan x(0)}$$
$$= \tan x$$

9.8 Practice B

1. $-2 + \sqrt{3}$ **2.** $\dfrac{\sqrt{6} - \sqrt{2}}{4}$ **3.** $\dfrac{-\sqrt{2} - \sqrt{6}}{4}$

4. $\dfrac{\sqrt{6} - \sqrt{2}}{4}$ **5.** $\dfrac{\sqrt{6} - \sqrt{2}}{4}$ **6.** $2 - \sqrt{3}$

7. $-\dfrac{171}{221}$ **8.** $-\dfrac{21}{221}$ **9.** $-\dfrac{220}{221}$

10. $\dfrac{140}{221}$ **11.** $-\dfrac{171}{140}$ **12.** $\dfrac{21}{220}$

13. $\tan x$ **14.** $\sin x$ **15.** $-\sin x$

16. The formula for $\sin(a + b)$ involves the product of sin with cosine, not sine with sine;

$$\sin\left(x + \frac{\pi}{2}\right) = \sin x \cos\frac{\pi}{2} + \cos x \sin\frac{\pi}{2}$$
$$= (0)\sin x + (1)\cos x$$
$$= \cos x$$

17. $x = \dfrac{7\pi}{6}, \dfrac{11\pi}{6}$ **18.** $x = \dfrac{\pi}{2}, \dfrac{3\pi}{2}$

19. $x = 0, \dfrac{\pi}{2}, \dfrac{3\pi}{2}, \pi$ **20.** $x = \dfrac{\pi}{4}, \dfrac{5\pi}{4}$

21. $\tan(a + b) = \dfrac{\tan a + \tan b}{1 - \tan a \tan b} = \dfrac{\dfrac{\sin a}{\cos a} + \dfrac{\sin b}{\cos b}}{1 - \dfrac{\sin a \sin b}{\cos a \cos b}}$

$$= \dfrac{\sin a \cos b + \sin b \cos a}{\cos a \cos b + \sin a \sin b}$$
$$= \dfrac{\sin(a + b)}{\cos(a + b)}$$

9.8 Enrichment and Extension

1. true; expand using identity for $\sin(a - b)$

2. true; expand using identities for $\cos(a + b)$, $\cos(n\pi) = (-1)^n$, and $\sin(n\pi) = 0$

3. false; It should be $(-1)^n \sin \theta$.

4. false; It should be $(-1)^{n+1} \sin \theta$.

5. $\cos u \cos v \cos w - \sin u \sin v \cos w$
$$- \sin n \cos v \sin w$$
$$- \cos u \sin v \sin w$$

Answers

6. $\dfrac{\tan u + \tan v + \tan w - \tan u \tan v \tan w}{1 - \tan u \tan v - \tan u \tan w - \tan v \tan w}$

7. Change the first term to $\sin(0 - u)$. Then use the difference formula to expand and simplify.

8. Change the first term to $\cos(0 - u)$. Then use the difference formula to expand and simplify.

9. Change the first term to $\tan(0 - u)$. Then use the difference formula to expand and simplify.

10. Change the first term to $\sec(0 - u)$. Use the fact that $\sec(0 - u) = \dfrac{1}{\cos(0 - u)}$. Then use the difference formula to expand and simplify.

11. The functions $y = \tan(x + \pi)$ and $y = \tan(x)$ are the same function. They coincide. The period of the tangent function is π.

9.8 Puzzle Time
STEREOTYPE

Cumulative Review

1. $-|4|, |7 - 8|, |-1 + 6|, |-6|$

2. $-|4 + 1|, |-4 + 3|, |-8 + 3|, |9|$

3. $\dfrac{|-6|}{|8|}, |2|, |-2 + 5|, |-6|$

4. $|-5 + 5|, \dfrac{|5|}{|-7|}, |4 - 9|, |-8|$

5. $|9 - 9|, |-6| - |4|, |8| + |-4|, |-7 \bullet -6|$

6. $|-4 + 6|, |-8| + |4|, |9 + 6|, |4 \bullet -4|$

7. $|7 - 5|, |3^2|, |9| + |-4|, |-2 \bullet -9|$

8. $|-7|, |-8|, |-4^2|, |7 \bullet 3|, |-6 \bullet -6|$

9. $(10, -3)$ **10.** $(-9, -13)$ **11.** $(0, 6)$

12. $(10, -6)$ **13.** $(-3, -2)$ **14.** $(0, 0)$

15. $(7, -16)$ **16.** $(-14, 6)$ **17.** $(0, 5)$

18. $(-2, -1)$ **19.** $2\sqrt{149}$ **20.** $3\sqrt{85}$

21. $3\sqrt{53}$ **22.** $5\sqrt{26}$ **23.** $\sqrt{10}$

24. $3\sqrt{10}$ **25.** $3\sqrt{85}$ **26.** $\sqrt{409}$

27. $5\sqrt{5}$ **28.** $2\sqrt{181}$

29. a. 5.7 ft **b.** 12 ft^3 **c.** 8 ft^3 **d.** \$9.52

30. $c = 20$ ft **31.** $b = 40$ km **32.** $a = 10$ in.

33. $b = 24$ mi **34.** $a = 13.5$ cm

35. $c = 6.5$ m **36.** $c = 24.4$ in.^{2}

37. a. 4.2 ft
b. 4.5 ft^3
c. 3.4 ft^3
d. \$8.47, or \$8.40, using exact value from part (c)

38. 44π in. **39.** 34π km **40.** 2π mi

41. 20π cm **42.** 6π ft **43.** 14π mm

44. 32π yd **45.** 24π m **46.** 24π cm

47. 36π mi^2 **48.** 9π in.^{2} **49.** 16π km^2

50. 484π yd^2 **51.** 225π ft^2 **52.** 49π cm^2

53. 4π m^2 **54.** 81π mi^2 **55.** 4π yd^2

56. a. $\dfrac{1}{27}$ **b.** 9 **57. a.** $\dfrac{1}{125}$ **b.** 25

58. a. $\dfrac{2}{27}$ **b.** 18 **59. a.** $\dfrac{1}{2}$ **b.** 16

60. a. $\dfrac{3}{125}$ **b.** 75 **61. a.** $\dfrac{193}{64}$ **b.** 19

62. a. $\dfrac{17}{8}$ **b.** 6 **63. a.** $-\dfrac{107}{27}$ **b.** 5

64. a. $-\dfrac{55}{8}$ **b.** -3

65. e^{-11} **66.** e^{14} **67.** e^3

68. $3e^5$ **69.** $-\dfrac{e^2}{2}$ **70.** $6e^7$

Answers

71. $8e^{-24x}$ **72.** $27e^{-27x}$ **73.** $9e^{12x}$

74. $4e^{6x}$ **75.** $6e^{2x}$ **76.** $3e^{5x}$

77. e^{7x+5} **78.** e^{-2x+9} **79.** e^{3x+4}

80. a. exponential decay
   b. 20% decrease
   c. a little more than 4 years

81. 5   **82.** 6   **83.** 4

84. 1   **85.** 2   **86.** 0

87. -5 **88.** -3 **89.** -3

90. -2 **91.** -2 **92.** -2

93. $\log_2 5 + \log_2 x$ **94.** $\log_7 8 + \log_7 x$

95. $\log_9 5 + \log_9 x$ **96.** $\log_4 8 + 3 \log_4 x$

97. $\log_2 4 + 5 \log_2 x$ **98.** $\log_2 3 + 4 \log_2 x$

99. $\ln 2 + \ln x - \ln y$

100. $\ln x - \left(\ln 5 + \ln y\right)$

101. $\ln 4 + \ln x - \left(\ln 3 + \ln y\right)$

102. $\dfrac{1}{2} + \dfrac{1}{2} \log_9 x$

103. $\dfrac{1}{3}\left(\log_8 x + 4 \log_8 y\right)$

104. $\dfrac{1}{2} + \dfrac{3}{2} \log_4 x$ **105.** $\log_7 66$

106. $\ln 2$ **107.** $\ln 42$

108. $\log_8\left(\dfrac{x^3}{y^2}\right)$ **109.** $\log_5\left(y^9 z^4\right)$

110. $\log_9\left(w^{10} x^8\right)$ **111.** $\ln\left(5^7 \bullet 4^6\right)$

112. $\log\left(\dfrac{4^7}{5^4}\right)$ **113.** $\ln\left(49x^7 y^9\right)$

114. $\log_4(5x)$ **115.** $\ln\left(\dfrac{z^3}{y^4}\right)$

116. $\log_3\left(25x^6 y^4\right)$ **117.** $\dfrac{4}{3x^2 - 1}, x \neq 0$

118. $\dfrac{x}{3x^3 + 4}, x \neq 0$ **119.** $\dfrac{x^3}{3x - 7}, x \neq \dfrac{7}{3}$

120. $\dfrac{x + 1}{x - 2}, x \neq -3, x \neq 2$

121. $\dfrac{x + 4}{x - 5}, x \neq 5, x \neq 7$

122. $\dfrac{x - 1}{x + 4}, x \neq -4, x \neq 3$

123. $\dfrac{x + 3}{x - 8}, x \neq 1, x \neq 8$

124. $\dfrac{x + 2}{x + 4}, x \neq -5, x \neq -4$

125. $\dfrac{(x + 3)^2}{x + 6}, x \neq -6, x \neq -3$

126. $\dfrac{(x - 2)^2}{x + 8}, x \neq -8, x \neq 2$

Chapter 10

10.1 Start Thinking

Sample answer:

1. *Sample answer*: It is not too likely that you will grab the number that matches your jersey. You have a 1 in 15 chance of choosing a matching pair of shorts.

2. *Sample answer*: Possible Outcomes: Jersey and shorts – 11 and 1, 11 and 2, 11 and 3, 11 and 4, 11 and 5, 11 and 6, 11 and 7, 11 and 8, 11 and 9, 11 and 10, 11 and 11, 11 and 12, 11 and 13, 11 and 14, 11 and 15

10.1 Warm Up

1. "H" for heads, "T" for tails, HHH, HHT, HTH, HTT, THH, THT, TTH, TTT

2. "B" for blue, "Y" for yellow, "G" for green, "R" for red, BB, BY, BG, BR, YY, YB, YG, YR, GG, GB, GY, GR, RR, RB, RY, RG

3. BH, BT, YH, YT, GH, GT, RH, RT

Answers

10.1 Cumulative Review Warm Up

1. $\sin\theta = \dfrac{4}{7}$, $\cos\theta = \dfrac{\sqrt{33}}{7}$, $\tan\theta = \dfrac{4\sqrt{33}}{33}$,

$\csc\theta = \dfrac{7}{4}$, $\sec\theta = \dfrac{7\sqrt{33}}{33}$, $\cot\theta = \dfrac{\sqrt{33}}{4}$

2. $\sin\theta = \dfrac{\sqrt{17}}{9}$, $\cos\theta = \dfrac{8}{9}$, $\tan\theta = \dfrac{\sqrt{17}}{8}$,

$\csc\theta = \dfrac{9\sqrt{17}}{17}$, $\sec\theta = \dfrac{9}{8}$, $\cot\theta = \dfrac{8\sqrt{17}}{17}$

3. $\sin\theta = \dfrac{5\sqrt{41}}{41}$, $\cos\theta = \dfrac{4\sqrt{41}}{41}$, $\tan\theta = \dfrac{5}{4}$,

$\csc\theta = \dfrac{\sqrt{41}}{5}$, $\sec\theta = \dfrac{\sqrt{41}}{4}$, $\cot\theta = \dfrac{4}{5}$

4. $\sin\theta = \dfrac{3}{8}$, $\cos\theta = \dfrac{\sqrt{55}}{8}$, $\tan\theta = \dfrac{3\sqrt{55}}{55}$,

$\csc\theta = \dfrac{8}{3}$, $\sec\theta = \dfrac{8\sqrt{55}}{55}$, $\cot\theta = \dfrac{\sqrt{55}}{3}$

5. $\sin\theta = \dfrac{4}{5}$, $\cos\theta = \dfrac{3}{5}$, $\tan\theta = \dfrac{4}{3}$,

$\csc\theta = \dfrac{5}{4}$, $\sec\theta = \dfrac{5}{3}$, $\cot\theta = \dfrac{3}{4}$

6. $\sin\theta = \dfrac{2\sqrt{14}}{9}$, $\cos\theta = \dfrac{5}{9}$, $\tan\theta = \dfrac{2\sqrt{14}}{5}$,

$\csc\theta = \dfrac{9\sqrt{14}}{28}$, $\sec\theta = \dfrac{9}{5}$, $\cot\theta = \dfrac{5\sqrt{14}}{28}$

10.1 Practice A

1. 8 outcomes; HHH, HHT, HTT, HTH, TTT, THH, THT, TTH

2. 9 outcomes; Pa, Pb, Pc, Ya, Yb, Yc, Ta, Tb, Tc, where "Pa" represents a purple balloon labeled *a*

3. $\dfrac{3}{14}$

4. a. 0.44   **b.** 0.50

5. red

10.1 Practice B

1. 4 outcomes; H-P, H-R, T-P, T-R

2. 3 outcomes; BBY, BYY, YYY

3. a. $\dfrac{1}{9}$ **b.** $\dfrac{8}{9}$ **c.** $\dfrac{5}{18}$ **d.** $\dfrac{1}{6}$

4. 0.170

5. always; Equally likely events have the same probability.

6. sometimes; The experimental probability could be greater than or less than the theoretical probability.

7. always; Together, the event and the complement of the event make up the entire sample space.

8. 0.027; about 1 defective dishwasher

10.1 Enrichment and Extension

1. T, T, T, T, T, H, H, T, T, H, H, H

2.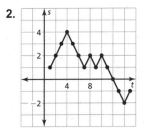

3.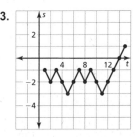

4.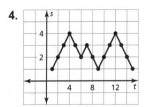

5. $t = 12$; 12 s   **6.** $t = 14$; 1 s

7. does not exist; 15 s

8. a. *Sample answer:* 80%

   b. *Sample answer:* 6 tosses

9. the financial status of a gambler; Graphing several random walks can help you visualize and better understand the random nature of a random process.

10.1 Puzzle Time

TIMES UP

Answers

10.2 Start Thinking

Abbey's softball team winning the district and state championships are dependent events because they cannot win the state title without winning the district title. Abbey being accepted at her favorite college is independent of the other two events because winning the championships should not affect whether she is accepted at the college and being accepted at college will not affect her chances of winning.

10.2 Warm Up

1. $\dfrac{5}{32}$
2. $\dfrac{35}{128}$
3. $\dfrac{73}{128}$

4. $\dfrac{55}{128}$
5. 1
6. 0

10.2 Cumulative Review Warm Up

1. $2(x + 2)(x - 2)$
2. $3(2x - 3)(3x + 4)$

3. $(2 - 3x)(4 + 6x + 9x^2)$

4. $(x^2 + 2)(x + 3)(x - 3)$

5. $5x^4(x + 1)(x^2 - x + 1)$

6. $x(x - 5)(x - 3)(x + 3)$

10.2 Practice A

1. independent; Because the first tool was put back in, it does not affect the occurrence of the second choice.

2. dependent; Because the first juice box is not put back in, it does affect the occurrence of the second choice.

3. yes; What you roll on a die does not affect what is next rolled on that die.

4. no; Selecting the thirty-year-old for the game affects the selection of the second contestant.

5. a. $\dfrac{1}{100}$ b. $\dfrac{1}{90}$

6. 48%

10.2 Practice B

1. dependent; Because the player was not put back in, it does affect the pick of the second player.

2. independent; The pick of a charm does not affect the pick of a piece of leather.

3. yes; The result of flipping the coin the first time does not affect the result of flipping the coin the second time.

4. no; The selection of one male does affect the selection of the next male.

5. a. $\dfrac{1}{676}$ b. $\dfrac{1}{650}$

6. 25%

10.2 Enrichment and Extension

1. 0
2. 0.0701
3. 0.1857
4. 0.4264

5. a. 0.25   b. 0.0667

6. 0.3265
7. 0.6232

10.2 Puzzle Time

A HOLE

10.3 Start Thinking

		Owns a Dog		
		Yes	No	Total
Owns a cat	Yes	6	8	14
	No	28	8	36
	Total	34	16	50

Sample answers: Some may prefer the Venn diagram because it is more familiar. The Venn diagram also clearly shows the overlapping circles indicating those who have both a cat and a dog. The number outside the circles clearly shows those students who do not have a dog or cat. Some may prefer the two-way table because it is similar to a binomial product set up, algebra tiles, and games like Battleship. The two-way table also shows totals that are not as clear in the Venn diagram; and with the totals, you can check your work.

10.3 Warm Up

1.

		Age Started Driving		
		≤ 16	> 16	Total
Gender	Male	28	5	33
	Female	14	8	22
	Total	42	13	55

Answers

10.3 Cumulative Review Warm Up

1.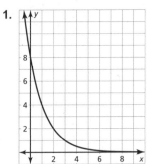

2.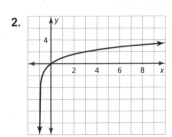

3.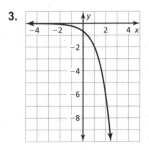

4.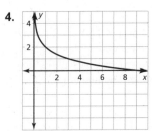

5.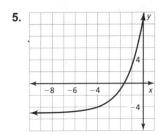

6.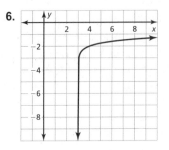

10.3 Practice A

1.

		Ran a Half Marathon		
		Yes	No	Total
Role	Student	12	112	124
	Teacher	7	151	158
	Total	19	263	282

2.

		Owns Dog		
		Yes	No	Total
Owns Cat	Yes	24	61	85
	No	107	34	141
	Total	131	95	226

3. a.

		Amount of Fresh Water Should Be Reduced		
		Yes	No	Total
Fish	Yes	98	12	110
	No	14	75	89
	Total	112	87	199

112 people agree; 87 people do not agree;
110 people fish; 89 people do not fish

b.

		Amount of Fresh Water Should Be Reduced		
		Yes	No	Total
Fish	Yes	0.49	0.06	0.55
	No	0.07	0.38	0.45
	Total	0.56	0.44	1

Answers

c.

		Amount of Fresh Water Should Be Reduced	
		Yes	No
Fish	Yes	0.89	0.11
	No	0.16	0.84

10.3 Practice B

1.

		Surfing Style		
		Regular	Advanced	Total
Gender	Male	0.42	0.12	0.54
	Female	0.38	0.09	0.46
	Total	0.8	0.2	1

2.

		Fishing License		
		Yes	No	Total
Hunting License	Yes	0.10	0.06	0.16
	No	0.29	0.55	0.84
	Total	0.39	0.61	1

3. a.

		Exercise Regularly		
		Yes	No	Total
Feel Tired	Yes	1	1	2
	No	4	20	24
	Total	5	21	26

2 people feel tired; 24 people do not feel tired; 5 people exercise regularly; 21 people do not exercise regularly

b.

		Exercise Regularly		
		Yes	No	Total
Feel Tired	Yes	0.04	0.04	0.08
	No	0.15	0.77	0.92
	Total	0.19	0.81	1

c.

		Exercise Regularly	
		Yes	No
Feel Tired	Yes	0.20	0.05
	No	0.80	0.95

10.3 Enrichment and Extension

1.

	Yes	No	Total
Adults	0.42	0.31	0.73
Students	0.21	0.06	0.27
Total	0.63	0.37	1

2. 22% **3.** 58% **4.** 63% **5.** 583

10.3 Puzzle Time

THEY BOTH DRIBBLE

10.4 Start Thinking

1. {White 1, White 2, White 3, Black 4, Black 5, Black 6}

2. $\dfrac{1}{6}$ **3.** $\dfrac{1}{2}$ **4.** $\dfrac{2}{3}$ **5.** $\dfrac{2}{3}$

10.4 Warm Up

1. $P(\text{green}) = \dfrac{11}{24}$ **2.** $P(\text{blue or green}) = \dfrac{5}{6}$

10.4 Cumulative Review Warm Up

1. $a_n = 3n - 3$ **2.** $a_n = \dfrac{n}{2n + 2}$

3. $a_n = (-2)^n$

10.4 Practice A

1. 0.6 **2.** $\dfrac{5}{6}$ **3.** 0.75

4. $\dfrac{2}{3}$ **5.** $\dfrac{2}{3}$ **6.** 15%

7. a. 0.65
   b. 0.70
   c. 0.65
   d. Door 2; Both the probability of winning the Grand Prize and the probability of winning either the Grand Prize or the Nice Prize are greater for Door 2.

10.4 Practice B

1. 0.575 **2.** $\dfrac{9}{20}$ **3.** 0.675

4. $\dfrac{5}{6}$ **5.** 1 **6.** 65%

Answers

7. $P(A) = 0.96$; $P(\overline{A}) = 0.04$; $P(B|A) = 0.92$;

$P(\overline{B}|A) = 0.08$; $P(B|\overline{A}) = 0.80$; $P(\overline{B}|\overline{A}) = 0.20$;

$P(B) = 91.52\%$

10.4 Enrichment and Extension

1. a. Given: $P(A) = 0.25$, $P(A \text{ or } B) = 0.35$,

$P(A \text{ and } B) = 0.05$. Determine: $P(B)$

 b. 15%

2. a. $\dfrac{1}{4} = \dfrac{2s}{5s + 6}$

 b. 16 songs

 c. $\dfrac{7}{8}$

3. 70%

4. a. 27 marbles

 b. 24 marbles

10.4 Puzzle Time

CLOGS

10.5 Start Thinking

24 possible outcomes; Each row represents a different event. Each branch represents a possible outcome; *Sample answer*: To determine the total number of outcomes from the tree diagram, you can count the outcomes (branches) in the bottom row. Another way to determine the total number of outcomes from the tree diagram would be to multiply the different outcomes represented in each row. For example, in this tree diagram you have 6 different outcomes in the first row, 2 in the second, and 2 in the third. Therefore, there are $6 \cdot 2 \cdot 2 = 24$ possible outcomes.

10.5 Warm Up

1. 3; PPO, POP, OPP

2. 6; TAP, TPA, ATP, APT, PAT, PTA

3. 6; NNOO, NOON, NONO, ONNO, ONON, OONN

4. 12; KEEP, KEPE, KPEE, EKEP, EKPE, EEKP, EEPK, EPEK, EPKE, PKEE, PEKE, PEEK

10.5 Cumulative Review Warm Up

1. $A = 30°$, $BC \approx 8.0829$, $AC \approx 16.1658$

2. $B = 40°$, $BC \approx 8.4265$, $AC \approx 7.0707$

3. $C = 53°$, $BC \approx 3.0142$, $AC \approx 5.0085$

10.5 Practice A

1. a. 6   b. 6

2. a. 24   b. 12

3. a. 120   b. 20

4. 24   5. 30   6. 8   7. 120

8. 15,120   9. 1   10. 2730   11. 0.0179

12. 10   13. 10   14. 6   15. 21

16. 1   17. 36   18. 462   19. 66

20. 56

21. combinations; The order in which you visit the stations does not matter; 28

22. permutations; The 7 logos are all distinct and the three chosen are being ranked, so the order matters; 210

10.5 Practice B

1. a. 120   b. 20

2. a. 720   b. 30

3. a. 362,880   b. 72

4. 360   5. 12   6. 604,800

7. 1   8. 600   9. 27,907,200

10. 5040   11. 0.0083   12. 15

13. 15   14. 9   15. 1

16. 210   17. 1716   18. 3003

19. 53,130

20. permutations; The order in which the three top athletes finish matters; 830,490

21. combinations; The order in which the 6 seniors are chosen does not matter; 7,059,052

22. $x^4 + 12x^3 + 54x^2 + 108x + 81$

23. $8m^3 - 60m^2 + 150m - 125$

24. $243s^5 + 405s^4t + 270s^3t^2 + 90s^2t^3 + 15st^4 + t^5$

10.5 Enrichment and Extension

1. 2160   2. 720   3. 2880

4. 1440   5. 479,001,600   6. 1,437,004,800

7. 48   8. 72   9. 24

Answers

10.5 Puzzle Time

IT KNEW WHAT WAS IN STORE

10.6 Start Thinking

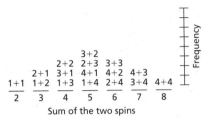

Sum: 2, Frequency: 1; Sum: 3, Frequency: 2; Sum: 4, Frequency: 3; Sum: 5, Frequency: 4; Sum: 6, Frequency: 3; Sum: 7, Frequency: 2; Sum: 8, Frequency: 1; *Sample answer*: It appears that the frequency chart has a vertical line of symmetry. The frequency starts at 1, climbs to 4, and then declines in a similar pattern back down to 1; {1, 2, 3, 4, 3, 2, 1}

10.6 Warm Up

1. 6   **2.** 7   **3.** 1   **4.** 126

5. 1   **6.** 11   **7.** 20   **8.** 45

10.6 Cumulative Review Warm Up

1. amplitude: 2; period: $\dfrac{2\pi}{3}$

2. amplitude: 1; period: 8

3. amplitude: $\dfrac{4}{3}$; period: $\dfrac{2\pi}{3}$

4. amplitude: 1; period: 2π

5. amplitude: $\dfrac{1}{2}$; period: 2π

6. amplitude: 3.8; period: $\dfrac{4\pi}{3}$

10.6 Practice A

1.

X	A	B	C
Outcomes	2	5	1
$P(X)$	$\dfrac{1}{4}$	$\dfrac{5}{8}$	$\dfrac{1}{8}$

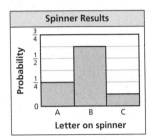

2.

F	Apples	Pears	Oranges
Outcomes	3	4	4
$P(F)$	$\dfrac{3}{11}$	$\dfrac{4}{11}$	$\dfrac{4}{11}$

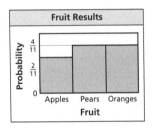

3. a. 2

   b. $\dfrac{5}{8}$

4. a. 6

   b. $\dfrac{1}{2}$

5. 0.0002   **6.** 0.0739   **7.** 0.0370

8. The exponents should sum to 6, the total number or rolls;

$$P(k = 4) = {}_6C_4\left(\dfrac{1}{6}\right)^4\left(\dfrac{5}{6}\right)^{6-4} \approx 0.008$$

Answers

10.6 Practice B

1.

V	1	2
Outcomes	15	11
$P(V)$	$\frac{15}{26}$	$\frac{11}{26}$

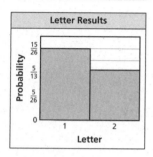

2.

X	1	2	3	4
Outcomes	3	6	22	4
$P(X)$	$\frac{3}{35}$	$\frac{6}{35}$	$\frac{22}{35}$	$\frac{4}{35}$

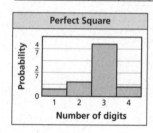

3. 0.0011   **4.** 0.0148   **5.** 0.0002

6. a.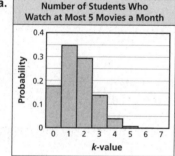

b. 1

c. 0.954

7. The number k is the number of successes (5), not the number showing on the number cube (4);

$$P(k = 5) = {}_6C_5\left(\frac{1}{6}\right)^5\left(\frac{5}{6}\right)^{6-5} \approx 0.006$$

8. a. not valid; The fifth box has the same probability (20%) as any other box of having a prize, and is not affected by the prize status of any previously opened boxes.

b. 0.4096

c. 0.32768

d. 0.00032

10.6 Enrichment and Extension

1. a. 4.8; 0.98

b. 0.34464

c. 0.90112

d. 0.7379

2. 20.28; 4.22   **3.** 2.4; 1.50   **4.** 40; 2.83

10.6 Puzzle Time

GRILLED HIM

Cumulative Review

1. $\dfrac{14}{80} = \dfrac{x}{100}; x = 17.5\%$

2. $\dfrac{x}{78} = \dfrac{74}{100}; x = 57.72$

3. $\dfrac{25.2}{35} = \dfrac{x}{100}; x = 72\%$

4. $\dfrac{9}{48} = \dfrac{x}{100}; x = 18.75\%$

5. $\dfrac{x}{63} = \dfrac{45}{100}; x = 28.35$

6. $\dfrac{15.68}{98} = \dfrac{x}{100}; x = 16\%$

7. $\dfrac{45}{120} = \dfrac{x}{100}; x = 37.5\%$

8. $\dfrac{x}{230} = \dfrac{32}{100}; x = 73.6$

9. $\dfrac{12.1}{55} = \dfrac{x}{100}; x = 22\%$

10. $\dfrac{57.8}{68} = \dfrac{x}{100}; x = 85\%$

Answers

11.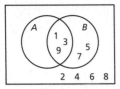

12.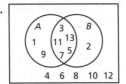

13.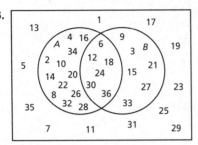

14.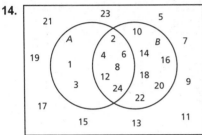

15.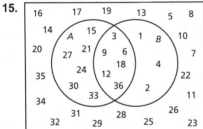

16.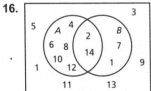

17. 87.3%

18. 8%

19. a. 82.9% **b.** 88.6% **c.** 5.7% better

20. translation 1 unit down

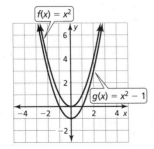

21. translation 9 units up

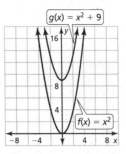

22. translation 5 units down

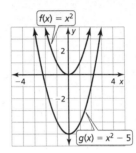

23. translation 3 units right

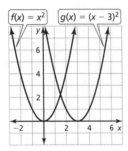

24. translation 6 units left

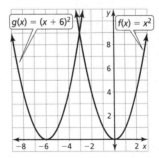

25. translation 4 units right

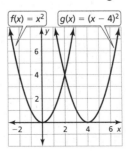

Algebra 2 A129
Answers

Answers

26. translation 9 units left and 3 units down

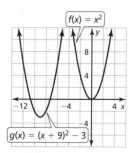

27. translation 2 units right and 6 units down

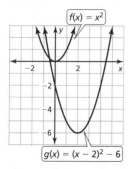

28. translation 5 units left and 8 units up

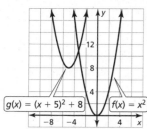

29. reflection in the x-axis

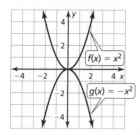

30. vertical stretch by a factor of 4

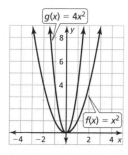

31. vertical stretch by a factor of 3 and a reflection in the x-axis

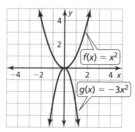

32. vertical shrink by a factor of $\dfrac{1}{4}$

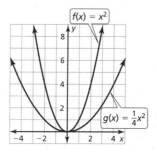

33. vertical shrink by a factor of $\dfrac{1}{2}$ and a reflection in the x-axis

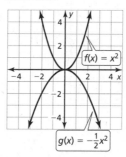

34. vertex: $(-5, 0)$, axis of symmetry: $x = -5$

35. vertex: $(9, 0)$, axis of symmetry: $x = 9$

36. vertex: $(0, 4)$, axis of symmetry: $x = 0$

37. vertex: $(0, -5)$, axis of symmetry: $x = 0$

38. vertex: $(-8, 1)$, axis of symmetry: $x = -8$

39. vertex: $(3, 8)$, axis of symmetry: $x = 3$

40. vertex: $(0, 7)$, axis of symmetry: $x = 0$

41. vertex: $(-1, -1)$, axis of symmetry: $x = -1$

Answers

42. vertex: $(6, -7)$, axis of symmetry: $x = 6$

43. vertex: $(8, -6)$, axis of symmetry: $x = 8$

44. $x = 4$ **45.** $x = 4$ **46.** $x = 5$

47. $x = 16$ **48.** $12i$ **49.** $7i$

50. $50i$ **51.** $-132i$ **52.** $40i\sqrt{5}$

53. $-24i\sqrt{2}$ **54.** $-1 - 9i$ **55.** $-9 - 8i$

56. $6 + 10i$ **57.** $8 - 23i$ **58.** $-2i$

59. $17 + 5i$ **60.** $-150 + 15i$ **61.** $48 - 30i$

62. $-42 - 134i$ **63.** $158 - 189i$ **64.** $-578i$

65. $-44 + 240i$ **66.** 3 **67.** 4

68. 5 **69.** 216 **70.** 36

71. 27 **72.** 2.08 **73.** 0.43

74. 9 **75.** 6.87 **76.** 8

77. 243 **78.** e^{10} **79.** e^8

80. $6e^9$ **81.** $3e^{18}$ **82.** $64e^{36x}$

83. $729e^{-12x}$ **84.** $8, 9, 10, 11, 12, 13$

85. $3, 2, 1, 0, -1, -2$ **86.** $-7, -6, -5, -4, -3, -2$

87. $1, 8, 27, 64, 125, 216$

88. $-1, 6, 25, 62, 123, 214$

89. $-2, 1, 6, 13, 22, 33$ **90.** $36, 25, 16, 9, 4, 1$

91. $4, 9, 16, 25, 36, 49$ **92.** 40

93. 285 **94.** 110 **95.** 123 **96.** -78

97. $\dfrac{208}{105}$ **98.** $\dfrac{565}{252}$ **99.** 12 **100.** 1785

101. **a.** \$12.75
    b. 264 days

102. **a.** $a_n = n + 2$
    b. 33 dancers
    c. 42 dancers
    d. 9 dancers

Chapter 11

11.1 Start Thinking

mean $= 75$

Score	Frequency
50–59	2
60–69	3
70–79	8
80–89	5
90–99	2

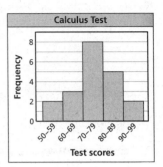

Sample answer: The histogram appears to have a reasonably symmetric distribution about the mean value of 75.

11.1 Warm Up

1. mean $= 18.1$, median $= 17.5$

2. mean $= \dfrac{855}{7} \approx 122.14$, median $= 120$

3. mean $= \dfrac{177}{40} \approx 4.43$, median $= 4.6$

11.1 Cumulative Review Warm Up

1. $g(x) = -|x - 1| + 3$

2. $g(x) = -\dfrac{1}{2}|x| - 5$

11.1 Practice A

1. 50%   **2.** 47.5%   **3.** 0.15%   **4.** 99.85%

5. 47.5%   **6.** 68%   **7.** 47.5%   **8.** 16%

9. a. 81.5%   **b.** 16%

10. The probability that x is from 15 to 27 was found instead of the probability that x is at least 15.

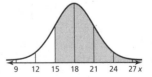

The probability that x is at least 15 is 0.84.

11.1 Practice B

1. 16%   **2.** 5%   **3.** 97.5%

4. 83.85%   **5.** 13.5%   **6.** 97.35%

Answers

7. 84%   **8.** 2.5%

9. a. 95%   **b.** 2.5%

10. The probability that x is from 18 to 24 was found instead of the probability that x is at most 24.

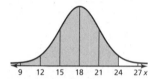

The probability that x is at most 24 is 0.975.

11.1 Enrichment and Extension

1. $P \approx -0.178$, so the distribution is approximately symmetric

2. $P \approx 0.381$, so the distribution is approximately symmetric

3. $P \approx 1.160$, so the distribution is skewed to the right

11.1 Puzzle Time

FISH AND SHIPS

11.2 Start Thinking

The theoretical probability is $\frac{1}{8}$; *Sample answers*:

Some students may find that it takes only one toss of the three coins to get all three to land heads up. However, as a group they should notice that the average number of tosses is somewhere around eight. The experimental probability will quite likely differ from the theoretical probability. However, as the number of tosses increases (sample size increases), the two probabilities should get closer together.

11.2 Warm Up

1. The sample space is the set of all 52 cards.

2. The sample space is the set given that includes all possible color combinations with two spins; {Red-Red, Red-Blue, Red-Yellow, Red-Green, Blue-Blue, Blue-Yellow, Blue-Green, Blue-Red, Yellow-Yellow, Yellow-Green, Yellow-Red, Yellow-Blue, Green-Green, Green-Red, Green-Blue, Green-Yellow}

3. The sample space is the set of all possible responses and may include, yes, no, and maybe.

4. The sample space is the set of all possible responses and may include, yes, no, and sometimes.

11.2 Cumulative Review Warm Up

1. $(4, 0)$

2. infinitely many solutions of the form $(x, x - 8)$

3. $(-2, 1)$ **4.** $\left(4, -\frac{3}{4}\right)$ **5.** $(4, 3)$ **6.** $(0, 0)$

11.2 Practice A

1. sample; There are more than 25 bags of popcorn.

2. population; degrees of every (all) employees

3. The population is all students at the university, and the sample is the 1641 students that were surveyed. Of the students surveyed, 479 of them do not know the name of their college's mascot.

4. The population is all people in the United States, and the sample is the 1000 households with at least one child that were surveyed. Of the households surveyed, 874 of them have two or more computers.

5. parameter; it is referring to all of the football players on the team

6. statistic; it is referring to only the surveyed utility bills

7. a. The maker's claim is most likely true.

   b. The maker's claim is most likely false.

11.2 Practice B

1. population; every student in the school

2. sample; more than 80 people could access the website

3. The population is every employee in the office building, and the sample is the 648 employees that were surveyed. Of the employees surveyed, 147 of them ride the subway to work each day.

4. The population is all homeowners in the State of Florida, and the sample is the 2500 homeowners that were surveyed. Of the homeowners surveyed, 1145 of them have switched their homeowner's insurance policy to a different company within the last 3 years.

5. statistic; it is referring to only the surveyed hockey players

6. parameter; it is referring to all the sold tickets

7. a. The maker's claim is most likely false.

   b. The maker's claim is most likely true.

Answers

11.2 Enrichment and Extension

1. **a and b.** Type I: Decide garlic is effective in reducing tick bites when it really is not effective; Consequence: People would consume more garlic but not have the protection against tick bites and could develop Lyme's disease (or some other disease carried by ticks); Type II: Decide garlic is not effective in reducing tick bites when it really is effective; Consequence: People would not use the garlic (a nontoxic treatment) to prevent tick bites, but have to use a toxic repellant.

   c. *Sample answer*: Type I is more serious because people could potentially develop a serious disease from tick bites.

2. **a and b.** Type I: Say that there are too many defects when in reality there are not; Consequence: You would stop the assembly process when there is no problem, wasting production time; Type II: Say that there are not too many defects when in reality there are; Consequence: You would continue with the assembly process, but have many defective products, which could cause you to lose money.

   c. *Sample answer*: The factory owner might consider Type I more serious because he loses production time for no reason, which could cause him to lose more money than the defective products.

3. **a and b.** Type I: It is decided that the shop is not meeting standards, when it is.; Consequence: The shop and state might be in trouble when it shouldn't be; Type II: The shop is certified as meeting standards when it is not; Consequence: Cars that are polluting the environment are being used.

   c. *Sample answer*: Either could be argued as worse depending on if you work for the state or care about the welfare of the environment.

4. **a and b.** Type I: The software seems like it helps (and the professor buys it) even when it really did not; Consequence: The students are wasting their time using the software, and it is a waste of money; Type II: The software doesn't seem to help (and the professor doesn't buy it) when it would have helped; Consequence: The students would be missing out on software that helps them.

   c. *Sample answer*: Either could be argued for. Because the software is expensive, Type I might be more serious, because the money could have been spent elsewhere.

11.2 Puzzle Time

ON A MAP

11.3 Start Thinking

1. *Sample answer*: Surveying 50 random students at your school may not give the school board good information in regards to allocating funds for a robotics team. Depending on the total number of students in the school, the 50 surveyed may be a very small percentage or a very large percentage of the entire school population. The school board could get better information by surveying all the students to determine exactly how many (what percentage) of the students are actually interested in participating in robotics.

2. *Sample answer*: If the Student Government Association wants to know if families would be interested in participating in a school carnival, they should probably survey the parents as well as the students.

11.3 Warm Up

1. *Sample answer*: Because the survey only includes pet owners, it is quite likely that they would want hotels to accept pets. It might be better to survey hotel guests in general rather than pet owners who are likely biased in favor of pets.

2. *Sample answer*: Shoppers in the mall are quite likely to be biased toward extended mall hours so that they can shop longer. A better option would be to survey shoppers along with mall employees and store owners, as well as people living in the neighborhood around the mall.

3. *Sample answer*: Students would most likely be biased in such a way to encourage a decreased homework load. Surveying teachers, parents, administrators, and students might give more reliable results.

4. *Sample answer*: Because the survey includes individuals inside an athletic club, they are probably more likely to exercise. Surveying a larger and more diverse group would give more reliable results.

11.3 Cumulative Review Warm Up

1.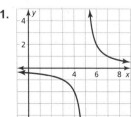

2.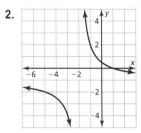

Answers

3.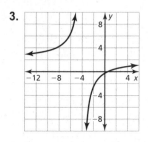

11.3 Practice A

1. self-selected sample   **2.** convenience sample

3. systematic; These customers shop at a locally-owned hardware store, so they would probably want the store to remain opened for business.

4. systematic; Members with last names that begin with the later letters of the alphabet do not get an opportunity to voice their opinion, and some of the first 20 members with the same last names might be related.

5. unbiased; The sample represents the population.

6. unbiased; The students are randomly selected.

7. A sensitive question is being asked. This type of question is better asked anonymously.

8. By saying "could be toxic," one would feel guilty if he or she did not agree. These words could be removed from the question and the individual could make his or her own judgment about lesions.

11.3 Practice B

1. cluster sampling

2. systematic sampling

3. cluster; The cluster was not randomly selected; People who own waterfront property will support lower taxes for those who own waterfront property

4. self-select; Those who are listening to the station probably prefer country music, so they are more likely to vote for country music

5. biased; Local fisherman are not likely to support the bill, because they would probably want to catch as many lobster as possible.

6. biased; Only one age group was surveyed.

7. People may hesitate to vocalize their agreement if they are standing next to employees at the plant. This question would be better asked anonymously.

8. The use of the words "far beyond" could influence someone to not disagree. The words could be removed.

11.3 Enrichment and Extension

1. Method 1: experiment; Method 2: survey; Method 3: observational study; Method 1 is most reliable; Method 2 and 3 depend on finding farms using the desired fertilizers, and different farms may use different amounts of fertilizer.

2. Method 1: experiment; Method 2: observational study; Method 3: survey. Method 1 is most reliable; Method 2 may not be random, and Method 3 relies on the drivers accurately remembering their battery usage.

11.3 Puzzle Time

TO UNWIND

11.4 Start Thinking

To determine if a spinner is fair, you could examine its design and make sure each space has the same area and that the spinner actually spins freely over each space. You could also test the spinner by recording the results of 100 or 1000 (or more) spins to see if each number/color came up about the same number of times. In a similar way, you could examine a coin to make sure that one side didn't seem to be weighted. Then you could test the coin by recording the results of 100 or 1000 (or more) flips to see if each side came up about the same number of times.

11.4 Warm Up

1. experiment   **2.** observational study

11.4 Cumulative Review Warm Up

1. $3^{1/3}$ **2.** 324   **3.** $9\sqrt{3}$

4. $\sqrt[6]{12}$ **5.** 2   **6.** $5^{1/2}$

11.4 Practice A

1. This study is a randomized comparative experiment. The treatment is the use of the computer for testing. The treatment group is the 150 students who test on the computer. The control group is the 150 students who test using paper and pencil.

2. This study is not a randomized comparative experiment because the people were not randomly assigned to a control group and a treatment group. The conclusion may not be valid. There may be other reasons why those who drank water had lower cholesterol.

Answers

3. This study is best done as an experiment. Half of the team is randomly assigned to yoga, and the other half is not.

4. This study is best done as an observational study because a time frame of 10 years is too long for an experiment of this type. After 10 years, the drugs may be obsolete. The effects of the drugs can be examined on those who have already taken them.

5. a. Muscle damage is more likely as one gets older. Thus, the breakdown according to age may affect the results. This study can be improved by just randomly assigning people to groups, regardless of age.

b. The experimental design is good. However a potential problem may be that injuries can occur.

11.4 Practice B

1. This study is not a randomized comparative experiment because the people were not randomly assigned to a control group and a treatment group. The conclusion may not be valid. There may be other reasons why those who switched were more satisfied with the condition of their pool.

2. This study is a randomized comparative experiment. The treatment is the use of the recyclables containers. The treatment group is the 75 customers who used the recyclables containers. The control group is the 75 customers who used the recyclables bins.

3. This study is best done as an observational study because the organization cannot force someone to donate 20% to charity. Job satisfaction can be rated for those who already give 20% to charity.

4. This study is best done as an experiment. The rancher randomly chooses half the cows to receive the new feed, and the other half do not.

5. a. The experimental design is good. However, a possible potential problem may be that someone dislikes the taste of diet soda.

b. A potential problem is the division based on exercise habits. Those who exercise regularly tend to eat less sugar, and may tend to drink more diet soda than the other group. Thus, their bodies may already be conditioned to the sugar cravings. This design could be improved by dividing the group randomly rather than based on exercise habits.

11.4 Enrichment and Extension

1. a. class size: small, medium, large; textbook: traditional, new

b. final grades

c. 6

d. The experiment could be blind or double-blind. The students might not know they are part of an experiment, but the teacher would probably know that he/she was part of an experiment. If they didn't, that would diminish bias, and it could be done.

2. a. watering: daily, three days a week; fertilizer: traditional, organic

b. average final heat rating for the plot at the end of the growing season

c. 4

d. The plants will not have bias. Blinding the botanist could occur so that he/she does not know which fertilizer each plot got, but as for watering, the botanist would know, so the experiment could be blind but not-double-blind.

3. a. new or old dog food

b. improvement in kidneys

c. 2

d. The experiment could be blind or double-blind. The dogs will not have bias. Blinding the feeder could be done and would diminish bias.

4. a. walking: using no device, a standard walker, or a rolling walker; responding (or not responding) to a signal while walking

b. Cadence was measured.

c. 6

d. The subjects don't need to be told what is being tested when they are directed to walk but it would be difficult to do a blind or double blind experiment.

5. *Sample answer*: Randomly divide the subjects into two groups of 50. Give 50 the inhaler and 50 the shot. Measure insulin levels three times a day. Compare the results.

11.4 Puzzle Time

WAVY

Answers

11.5 Start Thinking

The sample survey results show that 35% of the students have part-time jobs; *Sample answer*: Because the original prediction is 10 percentage points off, we may choose to change our prediction based on the sample survey. However, we may also decide to redo the survey with a greater number of students to make sure our sample was a good representation of the entire population.

11.5 Warm Up

1. 185.8   2. 4.8

11.5 Cumulative Review Warm Up

1. $x^5 - 15x^4 + 90x^3 - 270x^2 + 405x - 243$

2. $16x^4 + 160x^3 + 600x^2 + 1000x + 625$

3. $-128x^7 + 448x^6 - 672x^5 + 560x^4 - 280x^3$
$$+ 84x^2 - 14x + 1$$

4. $x^4 + 4x^3y^2 + 6x^2y^4 + 4xy^6 + y^8$

5. $64a^6 - 576a^5b + 2160a^4b^2 - 4320a^3b^3$
$$+ 4860a^2b^4 - 2916ab^5 + 729b^6$$

6. $x^{24} - 8x^{21}y^4 + 28x^{18}y^8 - 56x^{15}y^{12} + 70x^{12}y^{16}$
$$- 56x^9y^{20} + 28x^6y^{24}$$
$$- 8x^3y^{28} + y^{32}$$

11.5 Practice A

1. **a.** The sample mean is 9.3, so an estimate for the population mean would be 9.3.

   b. The sample proportion is approximately 0.233, so an estimate for the population proportion would be 0.233.

   c. The sample proportion is approximately 0.267, so an estimate for the population proportion would be 0.267.

2. Not very confident because the sample mean is an estimate of the population mean.

3. **a.** Based on your survey, 0.43 is just outside the margin of error, so you can conclude that the claim is probably incorrect.

   b. Based on your survey, 0.43 is within the margin of error, so you can conclude that the claim is probably correct.

   c. 95% of the time, a sample proportion should lie in the interval from 0.29 to 0.57.

11.5 Practice B

1. **a.** The sample mean is 5.825, so an estimate for the population mean would be 5.825.

   b. The sample proportion is 0.325, so an estimate for the population proportion would be 0.325.

   c. The sample proportion is 0.275, so an estimate for the population proportion would be 0.275.

2. Not very confident because the sample mean is an estimate of the population mean.

3. **a.** Based on your survey, 0.45 is outside the margin of error, so you can conclude that the claim is probably incorrect.

   b. Based on your survey, 0.45 is within the margin of error, so you can conclude that the claim is probably correct.

   c. 95% of the time, a sample proportion should lie in the interval from 0.31 to 0.59.

11.5 Enrichment and Extension

1. *Sample answer*: Should the school start a foreign language club?

2. *Sample answer*: yes; The type of club is specific and it is an easy yes or no answer.

3. The entire student population.

4. *Sample answer*: I will ask 100 students chosen randomly by ID number.

5. *Sample answer*: no; The sample is random.

6. *Sample answer*: yes; The sample is random.

7. *Sample answer*: yes; I may need to change the question to, "Would you join a foreign language club if it were offered?"

8. *Sample answer*: Yes, the results became more accurate the more people I surveyed.

11.5 Puzzle Time

A SWALLOW

Answers

11.6 Start Thinking

Sample answer: The company might produce a small amount of the sports drink in the suggested size bottle and see how the sales compare to the original size over a given period of time. They could do the same thing with a label change. They could test a small market with just a change in the label. And finally, they could produce a small amount of the sports drink with both a change in size and labeling. By comparing the sales within similar markets, they could determine if the label change or the change in size, or both, affect the sales in a positive or negative way.

11.6 Warm Up

1. mean of the control: 14.79; mean of the treatment: 15.02; difference: 0.23

2. mean of the control: 59.6; mean of the treatment: 55.4; difference: −4.2

11.6 Cumulative Review Warm Up

1. 1

2. $\tan^2 x$

3. $2\csc x$

4. $\cos x$

5. $\sec x$

6. $\cos x - 1$

11.6 Practice A

1. a. 3.625

   b. 5.375

   c. 1.75

   d.
   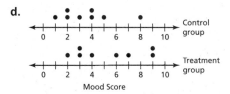
   Mood Score

   e. The plot of the data shows that the two sets are fairly symmetric. The control group may have a possible outlier, but it is a valid data item. So, the mean is a suitable measure of center. The mean score of the treatment group is 1.75 higher than that of the control group. It appears that mood therapy might be slightly effective, but the sample size is small and the difference could be due to chance.

   f. *Sample answer*:

	Mood Score							
Control Group	5	9	2	3	3	7	8	4
Treatment Group	1	3	4	2	6	9	2	4

g. *Sample answer*: 5.125

h. *Sample answer*: 3.875

i. *Sample answer*: −1.25

11.6 Practice B

1. a. 3.35

   b. 2.425

   c. −0.925

   d.
   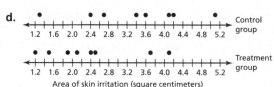
   Area of skin irritation (square centimeters)

   e. The plot of the data shows that the two sets are fairly symmetric and have no extreme values. So, the mean is a suitable measure of center. The mean score of the treatment group is 0.925 lower than that of the control group. It appears that photo therapy might be slightly effective, but the sample size is small and the difference could be due to chance.

   f. *Sample answer*:

	Area of Skin Irritation (square centimeters)							
Control Group	4.1	2.5	5.1	1.2	3.4	3.7	2.7	1.3
Treatment Group	4.2	2.1	3.6	2.4	1.5	1.9	2.4	4.1

g. *Sample answer*: 3

h. *Sample answer*: 2.775

i. *Sample answer*: −0.225

11.6 Enrichment and Extension

1. Because zero is not in the interval, there is sufficient evidence to suggest beef hotdogs have a higher fat content than meat.

2. Because zero is in the interval, there is insufficient evidence to suggest route A is faster than route B.

3. Because zero is not in the interval, there is sufficient evidence to suggest front loading washers take longer than top loading washers.

4. Because zero is not in the interval, there is sufficient evidence to suggest children's cereals have more sugar than adults' cereals.

Answers

ROCKET

Cumulative Review

1. mean: 12, median: 14, mode: 14

2. mean: 45, median: 46, mode: 46

3. mean 69.7, median: 68, mode: 80

4. mean: 44.1, median: 44, mode: 43 and 47

5. mean: 13.3, median: 16, mode: none

6. mean: 15.4, median: 15, mode: 14 and 15

7. mean: 59.6, median: 59.5, mode: none

8. mean: 8.1, median: 10, mode: 10 and 11

9. 4.3; *Sample answer*: The typical data value differs from the mean by about 4.3 units.

10. 2.6; *Sample answer*: The typical data value differs from the mean by about 2.6 units.

11. 6.6; *Sample answer*: The typical data value differs from the mean by about 6.6 units.

12. 1.6; *Sample answer*: The typical data value differs from the mean by about 1.6 units.

13. 2.6; *Sample answer*: The typical data value differs from the mean by about 2.6 units.

14. 3.8; *Sample answer*: The typical data value differs from the mean by about 3.8 units.

15. inverse variation

16. direct variation

17. neither

18. neither

19. direct variation

20. direct variation

21. $y = \dfrac{7}{x}; \dfrac{7}{3}$

22. $y = -\dfrac{40}{x}; -\dfrac{40}{3}$

23. $y = -\dfrac{7}{x}; -\dfrac{7}{3}$

24. $y = -\dfrac{10}{x}; -\dfrac{10}{3}$

25. $y = \dfrac{56}{9x}; \dfrac{56}{27}$

26. $y = \dfrac{3}{2x}; \dfrac{1}{2}$

27. $y = \dfrac{4}{5x}; \dfrac{4}{15}$

28. $y = \dfrac{8}{3x}; \dfrac{8}{9}$

29. mean: 84.7, median: 85, mode: 71, 75, 77, 92, and 95

30. $\dfrac{1}{2x - 9x^4}$

31. $\dfrac{6 + 2x^3}{3}$

32. $\dfrac{x - 4}{x + 5}$

33. $\dfrac{x + 9}{x + 4}$

34. $\dfrac{x - 9}{x + 6}$

35. $\dfrac{x - 5}{x + 3}$

36. $\dfrac{y^4}{3x^4}$

37. $\dfrac{y^2}{6}$

38. $\dfrac{x^2 - 6x + 8}{x}$

39. $\dfrac{x + 2}{x - 10}$

40. $\dfrac{x - 2}{x + 7}$

41. $\dfrac{x + 3}{x - 10}$

42. $\dfrac{20}{7x}$

43. $\dfrac{x - 3}{2x^2}$

44. $\dfrac{8 + 3x}{x - 2}$

45. $\dfrac{3x^2 - 1}{x + 5}$

46. $\dfrac{-7x}{3x + 4}$

47. $\dfrac{x^3 + x^2}{x^2 + 1}$

48. $\dfrac{-x^2 + 4x + 18}{x^2 + 3x - 40}$

49. $\dfrac{x^2 + 2x - 38}{x^2 - 12x + 35}$

50. $\dfrac{3x^2 - 27x - 68}{x^2 - 12x + 11}$

51. $\dfrac{x^2 + x + 62}{x^2 - 11x - 12}$

52. a. $P = 10x + 32$

   b. $A = 6x^2 + 39x + 63$

   c. 52 in.; 165 in.^{2}

53. $\sin \theta = \dfrac{3}{5}, \cos \theta = \dfrac{4}{5}, \tan \theta = \dfrac{3}{4}, \csc \theta = \dfrac{5}{3},$
$\sec \theta = \dfrac{5}{4}, \cot \theta = \dfrac{4}{3}$

54. $\sin \theta = \dfrac{3}{5}, \cos \theta = \dfrac{4}{5}, \tan \theta = \dfrac{3}{4}, \csc \theta = \dfrac{5}{3},$
$\sec \theta = \dfrac{5}{4}, \cot \theta = \dfrac{4}{3}$

55. $\sin \theta = \dfrac{3}{7}, \cos \theta = \dfrac{2\sqrt{10}}{7}, \tan \theta = \dfrac{3\sqrt{10}}{20},$
$\csc \theta = \dfrac{7}{3}, \sec \theta = \dfrac{7\sqrt{10}}{20}, \cot \theta = \dfrac{2\sqrt{10}}{3}$

56. $\sin \theta = \dfrac{4\sqrt{137}}{137}, \cos \theta = \dfrac{11\sqrt{137}}{137}, \tan \theta = \dfrac{4}{11},$
$\csc \theta = \dfrac{\sqrt{137}}{4}, \sec \theta = \dfrac{\sqrt{137}}{11}, \cot \theta = \dfrac{11}{4}$

Answers

57. $x = 12$ **58.** $x = 7\sqrt{2}$

59. $x = 3\sqrt{3}$ **60.** $x = 4$

61. *Sample answer:* $-272°$ and $448°$

62. *Sample answer:* $-665°$ and $55°$

63. *Sample answer:* $-\dfrac{11\pi}{4}$ and $\dfrac{5\pi}{4}$

64. *Sample answer:* $-\dfrac{7\pi}{6}$ and $\dfrac{17\pi}{6}$

65. *Sample answer:* $-300°$ and $60°$

66. *Sample answer:* $-\dfrac{10\pi}{3}$ and $\dfrac{2\pi}{3}$

67. $\dfrac{11\pi}{18}$ **68.** $\dfrac{31\pi}{18}$ **69.** $-240°$

70. $150°$ **71.** $-\dfrac{\pi}{3}$ **72.** $-135°$

73. $\sin 180° = 0$, $\cos 180° = -1$, $\tan 180° = 0$,
$\csc 180° = $ undefined, $\sec 180° = -1$,
$\cot 180° = $ undefined

74. $\sin 495° = \dfrac{\sqrt{2}}{2}$, $\cos 495° = -\dfrac{\sqrt{2}}{2}$,
$\tan 495° = -1$, $\csc 495° = \sqrt{2}$,
$\sec 495° = -\sqrt{2}$, $\cot 495° = -1$

75. $\sin\left(-\dfrac{\pi}{3}\right) = -\dfrac{\sqrt{3}}{2}$, $\cos\left(-\dfrac{\pi}{3}\right) = \dfrac{1}{2}$,
$\tan\left(-\dfrac{\pi}{3}\right) = -\sqrt{3}$, $\csc\left(-\dfrac{\pi}{3}\right) = \dfrac{-2\sqrt{3}}{3}$,
$\sec\left(-\dfrac{\pi}{3}\right) = 2$, $\cot\left(-\dfrac{\pi}{3}\right) = -\dfrac{\sqrt{3}}{3}$

76. $\sin\dfrac{\pi}{6} = \dfrac{1}{2}$, $\cos\dfrac{\pi}{6} = \dfrac{\sqrt{3}}{2}$, $\tan\dfrac{\pi}{6} = \dfrac{\sqrt{3}}{3}$,
$\csc\dfrac{\pi}{6} = 2$, $\sec\dfrac{\pi}{6} = \dfrac{2\sqrt{3}}{3}$, $\cot\dfrac{\pi}{6} = \sqrt{3}$

77. $\sin(-120°) = -\dfrac{\sqrt{3}}{2}$, $\cos(-120°) = -\dfrac{1}{2}$,
$\tan(-120°) = \sqrt{3}$, $\csc(-120°) = -\dfrac{2\sqrt{3}}{3}$,
$\sec(-120°) = -2$, $\cot(-120°) = \dfrac{\sqrt{3}}{3}$

78. $\sin\dfrac{7\pi}{4} = -\dfrac{\sqrt{2}}{2}$, $\cos\dfrac{7\pi}{4} = \dfrac{\sqrt{2}}{2}$, $\tan\dfrac{7\pi}{4} = -1$,
$\csc\dfrac{7\pi}{4} = -\sqrt{2}$, $\sec\dfrac{7\pi}{4} = \sqrt{2}$, $\cot\dfrac{7\pi}{4} = -1$

79. 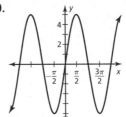   **80.**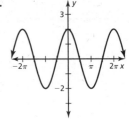

81. 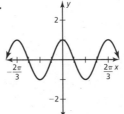   **82.**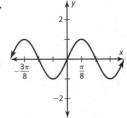

83. 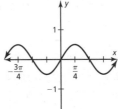   **84.**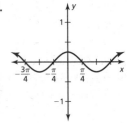

85. 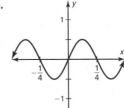   **86.**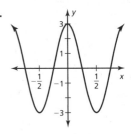

Answers

87.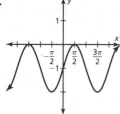

88.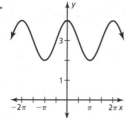

89.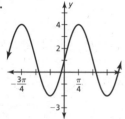

90.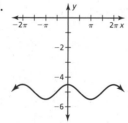